The American Presidency

THE
AMERICAN
PRESIDENCY

RICHARD M. PIOUS

BASIC BOOKS, INC., PUBLISHERS

NEW YORK

Library of Congress Cataloging in Publication Data

Pious, Richard M   1944–
    The American Presidency.

    Bibliography: p. 436
    Includes index.
    1. Presidents—United States. I. Title.
JK516.P55   353.03′13   78–19808
ISBN: 0–465–00183–1
ISBN: 0–465–00184–X pbk.

For my Mother and in Memory of my Father

of policy making: budgeting and fiscal management, foreign policy and national security management, legislative initiative and congressional relations, etc.

In developing this challenging and controversial thesis the author, drawing on the very latest scholarly research, covers all aspects of the modern American presidency, including many, such as fiscal policy making, that are usually ignored. The result is a unique book —at once rich in scholarship and a pleasure to read—that is bound to become the standard work about a political institution on which, for good or ill, the future welfare of this country and the peace of the world so largely depend.

he executive are unity; dura-
npetent powers. The ingredi-
se are a due dependence on

ALEXANDER HAMILTON

tion. The interest of the man
of the place. It may be a re-
d be necessary to control the
self but the greatest of all re-
s, no government would be
external nor internal controls
a government which is to be
ty lies in this: you must first
nd in the next place oblige it
10 doubt, the primary control
kind the necessity of auxiliary

JAMES MADISON

is adopted by the Convention
ude the exercise of arbitrary
it by means of the inevitable
ntal powers among the three

LOUIS BRANDEIS

spensable contribution to the
er make a contribution just as

JOHN KENNEDY

RICHARD M. PIOUS is Assistant Professor of Political Science at Barnard College. He is the author of *Civil Rights and Liberties in the 1970s* (1973).

CONTENTS

9:   Economic Policymaking

10:   Foreign Policymaking

ACKNOWLEDGMENTS

I THANK COLLEAGUES at Barnard College and Columbia University for reading chapter drafts, including Demetrios Caraley, John Chambers, Flora Davidson, Gerald Finch, Thomas Horne, Peter Juviler, Richard Rubin, and Catherine Yatrakis. Bruce Feld and Harvey Mansfield were helpful on program innovation, and Richard Rubin provided data on presidential primaries. Friends who read chapter drafts include Caren Dubnoff, Michael Goldstein, Robert Lamb, Robert Mutch, David Pass, Steven Singer, and Susan Weil. Daniel Traister provided invaluable editorial assistance.

I have clarified my arguments by participating in several conferences, including "Congress Against the President," sponsored by the Academy of Political Science in 1975, the 1976 New Paltz, SUNY Conference on Martin Van Buren, and the 1976 Columbia–CUNY Conference on Political Economy. I appreciate criticisms of my papers and presentations by scholars at these events.

Conversations with Louis Fisher and Thomas Cronin about textbook writing and a brief correspondence with Arthur Schlesinger, Jr., about constitutional standards for the exercise of war powers have been useful. A brief exchange with Robert Reischauer about the effectiveness of the Congressional Budget Office has clarified some of my ideas about collaborative government. Ronald Moe and Herbert Parmet have given me useful insights on congressional-executive relations. Duncan Foley, Gordon Adams, John Prados, Don Scharf, and Gerald Benjamin have provided me with useful sources. Stephen Solarz has discussed with me the efforts that he and his colleagues on the House International Relations Committee made to amend the War Powers Resolution. Those of us who served as teaching assistants to the late Eaton Professor of Public

Administration Wallace Sayre have gathered informally on several occasions to discuss his theories, and two of Sayre's colleagues, Herbert Kaufman and Bruce L.R. Smith, made comments about administrative oversight that were useful to me. I have also benefitted from James S. Young's ideas about decentralization of executive branch functions.

I am indebted to Wallace Sayre, Richard Neustadt, Alan Westin, Roger Hilsman, and Louis Koenig, whose lectures at the Graduate School of Arts and Sciences of Columbia University in 1964–65 introduced me to the central issues involved in the use and abuse of presidential power. The hope is that this work has enough new ideas to justify their investment in my education, but not so much that is different that there would be doubt that I learned anything at all.

The research of several students is incorporated in this book, including the senior essays of Marion Burnbaum, Nancy Cohn, Molly Heines, Joseph Moodhe, and Matthew Nemerson on the budgetary process, Russell Berman on transitions, Victoria de Ganon on the Watergate special prosecutor, David Friend and Lori Root on surveillance, Joel Bennett on the *Mayaguez* incident, Joyce Perlmutter and Ed Ferguson on war powers, Raymond Gietz on the Panama Canal treaties, and the senior scholar thesis of Diane Wallerstein on presidential election campaigns. Nancy Cohn and Shawn McDaniel provided research assistance. Drafts of this book have been tested for several years, and I am grateful to the Barnard and Columbia students who made substantive or stylistic suggestions.

Robert Connery, Demetrios Caraley, and Maryanne Epstein made available to me the collections of the Academy of Political Science. The reference librarians at Barnard and Columbia obtained materials for me, and I appreciate their efforts.

Barnard College awarded me a modest research grant. As always in such cases it is primarily the thought that counts. I am especially grateful to the Donner Foundation for a grant enabling me to put the presidential system in comparative perspective.

James Q. Wilson and Thomas Cronin read the completed manuscript and offered suggestions about style and format for which I am grateful.

Paul Neuthaler helped me conceive this book, and Martin Kessler helped me to complete it. To both of them my thanks for the opportunity to carry the project through. Libby Bruch served as project editor and saved me from many errors.

Credit for the merits of this work I share gladly with colleagues, friends, and former students. In taking responsibility for its defects, the buck stops here.

Morningside Heights
New York City
1979

The American Presidency

Introduction:

Is Presidential Power

Poison?

AMERICANS are ambivalent towards the presidency. We consider the office a unique contribution to the art and science of constitutional democracy. We give the president the authority of chief of government but surround him with checks and balances and competing institutions. We claim he represents the people, but the low turnout of voters in presidential elections makes the definition of *president* in Ambrose Bierce's *Devil's Dictionary* seem apt:

President, n. The leading figure in a small group of men of whom—and of whom only—it is positively known that immense numbers of their countrymen did not want any of them for President.

I

Celebrity and Sun King

Presidents, like the Tibetan Dalai Lama, are rulers in whose name the government acts. We hang their portraits in public buildings, engrave their images on currency and stamps, and name our public works for them. We make shrines of their graves and tourist attractions and national monuments of their homes. We build libraries for their papers under provisions of the Presidential Libraries Act of 1955. The first family becomes part of our popular culture. Children of presidents gravitate toward careers in the media. The White House wives serve as "First Ladies," and Betty Ford became the "First Mama" of the truckers with their citizen band radios. The 1976 Gallup poll of "most admired women" listed Betty Ford first, Mamie Eisenhower seventh, Jacqueline (Kennedy) Onassis tenth, Patricia Nixon twelfth, Rosalyn Carter fourteenth, and Lady Bird Johnson sixteenth. Observing the postelection publicity in 1977, columnist Harriet Van Horne pointed out "We all have our favorites in the most dazzling drama of our time—Jimmy Carter goes to Washington."[1]

We reach out to presidents, whether to touch them at an airport reception or line their route at a motorcade. More than nine million people called the White House during Carter's "Dial-a President" day, and in his first few months in office he was averaging more than twenty thousand incoming calls to the White House daily. Room 59 of the Executive Office Building hums with twelve magnetic-tape selectric typewriters and signature machines finishing form letters responding to incoming mail. Twenty or more "mail analysts" punch up computerized letters, such as PR-70 (responding to prayers for the president and his family) and P-8-14 (replying to chatty letters from children). Tourists troop through the White House at the rate of 1.5 million yearly.

The president's civil service classification is Executive I, entitling him to a salary of $200,000 and $50,000 for expenses. He has at his disposal Air Force One, more than a dozen Boeing 707s and Lockheed Jetstars, eight VH-3 helicopters, and specially constructed Lincoln Continentals with armor plating. Transportation is arranged by the White House Transportation Office, the Secret Service, and the Special Missions Fleet of the 89th Military Airlift Wing at Andrews Air Force Base, whose sole function is to take administration officials anywhere on the globe.

White House grounds are maintained by thirty gardeners, who care for its 18.7 acres, and craftsmen from the National Parks Service who maintain its 123 rooms. Maintenance costs for the mansion came to $2,159,000 in 1978. Recently $5 million was raised by Clement E. Couger, the "Grand Acquisitor" of the curatorial staff, to refurbish twenty-one rooms and restore them to the elegance of the early nineteenth century. The president also uses 180-acre Camp David in the Catoctin Mountains, served by 150 Naval personnel, complete with its heated pool, skeet range, and tennis courts. In recent years the Secret Service and General Services Administration approved large expenditures to upgrade the homes of several presidents for security reasons, although guidelines have been tightened after criticism involving the $3,690,902.80 spent on Nixon's San Clemente and Key Biscayne homes.[2]

Ex-presidents are given a retirement pension of $66,000 annually with an additional nontaxable $96,000 for staff support. The transition from office is eased with a special $1 million grant to cover expenses for the first six months. Ex-presidents and their families receive Secret Service protection, mailing privileges, and government transportation, and may use an official residence at 716 Jackson Place on LaFayette Square, just next to the White House.[3] The ex-president functions in the *ex-presidency*, a quasi-official position supported by public funds that enables him to perform public service, offer advice during crises, or address the Senate.[4] But ex-presidents who have gone into business have been subject to severe criticism for "cashing in" on their careers; once placed upon a pedestal the public prefers that they remain there.

But no president, despite the veneration of the office, ever becomes an absolute monarch or "Sun King" in the manner of French royalty. Americans have a healthy strain of democratic skepticism and even contempt for their leaders. In 1789 proposals for royal salutations, such as "His Highness, the President of the United States of America, Protector of their Liberties," were rejected in favor of the simpler title "Mr. President." Court etiquette was adopted by Washington, but was criticized by anti-Federalists and abandoned by Jefferson. Aristocratic airs proved fatal to John Quincy Adams and Martin Van Buren, each of whom was defeated for reelection by a candidate with the common touch. Presidents are mindful of the observation made by Alexis de Tocqueville over a century ago that "public officers themselves are well aware that the superiority over their fellow citizens which they derive from their authority they enjoy only on condition of putting themselves on a level with the whole community by their manners."[5]

The people will bestow perquisites lavishly on incumbents and ex-presidents, but will not tolerate a president who claims them by right. Nixon's successor referred to himself as "a Ford, not a Lincoln" and hung a portrait of the great commoner Harry Truman in the Oval Office. Carter installed his relative Hugh Carter (nicknamed "Cousin Cheap") as a White House aide with the assignment of "de-pomping" the presidency. The new post-Watergate mood was captured by *Shipmate*, the alumni magazine of the U.S. Naval Academy, which noted that one of the members of the class of 1947 "has accepted a position with the Federal Government . . . appears very pleased with his new position and has indicated that he and Rosalynn expect to be at their new address for at least four years."

While we respect our presidents, we often send them to retirement with sharp public criticism. The most active and successful administrations have had allegations of misconduct, maladministration, or corruption directed against them, including the early presidents whom we now venerate as the fathers of our country. Most incumbents have been charged with negligence, indecision, or even coverups of the wrongdoings of associates.[6] Modern presidents have fared worse. Lyndon Johnson, almost a political outcast after his term of office, retired to his Texas ranch to brood and write his memoirs. In his isolation he might well have reflected on his remark to the Senate many years earlier that "the American people still look to an ex-president for advice, for counsel, and for inspiration in their moments of trial."[7] Richard Nixon, forced to resign from office, was given a presidential pardon as his monument, and to prevent further tampering his presidential papers were removed from his custody and placed in charge of the General Services Administration under the Presidential Recordings and Materials Preservation Act of 1974.[8] The American people can treat their leaders less like Louis XIV and more like King Farouk.

Symbol of the Nation

Our childhood political socialization encourages us to look to the presidency for leadership, especially in crises, and to assume that he represents the nation. Children are taught to recognize the president as an authority figure, on a par with parents or police. The president runs the nation, makes the laws, helps people in trouble, and relies on Congress and the courts as his helpers—at least that is the view from the second grade. He is a combination Washington-Lincoln, making wise decisions, keeping his promises, and working harder than most people. Only children from some poverty subcultures and those interviewed in the immediate aftermath of Watergate revelations offered a picture of the president as malevolent.[9]

We discard adult overlays of skepticism to return to childhood images in times of national emergency. We then seek presidential leadership at once sympathetic and strong. Yet we are not always prepared to follow presidents, especially if we suspect a crisis to have been manufactured or overblown. Following decisions to use force in South Korea and South Vietnam, two presidents divided the nation, weakened their parties, dropped in the polls, declined to run for a second term, and yielded the White House to the opposition. The nation did not rally around Nixon in the recession or Ford or Carter during the energy crisis. Since Watergate the "Hail to the Chief" attitude is mixed in with a "Jail to the Chief" cynicism. Restoring "faith" in the presidency as a symbol of national unity and as an instrument of constitutional government was high on the Ford and Carter agendas.

The Assassination Syndrome

Nothing so vividly demonstrates the central place of the presidency in the political culture as the impact upon us of assassination. When the symbol of national unity is killed, surface attitudes give way to shock, disbelief, anger, and disorientation. Within ninety minutes of the assassination of John F. Kennedy nine-tenths of the public knew that he was dead.[10] Most people felt nervous, tense, dazed, or numbed. Only one-fifth could carry on with their daily routine. Almost half the population reported trouble sleeping for several days. A mother from Houston recalled, "When my little girl came out of school she told me someone killed the President, and her thoughts were—since the President was dead, where would we get our food and clothes from?"[11] People could not believe that such a thing was possible, although Lincoln, Garfield, and McKinley had all been killed, and attempts had been made on the lives of Jackson, both Roosevelts, and Truman. "This just doesn't happen in 1963," a Wesleyan University student told his professor, and a second added, "This sort of thing just isn't done in these United States," comments that say more about the teaching of American history than about what actually happens.[12]

To cope with shock people managed feverish bursts of activity: pollsters began polling, journalists covered "the story" until they dropped with exhaustion, performing artists gave impassioned performances in Kennedy's memory. The public stayed glued to television: 70 percent of sets were tuned to the arrival of Air Force One at Andrews Air Force Base; 85 percent tuned to ceremonies at the Capitol Rotunda; 93 percent tuned to the funeral ceremonies.[13] In effect the American public attended the funeral, permitting a catharsis of grief and anxiety. Former presidents Truman, Eisenhower, and Hoover sat with Lyndon Johnson in church, performing as visible symbols of continuity of political leadership to reassure the public of the stability of the government.

Even when a president dies peacefully in office there are traumatic effects. At the death of Franklin Roosevelt CBS newscaster Robert Trout remarked, "The news is known, but the brain does not quite grasp it," while an obscure Texas congressman, Lyndon Johnson, remembered that "he was just like a daddy to me always; he always talked to me just that way."[14] Roosevelt's biographer James MacGregor Burns, has described the scene in New York City: "At the time of Roosevelt's funeral service in the White House, New York City news presses stopped rolling, radios went silent, subway trains came to a halt, police held up traffic."[15] Nothing in the American experience comes closer to the apocalypse than the death of a president in office.

A presidential assassination may have disruptive effects on the political culture. The Warren Commission concluded that Lee Harvey Oswald acted alone, for irrational reasons, in assassinating Kennedy. But other investigators have found flaws in the investigation and have posed the possibility of a conspiracy. In 1976 Congress reopened the inquiry by establishing the House Select Committee on Assassinations—after revelations by the Senate Committee on Intelligence that the FBI and CIA had withheld important information from the Warren Commission. Notions that Kennedy might have been killed by conspirators are prevalent: Gallup polls conducted in the fall of 1976 indicated that 81 percent of respondents believed that the assassination was committed by more than one person: favorites included Cubans (15 percent), the CIA (4 percent), the Mafia (3 percent), or the Russians (3 percent).[16] The unanswered question—Who killed Kennedy?—remained the time bomb of American politics.

And thirteen years after his assassination, Kennedy topped a poll that asked Americans to name the greatest presidents, closely followed by Lincoln and Franklin Roosevelt.[17]

The Breach of Faith

Politics is the secular religion of America, its martyred presidents are the saints, and the incumbent is the high priest. As Theodore White notes, Americans believe "that no matter how the faith may be betrayed elsewhere, at one particular point—the Presidency—justice will be done beyond prejudice, beyond rancor, beyond the possibility of a fix."[18] Nixon betrayed this trust and shattered the myth, and for that his presidency was destroyed. But faith in the office itself was so strong that it shielded him long after the facts pointed to his complicity in Watergate.

The White House press corps conducted no serious investigation of the break-in prior to the 1972 election, even though a connection had been established between Donald Segretti, the "dirty tricks" operative, and presidential assistant Dwight Chapin. (The reporters who eventually broke the story, Robert Woodward and Carl Bernstein, worked on the metropolitan staff of the *Washington Post*.) Those closest to the president did not insist on hearing the tapes. Not until the Supreme Court ordered the president to turn the tapes over to the special prosecutor did his attorneys hear the conversation of June 23, 1972, the "smoking gun" tape that provided evidence that Nixon had conspired to have the CIA impede the investigation. Only then did Haig, Buzhardt, Buchanan, and other aides persuade the president to resign. For lower-level aides the revelation of Nixon's guilt was "like reading a document and discovering that your own father was not your father."[19]

Congress was reluctant to investigate. A preliminary inquiry into laundered funds conducted by the House Banking and Currency Committee during the election campaign was ignored by most members; Minority Leader Gerald Ford worked with the White House to bury the investigation in the House, convinced that it was being sponsored by Democrats for partisan reasons. Not until Judge John Sirica began to impose lengthy provisional sentences on the Watergate burglars and newspapers began to unearth the story did the Ervin committee in the

Senate conduct hearings. Only after Nixon tampered with the independence of the special prosecutor, forcing the resignation of Attorney General Elliot Richardson, firing Deputy Attorney General Ruckelshaus, and dismissing Special Prosecutor Archibald Cox, did members begin to think in terms of impeachment. Most Republicans informed their leaders after the White House tapes were released that they did not want to vote on an impeachment—at least not before the midterm congressional elections, which were more than one year away.

Members of the House Committee on the Judiciary, assigned to investigate and possibly to report articles of impeachment, agonized over their duty. "I wake up nights," Walter Flowers told his colleagues, "at least on those nights I have been able to go to sleep lately, wondering if this could not be some sordid dream. Impeach the President of the United States!"[20] Most Republicans on the committee defended Nixon, for as Wiley Mayne explained, "the President did try, according to his best judgment, to protect the national security of this country, and the mere fact that he didn't do it perfectly, and got an inexperienced group in there who certainly botched the job and were a great discredit to our country in every respect, that does not mean that he was guilty of a high crime or misdemeanor for which he should be impeached."[21]

The public was also reluctant to drive Nixon from office. In August 1973, after malfeasance of White House staffers had been revealed, polls showed that 60 percent of the public wanted Nixon to remain in office, 20 percent favored resignation, and only 10 percent wanted impeachment. In November 1973, following the resignation of Attorney General Richardson and the firing of Cox, 49 percent wanted the president to remain in office, 29 percent favored resignation, and only 10 percent called for impeachment. Only after the White House released its own version of the tapes in a published transcript, damning Nixon with what Senate Republican Minority Leader Hugh Scott called a "deplorable, disgusting, shabby, immoral performance" did public opinion turn against the president, with a majority, 49 percent to 41 percent favoring his removal from office.[22] As late as February 1975 only 66 percent of the public approved of the Judiciary Committee vote for articles of impeachment.[23] One-third of the public believes that "Nixon's political enemies unfairly exaggerated his actions in order to force him out of office."[24] Would the American people delay judgment so long for the incumbent in any other office?

II

The Ordeal of Power

Even after Watergate, most Americans still favor strong presidential leadership. Walter Mondale, while serving in the Senate, could argue in a book published shortly after Watergate that the president "can become the moral, almost spiritual leader of our country."[25] Theodore White expressed his fear that reforms proposed might make the office too weak, and concluded, "If he [Nixon] has indeed destroyed the powers of a President to lead, he has destroyed all."[26] The columnist Russell Baker represented the viewpoint of a minority when he wrote pointedly at the beginning of the 1976 presidential primary season, "Although Watergate has ruined men, the apparatus of the Superpresidency (along with the machinery of normal government) is still there, and public expectations of the office still seem to make Americans hunger for an ideal man to fill it, which, finally, is what makes our Caesars fatten."[27]

Did we have a Sun King? Was Nixon an aberration, or was he the culmination of the expansion of the presidency well beyond its constitutional boundaries? Do Americans hunger for a Caesar? Do presidents wish to cross a Rubicon?

Americans remain of two minds about the powers of the presidency: excited by its potential for good, yet fearful of the abuse of power. Between 1964 and 1970 the public registered sharp dissatisfaction with the policies of the executive branch, not a surprising finding in view of the rapid pace of social change and the problem of fighting a limited war against intractable foes.[28] In the 1970s dissatisfaction about policies was superseded by a pervasive mistrust of leaders and a questioning of their uses of power. People wondered about the legitimacy of the system: were officials fair? Did they act within the confines of the Constitution and the laws? A segment of the public believed that the conduct of officials at the highest level was *normless*: fundamentally outside of and apart from the constitutional process. Between 1966 and 1971 pollster Louis Harris reported a drop in answers indicating "a great deal of confidence" in the executive branch from 41 percent to 23 percent. At the end of Carter's first year in office he found that a 44 percent to 43 percent plurality believed the White House to be "mostly out of touch" with the country. Similarly between 1972 and 1974 other polls conducted during the Watergate crisis found drops in positive answers to the question, "How much trust and confidence do you have in the executive branch of the federal government?" down from 76 percent to 42 percent.[29]

Americans pay heed to the warning of the Supreme Court over a century ago that "wicked men, ambitious of power, with hatred of liberty and contempt of law, may fill the place once occupied by Washington and Lincoln."[30] The words of historian Henry Adams remain apt: this son and grandson of presidents took notice of the corrupt cabinet of spoilsmen assembled by Grant and remarked that "the progress of evolution from President Washington to President Grant was alone evidence enough to upset Darwin."[31] "Your President is not a crook," insisted Nixon, but a more accurate assessment comes from the *London Spectator*, which observed that Americans had gone from "George Washington, who could not tell a lie, to Richard Nixon, who cannot tell the truth."[32] Many Americans believed that several presidents could not tell the difference.

The institution of the presidency is a bit like the White House itself. On the outside it is a gleaming white palace, its elegant lines and carefully tended gardens and lawns the showpiece of the nation, radiating an impression of positive and decisive government. But the mansion smells of the rot of a building approaching the end of its second century of use: periodically it is surveyed and found to be infested with insects and vermin.[33] The presidency no less than the mansion should be inspected and renovated every so often.

"What this country needs," former White House assistant Arthur Schlesinger advises us, is "a little serious disrespect for the office of the Presidency."[34] Commentary about the office runs in cycles. Just a few short years after Abraham Lincoln had been "canonized," Henry Adams could look at Grant's conduct and claim that "power is poison" and "its effects on Presidents has always been tragic."[35] Like keystone cops in the silent movies, the whole pack of political scientists, historians, journalists, and former presidential aides first praise and then damn the presidency, depending on current fashion. In 1963 Theodore Sorensen celebrated the decision-making processes of the Kennedy White House, but by 1975 warned of "Camelot-like glorifications of the Presidency."[36] Other White House aides, including Schlesinger, have offered their own mea culpa.

Yet one recurring theme remains: the presidents who go down in the history books as "great" are those who reach for power, who assert their authority to the limit. The incumbent remains the Great White Father, the Leader of the Free World, and as Clinton Rossiter notes, he carries on his shoulders certain expectations because he follows the path of presidents who came before:

Lincoln is the supreme myth, the richest symbol in the American experience. He is, as someone has remarked neither irreverently nor sacrilegiously, the martyred Christ of democracy's passion play. And who, then, can measure the strength that is given to the President because he holds Lincoln's office, lives in Lincoln's house, and walks in Lincoln's way? The final greatness of the Presidency lies in the truth that it is not just an office of incredible power but a breeding ground of indestructible myth.[37]

The myth is indestructible but the successor incumbents are not. The ghosts of presidents past haunt incumbents. How can any president live up to Lincoln's myth. Who can follow a martyred Christ? Eisenhower chafed under comparisons with Franklin Roosevelt, Johnson became enraged when compared with Roosevelt, Truman, or Kennedy. "What do they want—what really do they want?" he complained to his court historian, Eric Goldman, "I am giving them boom times and more good legislation than anybody else did, and what do they do—attack and sneer."[38] Always there is the burden of office, which takes its toll on the health and well-being of the incumbent. Men spend their lives seeking the presidency, only to complain of its burdens once in the Oval Office. The incumbent always must defend the institution and leave it stronger than he found it, lest he be thought less than "presidential." The line between a leader of a democracy and an imperial Caesar may become blurred, especially when myths of past presidents intersect with exigencies of current crises.

III

The Textbook Presidencies

We identify the presidency with the resolution of great crises: Roosevelt—the Depression and the Second World War; Truman—the use of the atom bomb, the Marshall Plan and the Berlin Airlift, the Korean War; Eisenhower—the Korean armistice, the Suez and Hungarian crises, the summit conferences; Kennedy—the Berlin Wall, the Bay of Pigs, the Missile Crisis, the Test Ban Treaty; Johnson—the Vietnam War, the Civil Rights Movement, the Six Days War; Nixon—the visit to China, detente with the Soviet Union, the escalation of the war in Vietnam, the Cambodia invasion; Ford—the evacuation of Vietnam, the Mayaguez, the Vladivostok Summit. Carter—the Camp David accords, college textbooks, and general treatments of the presidency tend to focus on these major events. They adopt either a benevolent or malevolent model of the presidency, and at this point it is useful to describe the major assumptions underlying each model.

The Benevolent President: Nominated by the party rank-and-file and elected by a popular majority, the president prepares a program based on his campaign themes. He relies on persuasion and influence to enlist various economic, geographic, and public interest groups to support his programs. He governs by consensus rather than relying on his formal powers, preferring to persuade rather than mandate. He persuades others in government to act on their own authority in ways compatible to his purposes. As the only official elected by the nation, he governs from a unique vantage point, blending political considerations with the expertise of the departments to make decisions in the national interest. His decisions are viable and pragmatic, and worthy of public support. His choices are made after vigorous debate among the best minds in the nation, whom he has attracted into his advisory system. The president remains accountable to the people because he is ennobled by the responsibilities of the office, and accepts democratic values. He is the protector of civil liberties at home and human rights abroad, and is the symbol of the nation and the liberty and justice for which it stands.[39]

The Malevolent President: Nominated by media manipulation in the primaries and deals at the convention, the president's platform and public statements represent neither his past record nor his future purposes accurately. He is backed by special interest groups seeking to gain advantage from his election. The contest is a parody of democracy, since the winner is chosen by a small percentage of the eligible electorate which has been brainwashed by the media. The incumbent rules through assertion of his prerogatives, carrying them beyond the limits set by the Constitution. He relies on command rather than persuasion, and cares little about bargaining or consensus-building. He often acts against the recommendations of the advisory system and isolates himself from cabinet and congressional leaders. He centralizes power in the White House staff, which in turn imposes a chain of command on the departments. He successfully uses surveillance, intimidation, secrecy systems, and dirty tricks to destroy his political enemies, converting the FBI, CIA, and IRS into secret "political police." He is secretive, deceitful, and governs by fait accomplis. He does not internalize democratic norms, nor does he look for public support. He is neurotic and possibly psychotic. His ambitions are imperial: he converts colleagues into subordinates and foreign allies into dependencies. He tries to overthrow or even assassinate leaders of unfriendly nations. While outward constitutional forms are maintained, they are perverted in practice and the office becomes an "imperial presidency."[40]

These are the two main models of the presidency, but there are several others that should be noted. In the model of the *co-opted* president the White House is controlled by national security managers recruited from the corporate-military-university "power elite" that controls national security policy. The elite makes the crucial decisions, and the president's major function is to serve as their "front man" and win public support for their initiatives.[41] Then there is the model of the *amateur*: the president is passive in office, and power flows to his aides or to strong members of the cabinet who may function as "prime ministers" for foreign or domestic affairs. The president has no stomach for political infighting, has no appreciation for the sources of his power, and prefers to delegate authority and share it with the other branches. He presides over the government but does not run it, and officials, abhorring the vacuum, move to take charge.[42] Both the co-opted president and the amateur president are *irrelevant*—however personally benevolent they might be as individuals.

Presidential Power

No single model of the presidency is accurate. Consistency is not the chief trait of presidents; nor, it might be added, is it the trait of those who would write about them. Most textbook literature generalizes from short-range trends. Eisenhower was perceived to be a weak president, either amateur or co-opted, so commentators focused on ways in which a president could increase his power by relying on influence and reputation. In the midst of the Kennedy and Johnson administrations, analysts argued that presidents could be effective catalysts for social change and urban reconstruction. In the later stages of Johnson's presidency, and during Nixon's presidency, the office was described as swollen with excess personnel and imperial powers. With Carter, observers have come full circle, concentrating less on curbing abuses of power and more on discovering sources of influence with a seemingly intractable legislature and bureaucracy.

No one model of the presidency, no one notion of its "evolution" as an office, can explain how incumbents function or how the office works. The presidency may be an instrument for representative democracy, benevolent autocracy, or malevolent Caesarism—depending on the interplay of constitutional interpretation, institutional competition, and personality and leadership qualities of the incumbent.

While no model is likely to work in all circumstances, it is possible, by carefully describing the powers and processes, to construct generalizations about the *probabilities* of power: the conditions under which the president will have influence, the circumstances in which checks and balances are likely to be employed, the periods in which the party system and public opinion will support or desert him. It is a hopeless enterprise to attempt to construct a single grand theory of presidential power on a deterministic basis; however, it is within our powers to offer important generalizations that offer a high degree of probability in specific circumstances.

To develop these generalizations it is necessary to consider the following issues:

1. *The Sources of Power*: Of what does presidential power consist? Constitutional authority? Powers delegated by Congress? A mandate from the people? Powers of persuasion?
2. *The Accountability of Power*: To whom is the president accountable? The electorate? The legislative party? Can he claim his election was a plebiscite, permitting him to take whatever actions he thinks necessary in the national interest?
3. *The Limits of Power*: How well does the system of checks and balances

work? Can we rely on the cabinet, legislative party leaders, and career officials to serve as "extraconstitutional" checks? Under what circumstances should the president deploy emergency powers?

4. *The Uses of Power*: What do presidents do well? What functions might better be performed by other institutions? Do the advisory systems serve the president adequately? How can the president improve his management of general government? How can he better manage economic and foreign affairs?

5. *The Locus of Power*: Who governs? Does the president make decisions, or is he a "clerk" for officials who use his formal powers for their purposes? Is there a "power elite" that controls national security policymaking, especially decisions concerning peace or war?

Towards a Theory of Presidential Power

To provide an updated description of the presidency this book builds upon recent scholarship in political science, other social and behavioral sciences, history, and constitutional law. Advances in the methodology of the behavioral sciences, especially for voting and public opinion studies, enables us to specify the relationship between presidential power and electoral and public support for the incumbent. Constitutional lawyers and historians have provided major studies of the formal powers of the office, and recent events have forced the reconsideration of interpretations involving impeachments, impoundments, executive privilege, delegation of powers, vetoes, and war powers. The Pentagon papers and White House transcripts, coupled with the memoirs of officials in the Kennedy, Johnson, and Nixon administrations, offer new insights into the functioning of the presidency in crises, and the routine workings of the Executive Office agencies and the White House Office have been studied in great detail by political scientists and various commissions. Detailed research by political scientists on the programming, legislative clearance, budgetary, enrolled bill, and administrative processes have all been utilized here to provide a full description of how the presidency functions.

This book also develops a new theory of presidential power. Prior works emphasized one of three approaches: some used a historical approach and dealt with power as a consequence of the political position of the incumbent, focusing on electoral results, partisan lineups in Congress, and the mobilization of public opinion; others used the methods of the constitutional lawyers and dealt with the formal powers of the office, placing presidential power in the context of the system of checks and balances, and providing a listing of the formal authority of the president, including a statement of the limits that the constitution or laws placed on his powers; still other works used case studies or psychological approaches and considered leadership and personality factors, focusing on those characteristics that might enable a president to lead Congress and his administration by persuasion and influence.

The argument here is that the political factors are least significant in determining what a president can accomplish. Election results, party lineups in Congress, the mobilization of public opinion—these factors all affect presidential power at the margins, but do not determine its use or set its limits. This book uses the public law and case study approaches and combines them with fairly detailed analysis of various processes, in order to develop a dynamic model that specifies circumstances under which the authority of an incumbent will increase or decrease, and the conditions that must obtain for presidential power to be institutionalized and incorporated into the workings of the political system.

The theory here specifies that the key to an understanding of presidential power is to concentrate on the constitutional authority that the president asserts unilaterally through various rules of constitutional construction and interpretation, in order to resolve crises or important issues facing the nation. In response to the presidential use of prerogatives, Congress and the courts may acquiesce in the context of an authentic emergency. But the other branches may also react negatively under certain circumstances. If they do, the courts may check the president (though this is rare), and Congress may strengthen the system of checks and balances by legislating a new set of processes (under its own constitutional authority) that forces the president to interact and collaborate with the legislature. In certain exceptional cases the president will confront congressional majorities intent on limiting his prerogatives, and the result of the conflict may involve the collapse of the administration and a fundamental restructuring of the relationships between the branches of government.

The president's use of his constitutional prerogatives, as he himself defines them, sets the stage for Congress, the courts, and the party system to provide "feedback" that may profoundly alter the contours of the presidential office—either by expanding or contracting the limits of the formal powers—and that may also result in fundamental restructuring of the programming, legislative, budgetary, and administrative processes. The theory developed here attempts to provide an explanation for changes in processes and functions of the presidency by placing these changes primarily in the context of the constitutional authority of the office rather than by focusing on the relatively less significant electoral and partisan factors.

The sources of presidential power are considered historically in chapter 1, which focuses on the creation of the presidency in 1787. The framers did not confine or limit presidential power, which left the way clear for incumbents to assert, unilaterally, constitutional authority to resolve the most important issues facing the nation. The pattern that has developed is explored in chapter 2, which explores the tension between *prerogative government* that presidents may establish to deal with crisis situations, and the checks and balances system that Congress may apply in reaction to what it considers to be presidential excesses. It is the thesis of this chapter that the fundamental and irreducible core of presidential power rests not on influence, persuasion, public opinion, elections, or party, but rather on the successful assertion of constitutional authority to resolve crises and significant domestic issues. The conditions under which presidents succeed or fail in deploying their prerogatives are also considered.

The failure of the president to exploit other sources of power, and his weakness as a popular, party, legislative, and administrative leader are examined in chapters 3–7. The central argument here is that presidents must rely on their constitutional prerogatives because they cannot obtain an electoral mandate, do not gain control of party machinery, fail to lead their legislative parties, and cannot obtain expertise from the advisory systems that would permit them to lead Congress and the nation by force of argument.

The concluding chapters, 8–11, explore presidential influence and leadership in the budget process, fiscal policymaking, the management of foreign relations, and war making. The purpose of this exploration is to examine the interplay of prerogative government with the checks and balances system, and to see how presidential initiatives have been matched by congressional and departmental responses. Much restructuring of the decision-making processes has occurred in recent years, which has affected the influence of the president and the contours of the presidential office. The concluding chapter will examine some of the constitutional and institutional dimensions of these changes and offer a forecast of things to come.

The Creation

of the Presidency

THE thirty-nine signers of the Constitution and the hundreds of state convention delegates who ratified it did not promote a new form of government to satisfy an abstract political theory. The framers were men of affairs, who sought to advance their fortunes and careers as well as the interests of their states. They proposed a new form of government because they were convinced that the existing one could not preserve the states and territories against European powers, maintain domestic order and protect private property, promote commerce among the states and with other nations, or defend settlements and encourage industry.

The Constitution was an experiment crafted by politicians who made pragmatic accommodations to achieve common purposes. Within this experiment was contained another: the presidential office, embodying civil, secular, executive power without recourse to monarchy. The creation of the presidency was a response to the failure of the Articles of Confederation, which provided no real executive branch. It was also firmly grounded in almost two hundred years of colonial and state experience with the use and abuse of executive power. The presidency was an experiment, but the ideas about power on the basis of which it was formed represented a distillation of the best of the American political tradition.

I

Failure of Confederation

"Our situation is becoming every day more and more critical," James Madison wrote to Virginia's Governor Randolph from the Continental Congress. "No money comes into the federal treasury; no respect is paid to the federal authority; and people of reflection unanimously agree that the existing confederacy is tottering to its foundation."[1] In the Northwest Territory the British had not evacuated their garrisons according to the treaty ending the Revolutionary War, and they sent no envoy to the Confederacy, not recognizing it as a sovereign state. The Spanish in Florida concluded alliances with Indian tribes and threatened settlers in Georgia. After the British incited tribal attacks on western settlements, Congress, pleading lack of funds, turned down a proposal from the secretary of war to build forts for defense.[2] Pirates in the Mediterranean menaced Yankee shipping with impunity, for there was no American navy to punish them. The talk among politicians in 1786 was of three regional confederacies, linked to each other by treaties, in place of the Confederation.

The government could not maintain order. In 1782 army units quartered at Newburgh, New York, threatened to mutiny over back pay. In 1783 other troops ransacked arsenals in Philadelphia and forced Congress to flee to Princeton while the Pennsylvania militia put down the mutineers.[3] So long as pay claims remained unsettled, the army would remain a volatile force, but Congress could not devise a funding plan acceptable to the states. Officers might take bribes from foreign powers; the highest-ranking army general, James Wilkinson, was in the pay of the Spanish.

Without a reliable army, Congress could not intervene decisively in struggles between debtors and creditors, such as the armed conflict in Massachusetts in 1786. The state legislature passed laws that made hard currency the sole legal tender and that empowered the judiciary to enforce judgments for debt against farmers in the western part of the state. Debtors prevented the state court from sitting in the west to render judgment, and at Springfield, twelve hundred followers of Captain Daniel Shays, a hero of the revolutionary war, faced down nine hundred troops of the state militia. Both sides withdrew from the area after an agreement was reached that the state judges would return to Boston without rendering decisions against debtors. Eventually militia from several states combined to put down this "rebellion," but not before the national government had demonstrated its impotence. Congress did not have funds to pay for a military force to defend the national arsenal at

Springfield, which almost led to its capture by Shay's forces. The only help Congress provided was the loan of rifle and cannon from the arsenal to the Massachusetts militia, and even then the War Department insisted that the state pay for cleaning and storing the weapons after their use.[4]

The performance of Congress had a profound effect on men of property. Washington, responding to a plea from Congress that he use influence with Shay to end the rebellion, replied, "I know not where that influence is to be found, or if attainable, that it would be the proper remedy for the disorders. Influence is no government. Let us have one by which our lives, liberties, and properties will be secured, or let us know the worst at once."[5] Disorders in several states in 1786 spurred political leaders to correspond with one another to consider changes in the governmental system. As Washington wrote to Jefferson just prior to the convention, "The situation of the General Government (if it can be called a government) is shaken to its foundations and liable to be overset by every blast—In a word, it is at an end, and unless a remedy is soon applied, anarchy and confusion will inevitably ensue."[6]

Throughout the 1780s men of continental vision had proposed a stronger central government, for they intended to promote commerce among the states by ending state import duties. They also favored a tax system that would provide revenues for a navy to protect shipping and promote exports and a protective tariff that would discourage imports of manufactures. Land speculators like Washington expected a new national government to protect western settlers, thus increasing the values of their properties. Speculators in national and state securities hoped a new government would assume these obligations at face value. Some financial interests wanted a national banking system: a struggle in Pennsylvania between 1783 and 1787 over the rechartering of the Bank of North America convinced them that only a strong national government, empowered to create a national bank, could provide for the needs of industry and commerce.[7]

Most of the authority to implement these economic goals would be given to Congress if a new form of government were instituted. But some of the confederation's problems were due to the absence of a strong executive, and by 1787 many politicians representing landed, commercial, and financial interests, were prepared to create an executive branch. Washington corresponded with several national leaders in 1786–87, asking them to propose ideas for a new national government. He was particularly impressed with ideas submitted by Secretary of War Knox and by John Jay, both of whom called for the creation of an executive branch led by a "Governor General."[8]

Executive Power in the Confederation

The Articles of Confederation and Perpetual Union, adopted in 1781, made no mention of an executive branch. In 1777 the Continental Congress had specifically *rejected* a plan for an executive proposed in the "Dickinson Draft." That plan would have provided for a "Council of State" appointed by Congress and for other officers "for managing the general affairs of the United States." The council would sit while Congress was in session and continue during its recesses, exercising broad powers: command of the military, administration of finances and diplomacy, and "the Execution of such Measures as may be resolved on by the United States."[9]

The version of the Articles that the Continental Congress adopted provided for a weak Congress and no executive. Almost as an afterthought the Articles provided for a "Committee of States" to sit only when Congress was in recess. The powers of the committee were limited: it was "to execute in the recess of Congress, such of the powers of Congress as the United States, in Congress assembled, shall by the consent of nine states, from time to time, think expedient to vest them with . . . ."[10] The committee was prohibited from exercising military, diplomatic, or fiscal powers.

Government operations were left to ad hoc or standing committees of Congress, supplemented by boards operating under their direction. The Marine Committee dealt with the navy, the Board of War and Ordnance with the army, the Committee of Secret Correspondence handled diplomacy. Men who wished for energetic administration, like James Duane and Alexander Hamilton, proposed establishing departments with single secretaries, but at first Congress resisted, even replacing the superintendent of finance, Robert Morris, with a treasury board. Hamilton wrote to Duane in 1780 that "Congress is properly a deliberative corps, and it forgets itself when it attempts to play the executive."[11] By 1781 several departments were created, among them Foreign Affairs, War, Marine, and Treasury, but no executive or council gave direction to the departments, boards, and agencies, and results remained chaotic. Congress insisted that the secretaries report to it and take its directions. The secretary of war was "to give his opinion on all such subjects as shall be referred to him by Congress," the superintendent of finance was "to digest and report plans for improving and regulating the finances and for establishing order and economy in the expenditure of the public money," while the secretary of foreign affairs was to "report on all cases expressly referred to him for that purpose by Congress."[12] The departments were mere appendages of the legislature, not an executive branch. Presidents of the congresses were simply presiding officers of the legislature: the common use of the term *president* in the eighteenth century emphasized this function, almost to the exclusion of any executive powers. Presidents served one-year terms, and they were usually men whose talents and reputations matched their office.

The Experience of the States

While government under the Articles was, according to Noah Webster, "but a name, and our confederation a cobweb," the mechanisms of colonial and state government provided several alternatives.[13] State politicians could draw on their experiences in using systems of separation of powers. The fifty-five delegates to the Constitutional Convention were immersed in that experience: thirty-nine had served in the congresses, forty had been state officeholders (including seven chief executives and ten judges), and eight had played major roles in drafting state constitutions. They were aware of the works of leading European political theorists such as John Locke and Baron de Montesquieu, who justified the separation of powers as a bulwark against tyranny.[14]

Separation of powers evolved in the provincial governments in the seventeenth century because governors could not simultaneously represent the interests of the Crown, the wealthy proprietors, and colonists. Governors and judiciaries took the part of the Crown, while assemblies represented settlers. Between 1660 and 1730 different institutions began to exercise different powers; the assemblies began to sit apart from the governors and passed legislation on their own initiative. Between 1730 and 1750 the governors' councils constituted themselves into "upper houses" of the legislatures (the assemblies becoming the "lower houses"), primarily to represent the interests of landed gentry and merchants. By 1750 the representation of social and economic interests through separate political institutions exercising different functions was well established.

Colonists also developed a system of checks and balances.[15] Legislation was subject to absolute veto by the governor. Clashes between governors and assemblies over appointments and direction of the militia were regular features of colonial politics, and governors often traded their formal powers for funds needed to carry on their administrations. A governor who ignored the assembly in filling offices might find that it had refused to vote funds to pay salaries—including his own. Although the governor was captain-general and vice admiral of the colony's forces, the assemblies often placed officers of their choice in command and determined military strategy in wars against the Indians and French. But as Benjamin Franklin recounted at the Constitutional Convention, governors also had powers:

No good law could be passed without a private bargain with him. An increase in his salary, or some donation, was always made a condition; till at last it became the regular practice to have orders in his favor on the Treasury presented along with the bills to be signed, so that he might actually receive the former before he signed the latter.[16]

Colonists were familiar with a system of legislative supremacy. The period between 1763 and 1774, during which governors carried out British tax and regulatory policies based on "Orders in Council" issued by the Crown, was a departure from the established norm. During the Revolution the pattern of legislative dominance reasserted itself in the formation of the state governments.[17] Framers of state governments provided for weak executive branches, which were restricted to carrying out the will of the legislature. The Virginia Constitution of 1776 restricted the powers of the governor in the following provision:

He shall, with the advice of a Council of State, exercise the executive powers of government, according to the laws of this Commonwealth, and shall not, under any pretence, exercise any power or prerogative, by virtue of any law, statute, or custom of England.

In Massachusetts the governor was checked by a nine-member privy council, whose assent was required for appointments, vetoes, and disbursements of funds. In most states the governor had no veto or appointment power, and in all he was checked by a council. In New England states and in New York, governors were elected by the voters, but in other states they were elected by the legislature. All states provided for removal of the governor by impeachment.

State constitutions did provide that the governor and executive department constituted a separate branch of government with some independent powers. Governors had a veto over laws, and some had the power of appointment. New York gave its governor "the Supreme Executive Power and Authority" and New Jersey granted its governor "the Supreme Executive Power." In New York, Pennsylvania, and Vermont they were required to faithfully execute the laws. In every state they were commander-in-chief of the militia, although legislatures made the appointments and promotions to military office.

Delegates to the Constitutional Convention were most impressed with the New York Constitution of 1777, for it provided for a strong governor. He was elected by freeholders rather than chosen by the legislature; served for three years and was eligible for reelection. He could exercise, in conjunction with a Council of Revision, a veto over legislation he thought "inconsistent with the spirit of the Constitution or with the public good." Governor George Clinton used this power to veto fifty-eight bills, at one point using his constitutional power to dismiss the legislature. By dominating the Council on Appointments, Clinton controlled patronage and thus the executive departments. He commanded the militia effectively and helped put down both Shay's Rebellion and the "Doctors' Riots" in New York City.

Not coincidentally, the drafters of the New York Constitution—

Gouverneur Morris, John Livingston, and John Jay—were among those politicians most in favor of a strong executive branch for the national government. Similarly, men of property in Pennsylvania, the "Republican" faction in state politics, led by James Wilson and Robert Morris, attempted to revise their state constitution to provide for a "principal executive magistrate" to replace the existing Executive Council. They failed to win their point, but were to exert considerable pressure at the Constitutional Convention in favor of a strong presidency. These men and others had come to believe that a strong executive was needed at both the state and national levels. These men recognized that executive power, when checked and balanced, might guard against autocratic rule. John Adams in 1785 could defend the separation of powers embodied in state governments against the attacks of European commentators by pointing with pride to the creation of "a multitude of curious and ingenious inventions to balance, in their turn, all those powers, to check the passions peculiar to them, and to control them from rushing into the exorbitancies to which they are most addicted."[18]

Rejection of Monarchy

The monarchical form was the obvious model for executive power on a national scale. But George Washington, the obvious choice to be king, demonstrated his fidelity to republican principles by spurning the invitation to lead the Newburgh Mutiny and by warning his followers, especially his former military aide Alexander Hamilton, against monarchist intrigues.[19] No American pretender or European prince could establish himself without the support of the army, the ex-officers of the Society of the Cincinnati, and the state politicians, all of whom looked at Washington. A monarchy would require an established church and a titled nobility, neither of which existed in America. The radicals, debtors, and others who had insisted on weak central government would be unlikely to suffer patiently the ceremonial extravagance of transplanted royalty and nobility. For that matter, neither Yankee merchant nor Tidewater planter would relish paying taxes to support a royal court. What monies could be raised by Congress would be needed for the assumption of debts and the settlement of the back pay issue with the army. The men of property in America intended to make their fortunes through commerce, finance, speculation, and agricultural development. To institute a monarchy would mean a return to feudal privilege and franchises, which would be controlled by a king and his court. The American elites preferred elective politics and capitalist enterprise rather than monarchy and mercantilism.

WASHINGTON REJECTS MONARCHY

What astounding changes a few years are capable of producing. I am told that even respectable characters speak of a monarchical form of government without horror. From thinking proceeds speaking; thence to acting is often but a single step. But how irrevocable and tremendous! What a triumph for the advocates of despotism to find that we are incapable of governing ourselves, and that systems founded on the basis of equal liberty are merely ideal and fallacious! Would to God that wise measures be taken in time to avert the consequences we have but too much reason to apprehend.

George Washington to John Jay, August 1, 1786.

II

Choices for the Convention

The framers had several alternatives. One was to create a "Council of States" as a plural executive to administer departments. Such a weak executive would be part of a system of legislative supremacy in the national government. As Roger Sherman put it,

He considered the Executive Magistracy as nothing more than an institution for carrying the will of the legislature into effect, that the person or persons ought to be appointed by the acceptible to the legislature only, which was the depository of the supreme will of Society.[20]

Another was to create an executive branch that would share power with the legislature subject to a system of checks and balances. Finally, a strong executive might be given independent grants of power and assume the function, if not the shape, of a monarchy, invested with prerogative powers of the British Crown. Most delegates were prepared to go beyond the first alternative and consider a system of separated institutions. But as the convention opened few were prepared to give such a branch an equal share in governing powers with the legislature, and hardly any expected that the executive would exercise prerogative powers.

Some convention leaders favored a greatly strengthened executive. George Washington well knew the difficulties of dealing with Congress in matters of war and diplomacy. His host at the convention, Robert Morris, had had difficulties in dealing with the legislature as superintendent of continental finances. Alexander Hamilton believed that the British Constitution was "the best in the world," and hoped to provide the executive with some crown prerogatives.[21] Hamilton worked with Gouverneur Morris (his partner in founding the Bank of New York) and James Wilson (counsel for the Bank of North America) in obtaining support of financial elites for a strong executive. In 1786 these men founded the Society for Political Inquiries to consider the problems of the confederation. Now they were ready to put into action their plans for fundamental reform.

Other delegates were less sure of their position on executive power. James Madison, the "father" of the Constitution, was attracted to a system of checks and balances in which a stronger executive would remain subordinate to the legislature. Under the prodding of Washington and Wilson he moved in the direction of a stronger executive. Eventually he was to warn of "a tendency in our governments to throw all power into the legislative vortex," which was reason to strengthen the executive as a check against congressional autocracy.[22]

A majority of the convention delegates were "congressionalists," skeptical of arguments of men like Wilson and Hamilton. These men included Virginia Governor Edmund Randolph, Elbridge Gerry of Massachusetts, and John Dickinson of Pennsylvania. They intended to expand the powers of the national legislature rather than provide new authority to an executive branch. They would be outmaneuvered at the convention, especially on the committees drafting Article II, until by the close of the proceedings a greatly strengthened executive branch had been included in the Constitution.

Popular Connections

Convention deliberations began with Robert Morris's motion, carried unanimously, to elect Washington the presiding officer. At Hamilton's suggestion the motion was adopted that the convention deliberate in secrecy. The result of these motions was that the delegates could consider major changes in the form of government without being influenced by public opinion. It was obvious from the start that the delegates expected Washington to lead the new government. All deliberations about the form of a new executive branch were debates in part over powers to be accorded Washington. Pierce Butler, a "congressionalist" delegate, later observed that the powers of the presidency would not have been so great "had not many of the members cast their eyes toward General Washington as President; and shaped their ideas of the Powers to be given a President, by their opinions of his Virtue." Washington lobbied delegates for a strong executive, and his votes as a member of the Virginia delegation always supported proposals granting the executive maximum authority.

The convention began work with the "Virginia Plan," which increased

7. Resd. that a National Executive be instituted; to be chosen by the National Legislature for the term of _____ years, to receive punctually at stated times, a fixed compensation for the services rendered, in which no increase or diminution shall be made so as to affect the Magistracy, existing at the time of increase or diminution, and to be ineligible a second time; and that besides a general authority to execute the National laws, it ought to enjoy the Executive rights vested in Congress by the Confederation.

8. Resd. that the Executive and a convenient number of the National Judiciary, ought to compose a council of revision with authority to examine every act of the National Legislature before it shall operate, & every act of a particular legislature before a Negative thereon shall be final; and that the dissent of the said Council shall amount to a rejection, unless to Act of the National Legislature be again passed, or that of a particular Legislature be again negatived by _____ of the members of each branch.

the powers of the legislature, provided for a congressional veto over state laws (a proposal designed by Madison), and created a "National Executive" consisting of several officials elected by Congress. The authority of the executive would derive solely from "the Executive rights vested in Congress," so the executive would be simply an agent of the legislature with no independent authority. Its only check on Congress would be the veto over laws passed (and over the "negative" that Congress exercised over state laws), but even this power was to be shared with a Council of Revision consisting of members of the judiciary. Congress could repass the law or the negative over the veto, and it would then go into effect. The plan provided for a seven-year term of office with no reelection. In theory the executive would have no incentive to conspire with factions in the legislature to ensure reelection. But the executive would not be accountable to the legislature or to the people.[23]

The "presidentialists" tried to replace the plural executive with a single official. James Wilson argued that a single executive would promote responsibility for administration and clear accountability for conduct in office. This proposal alarmed diehard congressionalists; Edmund Randolph remarked that "he regarded it as the foetus of monarchy," while after the proposal passed Colonel Mason warned, "We are not indeed constituting a British Government, but a more dangerous monarchy, an elective one."[24] After two weeks of debate the convention approved an article calling for a single executive, chosen for a seven-year term by Congress, ineligible for reelection, with powers derived solely from the legislature and a veto that could be overridden only by a two-thirds vote of each house.[25]

James Wilson and Gouverneur Morris fought to make the president accountable to the electorate. They argued that legislative election opened the unpleasant possibility of foreign or domestic conspiracy, for as Morris pointed out, "If the legislature elect, it will be the work of intrigue, of cabal, and of faction: it will be like the election of the Pope by a conclave of cardinals; real merit will rarely be title to the appointment."[26]

Presidentialists proposed that the president be given a shorter term, be made eligible for reelection, and be made accountable to a popular electorate. But no plan calling for direct election by propertied freeholders (the restricted electorate the framers referred to when talking about "the people") could pass the convention, although as Morris hinted, "If the people should elect, they will never fail to prefer some man of distinguished character, or services; some man, if he might so speak, of continental reputation."[27] Even this reference to Washington did not move the convention. Colonel Mason of Virginia expressed the prevailing sentiment when he cracked that "it would be as unnatural to refer the choice of a proper character for chief magistrate to the people, as it would to refer a trial of colors to a blind man."[28]

Wilson's solution was to entrust the selection of the executive to *electors* chosen by the states. The election would be removed from Congress, ensuring executive independence, and from the people (this gave the proposal a chance to pass the convention). But a coalition of small-state and congressionalist delegates defeated proposals for an "electoral college."[29] Those who favored such a system found a way to break the coalition: they proposed that instead of each *state* casting a vote in Congress to elect the president, each legislator in the House would cast a vote, thus ensuring a majority for the large states if the system of legislative election of the executive were retained. The small-state delegates then declared their opposition to legislative election, and the issue was referred to a Committee on Postponed Matters for resolution.

The committee was dominated by delegates favoring a strong executive. It reported its compromise to the convention: a college of electors, meeting separately in each state, would choose the president. In the event no candidate received a majority, the final choice would be made by the Senate, where each state would cast an equal number of votes.[30] The convention delegates assumed that after the certain election of Washington, no candidate would subsequently obtain a majority of the electoral college vote, and they calculated that elections would be decided by the Senate. In effect the electoral college would nominate five contenders, and the Senate would then choose the president from among them. The convention approved the plan, but replaced the Senate with the House, where each state delegation would cast a single vote in the contingency election of the president.[31] The convention had finally cut loose from the notion that the president should be politically accountable to the legislature rather than to the people.

Enumerating the Powers

Presidentialists tried to provide the office with general and specific enumerated powers granted directly by the Constitution. The president must be able to act on his own authority, for otherwise Congress could cut him down. In addition to the veto power of the Virginia Plan, the subsequent New Jersey proposals added that the executive "would appoint all federal officers not otherwise provided for" and would "direct all military operations."[32] Later the Committee on Detail, chaired by James Wilson, provided several enumerated powers. The president was to appoint officers otherwise not provided for, give Congress information on the state of the union and recommend measures for its consideration, receive ambassadors, grant reprieves and pardons, convene Congress on extraordinary occasions, take care that the laws be faithfully executed, command the armed forces, and command the militia when called into federal service.[33] These provisions were authored by Wilson, and based in part on a draft written by Charles Pinckney, which in turn had been inspired by the provisions of the New York State Constitution.[34] The Committee on Postponed Matters added the power to appoint, by and with the advice and consent of the Senate, ambassadors and justices of the Supreme Court, and provided that the president "may require the opinion in writing of the principal officer in each of the executive departments, upon any subject relating to the duties of their respective offices."[35] No longer would department heads report only to Congress.

Just as important as these enumerated powers was the provision offered by the Committee on Detail that "the Executive Power of the United States shall be vested in a single person." Gouverneur Morris, chairman of the Committee on Style, later revised this into the opening words of Article II, "The Executive Power shall be vested in a President of the United States of America." This version made it clear that the powers of the office, especially the enumerated powers that followed, were derived from the Constitution, not derived from or limited by the legislative powers granted Congress in Article I. The powers of the president were not those of Congress to confer upon the executive, nor could they be modified or rescinded by congressional action.

The phrase "The Executive Power" was a general term, sufficiently ambiguous so that no one could say precisely what it meant. It was possible that the words referred to more than the enumerated powers that followed, and might confer a set of unspecified executive powers. Early in the convention Wilson had proposed limited executive authority when he observed that "he did not consider the prerogatives of the British Monarch as a proper guide in defining the Executive power . . . the only powers he conceived strictly executive were those of executing the laws and appointing officers not appertaining to and appointed by the legislature."[36] But Wilson had been disingenuous: he had conceived of many additional executive powers in the Committee on Detail, and when he and Gouverneur Morris used the term "The Executive Power" they were seeking deliberately to build into the Constitution an open-ended clause useful to expand the powers of the presidency. Indeed, the common rules of constitutional construction that then prevailed assumed that general terms might imply more than the enumerated powers that followed.

The convention, in creating a system of separate institutions for legislative and executive powers, labored under the delusion that it was adapting to American usage one of the best features of the unwritten British constitution. In theory the Crown and Privy Council exercised royal prerogatives and administered laws passed by Parliament, with administrative authority stemming primarily from the monarch. Ironically, the Americans adopted the principle of the "balanced" Constitution as the British abandoned it. Throughout the eighteenth century the Hanoverian monarchs used "places and pensions" (patronage and bribes) to corrupt Parliament. After the loss of the American colonies a struggle broke out between Crown and Parliament. The House in 1782 condemned "farther prosecution" of the war, and when the king's ministers ignored this warning, a resolution stated that the house "will consider as enemies" those ministers favoring reduction of the revolution by force. Faced with this threat of impeachment, the king's prime minister, Lord North, informed the king that he could not govern since he lacked the confidence of the House of Commons. This was a step toward the system under which the prime minister and cabinet, while formally appointed by the Crown, owe their appointment to the support of a parliamentary majority. In turn, the new system marked the beginning of the end of the separation of powers in Britain; by the 1830s cabinet government based on party competition had eclipsed the king and Privy Council, ending the separation of legislative and executive powers and fusing crown prerogatives with parliamentary powers.

Although American politicians looked to some extent to the British constitution to support their proposals, they misunderstood developments. Madison analyzed the fall of Lord North's ministry in 1782 and the subsequent accession of Whig leaders opposed to the Crown's policies as a sign of the vitality of the doctrine of separation of powers. These events demonstrated to him the utility of separate institutions acting as checks on one another, for the checks and balances of the British system had led to an end of the revolutionary war once the king lost the confidence of the House of Commons. For Hamilton the significant event was the smashing victory that Pitt, a member of the Tory party (promonarch) won over the Whigs in the succeeding elections, which seemed to demonstrate that the Crown could continue to dominate Parliament and royal prerogatives would remain the dominant factor in the British constitution. In fact, neither checks and balances nor royal prerogatives were to have much influence on British political development in the next century. Had the American convention been delayed by twenty years, delegates would have seen clearly that the Crown no longer ran the government. Americans might then have considered cabinet government and the *fusion* of legislative and executive powers rather than concentrating on the *fission* of powers.

III

Checks and Balances

Once the presidential office had been created the framers had to consider how to prevent abuses of power. One technique was to provide for collaborative exercise of powers: the Senate would advise and consent to nominations to office and to treaties. The president was commander in chief, but Congress declared war and provided rules for the regulation of the armed forces. Another technique was to provide for checks and balances: the president could veto laws passed by Congress, and such vetoes could be overridden only by a two-thirds vote of each house. (Although the convention did not accept the "presidentialist" proposal for a three-fourths vote to override the veto, the delegates defeated on four separate occasions Madison's proposals that the president share the veto power with a Council of Revision.)[37]

Madison wanted to provide a system of checks and balances within the executive branch. He proposed a council to share in the executive powers, and gathered a roster of supporters including James Wilson, Oliver Ellsworth, George Mason, John Randolph, and Benjamin Franklin, a group bridging the presidentialist and congressionalist factions. To forestall Madison, Gouverneur Morris and Charles Pinckney proposed a "Council of State" to consist of the president and several department officers. The council would have had advisory powers, with no checks on the president. The plan also provided a detailed enumeration of the powers of the departments.[38] Many delegates correctly recognized the proposal as a ploy to place in the Constitution a detailed blueprint for an executive branch with vast powers. Morris and Pinckney sought to create the departments at the convention, in effect minimizing the role of Congress in organizing the government once the new Constitution was approved. In any event, neither the Committee on Detail nor the Committee on Postponed Matters reported to the convention any plans for a council. An attempt by Madison, Randolph, and Mason to create a six-member council consisting of two members each from northern, central, and southern states was defeated at the end of the convention, ending the last attempts to provide internal checks within the executive branch.

Impeachment

The delegates provided a means of removing the president upon conviction on an impeachment charge. The system they adopted owed something to British precedents, but adapted to American needs, it was in some respects a major improvement on British practice. In Britain, impeachment had been used as a vote of "no confidence" in the policies of the king's ministers. But the actual proceedings were conducted not as a vote on a motion, but rather as a trial in the House of Lords; and conviction could lead to stiff fines or even imprisonment. It was an unsatisfactory method of dealing with political disputes: between 1660 and 1717 many impeachments were voted, but not one resulted in a guilty verdict. In the late eighteenth century the only important trial was that of Warren Hastings, the British governor of India, which began in 1788. After 1782 the British substituted the parliamentary motion of no confidence for impeachment in order to remove ministers from office.

Americans reversed several aspects of British practice. First, the convention rejected the attempt to provide mechanisms to remove the president on political grounds. One proposal was to make the executive removable by a majority of the state legislatures; another would make him removable on the application of a majority of the state governors. By refusing to provide for the removal of the president simply because he lacked political support in state governments, the convention signaled that the function of the impeachment process would not be related to holding the confidence of another branch or level of government.

But the convention wanted to remove a president who abused his power. George Mason, an opponent of the strong presidency, gained support for an impeachment mechanism when he asked, "Shall any man be above justice? Above all shall that man be above it, who can commit the most extensive injustice?"[39] Few delegates supported Rufus King, who warned that impeachment would destroy the separation of powers, or Gouverneur Morris, who argued, "If he is to be a check on the legislature, let him not be impeachable."[40] Morris and Pinckney proposed to strike an impeachment provision from the Virginia Resolutions. Madison and other delegates defended impeachment. Morris realized, as the debate continued, that the only way to win the delegates over to a strong presidency was to reassure them that abuse of powers would be punished. Shifting his ground, he agreed with Madison's comment that a president "might lose his capacity after appointment. He might pervert his administration into a scheme of peculation or oppression. He might betray his trust to a foreign power."[41] Morris suggested that "the Executive ought therefore to be impeachable for treachery; corrupting his electors and incapacity were other causes of impeachment."[42]

The Committee on Detail placed the impeachment power in the House and the power to try the impeachment in the Supreme Court. Grounds were limited to "treason, bribery or corruption." The Committee on Postponed Matters, as part of a compromise with small states designed to increase the powers of the Senate, removed the power to try impeachments from the Supreme Court and placed it in the Senate. The committee removed "corruption" as grounds for impeachment when the delegates realized that a president would use patronage and influence as a legislative leader. Debate further defined the purposes of impeachment. Mason proposed adding "maladministration" to the list of impeachable offenses.[43] Madison, sensing that this vague phrase was designed to increase legislative control over the presidency, argued that "so vague a term will be equivalent to tenure during the pleasure of the Senate."[44] Mason compromised and moved that the phrase "other High Crimes and Misdemeanors" be substituted.

Mason's phrase, adopted by the convention, referred to certain offenses charged by the British House of Commons in impeachments. These offenses were not found in criminal laws of England, but included the following charges against officials acting in their public capacity: misapplication of public funds; abuse of authority; criminal conduct; corruption; encroachment upon the prerogatives of the legislative branch.[45] The phrase dealt with offenses of a serious nature committed in an official capacity, but was not limited to a criminal act under ordinary criminal law. The convention adopted this phrase so that abuse of power, rather than ordinary criminal behavior, would be grounds for impeachment. The language was a compromise: presidentialists favored the restrictive ground of criminal offense, while congressionalists wanted a provision similar to a "vote of confidence" to remove the executive on political grounds.

The impeachment provision reversed a second British practice. Conviction did not result in criminal penalties, but only in removal from office and possible disqualification from holding office in the future. If the offense involved a crime, judicial proceedings could be instituted after removal from office. The framers did not intend impeachment to mete out ordinary criminal justice, but rather to serve as part of the checks and balances system.

IV

Sovereign Powers

The new Constitution was designed to limit the power of the states: no state could coin money or pass a law impairing the obligation of contracts, two provisions that would benefit men of property. If debtors gained control of state governments, then the army or state militia called into national service could be used by the president to enforce orders of federal courts enjoining certain state actions. The federal judiciary could protect property holders from adverse state legislative action. The president would then uphold Article VI, the supremacy clause, providing that the Constitution, laws, and treaties of the United States are the "supreme law of the land." Congress, under Article I, could specify by law the procedures and circumstances under which the president could call forth the militia to enforce national laws and suppress domestic violence. The framers remedied a major defect of the confederation—the lack of a specific institution to enforce the laws and preserve domestic tranquillity.[46]

The president was given the "power to grant reprieves and pardons for offences against the United States, except in cases of impeachment." This power, proposed by Hamilton, was included by the Committee on Detail. The convention defeated a motion requiring the senate to consent to the exercise of the pardon power. It also defeated a motion to limit pardons to persons already convicted of a criminal offense. James Wilson argued that it should extend to persons not yet convicted, for the purpose of obtaining confessions that could be used in other prosecutions. He also blocked a proposal that would have prevented the president from pardoning in cases of treason.

Hamilton proposed the power, and Wilson fought against limitations on it, because they saw the pardon power as an instrument of statecraft. It could be used to put down insurrections, for as Hamilton explained,

The principal argument for reposing the power of pardoning in this case in the Chief Magistrate is this: in seasons of insurrection or rebellion, there are often critical moments when a well-timed offer of pardon to the insurgents or rebels may restore the tranquillity of the commonwealth; and which, if suffered to pass unimproved, it may never be possible afterwards to recall.[47]

War Powers

The confederation required the votes of nine states in Congress to determine for war. The convention considered whether to continue that precedent or to adopt the British system of confiding the decision to the executive. But outright adoption of British practice was unacceptable to most Americans, who viewed this particular royal prerogative with extreme distaste. They assumed that George III had initiated and prosecuted the war, and they sympathized with the Whigs who stressed the war powers of parliament and had finally forced the king to end hostilities.

Neither the Virginia nor New Jersey plans mentioned war powers, since their authors expected no change in the existing system under the Articles of Confederation. But when the Committee on Detail submitted its draft, it borrowed from the New Jersey plan the provision that once war had been declared, the remaining war powers involved in prosecuting the war were to be divided between Congress and the executive, with the president functioning as commander in chief.

The draft language that Congress would "make war" left certain issues unresolved. Did it mean that Congress would make the decision for peace or war? Would Congress control the conduct of war once begun? When the delegates debated the issue, Pinckney proposed that the power to make war be lodged in the Senate, while Butler "was for vesting the power in the President, who will have all the requisite qualities, and will not make war but when the Nation will support it."[48] Speakers in the debate appear to have used the word "make" in the broad sense of conducting as well as declaring hostilities. To clarify matters, Madison and Elbridge Gerry "moved to insert 'declare,' striking out 'make' war; leaving to the Executive the power to repel sudden attacks."[49] This motion left the president with the power to repel invasions on his own initiative.

The delegates intended to leave the *decision* for peace or war with Congress, except in the case of invasion. Convention leaders agreed on that point.[50] It was not clear whether the new wording would limit congressional power to *conduct* a war. Had the change from "make" to "declare" reduced the congressional role? Perhaps the president had the power to determine war policies based on the commander in chief clause. Equally likely the powers of Congress delineated in Article I left responsibility for the conduct of hostilities with it. Had the delegates cared to settle the issue, they could have followed the Massachusetts constitution and provided enumerated powers after the commander in chief title; since they did not, both branches of the national government could compete for war powers.

During the debate, Butler proposed to give the legislature the power to make peace, but the proposal was defeated.[51] Madison then proposed that the Senate, by two-thirds vote, could make a peace treaty without the concurrence or participation of the president. Gouverneur Morris led the opposition that defeated this motion. The convention twice refused to lodge any peace powers with the Senate or Congress, instead providing that the branches use the treaty power in a collaborative manner to make peace.

Diplomatic Powers

The framers had to deal with the question of which branch of government should be assigned primary responsibility for conducting diplomacy. The convention left the issue unresolved through ambiguous constitutional language.

The president was given the power to receive ambassadors and ministers. Most delegates thought of this as a ceremonial function without significance. They intended to assign the power of recognition to the president and senate, who were jointly to agree on the nomination of ambassadors. The collaborative pattern was extended to the negotiation of treaties, which was confided to the president with the advice and consent of the Senate. The president was to permit the Senate to participate in the negotiations; the convention did not assume that the president would simply lay the completed draft of a treaty before the Senate for its consent. The Constitution also assigned Congress jurisdiction over tariffs and commerce with foreign nations. From these limited grants of authority the two branches would find it necessary to construct a set of diplomatic powers, and the president would ultimately find his greatest authority from the silences of the Constitution.

V

Prerogative Power

Delegates who proposed a strong executive at the Convention had reason to be pleased with its work, yet some had been prepared to go much further, and among them Alexander Hamilton had particular reason to be disappointed. Hamilton had proposed a plan to the delegates that involved no less than the creation of an elected monarch exercising prerogative powers. His plan was presented in the course of a rambling speech on the principles of good government quite early in the convention. It bore a striking resemblance to the *Instrument of Government* instituted in England by Oliver Cromwell in 1653. The dictator had named himself "Protector for Life"; Hamilton's proposed "Governour" would be chosen by electors to serve "on good behavior." The protector had the "exercise of the chief magistracy and the administration of the government"; Hamilton's plan gave the "Supreme Executive Power" to the governour. Cromwell provided himself with a veto effective for twenty days against laws passed by Parliament; Hamilton went even further and gave his governour an absolute "Negative" against all laws passed, or about to be passed, by Congress.[52]

IV. The supreme Executive Authority of the United States to be vested in a Governour to be elected to serve during good behavior—the election to be made by Electors chosen by the people in the Election Districts aforesaid—The authorities & functions of the Executive to be as follows: to have a negative on all laws about to be passed, and the execution of all laws passed, to have the direction of war when authorized or begun; to have with the advice and approbation of the Senate the power of making all treaties; to have the sole appointments of the heads or chief officers of the departments of Finance, War, and Foreign Affairs; to have the nomination of all other officers (Ambassadors to foreign Nations included) subject to the approbation or rejection of the Senate; to have the power of pardoning all offenses except Treason; which he shall not pardon without the approbation of the Senate.

VI. The Senate shall have the sole power of declaring war, the power of advising and approving all Treaties, the power of approving or rejecting all appointments of officers except the heads or chiefs of the departments of Finance, War, and Foreign Affairs.

Records of the Federal Convention of 1787, vol. 1.

Hamilton drew on the prerogative powers of the British Crown in fashioning his plan. As a sophomore at King's College (now Columbia College) Hamilton had studied William Blackstone's *Commentaries on the Laws of England,* and he had reviewed this work while studying law in 1781. Hamilton was familiar with Blackstone's volume on the British Constitution, since his revolutionary pamphlets in 1774, and his major speech to the convention in 1787, rely heavily on the structure and phrasing of Blackstone's chapters "On Parliament" and "The Royal Prerogative."[53] Hamilton was attracted particularly to Blackstone's description of the Crown prerogatives. With the exception of the taxing power, granted to Parliament, Blackstone assigned almost all important governing powers to the monarch: war powers and command of the armed forces, the power to raise fleets and armies, to enforce embargoes, to make treaties, to make peace, to recognize foreign nations, to exercise other diplomatic powers, to coin money, to erect corporations, to arbitrate commerce, to pardon offenses, to create offices. The Crown exercised an absolute veto on legislation, supervised the courts, and appointed judges. Although in no sense an accurate description of British constitutional practice in the eighteenth century, the work of Blackstone could serve as a model of executive power in its most extreme form.

Most Americans would not have tolerated explicit recognition of prerogative power for the president in the Constitution. Madison, particularly, had warned delegates of the necessity "to fix the extent of the Executive authority," which "should be confined and defined."[54] Hamilton could not expect delegates to vote openly for prerogatives. His speech to the convention was tactical; it was designed to shock, and it did. In turn, other presidentialists like James Wilson appeared moderate; Hamilton's speech had the intended effect of giving his allies some room to maneuver in expanding enumerated powers.

Hamilton did not write most of the language of Article II, and he was absent from the convention while many of the enumerated powers were being drafted. But he and Gouverneur Morris (together with Hamilton's protégé, Rufus King) were members of the Committee on Style, and they shaped the language of Article II so that some phrases might later be used to justify the exercise of vast powers. Morris placed the words "The Executive Power shall be vested in a President of the United States of America" at the beginning of Article II. The committee left the commander in chief clause without a subsequent enumeration of duties. Silences about war, peace, diplomatic powers, and control of departments could provide the president with the opportunity to construe his powers expansively. While Madison argued for a presidency that was checked, limited, and precisely defined, Hamilton, Morris, Washington, and Wilson gained a version that provided the opportunity for the exercise of a residuum of unenumerated power.

The founders had not resolved the issue of prerogative power in the Constitution that they adopted. They had not determined whether they expected the president and Congress to collaborate or to check each other in the exercise of sovereign powers. While the framers were brilliant politicians, they were cautious draftsmen. At key points the Constitution was ambiguous, incomplete, underdefined, or silent. Much of the subsequent history of the presidency would involve the incumbent's claim that he had the power to act, and his critics' counterclaim that his exercise of authority was unconstitutional.

VI

Ratification

The unsettled issue of presidential power was to trouble many of the delegates to the state ratifying conventions. "Your president may easily become a king," thundered Patrick Henry in Virginia, and he predicted, "There will be no checks, no real balances in this government. What can avail your specious, imaginary balances, your rope-dancing, chain-rattling,

ridiculous ideal checks and contrivances?" James Monroe gloomily foresaw a president who might be reelected for life. George Mason, who
refused to sign the Constitution, warned of a dangerous combination
between the president and Senate that could "destroy all balances" unless
a council of state were provided by amendment. In Paris Thomas
Jefferson noted tartly after receiving a copy of the draft that "their
president seems a bad edition of a Polish King" since he could be reelected
indefinitely and commanded the armed forces.[55] Ironically, the New York
Governor, George Clinton, attacked the presidency because it resembled
the New York Governor. It was one thing, he argued, to have a strong
governor for a state, and quite another to have a strong president for the
nation. "This government is no more like a true picture of your own," he
warned New Yorkers, "than an Angel of Darkness resembles an Angel of
Light."[56] The Virginia and North Carolina conventions submitted proposed amendments to limit tenure in office to eight years in any sixteen
year period.

Defenders of the presidency, for tactical reasons, stressed legislative
supremacy in the new form of government. In their propaganda for
ratification they pointed out that the president could not become a king
because the nation lacked an established church or nobility. The president
did not appoint the Senate and was unlikely to combine with them in a
conspiracy. He had no hereditary income or honors. He had no royal
prerogatives and his limited diplomatic authority was subject to check
by the Senate. He would be nominated and elected by the electoral college
and (probably) the House of Representatives. As James Wilson pointed
out to Pennsylvania delegates:

The President, sir, will not be a stranger to our country, to our laws, or to our
wishes. He will, under this Constitution, be placed in office as the President of
the whole Union, and will be chosen in such a manner that he may be justly
styled the man of the people.[57]

Presidentialists reassured state convention delegates that the executive
would possess no royal prerogative powers. Wilson and Hamilton pointed
out that the executive power would extend only to the faithful execution
of the laws and was not intended to give the president additional powers.
But, as Hamilton reminded the New York convention:

When you have divided and nicely balanced the departments of government,
when you have strongly connected the virtue of the rulers with their interest, when, in short, you have rendered your system as perfect as human
forms can be, you must place confidence, you must give power.[58]

To influence delegates in New York, Madison, Hamilton, and Jay
wrote a series of essays, known collectively as *The Federalist Papers*.
Madison reassured his readers that the checks and balances system resembled state practices, and that each of the branches had "the necessary
constitutional means and personal motives to resist the encroachments of

the others."[59] Hamilton took great pains to point out the *dissimilarities* between the president and the British monarch, going so far as to list the prerogative powers of the Crown (as Blackstone had listed them) in order to *deny* that the president possessed them.[60] Hamilton was guilty of deliberate deception on two counts: by using Blackstone's seventeenth-century description of royal powers rather than eighteenth-century British practice he overstated the powers of the British Monarch; he then understated the powers of the president by sliding over the ambiguous language of Article II and misstating his position on "The Executive Power." Since the convention proceedings were kept secret, the public was not aware that Hamilton had supported a plan for an elective king, or that he had pressed a version of the plan on Madison at the very end of the convention. As a pragmatic politician Hamilton was supporting the Constitution as the best form of government that could be achieved under the circumstances, and in *The Federalist Papers* he supported precisely those limitations on presidential power that he and other delegates had previously fought and voted against.

Hamilton had not really abandoned the notion of prerogative powers. In *Federalist* 72 he defined the administrative powers of the president so expansively that in effect he smuggled the notion of prerogatives back into the office:

The actual conduct of foreign negotiations, the preparatory plans of finance, the application and disbursement of the public monies in conformity to the general appropriations of the legislature, the arrangement of the army and navy, the directions of the operations of war—these, and other measures of a like nature, constitute what seems to be most properly understood by the administration of government.

Hamilton had simply recast the argument. By denying prerogative powers he reassured state convention delegates. By expanding the definition of administration to encompass many of these royal powers he left the way clear for future presidents to claim them.[61]

The Constitutional Experiment

Readers of the convention debates are struck by the experimental nature of the enterprise. The politicians who made the historic compromises were disappointed in their work. Madison, who had not won his council of state, proportional representation in the Senate, his proposal for a congressional "Negative" over state laws, wrote in disgust to Jefferson that "the plan should it be adopted will neither effectually answer its national object nor prevent the local mischiefs which everywhere excite disgusts against the state governments."[62] Hamilton, disappointed with the presidential article, thought about the possibility of establishing an American branch of the Hanoverian monarchy if the states rejected the proposed Constitution. "The most plausible shape of such a business," he wrote in his diary shortly after the convention ended, "would be the establishment of a son of the present monarch in the supreme government of this country with a family compact."[63]

As George Washington assumed office in 1789, no one could foresee whether the Union would survive or the presidency would work. The new president expressed the mood of the people when he referred to this "republican model of government" as "an experiment entrusted to the hands of the American people."[64] And the presidential experiment would now be carried out by the politicians who had created it and the people to whom they would be accountable.

APPENDIX:
RULES OF CONSTITUTIONAL
CONSTRUCTION

This appendix provides a brief introduction to the techniques that presidents use to interpret the Constitution, derive extraconstitutional sources for the exercise of power, and claim emergency powers.

Extraconstitutional Powers

There are powers that may be exercised by the United States even if not specifically mentioned in the Constitution. Under the theory of *sovereign powers* the national government may exercise all the authority of a sovereign nation, including powers granted by the Constitution, the customs and usages of nations, international law, treaties, and membership in international organizations. Under the contrasting *federal powers* theory the source of national sovereignty was the states, which ceded to the national government only those powers necessary for their protection: therefore the national government may exercise only those powers specifically mentioned by the Constitution.

The president applies the sovereign powers theory for his own purposes: he claims that other branches of government have only those powers defined, enumerated, and assigned to them by the Constitution, but that he alone exercises the residuum of sovereign powers not mentioned in the Constitution. He relies on his oath of office and his obligation to faithfully execute the laws as a duty to uphold the powers and duties of the United States as a member of the family of nations.

Expansive Rules of Construction

The president applies the Constitution to justify his use of prerogative powers. He begins with the *plain meaning* of provisions that confer powers: he nominates high officials to office and vetoes laws passed by Congress. If the plain meaning of a phrase does not suit him he applies one or more of the following rules:

A. *Textual Definition.* The phrase is examined in the context in which it appears. The president may be removed from office "on impeachment for, and conviction of treason, bribery, or other high crimes and misdemeanors." But what are these high crimes and misdemeanors, a phrase unknown in ordinary criminal law? Since the words appear in the context of corruption and bribery, it may be assumed that they refer to the abuse of power rather than ordinary criminal violations.

B. *General Terms.* A general term that follows the enumeration of specified powers comprehends only the powers that preceded it. But in Article II a number of general terms, such as "The Executive Power," are used without prior or subsequent enumeration. The president argues that such terms confer grants of authority, taking both "The Executive Power" and the "commander in chief" clauses as such grants. Those who wish to minimize presidential power describe such phrases as mere titles rather than grants of power.

C. *Functions.* The president claims implicit authority under the general term "The Executive Power" to carry out functions assigned to him by the Constitution or laws. Although he has no removal power, he claims it as part of "The Executive Power" and as necessary to see the laws faithfully executed. The notion that he has an implied "necessary and proper" clause is open to dispute. The framers explicitly provided for such a clause when dealing with Congress, and had they wished, they could have put such language in Article II. The president claims a diffuse responsibility to function efficiently that serves to expand his powers within the executive branch.

D. *Combining Powers.* The president combines constitutional provisions to create "resulting powers." Lincoln combined the commander in chief clause with the duty to faithfully execute the laws and with the oath of office to create "war powers" enabling him to take emergency actions during the Civil War. Wilson and Roosevelt combined "The Executive Power" with the commander in chief function to mobilize the domestic economy during the World Wars. The president claims to be the "sole organ of communication" in foreign affairs by combining the commander in chief function with "The Executive Power," the oath of office, the power to receive foreign ambassadors, the treaty powers, the duty to faithfully execute the laws, and the power to nominate ambassadors.

E. *Separating Obligations.* Presidents argue that their oath of office—

which does not mention an obligation to uphold the laws—should be separated from their obligation to faithfully execute the laws. In emergencies they may find it necessary to disregard a particular law in order to protect and defend the Constitution. Congress argues on the contrary that the oath must be combined with the "take care" clause, and that the president is required under all circumstances to execute the laws. Combining powers would limit presidential discretion, while separating obligations lifts a check on his powers.

F. *Silences.* Presidents may act even if they cannot cite a specific provision of the Constitution by claiming *inherent powers*, based on the sovereignty of the American nation under international law. They may take any action in the field of national security that is not expressly prohibited by the Constitution or laws of the United States. In contrast there is the *delegated powers* theory, best expressed by William Howard Taft:

> . . . the President can exercise no power which cannot be fairly and reasonably traced to some specific grant of power or justly implied and included within such express grant as proper and necessary to its exercise. Such specific grant must be either in the Federal Constitution or in an Act of Congress passed in pursuance thereof. There is no undefined residuum of power which he can exercise because it seems to him to be in the public interest.

Presidents who rely on delegated rather than inherent powers attempt to find a constitutional provision that can justify the exercise of powers. For Taft, powers that were "implied" and that were "necessary and proper" could be exercised, which is a broad reading of Article II and offers ample scope for the assertion of prerogative powers.

G. *Inclusions.* The express mention of a power in Article II is an invitation to the president to exercise all related powers. Silences about related powers is taken by the president as a decision by the framers not to limit his authority. The power to receive foreign ambassadors is interpreted as license to exercise all related powers of diplomatic recognition, although most are not mentioned in the Constitution or assigned to any branch.

H. *Exclusions.* The express mention of a power in Article I is interpreted by the president as a limitation on Congress to restrict itself solely to the enumerated power. Silences about related powers is taken by the president as a decision by the framers to limit the authority of Congress. The president argues that the opening words of Article I, "All legislative powers herein granted," indicates that the Constitution intends that only expressly enumerated powers are to be exercised by Congress, and that all remaining functions, powers, and duties are exercised by the president under doctrines of inherent powers, resulting powers, sovereign powers, and inclusions.

I. *Sole Exercise.* The president argues that a power assigned to him is exercised by the executive branch alone. The power of recognition, once conceded to the president, cannot be exercised by Congress as well.

J. *Concurrent Exercise.* Under this rule a second branch of government may exercise a power assigned to the first branch, provided there is no express constitutional prohibition and there is a reasonable constitutional construction that permits the exercise of the power. The president uses sole exercise doctrine to say, "What's mine is mine," and the concurrent exercise doctrine allows him to add, "And what's yours is also mine." Presidents have used concurrent powers over habeas corpus, over regulation of foreign commerce (through quarantine and blockade), and for creation of executive branch agencies. They have also engaged in wars without congressional declaration.

K. *Subordinate Powers.* The president argues that in national security affairs other branches of government should exercise their powers in support of his decisions. He expects the Senate to consent to his treaties and Congress to pass appropriations to implement the obligations of the United States to other nations.

L. *Coordinate Powers.* The president argues that the executive branch is not constitutionally bound to support decisions taken by another branch as expressed in laws or resolutions that infringe on his constitutional responsibilities. Presidents may ignore provisions in laws that they believe infringe upon their authority as commander in chief, especially in wartime.

M. *Symmetry of Privileges.* The president assumes that any privilege that exempts one branch from the checks and balances of the others should apply to the executive branch. The Constitution makes explicit mention of legislative secrecy, by providing that each house of Congress may keep the journal of its proceedings secret. Although the Constitution makes no mention of executive secrecy, presidents have argued that they have an executive privilege against making known their deliberations to the other branches.

Emergency Powers

Presidents may claim that in crises the Constitution permits them to exercise legislative and judicial powers granted to the other branches, in effect fusing all governmental power in the executive branch for the duration of the emergency. Lincoln justified actions he took after the outbreak of the Civil War by claiming that the emergency made it necessary for him to exercise legislative powers until he could call Congress into session. Franklin Roosevelt threatened that unless Congress repealed a certain provision in a wartime economic measure, he would treat the law as if it had been repealed for the duration of the emergency, in effect threatening Congress with the loss of its legislative powers.

The doctrine of *emergency powers* assumes that the president must go beyond the bounds set by the Constitution or laws to preserve the union.

This doctrine is a variation of what the framers knew as Lockean Prerogative, named after the argument made by the seventeenth-century English political theorist John Locke. In dire emergency, he claimed, "the laws themselves . . . give way to the executive power, or rather to this fundamental law of nature and government, viz., that, as much as may be, all the members of society are to be preserved." This prerogative, Locke went on to say, permits the executive to "act according to discretion for the public good, without the prescription of law, and sometimes even against it."

No emergency powers were included in the Constitution: there is no mention of a Lockean prerogative. Yet the president's oath of office requires him to "preserve, protect, and defend" the Constitution, as well as to uphold its provisions, and does not mention an obligation to faithfully uphold the law. If the framers did not grant the president a Lockean prerogative, neither did they foreclose its exercise.

The Intentions of the Framers

In construing the Constitution, the president often applies the rule that the interpretation should be consistent with the problem the framers wished to solve when they adopted it. Since the framers faced the problem of suprise attacks on the frontiers, and they permitted the president to repel attacks and invasions without a declaration of war, the president construes the power of his office to permit him to defend the nation in limited wars or threaten the use of the nuclear deterrent without congressional participation in the decisions.

There are several sources that constitutional scholars use to determine the intent of the framers:

1. English constitutional theory and practice, as described by commentators such as Lord Blackstone and as understood by delegates to the convention.
2. Practices of colonial and state governments, as described in state constitutions and statutes and in decisions of state courts.
3. The Articles of Confederation and the customs and usages of the Congresses that convened under the Articles.
4. Writings of leading members of the convention such as Washington, Hamilton, Wilson, and Madison.
5. Proceedings of the convention, especially the records of debates kept by Madison and several other delegates. These are often sketchy and incomplete.
6. Proceedings of ratifying conventions. Debates often deliberately misstated provisions of the Constitution and cannot be read literally.
7. Essays written for the Constitution, such as *The Federalist Papers*. These sources are propaganda first and foremost and must be used with care.
8. Debates of the first Congress that convened under the Constitution. Many delegates to the convention served in this Congress, and their debates sometimes involved the meanings of the Constitution and shed light on the intentions of the framers.

These sources rarely provide complete answers. Framers often modified state or colonial or British practices deliberately. Convention and ratifying convention debates are incomplete. Essays involved as much propaganda as analysis. Commentaries and debates after 1789 involved struggles for power, and theorists such as Madison and Hamilton often reversed themselves on constitutional issues once in power. Historical reconstruction often provides no definitive interpretation of the Constitution.

Precedent and Usage

Presidents prefer to interpret the "living Constitution," which is based on the experience of almost two hundred years of governance. To determine the current meaning of a provision, the materials of public law are used:

1. Law reviews and historical journals interpret particular provisions in the light of usages.
2. Presidential interpretations are found in speeches, messages to Congress, veto messages, proclamations, executive orders, and the briefs of White House counsel. Departmental interpretations are prepared by the Departments of State and Defense, and by the attorney general and solicitor general of the Justice Department for significant constitutional issues.
3. Congressional views are found in floor debates, committee hearings and reports, resolutions expressing the sense of a chamber or of the Congress, proposed resolutions of censure or impeachment, and proposed Constitutional amendments affecting presidential powers. Laws may attempt to define or limit presidential power, or may delegate vast legislative authority to the executive.
4. Litigation by members of Congress or by private parties may result in opinion of federal courts, which construe presidential powers.

Presidents do not always consider themselves bound by precedent, custom, or past usage, especially if prior controversies over the scope of their powers have resulted in limitations. New conditions may impel a president to assert a revised interpretation of his authority. Most public law treatises serve a useful function as a description of how past conflicts over prerogatives were resolved; but they are not useful as predictive devices, for they cannot forecast what authority the president will claim in the future or how other institutions will respond to that claim.

Prerogative Powers

PRESIDENTS who claim constitutional authority to unilaterally make the most important domestic and national security policies in effect institute *prerogative government*. Several features distinguish such governance: presidential decisions are made without congressional collaboration, often in secrecy, and announced as faits accomplis; decisions are implemented by subordinate executive officials, and commands from the president are often self-executing, requiring compliance only from high-level officials to put them into effect with no discretion necessary; events are managed by the White House rather than by the departments. The president justifies his decisions on constitutional grounds, on powers enumerated, or on those claimed or created by his application of rules of constitutional construction. When his expansive interpretation is challenged, he appeals to the public for support by defining his actions in terms of "national security" or "the national interest."

Great presidents have always interpreted their powers expansively, far beyond the enumeration of specific powers in Article II. Theodore Roosevelt, bypassing the Senate to lead America into the responsibilities of a world power at the turn of the century, wrote a defense of his conduct at the end of his term to the British historian Sir George Otto Trevelyan, which expressed the fundamental spirit presidents bring to the office:

While President I have *been* president, emphatically. I have used every ounce of power there was in the office and I have not cared a rap for the criticisms of those who spoke of my "usurpation of power"; for I know that the talk has been all nonsense and that there had been no usurpation. . . . in showing the strength of, or in giving strength to, the executive, I was establishing a precedent of value.[1]

I

Legitimizing Presidential Prerogatives

The president claims that his office represents the will of the sovereign people. He is more than a broker of constituent interests, more than a champion of the majority against the minority, and more than a symbol of bipartisan national unity. Woodrow Wilson suggested the essence of the popular connection that legitimizes prerogative government in the Blumenthal Lectures he gave at Columbia University:

His is the only national voice in affairs. Let him once win the admiration and confidence of the country, and no other single force can withstand him, no combination of forces will easily overpower him. His position takes the imagination of the country. He is the representative of no constituency, but of the whole people.[2]

The president represents the national interest rather than simply the sum total of individual preferences or the interests of the electoral coalition that placed him in office. He represents, in short, "the people" of the Constitution. Therefore he may exercise the sovereign powers of the nation, including the residuum of powers that are neither enumerated nor assigned to any branch. As Theodore Roosevelt argued,

My view was that every officer, and above all every executive officer in high position, was a steward of the people. . . . I declined to adopt the view that what was imperatively necessary for the Nation could not be done by the President unless he could find some specific authorization to do it. My belief was that it was not only his right but his duty to do anything that the needs of the Nation demanded unless such action was forbidden by the Constitution or by the laws.[3]

Because of the bonds between the people, the president, and the Constitution, the president need not subordinate himself either to his party or to the majority sentiment in Congress. James Buchanan once responded to a communication from the House of Representatives by noting that he was "the only direct representative on earth of the people of all and each of the sovereign states. To them, and them alone, is he responsible whilst acting within the sphere of his constitutional duty, and not in any manner to the House of Representatives."[4] Or as John Adams, harassed by a hostile legislature, had put it, presidents "will act their own independent judgments, and not be wheedled or intimidated by factious combinations of senators, representatives, heads of departments, or military officers."[5] When even the weakest of presidents assert their independence from the legislature, the strongest may be expected to exploit the popular connection fully.

These ideas—that the president acts for the sovereign people and performs his duties without holding himself accountable to party or Congress—have been echoed by all modern presidents. Although few have argued for the inherent powers of the "steward," most have accepted the principles laid down by William Howard Taft, in a speech delivered at Columbia University after his retirement from the presidency:

The Constitution does give the President wide discretion and great power, and it ought to do so. It calls from him activity and energy to see that within the proper sphere he does what his great responsibilities and opportunities require. He is no figurehead, and it is entirely proper that an energetic and active clear-sighted people, who, when they have work to do, wish it done well, should be willing to rely upon their judgment in selecting their Chief Agent, and having selected him, should entrust to him all the power needed to carry out their governmental purpose, great as it may be.[6]

The president is the agent of the people for the work they wish to perform. The people entrust to the president not simply the freedom to act, but also the power to define the scope of his authority, subject to subsequent challenge by Congress or the decision of the courts. The crux of the problem of presidential power is this: to use prerogatives effectively the president must first stake out his claims to them. Like Excalibur's sword, he must wrest his powers from the Constitution before he can wield them.

Constitutional Issues

A close look at Article II reveals some of the problems the framers bequeathed to the president, for the Constitution in only the roughest sense provides a blueprint for the mechanisms of government. Does the opening phrase, "The Executive Power shall be vested in a President of the United States of America," confer any powers on the president, or is it simply the designation of the incumbent as the officer who exercises the enumerated powers contained in Article II? If an "executive power" exists, of what does it consist and where lie its limits? Is it simply a reference to the general superintendence of the departments? Does it merely empower the president to exercise powers delegated to him by laws? Or does it comprehend emergency powers?

Consider the obligation of the president to faithfully execute the laws. Is this to be taken as an instruction to follow the intent of Congress in all matters? Or is it instead to be construed as a kind of "necessary and proper" clause that allows the president to take extraordinary actions in defense of the nation? Is it an invitation to Congress to monitor the performance of the president and his subordinate officials? Or was it intended to create a boundary between the branches, making it the responsibility solely of the president to ensure that the departments follow the letter of the laws? Does this provision give the president the power to issue orders to the secretaries and monitor departmental business? Does it give the president the power to remove officials who may have been appointed by and with the advice and consent of the Senate? Although the president must faithfully execute the laws, must he do so if he believes that a law passed by Congress violates the Constitution?

Does the commander in chief title confer war powers on the president? May he order troops into combat without a congressional declaration of war? Does he define war aims? Is the prosecution of a war a constitutional responsibility of the president, or is he delegated this responsibility through a declaration of war that may define the aims and the means of the hostilities?

Constitutional ambiguity is at the heart of the problem of presidential power. Presidents create controversy when they use their prerogatives to resolve issues. The purpose here is to examine the constitutional dimensions of the presidency by examining several crises. The focus is on authority and legitimacy—how to obtain it. There are three possible outcomes when presidents institute prerogative government. First, there is the *frontlash effect*: the crisis is managed successfully, Congress and the courts acquiesce in his actions and claims of authority, and the "living presidency" of custom, usage, and precedent grows stronger. This outcome occurs most often when national security issues are involved. Second, there is the *backlash effect*: the crisis is managed successfully, but the president's interpretation of his powers is challenged by other branches, events in the party system erode popular support for his initiatives, and his successors find their authority limited by laws, judicial decisions, or public opinion. This outcome is likely when prerogative powers are used to resolve domestic issues. Third, there is the *overshoot and collapse effect*: the president is checked by one or more branches, his prerogative government sets off a major constitutional crisis, his legitimacy as a national leader is ended, and he is censured or brought into the impeachment process. This outcome is possible when the president acts as if major national security issues were at stake in what is essentially a domestic political situation.

To explore the theme of prerogative government, several case studies will be presented. Each involves the president's search for constitutional authority to solve a crisis central to the nation's concerns and his own political fortunes. Several involve great success or good fortune for the president and the nation; others deal with the spectacular failures of administrations. The aim here is to demonstrate why presidents felt compelled to substitute constitutional claims for more routine methods of persuasion and influence.

II

Frontlash: Diplomatic Powers

National security was the most important issue for Washington. The 1778 Treaty with France left the United States committed to guarantee French possessions in the Americas. The British retained their forts on American soil, intrigued to get Vermont to join the Canadian Confederation, and incited Indians on the frontiers. Between 1784 and 1788 the Spanish cut off navigation rights on the Mississippi and then restored them under a system that left settlers at their mercy. Spanish territorial claims included parts of Georgia and what were to become Tennessee, Kentucky, Alabama, and Mississippi. The Spanish encouraged secessionists in Kentucky Territory.

To end the encirclement of the union and extricate it from the conflicts of the great powers Washington had to engage in subtle maneuvers. His diplomacy could not be carried out openly, for the population was violently anti-British, and no one knew who in Congress was in the pay of foreign powers or who could be trusted with secrets. The administration could not be sure of support in Congress for its diplomacy. So Washington used prerogative powers to pursue his foreign policies, and in doing so he developed precedents that amounted to the successful assertion of full presidential authority in the conduct of foreign relations.

One of Washington's most important decisions was to remain neutral in the war between the British and the French. The French wanted America to honor its treaty and engage the British in naval warfare. Secretary of State Jefferson and other pro-French Americans proposed instead a "benevolent neutrality," which, while keeping the Union out of hostilities, would permit the French to raise money and troops in the Union and outfit privateers to harass British shipping. Secretary of the Treasury Hamilton and pro-British Americans called for strict neutrality. Washington issued a Proclamation of Neutrality that favored Hamilton's pro-British position, a highly unpopular decision, for Vice-President John Adams recounted that "ten thousand people . . . day after day threatened to drag Washington out of his house and effect a revolution in the government."[7]

The proclamation touched off a sharp constitutional debate. Did the president have the authority to issue a proclamation of neutrality? Hamilton, under the pen name Pacificus, argued that diplomacy is inherently an executive function and that all diplomatic powers, except those specifically enumerated in Article I, were to be exercised by the president: "The general doctrine of our Constitution then, is that the executive power of the nation is vested in the President, subject only to the exceptions and qualifications which are expressed in the instrument."[8] Hamilton was arguing for "inherent powers" to conduct diplomacy, and claiming all the silences in the Constitution for the president. "It belongs to 'the executive power'" he argued, "to do whatever else the law of nations, cooperating with the treaties, of the country enjoins in the intercourse of the United States with foreign powers." Madison, using the pen name Helvidius, could not let this expansive interpretation of "the executive power" remain unchallenged. He argued that the president had not been given any specific enumerated power to declare neutrality. Since Congress was given the decision for peace or war in Article I, it had the power (through the necessary and proper clause) to determine whether to honor the treaty with France (in effect a decision for war) or remain strictly neutral (a decision for peace). To have the power to declare war, he argued, comprehends the power to determine treaty obligations that might lead to war, and to conduct diplomacy that might safeguard peace. Thus Madison counterbalanced the construction of an *implied* congressional power against Hamilton's projection of an *inherent* executive power.

Madison lacked the votes in Congress to challenge the administration, and the proclamation was enforced. By 1794 the administration obtained passage of neutrality legislation. The pattern was set: a presidential fait accompli followed by congressional implementing legislation to give it effect. By 1795 Washington had asserted several other prerogatives: the power of recognition of foreign governments; the power to break relations by recalling American ambassadors or demanding the recall of foreign ambassadors. He also established the practice that the president negotiates treaties unilaterally. John Jay was dispatched to London to negotiate a treaty with the British; although leading senators were kept informed, the president only consulted with the entire Senate to ask its consent once the draft had been concluded. It narrowly passed in the Senate despite popular opposition. The House, controlled by antiadministration forces, argued that the treaty regulated commerce with a foreign nation, a power that the Constitution confided to Congress, and required American payments to satisfy British claims, infringing on the congressional appropriations power. So the issue was raised: does a treaty to which the Senate has given its consent *require* Congress to implement its terms? The House did pass the necessary measures, but it resolved:

And it is the constitutional right and duty of the House of Representatives, in all such cases, to deliberate on the expediency or inexpediency of carrying such a treaty into effect, and to determine and act thereon, as, in their judgment, may be most conducive to the public good.[9]

By insisting that it might not back a presidential initiative, the House left open the possibility that the president would also assert a doctrine of coordinate powers and refuse to heed a congressional resolution or law, instead acting according to his own judgment of the public good.

Washington's prerogative government in diplomatic affairs was crowned with success. For the first time in more than a century war was averted in North America when European powers were in conflict. The Northwest Territory was secured as the British evacuated their posts. A treaty concluded with the Spanish opened up the Mississippi for commerce and settled the boundaries of Spanish Florida. The government could now borrow from European investment houses and was able to stabilize its finances, setting the stage for economic development.

Franklin Roosevelt and the Atlantic Alliance

A second case, almost a century and a half later, involves a reversal of roles: congressional majorities were intent on preserving strict neutrality while the president wished to institute a "pro-British" neutrality at the outbreak of World War II. Congress adopted an isolationist foreign policy in response to the rise of totalitarian regimes in the 1930s. In 1933 Roosevelt requested legislation that would permit him to embargo arms sales to aggressor nations but permit sales to their victims. Instead, Congress passed a Neutrality Act instructing the president to declare (at his discretion) an embargo against all belligerents. A law passed in 1936 required an arms embargo against all third parties entering hostilities and forbade loans to belligerents—by joint resolution Congress extended this law to both sides of the Spanish Civil War. In 1939 Congress provided that the provisions of the laws could be invoked either by the president or by its own concurrent resolution, further weakening presidential diplomacy.

When war began in Europe Roosevelt proclaimed neutrality and imposed the arms embargo. But in November 1939 Congress passed his proposal for a neutrality act that would permit "cash and carry" sales to the British and French. In March 1940 he proposed a program of "lend-lease" military assistance for the allies, but for months his program remained stalled in Congress. In June 1940, after the fall of France, the president declared an "unlimited national emergency" and under statutory authority mobilized the economy and began spending $17 billion appropriated for preparedness. After Poland and France fell he refused to concede that hostilities had ended, in gestures of solidarity with the vanquished nations. But Congress was in a defensive mood, matching the sentiments of the public; if Roosevelt wished to confront the Axis powers with military force, he would have to rely on his own constitutional authority.

Roosevelt was prepared to use prerogative powers to bypass the isolationist majority in Congress. By executive agreement (not requiring Senate or congressional consent) signed within the Pan American Union, the nations of the Americas provided for creation of provisional governments in Latin America for former French possessions to keep them out of the hands of the pro-Nazi "Vichy" government. Also by executive agreement a Permanent Joint Board of Defense involving Canadian and American military staffs was established.

These agreements were a prelude to the most controversial action Roosevelt took: the destroyer deal with Great Britain. By executive agreement the American navy transferred fifty overage destroyers to the British navy, in return for several Caribbean naval bases. The administration in effect concluded an alliance with the British, by circumventing the Senate treaty power and by ignoring the letter and spirit of several laws. The 1940 Neutrality Act prohibited the transfer of usable military equipment to other nations and required the chief of Naval Operations to certify the uselessness of equipment. Administration pressure on the chief secured his assent to the deal, although the destroyers were obviously useful—why else would the British have asked for them? A 1917 law prohibited the use of American warships by a belligerent power. But Roosevelt offered a peculiar interpretation of that law, claiming (in a brief prepared by Attorney General Jackson) that it only prohibited the use of ships built specifically for a belligerent power, but did not prohibit the transfer of ships built originally for the American navy. According to Jackson, the president as commander in chief had the power not only to dispose the armed forces, but also to dispose *of* them. By construing constitutional authority expansively and the statute so restrictively that it defied common sense, the president was able to consummate the deal. Jackson further argued that the agreement involved a single act, with no further obligations on either party, therefore not suitable for the treaty process, since treaties involve ongoing obligations. While such a distinction between agreements was well known in international law, it did not exactly fit, since both Roosevelt and Churchill used the agreement to cement a diplomatic and military alliance between the two nations. More to the point was Jackson's reference to the "plenary powers of the President as Commander-in-Chief of the Army and Navy and as head of state in its relations with foreign countries"—the language of prerogative government.[10]

Roosevelt kept congressional leaders fully informed and consulted with them in advance of the deal. He gained the approval of the Republican presidential candidate, which kept the issue out of the elections. A majority of senators were pleased that Roosevelt let them off the hook, since they did not want to go on record in support or opposition to a proposed treaty.

The "frontlash" effect of the agreement was soon apparent. Roosevelt took other prerogative actions. In April 1941 an executive agreement signed with the Danish minister to the United States allowed American forces to occupy Greenland, and in July the United States took over the defense of Iceland, protecting shipping lanes across the Atlantic. In April

Roosevelt also ordered the Navy to protect convoys on the open seas; in May the orders were to sink Axis submarines, the beginning of the undeclared naval war. In July Axis assets worth over $7 billion were frozen (this under statutory authority). Roosevelt and Churchill met at sea and produced the Atlantic Charter with its "Four Freedoms" defining war aims of the democracies. In September, after several merchant ships were sunk, the president ordered the Navy and Army Air Corps to attack Axis ships near convoys anywhere in the Atlantic, instituting a "shoot on sight" policy. In October the merchant ships were armed, and the navy was given orders to destroy Axis ships, even if they were nowhere near British convoys. The lend-lease law passed by Congress specifically prohibited the navy from convoying allied ships: Roosevelt ordered the navy to provide "neutrality patrols," and argued with perfect logic that the ships had to sail near the allied convoys to protect them against Axis submarines, claiming they sailed near the convoys but not with them—a meaningless distinction to soften a clear violation of the law. In November he made an agreement with the Dutch government-in-exile to occupy Dutch Guiana. Presidential emissary Harry Hopkins made two trips to Moscow in January and July 1941 to arrange for $3 billion in lend-lease supplies for the Soviet Union, establishing a second, even more controversial alliance, again without involving the Senate.

Roosevelt was wise to bypass Congress. It took a year to pass the lend-lease program. A selective service act that narrowly passed the House in 1940 was almost repealed in August 1941, which would have left the nation defenseless. Construction funds for naval facilities in the Pacific were held up and administration requests for procurement of advanced arms were cut. It was not until the end of 1941 that neutrality legislation was repealed. Congress demonstrated no foresight, courage, or common sense. Prerogative government was vindicated during the Second World War as a means of saving the nation and the democratic system of the West in its gravest crisis. The "frontlash" effect continued throughout the war and into the postwar period for two decades: in effect American foreign policy became a presidential prerogative as a reaction to presidential successes and the pathetic congressional performance prior to Pearl Harbor.

Frontlash: Preservation of the Union

Presidents may claim emergency powers in order to save the Union. Lincoln applied several doctrines of constitutional construction in prosecuting the Civil War involving the application of prerogative government in the emergency.

Consider the contrast between James Buchanan, operating within the confines of the "literal" Constitution, and Lincoln, using prerogative powers, just prior to the outbreak of hostilities. After Lincoln's election the slaveholders of the Lower South made plans to secede. Buchanan ruled out the use of force, although he declared that any secession would be unconstitutional. Delegates to a convention at Charleston, South Carolina, resolved that "the Union now subsisting between South Carolina and other States under the name of 'The United States of America' is hereby dissolved," and Georgia, Florida, Alabama, Mississippi, Louisiana, and Texas joined with South Carolina to form the Confederate States of America in February 1861. Buchanan reinforced federal forts in the region but gave no indication that he would put down the secession. He refused to enforce the Fugitive Slave Law against the North or the National Supremacy Clause of the Constitution against the South. But this caused each section to misread his actions and mistrust his intentions. Buchanan proposed a constitutional convention that would adopt amendments to guarantee slavery in the existing states and in future slave states, and in a message to Congress argued "that justice as well as sound policy requires us to seek a peaceful solution of the questions at issue between the North and the South."[11]

Even prior to his inauguration Lincoln intended to pursue a firmer course of action. He argued that all military positions in South Carolina should be fortified or retaken. He did not oppose replacement of the low tariff of 1857, favorable to the South, with the high Morrill Tariff of 1861, sure to increase regional tensions. Lincoln opposed the Crittendon Compromise, a plan to extend slavery to the Pacific below the 36° 90' latitude. He refused to endorse Buchanan's call for a constitutional convention to consider the plan. To Seward, his designee for Secretary of State, he confided, "I am for no compromise which assists or permits the extension of the institution [slavery] on soil owned by the nation."[12] Lincoln met with leaders of a "peace convention" involving delegates from twenty states held in Richmond, Virginia, but offered them no encouragement, and the convention disbanded a week before his inauguration.

At the inaugural Lincoln spoke favorably of a plan that Seward and the House Committee of Thirteen had developed that involved passage of a constitutional amendment to guarantee slavery in states where it already existed. But he insisted that the laws must be faithfully executed, that revenues of the United States must be collected at southern ports, and he warned secessionists, "You have no oath registered in Heaven to destroy the government, while I shall have the most solemn one 'to preserve, protect, and defend' it. You can forbear the assault; I can *not* shrink from the *defense* of it."[13]

For Lincoln to pursue his course he would have to institute prerogative government. Congress in the winter of 1860 had refused to confirm Buchanan's nomination of a customs collector in Charleston, so that there would be no federal official who could call for the militia to enforce the federal revenue laws, thus avoiding confrontation with the secessionists.

Congress also refused to pass a force bill (requiring the president to enforce federal laws), and it killed militia bills that would have authorized the call-up of troops to deal with the secession. It made no appropriations for military preparedness.

Initially Lincoln used his "executive power" to keep his cabinet in line. Secretary of State Seward was ordered not to grant an interview to commissioners from the Confederacy who arrived in Washington to arrange for peaceful dissolution of the Union. He rebuffed Seward's suggestions for a compromise with the South, to be followed by reunification of the Union and a war against Mexico to seal the reconciliation. He monitored department business, which enabled him to prevent Seward from sending a threatening note to Great Britain warning of war if it recognized the Confederacy—a scheme of the secretary to unify the estranged sections around anti-British sentiment. Seward pledged to Confederate President Jefferson Davis that Fort Sumter would not be reinforced; Lincoln overruled a majority of his cabinet and ordered the resupply of both Fort Sumter and Fort Pickens.

Had Lincoln not protected his constitutional authority, Seward would have acted as "prime minister" for the administration. He would have promoted his scheme to combine the Whigs of the South with the Republicans of the North into a new national party. The Union might have been preserved with this fragile compromise, but only at the cost of an aggressive war against Mexico or a pointless and possibly disastrous conflict against the British. Slavery would have been guaranteed by constitutional amendment and national supremacy replaced by a system of regional self-determination.

Most of Lincoln's career had been spent as a Whig, devoted to the principle of congressional supremacy. During the War of 1848 he had made his reputation as a member of Congress with a stinging attack on President Polk for his use of war powers to force the nation into hostilities against Mexico. But in the context of the emergency he exercised vast powers on an unprecedented scale; Lincoln in effect created a form of *constitutional dictatorship*: constitutional because the ultimate checks of elections and impeachment remained, but a "dictatorship" because he disregarded the proximate checks and balances in the emergency.

Once hostilities had begun Lincoln took unilateral action while Congress was out of session. He issued a proclamation calling forth the state militias and asked for 75,000 volunteers to aid in executing the national laws—a call that led to the secession of the states of the Upper South. Lincoln sent weapons to loyalists in Virginia, who then established the state of West Virginia. He proclaimed a blockade of southern ports, in effect an act of war without congressional declaration. He raised 42,000 army and 18,000 navy volunteers and increased regular army strength by 22,000, all of which violated ceilings in existing laws and disregarded the constitutional power confided in Congress to raise and maintain the armed forces. He accepted 188,000 volunteers from the militia for three years of service, created ten regiments, and authorized the construction of nineteen warships. He instructed the Treasury to pay two secret agents $2 million to purchase military supplies, a violation of the constitutional provision that requires all expenditures to be made in pursuance of appropriations. Six presidential proclamations authorized the commanding general of the armed forces to suspend the privileged of the writ of habeas corpus so that rebel sympathizers and insurrectionists in Maryland could be arrested and communications secured from the District of Columbia to the north.

Lincoln defended his rule by decree when he called Congress into session on July 4, 1861. "These measures," he told them, "whether strictly legal or not, were ventured upon, under what appeared to be popular demand and a public necessity, trusting . . . that Congress would readily ratify them. It is believed that nothing has been done beyond the constitutional competency of Congress."[14] Congress later ratified Lincoln's fusion of executive and legislative powers into an emergency prerogative by passing an appropriations act that specified the following:

That all the acts, proclamations, and orders of the President of the United States after the fourth day of March, eighteen hundred and sixty-one, respecting the army and navy of the United States, and calling out or relating to the militia or volunteers from the States, are hereby approved and in all respects legalized and made valid, to the same effect as if they had been issued and done under the previous express authority and direction of the Congress of the United States.[15]

Congress also ratified other presidential measures: in 1862 it passed legislation giving the president authority to censor telegraph lines, a power he had already exercised; the Militia Act enabled him to draft an additional 300,000 troops, and in 1863 a draft law had the effect of retroactively sanctioning prior drafts; also in 1863 a law permitted the president to suspend the privilege of the writ of habeas corpus. And in the first challenge to the presidential exercise of war powers the Supreme Court in a five to four decision ruled that the war had constitutionally begun.[16]

The "frontlash" effect of Lincoln's measures can be demonstrated by examining the circumstances involving his proclamation of emancipation. Lincoln viewed it as a war measure to strike at enemy property. He relied on his authority as commander in chief when he issued the proclamation. But slavery had been explicitly protected by the Constitution, and its regulation entrusted to Congress. Under the Fifth Amendment no citizen of the United States could be deprived of property without due process of law, even in areas in secession. If Lincoln wished to argue that emancipation was a war measure, then under the rules of international law the property of enemy citizens on land was exempt from seizure without compensation. Many in Congress argued that the proclamation

LINCOLN'S WAR POWERS: TWO VIEWS

5. RESOLVED: That we approve and applaud the practical wisdom, the unselfish patriotism and the unswerving fidelity to the Constitution and the principles of American liberty, with which ABRAHAM LINCOLN has discharged, under circumstances of unparalled difficulty, the great duties and responsibilities of the Presidential Office; that we approve and indorse, as demanded by the emergency and essential to the preservation of the nation and as within the provisions of the Constitution, the measures and acts which he has adopted to defend the nation against its open and secret foes; that we approve, especially, the Proclamation of Emancipation, and the employment as Union soldiers of men heretofore held in slavery; and that we have full confidence in his determination to carry these and all other Constitutional measures essential to the salvation of the country into full and complete effect.

Republican Party Platform, 1864.

RESOLVED, that the aim and object of the Democratic Party is to preserve the Federal Union and the rights of the States unimpaired, and they hereby declare that they consider that the administrative usurpation of extraordinary and dangerous powers not granted by the Constitution—the subversion of the civil by military law in States not in insurrection; the arbitrary military arrest, imprisonment, trial and sentence of American citizens in States where civil law exists in full force; the suppression of freedom of speech and of the press; the denial of the right of asylum; the open and avowed disregard of State rights; the employment of unusual test oaths; and the interference with and denial of the right of the people to bear arms in their defense is calculated to prevent a restoration of the Union and the perpetuation of a Government deriving its just powers from the consent of the governed.

Democratic Party Platform, 1864.

went beyond the president's constitutional authority. Congress had already legislated on the subject in the Confiscation Act of 1861, freeing slaves put to hostile use, by an act freeing slaves who crossed over to Union lines, and by a law emancipating slave-soldiers fighting for the Union who were owned by secessionists.

Lincoln fused legislative power with his own executive authority, but he did not rule without the consent of the governed. Congress freely ratified his actions, and at any time could have impeached and removed him from office. Elections in 1862 increased Democratic representation in Congress, and a hotly contested presidential election in 1864 was fought largely over the issue of presidential prerogatives. Lincoln did not destroy legitimate, loyal political opponents. Throughout the war much domestic policymaking was left to Congress, including the tariff, currency, western lands, education, and banking.

Lincoln's prerogative government rested on the consent of the governed. If the framers had not anticipated the exercise of emergency powers, they had provided a system of government supple enough to accommodate both their assertion and their use in authentic crises.

III

Backlash: Domestic Policymaking

Prerogative government may be criticized when presidents use it to resolve domestic issues. The party system may not accommodate itself to presidential claims, or checks and balances wielded by Congress or the judiciary may weaken the incumbent politically and establish precedents that weaken the office. The cases that follow illustrate this "backlash" effect.

Andrew Jackson and the National Bank

Andrew Jackson used two prerogatives, the removal and the veto, to defy hostile congressional majorities determined to control economic policy. Congress rechartered the Second Bank of the United States in 1832. The president, opposed to a national bank, vetoed the recharter bill, dooming the bank to expire in 1836. The veto was controversial: only six of the twenty-one prior presidential vetoes had been cast for other than constitutional reasons. Jackson claimed that a president could exercise the veto power on policy grounds, in effect a challenge to congressional primacy in economic policymaking. Jackson claimed that he could decide on the constitutionality of legislation, denying the contention of his critics that he should have signed the recharter bill because the Supreme Court in 1819 had ruled that a national bank was a constitutional exercise of legislative powers.[17]

Jackson ordered Secretary of the Treasury William Duane to remove deposits from the national bank and place them in state banks. Duane refused, claiming that the Treasury was under congressional as well as presidential superintendence. Jackson insisted that "the executive power" provided him with authority over the Treasury and dismissed Duane while the Senate was in recess. He appointed his attorney general, Roger Taney, as treasury secretary (an interim appointment that did not require Senate consent), and Taney drew down the federal account at

THE SENATE CENSURES JACKSON

Resolved, That the President, in the late Executive Proceedings in relation to the public revenue, has assumed upon himself authority and power not conferred by the Constitution and laws, but in derogation of both.

Journal of the Senate, March 28, 1834.

JACKSON REPLIES TO CENSURE

. . . the resolution of the Senate is wholly unauthorized by the Constitution, and in derogation of its entire spirit. It assumes that a single branch of the legislative department may for the purposes of public censure, and without any view to legislation or impeachment, take up, consider, and decide upon the official acts of the Executive. But in no part of the Constitution is the President subjected to any such responsibility, and in no part of that instrument is any such power conferred on either branch of the Legislature.

. . . It has already been maintained . . . that the Secretary of the Treasury is the officer of Congress and independent of the President; that the President has no right to control him and consequently none to remove him. With the same propriety and on similar grounds may the Secretary of State, the Secretaries of War and the Navy, and the Post-master-General each in succession be declared independent of the President, the subordinates of Congress, and removable only with the concurrence of the Senate. Followed to its consequences, this principle will be found effectually to destroy one coordinate department of the Government, to concentrate in the hands of the Senate the whole executive power, and to leave the President as powerless as he would be useless—the shadow of authority after the substance had departed.

From James D. Richardson, ed., *Compilation of the Messages and Papers of the Presidents, 1789–1897,* vol. II (New York: Johnson Reprint, 1969), pp. 79–80.

the national bank and made new deposits into state banks, in effect transferring federal funds as Jackson wished. Duane's removal touched off a controversy, for nowhere in the Constitution is the removal power vested in the president. Jackson argued that it was incidental to "the executive power" and that it was necessary for him to meet his duty to see that the laws were faithfully executed. The Senate, when it reconvened, responded to this argument (first made by Madison in 1789) by passing two resolutions charging that Jackson had acted unconstitutionally in dismissing Duane. Jackson challenged the House to impeach and the Senate to try him, knowing that the House was controlled by his forces and would never impeach.[18] The Senate refused to consent to Taney's nomination, marking the first time that a cabinet nomination was rejected.

Despite Jackson's success in destroying the national bank, his presidency was not strengthened. His assertions of prerogatives were not institutionalized, if by that term we mean that a set of precedents about the scope of presidential power had been accepted by the nation. The party system did not accommodate itself to prerogative government for domestic policymaking. The opposition Whigs expounded the doctrine of legislative supremacy. Their position was summed up by Sen. Henry Clay:

On principle, certainly, the executive ought to have no agency in the formation of the laws. Laws were the will of the nation authoritatively expressed. The carrying out of those laws into effect was the duty which ought to be assigned to the executive, and this ought to be his sole duty, for it was an axiom in all free governments that the three great departments, legislative, executive, and judicial, should ever be kept separate and distinct.[19]

Whigs were for a national government directed by Congress. They expected the president to take direction from legislative leaders, and to use his appointment powers for the benefit of his party. The veto was to be exercised solely on constitutional grounds. Whigs denied that "the executive power" was a grant of authority, for as Sen. Daniel Webster argued, "enumeration, specification, particularization, was evidently the design of the framers of the Constitution. . . . I do not, therefore, regard the declaration that the executive power shall be vested in a President as being any grant at all."[20] Cabinet secretaries would be transplanted congressional leaders such as Daniel Webster and John Calhoun, serving temporarily in an administration before returning to Congress. They would follow congressional intent as expressed in detailed laws and appropriations. As the Supreme Court observed in an 1837 case that rebuked Jackson,

It would be an alarming doctrine that Congress cannot impose upon any executive officer any duty they may think proper, which is not repugnant to any rights secured and protected by the Constitution; and in such cases, the duty and responsibility grow out of and are subject to the control of the law, and not to the direction of the president.[21]

Whigs assumed that presidents would serve one term and not seek reelection. The two Whig presidents went even further than party doctrine demanded and died in office. It is only a slight exaggeration to suggest that government-by-corpse was the logical extension of Whig principles.

Yet even Democrats reacted negatively to Jacksonian prerogatives. Virginia Sen. John Tyler quit the party in 1837 after refusing to follow instructions from his state legislature to vote for a motion to expunge the resolution of censure against Jackson from the Senate records. Another Democrat, Abel Upshur (later to become Tyler's secretary of state) wrote a major treatise on constitutional law in 1840, which discussed the presidency in the following passage:

The most defective part of the Federal Constitution, beyond all question, is that which relates to the executive department. It is impossible to read that instrument without being forcibly struck with the loose and unguarded terms in which the powers and duties of the President are pointed out. . . . the convention appears to have studiously selected such loose and general expressions, as would enable the President, by implication and construction, either to neglect his duties or to enlarge his powers.[22]

Upshur argued that the Senate must consent to the president's removal of any official to whose appointment it had originally been required to assent. He called for a constitutional amendment that would enable Congress to override a veto by a majority vote. He suggested that a simple majority of the Senate be sufficient to convict on an impeachment, and proposed a one-term limitation for the presidency.

Tyler Against the Whigs

The irreducible core of presidential power rests with the constitutional prerogatives of the office. This is the lesson that may be drawn from a brief examination of the Tyler administration. In 1840 Tyler, the Democrat who had broken with Jackson, ran for vice-president on the Whig ticket with Harrison and was elected. After Harrison's death he succeeded to the presidency and faced a dilemma: should he permit the Whigs in Congress to pass their economic program, or should he base his administration on his own Democratic domestic program? To oppose the Whigs he would have to rely on the very prerogative powers which had precipitated his decision to leave the Democratic party.

Tyler began his administration in an awkward position. It was not clear from the wording of the Constitution whether the vice-president succeeded to the office of president or only exercised the "powers and duties" of the office, serving as "acting president" in the case of a vacancy. Tyler took the presidential oath and issued a statement to the people couched in the form of an inaugural address. The House promptly passed a resolution referring to him as president, while the Senate defeated a resolution referring to him as vice-president.[23] But much of the nation referred to him as "His Accidency" and did not concede his legitimacy in the presidential office.

The Whig cabinet moved to take control of the administration. At the first cabinet meeting Secretary of State Webster told Tyler that his predecessor had settled questions by majority vote. Tyler refused to place his presidency "in commission," and responded,

I, as President, shall be responsible for my administration. I hope to have your hearty cooperation in carrying out its measures. So long as you see fit to do this, I shall be glad to have you with me. When you think otherwise, your resignation will be accepted.[24]

Tyler called a special session of Congress. The Whigs brushed aside the president's proposal for a national bank, and instead passed a much stronger version, which the cabinet urged him to sign. Tyler vetoed the bill, and the Democrats in the Senate sustained the veto. A second bill was passed by the Whigs and a second veto exercised and sustained. The Whig cabinet (with the exception of Webster, involved in treaty negotiations with the British) resigned, and when Congress adjourned, the Whigs issued a statement disassociating their party from the administration. Tyler now occupied the White House without an electoral mandate, a cabinet, or affiliation with a party. The Whigs demanded that he resign, to be succeeded by the Whig president pro tem of the Senate as "acting president." Under the existing succession law a special election would then be held. Instead, the president remained in office and formed a cabinet of Democrats through recess appointments. When the Senate reconvened, it eventually confirmed a cabinet. Senate Democrats provided support for Tyler that made his removal on an impeachment impossible.

Tyler demonstrated that a president without popular or party support could exercise Jacksonian prerogatives. The Whigs could not obtain a national bank or board of exchequer, they could not pass a high tariff, and they could not win their distribution bill to give the proceeds of the sale of public lands to the states for internal improvements. Led by former president John Quincy Adams, a Whig-dominated House Select Committee investigated the conduct of the president and reported that he had misused his veto power. Henry Clay proposed a constitutional amendment to permit Congress to override the veto by a majority vote. Neither this amendment nor resolutions to impeach the president passed the House. Instead, a censure resolution was passed in a feeble replay of the conflict involving Jackson and the Senate a decade earlier.

Tyler was a political failure. He did not obtain the Democratic presidential nomination in 1844. His use of prerogatives was not well received by constitutional commentators or by members of the Democratic party. Historians generally rated him an ineffective president as a result of the deadlock in domestic policymaking during his term of office. But he had demonstrated conclusively that a president without a shred of popular or party support could wield prerogative power and by doing so reduce his congressional opponents to complete ineffectiveness in policymaking.

Truman and the Steel Seizure

Another "backlash" effect occurred more than a century later during the Korean War. Truman used prerogative powers to seize the steel mills during a strike. The companies challenged his actions, and the Supreme Court (for the first time since 1866) used its power of judicial review to declare unconstitutional a presidential action.

After Truman sent forces to Korea, Congress passed the Defense Production Act of 1950, and although the administration had not requested it, provided for a "standby" system of wage and price controls. Eventually Truman established such a system: at the top was the Office of Defense Mobilization (ODM), which coordinated the wartime economy; underneath was an Economic Stabilization Agency, which had responsibility for wage and price policies; wage settlements were recommended by a Wage Stabilization Board and prices set by an Office of Price Stability.

In 1952, when the steel union was negotiating with the companies for an industry-wide settlement, the Truman administration wanted to give the workers somewhat higher wages, while limiting an increase in prices as an antiinflationary policy. The Wage Stabilization Board recommendations were accepted by labor but rejected by management, which wanted to maintain its high profits and linked any increase in wages to a large hike in steel prices. To placate the industry the ODM pressured the Office of Price Stability to raise prices, but that agency intended to limit increases to an adjustment of higher costs incurred between June 1950 and June 1951 under the terms of a bill passed by Congress. Backed strongly by his council of economic advisors, Truman sided with the Office of Price Stability. The director of the ODM, Charles Wilson, a former president of the General Electric Company, resigned in protest and charged that the president had not backed his efforts to obtain a settlement. With the administration just as divided as management and labor, talks on a new contract stalled, and after twice postponing a strike, the steelworkers finally went out.

If Truman granted the steel companies a large price boost, it would cripple his antiinflationary policy. He wanted to back the Office of Price Stability as a clear signal to other corporations that they could not pressure his administration. On the other hand he could not let the strike continue. Defense Secretary Robert Lovett warned of serious consequences to the war effort, and Secretary of State Acheson foresaw problems in meeting commitments to European allies for arms shipments.

The president considered applying the Defense Production Act to end the strike. Section 502 provided that management and labor could create an arbitration board and enter into compulsory arbitration, but only if the two sides agreed; no binding arbitration could be imposed from the outside, because section 503 provided that no measures taken under the act could be inconsistent with the Taft-Hartley law or other related statutes, none of which provided for compulsory arbitration.[25] Under the Selective Service Act of 1948 the president could seize factories if direct orders to the government were not fulfilled. This law might not apply to strikes. The government might first have to place direct orders with the companies and then wait until they were not fulfilled. The process would be cumbersome and time-consuming, and although the Justice Department was in favor of a seizure on these grounds, the Defense Department objected and pressed for more immediate action.

Truman could have applied the Taft-Hartley Act, which regulated peacetime labor-management relations. Under Title II, National Emergency Provisions, whenever a lockout or strike would, in the president's opinion, imperil national health and safety, he may appoint a board of inquiry to determine the facts, and may order the attorney general to seek a federal court injunction for a sixty-day "cooling off" period. Within fifteen days after that period ended, the National Labor Relations Board would conduct a secret vote of workers on the last offer of the employers. If the strike still could not be settled, the president would submit a record of his actions to Congress, with or without a request for legislation to settle the strike.

Truman did not wish to use the Taft-Hartley law. Wildcat strikes might occur. Members might obey the injunction and work for existing wages, which would benefit the companies. The sixty-day cooling-off period could not ensure continued war production. The courts might not even grant the injunction. The president had originally vetoed the bill in 1947, and it was opposed by his party and by the labor movement. Even if he did apply the law, it was doubtful that Congress would pass special legislation to impose a settlement if the mechanisms did not work. Truman could not even use the prestige of the office, for his popularity had plunged, and less than one-fourth of the electorate approved his performance in office as the unpopular Korean War dragged on.

But Truman had a combination of constitutional and statutory authority, an "aggregate of powers," that he might use. There were precedents for presidents' intervening with troops in labor disputes: at least twenty-six between 1902 and 1946.[26] And there were precedents for the seizure of factories in wartime. Since the Civil War, Congress had passed at least sixteen statutes authorizing seizure of private property in wars.[27] Presidents had also seized property without statutory authority, as Wilson had done in World War I. Prior to Pearl Harbor Roosevelt had seized three plants and had ordered twelve seizures before Congress passed the War Disputes Act. After he seized the North American Aviation Plan at Inglewood, California, Roosevelt had Attorney General Robert Jackson argue that the "aggregate of the President's powers derive from the Constitution itself and from statutes enacted by Congress." The president, Jackson argued, could seize plants to keep war production continuing, since that production had been ordered by Congress; he was, therefore, observing his duty to faithfully execute the laws, based on his "duty constitutionally and inherently resting upon the president to exert his civil and military, as well as his moral, authority to keep the defense efforts of the United States a going concern."[28] In 1943 Congress "ratified" this seizure by passing the War Labor Disputes Act; the moral for Truman seemed to be "seize first and answer questions later." After the war Truman himself had used these statutory powers to seize coal mines and the railroads during strikes. But the laws had expired, and there was no existing law that gave the president broad seizure powers. In fact, Congress had considered and had specifically rejected provisions for permanent injunctions, binding arbitration, and seizure when it passed the Emergency Provision of the Taft-Hartley Act.

Truman decided to use his constitutional authority to seize the steel mills and end the strike. He issued Executive Order 10340, which directed his secretary of commerce "to take possession of and operate the plants and facilities of certain steel companies," basing his authority on the wartime emergency and "as President of the United States and Commander in Chief of the Armed Forces." The president knew that the companies would challenge the seizure in the courts, but he calculated that his actions would be upheld. Not since 1866 had the Supreme Court decided against a president in the exercise of prerogative power—and in that case, the president against whom the decision was directed, Abraham Lincoln, was already dead. The justices would be sympathetic to the president. Justice Jackson had written the Opinions of the Attorney General for both the Destroyer Deal and the Inglewood Seizure, demonstrating support for prerogative powers as well as an ability to get around statutory obstacles. Justices Black and Douglas were sympathetic to labor. Justices Clark, Minton, and Burton had been appointed by Truman.

But Truman's speech to the American people justifying the seizure was harsh and frightened many citizens, and it was effectively refuted by spokesmen for the industry, who warned of a usurpation of power and of a political payoff to the unions. Industry won the battle for public support, with 43 percent opposing and 35 percent supporting the president.[29] In federal district court the Justice Department attorney made sweeping claims based on prerogative powers, and the flavor of the argument is captured in the following exchange:

The Court: So you contend the Executive has unlimited power in time of an emergency?
Mr. Baldridge: He has the power to take such action as is necessary to meet the emergency.
The Court: If the emergency is great, it is unlimited, is it?
Mr. Baldridge: I suppose if you carry it to its logical conclusion, that is true. But I do want to point out that there are two limitations on the Executive power. One is the ballot box and the other is impeachment. . . .
The Court: And that the Executive determines the emergencies and the Courts cannot even review whether it is an emergency.
Mr. Baldridge: That is correct. . . .[30]

The Justice Department was arguing that the president had inherent, residual powers to do good, to meet emergencies with emergency power. The federal judge questioned this assumption, and the following exchange ensued:

The Court: So, when the sovereign people adopted the Constitution, it enuerated the powers set up in the Constitution but limited the powers of the

Congress and limited the powers of the judiciary but it did not limit the powers of the Executive. Is that what you say?

Mr. Baldridge: That is the way we read Article II of the Constitution.[31]

Truman had the Justice Department retreat from this extreme position, claiming that his emergency powers flowed directly from specific constitutional provisions, but the damage was done. The president only compounded his problems when he remarked, just before the Supreme Court was to decide the case, "The President has the power and they can't take it away from him." When reporters at the news conference asked the president if he meant the courts, he added, "Nobody can take it away from the President, because he is the Chief Executive of the Nation, and he has to be in a position to see that the welfare of the people is met."[32]

After complicated maneuvers in district court and in the court of appeals, the case was decided by the Supreme Court. Only three justices, Chief Justice Vinson, and Justices Reed and Minton, were impressed with the president's argument that he had an "aggregate" of constitutional and statutory powers which he could use to seize the mills to ensure continuation of defense production. These justices emphasized the circumstances surrounding the seizure: the global conflict with communism, the warfare in Korea, commitments to allies. Citing Lincoln's actions during the Civil War and Roosevelt's destroyer deal, Vinson argued, "It amply demonstrates that presidents have taken prompt action to enforce the laws and protect the country whether or not Congress happened to provide in advance for the particular method of execution."[33] But a majority of justices, in separate opinions, ruled against the president. Each emphasized that Congress had legislated on the subject of strikes and seizures, thus preempting the field. Congress had rejected seizure as a method of settling disputes when it passed the Taft-Hartley Act, and had not provided for it in the various laws it passed for economic stabilization. Justice Jackson offered a test for weighing presidential powers against congressional action:

When the President takes measures incompatible with the expressed or implied will of Congress, his power is at its lowest ebb, for then he can rely only upon his own constitutional powers minus any constitutional powers of Congress over the matter. Courts can sustain exclusive presidential control in such a case only by disabling the Congress from acting upon the subject. Presidential claim to a power at once so conclusive and preclusive must be scrutinized with caution, for what is at stake is the equilibrium established by our constitutional system.[34]

Black argued in his opinion that the executive order that Truman had issued was a substitute for a statute that only Congress could pass, and that it could not be sustained as part of the president's authority as commander in chief because that phrase does not provide the president with lawmaking power. Frankfurter argued that the "take care" clause limited Truman to faithful execution of the laws Congress had passed on the subject of seizures, and in this case to the provisions of the Taft-Hartley Act. If Truman wished to seize mills, he must ask Congress to pass new legislation authorizing him to do so. Burton and Clark cited specific procedures that Congress had designed to support their view that the legislature had preempted the field.

The Supreme Court forced Truman to return the mills, because in Jackson's words, he had taken the commander in chief clause and had "turned inward, not because of rebellion, but because of a lawful economic struggle between industry and labor." Such a struggle could not be decided by prerogative government, but rather by the statutory procedures passed by Congress. The power of the commander in chief must yield both to legislature authority and to the protection of property included in the Fifth Amendment. As Jackson concluded, disposing of the "emergency" arguments, "Congress can grant and has granted large emergency powers, certainly ample to embrace this crisis, I am quite unimpressed with the argument that we should affirm the possession of them without statute."[35]

Not only had Truman been checked by the courts, but subsequent presidents would not be able to use the threat of seizure as a weapon. In steel strikes in the 1950s and in the coal strike of 1978, presidents could not make seizure a credible threat against companies—at least not without asking Congress for emergency legislation. Instead, all relied on collective bargaining or the Taft-Hartley procedures, and nothing in the American experience in labor-management negotiations suggested that faith in these statutory mechanisms was misplaced.

IV

Overshoot and Collapse

At its limits prerogative government is useful for presidents in the context of authentic national emergencies. Used past those limits to deal with domestic crises it produces severe "backlash." And when used to subvert the laws of the land and the democratic "rules of the game" prerogatives becomes a two-edged sword that can cut a president to ribbons. Two incumbents destroyed their administrations by overshooting the constitutional limits, abusing their powers, violating their oaths of office, and failing to faithfully execute the laws. In both cases their party was subsequently defeated in the presidential elections, and the collapse of their presidencies was followed by declines in the institutional powers of the office.

Andrew Johnson and Reconstruction

The central issue once the North had defeated the South in the Civil War involved reconstruction: on what terms would the South be permitted to rejoin the Union? With the accession of Andrew Johnson to the presidency, a struggle between Congress and the president over the terms of reconstruction that had simmered during the last stages of the war suddenly became a major institutional crisis. A "Union Democrat" who had been born in North Carolina and raised in Tennessee, Johnson ran with Lincoln in 1864 as a symbol of reunification. Republicans expected him to uphold the doctrine of legislative supremacy, since he was aware that Congress intended to control reconstruction. But he refused to bow to the legislature and set two goals calculated to infuriate Republicans: to weaken and destroy the Freedmen's Bureau, created in 1865 as a War Department agency to protect blacks through use of military courts; and to bring Southern states back into the Union and seat their delegations in Congress (which Republicans had refused to do in 1865).

Johnson declined to call Congress into special session following his accession to the presidency, and instead relied upon his powers as commander in chief to control reconstruction. He retained Lincoln's cabinet but made policy himself. He prevented Secretary of War Stanton from administering reconstruction so that blacks could participate effectively. He issued a proclamation enabling whites to elect state constitutional convention delegates without participation of black freedmen. He recognized the governments of Arkansas, Louisiana, Tennessee, and Virginia. He reported to Congress when it convened at the end of 1865 that he had recognized state governments formed by conventions chosen by 10 percent of the prewar electorate (following Lincoln's policy), that provisional governors had been appointed and state legislatures assembled, and that congressional delegations had been elected. Congress responded by refusing to seat the Southerners and by striking the names of the states from the rolls. It created a Joint Committee on Reconstruction to wrest control of the South from the president.

Republicans opposed the formation of the state governments, even though they had been required to repeal their secession ordinances, ratify the Thirteenth Amendment abolishing slavery, and repudiate Confederate debts. These states had adopted "black codes," which denied civil rights to black freedmen; they could not be litigants or witnesses in state courts in cases involving whites, nor could they enforce contracts. Even Johnson's Attorney General James Speed admitted, "It is the old slave code minus the slaveowners responsibilities—poor as they were."[36] The new governors issued pardons and appointed former secessionists to high positions in their administrations.

Johnson did not enforce the law that disqualified former Confederate

THE RADICAL REPUBLICANS CHALLENGE THE PRESIDENT

In this country the whole sovereignty rests with the people, and is exercised through their representatives in Congress assembled. The legislative power is the sole guardian of that sovereignty. No other branch of government, no other department, no other officer of the government, possesses one single particle of sovereignty of the nation. No government official, from the President and Chief Justice down, can do any one act which is not prescribed and directed by the legislative power.

. . . Since, then, the President can not enact, alter, or modify a single law; cannot even create a petty office within his own sphere of duties; if, in short, he is the mere servant of the people, who issue their commands to him through Congress, whence does he derive the constitutional power to create new States; to remodel old ones; to dictate organic laws; to fix the qualifications of voters; to declare that States are republican and are entitled to command Congress to admit their representatives? To my mind it is either the most ignorant and shallow mistake of his duties, or the most brazen and impudent usurpation of power.

. . . Though the President is commander-in-chief, Congress is his commander; and, God willing, he shall obey. He and his minions shall learn that this is not a government of kings and satraps, but a government of the people, and that Congress is the people. . . .

Representative Thaddeus Stevens, January 3, 1867.

leaders from holding state office. He did not enforce the Confiscation Act of 1862, and thereby delayed land reform that would have aided freedmen. Johnson vetoed the rechartering of the Freedmen's Bureau, requiring Congress to pass a new measure reestablishing it. Congress passed a civil rights act that made freedmen citizens; that gave them the right to make and enforce contracts, sue and be sued, give evidence and bear witness; and that offered them "full and equal benefit to all law and proceedings." All of these rights would be enforced by federal courts. The president vetoed the measure, but Congress overrode it.

In the congressional elections of 1866, Johnson allied himself with the Democrats, encouraged the southern states not to ratify the proposed Fourteenth Amendment, and took a consistently antiblack position in public speeches. Republicans won a great victory in these elections, and three cabinet members resigned, signaling a Republican break with the president.

Congressional Republicans themselves were split on reconstruction. The radicals wanted the national government to administer the defeated territory, with southern states assuming probationary status. They wanted land reform, free public education, and suffrage rights for freedmen. The conservative Republicans were willing to permit southern states to manage their own affairs, but proposed a national civil rights law and the Fourteenth Amendment to protect the freedmen. They would also prohibit black codes and guarantee blacks access to federal and state courts. The Freedmen's Bureau would protect blacks until the state governments had demonstrated good faith.

Led by its conservative wing, the Republicans passed a moderate Reconstruction Act, then repassed it over Johnson's veto.[37] The bill placed state governments in provisional status, created five military districts with military courts, required the states to ratify the Fourteenth Amendment, and required that a majority of the state electorate choose delegates to state conventions in elections supervised by the War Department. A rider on an army appropriations bill provided that all orders to military commanders were to be channeled through General of the Army Grant, and that "he shall not be removed, or suspended or relieved from command or assigned to duty elsewhere without the approval of the Senate." Secretary of War Stanton was also insulated from Johnson's control, for Congress passed a Tenure of Office Act (over the president's veto). The act provided that an official who had been appointed by and with the advice and consent of the Senate was to hold office until a successor had been appointed in like manner. The president could not remove Stanton until the Senate confirmed his successor; so long as the Senate wanted Stanton to supervise reconstruction, the president could not control him.

Johnson fought back against this dilution of "the executive power." His attorney general, Stanbury, provided him with a legal opinion on the Reconstruction law, which argued that military commanders had the power to keep the peace and punish criminal acts, but could not enforce the Civil Rights Act or remove officials of the provisional state governments. The president insisted that he retained authority over military commanders and could issue orders to them without going through Grant. In the midst of the controversy Grant issued his own instructions to the commanders, telling them in effect to be guided by their own interpretations of the Reconstruction law, and not to follow presidential orders if they conflicted with the Reconstruction or civil rights laws.

The situation was untenable. Either the president or Congress must control the armed forces. After Congress adjourned, Johnson asked Stanton for his resignation, and when he was refused, the president, seemingly acting under the provisions of the Tenure of Office Act, suspended him and authorized General Grant to act as secretary of war. Johnson had outmaneuvered Congress, for he used a provision in the law that permitted him to suspend a department secretary until the Senate reconvened. His appointment of Grant seemed to signal military support for him; it would be difficult for the Senate to refuse to confirm Grant when it reconvened. But Grant, with his own ambitions for the next Republican presidential nomination, passed the word to congressional leaders that he would not be part of a confrontation: when the Senate reconvened, it reinstated Stanton, and Grant turned over his offices at the War Department to the secretary.

Johnson now made a supreme gamble. He announced plans to create an Army of the Atlantic, with General Sherman in command, to be headquartered in the District of Columbia. But Sherman would have no part of a maneuver to intimidate the Senate, and asked that his name be withdrawn and his nomination removed from the Senate. Johnson would play the remainder of his hand without military cards.

Now the president acted for the first time in apparent violation of the Tenure of Office Act: he removed Stanton while the Senate was in session and appointed General Lorenzo Thomas secretary of war. The House thereupon voted to impeach Johnson for violation of the Tenure of Office Act. Although the charges were narrowly drawn, in reality the impeachment was over a policy disagreement involving the terms of reconstruction. Yet if it had been a simple disagreement, there would have been no grounds on which to impeach the president. In truth the president had obstructed enforcement of Reconstruction and civil rights laws, used patronage and removal powers to encourage subordinate officials to obstruct and violate laws, and encouraged southerners, many of them former secessionists, to flout federal laws. Had the question of the Tenure of Office Act not been at issue, there were more than enough legitimate reasons to remove Johnson from office. But the charges dealt specifically with the removal power of the president, and that proved a saving factor for him.

To begin with there was considerable doubt that the Tenure of Office Act was constitutional. Both president and Congress agreed that a removal power existed (though not mentioned in the Constitution). The president argued that it was his prerogative, and even Stanton had supported Johnson's veto of the act on the grounds that Congress had infringed upon presidential authority. Members of Congress argued that they had the power to enact laws specifying the procedures by which officials were to be removed from office. Such authority, they claimed, derived from legislative power under the "necessary and proper" clause to organize the departments and determine the duties of officials. Congress by law could vest the removal power in the president and Senate.

Even assuming the act was constitutional, Johnson could claim that his removal of Stanton was not covered by the law. Stanton had been appointed by Lincoln; Johnson argued that the law could not prevent a president from removing an official nominated by his predecessor, but covered only those nominations he himself had made. In removing Stanton he had not violated the law, but had simply exercised a power that was not covered by the statute.

Even if it were assumed that Johnson had violated the law, that in itself might not be grounds for impeachment, if the president thought the law itself was unconstitutional. To disobey a law might be the only way to bring the matter to the courts. For the purpose of making a case the president should be able to violate the law without the threat of an impeachment, especially when his own prerogatives were being challenged in the statute.

Johnson was acquitted by the Senate by a one-vote margin. He was "saved" by seven conservative Republicans who voted with twelve Democrats. Some of them believed Johnson had not violated the act. Others doubted the act was constitutional. The conservatives may not have wanted Benjamin Wade, the president pro tem of the Senate, to assume the presidency, for they opposed his tariff and currency policies. They favored the nomination of General Grant and voted to acquit so that Wade could not make a run for the nomination from the White House. The president offered assurances during the Senate trial that he would end his attempt to control Reconstruction, and he named General Schofield, a man favored by the Republicans, as secretary of war in a gesture of conciliation.

It is absurd to contend that Johnson's acquittal strengthened the presidency. True, Stanton surrendered his office and the presidential removal power was sustained, with most of the provisions of the Tenure of Office Act repealed during the Grant administration. But by the time the House voted its impeachment, control of the departments already rested in the hands of congressional leaders. They instituted a system of congressional supremacy, involving a close connection between department secretaries and committee chairs, which remained in effect for the remainder of the century. By the 1880s it seemed to many observers that the decline of the presidency was irreversible and that the nation was headed for parliamentary government. Woodrow Wilson made his academic reputation as a political scientist with a description of how congressional committees controlled departments, and urged adoption of cabinet government to bring order out of the chaos the rival committees had created.[38] The Pendleton committee, created by congressional reformers, recommended that cabinet secretaries sit in Congress and participate in question periods, a first step towards parliamentary government.[39] Henry Lockwood, a member of the New York City bar, captured the public mood in a book called The Abolition of the Presidency, which suggested instituting cabinet government by constitutional amendment.[40] Harvard professor Albert Bushnell Hart confidently predicted in 1891 that "since the legislative department in every republic constantly tends to gain ground at the expense of the executive, the Speaker is likely to become, and perhaps is already, more powerful, both for good and for evil, than the President of the United States."[41] Journalist Henry Jones Ford, in his classic book on the evolution of the American system of government, forecast that the management of government would pass to the departments and the career service operating under the general superintendence of Congress, led by the Speaker, while "the Presidency will tend to assume an honorary and ceremonial character, and will find therein its most satisfactory conditions of dignity and usefulness."[42] Predictions of the demise of the presidential office proved premature, the wisdom of Harvard notwithstanding, but until the turn of the century and the revival of presidential power in foreign affairs, it was touch and go for the future of the institution.

Watergate Prerogatives

More than a century after Johnson violated the Constitution, the Nixon administration ordered the burglary of the headquarters of the Democratic National Committee, break-ins and burglary of the office of Daniel Ellsberg's psychiatrist, and the violation of various statutory and Fourth Amendment prohibitions against illegal searches and seizures against a variety of individuals. Nixon may or may not have personally ordered these actions, but he certainly conspired to impede criminal investigations of these crimes by ordering the CIA to act in such a way as to remove the FBI from the investigations, by suborning perjury or silence through the payment of "hush money," by hinting of pardons to the Watergate burglars, and by conspiring with his chief aides to place the blame on Attorney General John Mitchell.

Evidence on White House tape recordings could establish whether or not the president was part of the original Watergate conspiracy, whether he was part of a coverup, or whether, as he claimed, he took legitimate action and was deceived by his aides and subordinates. The president claimed *executive privilege*—the right to refuse information to other branches of government—against the demands of the Senate Select Committee, the Watergate grand jury, the office of special prosecutor, and the House Committee on the Judiciary. By invoking executive privilege, Nixon created a "boundary dispute" with the other branches: his claim would be weighed against the need of a congressional committee for information necessary to legislate, a grand jury to obtain evidence in criminal proceedings, and the Judiciary Committee for information necessary to frame articles of impeachment against the president.[43]

The term *executive privilege* is not mentioned in the Constitution. The president constructs this prerogative, first, by arguing that it is "necessary and proper" in the exercise of "the executive power" to maintain confidentiality in his dealings with assistants, and second, by invoking a rule of symmetry (see Appendix: "Rules of Constitutional Construction"). "No president could function if the private papers of his office, prepared by his personal staff, were open to public scrutiny," Nixon wrote to

Senator Sam Ervin, chairman of the Watergate committee.[44] When Judge John Sirica asked Nixon's attorney, "What is the public interest served in the withholding of these tapes?" Charles Wright responded, "The public interest in having the President able to talk in confidence with his closest advisors."[45]

The office of special prosecutor sued Nixon to obtain tapes necessary for criminal prosecutions. Nixon argued that he had a general supervisory authority over the Department of Justice and therefore over the special prosecutor; thus the courts should not interfere in an "intra-branch" dispute. Based on his authority as "chief law enforcement officer" the president claimed powers of a "prosecutor-in-chief": he would make the determination about what information should be made available to the grand jury. In his brief the president argued that he "has the power and thus the privilege to withhold information if he concludes that disclosure would be contrary to the public interest."[46] To require the president to obey a court order compelling him to produce the tapes, Nixon argued, would "destroy the status of the executive branch as an equal and coordinate element of government."[47]

Special Prosecutor Leon Jaworski challenged Nixon's interpretation of his prerogatives. He argued that the grand jury was gathering evidence about criminal conspiracies. It had a right to every person's evidence, and the president was obliged to provide material evidence in his possession. The interest in confidentiality had to yield to the need for evidence, since there was reason to believe that crimes had been committed, and since close aides of the president, and even the president himself, were under suspicion of having committed them. The claim of executive privilege cannot be used to obstruct justice. Even if the president were to be considered chief prosecutor, he could not impede or terminate a grand jury investigation, nor restrict its demand for evidence, since no prosecutor has such powers.

Jaworski also argued that he was not a subordinate of the president; therefore the dispute was not "intra-branch." By statute Congress vested the power to conduct criminal litigation directly with the attorney general, who in turn had the authority to appoint subordinate officers such as the special prosecutor (in whom he vested the power to prosecute offenses arising out of Watergate).[48] When the first special prosecutor, Archibald Cox, was named to the post, the Senate guidelines for his position specified that "The Attorney General will not countermand or interfere with the Special Prosecutor's decisions or actions."[49] Following the intent of the Senate, the attorney general gave Cox full independence "consistent with the Attorney General's statutory accountability."[50] After Nixon fired Cox and nominated Leon Jaworski for the position, an "accord" was reached between the president and the Senate, which provided that the "substantial concurrence" of the majority and minority leaders, the Speaker and minority leader of the House, and the chairmen and ranking minority members of the House and Senate Judiciary Committees would be necessary for the president to dismiss the prosecutor. Had such an accord not been reached, the Senate would not have confirmed Jaworski, and instead it would have appointed its own prosecutor through new legislation. Jaworski argued that he was, therefore, an independent officer of government, accountable to Congress and the courts as well as to the attorney general, and vested with full authority and discretion to conduct the prosecutions. Because the president had agreed to conditions on his removal power, Jaworski argued, he "has ceded any power that he might have had to control the course of the pending prosecution."[51]

The special prosecutor argued that the courts could compel the president to produce evidence. To yield such authority to the president would itself constitute a violation of the separation of powers, for "the President cannot be a proper judge of whether the greater public interest lies in disclosing evidence, when that evidence may have a material bearing on the guilt or innocence of close aides and trusted advisors."[52] The judiciary alone determines the validity of the claim of executive privilege.

Nixon lost his case against the special prosecutor. The district court, the appeals court, and finally the Supreme Court determined that the courts, not the president, would make the final determination on the claim of executive privilege. The president was not to be the sole judge of the nature of, or limits on, his constitutional prerogatives, for if such were the case, then any presidential decision or action could be shielded from judicial review by cloaking it in the executive privilege. To protect its own powers in the checks and balances system the court had to rule against the president's claims.

In so doing, the courts denied that the president represented the sovereign interests of the United States in the litigation. As the appeals court made clear, "Though the President is elected by nationwide ballot, and is often said to represent all the people, he does not embody the nation's sovereignty."[53] Instead, the courts upheld Jaworski's contention that the special prosecutor was invested with the sovereignty of the United States for the purpose of litigating against executive branch officials who might have committed crimes. The courts also denied the president's contention that the dispute was "intra-branch," by noting that the special prosecutor had explicit power to contest the invocation of executive privilege by the president.[54]

The Supreme Court agreed with the president that executive privilege was necessary to preserve "the valid need for protection of communications between high government officials and those who advise and assist them in the performance of their manifold duties," the first time the courts had upheld any claim of executive privilege. But the court brushed aside Nixon's argument that the privilege could be applied in criminal proceedings where no issues of national security were involved. It held, instead, that absent the claim of national security, "the generalized assertion of privilege must yield to the demonstrated, specific need for evidence in a pending criminal trial."[55]

After the decision, Nixon listened to several tapes that he had been withholding from the prosecutor. Close aides who heard several incriminating conversations persuaded him to resign from office. When Nixon's supporters on the House Judiciary Committee heard the conversations on the copies of the tapes that the White House provided, they conceded, "The charges of conspiracy to obstruct justice, and obstruction of justice . . . may be taken as substantially confessed by Mr. Nixon," and they concluded in their report, "Richard Nixon, as President, committed certain acts for which he should have been impeached and removed from office."[56]

The Law of Impeachment

What constitutes an impeachable offense? Were Nixon's actions "well within the President's inherent constitutional powers," as John Ehrlichman argued when he defended the Ellsberg break-in, or were they part of a squalid conspiracy involving the abuse of power, reflected in John Dean's memorandum, which asked, "How can we use the available federal machinery to screw our political enemies?"[57]

Most Republicans on the Judiciary Committee argued that for an offense to be impeachable, there must be probable cause to believe that a serious criminal act under the Constitution or laws had been committed. As Nixon stated at a press conference, "You don't have to be a constitutional lawyer to know that the Constitution is very precise in defining what is an impeachable offense . . . a criminal offense on the part of the President is the requirement for impeachment."[58] Although Nixon might be indicted on several counts, the evidence was inconclusive—especially since the president had not made a full record of tapes and documents available to Congress. The narrow grounds for impeachment were related to the Republican view of the function of impeachment: in the words of Nixon's lawyers, it was meant only "to check overt criminal actions as they are defined by law."[59]

Committee Democrats argued that "the Framers intended impeachment to be a constitutional safeguard of the public trust," rather than simply a procedure to punish criminal misconduct. A staff memorandum argued that "State and Federal criminal laws are not written to preserve the nation against serious abuse of the presidential office, but this *is* the purpose of the constitutional provision for the impeachment of a President and that purpose gives meaning to 'high crimes and misdemeanors.'" The memorandum concluded that grounds for impeachment included violation of the oath of office, failure to faithfully execute the laws, "exceeding the Constitutional bounds of the powers of the office in derogation of the powers of another branch of government," and "behaving in a manner grossly incompatible with the proper function and purpose of the office."[60] Democrats followed Madison's argument that the president was responsible for the actions of his subordinates. In arguing for a presidential removal power in 1789, Madison observed, "It will make him, in a peculiar manner, responsible for their conduct, and subject him to impeachment himself, if he suffers them to perpetrate with impunity high crimes and misdemeanors against the United States, or neglects to superintend their conduct, so as to check their excesses."[61]

The irony was that the Democrats attempted to have it both ways. They supported Leon Jaworski in his request for tapes and documents, arguing that the president had qualified his removal power, yet they also argued that the presidential removal prerogative could be intimately linked to a broad view of the impeachment process. In each case an interpretation of the removal power proved a blow to the president's defense.

Democrats tried to distinguish their "broad grounds" from simple partisan opposition to a Republican president. They framed their charges narrowly and did not mention the administration's refusal to spend appropriated funds, its dismantling of legislated programs, its secret bombing of Cambodia. They did not charge Nixon with defrauding the United States on his income tax returns. Instead, they focused on two issues: obstruction of justice and abuse of power. As Representative George Danielson emphasized, they were dealing with "crimes or offenses against the very structure of the state, against the system of government."[62]

Seven Republicans joined the Democrats on the Judiciary Committee to vote for impeachment articles. These men had supported Nixon's political program, but the misfeasance and malfeasance of agencies such as the CIA, the FBI, and the IRS, powerful organizations with potential for subversion of the democratic process, led them to desert the president. As Rep. Robert McClory argued, "the acts and conduct upon which I feel an article of impeachment should be presented to our colleagues is strictly constitutional, which relates narrowly and directly to the President himself and his personal oath of office."[63] Five years after the burglaries had occurred, Nixon told a television audience, "When the President does it, that means it is not illegal," but the Judiciary Committee had created a set of different standards, not only for the disgraced president, but also for all presidents who might abuse their powers in the future.[64]

The Judiciary and Executive Power

The Nixon White House used its secret police force of "plumbers" to place under surveillance high-ranking officials in sensitive national security positions and newspaper and television reporters, ostensibly to prevent leaks of classified information. The surveillance program was initiated in 1969 after several accounts of administration decisions involving Vietnam, North Korea, and Cambodia appeared in the *New York Times*. National Security Advisor Henry Kissinger met with FBI officials and asked them to determine how correspondent William Beecher had obtained his information. Hoover speculated that information had been leaked by officials on the staff of the National Security Council (NSC). Since Nixon, Mitchell, and Hoover had already authorized electronic surveillance to prevent leaks, Kissinger and his deputy, Alexander Haig, submitted to the FBI the names of several NSC staff members who had access to the secret information. FBI agents later recounted that Haig stated that the request to tap the names on the list "was being made on the highest authority," phrasing that indicated a presidential decision.[65] Attorney General Mitchell signed the orders for warrantless wiretaps prepared for him by the FBI. In the two years the program was in effect, taps were placed on NSC staff members, White House presidential assistants, and several correspondents. At various times Kissinger, Haig, Mitchell, and Nixon submitted names to the FBI. Kissinger and Haig also recommended that taps be discontinued, which was done.[66] Hoover sent reports to Kissinger and Haig and later directly to the White House.

What may the president order in the name of national security? Is he permitted to order warrantless wiretaps on his own authority? In a letter he later sent to the Senate Foreign Relations Committee Nixon stated,

I ordered the use of the most effective investigative procedures possible, including wiretaps, to deal with certain critically important national security problems. Where supporting evidence was available, I personally directed the surveillance, including wiretapping, of certain specific individuals. . . . I wish to affirm categorically that Secretary Kissinger and others involved in various aspects of this investigation were operating under my specific authority and were carrying out my express orders.[67]

But Nixon claimed that he had no recollection of ordering taps on specific individuals, and that the lists were submitted by Kissinger and other officials.[68] When Kissinger was asked who had supplied certain names, he responded:

At the Oval Office meeting of April, 1969, President Nixon authorized an electronic surveillance to be conducted. . . . While his authorization was in general terms and not limited to specific individuals, my understanding was that he then directed surveillance of Morton Halperin and certain others.[69]

The surveillance and wiretapping had only a tenuous connection to national security. They were techniques of "palace guard" politics. Attorney General Mitchell used a tap to keep tabs on John Sears of the White House staff, an old adversary. Kissinger submitted names of several State Department and one Defense Department official, to monitor responses in the departments to his policies. Haldeman and Nixon ordered taps on newspaper reporters for political reasons. The taps had little use, for as Nixon observed, "They never helped us. Just gobs and gobs of material. Gossip and bullshit . . . the tapping was a very unproductive thing."[70]

But some taps had political uses. The taps on two former NSC officials, Morton Halperin and Anthony Lake, were continued even after they left government service. Both men served as advisors on foreign policy to the Muskie presidential campaign in 1972, so surveillance enabled the White House to obtain advance information on Muskie's campaign strategy. Erlichman wrote a memorandum to Haldeman noting, "This is the kind of early warning system we need more of. Your game planners are now in an excellent position to map anticipatory action."[71]

Hoover recognized that the surveillance might be unconstitutional. He ordered his deputy, William Sullivan, to direct the field office handling the taps to "keep no permanent records of the wiretaps either in writing or on tapes."[72] Only one copy of the log of each tap was to be made and sent to FBI headquarters. Hoover instructed Sullivan "not to put any of this material in the FBI filing system or records division and not to have any of the names indexed; that he would keep the mail in his own office."[73] Following this procedure would enable Hoover and Sullivan to be able to testify "truthfully" in Congress or the courts that there was no evidence of a surveillance program in FBI files. The FBI also circumvented a Justice Department regulation that required a department evaluation of taps every ninety days. No such review was undertaken.

Kissinger seems not to have played a part in the partisan aspects of the program. The Senate Foreign Relations Committee, after investigating the program, found that "Dr. Kissinger's role in the wiretapping of 17 government officials and newsmen did not constitute grounds to bar his confirmation as Secretary of State."[74] But the Senate assured his exoneration because of the circumstances: the investigation was held immediately after his successful Middle East "shuttle," and just at the time the Nixon administration was crumbling because of Watergate revelations. Most Americans, accordng to surveys, wanted Kissinger to remain as Secretary of State even if Nixon were impeached or resigned. Just before the Senate committee began its investigation, fifty-two senators, including Mike Mansfield and Hugh Scott, the party leaders of the Senate, signed a resolution in praise of the secretary, finding him "an outstanding member of this Administration, as a patriotic American in whom it has complete confidence, and whose integrity and veracity are above reproach."[75]

Morton Halperin, tapped for twenty-one months, brought a lawsuit against Kissinger, Haig, Hoover, Mitchell, and Nixon. The president had two defenses for his conduct. Justice Department lawyers argued that Nixon had an "inherent executive power" to tap for national security purposes. The law regulating wiretapping that Congress passed, the Omnibus Crime Control and Safe Streets Act of 1968, provides an exception to the requirement for warrants that recognizes "the constitutional power of the President to take such measures as he deems necessary to protect the United States against the overthrow of the Government by force or other unlawful measures, or against any other clear and present danger to the structures or existence of our Government."[76] The federal judge who decided the case exonerated Kissinger and Haig because although they furnished names to the FBI, "they regarded the 'triumverate,' in Haig's words—Nixon, Mitchell, and Hoover—as responsible for determining when to terminate the wiretap."[77] The court was prepared to concede that Kissinger and Haig, on national security grounds, had reason to furnish names of those suspected of leaking information to the FBI for investigation and possible warrantless surveillance.

But the court found Nixon and others in his administration liable for violating Halperin's Fourth Amendment rights. The taps invaded his privacy and infringed upon his freedom of expression. Nixon initiated the program. Attorney General Mitchell failed to carry out a review of the tap during the twenty-one month period of surveillance. Haldeman was liable "for having reviewed the wiretap material for over a year without recommending termination and for having disseminated the material for purposes unrelated to the tap's original justification."[78] The length of the surveillance, the indiscriminate nature of the materials compiled, and the purposes to which they were put were unconstitutional. Although the court agreed with Nixon that "there was justifiably grave concern in early 1969 over the leaking of confidential foreign policy information," it held the wiretaps unconstitutional under the Fourth Amendment requirement that a warrant must be issued by a neutral magistrate on probable cause to assure that citizens will be subject only to "reasonable searches and seizures." Taps placed for political purposes could not be used without meeting the warrant requirement.

The court awarded Halperin compensatory damages. He asked for a substantial amount, based on the formula Congress had passed in the law regulating wiretapping. He also requested punitive damages to ensure that no official would violate rights in the future. But the court, although willing to restrict presidential prerogatives, did not wish to award significant damages. Instead, it awarded the nominal sum of one dollar from each liable defendant, and refused to award punitive damages, noting that the conduct of the defendants "cannot fairly be characterized as a wanton, reckless, or malicious disregard of plaintiff's rights justifying the imposition of punitive sanctions."[79]

In its decision the court took a middle ground. It did not wish to legitimize the prerogative to tap without a warrant, nor did it wish to grant the president and his aides immunity from damages. On the other hand the court did not wish to adhere to a hard and fast rule based on a formula, for who in elective or appointive office would be prepared to act decisively in a genuine national emergency if the consequences might be costly in a subsequent court case? Had the formula established by Congress been used by the court, each defendant would have been liable for approximately $300,000. Such a decision would have prompted Congress to pass a statute either indemnifying or immunizing executive branch officials in future cases. The result would have been to insulate the executive branch from any deterrent.

The court's decision left it with maximum flexibility. It exonerated NSC officials who acted on national security grounds. It punished the president and several aides for political use of taps. In a different set of circumstances, a court might yet impose massive fines, especially since the court had now put the executive branch on notice that political use of taps would not be tolerated. While checks and balances had been imposed, the presidency was still free to act in legitimate espionage cases. The Carter administration used electronic surveillance of Ronald Humphrey, suspected of spying for North Vietnam, without obtaining a warrant, and the president based his prerogative action on his oath of office. A statement issued by the Justice Department noted that the courts had "expressly confirmed the president's authority to authorize warrantless electronic surveillance when national security is threatened by a foreign power or its agents."[80] Just as significant, perhaps, was the fact that Carter's Justice Department joined in the appeal to the Supreme Court against the Halperin decision, arguing that lawsuits entertained against a president acting in good faith would have an inhibiting effect on the incumbent's conduct in office. The courts retained flexibility. Carter claimed power to tap and the issue of prerogative power remained open.

V

Emergency Prerogatives

The cases illustrate one central point: presidents employ prerogative power out of weakness rather than strength. No president wants the controversy that ensues when he construes his authority broadly, and none prefers to take actions that might result in censure or even impeachment. But prerogative government will be employed when the president calculates that Congress will not provide him with authority that he seeks, or that Congress will control policymaking, or that Congress and the courts will check his actions.

A distinction may be drawn between emergency prerogative government and Caesarism. The former is instituted in times of grave danger to maintain the rule of law and the fundamentals of the constitutional system, and it is invoked only when crisis has reached such proportions that the very life of the nation is at stake. The latter is used to justify faits accomplis that circumvent the principles of checks and balances, and involves replacement of the rule of law by presidential fiat in the name of the people. Certain standards of behavior may help to clarify the distinction between the two governmental forms:

1. The exercise of power should not involve personal or partisan advantage, nor should it interfere with the constitutional processes of election or succession to office.
2. The powers must be exercised in a national emergency, when the continued existence of the Union and the physical safety of the people is at stake, when delay might prove fatal, and when traditional constitutional procedures would involve such delay.
3. The powers are exercised when no statute or precedent provides a viable alternative procedure, and nothing in the Constitution or laws of the land expressly prohibit the actions.
4. Use of prerogative powers should be preceded by the widest possible consultation within the government, including senior officials in the departments, and when possible, leaders of Congress. The president should try to create a consensus that emergency government must be instituted.
5. The president should make available to Congress and the judiciary a full record involving his actions as soon as practicable during or after the emergency. Courts should make the final determination if he claims executive privilege.
6. Once the emergency has passed Congress should legislate to routinize procedures, placing powers on a statutory basis, and should provide for legislative and judicial review if appropriate.
7. The checks and balances system must function throughout the emergency, permitting possible resolutions of censure or an impeachment proceeding.

No set of standards for the exercise of emergency prerogatives can provide an absolute guarantee against Caesarism. But if one assumes that in the future presidents may find it necessary to rely on their prerogatives in emergencies, these standards provide the criteria for judging their use. Safeguarding the integrity of the electoral process, forcing the disclosure of information about the emergency, maintaining the system of checks and balances—these precautions can confine emergency prerogative government to *emergencies*, and maintain it as the ultimate safeguard of our democracy and Union.

The

Popular Connection

ELECTIONS provide presidents with constitutional legitimacy. They establish *polyarchy*, a system through which the electorate periodically and freely chooses from among politicians of competing parties to determine who will govern for a limited term of office. In James Madison's words, election results are always a "mark of confidence" from the people.[1]

Presidents emphasize the personal victory they have achieved: the will of the people has been expressed; the leaders will now guide the nation through crises; the presidency is an instrument of government elected by a national constituency and therefore the incumbent has heard, in Washington's phrase, "the voice of my country."[2] Incumbents consider the elections a *plebiscite* on the choice of ruler, and the winner is permitted to make policy under the old Roman principle: *vox populi legati suprema lex est*. As Harry Truman once summed up the relationship between popular accountability and the exercise of prerogative powers:

As the president came to be elected by the whole people, he became responsible to the whole people. . . . Every hope and every fear of his fellow citizens, almost every aspect of their welfare and activity, falls within the scope of his concern—indeed, it falls within the scope of his duty.[3]

The president emphasizes a mandate based on an undifferentiated majority—no matter how narrow the victory. The "voice of the people" may not have offered a mandate on issues in a clearcut campaign, but that does not prevent presidents from claiming to act in the name of the people. As Jimmy Carter analyzed the election results the day after his victory, he glossed over the narrow margin to promise, "I'll be very aggressive in keeping my promises to the American people," adding "I think the fact that I won and had such a broad base of support throughout the country and a clear majority is a good indication of support."[4]

Elections are not true plebiscites and do not provide presidents with real mandates. There is no close connection between strength in the office and the use of prerogatives on the one hand and the margin of victory on the other. Lincoln, Wilson, and Nixon, elected to their first terms with less than half the popular vote, acted in office more decisively than their contemporaries, Grant, Harding, and Eisenhower, all elected by landslides. Coversely, the great victories of Roosevelt in 1936 and Nixon in 1972 were followed by spectacular collisions with Congress and stalemates or defeats in domestic policymaking. Strong presidents need not even be elected, as the first-year performances of Theodore Roosevelt, Harry Truman, and Lyndon Johnson demonstrate.

The assumption that prerogative government requires an electoral mandate for its operation is incorrect. The processes by which a president is nominated and elected preclude his control over party or legislature and serve to maintain the checks and balances system; provide only a tenuous connection to voter sentiment; and do not provide the president with either a mandate on issues or a plebiscite on his leadership. It is the weakness of the popular connection that forces the president to rely on the resources of his own office and the prerogatives he can discover in the Constitution; yet that same electoral weakness will make it difficult for the president to assert all his prerogatives successfully.

I

Eligibility and Contention

To run for president one must be a natural-born citizen, thirty-five years of age upon assuming office, and fourteen years a resident of the United States. There are no religious, racial, or sex bars. Although most adult Americans may run for the office, lack of "social acceptability" makes it almost impossible for members of many groups to win a place on a major-party ticket, including non-Christians, women, blacks, Orientals, Hispanics, and native Americans. Most candidates are of Anglo-Saxon, Irish, German, or Dutch ancestry.

Of the millions of Americans who are socially acceptable for the

PRIOR PUBLIC POSITIONS OF PRESIDENTS: 1789–1978

OFFICE	NINETEENTH CENTURY (24)	TWENTIETH CENTURY (14)
Vice-president	7	7
Cabinet secretary	7	2
Subcabinet official	1	5
U.S. representative	13	4
U.S. senator	8	5
U.S. Supreme Court Justice	–	–
Federal judge	–	1
Governor	11	5
State legislator	17	5
State executive	10	2
State judge	1	3
Mayor	2	1
City government official	1	3
Diplomat, ambassador	7	1
General	5	1

nomination, only a handful ever achieve *contender-status*. Between 1936 and 1972 only sixty-two Democrats and forty-seven Republicans received more than 1 percent support in prenomination Gallup polls.[5] Nominees of the major parties are always chosen from a tiny group of career politicians, or in exceptional cases from military ranks.

Neither party maintains an orderly system of apprenticeship for the nomination or has a clear line of succession to it. Nor is there a group of "kingmakers" who can determine which contender will receive the nomination. Instead, contenders compete in state contests that narrow down the field to a front-runner and perhaps one or two rivals just prior to the nominating convention. These preconvention contests are divided into three efforts: fund-raising, media manipulation, and competition for convention delegates.

Campaign Finance

A contender must have money to create an organization and communicate with the voters. Raising funds requires the services of an organization that can make computerized direct mail solicitations. The initial goal of a contender is to develop a list of contributors who can fund the early stages of the primary campaign. Until the 1976 election year, contenders were able to rely on a few large donors to launch their candidacies. To encourage George Romney to run in 1968, Nelson Rocke-

A CANDIDATE'S OPINION OF CAMPAIGN FINANCING

Campaign financing is a curse. It's the most disgusting, demeaning, disenchanting, debilitating experience of a politician's life. It's stinky, it's lousy. I just can't tell you how much I hate it. I've had to break off in the middle of trying to make a decent, honorable campaign and go up to somebody's parlor or to a room and say "Gentlemen and ladies, I'm desperate. You've got to help me. My campaign manager is here and I'm going to step out of the room."

And you see people there—a lot of them you don't want to see. And they look at you, and you sit there and you talk to them and tell them what you're for and you need help and, out of the twenty-five who have gathered, four will contribute. And most likely one of them is in trouble and is somebody you shouldn't have had a contribution from.

Hubert H. Humphrey, the *New York Times*, Oct. 13, 1974.

feller arranged for several associates to contribute $750,000. Nixon began his campaign that year with a $4 million war chest contributed by a group of businessmen known as Richard M. Nixon Associates. On the Democratic side Eugene McCarthy started with a $2.5 million fund collected from fifty backers.[6] Until 1976 initial funds were raised from wealthy patrons contributing for personal or ideological reasons, or from speculators hoping to gain influence in government. Candidates with personal fortunes had advantages over other politicians. Most contenders sought the backing of the "superrich," the families of inherited wealth and control of interlocking corporate empires, such as the DuPonts, Lehmans, Mellons, Schiffs, Whitneys, Pews, Harrimans, Rockefellers, Vanderbilts, Loebs, and others. The primaries were expensive, and large campaign contributions were crucial. In 1968 Nixon spent $9 million, Rockefeller $8 million, and McCarthy $8.6 million; Kennedy spent almost $5 million and Humphrey over $4 million. In 1972 the eighteen Democratic contenders spent a total of $32 million; the Republican primaries were hardly contested, accounting for the low figure of $3 million. In 1976 thirteen Democrats spent $42.8 million and two Republicans spent $30 million (although some of the 1976 totals involve Treasury funds).[7]

The Federal Election Campaign Amendments of 1974 changed the system of preconvention financing. It placed a limit on each contender of $10 million in preconvention expenditures (plus an inflation adjustment and an additional $2 million for expenses). No candidate could spend more than $50,000 in personal funds (a provision later ruled unconstitutional by the Supreme Court). No person could contribute more than $1,000, and no labor or corporate "political action committee" could contribute more than $5,000 in the preconvention period.[8] Each contender was eligible for up to $5 million in matching funds from the Treasury if he qualified by raising, in each of twenty states, $5,000 in contributions of $250 or less. The Treasury would then match, dollar for dollar, all contributions up to $250 (which would encourage small donations rather than the $1,000 maximum). As a result of the Supreme Court decision, a candidate who chose not to accept matching funds was not limited to the $10 million ceiling.[9]

The spending limits placed a premium on intelligent allocation of funds and on advance planning for each state contest. To be successful, contenders had to demonstrate an ability to raise funds from the grass roots, to develop a campaign strategy, and to budget properly for it— qualities useful for a future president and his assistants. In 1976 all contenders took advantage of the matching fund provisions, small contributions were encouraged, and the impact of the "superrich," the speculators, and the corporate and labor committees was significantly reduced. But these reforms increased the separation of the contender from state and local party organizations. Seed money for contenders was raised not by party leaders, but by professional fundraisers hired by the contenders. These fundraisers were not party workers and owed their allegiance solely to the contender. The separation between presidential government and party organizations begins at this early and crucial stage in the electoral process, as candidates create their own campaign organizations rather than rely on the resources of their parties.

Media Politics

Contenders must create a campaign organization, which in turn develops the media image. Money can be converted directly into a media campaign because of three developments in political communication:

1. Technology permits mass communication via radio, television, telephone, and mail from the candidate directly to the voter, without the use of party organizations to canvass the electorate.
2. Campaign consulting firms possess demonstrated expertise in organizing and running media campaigns and work directly for candidates who can afford them.
3. Advances in the social sciences, especially statistics, demographics, social psychology, and political science enable campaign firms to "target" different messages to different kinds of voters to influence their electoral choice.

These developments in media politics have removed party professionals from the center of presidential campaigns and made the contender's media specialists the key factor. Illustrative of the changes is the ironic note Jimmy Carter sent to his chief advisor, Gerald Rafshoon, after the election, in which the president-elect noted facetiously, "I'll always be grateful that I was able to contribute in a small way to the victory of

PROJECTING THE CANDIDATE'S IMAGE

The first phase of any Carter campaign should be to formulate a heavyweight program and project a heavyweight image, all at the same time, trying to infect other southern states and other regions with the Jimmy Carter "good guy" brand of populism.

. . . In general, I see the publicity phases as follows:

Phase I 1973: Projection of the Carter record and knowledge.

Phase II 1974: Carter as a leader in the Democratic Party and someone involved in bringing it back.

Phase III 1975: Carter as a heavyweight thinker, leader in the party (denote in Phases One and Two) who has some ideas for running the country and is going around the country talking about them and who may have presidential ambitions.

Phase IV 1976: Carter—a presidential candidate.

Each of these phases runs into the succeeding phase and is an integral part of the overall buildup. They all cannot be accomplished at the same time but they all must be accomplished at the time allotted in order to evolve into the next phase.

Gerald Rafshoon Memo to Hamilton Jordan, in Martin Schram, *Running for President*, 1976, pp. 52–53.

the Rafshoon agency." Joseph Napolitan, a leading media consultant, explains that he practices "the art of communicating a candidate's message directly to the voter without filtering it through the party organization."[10] Market researchers, social psychologists, demographers, and pollsters can "pretest" themes like a detergent or breakfast cereal, and make adjustments. The contender himself is often packaged: restyled hair, new wardrobe, makeup, speech lessons.

The contender uses his media advisors to project an image in the primaries: the underdog battling front-runner; the outsider struggling against Washington; the statesman uniting the party; the liberal or conservative as pragmatic problem-solver; the pragmatic leader as spiritual leader. The image is always a simplified depiction of reality, for as Ray Price once argued in a memo to Nixon, "It's not what's there that counts, it's what is projected—and, carrying it one step further, it's not what he projects but rather what the voter receives."[11] Charles Kirbo, a principal Carter advisor, recalls that "I told [Carter] not to run his campaign on an intellectual approach to issues, but on a restoration of confidence in government. I thought people would buy that."[12] The audience must not be overloaded with information or confused with ambiguities or complexities. The image must be vague enough so that the voter can fill it in: conservatives should be able to see the candidate as a conservative, and liberals as a liberal. The trick is to appeal to all voters without seeming insincere.

Media messages rarely deal with important issues seriously. Napolitan admits, "I have no interest in government and don't know anything about it."[13] Symptomatic of the problem is the advice given to Carter by his pollster, Patrick Cadell, during the transition, when he urged the president to rely on media politics in running the government, warning, "Too many good people have been beaten because they tried to substitute substance for style."[14] Issues in primaries are dealt with superficially. Most television viewers pay little attention to "talking heads"— contenders discussing issues in detail and at length, so to keep viewer attention contenders must create "pseudoevents" to capture time on the evening news. These events have the following characteristics:[15] interesting visual effects, easily digestible copy in the form of pungent quotes and slogans, and themes calculated to identify the contender with the hopes and fears of the electorate, providing emotional rather than cognitive impact. Each election offers a new "gimmick"; in some all the candidates appear in shirtsleeves, in others they walk the streets, and in the most recent elections they gave the appearance of listening to the voters rather than talking to them. A contender is successful if he receives news coverage, for as Robert Kennedy said, in assessing the importance of this kind of campaigning, "Three minutes on the six o'clock news is worth all the rest of the publicity you can get."

Party professionals in state and national organizations are excluded from this media campaign. Most have contempt for the new politics of media manipulation and for its slick practitioners. As former Democratic National Chairman Lawrence O'Brien asked, "If you figure that by setting up a twenty-five million dollar budget, and making a game of who gets the best time slots and who hired the most creative media talent—and if you elect a President that way, what the hell's the country coming to?"[16]

Contender Strategies

There are several different strategies a contender may use to try to win the nomination. The *incumbent* emphasizes his record and experience as president. He uses patronage to obtain the backing of state and local party leaders. He attempts to change party rules to make it difficult to challenge him in primaries. He warns that primary opposition will split the party and permit the other party to win the White House. He controls the agenda of government: Nixon took trips to China and Russia in 1972 to emphasize his position as world leader; Ford took a hard line on Cuba just prior to the 1976 Florida primary and announced reforms of the CIA just before the New Hampshire contest. But the president's major disadvantage is his record. Truman and Johnson withdrew rather than risk primary defeats defending their foreign policies. Ford did poorly in several southern primaries partly because of his position on negotiations

THE MYTH OF THE TWO-TERM PRESIDENT: 1896–1976

Gerald Ford	Defeated for first elective term.
Richard Nixon	Resigned during second elective term.
Lyndon Johnson	Declined to run for second elective term.
John Kennedy	Did not complete first elective term.
Dwight Eisenhower	Completed two elective terms.
Harry Truman	Declined to run for second elective term.
Franklin Roosevelt	Did not complete fourth elective term.
Herbert Hoover	Defeated for second elective term.
Calvin Coolidge	Declined to run for second elective term.
Warren Harding	Did not complete first elective term.
Woodrow Wilson	Completed two elective terms.
William Taft	Defeated for second elective term.
Theodore Roosevelt	Declined to run for second elective term.
William McKinley	Did not complete second elective term.

for a new Panama Canal Treaty and partly because of his policy proposing an end of the minority white government in Rhodesia. Ford almost lost the nomination to Ronald Reagan. The incumbent may claim that his renomination would ensure a victory in the general election, but eight incumbents have lost. The assertion that presidents automatically win renomination isn't true (losers include John Tyler, Andrew Johnson, Franklin Pierce, Millard Fillmore, James Buchanan, and Chester Arthur); and presidents do not always serve out two terms. Still, incumbents have won seven of the nine most recent contests in which they ran.

An incumbent who declines to run for a second term or is barred from a third term may support a contender as *heir designate*. Truman was helpful to Stevenson, and Johnson's support was crucial for Humphrey. But the heir cannot guarantee the party a victory in the general election, as Stevenson, Nixon, and Humphrey all discovered. The heir must fight for the nomination against other challengers.

The *celebrity* contender demonstrates his popularity with the party rank-and-file in primaries and polls. He argues that he alone can win the general election. Like Kennedy or Carter, he must do well in the early primaries to gain media recognition as a front-runner. He campaigns in "media states," where weak party organizations are not an important factor and an effective new politics media campaign can carry the day. John Kennedy began with endorsements in organized labor and support of some urban machines. He put together a combination of old-line bosses, reform activists, and delegates won in the primaries to sew up the nomination. His theme was that he was a Washington "insider" experienced in domestic and world affairs who could provide effective leadership. Sixteen years later Jimmy Carter used a different approach: with almost no labor support or help from party organizations, he presented himself to the voters as an "outsider" untainted by the "mess" in Washington. He entered delegate contests in every state except one and steadily accumulated delegates even when he lost primaries.

Early polls are not decisive. In 1952 Stevenson trailed Kefauver and in 1959 Kennedy trailed Stevenson; in 1971 McGovern was far behind Edward Kennedy, Edmund Muskie, George Wallace, and Hubert Humphrey; in 1975 Carter was not even listed in most polls, whereas after five primaries the following year he was running even with Humphrey. Early primary successes, which get exaggerated media coverage and impact, lead to a surge in poll support and a bandwagon effect in later primaries. It is more important to do well in early primaries than in early polls, for being a front-runner in the polls has no effect on the primary results.[17]

The *factional* contender raises issues that he hopes will polarize the party rank-and-file, enabling him to win the nomination on the basis of an ideological appeal. As Gary Hart, manager of McGovern's 1972 campaign explained, "When you come to the nomination in the Democratic Party there is, for all practical purposes, no center," adding that "we always knew it would be a two-man race between a liberal and a conservative."[18] Some factional candidates hope to capture the party and convert it into a vehicle for their ideology. But these candidates fare poorly: Goldwater was soundly defeated in 1964 and McGovern in 1972; both Eugene McCarthy and Ronald Reagan lost their nomination bids to centrist candidates.

Unifiers start with support in one wing, then reach out to build coalitions with other factions. Nixon in 1968 mastered this strategy: he was still Eisenhower's protégé, he won some primaries and erased his image as a loser, he scored high in public opinion polls, he gained support from some conservative and liberal leaders, and finally he worked with southern delegates to head off Reagan. But in 1972 Humphrey failed to win the Democratic nomination with a similar strategy, and in 1976 both Humphrey and Jackson failed to put together coalitions that could stop Carter.

The strategy of the *dark horse* is based on the hope that the convention will deadlock, and from a smoke-filled room the party leaders will choose an unknown. In 1844 Polk was chosen on the ninth ballot; in 1852 Pierce emerged after forty-nine; in 1880 Garfield was chosen after thirty-six; in 1920 Harding was picked after ten; and in 1924 Davis was nominated after one hundred three ballots. Since then, no dark horse has emerged. Since 1928 the Democrats have had only two conventions that lasted more than one ballot (1932 and 1952) and the Republicans have also had only two (1940 and 1948).

The function of the convention is now to register the decisions that have been made in the preconvention contests: it serves a function not dissimilar to the electoral college. Unifiers, dark horses, and heirs apparent do not fare well in such a situation; increasingly the field has been left to those celebrity and factional candidates who will fight for delegates in state contests.

Primaries

The contenders compete to eliminate rivals from the same wing of the party in early "shakeout" primaries; then to eliminate others in the large states and demonstrate national appeal; and finally to win several of the last contests to gain momentum and knock the last rivals from the race. The importance of primaries has increased as more states adopt this system to choose national convention delegates: primaries were held in seventeen states in 1968, accounting for 37.5 percent of the Democratic and 34.3 percent of the Republican delegates; in twenty-three states in 1972, accounting for 60.5 percent of the Democratic and 52.7 percent of the Republican delegates; and in thirty states in 1976, accounting for 72.5 percent of the Democratic and 67.9 percent of the Republican delegates.[19] In past elections they have often had little impact, either confirming the front-runner or yielding ambiguous results.[20] A candidate who won all the primaries could not sweep the state delegations for several reasons:

1. Some primaries are "beauty contests" in which no convention delegates are chosen (delegates being selected by caucuses or state conventions). In 1976 seventeen of the thirty primary states had binding primaries rather than beauty contests.
2. In some states the contest for delegates is separated from the presidential preference ballot, so that a contender may win the primary while an opponent wins the contest for delegates.
3. Many contests provide either for proportional representation or for district election of delegates, which makes it unlikely that a contender can win most of the delegates.

A string of primary victories may create a "bandwagon" psychology enabling a contender to pick up support among uncommitted delegates and win caucus and state convention contests. Carter received 39 percent of the popular vote in primaries, and his delegate total from those states left him short of the nomination, but his delegates from nonprimary states made him unbeatable after the primary season had ended.

In the past, candidates have lost a majority of primaries or chosen not to run in them and been nominated by their party, including Wilson and Taft in 1912, Hughes in 1916, Harding and Cox in 1920, Davis in 1924, Hoover in 1932, Landon in 1936, Willkie in 1940, Dewey in 1948, Eisenhower and Stevenson in 1952, and Humphrey in 1968. But the large number of delegates chosen in primary states since 1972 makes it unlikely that in the future a contender will be able to remain out of them or lose most of them and still hope to be the nominee.

Primary winners claim to be the popular choice, but that is not really the case. In 1976 there were approximately 150 million persons in the voting age population. Of these, approximately 40 percent were Democratic identifiers as 20 percent Republican identifiers: sixty million potential Democratic primary voters and thirty million potential Republican primary voters. Yet perhaps one-third of these potential voters did not register.[21] Only 28,925,000 persons voted in the 1976 primaries. Only three-fifths of the states held primaries. Not all contenders appeared on all ballots. Fourteen states, such as Texas, Indiana, and Michigan, permitted "crossovers" in the primaries, so that members of one party could vote in the primary of the other party. Ronald Reagan defeated Gerald Ford in several states by winning votes from Democratic supporters of George Wallace who crossed over, although Ford was the choice of a majority of registered Republicans.

Turnouts in primaries have been low. Although in 1972 and 1976 a slight majority of the *registered* voters turned out in "closed" primary states (those in which crossovers from the other party are not permitted), a majority of party identifiers in the voting-age population does not vote.[22] Those who do vote are better educated, wealthier, more partisan, and better informed than those who do not. Their vote may not be representative of the sentiments of all party identifiers.[23] The turnout in primaries since 1952 has ranged between one-fifth and one-quarter of the eligible voters, reaching 28 percent in 1972 and 1976. But these figures mask significant differences between the two parties. In 1968 and 1972 Democratic turnouts increased dramatically with no corresponding jump on the Republican side, whereas in 1976 Democratic turnouts fell slightly and Republicans registered major gains.[24] In states with "closed" primaries and a long history of primary contests, the trend in turnout is increasing for both parties. In the future, assuming there are serious contests for the nominations, the "socialization" of the electorate into mass primary participation will yield ever-higher turnouts, as the majority of voters become accustomed to participating in these contests. As turnouts increase, primaries should become a more representative method of selecting delegates.[25]

Primaries do not give the nominee a mandate from the party. Contenders may receive support from liberals in one state, moderates in another, and conservatives in a third, like Jimmy Carter in 1976. Ford received majorities from conservatives, moderates, and liberals in several states, whereas in others dissident Democrats crossing over into Republican primaries helped to defeat him.[26] Antiwar candidate Eugene McCarthy received the support of hawks and doves in the 1968 New Hampshire primary, since neither group supported Johnson's conduct of the war. Supporters of conservative George Wallace voted for the liberal Robert Kennedy in many of the 1968 Democratic primaries as a form of "protest" with conditions. Primaries offer voters a jumble of issues, some local and some national, some transitory, and some enduring, and the electorate often chooses on the basis of personality. Rarely do primaries offer a contest between two candidates diametrically opposed to one another; even when that situation occurs, rarely do primary voters give a clear indication of which policies they prefer when they make their choices.

Primary victories do attract funds and volunteers to a campaign. They provide media exposure and improve the contender's poll ranking.[27] They eliminate rivals from the field. They may also put to rest damaging issues, such as Kennedy's religion, Nixon's "loser" image, or Carter's southern background. But the primaries expose the weaknesses of contenders who cannot put together an organization, raise funds, speak effectively, or develop successful media campaigns.

Whether the nominee has won primaries or not, he almost always represents the final preconvention sentiments of the party rank-and-file as expressed in public opinion polls. Between 1936 and 1976, of the twenty-two major party nominations, the poll leader was nominated in all but two cases, the exceptions being Kefauver in 1952 and Scranton in 1964. In nineteen of these cases the poll leader prior to the primaries won the nomination. In some cases the primary system seems to be responsive to popular sentiment; in others victories in the primaries seem to change public opinion.[28] The nominee is almost always the choice of a plurality of county party leaders as well. Between 1960 and 1972 only George McGovern did not have such support. Humphrey, although not even entered in the primaries in 1968, had the support of 70 percent of the county leaders; Goldwater, although not the choice of the rank and file in the polls in 1964, did have a 48 percent plurality of the leaders. It is just as important to have the support of the leaders as it is to win primaries: primary winners who did not have such support and lost the nomination include Champ Clark in 1912, William McAdoo in 1924, Thomas Dewey in 1940, Harold Stassen in 1948, Estes Kefauver in 1952, Robert Taft in 1952, and Eugene McCarthy in 1968.

Reformers have suggested changes in the primary process. Woodrow Wilson proposed a single national primary. Estes Kefauver proposed a constitutional amendment to require that all delegates to a national convention pledge their votes to primary candidates, with each contender receiving a proportion based on the votes he won in each state. Contenders could release their delegates at the convention, and after ten ballots all delegates could vote for one of the top three candidates. The Mansfield-Aiken proposal for a constitutional amendment provided that state primaries be held on the same day, in effect creating a single national primary day. These reforms would hold the convention delegates directly accountable to rank-and-file party sentiment. They would limit the role of state party organizations in choosing delegates, and increase even more the importance of media election techniques. A single national primary would be a one-shot affair, with no change to expose shallow or inept contenders, with no opportunity to see how they fare over a long and grueling primary season, with no chance for candidates to revive fading candidacies. Front-runners would always be favored and "outsiders" would stand little chance of success. The present system at least provides a revealing picture of the character and stamina (if not the intelligence) of the contenders.

One reform is taking place. Several small states in each region in 1976 held their primaries on the same day or in the same week to increase the incentive for contenders to campaign. Such an emerging system of "regional" primaries represents a sound modification of the present system. It minimizes the travel burden, while at the same time preserving the strength of the present system with its unfolding sequence of contests. Another reform would be to hold the small-state primaries early, which would enable contenders starting late or lacking funds to have a reasonable chance to demonstrate popular appeal; later contests would shift to the large "media-states" for final eliminations.[29]

An incumbent president has no incentive to support party rules for an open primary season. In 1977 the Democrats on the "Winograd" commission in charge of making the rules for the 1980 contest were pressured by representatives from the White House to (1) shorten the primary season to thirteen weeks and (2) increase the minimum proportion of votes a contender would need to win delegates from 15 percent to 20 percent in the early contests and up to 25 percent in the later primaries. As political scientist William Crotty pointed out:

The effort represents a cynical attempt to reverse the work of a decade and to close the Democratic nomination to all but the incumbent. The thinking is that Carter, the best known of the candidates early on, should win the opening tests. As his opponents become better known and are in a position to offer a stronger challenge, the proportion of votes that they would need to get any delegate support at all would be made increasingly difficult.[30]

Having successfully used the outsider celebrity strategy in 1976, Carter intended to make it difficult for anyone else to use it against him in 1980.

State Caucuses and Conventions

One-fourth of the national convention delegates are chosen by caucuses (meetings of party members at the local level) or at state or congressional district conventions. Some states, including primary states, also provide that some national delegates be chosen by the state party organization. Each of these procedures increases the influence of party professionals and minimizes the impact of media politics.

Caucuses are the least-representative system of choosing delegates. Turnout is low, and the mean proportion of the voting age population attending them in twenty-one states in 1976 was 1.9 percent.[31] Turnouts range from slightly less than one thousand to slightly more than a hundred thousand for the state. Contenders work with regular party organizations or special interest groups (labor, farmer, ethnic, ideological, and environmental) to "flood" caucuses and control their proceedings. These contests set groups of activists against each other, with no mass involvement. At times state and local party organizations remain neutral; at other times they field "uncommitted" delegates. In the states with strong party organizations, the largest proportion of delegates will be "uncommitted" at the national conventions; in western states where party organizations are weak, the contenders may "blitz" the state with a makeshift local organization to capture delegates. These techniques worked successfully for McGovern in 1972 and Goldwater in 1964. Contenders pay special attention to the early caucuses that are held prior to the primaries. The media will cover these tiny contests as a first indication of how campaigns are progressing. A "victory" may be won with just a few thousand followers participating in local meetings: Carter's much-heralded victory in Iowa involved the support of 13,000 Democrats out of a total of 455,000 registered in the state.

National Conventions

The traditional pattern at national conventions has been for delegates to be controlled by delegate brokers representing state and local party organizations. As former Manhattan County Leader Edward Costikyan once explained, "The first thing a candidate who wants the nomination should recognize is that the delegates are not free agents, nor are they subject to persuasion. The delegate is the property of his leader."[32] Most delegates were party hacks whose convention participation was a reward for services rendered to the organization—a paid vacation. They took neither their duties nor themselves seriously, leaving the real business of the convention to their bosses, who worked behind closed doors, where state and local party leaders would negotiate with each other and construct coalitions with the managers of the contenders.

The purpose of the coalition building was to win a say in the distributions and patronage that the White House could make available after the election. These included cabinet and subcabinet appointments, judgeships, appointments as U.S. attorneys and marshalls, and awards, contracts, and subsidies. Sections might press for commitments on the vice-presidency or on important issues.

Modern conventions depart from traditional practices in several respects. Delegates are no longer the property of leaders. They hold themselves accountable to electorates in primary states and are bound by pledges they made in primaries. State delegations are no longer cohesive, to be bartered by leaders in return for promises of patronage. New groups have arisen to barter with contenders, including caucuses of women, blacks, labor union delegates, and environmental groups. These caucuses have yet to dominate a convention, and observers found them inexperienced in 1972, but they are likely to be strongly influenced by commitments made by contenders, which in turn reduces the influence of local party organizations and bosses.[33] In the classic convention the "unit rule" permitted the state delegation to vote as a bloc in accord with the will of the majority, and leaders voted the proxies of absent delegates. These rules ensured that minority factions would have little influence in the delegation. In 1972 Republicans and Democrats changed convention rules to eliminate these practices. Democratic rules in 1976 provided that all state delegations chosen on a statewide basis reflect the strength of candidates who had received at least 15 percent of the primary or state convention votes. The rules made it likely that delegations would consist of supporters of several candidates, and that these delegates could fragment the unity of the state delegation and vote for the contenders of their choice. The effect of the rules was to decrease the incentive of campaign managers to bargain with state delegate brokers, and increase their incentive to mount contests in each state to win their own share of delegates. Since candidates can use new politics techniques to communicate directly to state electorates, the separation of contenders from state and local party leaders has increased. Media politics techniques could even be applied at the convention itself to communicate to delegates, and increasingly the individual delegates were "candidate oriented" rather than party oriented: their concern about personalities and issues was increasing, while their interest in the fortunes of state and local party organizations was decreasing.[34]

These recent developments, which have weakened the power of party leaders at conventions, should be contrasted with proposals made by some political scientists to strengthen the parties. In 1950 a Committee of the American Political Science Association recommended that half the delegates to the national conventions consist of members of Congress and party leaders. Such a convention would make contenders accountable both to the legislative party and to state and local organizations.[35] The recent rules changes do precisely the opposite: they strengthen the contender and his personal following at the expense of all other segments of the party—the rank and file, who can be manipulated in primaries; the party leaders, who can no longer deliver unified state delegations; the congressional party, which is hardly represented at the convention and has no working relationship with the candidate's organization.

The Party Platform

No mechanism forces the successful candidate to honor his party platform, or even run his campaign on it. Although one study found that presidents redeem slightly more than half their platform commitments and ignore only one-tenth, no causal relationship should be inferred.[36] Platforms are so general that any action the new administration takes is likely to redeem a commitment. The planks are usually adopted to unify the party, but candidates often revise them once they have won the nomination. Eisenhower reached an agreement on campaign principles with Robert Taft in the "Morningside Heights" pact of 1952, in effect repudiating part of his own platform. Nixon in 1960 hammered out the "Fifth Avenue Accord" with Nelson Rockefeller, taking a more hawkish line in foreign policy than the platform. Hubert Humphrey changed his position on the bombing of North Vietnam near the end of his 1968 campaign, jettisoning a controversial platform plank that his supporters had won over the "doves." In 1972 McGovern's important proposals were frantically improvised, modified, and even discarded during the campaign, with little reference to the platform. In 1976 Carter began his campaign with a conservative fiscal program and hardly mentioned the Democratic platform, except to disavow its abortion plank in a highly publicized meeting with six Roman Catholic bishops. Ford disregarded a platform that had been written in large part by the Reagan forces, which contained language that disavowed his own foreign policy initiatives. The nominating convention does not serve as a link between voters, congressional party, or the president—it seems instead to provide the nominee with every incentive to disregard the party in developing his general campaign themes.

II

The General Election

The election continues the separation of the presidential nominee from the national and state party organizations. Once nominated, the candidate does not disband his personal following and rely on the national committee to run his campaign. Hugh Scott, a former Republican national chairman, was bluntly told during Thomas Dewey's 1948 campaign by one of the candidate's managers: "You keep the party happy. Brownell runs the campaign."[37] Nixon created his own campaign committee and used his own staff for all of his campaigns. Carter ran his entire operation from rented office space in Atlanta, Georgia, with little communication with the national party headquarters in Washington.

Election Finance

Money cannot buy the election, but large amounts are necessary in media campaigns. Combined expenditures in the postconvention period of the parties were over $13 million in 1956, $20 million in 1960, $25 million in 1964, $44 million (for three parties) in 1968, and $104 million in 1972.[38] These reported amounts significantly understate actual expenditures, since reporting systems were not taken seriously, many illegal contributions were not reported, and various nonparty groups donated labor or funds not included in these totals.

Most of the funds were not raised by party organizations, which concentrate on state and congressional elections. Instead, funds were raised by the candidate's own finance committees, which received contributions from special committees incorporated in the states. Until 1972 names of contributors to most of these committees could be concealed, since state laws did not require extensive record keeping. Through transfers between committees, funds could be "laundered" so that donors remained anonymous. Gulf Corporation, for example, covered up a $5 million fund for illegal political contributions by transferring funds through a subsidiary corporation, the Bahamas Exploration Company of Nassau, which in turn made contributions to Richard Nixon, Lyndon Johnson, and Gerald Ford (in his congressional campaigns).[39] In 1972 ex-Governor Tim Babcock of Montana, then a vice-president of Occidental Petroleum, served as a "front" for an illegal corporate contribution of $54,000, ordered by Occidental's chairman, Dr. Armand Hammer, to the Nixon campaign.[40] Lax reporting laws and poor auditing systems enabled Nixon and his principal aides to control discretionary funds: Herbert Kalmbach controlled a $2 million fund and H. R. Haldeman a $350,000 account.[41] The system of private financing of general election expenses allowed financiers, speculators, fronts for organized crime syndicates, stock swindlers, and others hoping to gain protection from the laws ample scope to buy influence and "protection."

Nixon carried the mortgaging of government to its lowest levels. As early as 1968 he accepted an illegal $50,000 corporate contribution from Phillips Petroleum.[42] Robert Vesco, a financier, gave Nixon's 1972 campaign $200,000 in order to avoid prosecution in an investigation conducted by the Department of Justice but eventually fled the country to avoid court proceedings. Milk cooperatives, in violation of the law, used corporate funds for gifts to the Nixon campaign in order to gain a rise in the price of milk after the elections.[43]

The administration continued the traditional system of "auctioning" ambassadorships in return for large, legal, personal contributions. Kennedy in 1961–62 had nominated seven contributors; Johnson in 1964–65 had nominated ten; Nixon in 1969–70 made fifteen such nominations. After the 1972 campaign it turned out that Ruth Farkas had contributed $300,000 to Nixon to obtain a European embassy, and she was reportedly miffed when offered Costa Rica instead.[44]

Significant legal contributions to the Nixon campaign included over $5.4 million from executives of the one hundred largest defense-contracting firms and almost $5 million from executives of the one hundred seventy-eight largest oil companies. But some corporate contributions were in direct violation of federal laws prohibiting direct contribution of corporate funds in presidential campaigns. The American Ship Building Company, headed by New York Yankees owner George Steinbrenner III, funneled $40,000 in corporate funds to several committees to reelect Nixon. American Airlines, applying to the Civil Aeronautics Board for a merger with another airline, was asked for $100,000 and made an illegal $55,000 contribution. The Amarada Hess Corporation gave $250,000. The list of corporations making such illegal donations to Nixon includes Ashland Oil, Braniff Airways, Diamond International Corporation, Goodyear Tire and Rubber Company, Hertz Corporation, Minnesota Mining and Manufacturing Company, Northrop Corporation.[45] Many of the contributions were solicited by White House aides, who cross-checked potential donors against lists of corporations facing regulatory or legal actions prior to making their "pitch" for contributions for executives.

Illegal contributions of corporate funds could be made by company executives using any or all of these methods:[46]

1. Corporate services to the campaign could be provided free, at a discount, or on the understanding that bills for such services would not be paid.
2. Personnel working on company time and salary could be donated to a campaign (a system also used by unions).
3. A company could reimburse executives who made large donations by raising their salaries, giving them special bonuses, or allowing them to pad expense accounts.
4. Customers served by the company could be underbilled with the understanding that the customers would donate to a campaign.
5. The company could allow itself to be overbilled by law firms, advertising agencies, or others from whom it purchased services, with the understanding that the firms would contribute to a campaign.

Congress in 1974 passed reform legislation to end these abuses.[47] Each major party candidate was to be limited in 1976 to $21.8 million (plus $4 million in administrative costs) for the postconvention election period. The party national committees could spend an additional $3.2 million on the campaign, and as much as $4.5 million could be spent on a presidential candidate's behalf by state and local party committees. The nominees could raise these funds from private sources (in which case the Supreme Court ruled that spending limits would not apply) or they could finance their activities entirely from public funds. Individual contributors were limited to $1,000 and political action committees to $5,000 during the general election period. However the contributors could give up to $20,000 to the national committees—a large loophole in the law.

To some extent the reforms increase the separation of the candidates from party organizations. If they accept full public funding for the general election, they have little incentive to work closely with the party to raise funds. But the expenditure ceilings do offer candidates an incentive to use the resources of the parties. The Federal Election Commission ruled that local committees might pay the cost of party headquarters that promote the national ticket as well as the local candidates, without expenses being charged to the national spending limit. Each state and local party committee can spend up to $1,000 for the national ticket without being charged on the ceiling. The party national committee can spend millions of dollars for voter registration drives, which might help the ticket in the large states. It may be too early to gauge the full impact of the reforms in financing on the relationship between candidate and party organization. But it does seem as if the thrust of the new law is to lessen the reliance of the national ticket on party professionals and on interest groups. In ending the system by which candidates relied excessively on large contributors, some accountability to the party organizations may have been sacrificed.

Voter Mobilization

Presidential candidates use media politics to communicate with the voters. They supplement the media campaign with efforts by interest groups to mobilize voters. And they also use state and local party organizations who want to work for the ticket, although they have no way of ensuring that these local units will do so. They use the $3.2 million in national committee campaign funds from the Treasury to pay some campaign expenses of the state and local parties. Together with volunteer groups, these organizations "pull" voters to the polls. Perhaps the best description of such an operation was given by Lincoln when he instructed his supporters in his congressional campaign of 1848:

The whole state must be so well organized that every Whig can be brought to the polls. So divide the county into small districts and appoint in each a committee. Make a perfect list of the voters and ascertain with certainty for whom they will vote. . . . Keep a constant watch on the doubtful voters and have them talked to by those in whom they have the most confidence. . . . On election day see that every Whig is brought to the polls.[48]

Some parties are a great help. Kennedy would not have won the election in 1960 were it not for the votes mobilized in large urban areas by the party machines. But regular party units do not perform well in most of the 178,159 precincts in the nation, because they lack the personnel to man them and perform the tasks Lincoln suggested. Only one in five voters is contacted in a presidential campaign. Most organizations are more interested in state or local contests than in presidential elections, and some may actually defect or sit out the contest. There are no "armies" of party workers the candidate can use to mobilize the voters.[49]

In recent campaigns, candidates have emphasized media politics. Their campaigns have several goals:

1. Activating and reinforcing decisions of party identifiers to vote for the ticket by appeals to party loyalty
2. Gaining the support of independent voters with broad thematic appeals, pseudoissues and psuedoevents, and personality appeals
3. Raising issues for those in the electorate who will vote on them
4. Making inroads into the traditional voter coalition of the opposition party by emphasizing thematic or personality appeals calculated to win the approval of their weak identifiers

Republicans, with fewer party identifiers, must move beyond the ranks of their traditional supporters; they try to appeal to independents and promote the defection of Democrats by "cross-pressuring" union members, suburban Catholics, and southerners, often with great success. Some campaigns emphasize personality ("I like Ike"), and others, like the 1968 Nixon campaign, play on the fears of the electorate by scapegoating such groups as the "New Left" and the antiwar movement and rallying a "Silent Majority" from both parties. Ford's 1976 campaign was geared to cross-pressuring the Democratic coalition, for a campaign memo indicated that

. . . the target constituency in the suburbs for the President is the upper blue collar and white collar workers, often from a family which has risen in mobility in the last generation. These are independent minded voters, many of whom are Catholic. In addition, there is a weakness in Carter's support among Catholics and also among Jews.[50]

If issues are raised they must coincide with the predisposition of potential party switchers—a campaign is no time to try to change peoples' minds.

Democrats enjoy more than a two-to-one margin in the number of party identifiers. They concentrate on unifying their party after the nomination. They emphasize party identification and try to counter any cross-pressuring of their supporters that Republicans attempt.[51] In half the campaigns since 1952 they have failed to maintain their initial advantage or keep their coalition intact: Republicans often succeed in gaining as much as half the southern, union, and Roman Catholic voters. In 1976 though, Carter managed to retain the support of traditional

Democratic identifiers, winning 80 percent of the Democratic vote, including 68 percent of the Jews, 55 percent of the Roman Catholics, 62 percent of the poor, and 75 percent of the liberals. There was more voting along class and party lines than in most elections of the 1950s or 1960s.[52]

Although candidates use media politics techniques, they may not be able to manipulate voter choice as much as they believe. In elections in which party identification is a major factor, media politics at best reinforces a predisposition to vote for the party candidate. Issue voters are most likely to obtain information from newspapers rather than from television news and commercials, since the broadcast media emphasizes the "contest" almost to the exclusion of the content of the campaign.[53] Debates that are televised are used more than any other source of information by less-sophisticated voters. The free-for-all debates cannot be fully controlled by the media advisors of the candidate: at times the voters catch a glimpse of the real personalities, and this may change the direction of a campaign.[54]

Political scientists disagree about the effectiveness of media campaigns. In a controversial study by Thomas Patterson and Robert McClure of the 1972 campaign, the authors concluded that "all the careful image planning—the coaching, the camera work, the calculated plea—counts for nothing."[55] There must be something to this argument, for if a pleasing personality were all that were required, Johnson might have lost in 1964 and Nixon in 1972. In those years voters seemed aware of major issues and able to choose between the candidates on the basis of their positions. In 1976 the Ford campaign constructed "perceptual maps" to find out what voters thought, and then tried to move the Ford "image" closer to these perceptions, while shifting the public impression of Carter away from them. The attempt to do this failed. Yet Carter's standing among voters dropped whenever people suspected that he was attempting to be all things to all people, and some of his media campaign seemed to backfire. The 1976 election results seemed to be little more than an indication of which candidate voters mistrusted least.

To use the media without appearing manipulative, candidates have resorted to several new techniques. They make "documentary" commercials that have the appearance of evening news broadcasts. They appear in staged "news conferences" and are asked questions by recognized broadcasters (being paid by the campaign), and these "shills" feed them easy questions. Instead of using the media to lead on the issues, they record commercials that simply reflect voter sentiment back to the electorate. People are expected to vote on the basis of a shared sentiment or emotion (the tax system is a disgrace, crime rates are too high) rather than on a position the candidate presents to solve the problem.

The Incumbency

It is difficult to run against a sitting president, unless he has stumbled into war or recession. A president wins some votes simply because he occupies the office. Nixon in 1972 called his campaign organization the Committee to Re-Elect the President to exploit this tendency. The incumbent uses the federal grant system and patronage powers to build his campaign organization. Nixon acted as all presidents do when he ordered "Operation Responsiveness," a program of federal grants and loans to be made available to minority businesspersons in the election year. Ford used a photograph of the highest-ranking black civil servants in his administration, supposedly for a bicentennial brochure, but actually used in campaign literature to create the false impression that they supported his campaign. A president can meet with foreign leaders in summits to proclaim peace and prosperity. He can sign symbolic accords if he cannot conclude serious agreements for detente. Or he can revive the cold war. He can share in the glory of the astronauts, announce grandiose development plans for the inner cities, and promise large tax cuts. Surrounded by the trappings of office, he seems more "presidential" than his opponent. When faced with difficult questions about his foreign policies, he can hint of secret information, warn of irresponsible opposition to his programs, and complain of the vast burdens of office.

Dirty Tricks

Most campaigns have a few "spies" planted in their rivals' headquarters, and disruption of campaign activities by the opposition is an old tradition, especially at the local level. But in only a few elections are tricks so significant that they determine the outcome. The election of 1876 was stolen by the Republicans, who used federal troops in several southern states to force ballot recounts, and then made a corrupt bargain with southern Democrats in Congress to ensure that the findings of a special commission to count electoral college ballots would be accepted.[56] In 1960 some Republicans charged that widespread vote fraud in Texas and Illinois enabled Kennedy to win, but Nixon refused to ask for a recount or an investigation. At worse the alleged activities in 1960 were commissioned by local party leaders, and took place without the complicity of the national ticket.

The "dirty tricks" of 1972 were of a different order of magnitude. Nixon's campaign was not a contest against opponents, but rather a *war* against enemies. His goal was not merely to defeat them, but to destroy and discredit them.[57] He ordered covert operations, relying on persons who had worked for law enforcement and national security agencies. The illegal covert activities were central to the campaign. They were paid for and covered up with funds extorted from corporations illegally. The media were threatened with FBI investigations of reporters, tax audits, and loss of licenses for radio and television stations by the White House Office of Telecommunications Policy.[58] Nixon's special counsel Richard Moore testified that White House operatives harassed Democratic contenders in the preconvention period in order "to create such confusion among the primary candidates that it would be difficult for the Democratic party to come back together after the convention."[59] The chief targets were Edmund Muskie and Edward Kennedy. White House staff members Dwight Chapin, Gordon Strachan, and Donald Segretti used at least $100,000 in campaign funds to hire agents to disseminate false information to newsmen, distribute false campaign literature purportedly coming from the contenders' campaigns, provide pickets, cancel contenders' speaking engagements, place stink bombs at rallies, and spread rumors about their private lives. Investigators were sent to tail Edward Kennedy in the hope of uncovering damaging information about his private life. Before the general election the Democratic National Committee offices in the Watergate apartment complex were placed under electronic surveillance and documents were photocopied by burglars under the direction of the White House "plumbers" unit. White House crimes didn't pay: the coverup of the Watergate break-in was exposed and ultimately forced Nixon's resignation from office. But the dirty tricks revealed possible abuse of office by incumbents that must be guarded against in future elections.

III

The Myth of Majority Rule

A presidential election never gives the incumbent support from a majority of eligible voters. The only majority the winner receives comes from the electoral college. In recent elections the number of eligible voters who did not turn out was greater than the number who voted for the winner: in one sense the popular choice is "no preference," and second choice in the election is the winning candidate (see figure 3.1).

Since only one-quarter to one-third of the eligible electorate votes for the winning candidate, the legitimacy of elections does not derive from the principle of majority rule. In the close election of 1976, of approximately 150 million persons in the voting age population, Carter received votes of slightly over 40 million—a bit better than one-fourth of the electorate. Under the present system a candidate may be elected without

PRESIDENTS WHO GOVERNED WITHOUT POPULAR MAJORITIES

YEARS	PRESIDENT	PERCENTAGE OF VOTE
1825–29	Adams	30.5
1841–45	Tyler	None
1845–49	Polk	49.6
1849–50	Taylor	47.3
1850–53	Fillmore	None
1857–61	Buchanan	45.3
1861–65	Lincoln	39.8
1865–69	Johnson	None
1877–81	Hayes	48.0
1881	Garfield	48.3
1881–85	Arthur	None
1885–89	Cleveland	48.5
1889–93	Harrison	47.9
1893–97	Cleveland	46
1901–05	Roosevelt	None
1913–17	Wilson	41.8
1917–21	Wilson	49.3
1923–25	Coolidge	None
1945–49	Truman	None
1949–53	Truman	49.5
1961–63	Kennedy	49.7
1963–65	Johnson	None
1969–73	Nixon	43.4
1974–77	Ford	None

a majority of the votes cast, and even without a plurality of the vote. Many presidents have governed with less than half the total vote cast, including Lincoln, Cleveland, Theodore Roosevelt, Wilson, Truman, Kennedy, and Nixon.

Presidents do not receive mandates in elections, in part because of the way they run campaigns, in part because of the way voters respond to their campaigns:

1. Candidates may appeal to voters on the basis of party identification, personality, or competence. They may take similar centrist positions on many issues and not offer the voters a choice.[60]
2. Candidates may not offer the voters a choice on issues. Since each candidate may choose to take a clear stand or a vague one, there is only one chance in four that the candidates will directly oppose each other on any issue.[61]
3. A candidate's supporters may differ on issues. In 1960 Kennedy was supported by northern blacks and southern segregationist whites. Nixon in 1968 won votes from hawks and doves. Carter in 1976 received support from those favoring and those opposing detente with the Soviet Union.[62]

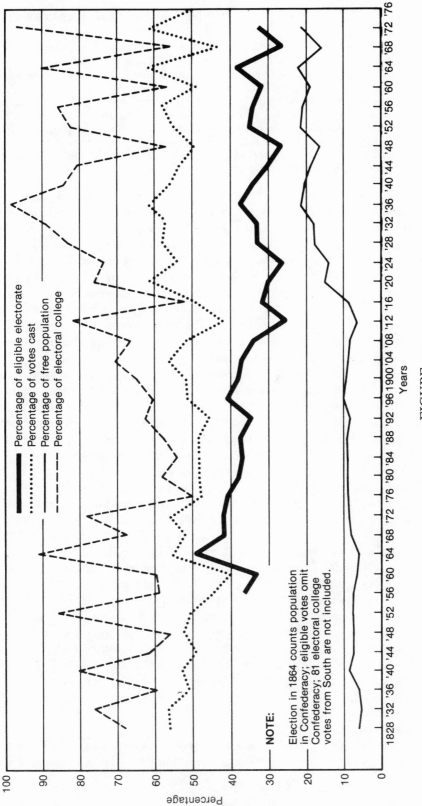

NOTE:

Election in 1864 counts population in Confederacy; eligible votes omit Confederacy; 81 electoral college votes from South are not included.

Percentage of eligible electorate
Percentage of votes cast
Percentage of free population
Percentage of electoral college

Percentage

1828 '32 '36 '40 '44 '48 '52 '56 '60 '64 '68 '72 '76 '80 '84 '88 '92 '96 1900'04 '08 '12 '16 '20 '24 '28 '32 '36 '40 '44 '48 '52 '56 '60 '64 '68 '72 '76

Years

FIGURE 3.1

4. Voters with similar positions on the issues may back different candidates. In 1972 a majority of Nixon and McGovern's supporters favored a pullout from Vietnam, an end to wage-price controls, more jobs for the unemployed, and harsher treatment of criminals.[63]

5. It is improbable that a coalition of voters agrees with the candidate on all or most of his expressed positions on issues. At best a voter can express his own preferences on one or two major issues in his choice for president. The electorate that voted for Roosevelt in 1940 opposed elements of his foreign policy; Truman's supporters were split on his civil rights program; Eisenhower's coalition opposed many Republican domestic proposals.[64]

In most campaigns the majority of voters do not choose between the candidates primarily on the basis of issues. Surveys conducted between 1952 and 1960 indicated that many voters were influenced primarily by party identification, secondarily by personality factors of candidates, and to some extent by identification with groups that tended to vote for a particular party.[65] Issue voting increased in the 1964, 1968, and 1972 elections, when clear choices on some major issues were offered by factional candidates. Even so, recent studies of voting behavior indicate that many voters are still not susceptible to issue-oriented campaigning.[66] At best voters send "messages" to candidates, indicating general support or opposition to their media themes.

More important than the increase in issue voting is the weakening of party identification as a cue for voting—especially between 1964 and 1972. In recent elections the personality factor and the claim of competence have been more significant as the importance of party identification has decreased.[67] Carter waged his 1976 campaign on issues involving trust, candor, honesty, and character, in the culmination of trends evident since 1964. Speaking tongue-in-cheek to the National Press Club at its annual congressional dinner a week after his inauguration, the president admitted that "when we were all elected, we were fuzzy on the issues, which is proven by the fact that we did get elected."[68] The key factors in voter choice in that election turned out to be party identification and the liberal-conservative dimension. It may well be that the 1976 results mark a comeback for party-oriented and issue-oriented appeals, but it is too early to generalize on the basis of a single election.[69]

A president may interpret his mandate as he sees fit. It has whatever value he chooses to assign to it, no more and no less. He weighs the interests of voting blocs that supported him and assigns priorities in meeting their claims on him as he wishes. The electorate that perceived Carter as slightly left of center in the November elections, and voted for him on that basis, considered him somewhat to the right of center just nine months later: even if there was a "mandate" in the election, the president did not seem to be bound by it in presenting his administration's programs.[70]

To preserve his freedom of action a president claims a general mandate to act in the name of the people, but denies the claims of any specific group to act in its interest. The president may simply walk away from preelection commitments. Republican presidents are notorious for submitting deficit budgets when they have promised balanced ones, and for increasing welfare and human resources expenditures in spite of promises to cut in these areas. Democrat Carter delayed the initiation of a welfare reform proposal and new aid to cities until prodded by black organizations and liberals in Congress. He publicly warned such black leaders as Vernon Jordan, directer of the Urban League, that pressure on the administration would not be productive. At best the election results offer a president clues about the hopes and fears of the people. But they cannot tell him what direction to take. People are better at voting against what they dislike than they are at voting for what they like; their vote may register dissatisfaction, and they may desert their party if its candidate's vision of the future is at odds with their own. In effect, elections are often a "veto" on existing politics and policies, as the defeats of the Democrats in 1968 and the Republicans in 1976 seem to indicate.

Without a mandate on issues, the temptation is for the president to claim a general mandate on leadership. Instead of responsible parties offering alternative programs to the voters, candidate-centered campaign organizations use media politics to present themes involving personality, competence, and "charisma." To some extent the election may be viewed, at least by the winner, as a *plebiscite*: the president may be tempted, once in office, to rely on "the voice of the people" as justification for actions, particularly prerogative actions, he wishes to take. He may act as if his election were *carte blanche* to act in the name of the people. Ironically, the only check against such a theory of plebiscitary democracy is the low rate of participation in elections. So long as slightly less than half the eligible electorate chooses not to vote, and so long as presidents are elected with between one-fourth and one-third of the votes of the eligible electorate, no incumbent can claim to represent the will of the majority.

IV

The Electoral Vote System

The electoral college distorts the popular vote and magnifies the impact of some groups and states in presidential elections. The campaign for president is only secondarily for popular votes: it is first a set of fifty-one contests for the electoral votes of the states and the District of Columbia. Each of these separate contests (with the exception of Maine's district system) is conducted on a winner-take-all basis, so the candidate who receives a plurality of the popular vote in a state wins all its electoral votes.[71] Candidates concentrate on states that are competitive, especially large states where the prizes are greatest.[72]

The electoral vote system is unrepresentative. It gives a slight numerical advantage to smaller states. Since the number of votes cast in the electoral college is based on the congressional apportionment and Senate representation, and *not* on the turnout, states with low turnouts are rewarded rather than penalized. The South receives a disproportionate number of electoral votes when compared with its proportion of the actual vote. Because the number of electors a state receives is based on apportionment, which in turn is based on data from the decennial census, states that have suffered relative populating declines receive an advantage over states growing in population until Congress reapportions itself. This recently has benefited the Northeast and Midwest at the expense of the South and Southwest. But these are minor arithmetic distortions, and with increased turnouts in the South the only serious problem has been almost eliminated.

The real problem involves the winner-take-all system. It disenfranchises those who voted for the loser in the state, since all the electoral votes are cast for the winner—in effect permitting the majority to cast their own votes as well as those of the losers for their candidate. Some political scientists argued that racial and religious minorities, especially blacks, urban Catholics, and Jews, held a "balance of power" in the large industrial states. To compete for votes of these minority groups, candidates would be responsive to liberal and urban constituencies.[73] But this theory has had little validity since the 1970s. Blacks are predominantly Democratic in all states and do not hold any balance of power between the parties. In 1976 black leaders complained that Democratic politicians were taking them for granted and making no effort to meet their demands, a clue that their votes were not a decisive factor.[74] In the 1950s it seemed that liberal and labor-oriented Catholic and Jewish voters in urban areas were "swing" voters, but by the next decade they too were solidly in the Democratic camp. The real contest between the two parties was for the "backlash" Democrats, of whatever religion, who were conservative on racial and social issues and willing to defect and vote Republican in presidential elections. The more conservative Democrats, not the liberals, were the ones who could be "switched," as Nixon demonstrated in 1972: a Republican presidential candidate swept the industrial states without favoring civil rights or a liberal domestic program, and without winning a significant proportion of black or liberal votes.

In the most recent elections no voting blocs have held a "balance of power" in the large states. With the exception of blacks and liberals, no groups are securely in the camp of either party. It can be demonstrated mathematically that the winner-take-all system in the electoral college gives a disproportionate share of voter choice to urban and suburban dwellers, blue-collar workers, and members of racial and religious minorities in the large states.[75] But the magnitudes are so small as to be virtually meaningless in the real world. There is no liberal, conservative, or "urban" bias in the system, and certainly none for the candidate who might want to do something about urban problems. Many of the groups "advantaged" by the electoral college system are susceptible to conservative appeals, and many live in suburbs rather than the inner cities.

The mechanics of the electoral college may create problems. Under the system electors assemble in their state capitols, cast ballots for president and vice-president, and the lists are certified and sent to Congress. The vice-president, before a joint session of the new Congress, announces the winner of the election. The Constitution does not *require* electors to comply with the results of the state contest, it merely permits such an elector to cast ballots for president and vice-president. In fact the framers expected the electors to exercise their independent judgment. Today we expect them to abide by the vote in their state. Sixteen states have laws that pledge electors to vote for the nominee of their party, and the Supreme Court has upheld the constitutionality of these laws, but it is not clear that anything can be done about the "faithless elector" who casts his ballot for someone else. In 1796 a Federalist named Samuel Miles voted for Jefferson instead of John Adams, prompting one of his supporters to exclaim, "What, do I chuse Samuel Miles to determine for me whether John Adams or Thomas Jefferson shall be President? No! I chuse him to act, not to think."[76] In 1820 an elector voted for John Quincy Adams instead of James Monroe; in 1956 for Walter Jones rather than Adlai Stevenson; in 1960 for Harry Byrd rather than Richard Nixon (and Byrd also won six unpledged ballots in Alabama and eight in Mississippi, even though Kennedy won the popular vote in Alabama); in 1968 for George Wallace rather than Richard Nixon; and in 1976 for Ronald Reagan rather than Gerald Ford. The "faithless elector" remains a problem.

The winner of the popular vote may lose in the electoral college. In 1824 Andrew Jackson won a plurality but lost to John Quincy Adams in a House contingency election. That House had itself been elected two years before, and was a "lame duck" session not at all representative of popular sentiment. In 1876 Hayes was elected with a minority of the popular vote, as was Benjamin Harrison in 1888. In 1960 Kennedy received fewer popular votes than Nixon, 34,049,096 for Kennedy and 34,108,157 for Nixon. The Kennedy figure is calculated by subtracting from his Alabama total the votes that were cast for the six electors that voted for Byrd in the electoral college.[77]

Although on only two occasions have elections gone to the House, and on only four occasions has the winner of the popular vote failed to win the election, there have been many occasions in which either of these results almost occurred. The shift of only a small number of popular votes in

TABLE 3.1

Some Near Misses in the Electoral College

YEAR	STATES SHIFTING	NEW RESULT
1836	1	Harrison
1844	1	Clay
1848	3	Cass
1860	1	Contingency election
1876	1	Tilden
1880	1	Hancock
1884	1	Blaine
1888	1	Cleveland
1916	1	Hughes
1948	3	Dewey
1968	2	Contingency election
1976	2	Ford

one or two states might have resulted in different outcomes in many elections. The probability of a discrepancy between the popular and electoral college results is one in three if the popular margin in an election is under 300,000, and one in four if the popular vote margin is less than 1.5 million, so it is possible that under the present system such discrepancies will occur in the future. In 1976 the shift of only 4,000 votes in Ohio and Hawaii would have given the election to Ford.

The system almost broke down completely in 1968. George Wallace, candidate of the American Independent Party, hoped to throw the election into the House. If 0.5 percent of the voters in Ohio and Missouri had shifted away from Nixon, the strategy would have worked. Democrats controlled twenty-six House delegations and the Republicans nineteen, with the rest evenly divided, so presumably the Democrats could have elected Humphrey. But in South Carolina and Virginia, Democrats running for Congress had pledged during their own campaigns that in the event of a House contingency election they would vote for whichever presidential candidate had carried their congressional districts. Had they honored this pledge, the results would have been twenty-four states ·for Humphrey, twenty-one for Nixon, and four ties.[78] Nixon or Humphrey would have had to withdraw in favor of the other to end the deadlock. If neither withdrew and the House could not produce a majority, Edmund Muskie, who would have been elected by the Senate in its contingency election as vice-president, would then have had to become acting president on inauguration day, in the absence of a constitutionally qualified president! Such are the absurd outcomes that might occur under the present cumbersome and archaic system.

Reforming the Electoral College

One reform, the "Automatic Plan," would end the problem of the faithless elector by providing for an automatic count of the electoral college vote and by abolishing the office of elector. A more significant change would end the winner-take-all system in favor of a return to district contests in use in the early 1800s: Michigan did this for the 1892 election, and Maine provided that two of its electors would be chosen on a district basis for the 1972 election. Under the *district plan,* electors would be chosen from congressional districts, with two picked by the entire state. A simpler and more equitable reform, the *proportional plan,* would abolish the electoral college and simply distribute the state electoral vote in direct proportion to the popular vote. In one version, the Lodge-Gosset plan (which passed the Senate in 1949 but was defeated in the House in 1950, the first step toward passage of a constitutional amendment) a 40 percent plurality of electoral votes would be sufficient to elect a president; if no candidate won, Congress would choose from among the two highest.

Proposals have been made to abolish the electoral college entirely and provide for direct popular election of the president. Carter proposed such a plan in 1977. In the event that no candidate received 40 percent of the vote, a runoff election would be held between the two top candidates.[79] Such a plan penalizes states with low turnout rates, unlike proposals that retain electors and merely apportion them according to the percentage of votes gained by each party, and therefore the popular election plan provides an incentive for politicians to mobilize the maximum number of voters.

Defenders of the present system claim that the electoral college favors urban and liberal constituencies and minority groups. They argue that this is good and reasonable because it provides these groups with representation they cannot obtain elsewhere. But it is not true that the present system has an urban and liberal bias. And it is also not true that urban and liberal constituencies do not gain fair representation elsewhere, especially since the reapportionment of congressional and state legislative districts on the basis of "one person, one vote" instituted by the courts in the 1960s. A defense of the inequitable electoral college on the grounds that it has served to balance out other inequities is unreasonable grounds for its continuance. The constitutional remedy for an inequity is to eliminate it rather than to balance it off. In any event, under a system of popular voting for president the candidates would still concentrate on urban areas in large states, for the obvious reason that a small margin of victory in areas with large populations tends to produce more votes than a larger margin of victory in less-populated areas.

The second argument for the present system is that the winner-take-all mechanism discourages third parties from mounting serious campaigns. The popular-vote system, critics claim, would weaken the two-party system and encourage many small parties to siphon votes from major-party candidates, thus requiring a runoff election. But the present system encourages third parties to form in order to deadlock the electoral college, as Wallace tried to do in 1968 and McCarthy in 1976. Third parties would have no more influence under a system of popular election. Minor parties would have an incentive to bargain with the major parties, resulting in the endorsement of major-party candidates, and the result would be broad coalitions of smaller parties supporting two major-party candidates in the initial election. Minor parties would stimulate voter turnout and force major-party candidates to clarify their positions on the issues in order to win endorsements in the initial races. The runoff election, should it prove necessary, would provide the president with a clear majority of the vote; under the new system no president could be elected with less votes than his opponent.

V

Succession to Office

Procedures to fill the presidency in the event of death, disability, or resignation emphasize constitutional rather than democratic values. Instead of holding elections to fill the vacancy, a set of elaborate constitutional and legal procedures are used for the succession. On the death of a president, the vice-president takes the oath and succeeds to the office of president. He fills out the remainder of the term. The same procedures hold if the president resigns. If a president is disabled, under provisions of the Twenty-Fifth Amendment the vice-president acts as president until the incumbent resumes the duties of the office. The president can declare he is disabled and invite the vice-president to act as president, or the vice-president and cabinet can find the president disabled. In either case the president determines when he is fit to resume the duties of the office. If the vice-president and cabinet disagree with him, the final determination is made by Congress.

The Twenty-Fifth amendment also resolves the problem of a vacancy in the vice-presidency. Six vice-presidents have died and two have resigned from office. Nine others have succeeded to the presidency. In each case the vice-presidential office remained vacant, and if the president then died, both offices would be vacant. The framers anticipated that in the case of a double vacancy an officer of Congress would serve as acting president. They rejected language that the acting president would serve "until the time for electing a President shall arrive." The language of the Constitution, that the powers of the office would be exercised "until a President shall be elected" meant until an *interim* election could be held. The Succession Act of 1792 confirmed this understanding by providing that in the case of a double vacancy the president pro tem of the Senate would serve as acting president until an interim election was held. The Succession Act of 1886 provided that the secretary of state would serve as acting president "until a president shall be elected," although in this measure no specific provision was made for a contingency election. Instead, the act required the acting president to convene Congress within twenty days, presumably so that a special election could be called. The Succession Act of 1947 provided that in the event of a double vacancy the Speaker of the House would act as president "until the expiration of the then current presidential term," an explicit choice to provide continuity in office rather than a special election to fill the vacancies.[80]

The Succession Act of 1947 was far from an ideal solution. Putting the Speaker of the House (followed by the president pro tem of the Senate) in line for the succession left the possibility open that a member of the opposition party might succeed to the presidency in the case of a double vacancy. These two congressional leaders were not "officers" of the United States and therefore might not even be eligible under the succession provisions of the Constitution. If they were to be considered "officers" for purposes of succession, several constitutional problems remained. The intent of the succession provision was that the "acting president" would be an officer of the United States who would retain his office while acting as president. It would be impossible for the Speaker or president pro tem of the Senate to retain congressional office and simultaneously serve as "acting president," for to do so would be to hold legislative and executive branch positions simultaneously, which would be a violation of the Constitution.

The Twenty-Fifth Amendment unties these constitutional knots by eliminating the possibility that a double vacancy will exist. In the event that the vice-presidency is vacant, the president's nominee for the office may be confirmed or rejected by a majority in each chamber of Congress. Although the amendment was intended to deal with death, disability, or succession to the presidency, it was first used after Vice-President Spiro Agnew resigned and pleaded *nolo contendere* ("no contest") to charges of income tax evasion and accepting bribes while he was Baltimore county executive and governor of Maryland. Had the amendment not been in effect the Democratic House Speaker would have been in line to succeed to the presidency during the Watergate crisis: Watergate might then have become a more partisan issue, and inhibited some Republicans on the House Judiciary Committee from recommending articles of impeachment.

Under the procedures of the amendment, after Agnew resigned Nixon consulted various congressional leaders. They indicated they would prefer a "caretaker" vice-president who would not run on the national ticket in 1976.[81] Nixon nominated House Minority Leader Gerald Ford, with the advance approval of congressional leaders from both parties and of the Republican National Committee. In both the House and the Senate the system of hearings and voting on the nomination involved a "confirmation" of the presidential choice rather than an election, for members of Congress agreed with Democrat Howard Cannon that the president had the right to choose someone "whose philosophy and politics are virtually identical to his own."[82] Democratic Senator Birch Bayh, the author of the Twenty-Fifth Amendment, added that its intent "was to get a Vice President who would be compatible and could work harmoniously with the President."[83] The congressional vote was almost unanimously in favor of Ford.

Once Ford assumed the presidency after Nixon's resignation the vice-presidency was again vacant. Ford nominated former New York Governor Nelson Rockefeller, but without advance consultation with congressional leaders or the Republican National Committee. Ford also insisted that his nominee be someone of "presidential calibre" rather than a caretaker, and his choice indicated that he wanted someone with whom he could run on the national ticket in 1976. The Democrats responded to a partisan maneuver in a partisan way. Hearings on the nomination dragged on so that the Democrats could score political points. They accused Rockefeller of owing taxes, of paying author Victor Lasky to "smear" political opponent Arthur Goldberg during a New York gubernatorial election, and of making large loans and gifts to public officials in New York State while governor. Ultimately Rockefeller was confirmed, although many Democrats voted against the nomination. The final vote took place after the 1974 congressional elections, by a lame-duck Congress, rather than by the newly elected membership.

President Ford and Vice-President Rockefeller exercised the duties of their offices based on constitutional rather than electoral legitimacy. As Senator Pastore noted in the hearings, "For the first time in the history of this great nation the President and Vice-President will both be appointed —not elected by the people and not responsive to any mandate from the citizens."[84] But constitutional legitimacy was preserved because the procedures of the Twenty-Fifth Amendment rested on principles of limited government and polyarchy: power was to be exercised for a fixed term; succession occurred according to procedures established by the Constitution, with no irregularities; the incumbents would be accountable to the electorate in future elections, should they choose to run for office. The electoral process had a prospective application to the incumbents. Rockefeller was dumped by Ford after opposition developed within the Republican party to his nomination for the 1976 election; Ford himself faced a stiff fight to win renomination and subsequently lost the election.

The Twenty-Fifth Amendment functioned well under difficult circumstances. Nixon had received the support of a large majority of voters, and the continuity Ford provided was more legitimate than the partisan change caused by the accession of a Democratic Speaker would have been. A breathing period of two years prior to the next presidential election was beneficial; it permitted the Ford administration to make its record, allowed the nation to place Watergate in perspective, and permitted the Republicans to campaign effectively. Ford and Rockefeller were confirmed as vice-presidents by both houses of Congress. Can it be argued that the Speaker of the House, elected by a single congressional district, would be more representative of electoral values than a vice-president chosen by the entire Congress who succeeds to the presidency?

The Twenty-Second Amendment also emphasizes constitutional and procedural values at the expense of the electoral process. It limits the president to two terms, and limits a vice-president who succeeds to the office and who serves more than half of his predecessor's term to only one elective term in office. The framers provided for indefinite eligibility as part of the popular connection, thrashing out the matter thoroughly at the Convention and at state ratifying conventions. Washington and Jefferson set the precedents that the president would serve no more than two terms, and prior to the Civil War the Whigs almost won the point that a one-term presidency was sufficient. Franklin Roosevelt broke with tradition by winning the presidency four times. In response, congressional Republicans sponsored the Twenty-Second Amendment, ratified in 1951. Its provisions were first applied to a Republican, Dwight Eisenhower, barred from running in 1960, although if he could have run he would have easily won renomination and election. The amendment is clearly undemocratic, for it restricts the choice of the party and of the electorate. And if the nation is in the midst of war or domestic crisis, it forces a rotation in office just when the people may wish for continuity. Yet it, like the succession amendment, demonstrates that the fundamental core of the constitutional processes for selection and retention in office emphasizes constitutionalism rather than the popular connection.

Conclusion

The nominating, election, and succession processes are primarily exercises in constitutionalism, and only secondarily are they instruments to forge a popular connection between the president and the electorate. Their purposes are to provide a peaceful and orderly contest for power within and between parties, and to provide for polyarchy and accountability rather than to confirm mandates and popular majorities. The president at best forges a link with the people by asking for their trust and support and by offering them his leadership. If the purposes of these processes is understood correctly, then the assessment of the results will be high, for peaceful change does result, the competition for power is contained in constitutional channels, and in most cases due accountability to the people characterizes campaigns. To the extent that pure democratic values become the yardstick for measurement these processes will be evaluated less favorably. The nominations do not measure party sentiment well, and primary electorates seem particularly susceptible to manipulation by media campaigns. General elections dissassociate the candidates from their national and state party organizations. Elections rarely result in a mandate on the issues for the winning candidates.

A president enters office without resources necessary to fulfill the expectations he has raised during his campaign. He has no organization to link him to state and local parties or to his legislative party. Without the backing of a majority of the eligible electorate, he claims a mandate from "the people." The temptation for him is great to claim by right what has not been granted in fact—leadership of the nation. His victory provides him with office but not with a party or popular connection to help him govern. No claim of mandate substitutes for the effort he must make once in office to forge the connections to the legislative party that will enable him to govern wisely and well.

Party Leadership

To RULE rather than reign, to govern rather than preside as head of state, a president must bridge the separation of powers and lead his congressional and state parties. But no president is an effective party leader. In the most fundamental sense, existing structures and mechanisms of the national and state parties are *antipresidential*: they prevent incumbents from dominating Congress and they decentralize power throughout the federal system. Considering the undisciplined organizations with which he must work, a president might relish the story told about the Duke of Wellington, who, upon reviewing his troops for a campaign, was asked by an aide if he thought they would frighten the enemy; Wellington replied, "I do not know if they will frighten the French, sir, but by God they frighten me."

But if the president does not control his party, neither does his party control him. The president has both the incentive and the opportunity to institute prerogative government, or to embrace the principles and programs of the opposition party if it suits his purpose. No party mechanisms constrain him in the exercise of his constitutional powers or political influence.

I

Titular Leadership

The president is the titular leader of his party. He has the aura of the winner about him as he enters office. Alliances he has made with party organizations during the primaries and in the elections may be strengthened. Some presidents, including Nixon, Ford, and Carter, campaigned in midterm congressional elections for their party prior to their elevation as president, and there may be members in the legislature grateful for their help. His party members have an incentive to work with him, since the public considers the president chief spokesman of the party. Politicians want to be considered his confidant, in his inner circle, so he may "stroke" them with invitations to social events or call them in for private (but well-publicized) tête-à-têtes. The incumbent chooses the national chairperson, and usually a majority of the national committee members will support him. He offers patronage to his allies and raises funds for the party by speaking at dinners.

These assets as titular leader do not amount to much. At best the president obtains a brief intraparty "honeymoon" before his program is challenged by factions in his congressional party and by governors in his state parties. A few presidents, including Jefferson, Wilson, Franklin, Roosevelt, and Lyndon Johnson, have managed to lead their congressional parties for any length of time; not coincidentally, these same presidents also managed to alienate many of their followers, and lost the support of congressional party leaders, leading to their defeat on some of the most crucial issues facing their administrations. Jefferson, the founder of his party, was unable to win the Senate conviction in the impeachment trial of Supreme Court Justice Samuel Chase, gain passage of a treason bill, or maintain his policy of neutrality in the Franco-British wars. Wilson was unable to hold his congressional party together after his unsuccessful fight for the Treaty of Versailles. Franklin Roosevelt, after a smashing election victory in 1936, lost his bid to "pack" the Supreme Court when Congress refused to pass his proposal, and with it his working majority in Congress, thus ending chances for passage of most New Deal bills after 1937. Opposition to the Vietnam War split the Democratic party and led to the delay, modification, or outright defeat of much of Johnson's program after 1966. Congressional Democrats split with Carter in his first months in office when he announced a goal of a balanced budget in 1981. The Democratic Speaker of the House, Tip O'Neill, warned, "I don't think any President can be a good President if he doesn't have the backing or the support of his party. You don't become a great president by opposing the Congress. I have told that to Jimmy Carter a half-dozen times."[1]

Presidents find the role of partisan leader incompatible with both their responsibilities and their political instincts. As Taft observed, "The longer I am President the less of a party man I seem to become."[2] They define their office in nonpartisan terms:

William McKinley: I can no longer be called President of a party; I am now President of the whole people.

Theodore Roosevelt: No man is fit to hold the position of President of the United States at all unless as President he feels that he represents no party but the people as a whole.

Franklin Roosevelt: No man can occupy the Office of President without realizing that he is President of all the people.

Dwight Eisenhower: I have the conception that although elected by only part of the population, as is evident, anybody occupying this office is President of all the people.[3]

The lofty nonpartisan pose that presidents assume once in office belies the fierce intraparty struggle in which they engage to attain it. The president becomes the titular leader of his party and "president of all the people" only by virtue of his nomination and election to office. Prior to the nomination he is simply one of the contenders, with no greater claim than anyone else in the pack to be called leader. The "out" party has no formal office of "opposition leader" as is common in most parliamentary democracies, and no member of the party can claim the nomination by right. Normally a party splits into several factions, with various rivals attempting to articulate its principles and serve as its voice. In the 1950s Democrats were "led" by congressional leaders, the national chairman, and splinter groups such as Americans for Democratic Action. After Goldwater's 1964 debacle the Republican Governors Association was created; and the Senate Republican Policy Committee played a major role in opposition to the "Great Society" programs of the Democrats. In 1969, after Humphrey's defeat, congressional Democrats created the Policy Conference; the party's mayors also took positions against Nixon's programs.

Eventually the "outs" will win the presidency, but since their party has not been unified, the mad scramble prior to the nominating convention creates problems for the president. The defeated elements of his party may consider him somewhat akin to Attila the Hun. The increasing number of "purists" who are committed to particular candidates and issues and uninterested in party unity strengthens the tendency for friction between the president and defeated factions of his party.[4] He may be scorned as an "outsider" or "novice" in national campaigning if he is a governor or military hero rather than a Washington insider. The sudden elevation of a factional leader to the White House is calculated to arouse the envy of his former peers, and most will be quick to take offense for slights real or imagined. George McGovern, chafing for several months under Carter's leadership, finally expressed his pique at the priorities of the new administration by observing, "in reviewing economic policy this Spring it sometimes seems difficult to remember who won last fall."[5]

Most vice-presidents who succeed to the presidency also fail as party leaders. They may have been picked to balance the ticket, so upon their elevation they are surrounded by a White House staff and cabinet that owe them no loyalty and may even have been instrumental in frustrating their own ambitions to win the party nomination. Truman was never accepted by the liberal wing of his party, and had the Democrats been able to convince Eisenhower to accept their nomination in 1948, they surely would have dumped Truman. Lyndon Johnson feared the Kennedy loyalists would try to replace him with Robert Kennedy in 1964. He used White House aides personally loyal to him to conduct his political business, and one of them, Joseph Califano, later recalled, "In my years on Lyndon Johnson's White House staff never once did I hear him say that he wanted to leave behind a strengthened Democratic party."[6] In 1976 Gerald Ford was almost overthrown by conservatives backing Ronald Reagan for the nomination. He was forced to accept a party platform that in effect repudiated the foreign policies of his administration.

The bruising struggle for the nomination may leave the president with suspicions about the loyalties of state party leaders. Eisenhower preferred to work with "Citizens for Eisenhower" groups during the campaign, which antagonized the regulars. His campaign aide Sherman Adams later referred to state leaders who "clung jealously to their authority to the exclusion of new and younger blood."[7] Kennedy did not get along well with most of the southern state chairmen and Nixon had his problems with chairmen in the east. Carter alienated Kennedyites, liberals favoring Udall or McGovern, hawks favoring Henry Jackson, and supporters of Jerry Brown.

The conduct of the presidential campaign does not give the president control of his party once he has won the election. As a candidate he inserts "outsiders" to coordinate the state campaigns, which creates friction with local leaders. The campaign coordinators remain in the state just long enough to antagonize the locals (and ride roughshod over them in making strategy). After the election they disappear from party machinery, so the president must function with few loyalists in the party at the state and local level. Carter ran his campaign from Atlanta using his own entourage and brooked no interference from the Democratic National Committee. His one concession to the party organizations was to permit the national committee to spend approximately $1.9 million on "Target 76"—a voter registration campaign that pumped funds into the state and local parties (a form of campaign "revenue sharing").[8]

Some state committees in the past have received funds intended for presidential campaigns and diverted them to state contests. In the aftermath of the 1976 election, Carter proposed legislation to give the presidential candidate the right to appoint his own campaign committee in each state to receive and expend funds. Congress substituted a proposal in committee consideration that would vest the power to designate the state committee with the party national committee. The pervasive friction between the president and state parties remains.[9]

Party Machinery

Once in office the president has no control over party machinery, because for all practical purposes such machinery does not exist. American parties are in a state of arrested organizational development, at least by comparison to their European counterparts. They do not have dues-paying memberships participating actively in party affairs, they do not control their membership rosters (since anyone may register in either party), they have no cadres of workers operating under the supervision of a secretariat, and there is no centralized control of party nominations or finances. Instead, local machines disintegrate, bosses lose power to elected officials or are challenged by reform and factional groups, precincts go unmanned by workers, and the organizations no longer monopolize nominations to elective office or even finance the campaigns of contenders.[10]

The sovereign body of the national party is the national convention, which meets for less than one week every four years. Most of its delegates come from state and local parties and have little knowledge of national party affairs. In 1972 only 12 percent of the Democratic and 20 percent of the Republican delegates had ever held national party office and only 2 percent of the Democratic and 4 percent of the Republican delegates had ever held a national public office in their careers.[11] Members of the national committee who represent state parties are chosen by those parties, and not by any central organ or by the president.[12] The national committees are dominated by state organizations, not by presidentially oriented operatives or a national secretariat, and each party is *federalized* rather than nationalized.

The national committees prepare for the national conventions, develop procedures for selection of convention delegates and monitor compliance with party rules in the delegate selection contests, and raise funds for congressional elections and voter registration drives. During presidential election years their staffs swell to seventy-five or more, and their budgets may soar to $3–4 million. But several presidents, including Franklin Roosevelt, Lyndon Johnson, and Jimmy Carter, pressured the national committee to cut back on staffing after the election to reduce party deficits. Califano recalls that "shortly after his 1964 election it became clear that Johnson regarded the Democratic National Committee as a debt-ridden, and presidentially irritating and irrelevant encumbrance."[13] In 1976, acting on Carter's recommendation, Democratic chairman Robert Strauss reduced the size of the Democratic National Committee's staff by 70 percent, down to only twenty fulltime employees.

The national committees used to pay for the transition expenses of the president-elect. In 1952–53 the Republican National Committee spent over $200,000 on the Eisenhower transition, and in 1960–61 its Democratic counterpart spent over $360,000 for the Kennedy transition. But the Presidential Transition Act of 1963 provides the president-elect with office space and funds for staff, travel, and consultants.[14] Now that the responsibility for funding the transition involves the government, the president needs his party even less than before, so he may pay less attention to its leaders in this critical period.

The president picks the national chairperson and may also select other party officials. Most party officials remain in office a short time, for the positions are not well paid and do not constitute a career for anyone with real ambition. Between 1967 and 1978 there were eight Democratic and six Republican national chairpersons. Often the office is held on a part-time basis. The president discourages party officials from speaking for the administration, and as Robert Strauss, former Democratic chairman observed, "If you're Democratic party chairman when a Democrat is president, you're a goddamn clerk."[15] After Carter was elected Strauss resigned and went to work at the White House. Within a year he was playing a major role in legislative liaison and political matters, and handling sensitive trade negotiations with other nations. His replacement as chairman was former Maine Governor Kenneth Curtis, hardly a heavyweight in Democratic politics. Curtis initially was self-effacing and noted that "the president and the members of Congress are elected by the people; the chairman of the DNC and the national committee are not."[16] But Curtis later feuded with White House political operatives who interfered with party affairs and eventually resigned in disgust. Political influence comes from being in the White House inner circle, assigned to the White House staff—not from running the national committee.

The president's choice of national chairman will please some in the party and antagonize others. When Nixon fired Ray Bliss, a seasoned but colorless former chairman of the Republican National Committee, he upset many chairpersons who viewed Bliss as one of them.[17] Perhaps the best solution to the problem is to appoint a nonentity to the position, downgrade the job, and humiliate the incumbent. That, at any rate, is how presidents usually operate.

Party officials want to be dealt in on patronage and other political matters. For his part, the president resents such pressure, views the national committee as a nuisance, and keeps his distance from it. Republican chairman Robert Dole, after trying to get an appointment with Nixon for months, was told by a White House aide that the way he could "see the President" was by turning on his television when Nixon was making a speech. A White House staff member refused to meet with a member of the national committee with the comment that he had no time to greet visitors.[18] The White House uses the national committee as a lightning rod to draw criticism: during the Kennedy administration White House assistant Lawrence O'Brien made sure that the president received credit for all patronage requests that were honored, while shifting the blame to national chairman John Bailey for all requests that were denied.[19] Before moving over to the Carter White House, Robert Strauss was reduced to begging that his own staff aides (about to be dismissed in the economy drive) be given positions in the new administration—hardly a condition to inspire confidence that the national committee could pressure the administration on patronage for the benefit of the state parties. Throughout 1977, while thousands of patronage positions remained unfilled, grumbling about Carter's leadership of the party increased, prompting Ann Campbell, head of the Association of Democratic State Chairman to admit, "We've raised the problem again and again with the White House but nothing happens."[20] To kick off the 1978 political campaign season Carter felt impelled to apologize publicly to the national committee for the neglect in his first year and promised to do better in working with them, and created an office of political coordination to channel party patronage requests to the bureaucracy.

National party officials may interfere with White House attempts to influence state and local elections. When Franklin Roosevelt supported Fiorello LaGuardia in his bid to become mayor of New York, Democratic chairman Ed Flynn backed the regular Democratic nominee, William O'Dwyer. In 1970 Nixon supported Conservative party Senate candidates James Buckley in an attempt to purge the Senate of moderate Republicans; at the same time, Republican chairman Rogers Morton endorsed Charles Goodell, the party's nominee.

The chairperson may even interfere in presidential nominating politics. In 1940 chairman Jim Farley made it known that he disapproved of a third term for Roosevelt. The two men broke, and as Farley recounted,

Almost before I knew it I was no longer called to the White House for morning bedside conferences. My phone no longer brought the familiar voice in mellifluous tones. Months dragged between White House luncheon conferences. . . . White House confidence on politics and policies went to a small band of zealots who mocked at party loyalty and knew of no devotion, except unswerving obedience to their leaders.[21]

In 1956 Republican chairman Len Hall backed Richard Nixon for a second term as vice-president, even though Eisenhower was dropping hints that Nixon might wish to accept an appointment as a cabinet secretary to gain executive experience. Hall became one of Nixon's "managers" in the successful campaign to keep Eisenhower from dropping Nixon from the ticket, and with the help of the GOP wheelhorses in the state parties, pressured Eisenhower into making a warm endorsement of his vice-president.

When the president wants to communicate with other politicians, he will use the White House staff or his own loyalists on the national committee. Roosevelt used the New Dealers so despised by Farley to try to "purge" disloyal members of Congress while the national committee remained neutral. Truman had several cronies on the White House staff, and Eisenhower relied on his chief of staff Sherman Adams and congressional liaison Bryce Harlow. Kennedy used the "Irish Mafia" of Larry O'Brien, Kenneth O'Donnell, and his brother Robert. Lyndon Johnson had a corresponding "Texas Mafia" headed by Marvin Watson. Nixon established a political section in the White House office and installed Harry Dent, a southerner with close ties to congressional conservatives. Carter relied on a principal aide, Hamilton Jordan, assisted by Mark Siegel (himself a former executive director of the Democratic National Committee) and staff assistants from Vice-President Mondale's office in maintaining contact with "The Network," the name given to the political operatives at the state level who worked in the Carter campaign. Funds necessary to communicate with the hundred thousand or so operatives and volunteers comes from the Democratic National Committee, which allocates $40,000 monthly for presidential political activities.

Kennedy, Johnson, and Carter each dismantled the political operation of the Democratic National Committee after their election. Haldeman told the Nixon staff that the Republican National Committee counted for nothing in the new administration.[22] The only recent instance in which a president beefed up the party political operation occurred after Watergate, when Nixon sent Dent over to the Republican National Committee as deputy counsel, giving major responsibility for party affairs back to national chairman George Bush.

Convention Pressures

Party conventions function primarily to nominate a presidential candidate, but they also serve as a pressure cooker where various factions and caucuses clash over policies. The Democratic nominee may expect pressure from organizations such as the National Women's Political Caucus, the Congressional Black Caucus, the Urban League, the Coalition of Black Trade Unionists, the AFL-CIO, the Labor Clearinghouse, the New Democratic Coalition, and Americans for Democratic Action. A Republican can expect similar pressures from groups such as the Ripon Society, Young Americans for Freedom, the National Conservative

Political Action Committee, and the Council for National Defense. Governors and mayors in each party have organizations to press for commitments on regional and metropolitan issues.

Both parties have changed their rules to favor selection of delegates committed to candidates and issues at the expense of those "regulars" who emphasize party discipline. The Democratic party has opened its conventions to grass-roots activists. Reforms proposed by the McGovern-Fraser Commission on Party Structure and Delegate Selection and adopted for the 1972 convention opened up the convention to all who wished to participate in delegate selection—Democrats, independents, and even in some states Republican crossover voters. It eliminated ex officio delegates (usually state and local party leaders and elected officials) and limited the number of delegates who could be named by state committees. State parties were required to "overcome the effects of past discrimination by affirmative steps," which required them to choose delegates "in reasonable relationship to their presence in the population of the State." These two rules (A-1 and A-2) led to a dramatic increase between 1968 and 1972 in the percentages of women, black, and under-thirty delegates.

The Republican Party Commission on Delegates and Organization proposed similar reforms, and in 1972 the party approved rule 32(a) calling for "positive action to achieve the broadest possible participation by women, young people, minority and heritage groups and senior citizens in the delegate selection process," and rule 32(c) proposing that "each state shall endeavor to have equal representation of men and women in its delegates to the Republican National Convention." While the Democrats could bar state delegations not in compliance with the rules, Republican parties were merely exhorted to open up their delegate selection process. Various ideological factions have been able to take advantage of the rules and the increased primary participation rates to end the domination by state leaders of the delegations.

In 1973 a new set of Democratic rules was proposed by the Mikulski Commission on Delegate Selection and Party Structure. To replace rules A-1 and A-2 the Commission proposed that "the goal of Affirmative Action shall be to encourage such participation in delegate selection processes and in party organizations at all levels of the aforementioned groups as indicated by their presence in the Democratic electorate." But it added, "This goal shall not be accomplished either directly or indirectly by the Party's imposition of mandatory quotas at any level of the delegate selection process or in any other Party affairs." The new rules also increased from 10 percent to 25 percent the proportion of at-large delegates permitted in a state delegation, "in order to encourage the selection of delegates including public officials, party officials, and members of traditionally underrepresented Democratic constituencies." Most important, the 1976 rules required that delegations represent in proportion to primary results supporters of contenders who received more than 15 percent of the primary vote, if held on a statewide basis. In 1976 these rules had the same effect as the 1972 version, by broadening participation to include all demographic groups, by giving delegates the opportunity to support candidates of their choice without being dominated by state and local party organizations.

New rules in both parties have converted the national party organization into a "referee" in intraparty primary and convention contests. The party now ensures that all groups, not just regular party organizations, participate in delegate selection processes. It encourages split delegations with support going to candidates, rather than unified delegations of "professionals" led by brokers prepared to bargain with campaign managers. The party maintains order between various factional and candidate-centered organizations as they contest for delegates in the states and as they meet to do battle at the convention. The new rules encourage the fragmentation of the parties and prevent the national organization from imposing any kind of discipline in the party.

Still another party development bodes ill for presidents. With much fanfare the Democrats held a midterm convention in 1974, which adopted a charter, supposedly converting it into a true national party.[23] But the various national organs that were created emphasize the referee function. The party rejected a proposal for national, dues-paying membership, and did not give the central organs significant powers. Instead, its reform proposals, including rules adopted for the 1976 convention, simply guaranteed that factional bloodletting would be the pattern in future conventions.[24]

One danger for a Democratic president is that the midterm party conference will examine and reject part of the administration record. By 1977, with Carter in the White House, the administration was attempting to stage-manage a party midterm convention that would simply endorse the president's record, and was opposing arrangements to make the party meeting truly representative of the sentiments of grass-roots activists. Proposals for a convention of over 2,000 delegates, a large majority of whom would be elected by the people from small districts, were defeated with approval of the White House.[25] Instead, the Executive Committee of the Democratic National Committee approved rules that guranteed that 45 percent of the delegates would be Democratic officeholders or chosen by state party leaders. The White House hoped that this group of professionals would be more amenable to a public show of party unity, however much they privately opposed parts of the president's program.

II

Autonomous Congressional Electoral Systems

The president does not control his congressional party because no national party mechanisms exist that bind it to him. Neither the president nor the congressional candidates need adhere to the party platform. Legislative leaders have their own priorities, distinct from the administration's, and may even sabotage the president's program. Sherman Adams recalled the problems Eisenhower faced:

The influential Republicans in Congress were for the most part, conservatives who did nothing to help Eisenhower get the nomination nor did they accept the fact that he virtually saved their party from a deepening oblivion. They gave him only intermittent support and considerable opposition and personal aggravation.[26]

The legislative party develops its own record to take to the voters. Its own finance and policy committees duplicate those of the national party. There is little to link the campaign mechanisms of the president and the candidates for Congress. After 1960 the Democratic National Committee and the congressional campaign committees agreed to coordinate their efforts, but by 1966 tensions between Johnson and the legislators was so great the effort was abandoned.[27]

The separation between the national committee and the legislative party is greatest when the party does not control the presidency. The legislators of the "out" party may promulgate a party philosophy or set of principles independently of the national committee, as Republicans did in 1945 and 1950.[28] Or legislators may become party spokesmen. In 1955, after Democratic chairman Paul Butler criticized Eisenhower's state of the union address, he was told by Senate Majority Leader Lyndon Johnson to adopt a lower profile, because Johnson intended to carry the public debate against the president.[29] The Democratic Advisory Committee, created in 1957 as a national policy organ, invited congressional leaders to join it. Speaker Sam Rayburn and Majority Leader Lyndon Johnson declined, for as Johnson wrote to Rayburn, "The American people will bitterly resent the idea that a group of appointive professional politicians are supervising the work of the men they have elected to Congress."[30] The Democratic Policy Council, created in 1969, had only five Democratic legislators—none from the leadership—on its sixty-six-member board, and stated that it would restrict itself to consideration of "long-term issues," by which it meant issues not being considered by Congress, in order to avoid friction with the congressional leaders.

The Republicans have similar problems. After their defeat in 1948,

National Chairman Hugh Scott proposed a Republican Policy Conference, but the suggestion was rejected by Robert Taft and other members of the Senate Republican Policy Committee. As Scott recalls, "I was hailed to the woodshed by Republican leaders of the Senate and put on notice that 'policy' was a congressional prerogative."[31] During the Kennedy administration the Republican congressional leaders, Everett Dirksen and Charles Halleck, produced the weekly "Ev and Charlie show" for television, which became the major Republican forum to denounce New Frontier programs. The national committee had far less influence. In 1977 when Republicans sponsored a televised response to the Carter energy proposals, they turned to Ronald Reagan and various congressional and state party leaders as spokespersons. Because congressional leaders are accustomed to representing their party when not in control of the White House, they do not always yield gracefully on policy matters to the president once their party has regained the White House.

The president does not determine the membership of his legislative party. He may suggest to his followers that they run for the House or Senate, and may give them an advance "buildup" by appointing them to visible executive positions in advance of their expected run for elective office. But he cannot ensure their nomination by the autonomous state and local parties. Most legislators do not owe their entrance to elective office to the promptings of presidents or other national party leaders. They are recruited by state politicians, Senate or House campaign committees, or local interest and constituency groups. Like Roosevelt or Nixon, a president may try to purge his party by seeing to the defeat of his enemies in the primaries. He may attack the incumbent and accuse him of party disloyalty, and encourage his opponent and arrange for financing of his campaign (with the promise of an executive appointment if the challenger fails); and he can cut off patronage to the incumbent and to any organization that backs him. But these methods are rarely employed: between 1913 and 1960 there were approximately 12,000 nominations to Congress, and presidents made only thirty-nine endorsements in contested primaries. In ten cases the opponent of the incumbent was endorsed, and in only five of those cases was the incumbent defeated.[32] Legislators win renomination with ease: between 1952 and 1972 of the 3,607 incumbents seeking the House renomination of their party, only 65 suffered primary defeats. Only 3 incumbents were ousted in primaries in the 1976 contests.

The president generally relies on the carrot rather than the stick. He may try to persuade an incumbent to retire, or may offer him a position in the executive branch. But any intervention with the legislative party is rare and usually unsuccessful. As James Farley observed after Franklin Roosevelt failed to purge most of the legislators on his list, "In pursuing his course of vengeance Roosevelt violated a cardinal political creed which demanded that he keep out of local matters," and added that "voters naturally and rightfully resent the unwarranted invasion of outsiders."[33]

Presidential coattails might once have provided an incentive for the legislative party to work closely with the president, for his next election attempt would have a bearing on their own prospects. But coattails have vanished. While the two-party vote for president fluctuates wildly from one election to the next, voting in congressional elections (especially in the House) is quite stable. The major determinants of voter choice in congressional elections are party identification (which gives the Democrats the advantage) and the incumbency effect.[34] Since party identification has weakened, the incumbency factor has played a larger role: most defections across party lines generally work to benefit the incumbent, keeping legislators of both parties well entrenched.[35] In presidential election years, between two-thirds and four-fifths of the party defections in congressional races have been toward the incumbent.[36] The lessening impact of presidential coattails is illustrated by the fact that the percentage of congressional districts carried by a president from one party that elect a member of the opposite party to the House has risen from 19.3 percent in 1952 to 44.1 percent in 1972.[37]

Most congressional districts are not competitive.[38] No matter which party wins the White House, the Democrats will retain large majorities in the House and Senate—at least until the next major party realignment occurs. Goldwater, Nixon, and Ford all wrote off the possibility of electing a Republican House in their presidential campaigns, a decision that did not bring them any closer to their congressional parties. Democratic presidents often run *behind* congressional candidates and receive a lower percentage of the two-party vote. Most members of the Democratic congressional party do not consider the president responsible for their own election victories. As Democratic Whip Percy Priest said in 1949 after Truman squeaked into office, "More than 100 or our 263 Democrats got more votes in their districts than Truman, and they felt they didn't owe him a damn thing."[39] But when Kennedy assumed the office, the House Democrats lost more than a score of seats, and many members blamed the presidential campaign for the losses. In 1976 Carter won the presidency with slightly more than 50 percent of the vote, while 208 of the 292 House Democrats received more than 60 percent of the total vote in their districts. Carter received a total of 40,828,587 votes, while the 435 Democratic candidates for the House won 41,749,411 votes, showing a greater enthusiasm for the legislative party. In all sections of the country Democratic House candidates scored higher margins of victory over their Republican opponents than Carter scored over Ford. Discounting any presidential coattails, Paul Pendergast, executive director of the Democratic Congressional Campaign Committee, noted that "national trends don't affect congressional races anymore."[40]

There are coattails on the Republican side, but not enough to overcome the Democratic advantage of incumbency and party identification. In 1972, when Nixon won by a landslide, thirteen additional House Republicans were elected, though Senate representation declined by two. The Republican percentage of the votes in the House contests was 48.6 percent, its highest level since 1920, and the better Nixon did in a congressional district, the better the Republican House candidate performed. Although the candidates did better, most could not overcome the Democratic advantage and actually win the seat. So though Nixon had a coattails effect, it was not strong enough to overcome Democratic advantages.[41] The result of the imbalance between the legislative parties seems to be that the Democrats don't need a strong presidential candidate and the Republicans cannot be helped significantly by one.

Legislative elections are constitutionally disassociated from presidential elections. The entire House is elected in the presidential year, but all members must run again two years later in the midterm elections. Each member must consider how he or she will win in the off-year election, when turnout will be much lower and national issues will not be a significant factor. Political scientists have measured the impact presidential performance has on House midterm elections. One study found that a change in presidential popularity of 10 percent in the Gallup polls is associated with a national change of 1.3 percent in the midterm congressional vote for candidates of his party. Furthermore, a change of $100 in real disposable income per person in the year prior to the midterm election is associated with a national change of 3.5 percent in the midterm vote for candidates of the president's party. The model was calculated for the 1938–70 off-year elections, but it worked well in predicting results for 1974.[42] Other studies suggest why the president's party usually loses House seats in midterm elections: disapproval of the president causes more defections from his party to the opposition than approval of him causes defections from the opposition to his party.[43] A president who does well will not help his congressional candidates, but an unpopular president will cause many defections from his party.

Presidents cannot help members of Congress retain marginal seats in off-year elections, as Wilson, Roosevelt, Johnson, Nixon, and Ford all discovered. With the exception of 1934, the party in the White House has always lost seats in the midterm election. Presidents may even be asked to stay out of congressional campaigns, especially if there is an unpopular war (Truman in 1950, Johnson in 1966) or a recession (Ford in 1974). Carter's problems began as early as 1977, when in six special House elections for vacancies, Republicans switched five House seats from the Democrats.

Presidents concentrate their efforts in the Senate, where elections are more volatile and where there are fewer safe seats. A Republican president can mount a media campaign for many candidates, since there are only thirty-three contests in any election. By electing only two or three Republicans the president may obtain a more "ideological" majority to the right of center, based on a coalition of Republicans and conservative Democrats, even though the Republicans remain the minority. Such a coalition enables a Republican president to check the Democratic House, and enables him to win support in the Senate for his nominations and for any treaties he negotiates.

In Senate elections a president may have a coattails effect. In 1972 Nixon won a smashing victory over McGovern, and seventeen Republicans were elected or returned to the Senate. In only six of these races did the Republican Senate candidate have a greater margin of victory than Nixon, and in only six races did the candidate receive more votes than Nixon. In all seventeen of these races Nixon received a total of 16,202,573 votes, while the Republicans elected received 14,844,354 votes, showing that the president had more popular support than the Senate party. In contrast, Democratic presidents suffer from a reverse coattails effect. Popular Democratic Senators often lead the ticket in their reelection attempts, and claim credit for carrying the state for the president. In 1976 Carter won a close election, and twenty-one Democrats were elected or returned to the Senate. In twenty of these races the Democratic candidate had a greater margin of victory than Carter, and in sixteen races the Democrat received more votes than Carter. The total Carter vote in these twenty-one states was 18,985,734, while the Senate candidates received 19,637,657 votes. Democrats in the Senate did not assume that Carter had aided them in their campaigns.

Those most likely to support the presidential program are, as one might expect, freshman members of the House who "turned" seats by defeating members of the other party in a presidential election year. They have an incentive to cooperate with the administration to obtain patronage and grants for their districts. During Lyndon Johnson's administration, freshmen from switched-seat districts provided the largest margin of support for presidential programs and the highest support for party positions.[44] Others likely to follow the president are those whose vote totals or margins of victory were lower than the president's. Evidence from the Johnson administration indicates that House members who lagged behind the president's vote supported him to a greater extent than those members who led their districts.[45] But the underlying factor was the tendency of northern liberal Democrats (likely to have lagged in vote totals and likely to have come from switched-seat districts) to support the Johnson Great Society program, and the tendency of southern conservative Democrats (likely to have lead in vote totals and not likely to have come from switched-seat districts) to defect from the administration program. Carter often had great trouble from freshmen members, even those from switched-seat and highly competive districts, when his proposals differed from their priorities (although this opposition to his program was more likely to be reflected in the House Democratic caucus and in the committees than in actual floor votes).

Members from safe seats are not likely to follow presidential leadership automatically. On the Republican side such members are generally more conservative than a Republican president, and as Eisenhower, Nixon, and Ford all discovered, they are prepared to sabotage the White House program. If they are Democrats, such members are in control of the committee and subcommittee structure of Congress and consider themselves to be autonomous policymakers who must be consulted closely by the administration. The committee leaders are the most insulated from electoral competition, and the president can neither purge them from the party nor remove them from their committee posts (see table 4.1).

TABLE 4.1

Insulation of Committee Leaders From Electoral Competition: 1952–1976

YEAR	HOUSE DEMOCRATS	SENATE DEMOCRATS	HOUSE REPUBLICANS	SENATE REPUBLICANS
1952	80.8	77.9	64.1	59.2
1956	83.7	77.0	62.4	56.2
1960	79.5	79.3	55.5	56.6
1964	76.6	70.8	58.4	57.0
1968	78.8	72.6	67.4	62.9
1972	76.8	62.9	67.0	59.6
1976	75.3	68.8	64.3	58.5

NOTE: Figures refer to mean percentage of total vote won by committee chairs and ranking minority members. House figures refer to election year indicated. Senate figures refer to most recent election of leaders.

Many legislators consider Congress a career, serving an average of over six terms in the House and over two in the Senate. In addition, most legislators are not invited to serve in the cabinet or in other executive positions, a sharp contrast to nineteenth-century practice when cabinets often contained several congressional leaders. Between 1810 and 1861 most cabinet members came from Congress; between 1861 and 1896 the percentage dropped to 37 percent; between 1897 and 1940 to 19 percent; between 1941 and 1963 to 15 percent; and since then only a handful of legislators have served at high levels in the administration.[46] Cabinet members are usually "outsiders" with no influence on the legislative party and little patience with its ways.

Legislators may be resentful that little money will be available from the national party for their congressional and senatorial campaigns.[47] When Kennedy was nominated in 1960, the party debt stood at $70,000; but by the time he was elected, it had climbed to over $4 million. After the 1972 Democratic defeat, the debt of the national committee was $2.4 million; during that campaign the committee and the McGovern organization fought over who would receive the proceeds of a telethon, since the committee was attempting to retire a $9.3 million debt from the unsuccessful 1968 Humphrey campaign. In 1976, after Carter's victory, the committee was saddled with $2.1 million in new debts and a total debt of $3.8 million. Although Carter helped the committee raise $1.3 million in the first six months of his presidency, the Republicans managed to raise $5.2 million in the same period, proving that control of the White House does not provide an advantage for the party in fund-raising.[48] In any event, party professionals need feel little gratitude for a presidential commitment to raise funds for the party; he is likely to be retiring the debt that his own campaign had created.

III

Autonomous State Electoral Systems

The president does not control the state parties, each of which has independence under national party rules. Most nominations for state and local office are made without presidential interference. When Carter was asked if he would support Mayor Abraham Beame (one of his early backers) in the New York City primary in 1977, the president responded, "My own inclination is to stay clear of Democratic primaries—let the Democrats in a particular state or jurisdiction make their own choice."[49] Elections for most state offices are held in non-presidential-election years to insulate them from national trends and issues. There are no coattails in these elections, nor do any exist in elections held in presidential years. In nonsouthern states, for example, the number of split-party results in gubernatorial elections has been increasing.

Gubernatorial Elections:1896–1976

YEARS	PERCENTAGE OF SPLIT-PARTY RESULTS
1896–1908	11.5
1912–1924	18.8
1928–1940	22.2
1944–1952	24.5
1956–1964	40.3
1968–1972	48.5
1976	41.6

SOURCES: For data through 1964, V. O. Key, Jr., *American State Politics* (New York: Philadelphia Book Co., 1956), p. 49; Joseph Kallenbach, *The American Chief Executive* (New York: Harper and Row, 1966), p. 104.

As with Senate elections, a Democratic presidential nominee may ride reverse coattails. In 1976 Carter led the ticket and Democratic candidates won two governorships, but in four states Carter won where the gubernatorial candidates led the ticket.

Democrats enjoy an overwhelming majority of state legislative seats. In 1976 they controlled 1,322 state Senate seats to the Republican 607, and 3,805 lower house seats to the Republican 1,760. These Democratic state legislative parties do not benefit from any presidential coattails. In 1976 Democratic state parties won majority control in legislative chambers in Kansas, North Dakota, and Vermont from the Republicans, while at the same time Ford defeated Carter by greater than 7 percent margin in each of these states. Some correlation seems to exist between prior Democratic control of the lower house of a state legislature and the prospects that a Democratic presidential nominee will carry the state. In the twenty-one states in which Democrats controlled the lower house by a better than 70 percent margin of seats, Carter won eighteen. In fourteen states in which the Democrats controlled the lower house by a margin between 60 and 70 percent, Carter won only five. He won only one state in which the Democrats had a margin of control lower than 60 percent or in which Republicans controlled the lower chamber. To the extent that coattails exist, the Democratic president rides on the prior successes of his state parties.

State party leaders are kept at a distance by the president once the campaign is over. One study reported that these leaders work closely with members of Congress and with their delegations on the party national committee, but that there are few contacts with the White House staff and hardly any with the president.[50] Eisenhower was so distant from these leaders that as Sherman Adams remembers, "A good many of the members of the National Committee were either lukewarm or openly hostile to the President."[51] After only three months of trying to work with Carter, the members of the Democratic National Committee unanimously passed a resolution rebuking the president for neglecting the state parties on patronage and appointments and for failing to help them with fund-raising.

Party leaders often take positions that conflict with the president. Kennedy was opposed by southern state parties against his civil rights efforts. Johnson faced a coalition of Democratic mayors and party leaders opposed to aspects of his "community action" programs. Carter was unable to persuade the Florida and North Carolina legislatures to pass the Equal Rights Amendment in 1977, engaged in a running dispute with New York Governor Hugh Carey on the timing and magnitude of welfare reform proposals, and outraged Democrats in the Bronx by ignoring them on his tour of urban slums in the borough, prompting some to label his visit a public relations gimmick. Carter's proposals for a system of election-day registration of voters met with strong resistance from many state governors and attorneys general of his own party, and the plan remained stalled in Congress during the first session.

Patronage and the State Parties

Presidential patronage has been the major weapon in the arsenal the White House possesses, but in modern times it has little impact on state parties. The highest cabinet and national security positions are filled without reference to state parties. Only a small fraction of the sub-cabinet-level positions are filled through their recommendations. In the 1930s and 1940s, Roosevelt and Truman did maintain some connection with the Democratic National Committee for "exempted" civil service positions, filled by state parties without competitive examination. During the Eisenhower administration, the "Willis Plan" was proposed, which would have linked the departments, the Republican National Committee, the state parties, and the congressional parties, but this plan was scuttled by White House aides. Instead, interest groups and careerists filled most political positions and party leaders were bypassed. After two years only 274 officials (of 10,000 appointed) had come from state party recommendations. As Sherman Adams recalled, Eisenhower "insisted on making the final decision on his own appointees and carefully avoided giving the Republican National Committee any responsibility in the selection of government officials, a duty the committee would have been happy to assume."[52] Kennedy used talent scouts to fill his administration, picking his "New Frontiersmen" from universities, business, and the professions. Lyndon Johnson often promoted from within the bureaucracy and re-cruited from interest groups that would benefit from the new programs he was passing. Nixon bypassed the party committee and instead chose careerists and loyalists from law and public relations firms, from the media, and from the ranks of management consultants.[53] Carter allowed his cabinet secretaries to fill most positions, and for the first several months relied on many Republican holdovers, prompting complaints from the Democratic National Committee.

Symptomatic of the presidential attitude was Kennedy's practice of appointing Republicans to the most sensitive national security positions, Nixon's attempt to persuade Democratic Senator Henry Jackson to serve as his secretary of defense, and Carter's appointment of James Schlesinger (a Republican who had served as Nixon's secretary of defense) as his energy advisor and first secretary of the new Department of Energy. Schlesinger in turn named as his second-in-command Thomas Reed, a Republican who had been secretary of the Air Force in the Ford administration and who had worked for Ronald Reagan in California and for Nixon's chief political operative, Harry Dent, at the White House. The key men in developing energy policy and in staffing an entire new department were Republicans, appointed by a Democratic president at the beginning of his administration. So much for the president as "chief partisan"!

Distributive Politics

The intergovernmental grant and contract system has grown greatly in size since the 1960s, and much of the funding is distributed on a discretionary basis. The president may attempt to manipulate the system to reward his followers, and work closely with state and local party leaders who are requesting grants. In 1968 Mayor John V. Lindsay of New York City seconded the nomination of Spiro Agnew for vice-president and campaigned hard among Republican liberals for the presidential ticket. The following year, when Lindsay was running for the Republican nomination for mayor, the White House returned the favor by announcing a series of grants and contracts, including the sale of the Brooklyn Naval Yard to the city for use as an industrial park, and the development of Breezy Point as the first urban national park.[54] Even so, Lindsay lost his nomination bid (although he was reelected on the Liberal line), demonstrating the weakness of a president, even when using patronage and distributions, in influencing local party contests. Nixon aided Republican Mayor George Siebels of Birmingham, Alabama, with large grants, in a tangible demonstration to the southern electorate of the advantages of electing Republicans to local office. In 1976 when James Buckley was attempting to win reelection as senator from New York, the Ford administration gave him help: the Environmental Protection Administration announced a $1.2 billion plan for sewage treatment facilities that would provide an estimated 14,000 jobs and increase the "gross city product" by an estimated $3 billion; the Department of Transportation announced approval of the Westway Highway project, which would cost over $1.4 billion and provide jobs; and the Department of Housing and Urban Development announced a $65 million mortgage guarantee for Battery Park City, an urban housing development. Buckley lost the election, in another demonstration of how little the grant process influences elections. Moreover, the man who defeated him, Daniel Moynihan, took pains to demonstrate to the Carter administration that far from being grateful for distributions to New York State, he believed that the state (and the entire Northeast) was being shortchanged by the national government, since far more tax dollars were leaving the region than grant dollars were returning.

IV

Party Reform

It is no coincidence that those who favor a strong presidency usually propose sweeping changes in the party machinery.[55] They suggest that the powers of the national committee be increased, that its staff be enlarged and professionalized, and that it gain control over the autonomous congressional campaign and policy committees. The national chairperson would become a presidential assistant with a White House office and would serve as the leader of the party on behalf of the administration.

Such proposals for sweeping reform will not be instituted. Instead of centralizing power in the White House, the reforms that parties have adopted in recent years have made the national committees larger and more unwieldy, and less likely to interfere with the autonomy of the state and congressional parties (except in the matter of delegate selection to the national conventions). Each national committee has created a small executive committee, and these have proved susceptible to presidential influence, but in turn these committees have run into trouble when they have acted on behalf of the White House.

Some party activists and political scientists have proposed that the parties bind themselves to the national platform, as prepared by nominating and midterm conventions. Such a reform now seems less likely than ever, for in 1976 both Carter and Ford abandoned or repudiated parts of the party platforms. Neither party is willing to give its national committee the power to withdraw the party label from candidates for public office who do not pledge support for the platform, and neither party will permit purges of members or elected officeholders who do not attempt to implement the national platform.

Proposals to centralize power in the party structure and impose discipline on elected officials has its appeal to academic reformers enamored of the idea of "responsible party government," but the party activists have moved in a different direction. They have made it easier for grassroots movements and candidate-oriented organizations to participate in nominating conventions and other party activities. The existing state and local organizations have been weakened and their connections with presidential contenders made tenuous. The national party is less a structure than it is a *process* for delegate selection to the convention. The party has become a battlefield on which contending armies struggle for position. Once the president has won his battles and occupied the White House, he find no party structure to control, no party to unite.[56]

Some reformers have suggested ways to restore presidential coattails in order to increase presidential influence with the legislative parties.

One proposal is that the Constitution be amended to provide a four-year term for representatives, who would then be elected only in presidential election years. Senators could be elected for either four- or eight-year terms to place all of them in the presidential election cycle. A popular presidential candidate might then sweep his party into control of both houses. Such a proposal has no chance of adoption. It goes against the intentions of the framers to provide for separate constituencies as a means of promoting the checks and balances system. Although the members of the House might prefer a four-year term, the Senate would never consent to holding all elections in a presidential year, for the present system enables its members to resist presidential pressures on nominations, treaties, and legislation. There is no chance that Congress will approve a constitutional amendment changing its terms of office.

Political scientist Charles M. Hardin has made the ingenious suggestion that the winner of the presidential election be given a majority of the House of Representatives by awarding his party "bonus" seats sufficient to ensure a partisan majority. The existing membership would be supplemented by an additional one hundred fifty at-large members, and the party winning the White House would choose one hundred. The opposition could choose up to fifty, less whatever number was necessary to ensure that the party in the White House maintained control of the chamber.[57] Such a proposal would dilute the power of the members, since it would create more competition for committee assignments, and more pressure for office space and perquisites of office. Members of the House are not likely to adopt a proposal that increases their numbers so drastically. Democratic congressional leaders might find that such a system endangered their influence and led to presidential domination of the legislative party.

There remains the possibility that a president could promote a realignment of the parties so that the Democrats would become the party of the liberals and the Republicans the party of conservatives. With ideology as a unifying factor, a president might lead his party by influence and example rather than by dominating it through a centralized structure. Presidents have never been successful when they have tried to realign the parties. Wilson hewed to a progressive line for several years, but then moderated his position until American entrance into the First World War put an end to his New Freedom program. His party was as diverse when he left the presidency as when he entered it, and subsequent Democratic nominees in the 1920s were conservatives. Franklin Roosevelt never had a coherent ideology, and by the end of his presidency his party had divided neatly along regional lines, with northern liberals confronting southern conservatives. Truman became a broker between these wings, and with no clear direction the party floundered, with progressives and dixiecrats both bolting in 1948 and running third-party candidates for the presidency. The Fair Deal program that Truman sponsored was stalled in Congress by a coalition of Republicans and Southern Democrats, an informal "Republicrat" majority that controlled Congress on many issues.[58]

On the Republican side Eisenhower encouraged the progressives in his party and referred to them approvingly as "Modern Republicans." But he made no attempt to purge the conservative wing, often worked closely with them, and at times sold out his own supporters. Eisenhower himself was more conservative than liberal on some domestic issues, such as housing and federal aid to education, and had no sympathy for civil rights programs.[59] At times Eisenhower thought about forming a new party by jettisoning the "Old Guard" congressional and state wheelhorses, but he never took any concrete steps.[60]

Neither Kennedy nor Johnson ever seriously considered attempting to expel the segregationists and conservatives from the party. Rather than attempting a dramatic realignment, they presided over a slower process of change as the South became a two-party region and the Democratic state parties were liberalized and opened up to black participation as a result of the Voting Rights Act of 1965. Both presidents placated the various wings of their party with patronage, distributions, and compromises. The culmination of the conciliatory policy occurred in 1976 when Jimmy Carter became the first president elected from the South in more than one hundred years. And under Carter no realignment of Democrats into a liberal party could take place, since the president himself appeared to be moderate or conservative on many domestic issues. If any transformation was occurring in the Democratic party, it seemed to be away from liberalism, not towards it.

Only Nixon seems to have considered forming a new party after his reelection in 1972. He had abandoned old guard Republican principles of the balanced budget and limited social welfare expenditures, and had replaced cold war rhetoric with the promise of "detente" with the Soviet Union and a new relationship with the People's Republic of China. His reelection victory was a personal triumph based on a "New American Majority" and not on traditional Republican themes. As president, Nixon had demonstrated his contempt for both the state parties and the national committee. He had even campaigned in the 1970 midterm election for such Senate Democrats as Eastland, Jackson, and Byrd. But Nixon hoped to infuse the legislative party with his own followers. He had recruited in 1970 a talented set of nominees for Senate seats, including George Bush, Lowell Weicker, and William Roth. In the aftermath of his own election victory in 1972, the Committee to Reelect the President had more than $3 million in unexpended funds. The president considered using these funds to recruit his own followers into the congressional party, by constructing an umbrella organization, run from the White House, that would stage-manage nominations for the congressional party and run the House campaigns in 1974. In turn, a successful congressional campaign would serve as a springboard for a realigned, perhaps even renamed, party of Nixon loyalists that would be created in 1976.[61]

Nixon turned from titular leader to scapegoat when the criminal activities of the Committee to Reelect the President and various White House aides were revealed. Again and again National Chairman George Bush disassociated his party from the Nixon campaign organization, and his theme was that "the Republican Party was not involved in Watergate." The financial assets of the Committee to Reelect the President were used to pay for the legal defenses of several of the conspirators, and to settle the Democratic Party's lawsuit (which cost the Committee $750,000). The president, preoccupied with his defense against the impeachment that might be voted by the House, could no longer make any plans for leading or realigning his party.

The 1974 midterm congressional elections resulted in a landslide defeat for congressional Republicans, and the hardest hit was the conservative wing. President Ford, struggling to win the presidential nomination, was in no position in 1976 to realign the party along conservative lines. He tried to win support from all factions. Even his challenger, Ronald Reagan, in a last-ditch attempt to win the nomination, concluded an alliance with liberal Pennsylvania Republican Senator Richard Schweiker in an effort to build a coalition that would cross ideological lines. After the 1976 elections, the party had lost the White House, controlled approximately one-third of the seats in Congress, controlled less than one-third of the state legislative seats and less than one-fourth of the governorships; and less than one-fifth of the eligible electorate identified themselves with the party. Conservatives argued that the party should be realigned by grass-roots activists, and various organizations raised large sums of money for "political action committees" in the 1978 congressional elections. The stage was set for a pronounced tilt to the right in Republican ranks, which would make the campaign of a presidential contender even more difficult. Such a contender would have to take a moderate position to build a successful electoral coalition; like Eisenhower and Nixon and Ford, a new Republican president would find his party less of a resource than a hindrance in governing.

Future prospects for party government are dim. In both parties the emphasis on intraparty democratic competition for nominations, and on grass-roots activism rather than organizational loyalty, make it unlikely that central party organs can impose discipline on presidents or legislative leaders. National committees will remain weak and their staffs ineffective. The national chairpersons will have problems in gaining access to the president and will be rivals for influence with the White House staff. Less and less patronage flows to the national and state parties, especially in the post-Watergate atmosphere in which investigative journalists stand ready to pounce on any perceived irregularities. Trends in voting behavior—the increased proportion of independents, the weakening of party identification as a clue for voting choice, the lessening of the coattails effect, the disassociation of state elections from the presidential election cycle—all make it unlikely that the legislative or state parties will coordinate their programs closely with the White House. No party mechanisms will develop to ensure that the president can control the nominations or finances or platforms of the legislative and state parties.

The question remains: would party government be desirable if it could be instituted? Clearly it would serve the president, since he could bridge the separation of powers and make the prerogatives of Congress his own, as in a parliamentary system. Our present decentralized and splintered party structures make it impossible for the president to command his fellow partisans. He must compromise with factions and even with partisan opponents to pass his programs. He must accommodate the interests of state and local leaders and elected officials by decentralizing programs rather than insisting on comprehensive national approaches to solve problems. The friction between president and Congress, and between national and state officials, slows down new initiatives, and the small amount of party loyalty that exists provides precious little lubricant to prevent the clanking of gears in the machinery of government.

But unity of purpose and speed in implementation of programs were *not* the principles on which the national government was founded under the Constitution. The framers were profoundly suspicious of "factions" and never intended that a party of "president's men" should dominate the other branches of government or the states. To check the abuse of power, the legislative party and presidential party should remain autonomous. To accommodate the diverse interests of a heterogeneous population, a federal system, and federalized parties with autonomy, are a necessity.

The party cannot "brake" the president—it cannot constrain him from taking certain prerogative actions. No party system can prevent a president from abusing his powers. But even in centralized party systems, such as the British system, it proves impossible to restrain the leadership, as those familiar with the experiences of the British during the ill-fated Suez invasion of 1956 will attest. No party system can prevent a government from taking ill-advised or even harebrained actions on its own initiative and authority. The great danger in all systems, not just the American, is that a leader will ignore his party associates and go off half-cocked.

In the final analysis the party system provides the president with great freedom, if not with governing resources. He is of his party but also above it. If he finds it necessary to transcend its interests, he may do so without damage to his principles or interests. He may choose bipartisan consultation and accommodation of interests for routine situations, and non-partisan emergency prerogatives for crisis situations. He may rally his party for his domestic program, but build liberal and conservative coalitions that cross party lines as it suits his purposes. He may shift from one day to the next: consistency may be the virtue of a party man or woman, but it is a presidential vice. To the extent that his legislative party collaborates with him without losing its autonomy, the system remains in tune with the original constitutional principles of checks and balances, and with the intentions of those who framed a system of limited constitutional government.

Domestic Program

Innovation

PRESIDENTS must move the nation. There are New Frontiers to be crossed, Great Societies to be built, and New or Fair Deals to be made. But without a mandate or a disciplined legislative party, a presidential program is difficult to develop or enact. The campaign organization that put the incumbent in the White House has none of the skills necessary to govern innovatively, or to monitor and evaluate existing programs in order to improve them.[1] Yet innovation can be good politics: the president wishes to redeem pledges made during the campaign and reward his voter coalition. By claiming expertise and invoking "the national interest," the president may try to substitute *wisdom* for his weakness as party leader, and to do so he must develop and use the resources of the institutionalized presidency.

I

The President as Initiator

The president sends up to Congress between one hundred and four hundred bills annually as his legislative program. Congress has come to expect such a program; it will criticize a president that does not offer one. As the chairman of the House Foreign Affairs Committee told an administration spokesman in 1953, "Don't expect us to start from scratch on what you people want. That's not the way we do things here. *You* draft the bills and *we* work them over."[2] Many legislators prefer to concentrate on constituent services, private bills, and oversight of agencies; for them the investment of time necessary to innovate may be greater than the anticipated return. By requiring the president to present a program, Congress avoids "start-up" costs and gains, as political scientist Richard Neustadt notes, "a menu whereby Congress can gain from the outside what comes hard from within: a handy and official guide to the wants of its biggest customer; an advance formulation of the main issues in each session; a work load ready to hand to every legislative committee."[3]

Congress has passed many laws that require the president or departments and agencies to submit either a program or an annual report: the Budget and Accounting Act of 1921 requires the president to submit an executive budget; the Employment Act of 1946 requires presentation of an annual economic report; and other laws require reports on energy, the environment, international economic affairs, foreign aid, and humanitarian assistance. By resolution, Congress can require the president or a department to present specific legislative proposals: in 1975 Robert Dole sponsored a resolution in the Senate that forced the Ford administration to propose modifications in the food stamp program for congressional consideration.

Congress does not always sit back and wait for the president to present his program. The House Foreign Affairs Committee, which in 1953 waited impatiently for the administration to send it bills, was in some senses atypical: it was under Republican control for the first term in several years and the majority was ill prepared to initiate its own program without awaiting communication from a newly elected Republican president; it was a weak committee with less prestige or expertise than its Senate counterpart; it dealt with subjects in which the president had classified information and a major interest. Other committees that deal with domestic programs often innovate prior to receiving proposals from the executive branch. In such cases the president sends up his program as part of a competition for power, and may try one or more of the following tactics:

1. Preempt a committee initiative so that he can claim it as his own and receive credit for its passage.
2. Substitute his version for the committee's, so that Congress will have options, and so that the ultimate compromise will be a bill that the president can sign.
3. Offer alternative proposals to those a committee has put forward, by raising new issues and priorities; such proposals will delay action on the committee bill and force a consideration of the presidential program.[4]

Presidents may claim credit for social security increases or hikes in the minimum wage that have already been developed in committee. They may send up tax reform bills to provide alternatives to proposals Congress is considering. The Ford administration proposed overhaul of the FBI and CIA to forestall congressional proposals for more drastic changes; Carter used this tactic in proposing a shift from plutonium reactors to alternative nuclear technologies, and in proposing a college-tuition loan program in place of a costly tax credit system that Congress was about to consider.

Presidents enhance their power in the executive branch when they take a major part in program formulation. They control the lines of communication between departments and committees, since proposals from agencies and bureaus must first be reviewed by the Executive Office of the President before being transmitted to Congress. With advance notice of what bureaus are proposing, a president can forestall initiatives that conflict with his own priorities. His response to departmental "laundry lists" submitted for his consideration provide the cabinet and the rest of the administration with his sense of direction. The president can reward or punish officials by supporting or opposing their proposals.

But presidents act intermittently as initiators. They ignore low-priority problems, allowing Congress and the departments to work things out. "I've often thought this country could run itself domestically without a President," Nixon once observed. "All you need is a competent cabinet to run the country at home."[5] Sometimes their proposals are simply political ploys: Harry Truman in 1948 proposed a civil rights program based on the recommendations of the President's Committee on Civil Rights. Although the program could not pass Congress, as Truman well knew, it was presented to win support of black voters in the north, a strategy that proved a key factor in Truman's win in the election. Truman later pushed through several civil rights measures by executive order as "payment" for black votes. Before the 1956 election the Eisenhower administration introduced a watered-down civil rights bill as a ploy to split southern Democrats from their northern colleagues.

A lame-duck president may try to embarrass his successor when the opposition party has won the White House. He will propose a balanced budget, large tax cuts, or popular new social programs. He may also propose things that are politically unpopular, since he can no longer suffer electoral consequences: Gerald Ford's proposed pay increase for the vice-president, members of Congress, members of the cabinet, and federal judges falls into this category. Lyndon Johnson made similar pay proposals at the end of his term to spare his successor the onus of public disapproval. A lame duck may also make a proposal that has no chance of being adopted simply to initiate public debate; Ford's proposal that statehood be offered to the Commonwealth of Puerto Rico is the most recent example.

Choices in Program Initiation

The administration must decide whether to focus on substantive or managerial proposals. *First-stage* policy initiation will occur when an administration takes a new innovation and makes a major effort to see the proposal enacted. First-stage initiation is more than a routine decision, more than an incremental adjustment in standard operating procedures of the bureaucracy; it involves a major break in standard routines, adds or subtracts from existing agency authority, and may change the mission, jurisdiction, or legal authority of one or more agencies or departments. After a major innovation has been implemented, feedback from its operations becomes available, derived from audits, legislative oversight, interest group pressure, and contracted research or evaluations. The president can then propose *second-stage* initiation: changing federal authority or jurisdiction over programs relative to that of state and local governments; increasing or decreasing clientele and interest group participation in program operations; modifying personnel practices and staffing patterns; resolving jurisdictional disputes through reorganization; improving decision-making through introduction of cost-benefit analysis, program and performance budgeting, management-by-objective, or zero-based budgeting.

An administration intent on promoting substantive change might, for tactical reasons, present it as a second-stage initiative. The abolition of many grant programs to aid urban areas was named New Federalism and billed as a procedural change by Nixon. Similarly, Nixon's attempt to expand coverage and payments in welfare programs for the elderly, blind, and disabled were presented as a simple administrative reorganization; it eventually shifted expenses of more than $2 billion annually from states to the national government.[6]

A president may discover that proposing a set of incremental innovations introduced over time will stand a greater chance of passage in Congress. Lyndon Johnson ordered the task forces drafting antipoverty programs in 1964 to limit themselves to no more than $500 million in new program proposals, which was less than $40 per poor person; the small size of the program ensured congressional approval.[7] In contrast, Vice-President Rockefeller's proposal for a $100 billion energy development agency sank without a trace in the Ford administration, while a series of minor modifications in energy policy were slowly moving through the legislative mill.

The president must make decisions about the timing of programs. Kennedy delayed submission of civil rights legislation for more than two years in order to gain southern Democratic support for his economic program. Nixon and Ford sometimes submitted programs in order to preempt Democratic congressional initiatives. Carter, in contrast, delayed submission of welfare, health, education, and urban programs for more than a year because his tax and energy bills were higher-priority items.

In an election year many program proposals contain "dipsy doodle" provisions: they confer benefits before the election and costs afterwards. The 1975 energy bill lowered gas prices at the pumps in 1975–76, but provided for increases after the election. Tax bills in an election year usually lower withholding rates, whereas the resulting inflation catches up to the electorate only after Congress has been returned. Social security payments are increased in election years, whereas the withholding rates go up afterwards.

The president must learn how to deal with interest groups that pressure him to take action. He may decide to act as "honest broker" for various interests. Conservationists, for example, proposed in 1977 that 114 million acres of Alaskan wilderness be preserved as national parks, wildlife refuges, and recreational resources. Alaskan state officials and various timber companies proposed that only 25 million acres gain protection, after prior "management" (exploitation) of these acres. The Carter administration took a middle course, proposing that some 80 million acres gain federal protection. In another case, Jewish organizations proposed an "anti-boycott" law to prevent American companies from complying with the terms of the Arab League boycott against Israel. The Ford administration decided to oppose these proposals. Carter again chose the "honest broker" approach. The Anti-Defamation League of the B'nai B'rith, a leading Jewish organization, held meetings early in 1977 with the Business Roundtable, a group consisting of heads of major corporations, under administration auspices, to see if a compromise could be reached. Eventually the groups agreed on a Joint Statement of Principles, which the administration then used to draft a bill to present to Congress. When the two sides split on an interpretation of the bill's provisions, Carter dispatched White House aides to bring the sides back into agreement. Ultimately the bill was supported by both groups, presented by the president to Congress, and passed into law.[8]

The president will concentrate on first-stage initiation during national or international crises involving economic issues. Urban unrest and rioting in the 1960s sparked proposals for antipoverty, job training, public works, community action, model cities, legal services, and civil rights legislation. A president faced with recession or depression can also rely on already-existing programs that provide funds (welfare, unemployment insurance, food stamps, medical reimbursement) and services (public housing, job training) or employment (public works and emergency employment) to those in need. The president may call for incremental modifications in these programs, including increased payment levels or increased coverage—techniques used successfully by Kennedy in the 1961–62 recession, and by Nixon, Ford, and Carter in the 1970s.

For several presidents foreign crises and wars have pushed domestic program initiation off their agendas. But sometimes a major international situation can spur domestic programming. The Soviet launch of the Sputnik satellite in 1957 spurred Eisenhower to promote a program of federal aid to education and the Kennedy administration to speed up the space program. The Interstate Highway System was "sold" to Congress in the 1950s as a national defense system, and much of the Kennedy domestic program was billed as a set of measures for outperforming the Soviet economy. The Ford administration used the energy crises to promote proposals for the deregulation of oil and gas, while some congressional Democrats used it to revive the proposal that integrated oil companies be broken up.

An overwhelming election victory produces two patterns:

1. A Democratic president will offer first-stage proposals after a landslide election. Provided the liberal wing of his party has also increased its representation, prospects for passage of a substantial part of the presidential program are good.
2. A Republican president will present second-stage proposals after a landslide election in order to preempt the Democratic congressional majority. Unless the president can create a bipartisan coalition, the chances Congress will pass his measures are poor.

The mood of the public may influence the timing of programs. John Kennedy was forced to submit civil rights bills to Congress after demonstrations by black leaders gained widespread public support. Later Lyndon Johnson identified with the demands of these groups and secured passage of the Civil Rights Act of 1964 and the Voting Rights Act of 1965. The Nixon administration was pressured into proposing a major expansion of the food stamp program after investigative reporters exposed widespread malnutrition among the nation's poor, and congressional committees began preparing their own proposals. Most consumer and ecology legislation that an administration introduces is preceded by public relations campaigns that force the president's hand.

But the public may become disillusioned about government programs. When it believes that tax dollars are being wasted, first-stage initiation may become politically unpopular. Nixon and Ford believed that many New Frontier and Great Society programs had high costs and low (or nonexistent) benefits for both the general public and the recipients of services. A rational strategy for a president is to propose first-stage initiation only when costs can be accurately calculated and when the new programs' worth are proven, so that benefits from the expenditures are certain and measurable. But when costs are high and benefits are low or not calculable, the president may prefer to retrench. Carter's initial proposals to reform health-delivery systems involved curtailment of services and benefits. He rejected his urban task force's initial recommendations as "more of the same" and seemed as skeptical of many social programs as Nixon and Ford had been. Rather than proposing major new initiatives, some presidents may capitalize on the public mood to present themselves as "curtailer in chief."

Economic conditions influence presidential choices. In the New Frontier and Great Society, Kennedy and Johnson calculated that new programs could be funded painlessly from projected surpluses in the budget that would occur as the economy advanced. New programs were even fiscally necessary, according to some economists, to use up the anticipated surpluses and prevent a "fiscal drag" that might slow down economic growth. Even after the nation became involved in Vietnam hostilities, administration economists argued that once the war ended a "peace dividend" would be available for domestic programs. But the war dragged on, costing over $200 billion, and severely dislocated the economy. Available funds were allocated for payout programs such as social security, welfare, unemployment insurance, medicare, and pensions. The tax cuts of 1969 and 1971 cut into anticipated receipts, leading the Nixon administration to take a hard line on new spending proposals. The combination of recessions and tax cuts led to ever-larger deficits, and the Ford administration curtailed almost all domestic innovations except in areas of energy research and development.

The massive deficits of the 1970s forced presidents into a dilemma. New programs might cause greater inflation if total spending were increased. But if there were a spending ceiling, each new proposal would have to compete with existing programs, causing executive branch rivalry. In the absence of a major crisis, such as depression or urban violence, presidents sidestepped the bitter political struggles that major new initiatives would create, and instead emphasized control of inflation, movement towards balanced budgets, second-stage innovations, and incremental improvements in existing programs. To a large extent Congress was preoccupied with struggling over levels of benefit and coverage, and formulae for the distribution of goods and services to various regions, states, and urban areas.

In the 1980s, program innovation will involve new approaches. The politics of resource management will become central. Faced with severe and increasing shortages of energy and natural resources, government innovation will emphasize conservation and planned growth in selected areas, elimination of "frills" in the provision of social services, and control over the various "payout" programs to keep costs at a reasonable proportion of the gross national product. Presidents will not rouse the nation by emphasizing the perfectability of society through government programs, but rather will warn of wrenching dislocations and discontinuities in the American Way of Life unless significant departures from "business as usual" are made. New innovations are likely to be unpopular, since they will involve calls for retrenchment, conservation, and prudent management. In effect, these calls will constitute *third-stage* program initiation:

presidents will need great political skill and some courage to propose them and fight for them against interest and clientele groups pressuring them to propose expanded distributions, increased payouts and benefits, and operation of the economy without significant new planning mechanisms.

Personal Factors

Prospects for program initiation are affected by the background, experience, and personality of the president. Lyndon Johnson's firsthand experience with the quality of education in the South made him committed to a program of federal aid to education.[9] Nixon traced his decision to support the Family Assistance Plan to his own humble origins and the influence his mother had on him. As governors of New York, both Theodore and Franklin Roosevelt gained experience in dealing with the labor movement, and as presidents they were receptive to programs advanced by union leaders to regulate labor-management relations.

Prior career experiences may determine the receptivity of the president to proposals. Kennedy had been a senator with little influence, and his talents lay in raising issues rather than in passing laws. As president he pushed some domestic programs as much for their educational or partisan value as for their immediate passage; his idea was to educate the nation so that in his second term he could pass the far-reaching programs of the New Frontier. Lyndon Johnson had been majority leader of the Democrats in the Senate, and he was used to creating coalitions that gave something to everyone and ensured passage of laws. Carrying the skill of the broker into the White House, Johnson became "president of all the people" and accommodated as many interest groups as possible through consensus building. Both as legislative leader and as president he used an "inclusive" style, for he tried to provide all participants with a "piece of the action."[10] As minority leader of the House, Gerald Ford's function was to oppose the proposals of the Democratic majority. Republican leaders generally made it a rule to reject claims for special treatment by any faction of their party: only when a majority of House Republicans supported claims of an interest group would the party present a proposal.[11] This "exclusive" style, so opposite to Johnson's, carried over into the Ford administration. The president generally rejected claims of many interest groups for special treatment, and he used the veto to obstruct Democratic program proposals without necessarily proposing measures of his own.

The presidential temperament may also affect prospects for program initiation. Franklin Roosevelt was unafraid of failure, receptive to new ideas, and always willing to experiment and tinker. He saw nothing wrong with asking his advisors to combine apparently irreconcilable elements of different proposals into a speech or bill. He presented his initiatives as experiments, suggesting that if they didn't work he would introduce something else until he hit on something that did work.[12]

Recent studies of presidential personality suggest that incumbents with certain character traits may "freeze" in a crisis. Political scientist James Barber refers to such behavior as "rigidification," which he defines as continued adherence to a failing policy.[13] A president who is "active" in his conception of the office, wanting to make policy, but is "negative" in his feelings about work, and in Barber's phrase does not "give the impression he enjoys his political life," is a likely candidate for rigidification. Such a president digs his own grave: he works himself to exhaustion, isolates himself from political allies, turns on associates and friends with charges of betrayal and disloyalty, succumbs to self-pity, and looks for scapegoats in the worsening situation. Program initiation does not occur; instead, the president continues on his failing course.

Not all policy failures lead to rigidification. "Active-positive" presidents, those with sweeping conception of the powers of the office and a love for political rough-and-tumble (in which category Theodore Roosevelt, Franklin Roosevelt, and John Kennedy are classified) are likely to drop a failing line without damage to their political prospects. It can be argued that the New Deal consisted of one failure of innovation after another, none of which inhibited Roosevelt from sending up his next pet measure.

Idiosyncratic personality traits may affect program initiation. Kennedy was reputed to resent pressure from associates, and he would delay making decisions to show them he was still boss. Johnson had a passion for secrecy, and was known to reverse decisions when press leaks preempted his announcements of a new program. A president may lean over backwards to compensate for expected biases. Roman Catholic Kennedy opposed federal aid to parochial schools. Southern Protestant Lyndon Johnson led the struggle for civil rights legislation and aid to parochial schools. Army General Eisenhower reduced the size and role of the army, and Kennedy and Carter, navy men, did the same for that service.

II

Planning the Program

Policy initiatives come from many different sources.[14] Proposals to regulate political competition are usually based on work of constitutional lawyers and political scientists, and they are primarily initiated by congressional committees. The White House usually takes a secondary role on such reforms as the limitation of the president to two terms, elimination of the poll tax, the succession amendment, and campaign finance reform. Occasionally a president will take the initiative, as Johnson did with voting rights and Carter did with his major package of electoral college and voter registration bills. Even so, such proposals are most often a preemption of existing ideas.

Distributive programs—including grants, loans, contracts, public works, subsidies—to the private sector or to state and local governments, are usually developed by interest groups, state and local officials, congressional committee leaders, and the departments. The president will either adopt the proposal and make it his own or will, in a period of retrenchment, disapprove of his department's submission. Welfare-state distributions that involve contracts to public-interest groups and intergovernmental grants to state and local governments to provide goods and services to specified clientele groups are often initiated by an administration. In periods of retrenchment the president usually proposes second-stage initiatives.

Redistributive programs involve use of tax and social security funds to finance major income-transfer and maintenance programs. Initiatives often come from the presidency, but interest groups and congressional committees share second-stage initiation when they revise and amend programs in subsequent years.

The initiative for economic regulation and planning usually comes from the private-sector and from "public-interest" lobbies. Departments and presidential advisory agencies work closely with affected interests, and the president ultimately acts as a broker for coalitions of groups. A recent trend in energy planning is for the president to make his own proposals and try to rally public opinion for his program, even if it means taking on major corporate interests.

There is always a grab bag of social issues, including civil rights for various groups, laws involving drugs, consenting sexual behavior, status of illegal aliens, and so on. The president may be forced by public pressure to propose laws on issues he would rather avoid. At times a president will seek to sidestep issues: none in recent years seems to have formulated a position on abortion that has won popular support, and Nixon, Ford, and Carter each have attempted to steer clear of involvement in the controversy between planned parenthood and right-to-life groups.

Whatever the issue, a key factor in determining the extent to which the president gets involved is the *process* by which the issue is brought to his attention. The *transition* process occurs in the first six months after the election, when the president attempts to implement some of the proposals he had made in the campaign. Transition task forces, composed of academics, members of the campaign organization, lobbyists, former officials, and permanent careerists in the bureaus, help shape the first presidential program. Kennedy used twenty-nine such task forces, which submitted twenty-four reports at the beginning of his administration.[15] Carter started using task forces even prior to winning his party nomination, when he set up a "Policy Planning Office" in his campaign in the spring of 1976. By the time of the convention, he had received 135 policy reports, including studies on budget priorities, executive reorganization, and sources of staffing for the new administration. His transition teams included career officials and staff members of congressional committees as well as campaign advisors.

Presidential nominees in the departments or on the White House staff bring ideas with them. Frances Perkins, Franklin Roosevelt's secretary of labor, developed a program of comprehensive labor legislation and then sold it to her boss. Nixon's appointment of Daniel Moynihan as counselor for urban affairs and director of the Urban Affairs Council led to plans to reorganize manpower training and the welfare system. Department secretaries organize their own task forces to obtain new ideas; Carter's secretary of health, education and welfare set up a working group consisting of officials from a variety of agencies to submit new proposals for welfare reform. James Schlesinger, the White House energy advisor, used a task force to develop the plans for a new Department of Energy.

The president's legislative party provides much of his program. Many of the proposals developed in the campaign are borrowed from the congressional committees. Kennedy's transition teams relied heavily on programs that Democrats had tried unsuccessfully to enact in the 1950s, defeated either by presidential vetoes or by the conservative coalition.[16] Republican leaders pressured Nixon and Ford to emphasize second-stage initiatives they had proposed in the 1960s while Democrats were creating the Great Society. Carter's initial economic program was created after consultations with committee leaders. The specific task-force proposals were drafted by Laurence Woodworth, who after thirty years as director of the staff for the Joint Committee on Taxation became Carter's assistant secretary of the treasury for tax policy. Former congressional staff aides or legislators who move to the executive branch always have a major influence on policymaking, since at the beginning of an administration they are often the only people who have any idea of what program innovations can be fashioned into a workable program.

The State of the Union Address

Under Article II, section 3 of the Constitution, the president has the duty from time to time to "give to the Congress information of the State of the Union." In the nineteenth century, presidents followed the custom Washington established and simply listed in their annual message to Congress subjects on which new legislation might be required, without offering an administration position. Some presidents used the annual message to present summaries of departmental business and a roundup, country by country, of American diplomacy in the preceding year. These messages might run for forty or more pages, and they were sent to Congress rather than delivered in person. As a foreign observer, James Bryce, indicated, "the message is a shot in the air without practical results."

Twentieth-century presidents follow the precedent established by Theodore Roosevelt and make the message, known since 1945 as the State of the Union address, into a major statement of foreign and domestic goals. Wilson revived the custom that Jefferson had abandoned of addressing Congress in person, and in his first address requested that Congress pass his banking bill, adding, "I need not say how earnestly I hope for its early enactment into law." He also found it an "urgent necessity" for Congress to pass bills on agricultural credits, railway employers liability, and mine safety.[17] Franklin Roosevelt, in his 1935 message, informed Congress that he would submit detailed proposals on relief, public employment, regulatory agencies, and industrial recovery. Truman presented an entire "Fair Deal" program of civil rights, housing, and medical care. Even Eisenhower, with a limited domestic program, offered specific proposals in the second and third addresses of his first term.[18]

The State of the Union address is an action-forcing process. It is delivered each year at the beginning of the congressional session. The president asks the department to compile lists of potential new programs and legislative requests several months in advance of the address. The speech offers members of the administration the opportunity to convince the president that their proposals are worthy of support. Each address creates a contest among departments, and between department secretaries and officials of the various presidential agencies, to determine whether a proposal will be included in the speech.

Legislative Clearance

The competition for presidential attention and support involves the legislative clearance process. Legislative clearance involves the transmission of all agency and departmental requests for new laws to one or more presidential agencies for examination and recommendations to the president prior to transmittal to Congress. The clearance function is performed primarily by the Office of Management and Budget (OMB).* The function was instituted in 1921 during the Harding administration: the Bureau of the Budget (BOB) helped the president decide if department proposals should become part of a presidential program. Under

---

* Prior to 1970 the OMB was known as the Bureau of the Budget (BOB).

the second director, Herbert Lord, it was routinized in 1924 during the Coolidge administration.[19] The OMB now provides the president with several options:

1. He can identify the proposal as "in accordance with the program of the president" and submit it as a presidential program, modifying it as he sees fit.
2. He may allow the department to claim that its bill is "in accordance with the program of the president," but leave it as a departmental bill.
3. He may allow the department to submit its proposal to Congress without a presidential endorsement, letting officials "go into business" for themselves.
4. He may register his disapproval and prohibit officials from submitting the proposal to Congress or testifying in favor of the measure in congressional hearings.

Legislative clearance is an action-forcing process. Bills must be prepared by bureaus and departments according to timetables that enable clearance to occur in time for presidential budget submissions and the State of the Union address. Clearance enables the president to monitor department requests to ensure that they are not in conflict with his own. It forces interest groups to come to terms with the president should he object to their proposals.

Harding and Coolidge used clearances on bills involving spending authority and appropriations.[20] During the New Deal, Roosevelt established the National Emergency Council, which cleared substantive measures. After the council was phased out, Roosevelt assigned all clearance to the BOB.[21] In 1947 Truman assigned its Legislative Reference Division the responsibility for creating a presidential program taken from the submissions of the departments, a practice that Eisenhower extended.[22] In the 1960s White House staffs and councils assumed some clearance functions, especially for the more important programs that the president might suggest. The BOB was limited to routine clearance of departmental proposals rather than coordinating the submission of the presidential program.[23] The BOB lost influence because it had close ties with agencies it supervised and it suffered from "tunnel vision" and could see solutions to problems only along lines devised by departments. It had difficulty in analyzing programs that cut across jurisdictions or proposed major innovations. As one former official of the bureau noted, "Ideas are limited by the imagination of the old line agencies. They tend to be repetitive—the same proposals year after year."[24] The BOB served the president well only when he wished to be a broker of bureaucratic interests, for as another BOB official stated, "On the less important matters, we rely primarily on the compromises that can be negotiated out among the departments and their respective agencies. . . . In effect, a good proportion of the President's program consists of the compromises that are struck here."[25]

Nonetheless the BOB, by handling routine clearance, could free the White House agencies to work on the most important initiatives. The

BOB also provided continuity during transitions for new administrations, and an "institutional memory" so that the new president could use the experience of his predecessors in evaluating department proposals. The BOB often was the only agency that remembered "how things work" and could facilitate routine operations while the president and his aides learned the ropes. The BOB could combat "departmentalism" by organizing and participating in interdepartmental task forces to create new programs.[26]

In 1970 the Nixon administration abolished the Bureau of the Budget and replaced it with an Office of Management and Budget (OMB). The White House staff and newly created councils in the Executive Office of the President took primary responsibility for planning the president's program, while the OMB retained the responsibility to conduct routine clearance and oversee implementation of legislation. The Legislative Reference Division itself was challenged within OMB by a new political group of Nixon appointees, the Program Associate Directors (PADs), who vied with the division's civil servants for control of the clearance process. The careerists closely identified with the first-stage innovations that had been developed in the New Frontier and Great Society period (some even having worked in Fair Deal and Eisenhower programs); the Nixon appointees emphasized second-stage innovations. A July 1974 circular from Director Roy Ash to the executive branch departments noted, "Marginal and ineffective programs must be identified and eliminated wherever possible. . . . Proposed legislation will be necessary to reduce programs." The OMB no longer played the BOB role of "educating from below," since its career officials were insulated from the top levels of the administration by the new echelon of PADs. The OMB had little influence with senior presidential aides intent on dismantling many Great Society programs. No longer at the center of presidential program planning, the OMB has become a mechanism to reorganize or curtail programs.

The Programming and Advisory System

The president does not create a program simply by culling proposals from lists submitted by the departments. Routine legislative clearance is not sufficient, for as Lyndon Johnson argued, "The bureaucracy of the government is too preoccupied with day-to-day operations, and there is strong bureaucratic inertia dedicated to preserving the status quo."[27] To develop programs that cross departmental lines, that rely on new technological developments, and that involve second-stage innovation, the president must develop his own mechanisms for programming. Political scientist Stephen J. Wayne makes the useful distinction between *external programming*, relying on task forces, commissions, outside advisors, and transitional teams, and *internal programming*, based on White House agencies that oversee several departments in developing new ideas.[28] By the 1970s, the major units of internal presidential programming were in place.

The Council of Economic Advisors (CEA) has sometimes participated in programming. Created by Congress in 1946, it consists of a three-member board appointed by the president and confirmed by the Senate. Its members and staff participate in interdepartmental task forces and played a major role in developing New Frontier and Great Society domestic programs. In the Ford and Carter administrations, CEA members have served or chaired task forces dealing with deregulation of industry, energy policy, and international economic negotiations. The chairman plays a key role in domestic program development. According to Arthur Burns, chairman under Eisenhower:

He represented the Council at weekly Cabinet meetings, made frequent reports on current and emerging policy requirements, and participated actively in Cabinet debates on economic matters. He served as Chairman of various cabinet committees and used the opportunity to advance the Council's program. He worked closely with the Secretary of the Treasury and the Chairman of the Federal Reserve Board. He and his Council colleagues spent a good part of practically every day striving for a consensus on policy issues with representatives of the various departments and agencies. The Council thus fought tirelessly within the Executive establishment for the policies that it deemed necessary and proper.[29]

The president may use the CEA to prepare much of his domestic economic program, or he may rely on other units in the executive branch. Ford created an Economic Policy Board in 1974 to provide a cabinet-level forum in which economic expertise, political factors, and bureaucratic vested interests could clash in the debates among cabinet secretaries, White House advisors, and professional economists. Carter disbanded this organization and replaced it with a less-structured Economic Policy Group, which enabled him to counterbalance the advice of his economists against competing bureaucratic and political interests.

In both the Nixon and Ford administrations, the preparation of most new domestic programs was theoretically the responsibility of the Domestic Council. Created in 1970, the Council consisted of ten department secretaries and the heads of several presidential agencies.[30] It was one of a series of attempts to transcend the perspectives of the departments that presidents had initiated ever since Franklin Roosevelt had created the National Emergency Council. The function of the Domestic Council, as the U.S. Government Organization Manual described it, seemed all-encompassing:

The purpose of the Council is to formulate and coordinate domestic policy recommendations to the President. The Council assesses national needs and coordinates the establishment of national priorities; recommends integrated sets of policy choices; provides a rapid response to presidential needs for policy advice on pressing domestic issues; and maintains a continuous review of on-going programs from a policy standpoint.[31]

To perform these functions the council was equipped with a staff director and six working groups headed by an associate director in charge of a broad functional area (e.g., transportation, energy, agriculture), and it was assigned a small group of staff members.

The council was created after widespread criticism of the performance of presidential agencies in developing the Great Society. Not only had Lyndon Johnson been dissatisfied, but so too had officials who had participated on task forces. As William Carey, a former high-ranking BOB official, wrote in 1969:

In the main, the presidency is in the retail business when it comes to policy formulation; it reacts, responds, modifies, and tinkers with departmental policy and program thrusts, but it does not wholesale public policy in the sense of recasting priorities and evaluating the relationship of accrued commitments to long-term goals.[32]

The council was recommended to Nixon by the Ash Council, a task force that made far-reaching recommendations for the new administration, including the conversion of the BOB into the OMB and its reorientation away from first-stage and towards second-stage policy initiation. The Domestic Council was expected by the administration to aid the president in reorganizing Great Society programs.

But the council hardly ever met. Instead, it served as a vehicle for John Erlichman, its director, to push White House directives that affected departmental policies. For the most part it served as a "traffic cop" to expedite the flow of paperwork; in effect, it was little more than an extension of a cabinet secretariat that Eisenhower had used. Its task forces did not make effective use of outside consultants or the resources of the academic world. Instead, it created working groups involving officials from OMB, the departments, and the council staff. It rode herd or rough-shod over the career officials of the bureaucracy, and in turn the careerists used all the techniques they could to undercut the council staff. Frictions developed between council officials and with cabinet secretaries. As Ehrlichman observed, "Cabinet officers had no chance unless and until it was cleared through us to the President," noting that "they bitched continuously because Nixon wouldn't see them."[33] The council was supposed to present the president with all the options, much like its counterpart National Security Council. But unlike that body, the Domestic Council staff was unable to develop its own policies. Its staffers were often detailed by the White House for immediate problems, of a political nature, rather than for programming. They were used to gain control of the departments and often dealt in day-to-day operational issues.[34] John Ehrlichman used the staff primarily for "crisis management" rather than programming, and he also used the council's budget to fund Watergate activities. (One unit of the council, the "Plumbers," committed several felonies, including the break-in at the Democratic National Committee.) With more political operatives and plumbers than serious policy analysts, the council staff was never able to meet its responsibilities to plan a presidential program. After Ehrlichman's departure its size and influence sharply diminished. Its director, Kenneth Cole, lacked access to Nixon, and his staff therefore lacked any clout in dealing with the departments. OMB attempted to use the legislative clearance process to regain influence for program planning. Its Program Associate Directors developed an intense rivalry with the Associate Directors of the Domestic Council.[35] Instead of the amicable division of labor that the Ash council had anticipated, the reorganization of presidential agencies had resulted in a fierce competition for power.[36]

When Gerald Ford became vice-president, Nixon assigned him responsibility for presiding over council meetings, and Ford also assumed responsibility for coordinating the administration's domestic program. When Ford assumed the presidency, he in turn gave primary authority over the council to his vice-president, Nelson Rockefeller. In spite of opposition from the White House staff, Rockefeller named his key aides as director and deputy director of the council, and he used the resources of his own Commission on Critical Choices (a private organization that had been engaged in long-range planning—and of which Gerald Ford had been a member). The staff was reorganized and ten associate directors were to develop proposals in policy areas. It seemed at the time that the vice-president might institutionalize his role as "prime minister for domestic affairs" through control of the council. For several reasons this development never occurred. Ford did not support key Rockefeller proposals, including an energy development corporation. The White House staff, other presidential agencies, and the departments all undercut the work of the council. The OMB assumed a greater role in legislative clearance. Turnover on the council staff was high and expertise in domestic planning minimal. Most of the work of the Nixon council was dropped. The council had no "institutional memory," since it had no permanent career officials and the new president made a clean sweep of its senior staff. Rockefeller himself was perceived by many Republicans as a political liability, was dropped from consideration as a running mate for the 1976 campaign, and by December 1975 had returned control of the council to the White House staff.

Perhaps the council had become part of the institutionalized presidency about a decade too late. Had it been established in 1961, as proposed by a New Frontier transition team (but rejected by Kennedy), it might have coordinated the work of task forces and departments, and taken on the functions assigned to the Bureau of the Budget and the Council of Economic Advisors. But by the 1970s, with retrenchment the order of the day, it dealt with second-stage initiatives in selected areas, such as drug-abuse prevention, deregulation of industry, nuclear policy, mass transit, revenue sharing, housing, and crime. Long-range planning was de-emphasized. At times its studies could be cited as an excuse to hold up costly first-stage initiatives from the departments, especially in health care, housing, mass transit, and income maintenance. By referring such proposals to the Domestic Council, the administration could effectively study them to death. By 1976 the Domestic Council had been reduced to compiling proposals submitted by the departments for Ford's state of the Union address. It had ceased to do any serious program planning.[37]

Recognizing that the Domestic Council was in limbo, the Carter administration abolished it and established instead a large Domestic Policy Staff in the White House itself, headed by an assistant for domestic affairs and policy and staffed by eleven associate directors for specific policy areas. The purpose of this reorganization was to oversee the establishment of interagency teams and task forces that would be chaired by cabinet officers, and to provide a mechanism to communicate White House concerns to these groups. The staff did little program planning itself, but served primarily as a coordinating mechanism and clearinghouse so that all affected interests would have an opportunity to participate. In essence the system provided for an ad hoc, free-floating staff that was directed by senior White House aides in order to provide a counterweight to the department perspective. Unlike the Domestic Council, the aims of the staff were modest, and thus its record of accomplishment would likely be better.

Other policy councils have fared poorly in recent administrations. Some, such as the Council on Marine Resources, were foisted on the presidency by interest groups in order to protect their industry, and were discarded as soon as the president could have them moved into a department. In the Kennedy administration the Office of Science and Technology and the President's Science Advisory Committee were created. Nixon eliminated both units after they publicly opposed his plans for an American-built supersonic plane and an antiballistic missile system.[38] In the Carter administration a new scientific office was established, but the pendulum swung away from use of councils, as the president abolished the Domestic Council, the Council on International Economic Policy, the Office of Telecommunications Policy, the Federal Council, the Economic Policy Board, the Office of Drug Abuse Policy, the Energy Resources Council, and the Economic Opportunity Council.

The influence of councils and offices located in the White House has been limited, for the president has little time to consider their proposals and may wall himself off from officials who run them. He may become impatient with long-range planning and irritated at lack of consideration for his political problems. He may prefer to postpone consideration of issues that they believe important, especially if initiatives will be costly. As William Carey remarks,

I do know that very little of the advice emanating from most advisory bodies ever seeps through to the President himself. Most of it is lost through evaporation, some of it leaks out on staff advisors to the President, and no one can say with certainty how much of it feeds into policy decisions.[39]

The White House Office, which consists of the personal staff of the presidency, is a crucial link between president and sources of program initiatives. The president may encourage his aides to create "back channels" to him, bypassing routine clearance and budget processes and the work of his councils, in order to obtain access to innovative ideas at the formative stages. Alternatively, he may prefer to be shielded by his staff, and like Eisenhower and Nixon and Ford, work only with items brought to him through council mechanisms.

Although the memoirs of aides such as Robert Sherwood, Arthur Schlesinger, Jr., Theodore Sorensen, and William Safire maximize the influence of the White House staff on program initiation, their assessments are not representative of the quality of staff work.[40] Most aides are not involved in program initiation, and of those who dabble in it, most are literary historians, lawyers, journalists, public relations flacks, who are ignorant of technical, scientific, administrative, economic, or legal issues involved. Many work in the White House after campaign stints, and know more about media manipulation than about the workings of government. They emphasize short-range political considerations rather than long-range planning. Economists, systems and operations analysts, engineers and natural scientists, social scientists, and policy analysts— these people are rarely seen in White House precincts. Only 1 percent of White House aides employed by presidents from Truman to Nixon were scientists or engineers. Only 15 percent had received doctorates in any subject. About 15 percent came from business, 16 percent from law, 13 percent from journalism and public relations, and 11 percent from education. Expertise in the workings of government was supplied by the 29 percent recruited from nonelected governmental positions.[41] Friction occurs between council and departmental specialists on the one hand, and White House "generalists" on the other, because neither understands the other's language, values, or outlook. At best there is an uneasy truce, but it often masks mutual contempt. At worst, departmental officials try to sabotage White House initiatives and undercut White House aides.

The most constructive role the White House generalists can play is to bring diverse sources of information to the attention of the president and to brief him on the bureaucratic and political factors involved. White House assistant Joseph Califano set up forty-five task forces for President Johnson, and seventeen were organized for Nixon by Arthur Burns and Charles Clapp. Ford met with the heads of several study groups, and with intellectuals and academics at small informal dinners.

Some staff members may be brought into the White House to act as policy advocates. Nixon appointed two men with contrasting views on domestic policy, Daniel Moynihan and Arthur Burns, as his "counselors." No one expected these advisors to be neutral generalists: instead each used his command of the subject matter of various policies to propose specific new programs, providing the president with the opportunity to contrast arguments and weigh different proposals.

Presidents make use of several ad hoc organizations to develop new programs. National commissions are created either by law or by executive order to investigate specific problems and report to the president (and sometimes to Congress).[42] Presidents find their utility limited for several reasons. Although the president appoints some or all of the commission members, its staff is likely to consist of "activists" who will educate members to the dimensions of the problem under study. Commission members, often shocked by what they learn, often become "radicalized" and propose dramatic and costly solutions to solve the problems. If a president attempts to use a commission to buy time, to sweep a problem under the rug, or to propose incremental second-stage innovation rather than sweeping change, members of the staff may leak information to the media, charge the White House with attempting to influence commission findings, and mount a press campaign to discredit the administration.

Presidents prefer that commission recommendations follow the general outlines of policies they intend to pursue.[43] Most commissions are political liabilities, since they make recommendations that the president opposes or ignores. The Kerner commission (civil disorders) blamed "white racism" for riots in urban areas in the 1960s, a finding Lyndon Johnson disavowed. The Scranton commission (campus disorders) found many protests by students legitimate, causing Nixon to attempt to discredit the chairman and the report. The Commission on Marijuana and Drug Abuse held that penalties for possession of the substance were out of proportion with the problem, a finding rejected by Nixon. Presidents did not act on the central recommendations of the reports of these commissions, and in several cases they publicly took issue with commission reasoning and findings.

Outside "think tanks"—such as the Brookings Institution, the Rand Corporation, and the American Enterprise Institute—and individual academic consultants may investigate specific problems and make recommendations to presidential agencies. In 1975 the American Enterprise Institute employed former Defense Secretary Melvin Laird to chair its National Energy Project, former White House aide Bryce Harlow to chair its Program Priorities Committee, and former Council of Economic Advisors Charman Paul McCracken to chair its academic advisory board. Panels consulted with Ford administration officials on fiscal, monetary, and energy policies, and were behind the initiative to deregulate industry. The Brookings Institution has long played a similar role for both Democratic and Republican administrations. Two of its senior staff, Charles

Schultze and Harold Stein, held positions as chairmen of the Council of Economic Advisors. The institution's books generally made specific policy recommendations, often picked up by an administration, sometimes by former Brookings staff members who work in the departments or White House.

Departments also organize task forces, and they may participate in interdepartmental task forces. These are often chaired by White House aides or officials from presidential agencies, especially the CEA and the Domestic Policy Staff. The White House plays a role in working out the compromises between departments that lead to legislative proposals, and the president may become personally involved in major decisions. The president may also appoint a "czar"—one official with responsibility to develop a new program. Carter gave James Schlesinger the authority to develop the administration's energy program. Schlesinger then recruited aides, some of whom had worked for him previously when he had headed the Atomic Energy Commission, the Central Intelligence Agency, and the Defense Department. Schlesinger created a task force with these former aides and added a sprinkling of officials from OMB and several academics. This group acted outside the department structure, and none of the officials represented the "position" of an agency (so in that sense it was quite atypical of most interdepartmental groups). The task force became the nucleus for the new Department of Energy. Another example of the "Czar" system involves the "vice-presidential" task forces headed by Walter Mondale, which prepare various proposals for the administration. He too finds participants from various government agencies, and he uses their talents and expertise to prepare comprehensive proposals.

The advantage of task forces over other mechanisms is that they can be formed on an ad hoc basis to deal with specific issues (unlike policy councils and offices) and they can operate with a minimum of publicity (unlike national commissions). If they are run on the "czar" system rather than as interdepartmental groups, they can use comprehensive methods of policy analysis rather than negotiate around bureaucratic interests. The problem with using task forces is that they may "freeze out" departments, give the president a single point of view, and restrict his range of choice.

An unofficial advisory system also serves the president. Some first ladies, such as Eleanor Roosevelt, are a major source of innovation. Betty Ford and Rosalyn Carter seem to have influenced their husband's thinking on issues involving women's rights, including the Equal Rights Amendment, federal hiring practices, and enforcement of existing antidiscrimination laws.

Presidents also rely for advice on "in-and-outers," private citizens who have served several presidents at the highest levels and who are called on for their counsel even when they are out of government. Louis Brandeis played a major role in developing the New Freedom program of Woodrow

Wilson. In the New Deal the "Brains Trust" of Columbia University professors Raymond Moley, Rexford Tugwell, Adolph Berle, and Schuyler Wallace performed a similar function for Franklin Roosevelt. Harvard professor Felix Frankfurter sent Roosevelt various "bright young men" to staff New Deal agencies. Eisenhower consulted with Bernard Baruch, financier and self-proclaimed "advisor to presidents." Like Lyndon Johnson, they may ask for advice from sitting members of the Supreme Court, in spite of the "rule" that the justices remain out of political arenas.

In most administrations the vice-president plays a limited role in proposing new programs. He almost never chairs cabinet-level committees, task forces, or councils (the significant exception being Nelson Rockefeller's working control over the Domestic Council for one year). Most vice-presidents are assigned the liaison function with governors and mayors, and administer an Office of Intergovernmental Relations and one or two other minor committees. Perhaps the definitive statement on the role of a vice-president in policy initiation was given by Eisenhower during a news conference:

Q. We understand that the power of decision is entirely yours, Mr. President. I just wondered if you could give us an example of a major idea of his [Nixon] that you had adopted. . . .
A. If you give me a week, I might think of one. I don't remember. [44]

Vice-President Walter Mondale seems to be the exception to the general rule that vice-presidents are an insignificant part of an administration. Instead of being given narrow assignments, Carter named him a senior advisor, with concurrent authority over the entire White House staff. He became a principal advisor on domestic policy issues, including legislative strategy and party affairs. As Carter described Mondale's responsibilities at a press conference,

I see Fritz four to five hours a day. There is not a single aspect of my own responsibilities in which Fritz is not intimately associated. He is the only person that I have with both the substantive knowledge and political stature to whom I can turn over a major assignment. [45]

The President as Program Innovator

No shortage of ideas and program proposals exists. The president need not think things up all by himself. But he must know enough to reach out and use the clearance and advisory systems effectively. He must remain flexible and open without becoming overloaded. The present advisory system is useful if the president wishes to make it so. He can reach out in any direction for new ideas, draw on competing sources for expertise, match his departments against councils and advisors, and weigh competing values in making decisions. Neither party orthodoxy nor constraints of legislative party leaders can prevent him from developing his program as he wishes.

But the institutionalized presidency shares the problems that plague all planners of social and economic programs at every level of government. The president finds it difficult to forecast trends accurately, or to gather valid information that describes existing conditions. Social and economic models of human behavior are weak, both descriptively and predictively. The president cannot be sure that his advisors are correct in their assessments of conditions. Most councils and other advisory units lack an "institutional memory," which would enable the president to learn from the mistakes of his predecessors. Each administration seems to "reinvent the wheel" rather than pick up where its predecessor left off. Officials must be "educated from below" by careerists, who are often the only source of expertise on the mechanics of government. Their approach is likely to be incremental rather than comprehensive and short-range rather than long-range. Like everyone else, presidents find it difficult to distinguish effective innovations from patent medicines. Daniel Moynihan argued that Nixon coped with this problem well; lacking confidence in his social science advisors, he proposed the Family Assistance Plan precisely because it was necessary to begin experimenting. Other presidents may be just as skeptical, yet decide to hold back on innovations.

Proposals to strengthen the presidential advisory system move in two opposite directions: towards strengthening descriptive, forecasting, and planning capabilities; or towards decentralizing these functions and reducing the president's role as policymaker. Proposals to strengthen the advisory system include the following:

1. A Council on Social Policy, similar to the Council of Economic Advisors, which would prepare an annual social report for the president and Congress, and would propose new programs and evaluate existing ones
2. A Policy Planning Board, to replace the Domestic Policy Staff, equipped with a large secretariat to operate legislative clearance, forecasting, and planning a presidential program
3. A Policy Coordination Office, which would operate legislative clearance and preparation of the presidential program, and which would be staffed by policy analysts, economists, and social and natural scientists able to monitor adequacy of existing programs

The names of these agencies differ, but each would be located in the Executive Office, serve as a presidential agency, and perform essentially the same functions. Proposals to decentralize and diffuse power to innovate throughout the government include the following:

1. Strengthening the collective cabinet by providing a secretariat for clearance, and enlarging the policy planning staffs in each department
2. Relying on parties to develop policy by making the platforms serious statements, providing for yearly conventions that would revise and update the platforms, and developing central policy organs in Congress that would work with the president to implement his party's proposals

3. Decentralizing policymaking in the federal system, by strengthening regional administration, establishing regional planning agencies, expanding revenue-sharing and bloc-grants to enable states to develop their own programs, and providing new incentives for experimentation and innovation (especially second-stage) through the intergovernmental grant system

Those who propose these arrangements argue that no president is likely to devote sufficient time and energy on domestic innovation to make his participation worthwhile. Instead of attempting to centralize authority in the institutionalized presidency, the president would be better off recognizing that his major priorities are in national security and international economic matters, and in delegating responsibility for programming out to departments at the national level and decentralizing programming throughout the intergovernmental system.

III

Congress as Innovator

The president often appears to be the initiator of policies because media attention is focused on the White House and the work of one president is more dramatic and understandable than the work of 535 legislators operating the most complex representative body in the world. The president acts decisively and expertly in presenting his program, while the legislature that considers them often appears divided, indecisive, parochial, partisan, and dilatory. James Sundquist, in assessing the New Frontier and Great Society innovations, provides the standard portrait of the two institutions when he argues,

With the exception of anti-pollution measures, the major legislative impulses of the 1961–66 period came from a single source—the White House. Members of Congress could retard, accelerate, or deflect those impulses, and they could expand, limit, or modify the specific proposals initiated from the White House. But they could not set in motion the legislative stream itself.[46]

Because the president delivers a highly visible state of the Union address at the beginning of the congressional session, and Congress then responds to this speech and subsequent messages, one might assume that Congress plays no role in programming prior to these messages. When the executive is unsure of itself or modifies its proposals, it does so behind closed doors, in task forces and study groups, with little publicity; by the time the proposals are presented, the vast public relations apparatus of the executive branch is geared to create the impression that the proposals are solely the product of the vast expertise of executive branch officials. In contrast, when Congress fails to act, modifies and amends, and subjects bills to all the politics of the legislative process, it provides some evidence for the proposition that expertise is being diluted with "politics," that the national interest is being compromised, or that the legislature lacks the expertise to make sound judgments on complex technical and scientific issues. Even some members of Congress contribute to the stereotype of a "sapless branch," for as former senator Joseph Clark argued, "The Framers of our Constitution vested legislative powers in the Congress, but we have tended through the years to largely abdicate that responsibility and to confine ourselves merely to Executive recommendations."[47]

Some political scientists have argued that the president should have the major responsibility for program planning, and that Congress should confine itself to passing or defeating his proposals. This is no less than a reversal of constitutional roles, with the president acting as legislator and Congress exercising a "veto" power.[48] Congress could then increase its role in oversight of implementation of laws; some think it is better suited for this role than for innovation. What the proposed role reversal overlooks, however, is that in order to play a strong oversight role Congress must be able to pass laws of its own devising. The only reason that legislators can obtain information from officials and exercise oversight functions is that Congress controls statutory authority, funding authority, and appropriations for departments.

Congress will not abdicate its legislative powers, because it plays a dominant role in framing the bulk of the laws. The Constitution anticipates that Congress will play the major role in domestic policymaking. Under certain conditions it does, especially when—

1. the president is uninterested in the problem or preoccupied with crises;
2. interest groups have proposed new innovations and built coalitions of supporters in committees;
3. Democrats control both chambers of Congress and are interested in passing their own versions of bills when Republicans control the White House;
4. the president's veto threat is calculated as a bluff, since the innovation is part of a bill he wishes to sign.[49]

Committees and Innovation

The committee system, free of party or presidential domination, allows members to specialize in specific policy areas. Legislators who remain on a committee for a decade or more will develop expertise and an interest in affecting program development. Committee staffs now include "policy entrepreneurs" who are interested in innovation, evaluation, and legislative oversight.[50] Proposals are fed to legislators by informal networks linking staff aides, department officials, and interest-group lobbyists.[51] Some committees have gained a reputation for being major sources within the government for policy innovation, including the Joint Committee on

Internal Revenue and Taxation, the House Ways and Means and Senate Finance Committees, the Joint Committee on Atomic Energy (now abolished), and the House and Senate Budget Committees.[52]

Committees can tap experts by making them consultants and commissioning reports from them, or by obtaining their testimony at hearings. Members of departments may be detailed to serve on committee staffs to provide technical knowledge, a common situation for the Atomic Energy Commission and the Joint Committee on Atomic Energy in the 1950s. The Legislative Reorganization Act of 1970 provided that committees could contract for technical reports, and among groups now supplying such reports to committees are the National Academy of Sciences (through its Committee on Science and Public Policy), the National Academy of Engineering (through its Committee on Public Engineering Policy), the National Research Council, the Institute of Medicine, and the National Academy of Public Administration. The House Public Works Committee set up a science advisory panel. The Banking and Currency Committees use computer models of the economy to evaluate proposals involving the housing industry. The House and Senate Budget Committees developed fiscal models to test alternative policies prior to making budget ceiling resolutions. The Joint Committee on Internal Revenue Taxation uses computer "runs" provided by the Commerce Department, and also works with macroeconomic models developed by such private groups as Chase Econometrics, in order to calculate the economic impact of various tax reform proposals. Committees also rely on the same outside experts as the executive branch, such as the Brookings Institution, the American Enterprise Institute, and the Academy of Contemporary Problems (to name three of the many groups). Many national commissions report to Congress as well as to the executive branch. Their members often include legislators, who are likely to draw on their experience later in drafting proposals. In 1977 the Institute for Congress was created as a private "think tank" to provide policy analysis on selected issues.

The pooled resources of Congress have also been strengthened in recent years. The Congressional Research Service (until 1970 called the Legislative Reference Service) has expanded its staff to almost six hundred professionals and has developed its own computer models for economic issues. It created a Science Policy Research Division for technical and scientific issues. It holds seminars on various issues for members of Congress, and its personnel may be detailed to work with committees. It identifies issues for congressional committees to consider when requested. The Technology Assessment Act of 1972 established the Office of Technology Assessment (OTA), a congressional agency with more than ninety professional staff members. OTA works with committees on such subjects as continental-shelf development, oceanic exploration, solar energy, urban mass transit, and food assistance for developing nations. It contracts for scientific advice and uses panels of experts. A bipartisan Technology Assessment Board sets policy for the OTA, and an advisory council of scientists assists in setting its priorities. To implement the Intergovernmental Cooperation Act of 1968, which requires an assessment of grant programs every four years, the General Accounting Office (GAO), a congressional agency with over 3,600 professionals, created an Office of Program Review and Evaluation. The GAO now monitors the revenue-sharing, bloc grant, and intergovernmental grant programs, making recommendations for second-stage initiatives. As its 1971 annual report advertised:

The GAO professional staff is well acquainted with the programs and activities of most government agencies through on-site review and observation of agency operations. Consequently, the Office can provide the committee with independent advice and information on proposed legislation; often there may be no other available source for such well-informed comment.[53]

The Congressional Budget Office (CBO) established in 1974, is a counterpart of the OMB, and provides expertise and offers fiscal policy alternatives to the House and Senate Budget Committees. Two of its divisions, Natural Resources and Commerce, and Human Resources and Community Development, provide legislators with a stream of special reports focusing on specific policy-areas with recommendations for second-stage initiatives presented in the form of "options."[54]

Congressional Innovation Assessed

Congress often takes the lead in innovating through committee activities. Hearings are held, bills are marked up, interest groups are consulted, and the process has been described as an "incubation period."[55] Senator Carter Glass proposed a board to manage the currency prior to Wilson's introduction of such a measure. Senator George Norris promoted the Tennessee Valley Authority prior to its adoption by Franklin Roosevelt. The House had been considering revenue-sharing long before the Nixon administration discovered its merits. If a president acts as curtailer in chief and concentrates on second-stage initiation, the committees, with their "institutional memories," serve as convenient warehouses in which major program proposals can be stored until times favor new proposals. The Fair Deal programs that Truman proposed and a Republican Congress rejected lay dormant in the 1950s, but Democratic committees kept many of them under consideration until Kennedy and Johnson picked them up again in the 1960s.

Congress plays the major role in second-stage initiatives, even with programs originally promoted by the president, such as civil rights, voting rights, antipoverty, and urban legislation. The Voting Rights Act of 1965, for example, was significantly stronger than the version proposed by the administration, and subsequent five-year extensions of the act have also improved it.[56] Similarly, executive introduction of anti-poverty legislation in 1964 was followed by major revisions in 1966 and 1968 based on congressional evaluations of program effectiveness and the desire to increase services.[57]

In some areas of domestic policymaking Congress plays the major role in initiation. This is evident most clearly in the distributive programs: public works, area development, urban renewal, public housing, small business loans, disaster relief assistance, and educational loan programs. Congress takes the initiative in consumer legislation, including fair packaging, auto safety, and nuclear power safety. It has dominated the resolution of labor-management struggles over minimum wages, hours and safety, pensions, and open and closed shops. Collective bargaining is regulated by the National Labor Relations Board, itself an initiative of Senator Robert Wagner in the 1930s. The Taft-Hartley and Landrum-Griffin labor laws were developed by congressional committees rather than presidential agencies. Although presidents are usually initiators of major social welfare legislation, Congress can play an important role: in the New Deal it was primarily responsible for social security, in the Fair Deal for public housing, and in the Great Society for expansion of poverty programs. In the 1970s the conversion of the food-stamp program into a major income-maintenance program was due to congressional initiative. Congress has promoted new maritime technology, aid to airports, civilian uses of atomic energy, a nuclear shipbuilding program, the communications satellite, and air and water pollution legislation. It played a major role in developing the Amtrak and Conrail systems for the railroads. It pioneered developments in coastal zone planning and land use, and fought the Ford administration to a standoff on energy policy.[58]

Congress will continue to play a major role in domestic policy initiation whether the president acts as curtailer in chief and focuses on second-stage initiation or presents a full package of major new initiatives. The kinds of innovations that will be adopted in the next decade are those with which Congress has traditionally played a major role: regulatory actions involving the environment and civil rights, and promotion of industrial sectors, especially energy development. Congress will be able to play a major role because it has increased its committee and pooled resources, insulated itself from presidential domination of the legislative party, and equipped itself to deal with technical subjects. But like the presidency, Congress finds it difficult to develop *effective* domestic programs. The fragmentation of the committee structure parallels the "tunnel vision" of the departments: in both cases there is an inability to take a broad perspective and deal with interrelated subjects that cross committee jurisdictions. Few mechanisms similar to presidential councils offer committee leaders the opportunity to broaden their perspective and consider issues comprehensively. Congress has a tendency to promote particular programs and projects favored by coalitions of interest groups.

Legislators promote pet projects and emphasize distributions involved in new programs.

Harnessing both the executive and legislative branches to a common purpose, and improving policy analysis and innovation in both branches, cannot be achieved by simply instituting party government or centralizing presidential control over the legislative party. Processes that require the president to submit reports or draft bills, and then require a congressional response, are perhaps the best way to encourage both branches to innovate intelligently and expeditiously. Such mechanisms of collaboration encourage Congress to develop its expertise and rely effectively on pooled resources and outside experts.

Systems of collaboration now work with the budgetary process, fiscal policy, environmental legislation, tax legislation, and reorganization proposals. Mechanisms that require collaboration, yet permit each branch to innovate and initiate proposals autonomously, seem far more in tune with established constitutional principles of separation of powers and checks and balances than do proposals that invite the legislature to subordinate itself to the president, give up its constitutional responsibilities, and become a handmaiden of the executive branch.

6

Legislative Leadership

PRESIDENTS must lead Congress. They need Senate consent to
their nominations and treaties, and congressional assent to their legislative proposals, reorganization plans, and certain administrative actions.
They want Congress to appropriate the funds they recommend in their
executive budgets. But presidents rarely succeed as legislative leaders.
Lyndon Johnson could talk of "my Congress" after winning passage of
much Great Society legislation, but most presidents echo Theodore
Roosevelt, who pleaded, "Oh, if I could be President and Congress too
for just ten minutes," and his cousin Franklin, who remarked "I suppose,
if the truth were told, he is not the only President that has had that
idea."[1]

The Constitution permits the president to propose measures to Congress that he thinks expedient, address or otherwise communicate to it
on the state of the Union, call it into special session or adjourn it if the
two chambers fail to agree on a date, and use the suspensory or pocket
veto. Congress is assigned seventeen enumerated powers, the "necessary
and proper" power, and the right to override the suspensory veto. It
uses its constitutional authority to teach one president after another that
it is a coordinate rather than subordinate branch of government.

Each president asks for a marriage with Congress, but after an initial
honeymoon period each winds up filing for divorce. "It is much easier in
many ways for me," John Kennedy admitted, "when Congress is not in
town."[2] Much of Eisenhower's Modern Republicanism, Kennedy's New
Frontier, and Nixon's New American Revolution wound up the casualty
of the war between the branches. Lyndon Johnson had his tax program

delayed, reorganization plans stalled, and nomination for chief justice defeated by a legislature he supposedly dominated. After just two months of Carter's presidency, the majority leader of the Senate, Robert Byrd, told a news conference, "I wrote to the President that there's a great sense of frustration, the feeling on the part of members that they had not been consulted, brought into decisions before they were made."[3] By the fall the Senate had gutted the energy program, withdrawn the tax rebate bill, and stalled a package of political reforms. In an end-of-year television interview with several network correspondents, Carter admitted that as a novice in the ways of Washington he had a lot to learn about Congress, but that legislative leaders had taught him several hard lessons about consultation and compromise.

Congress insists on being treated as a partner. Party and committee leaders balk at prerogative government and react when presidents ride roughshod, take them for granted, or refuse to bargain with them. The opposition speaks of cooperation in the national interest but awaits any situation ripe for a partisan ambush. Always there are the complicated parliamentary procedures which a new administration must master in order to move its proposals along.

But Congress will accept strong presidential leadership because it simply is not very good at developing or passing comprehensive programs when left to its own devices. The so-called veto-proof Democratic Congress elected in 1974 fought President Ford to a standstill, but could not pass a coherent energy package, failed to reform the banking system, and did not pass proposals for structural economic reform. The president is best situated to propose comprehensive programs, articulate a conception of the national interest, and educate the public to the dimensions of national problems. A president who is weak as a leader does not, by his failure to lead Congress, create conditions for legislative policymaking: there is no "see-saw" effect. When the president cannot lead Congress the result is scattered innovation, incremental rather than comprehensive programming, or deadlock between the branches. Crisis then forces the president to assert prerogative powers, with all the resulting problems this may cause him. However hard it may seem, the president must make the effort to lead Congress, even though what Lord Chesterton once said of "sexual congress" applies equally well to his job: "the pleasure is temporary, the position is ludicrous, and the expense is damnable."

I

The Presidential Program

When a president sends a bill to Congress he usually asks for broad authority for his executives, for responsibility expressed in terms of goals rather than specific methods, and for any delegation of legislative power to be given to the president, who then subdelegates to subordinate officials, ensuring a "chain of command" from the White House to the departments.[4] Officials are to be given power to "legislate" the details of the law by issuing regulations. Bills generally provide for indefinite or long-term authorizations. In crises Congress often passes laws with these broad provisions, and even in normal times some bills may delegate authority in this way, as examination of some of the Great Society laws indicates. But most of the time Congress will modify presidential proposals. It will provide only narrow statutory authority for officials, include detailed descriptions of authorized activities, and include specific limitations and prohibitions on agency activities. Congress often rewrites and revises the statutory bases of agencies, placing administrative procedures and standards into the law, as well as agency regulations and directives as Congress itself interprets them. It delegates authority directly to sub-cabinet officials, some at the career level, limiting presidential authority to set policy for the agency. It may require detailed reporting to committees or the full chamber prior to action by officials, and certain administrative actions may even require committee or chamber approval from one or both houses of Congress prior to implementation. Often agencies are authorized to act for only one or two years. Authority may be delegated to agencies not controlled by the president, such as public corporations, regulatory commissions and boards, or autonomous units within departments that function as quasi-judicial commissions.

Presidents do not control distributive or "pork-barrel" measures. Congress usually rewrites various formulae governing grant distributions, because cleavages form on regional (e.g., sunbelt versus snowbelt) or county (e.g., urban versus rural) lines. Presidents do better in shepherding welfare legislation through the legislature. Their proposals involving fiscal policy, including appropriations and tax measures, are usually reworked substantially by Congress, and their priorities are often given short shrift (see chapters 8 and 9). Defense and national security bills provide a mixed picture: presidents have least influence in the distributions (e.g., military bases, procurement contracts); they are often defeated in amounts they request for foreign aid; and they must compromise when they attempt to reorganize the defense establishment. But they do obtain congressional resolutions backing them in crises, such as the

Formosa, Middle East, Berlin, Cuban, and Gulf of Tonkin resolutions. They have won in the past authorizations and appropriations to conduct undeclared wars in Korea and Indochina (see chapter 11). More recently Congress has placed restrictions on the conduct of presidential war-making, created a veto over arms sales and nuclear reactor sales abroad, prevented aid to an American-backed faction in the civil war in Angola, and placed some restrictions on Pentagon contracting and budgeting. No longer can a president count automatically on congressional backing for his diplomatic or military initiatives.

Presidents seem to have good records as legislative leaders, if one simply looks at the percentage of measures they support that Congress eventually passes—a figure that ranges from 50 percent to 90 percent. But the president often simply goes on record in support of department or legislative initiatives about which he cares little. Congress passes a far smaller proportion of the president's own program—generally between 25 percent and 35 percent when a Republican president faces a Democratic Congress, and between 40 percent to 60 percent when a Democratic president enjoys partisan majorities in both houses. Yet in only four years between 1961 and 1977 have over half the presidential programs been passed into law. Some measures that are passed actually represent defeats for the president: titles of his bills may remain after their content has been changed, with revisions designed to weaken his influence over policymaking. At times the program a president submits will have already been modified in anticipation of the reactions of Congress, so even if it is passed intact, it may still incorporate a "congressional" rather than a "presidential" position. Or a president may support or even introduce a bill that he does not care about, as part of an arrangement with a member of Congress whose cooperation on another issue he needs. It isn't often that a president wins passage of a bill he really wants in exactly the form he wants it.

II

Party Leaders

No president controls his legislative party. Its leaders, the Speaker of the House, the House leader and whips, and the Senate leader and whips, are not his lieutenants, for he neither chooses them nor do they serve at his pleasure. The legislative party chooses its leaders, and the president does not intervene because such intervention would violate the separation of powers and alienate the loser and his faction, and because most contests are already sewn up by a favorite.[5] The Speaker of the House is usually elected after more than twenty years' service in Congress, through an established succession from whip to leader to Speaker.[6] "When I'm talking about my party," Speaker "Tip" O'Neill observed, "I'm talking about the House," for it is to the legislative party that loyalties of the leaders run. In the Senate, party leaders may be elected as early as their first term, but they are also loyal to the chamber; in the words of Majority Leader Robert Byrd, "the role of the Senate is not to be a rubber stamp for any president."[7]

But sometimes a president may dominate the legislative party, and for brief periods the leaders subordinate themselves to White House domination. Usually friction between leaders and the president ends the brief foray into party government. Jefferson founded his party and personally led it: Speaker of the House Nathaniel Macon and chairman of the Ways and Means Committee John Randolph were his personal selections. Committees were packed with administration supporters, and Jefferson presided over a party caucus to set policy. Even so, the president could not maintain control of the party, which split along regional lines on several domestic issues and failed to back his foreign policy by repealing the neutrality laws. In 1806 Randolph split with him over an administration proposal for a secret fund to bribe the Spanish and French courts in order to acquire Florida, and Jefferson had trouble with a succession of other congressional leaders.

Woodrow Wilson, considered a strong party leader, fared even worse with the congressional leaders. At the beginning of his presidency, 114 freshmen Democrats looked to him for leadership, and Speaker Champ Clark and Ways and Means Chairman Oscar Underwood hoped to work closely with the president. Most of the committee chairmen came from the progressive wing of the party as a result of assignments Democrats had made when they won control of the House in 1911. Wilson might have been able to use the House caucus much as Jefferson had done, since in 1909 the Democrats adopted a rule that provided that members must back any position that won a two-thirds vote in the caucus. In the Senate Wilson's choice for majority leader, John Kern, replaced Thomas Martin, and the new leader appointed a Steering Committee dominated by progressives, which in turn reorganized committee assignments to give Wilson's allies key positions.[8] Given these initial circumstances, Wilson functioned for some time as an effective leader, with successes on the tariff, the Federal Reserve System, the Federal Trade Commission, a Department of Labor, workmen's compensation, and an income tax. But Senate Majority Leader Claude Kitchin opposed Wilson's foreign policies, and even voted against the declaration of war. On several major bills Wilson used Democrats on the Rules Committee to undercut Speaker Clark and his majority leader.[9] Wilson made a routine practice of using committee leaders to manage legislation, which weakened the position of party leaders and the usefulness of the caucus. Although he had begun his presidency as an advocate of party government, Wilson could not work well with his leaders, and actually promoted the centrifugal tendencies in Congress.

The Speaker of the House

Presidents want to work closely with the Speaker, especially if they are of the same party. But presidents also know that the Speaker is a potential rival to dominate policymaking. That this danger is not hypothetical is illustrated by the strong Speaker system that developed between 1880 and 1910. Rules changes gave the Speaker power to appoint members to committees, to appoint and chair the Rules Committee (giving him control of the legislative calendar and procedures for debate), to appoint committee chairmen, and to preside over his party caucus. The majority leader chaired the Appropriations Committee and the majority whip the Judiciary Committee, and the patronage they could bestow was used to ensure that the Speaker would dominate the party caucus. In the 1890s adherence to caucus decisions became an expected norm, and party discipline on roll call votes increased.

Some journalists and political scientists, observing these developments, predicted that the Speaker would soon become a "prime minister" running the government under a figurehead president. The Speaker and his committee chairmen would form a "ministry" that, through laws and appropriations, would direct the departments. The figurehead president would invite the Speaker and his "ministry" to sit with department secretaries in a "supercabinet" arrangement, with the Speaker presiding. Policy would be set by Congress and routine administration left to the secretaries. The president would remain ceremonial head of state, but the real contest for power would center around control of the House, for the party with the majority would elect the Speaker. Voters, in choosing members of Congress, would in effect be indicating their choice for a Speaker who would run the government through the "supercabinet."

For several reasons such a system never evolved. The majority party in the House sometimes dealt with a president from the opposition, and it would have been absurd to expect Cleveland or McKinley or Taft to invite a Speaker from the other party to control their administrations. The Senate also experienced centralization of power. In the 1890s the Republican Senate caucus permitted the majority leader to set the legislative agenda and make committee assignments. Party voting increased, and the Republican majority was dominated by men representing the great financial empires of the nation (William Allison, Nelson Aldrich, Mark Hannah, James McMillan, and Orville Platt), and these men were not about to relinquish the great constitutional prerogatives of their chamber in appointments and foreign affairs to a "superministry" dominated by the Speaker of the House. The president could play off the Senate against the House on issues involving taxes, tariffs, currency, and foreign policy. The House itself chafed under the Speaker's rule and eventually ended the system. In 1910 a coalition of Democrats and insurgent Republicans stripped Speaker Joe Cannon of the power to appoint and chair the Rules Committee, set calendars, and control floor debate. In 1911, when Democrats took control of the House, they took from the Speaker the power to appoint committee chairs, and soon both parties established special "committees on committees" to make these assignments. The majority leader lost the chairmanship of Ways and Means in 1921, and henceforth party and committee positions were left separated. No Speaker in modern times can accumulate enough power in the chamber to become a "prime minister," and no president is so weak that he would permit such a development.

Although power remains decentralized in Congress, some strengthening of party leadership occurred in the 1970s. The Democratic caucus began to hold a meeting every month, provided fifty members requested it, and in 1972 the caucus ordered Democrats on the House Foreign Affairs Committee to legislate an end of American combat in Indochina, in an attempt to force a confrontation with the Nixon administration. In 1973 the caucus debated Watergate, war powers, and budget bills; in 1974 it developed positions on energy and tax legislation; and in 1975 it voted to end assistance to South Vietnam. The caucus also gained some authority over the selection of committee chairmen. In 1973 it provided for secret voting for election of chairmen, and in 1975 it gave the function of making nominations to the Steering and Policy Committee of the caucus. When this committee recommended that two chairmen be deposed, the caucus went one better and deposed three. In 1977 it also ousted the chairman of an appropriations subcommittee. Henceforth no committee leaders could be assured of their positions if they defied express instructions of the caucus on a significant issue.

This centralization of party leadership might be useful to a Democratic president if he could persuade the caucus of the merits of his program. As Carter assumed office in 1977, however, the trend to strengthen party leaders seemed to increase his problems. Instead of following the White House line, leaders became even more responsive to sentiment within the chamber, and the caucus often took its own initiatives to pressure the administration to advance its scheduling of new measures. Committee leaders managed to retain independence from both caucus and president on most issues, while Carter was unable to dominate the caucus and make it an instrument of party leadership.

The Speaker presides over the House, assigns bills to committees, schedules floor debates, and if a Democrat, chooses the Democratic members of the Rules Committee. Since the House does not provide the president with a special calendar for executive proposals, the president must seek the cooperation of the Speaker on his terms. When the president does work closely with the Speaker, he finds that his program is facilitated. Speaker O'Neill's efforts on behalf of the Carter energy program are illustrative. The Speaker created an ad hoc energy committee to consider the program once the regular standing committees had completed their work. He used party leaders and his allies on the Rules Committee to make compromises among various party factions. He set deadlines, and the energy bill sailed through the House in less than one hundred days, in substantially the form that the president could accept. In another example, when Democrats were about to rebuff the president and restore funds he had cut from the B-1 bomber program, the Speaker made a speech urging Democrats who were thinking of defecting to "stay with the President of the United States, who is the leader of our party." Alluding to criticisms of the president, the Speaker continued, "I know there are those who believe that they haven't been treated right by this Administration. I know there are those who say, 'I haven't been able to get a job in my district. I haven't been able to get a dam.' Cast that aside. This is a national issue."[10] The Speaker managed to hold over two-thirds of his party in line and carried the day for the president.

Senate Democrats have never centralized power formally in the manner of their colleagues in the House, but in 1975 they provided for a secret vote for election of committee chairmen, and their caucus began to discuss issues. But since 1934 there has been no rule binding members to support the caucus position, and even when such rules existed in 1903–13 and 1933 they were never applied. Republicans also maintain a decentralized system. In neither party are committee chairs ousted from their positions for disagreements with a president of their party. Senate leaders confine themselves to scheduling, arranging floor debate, and persuading members to support the party consensus on floor votes. When a president has a hard time working with the leader, as Carter does, he may be abruptly "notified" that his major welfare reform and tax proposals and his Panama Canal treaty will be delayed for several months until the administration can round up more support.

The president consults with party leaders about the content and timing of his proposals. They sense the mood of the chamber and advise the president when to move ahead and when to lay back, when to make a dramatic gesture and when to adopt a low profile. They can advise the president on his choice of a sponsor for the bill and on his choice of a person to manage it in committee and on the floor. Party leaders also help choose members of the "conference committee" that reconciles the versions passed by the two chambers—the final stage of the legislative process when the president wants supporters revising the measure.

Neither the president nor the party leaders control Congress, but working together they can develop a strategy that offers the White House some chance of success.

Party Voting

Although the president cannot enforce party discpline, party voting in the chamber is usually high. Such cohesion cannot be ascribed to efforts the president or his party leaders make, nor to the limited authority of the caucuses. The president provides no "gravitational attraction" that induces members of his party to support his position on domestic issues. Kennedy did not change Democratic patterns in 1961, and Nixon did not change Republican patterns in 1969.[11] But the president may have some influence in foreign affairs and national security matters. Republican support for foreign aid programs rose sharply when Eisenhower was in office, and similar gains were recorded when Kennedy was president on the Democratic side.[12] Congressional party leaders have little influence and caucuses almost none.[13] If the president and an administrative agency disagree on a bill, legislators are likely to support the agency position, especially on authorizations and appropriations.[14] Party cohesion is high, primarily because members of the same party draw on similar kinds of voter coalitions and make similar appeals to the electorate. Different factions in the party that come from different regions or appeal to diverse constituencies have an incentive to logroll and compromise rather than defect to the opposition. These deals are facilitated by party leaders and the White House. Democrats especially encourage their leaders to arrange compromises to benefit each of the various factions in its turn, and this style of leadership results in high party voting.[15]

On important issues approximately 70 percent of the key roll call votes will put a majority of one party against a majority of the other. But even on these votes there will be defections: one study concluded that between 1949 and 1969 on only 13 percent of the votes did as much as 90 percent of the Democrats vote together, and on only 31 percent of the votes did 90 percent of the Republicans vote together.[16] Democrats win three out of four party votes, since they are almost always the majority in both houses. But when southerners defect and join with Republicans to form a conservative coalition on distributive or social welfare issues, a Democratic president may be defeated. The conservative coalition appeared on approximately one-quarter of the roll call votes between 1961 and 1976, winning as little as 35 percent of them in 1965 and as much as 83 percent of the votes in 1971.[17] The president relies on party leaders to try to forestall the emergence of such a coalition, or else he will be defeated on his urban-oriented welfare measures.[18] Republicans may split along conservative-liberal lines, or may fragment on a regional basis so that Republican presidents may lose enough votes to doom their program from the start. A conservative president may not be able to piece together a coalition if enough southern Democrats remain with their party. A Democratic president who can compromise with liberal Republicans may create a bipartisan majority sufficient to pass major parts of his program.

III

Coalition Building

The president must persuade and bargain with legislators to build working majorities in each chamber. Some presidents, like Franklin Roosevelt, are fierce partisans who work with the opposition only in crises. Others, like Eisenhower, prefer a bipartisan approach. Kennedy and Johnson combined partisan leadership with overtures to the Republicans when necessary. Kennedy rarely succeeded, but Johnson, working closely with Republican Senate Minority Leader Everett Dirksen, won passage of the Civil Rights Act of 1964, the Voting Rights Act of 1965, and foreign aid, minimum wage, and rent subsidy legislation.[19] Johnson made sure that credit was shared with Dirksen, so that "a hero's niche could be carved out for Senator Dirksen, not me."[20] Nixon and Ford tried to create a bipartisan conservative coalition. William Safire recalls that at a meeting of senior White House aides Nixon reminded them that "some Democrats support us better than some Republicans do."[21] The conservative coalition achieved some of its greatest successes in the Nixon and Ford presidencies.

Influencing the Committees

The key to success with Congress is influencing what happens in the committees. A sympathetic majority can speed consideration of presidential proposals, arrange for "friendly" hearings, and "mark up" the bill to reflect White House priorities. Its members can lead the floor debate and work with party leaders to create a coalition for passage. A hostile committee can pigeonhole the bill by refusing to report it to the chamber, delay hearings, or revise the measure so thoroughly that it no longer is a presidential bill. When a committee bottles up a measure it is almost impossible for the president to win its release. House procedures permit the discharge of bills from committees, but between 1910 and 1971, while thousands of bills were delayed, there were only 835 discharge petitions circulated and only 24 gained floor consideration. Only two of those measures ever became law. A hostile committee majority may also speed consideration of measures when the president prefers to wait.

Usually administration bills are revised thoroughly in the "markup" sessions, so that the committee version is reported to the chamber for consideration. The president must negotiate with committee and sub-committee leaders, who are not lieutenants of the president, do not necessarily represent the sentiment of rank-and-file members of the legislative party, and need not pay attention to the caucus under most circumstances. Committee leaders are specialists who identify with particular programs and are intimately familiar with the details of the laws they write. Most will support agencies in conflicts with the president. They have close ties with the bureaucracy and with the interest and clientele groups that government agencies serve. They come for the most part from safe districts and therefore are insulated from electoral pressure. They have the most seniority in Congress (uninterrupted service in the chamber) and the most committee seniority (uninterrupted service on the committee). Almost all of them become chairmen (or ranking minority members) through operation of the rule of seniority, which gives the position to the member of the party with the most seniority on the committee. The almost automatic operation of the seniority rule prevents the president from assembling his own team of loyalists whom he can install as committee leaders. Unlike Jefferson or Wilson, presidents now must take committee leaders and rosters as they find them.[22]

Once committee leaders were all-powerful, especially after the decline of the strong-Speaker system and weakening of caucuses. The autocratic chairman of the House Rules Committee, Charles Campbell, once told his colleagues, "You can go to hell; it makes no difference what a majority of you decide, if it meets with my disapproval, it shall not be done. I am the committee!"[23] But in the past few years a quiet revolution has taken place: chairmen must now obtain approval of majorities for everything from scheduling hearings to making subcommittee appointments; the subcommittees in turn have gained a "bill of rights" that gives them some autonomy from the full committees. Legislative power has been diffused, to encompass most senators and over one hundred representatives who chair such subcommittees. No longer can a president simply win over a committee chairman; he must now win over a majority. But an obstructive chairman is no longer an insurmountable obstacle: when Carter attempted to win House approval of his proposals for new reorganization authority, he faced opposition from the chairman of the Government Operations Committee in the House. Taking advantage of the new committee procedures, the president was able to build a majority coalition on the committee and win favorable action on his proposal.

Liaison and Lobbying

To build his coalitions the president must communicate with legislative leaders and rank-and-file members. Lyndon Johnson told his cabinet after the 1964 elections, "I want to be especially sure that each of you selects a top man to serve as your legislative liaison. Next to the cabinet officer himself, I consider this the most important position in the department."[24] Prior to the Second World War presidents were assisted by cabinet and subcabinet officials, especially those with prior congressional service. Wilson relied on his attorney general and also instituted the "Common Council Club," a group of thirty subcabinet officials (including Assistant Secretary of the Navy Franklin Roosevelt) to round up support on Capitol Hill for administration measures. Franklin Roosevelt used his postmaster general, and the position of assistant secretary of commerce was filled by an official in charge of White House lobbying efforts.

During the Second World War the War Department performed liaison for the administration, with over 200 officers assigned to its Legislation and Liaison Division. Several White House aides and the BOB's Legislative Reference Division also lobbied in Congress. After the war the Department of Defense created an assistant secretary for congressional liaison, the Department of State named an assistant secretary for congressional relations, and between 1949 and 1963 the other departments followed suit, assigning over five hundred officials to these units.

Departmental liaison offices were supervised by a White House unit. Truman assigned the lobbying function to two aides, and Eisenhower created the first formal office, headed by Jerry Parsons and Bryce Harlow, both of whom had operated within the original War Department office. Kennedy kept the unit and named Lawrence O'Brien to head it; Johnson retained O'Brien, and occasionally attended staff meetings to regale department liaison officers with anecdotes and to give them advice based on his long experience as a party leader in the Senate.[25] Bryce Harlow returned to serve under Nixon, and after he left, William Timmons served both Nixon and Ford. The Office of Congressional Relations (OCR) was enlarged and divided into a "Senate Staff," "House Staff," a group to service requests by legislators to the departments, and a group that circulated a "reporter" of committee and chamber schedules for hearings, markups, floor debates, and votes. Frank Moore headed Carter's operation, but the president also relied on Vice-President Mondale to develop strategy and contact key congressional leaders.

In every administration, OCR staff members have backgrounds as legislators, legislative aides, lobbyists, or public relations experts. Some move from departmental liaison offices to the White House. They rely on expertise to present the president's case. As Ralph Huitt, a political sci-

entist who was a department lobbyist in the Johnson administration
pointed out,

The most effective tool . . . is knowledge, expertise, a command of the business
at hand. The member wants to do his job well and succeed as a congressman.
The person who can help him do that, who knows how to solve a problem—
especially if he can offer a "little language," i.e. a well drafted provision that
can go into a bill—never has trouble getting access and a thoughtful hearing.[26]

Administration lobbyists work closely with interest groups. In support of
Johnson's 1965 aid to education bill, U.S. Commissioner of Education
Francis Keppel won support from Catholic lay organizations, Jack Valenti
at the White House maintained communication with the Vatican apostolic
delegate, Lee White worked with Jewish groups, Henry Hall Wilson
rounded up southern support, and Douglass Cater drummed up support
from the National Education Association.[27] Campaigning to raise the
debt ceiling, the Nixon administration mobilized defense contractors,
who called conservative Republicans and urged them to support the
measure on national security grounds. When Kennedy submitted a school
construction bill, White House aides worked to get Democratic votes,
and construction company lobbyists were dispatched to work on the
Republicans. White House aides work with the American Bar Association
on bills providing legal services, with the American Medical Association
when issues involve medical care, and with other professional organizations as the need arises.[28]

The administration will work with local and state party leaders, public
officials, and interest groups who might hold the key to how legislators
will vote.[29] During the fight to pass a federal aid to education measure,
a legislator offered a parochial school amendment that Kennedy opposed.
The White House contacted his local party leader, who then phoned the
Roman Catholic congressman and urged him to withdraw the amendment, asking, "Who sent you there, me or the Bishop? And who's going
to keep you there, me or the Bishop?"[30] In 1977 Vice-President Mondale
appealed to Democratic state party leaders to support Carter's ill-fated
tax rebate proposal at a luncheon for the Democratic State Chairmen's
Association—efforts that could not salvage the proposal. Just three days
after the Kennedy assassination Lyndon Johnson invited the governors
to the White House for a discussion of his legislative program, and convinced many of them to support his tax and civil rights proposals. The
governors in turn used their influence on congressional delegations.[31]
The Nixon administration lobbied with governors and mayors of both
parties to gain support for its revenue-sharing proposals, and they pressured a reluctant committee chairman, Wilbur Mills, to speed consideration of the measure.

The president will "stroke" important legislators. The master of the art,
Lyndon Johnson, noted that "there is but one way for a President to deal
with Congress, and that is continuously, incessantly, and without interrup-

tion," adding that "if it's really going to work, the relationship between the President and Congress has got to be almost incestuous."[32] The president meets with members of Congress for breakfast and luncheons, strolls with them in the White House Rose Garden, and may on exceptional occasions invite them to spend the weekend with him at Camp David or another retreat. Eisenhower invited the entire Congress to a series of luncheons and met regularly with Democratic leaders Rayburn and Johnson over drinks. Kennedy hosted cocktail parties, and Lawrence O'Brien invited members to brunches. Johnson held buffet dinners followed by briefings from cabinet members, and he would brief about one hundred members of his party the evening before a major new bill would be sent up. The president may offer certain key legislators unlimited access; Eisenhower gave Majority Leader Robert Taft the go-ahead to phone or visit at any time at the senator's convenience.

These techniques rarely change votes. At best they keep the president and his opponents on speaking terms, and let members who support the administration know that their help is appreciated. Eisenhower's luncheons were held amidst his feuds with the Republican right wing, and Taft was a fierce opponent of the president on many issues. Even Lyndon Johnson's "treatment," which involved bringing lawmakers into the White House for doses of flattery, bullying, and every possible psychological ploy, did not prevent Congress from obstructing much of his domestic program after 1966.

The institutionalization of legislative liaison provides an object lesson for anyone who would equate a large White House staff with effective use of presidential power. An aide needs immediate access to the president and the authority to speak for him, deal for him, and act in his name. Bryce Harlow has observed that "for real effectiveness a White House congressional man must be known on Capitol Hill as a confidant of the president; he must be in the know, he must have the stature to obtain immediate contact with the President, directly or indirectly, when emergency requires."[33] Aides like Harlow or O'Brien recount the times they have spoken in the name of the president during sensitive negotiations with congressional leaders, and how impressed these leaders were with the degree of access the liaison officers enjoyed. But the president can give such access and authority to only a few aides, for otherwise he would be under seige. No matter how large the office, only a few staff members have the stature and access to the president necessary to impress legislative leaders. Low-ranking aides can neither deal for the president nor bring him accurate information, for Lyndon Johnson notes that "the key to accurate head counts is personal knowledge or trust, and the ability to probe beneath the surface to see what individuals are really thinking and feeling."[34] Unless a liaison officer is close to the president, he will be unable to communicate presidential views to legislators, and they in turn will not confide their intentions to a low-ranking aide.

The liaison staff argues that to be effective it must serve as "counsel" to the president on legislative strategy. It therefore may attempt to influence the content of program proposals as well as advise on strategy and tactics. But if it claims a program "won't fly" in Congress, it may interfere with the interests of the OMB, the Domestic Policy Staff, the Council of Economic Advisors, and other White House aides, councils, or offices. The OCR is often involved in bureaucratic infighting and may contribute to conflict within the inner circle. When presidential bills are delayed, gutted, amended, or defeated, the OCR takes the heat, and other White House units are likely to argue that its performance (rather than the content of the measure) was responsible for the outcome.

No Office of Congressional Relations, however run, can substitute for intimate and sustained presidential involvement in the legislative process. The incumbent must know the mood in each chamber, and demonstrate some mastery of legislative strategy and tactics. He must know the details of the process that involves his bill—budgetary, fiscal, reorganization, nomination, treaty—or other measure. By mastering the details, he impresses his supporters with his personal commitment and his opponents with his ability. His legislative program will languish if he does not pay attention to it. Theodore Roosevelt, Woodrow Wilson, and Franklin Roosevelt had no formal liaison offices, yet each, by personally involving himself, won major victories.

Transactions

The presidential power to persuade legislators rests on more than expertise, lobbying, or "stroking." A president may offer tangible quid pro quos to win votes for his measures. As one congressman described how the Eisenhower administration sought to win passage of the Landrum-Griffin act regulating labor union activities, "If a man goes along, he gets money for his campaign; if he doesn't go along, he gets nothing. It's that simple."[35] Former White House assistant Doris Kearns reports that during the Johnson administration, Senate Minority Leader Everett Dirksen "would blatantly and without hesitation send long memos to the White House detailing his requests for that week: a judgeship in the fifth district, a post office in Peoria, a presidential speech in Springfield, a tax exemption for peanuts."[36] Such favors are useful for low-visibility (yet crucial) actions such as voting for a measure in committee or on votes prior to final passage of bills. Legislators can vote one way on final passage, shielding themselves from constituent reprisals, while at the same time helping the president move his program along prior to that vote.

The president can offer patronage. Most of the approximately five hundred federal district judges are nominated by arrangements with state and local party organizations through the custom of "senatorial courtesy," in effect making the president a "clerk" for members of the Senate from his party. The ninety-four U.S. attorneys and the marshalls are also chosen by party leaders. Some nominees for specialized and appellate federal courts are sponsored by members of the House and Senate Judiciary Committees.

The White House fills executive branch positions in consultation with members of Congress, who may sponsor aides or committee staff members for positions. Former legislators defeated in the elections may also be offered positions with the administration. The president may trade his appointment power for passage of a program. To win the support of Republican Senator Arthur Vandenburg for the Marshall Plan aiding Europe after the Second World War, Truman promised congressional Republicans that they could staff the program. They in turn pressed Truman to name corporate executives, rather than state department careerists, to run the program. Vandenburg himself nominated the director of the program.[37] Lyndon Johnson cleared nominations of black officials with southern senators; they opposed his choices but appreciated his courtesy in giving them advance notice.[38] Carter named several protégés of House Speaker O'Neill to high positions, including the Speaker's choice to run the General Services Administration, with its pork-barrel distributions.

Members of Congress may support the administration in return for assistance in expediting contracts or grants that will benefit their states or districts. But presidents share power over distributions with committee leaders, and legislation may limit the extent to which the White House can affect the awarding of grants. Some transactions backfire: Rep. Edith Green was outraged by what she considered to be a heavy-handed attempt to "buy" her support for an administration measure combating juvenile delinquency (through the award of a large grant to her district) and turned against the White House. Because she was a committee leader with jurisdiction over the subject, the result was a measure that incorporated her views rather than the White House proposals.[39]

Often presidents make transactions as part of a general strategy. Kennedy cultivated the southern wing of his party: he refrained from issuing an executive order ending racial discrimination in federally assisted housing for two years, and the order he finally signed included only a small fraction of future construction; he kept open unneeded military facilities in the South and made sure defense contracts were disproportionately placed there; he approved a manned space center for Texas; he proposed formulae for grant programs channeling funds to rural areas; he offered a farm program with high price supports for southern crops. In return for the accommodation of southern interests, Kennedy won support from legislators for his economic, military, and foreign assistance programs.

The president must know when to bargain and when to draw the line. Like Wilson or Franklin Roosevelt, he may pass the word that all patronage and distributions will be given near the end of the congressional session once loyalty to the administration has been demonstrated. Lyndon Johnson rewarded legislators who generally supported his program rather than dealing with individuals on each issue in a quid pro quo arrangement. Johnson recalled that with few exceptions, favors were "generally delivered by the White House staff after the fact, and on the basis of a pattern of voting, not by the President personally in exchange for a specific vote."[40] But at times a specific deal is absolutely necessary: Franklin Roosevelt saved his measure extending the draft just prior to American entry into the Second World War with a transaction that provided passage by one vote in the House. Carter preferred not to engage in payoffs, but after the defection of 101 Democrats in the House on his consumer protection bill, a meeting of 26 whips was arranged with the president, and he agreed to facilitate their requests for appointments, grants, and contracts.[41]

Sometimes presidential favors lead to tensions in the chamber. If partisan opponents are rewarded, the president weakens his position with his own party. Transactions merely whet the appetite of lawmakers, and as Johnson explained, "I could not trade patronage for votes in any direct exchange. If word spread that I was trading, everyone would want to trade and all other efforts at persuasion would automatically fail."[42] But a president who announces a "no deal" policy will find himself in trouble: President Carter decided to cut out funding for 19 water-development projects in his fiscal year 1978 budget. He announced that he would review the economic feasibility of another 320 such projects. Both the Senate and the House reacted by voting to require the president to spend any previously appropriated funds for these projects. After the firestorm of protest against the interference in the pork-barrel arrangements, the president backed down, releasing from his review 307 of the projects and restoring to funding 3 of the 19 he had dropped. Still later he restored most of the projects. Carter had damaged his relationship with Congress in a futile attempt to control these distributions, a setback that took him months to repair.

Hardball Tactics

Successful party leaders such as Speaker Sam Rayburn would advise new members "to get along, go along" but they would never ask a member to put his career in jeopardy or violate his conscience on a vote. A corollary of the Rayburn rule was developed by Lawrence O'Brien, who eschewed the hard sell for a softer approach. O'Brien later observed, "I never expected any member to commit political suicide in order to help the President, no matter how noble our cause. I expected politicians to be concerned with their own interests; I only hoped to convince them that our interests were often the same."[43] But at times presidents use rough tactics. Kennedy once lost a crucial Senate vote when West Virginia's Randolph voted against the administration measure. Kennedy ordered the Bureau of the Budget to drop a project that the senator had sponsored. But as White House aide Theodore Sorensen recounted, conservative senators supported Randolph by channeling new projects to his state through other pieces of legislation.[44] Johnson retaliated against Senate criticism of his war policies by cutting off projects in his critics' states, but this only hurt him in the Senate. During both the Haynesworth and Carswell nomination struggles, Nixon threatened senators who planned to vote against his choices for justices of the Supreme Court with opposition in their next primaries, a cutoff of national campaign funds, elimination of public works and grants, and an end to their access to the White House. Some senators were even threatened with an Internal Revenue Service audit of their tax returns. Both nominations were defeated.[45] Larry Pressler, a Republican congressman from South Dakota, charged during Ford's presidency that "a political threat was made to me by a White House lobbyist last week concerning my vote on the natural gas deregulation issue."[46] Two Maine Republicans, William Cohen and David Emery, charged that White House aides told them that if they did not vote to sustain a Ford veto, a former Maine governor would not be reappointed as chairman of the National Transportation Board. They didn't, he wasn't, and they leaked the threat to the press, which prompted Ford, after the public outcry, to send his liaison officials over to the Capitol to make a public apology to the representatives.[47] When the director of the Office of Management and Budget, Bert Lance, was being investigated by the Senate for alleged improprieties as a banker in Georgia, Carter's Press Secretary Jody Powell encouraged publication of a charge that Republican senator Charles Percy had been involved in a violation of the law in financing his 1972 reelection campaign. When Powell's "plant" of the rumor was made known, Carter had him apologize and admit that his action was "inappropriate, regrettable, and dumb."[48] Within a fortnight Lance had resigned, as the Senate continued its investigation into his affairs. In the post-Watergate climate, rough tactics were counterproductive, since there was more political profit to be made by revealing the pressure and standing up to it than there was in knuckling under to it and remaining silent. Neither Ford nor Carter had much success in using "dirty tricks" in their legislative campaigns.

IV

National Agenda Politics

If the president calculates that his attempts at persuasion, negotiation, coalition building, and lobbying will fail, he may move from the "closed" arena of legislative politics to an enlarged arena of the attentive and mass publics.[49] By gaining support for his program in the constituencies of the legislators, he hopes to pressure them to vote for his program. As Lyndon Johnson put it,

When traditional methods fail, a President must be willing to bypass the Congress and take the issue to the people. By instinct and experience, I preferred to work from within, knowing that good legislation is the product not of public rhetoric but of private negotiations and compromise. But sometimes a President has to put Congress' feet to the fire.[50]

The president "goes public" out of weakness, for if he had the votes he would pass the measure first and go to the public only for the bill-signing ceremonies. But public appeals are one of the few credible threats a president can make. Eisenhower threatened the party leaders who stalled his measures in 1953 that if they did so the next year he would take his case to the people. Only then did his bills begin to move through Congress.[51] Lyndon Johnson had to make an appeal to the people to obtain passage of his Civil Rights Act of 1964, Voting Rights Act of 1965, and Housing Act of 1968. Both Ford and Carter attempted to rally the public behind their energy programs.

The White House may attempt to make its proposals part of the "national agenda," consisting of matters that the public is interested in and that may influence voting behavior in subsequent presidential and congressional elections. (But only a handful of his bills will ever receive sustained public attention; for most of this a strategy cannot be employed.)

A presidential decision to "go public" galvanizes the White House pollsters, speechwriters, and media experts into action. The president must "package" his legislation prior to presenting it to Congress; decisions about substance may be influenced by media advisors. The president needs a theme for a national agenda proposal. Lyndon Johnson called his grab bag of community action, public works, and job training programs a "War on Poverty" because, as he put it, "I wanted to rally the nation, to sound a call to arms. . . ."[52] Other presidents have declared "wars" against crime, drugs, or disease. Some presidents present their initiatives in the context of the cold war. Kennedy sold the nation on high expenditures for space exploration by insisting that Americans had to beat the Russians in a manned lunar landing. In the Eisenhower administration, federal aid to education was billed as a way to surpass Soviet scientific achievements, and the program of highway construction was named the Interstate Highway Defense System, since it supposedly had some military value.

The president may package liberal programs in conservative wrappings. Revenue sharing was billed by the Nixon administration as a return to "states rights" and "grass-roots control" of programs. Job training and public works employment measures are promoted to get the "able-bodied" off welfare rolls and onto tax rolls, even though studies have shown that most welfare recipients are not presently employable. The Demonstration Cities proposal of the Great Society was hastily renamed Model Cities after rioting in urban areas gave a bad odor to the original title. The Nixon administration proposal for welfare reform was called the Family Assistance Plan to gain public support. Ford's energy program was called Operation Independence as a means to harness national pride to price decontrol measures.

The president may lose control of the definition of an issue. Truman's program of national health insurance was dubbed socialized medicine by the American Medical Association; after a multimillion dollar public relations campaign, public opinion turned against the plan and Congress never passed it. Also, the president cannot always control the timing of a national agenda issue. In 1961 Kennedy shelved plans to introduce civil rights legislation in Congress in order to gain southern congressional support for his economic and military programs. Black leaders took their followers to the streets in nonviolent demonstrations, and by 1963 the violent response to their activities had made civil rights the major domestic issue. Extensive media coverage was instrumental in placing public opinion on the side of the demonstrators. Kennedy and Johnson then introduced bills that eventually became the Civil Rights Act of 1964. Johnson had no intention of introducing more legislation, preferring a brief cooling-off period, but civil rights leaders again took to the streets, and the violence committed against them by law-enforcement officials in Selma, Alabama, again focused public attention on their cause. The administration then introduced a voting rights bill, which became law in 1965.

The president uses the same media politics techniques that helped him win the nomination and election to make an issue part of the national agenda and to control the debate. He can leave Washington and "work the country," making speeches at rallies and before local parties. White House staff members have worked in campaigns and are eager to replicate their election victory in a new campaign. Such efforts are institutionalized: in the Ford administration the Office of Public Liaison organized conferences between administration leaders and interest groups; the Office of Communications handled television and radio exposure; the Editorial Office coordinated most communications and speeches. Carter's efforts included an assistant to the president for political affairs (Hamilton Jordan), an assistant to the president for intergovernmental affairs (Jack Watson), an assistant to the president for public liaison (Margaret Costanza), a press secretary (Jody Powell), a media advisor (Gerald Rafshoon), a special assistant to the president for appointments (Tim Kraft) in charge of "advance" scheduling and transportation, and a director of White House projects (Gregory Schneiders) who arranged the "town meetings" and other media extravaganzas. In addition, Carter made extensive use of Vice-President Mondale and received advice from his pollsters and media advisors. While the names of these offices change from one administration to the next, the services they provide to the president remain the same.

The president presents national agenda issues in his state of the Union address, his annual budget message, and his economic message. He also may appear on television prior to submitting major programs to Congress, making a "need speech" to the public. He defines the issues, characterizes the program, presents a thematic title, and anticipates criticisms.[53] The White House television studio has a "warm" color camera ready to project the presidential image at a moment's notice. Each studio camera is equipped with a TelePrompTer two-way mirror, so the president can look straight at the camera while following his script. The White House requests air time from the three network news directors, who constitute themselves as an informal committee to consider the request. Each network, however, makes its own decision. Occasionally a network will deny a request or move it to a different time slot and show the speech on videtape.[54] Presidents argue that they have the right to preempt network schedules because what they say is inherently newsworthy, and the networks have an obligation to the public to broadcast their speeches. But the networks have maintained that theirs is a public trust, not a presidential one, and that the final decision on programming must be theirs to make. Although few requests are denied, the network committee may bargain with the White House over the time slot and the length of the speech.

The president has an advantage over his political opponents when he goes public. Between 1969 and 1975, Democratic congressional leaders requested air time eleven times, and were turned down on eight occasions. No group, under the law and the rulings of the Federal Communications Commission, has an automatic "right of reply" to a presidential speech. The FCC's "fairness doctrine" requires that the networks present other viewpoints, but it permits them to determine who represents responsible persons for opposing views, and allows them to determine the format in which these views are presented. At times congressional leaders or the national chairman of the opposition party has received free time to reply to a presidential address, but on other occasions they have been refused prime time and the matter has gone to the courts or to the FCC.[55]

The president always gets a larger audience share than his opposition: Ford's state of the Union address in 1975 was seen by 75 million viewers,

---

PRESIDENT FORD DRAMATIZES THE ISSUE

... I asked the Congress in January to enact this urgent ten-year program for energy independence within 80 days. ... Now what did the Congress do in February about energy? Congress did nothing. ... [tears page off calendar] What did the Congress do in March? [tears page] What did the Congress do in April about energy? Congress did nothing. ... [tears page]

So, What has the Congress done in May about energy? [tears page] Congress did nothing and went home for a 10 day recess. ... The Congress cannot drift, dawdle, and debate forever with America's future.

I need your help to energize this Congress into comprehensive action. I will continue to press for my January program, which is still the only total energy program there is. I cannot sit here idly while nothing is done. We must get on with the job right now.

President Ford, May 27, 1975 radio and television address.

---

whereas three broadcasts on separate evenings of the reply by Democratic congressional leaders drew a total audience of only 47 million. But the president can hardly resort to television for most of his program. His popularity will decline if he preempts prime time too often, and he will suffer from overexposure. Carter's 1978 Panama Canal "need" speeech drew only 48 million viewers, while a movie playing at the same time on CBS drew 35 million.[56] If a presidential appearance generates a temporary surge of public support, congressional leaders may delay consideration of the measure until the media effects wear off. Neither Ford nor Carter could time their use of television to coincide effectively with congressional consideration of their energy programs, and after brief flings with national agenda politics, both returned to the "closed politics" methods of bargaining and compromise.[57]

The president may use news conferences to build support for his programs. Originated by Wilson, conferences were held twice weekly by his Republican successors, dropped entirely by Hoover in the midst of the Depression, then revived by Roosevelt on a biweekly basis. Since then, the frequency has dropped: Truman held almost one a week, Eisenhower two a month, Johnson one a month, Nixon once every two months. In the post-Watergate atmosphere presidents have tried to become more accessible to the media: Ford held a conference approximately once a month, and Carter attempted to meet a schedule of one every two weeks.

The conferences may be keyed to pending legislation. Eisenhower often pressed Congress to take specific actions to move his program along.[58] Staff aides may "plant" a question with a reporter so that the president can comment on congressional committee actions. He may use the conference to signal willingness to compromise, or instead to rally the public to his line. Presidential statements made early in the day may then be circulated by party leaders on the floor to rally administration supporters in close votes. Eisenhower used this tactic to fight cuts in his foreign aid program in 1953, although it had little impact on the voting.[59] The president may even use a news conference to disassociate himself from proposals of his own departments. In 1957 Eisenhower was asked if he favored a provision of the civil rights measure that had been drafted by the Justice Department; his equivocation signaled to Congress that it could amend the measure. Asked in another conference if he supported the spending totals in his budget submitted to Congress, Eisenhower invited Congress to make additional cuts, thus signaling that he would not stand behind the requests of his cabinet secretaries.[60]

Held at the president's pleasure, the news conference enables him to project his strength when he is popular. He will postpone conferences when he is in trouble. He is under no obligation to respond to questions. Presidents generally follow the ground rules set by Franklin Roosevelt, who told reporters at his first conference, "There will be a great many questions, of course, that I won't answer . . . questions which for various reasons I do not want to discuss, or am not ready to discuss, or I simply do not know anything about."[61]

Presidents make remarks at conferences that sometimes do more harm than good. Truman called poll taxes, imposed by several states to discourage blacks from voting, a "states rights" issue with which the federal government should not interfere; later, after consulting with his political advisors, he reversed himself.[62] Eisenhower, after inviting Congress to cut his budget, later issued a strong defense of his original requests. Lyndon Johnson was so afraid of making slips that he refused to permit conferences to be televised for almost a year. After his foreign policies were challenged by reporters, he began to call conferences on weekends, often at his ranch in Texas, so that few foreign affairs specialists or reporters would be present, and so that reporters filing stories would be unable to verify details or obtain comments from congressional opponents of the war.[63] In the midst of a war, the president may find his news conference useless for purposes of pressuring Congress on legislation.

The president may cultivate editors, syndicated columnists, and network executives. Kennedy's press secretary, Pierre Salinger, describes such treatment of columnists:

A request from one of them to see the president personally was usually honored, and the White House staff members on the policy level like Ted Sorensen and McGeorge Bundy made sure that they had the administration's views on prevailing problems.[64]

The president may go over the head of a reporter or bureau chief to the editor or publisher in order to push the administration position on pending legislation, the tactics favored by Kennedy and Johnson. Or he may use "hardball" tactics favored by Nixon: dispatching his vice-president to make an issue of "media bias"; threatening to influence applications by television stations for license renewals before the FCC; having the IRS audit tax returns of reporters; and using White House plumbers to wiretap members of the press.[65]

Most presidents use the carrot more than the stick. Lyndon Johnson gave reporters a version of "the treatment," and as White House correspondent Hugh Sidey described it:

His idea of great flattery to a correspondent was to take the man under his arm, wine him and dine him and entertain him, treat him to a few innocuous secrets, and then suggest a story line. If it came out as Johnson wanted it to, he invited the fellow back for more intimate moments.[66]

For their favorites, presidents grant exclusive interviews and off-the-record briefings. Kennedy was famous for his "rocking chair" interviews. Johnson participated in a television interview with three network correspondents that was then edited under White House supervision. Nixon telephoned columnists to thank them for defending administration policies.[67] Lyndon Johnson gave publishers advance notice of his intention to develop an antipoverty program so that magazine articles and books appeared about poverty just about the time the program was sent to Congress. Then the president appealed to newspaper editors to mold public opinion through editorials. "Let them know," he told a group of editors and publishers, "that everybody is not eating three meals a day the way they are, that there are conditions in this country that are insupportable, and except for the grace of God they could find themselves in the same spot."[68]

But the president's opponents may use the media effectively. Many former White House political, public relations, editorial, and legislative liaison aides set up shops as lobbyists in the private sector once they leave government service. They know the techniques the White House will use to control the national agenda and can try to develop their own counters on behalf of their clients. Washington "superlawyers" are retained by interest groups to oppose legislation that the administration favors. The investigative media may have its own priorities: documentaries and news articles about malnutrition and hunger in America permitted senators to focus public attention on the indaequacies of the food-stamp program and allowed Congress to expand the program beyond the limits set by the Nixon administration.

The White House may use cabinet secretaries and lower-ranking officials to publicize its programs. During his second term Franklin Roosevelt had 203 officials make radio addresses extolling the accomplishments of the New Deal. Other presidents have dispatched officials around the country to fight for a controversial measure. If the president uses White House speechwriters to monitor addresses given by his secretaries, the press and his opponents may charge that he is "muzzling" the cabinet. But if he gives his secretaries free reign to speak on the issues, they may promote departmental priorities at the expense of his own. Truman fired Secretary of Commerce Henry Wallace for his public campaign to force the president into a reconsideration of his foreign policies. Ford fired James Schlesinger as secretary of defense when he attempted to make a national agenda issue of alleged Soviet arms build-ups in strategic and conventional weaponry just at the time Congress was considering the Pentagon's procurement requests. Carter's secretary of agriculture, Robert Berglund, took the side of the farmers and urged them to continue their "strike" until Congress passed measures to raise farm income—measures that the president did not support. The White House often must counter national agenda efforts made by its own departments. A constant flood of news releases, messages to Congress, letters to committee leaders, memoranda to cabinet officials, remarks at political functions, and meetings with interest groups—all serve as correctives to present the administration "line" and undercut secretaries who have staked out their own positions.

A president stands a better chance of success with national agenda politics when he takes his initiatives early in his term, or if his popularity increases due to a successful venture in foreign affairs. Every president begins his term with high ratings during the "honeymoon" period. Each, with the exception of Eisenhower, experienced a long-term decline in his approval rating, with a slight "rebound" effect near the end of his term.[69] The decline-rebound effect gives the "approval rating" as measured by public opinion polls a parabolic curve that appears natural and inevitable. Declines may often be sharp and can be traced in part to specific events, such as recession or scandal: recent examples include Watergate, Ford's pardon of Nixon, and Carter's problems with the Bert Lance affair. Presidential popularity may not be much of a resource for most presidents: Truman conducted much of his first and almost all of his second term with low ratings; Lyndon Johnson was unpopular after he escalated the war in Vietnam; and during Nixon's second term and Ford's care-taker term public approval ratings for presidents reached new postwar lows. Carter had not yet completed his first year in office when his ratings tumbled as a result of the Lance affair, and many polls found low levels of confidence in the executive branch that almost matched levels during the Ford administration (see figure 6.1).

Sometimes the making of a national agenda issue may be the unmaking of a president. Truman's agricultural program, the Brannan Plan, became a national agenda issue but proved unpopular with urban voters when they learned that its implementation would mean higher food prices. Nixon's attempt to curtail several Great Society education programs failed after education lobbies rallied grass-roots constituencies and even turned many Republican county parties off the plan. A Ford proposal to decontrol domestic oil prices ran into stiff opposition from motorists who

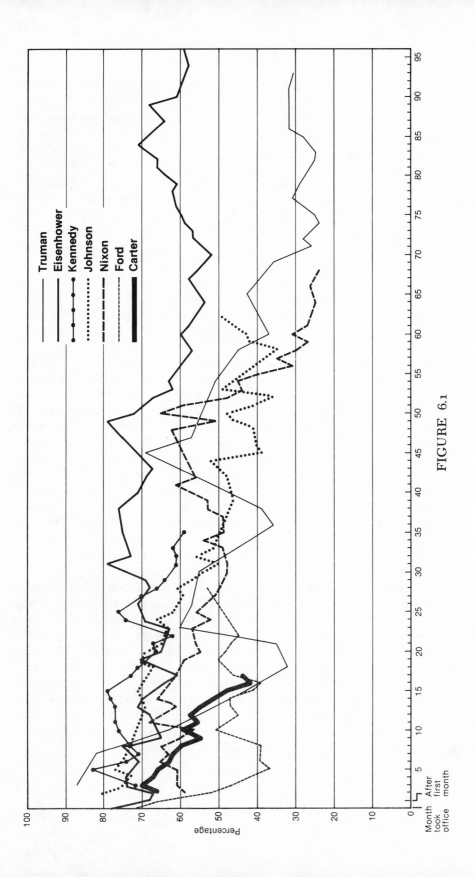

FIGURE 6.1

opposed higher prices at the gasoline pumps. Support for Carter's energy program tumbled soon after his nationwide television address in 1977.

To dramatize an issue a president may call one or both houses of Congress into special session.[70] He presents a program, often just before an election, and puts the opposition party on the defensive by forcing it to go on record in support or opposition to his measure. Truman used this tactic brilliantly by calling a session to force Republicans controlling Congress to vote against his Fair Deal measures. The sessions he called were "failures" in the sense that little legislation passed, but Truman then campaigned against a "do-nothing" Congress and was elected to the presidency in 1948, so in a political sense these sessions were a great success. No president since has used this tactic.

When the president raises a national agenda issue his opponents may counter with the charge that he is expanding the powers of the office beyond the constitutional limits. An appeal to the people always raises the danger of a *plebiscitary* presidency, and opponents of a measure may claim that they are preventing an "imperial presidency" from riding roughshod over the separation of powers. Woodrow Wilson was defeated in his attempt to win Senate consent to the Treaty of Versailles partly on these grounds, and it was not by chance that the "reservations" to the treaty introduced by its opponents in the Senate dealt specifically with the powers of the president to conduct foreign affairs or engage in hostilities with other nations. Franklin Roosevelt's bill to add additional members to the Supreme Court (one for each sitting justice over the age of sixty-five) was attacked by opponents who charged that he was attempting to "pack" the court and undermine its part in the checks and balances system. Many New Dealers broke with Roosevelt on this issue, and not only did he lose the measure, but his defeat marked a turning point for the New Deal; thereafter Congress passed on a small fraction of his domestic program, and control of the legislature passed to a coalition of Republicans and anti-Roosevelt Democrats.[71]

National agenda politics may be a useful tactic, but it has its drawbacks and is not always successful. It may be pointed out that Great Society laws were passed by Congress even though Lyndon Johnson was awkward and unsure of himself in dealing with the media, while the far slicker and glamorous Kennedy White House had a lesser success with Congress. It only states the obvious to point out that a president who has mastered legislative strategy and tactics, who has a "feel" for Congress and good rapport with its leaders, and who is blessed with large party margins in both chambers, is likely to have more legislative success than a president who relies on national agenda politics to make up for his weaknesses as a legislative tactician and party leader.

V

The Veto Powers

The president may always attempt to influence Congress by substituting prerogative government and the veto power for efforts at persuasion. He may use the veto to induce an antiadministration coalition to negotiate with him, or to frustrate the opposition party if it controls Congress. The veto is employed in the following situations:

1. When the president believes a measure is unconstitutional. Some presidents have vetoed bills that they thought infringed on their prerogatives.
2. To discourage "riders," which are nongermane amendments tacked on to popular measures such as appropriations bills. The president may call the congressional bluff and veto the bill rather than accept the rider. (The Legislative Reorganization Act of 1970 provides that riders are subject to a point of order, which then requires a two-thirds vote to attach it to the bill, thus eliminating the rider for most measures.)
3. To modify a bill through bargaining. On some occasions, the president vetoes a bill, and Congress then passes a version that he can sign.
4. To defeat a measure passed by Congress, often in order to define differences between the parties for forthcoming elections.

Political scientists have attempted to specify the conditions under which the veto is likely to be exercised. One study by Jong R. Lee, tracing the use of the veto from Washington through Nixon, found that Democratic presidents are more likely to wield the veto than Republicans, and that presidents with prior service in Congress are least likely to veto bills.[72] But for recent years these results are misleading. Democrats such as Kennedy and Johnson vetoed fewer measures than Republicans Eisenhower, Nixon, and Ford. And Ford, who had spent most of his political career in the House of Representatives, had no hesitation in using the veto to frustrate the will of Congress. He vetoed a foreign aid authorization in 1976 because he believed it infringed on his constitutional prerogatives, a housing bill in 1975 to force Congress to send him a more palatable version, a tax measure with rates he did not approve, and a series of appropriations bills to make the level of federal spending an issue in the presidential campaign of 1976. As Lee points out, the important factor underlying the statistical correlations is partisanship: in periods of split government, the veto is likely to be used more than it will be when one party controls both the White House and the Congress. Carter, for example, vetoed very few measures—though he used the veto threat frequently.

After a bill is passed by both houses, the enrolled copy, signed by the president of the Senate and the Speaker of the House, is processed and sent to the White House within ten days. If the president approves the bill, he signs it into law within ten days of its presentation to him. If he wishes he may hold a public signing ceremony. Johnson signed the 1965 education measure at a one-room schoolhouse in Texas, the voting rights measure in a room at the Capitol next to the chamber where Lincoln had signed the Emancipation Proclamation, and a new immigration law at the Statue of Liberty. But if the president opposes the bill, he may exercise one of these options:

1. He may withhold his signature for ten days, and the bill becomes law. He may issue a statement outlining his objections and indicating his reasons. He may take this action if a bill he favors has a rider attached, or if he opposes a measure but thinks it would be overridden by a large margin, or if he thinks a veto would damage him politically.
2. He can permit the bill to become law without his signature, but indicates that he will not enforce a section that he believes to be unconstitutional. He then forces his opponents to take him to court, which tests the constitutionality of the measure. He may, alternatively, enforce a section of the law in a way not intended by the majority that passed the measure.
3. He may take actions in the ten-day period after the bill is passed that limit the effect of the measure. Theodore Roosevelt established much of the National Forest System by executive order in the ten-day period, prior to signing a bill (which he wanted) that had a provision (of which he strongly disapproved) restricting the use of federal lands.
4. He may veto the measure within ten days of its presentation to him, sending it back to its chamber of origin with a message indicating his reasons. He may use this message to suggest changes Congress might make that would enable him to sign a revised version. (An incoming president succeeding to the office may sign bills presented to his predecessor within the ten-day period).

If, during the ten-day period, Congress adjourns, the president may still sign the measure into law. But if he chooses not to sign it, the Constitutional provisions regarding the *pocket veto* take effect. The president need not return the bill to either chamber, need not provide reasons for the pocket veto, or send a message to Congress. Most important, the legislature cannot override a pocket veto and enact the measure into law. Congress must pass a new measure in its next session, even one identical to the version pocket-vetoed, and present it to the president after it reconvenes from adjournment.[73]

The prerogative to pocket veto has been misused by several presidents, who prefer it to the regular veto because it cannot be overridden. They have killed measures when Congress adjourned or recessed for short vacations prior to the end of the legislative session. Both Nixon and Ford used the pocket veto during interim adjournments—Nixon to kill a health bill and Ford to kill vocational rehabilitation, farm labor, and wildlife refuge measures. Congress responded by recessing rather than adjourning for vacations, and by designating officers in each chamber to receive suspensory veto messages from the president, thus attempting to retain the ordinary veto and prevent the president from exercising the pocket veto. The Senate majority leader, as a further precaution, would wait until the Senate returned from short vacations before sending down bills to the president for his consideration. In August 1974, a U.S. Court of Appeals decision barred the president's use of the pocket veto during congressional recesses, provided an officer was appointed by the chamber to receive a suspensory veto message.[74] In 1976 Attorney General Edward Levi announced a new Ford administration policy; pocket vetoes would be used only for the period after the final adjournment of Congress at the end of its second session, and not during the vacation adjournments or for the period between the sessions of Congress.[75] Courts and Congress had combined to limit the misuse of prerogative government.

The Constitution provides that the suspensory and pocket veto provisions apply to "every order, resolution, or vote to which the concurrence of the Senate or House of Representatives may be necessary." But Congress has construed this presidential check on its actions narrowly. The president cannot veto constitutional amendments proposed by both Houses of Congress, nor must he sign them.[76] Although he may veto joint resolutions of Congress with the force of law, he does not veto concurrent resolutions of both chambers, or simple resolutions passed by a single chamber. (In theory such resolutions do not have binding force, but in practice Congress has used them either to institute or to prohibit activities involving reorganization, war powers, and the budget process.) The president cannot veto measures of the House or Senate that deal with internal organization, such as election of officers, assignments of members to committees, or establishment of rules. He may veto laws passed by Congress that deal with legislative reorganization, but under the principle of comity he gives his approval.

The veto power is employed as part of an action-forcing process involving review of enrolled bills. After presentation of every measure passed by Congress, the president has ten days to decide whether to sign the bill or exercise other options. White House aides, advisory councils, the OMB, the departments, legislative leaders, and lobbyists all offer advice to the president. The classic conflict is usually between a cabinet member who wants the president to sign a bill and the OMB or members of the staff who urge a veto. When the OMB urges the president to sign, he will almost always do so: between 1953 and 1960 Eisenhower approved 99 percent of the bills recommended by the Bureau of the Budget, and figures were also high in later administrations.[77] When the OMB recommends a veto, the picture is mixed. Eisenhower followed the BOB recommendation three-quarters of the time, while Johnson signed twenty-seven of sixty-two bills the Bureau wanted him to veto.[78] Nixon and Ford often faced situations in which the OMB urged a veto and other agencies and advisors urged them to sign—often the president sided with the departments and went against the OMB recommendation.[79]

The president and his advisors make the decisions on the key bills, but for the thousand or so other measures that reach his desk each year, the president must rely on staff work. In the 1930s the Bureau of the Budget began to submit "briefs" on bills that flooded the White House at the end of the session that were subject to the pocket veto. Gradually the Bureau assumed responsibility of preparing memoranda for bills during the session, and worked up drafts of messages approving or disapproving minor bills. By 1960 the Bureau was given responsibility to comment on all enrolled legislation within five days of its presentation to the White House.[80] In the 1970s the OMB maintained its role for low-level measures, but faced competition from the Domestic Council and other White House agencies in advising the president on more important bills. In determining whether to sign or veto measures, presidents obtain advice from every unit of the institutionalized presidency rather than simply from the OMB and its Legislative Reference Division.

The president uses the OMB, the Domestic Staff, and the other units of his office to intervene with a veto threat early in the legislative process, when committees are marking up administration measures. Timely warnings by the White House may induce committees to compromise with White House representatives. The negotiations involve calculations on the part of all participants about the likelihood that the president will actually employ the veto; it is said that Franklin Roosevelt occasionally asked his aides to find him "something I can veto" just to impress on Congress that he had the power to frustrate members bills. The actual use of the veto is often not a demonstration of presidential strength, but an indication that White House influence in Congress has eroded and the system of bargaining and accommodation has broken down.

The veto is always a credible weapon. The president must obtain the votes of only one-third of a *quorum* of a single chamber to defeat an override attempt.[81] Only about 4 percent of presidential vetoes have been overridden. But sometimes presidents lose on those issues that matter to them the most. Andrew Johnson's vetoes of civil rights, reconstruction, and tenure of office acts were overridden by a Congress determined to control postwar policies. Truman's vetoes of the Taft-Hartley labor law, McCarran immigration law, and internal security measures were overridden by a conservative coalition and constituted severe defeats for the Fair Deal president. Nixon's vetoes of curbs on presidential war-making were overridden. Ford's vetoes of education and health measures were overturned, and Congress twice voted to end military aid to Turkey over his veto in a significant rebuff to his conduct of foreign policy.

Conflict between the branches leads to proposals for constitutional amendments to strengthen or weaken the veto power. After Andrew Jackson frustrated the Whig economic program, the Whigs proposed to abolish the veto by constitutional amendment. After Tyler vetoed a bank bill, the Whigs proposed an amendment that would permit a majority in each house to override, in effect nullifying the veto. Following the im-

PRESIDENTIAL VETOES		
PRESIDENT	TOTAL VETOES	OVERRIDDEN
Washington	2	–
Adams	–	–
Jefferson	–	–
Madison	7	–
Monroe	1	–
Adams	–	–
Jackson	12	–
Van Buren	–	–
Harrison	–	–
Tyler	10	1
Polk	3	–
Taylor	–	–
Fillmore	–	–
Pierce	9	5
Buchanan	7	–
Lincoln	6	–
Johnson	29	15
Grant	93	4
Hayes	13	1
Garfield	–	–
Arthur	12	1
Cleveland	413	2
Harrison	44	1
Cleveland	170	5
McKinley	42	–
Roosevelt	82	1
Taft	39	1
Wilson	44	6
Harding	6	–
Coolidge	50	4
Hoover	37	3
Roosevelt	635	9
Truman	250	12
Eisenhower	181	2
Kennedy	21	–
Johnson	30	–
Nixon	43	6
Ford	66	12
Carter (through 9/1/78)	3	–

SOURCE: *Presidential Vetoes: 1789–1961* (Washington, D.C., U.S. Government Printing Office, 1961) p. iv.; *Congressional Quarterly Alamanc*, 1976, p. 28.

peachment and acquittal of Andrew Johnson, "presidentialists" suggested strengthening the veto in order to restore the prestige of the office. President Hayes, beset by "riders" attached to appropriations measures, recommended a constitutional amendment that would give him an item veto on appropriations, and between 1877 and 1888 several such amendments were introduced in Congress but never passed. Eisenhower also proposed an item veto in his 1959 budget message. But the item veto would strike at the heart of the system of transactions and payoffs that form the core of the legislative process. If the president could strike out specific provisions of laws or appropriations, no one in Congress could be sure that deals made with party or committee leaders would bring him benefits—especially if the president were not party to the arrangements. Committees would lose influence in the distributive process, and their leaders would lose power in the chamber. If the president exercised his item veto to strike out particular projects, members might think he was doing so for the benefit of some party or committee leader, and there would be charges of bad faith and double-cross in the chamber. What makes good sense to the president on fiscal grounds runs counter to the logic and politics of Congress. It is unlikely that proposals to strengthen the veto power will be adopted.

VI

The Reform Agenda

There are two schools of thought about making the president a more effective legislative leader: one suggests that a responsible party system be instituted; the other emphasizes modifications of the legislative process to speed consideration of the presidential program. Some reforms of the legislative process have been instituted. Although there is still no "executive calendar" in each chamber, reforms make it likely that some version of administrative bills can be brought to a vote in each chamber.

In the House, the problem for the president for many years involved the power of the Rules Committee. At one time an arm of the Speaker, the committee became autonomous after the 1911 reforms. After the Second World War it was dominated by conservatives who could kill measures reported to it by standing committees by refusing to grant a "rule" for floor debate. In 1960, after Kennedy was nominated by the Democrats, Congress reconvened at his urging to consider the Democratic convention program, including aid to education, extension of the minimum wage, and medicare. The Rules Committee blocked consideration of some of these measures, so Kennedy's election strategy of forcing Republicans to vote on these bills was frustrated. Once president, Kennedy encouraged Democratic liberals and party leaders in Congress to enlarge the committee to add members that would end conservative domination. By working closely with Speaker Rayburn, the administration won a vote adding three new members, which had the effect of unblocking the New Frontier legislative program. In 1975 the Democratic caucus gave Democratic Speakers the right to nominate members to the committee, in effect converting it into an arm of the leadership. The president, if a Democrat, can work with the Speaker to obtain the rule he wants for debate on his measures, which is the next best thing to obtaining an executive calendar.

In the Senate the problem for the president has been the filibuster. The tradition of unlimited debate may tie up the chamber for days or weeks. It was used to protect regional interests, especially southern concerns about race, and enabled the South to delay or kill civil rights legislation for decades. But it has also been used by liberals: in 1962 against the COMSAT bill for a corporation to develop space communications, and in 1977 against the Carter energy program. The filibuster is a formidable weapon, but debate may be ended under rule 22, instituted in 1917, which provides that a cloture motion may be passed. Until 1975 passage required two-thirds of the members present; since that time three-fifths of the entire Senate, sixty members, has been required.[82] The vice-president presides over the Senate and may make parliamentary rulings that favor the administration. In recent years presidents have defeated filibusters on many important issues, including the COMSAT bill of 1962, the Civil Rights Act of 1964, the Voting Rights Act of 1965, the Civil Rights Act of 1968, and the U.S.-Soviet Arms Agreement of 1972. After being defeated in 1977 by a filibuster of a measure to provide for public financing of Senate election campaigns, the Carter administration determined to weaken the filibuster still further. Vice-President Mondale made certain parliamentary rulings that led to a cloture vote. The irony was that cloture having been achieved, the Senate could then proceed to pass an energy bill that represented a substantial setback for the administration. But the principle had been won and the signal given that the administration was determined to continue the assault on the filibuster as a weapon to prevent consideration of the White House program.

The major procedural changes currently in progress involve strengthening of the checks and balances system through passage of various measures that provide for an ordered confrontation between the two branches.[83] Congress has created various action-forcing processes that require the president to submit a program and that set a deadline for various kinds of congressional responses. Several of these laws will be considered in succeeding chapters. They fit into the constitutional and political logic of the American system. The administration must present a program, work closely with party and committee leaders, and obtain majority support in the chambers. The processes created provide for an exchange of information and viewpoints as a prelude to bargaining and completion of transactions. They do not threaten the power of legislators in the distributive process. They require that actions be taken in specified time periods, ending the deadlock or inconclusive results that may plague an administration. They minimize the president's inclination and ability to act unilaterally through instituting prerogative government. Most important, operation of these processes does not require changes in the electoral process or a restructuring of the existing decentralized party system. The autonomy of Congress is maintained and strengthened, and with it the probability that the legislature can function effectively as a coordinate branch of government.

Administrative Powers

PRESIDENTS assume, in the words of Franklin Roosevelt, that "the Presidency was established as a single strong Chief Executive in which was vested the entire executive power of the National Government."[1] But this claim of plenary constitutional authority is not accepted by Congress, the judiciary, or the career officials of the executive branch. Arthur Schlesinger, a historian of the presidency and aide to President Kennedy, described what faced Kennedy's New Frontiersmen:

The presidential government, coming to Washington aglow with new ideas and a euphoric sense that it could do no wrong, promptly collided with the feudal barons of the permanent government, entrenched in their domains and fortified by their sense of proprietorship; and the permanent government, confronted by this invasion, began almost to function . . . as a resistance movement.[2]

After another invasion, this one by Nixon loyalists, political scientists found "a social service bureaucracy dominated by administrators ideologically hostile to many of the directions of the Nixon administration in the realm of social policy.[3] Presidents always face the problem that Franklin Roosevelt complained of:

The Treasury is so large and far-flung and ingrained in its practices that I find it is almost impossible to get the action and results that I want. . . . But the Treasury is not to be compared with the State Department. You should go through the experience of trying to get any changes in the thinking, policy and action of the career diplomats and then you'd know what a real problem was. But the Treasury and the State Department put together are nothing compared with the Na-a-vy.[4]

I

The Chain of Command

Presidents wish to establish a chain of command running from the White House through the department secretaries to their subordinates. In 1937 the Brownlow commission recommended the establishment of an Executive Office of the President for just such a purpose, and Roosevelt won approval from Congress for this unit in 1939. The 1949 Hoover commission (led by former president Herbert Hoover) called for measures instituting "a clear line of control from the President to these departments and agency heads and from them to their subordinates . . . cutting through the barriers that have in many cases made bureaus and agencies practically independent of the chief executive."[5] After a second Hoover commission (for Eisenhower), a Heineman task force (for Johnson), an Ash council (for Nixon), and a set of task force reports (for Carter) the reformers have no more succeeded in establishing that line of control than they did in 1949. Harry Truman, who received Hoover's recommendations, several years later contemplated his successor's fate: "He will sit here and he'll say, 'Do this! Do that!' And nothing will happen. Poor Ike—it won't be a bit like the Army!"[6]

It is neither possible nor desirable for the president to personally superintend every department and agency or the dozens of independent agencies, boards, commissions, and public corporations established outside the department structure. There are several hundred bureaus within the departments, each responsible for several programs, and no president can know enough about the activities of most of them to superintend their affairs. It takes a few weeks for a new administration to learn how to intervene in the affairs of a bureau; it may take a few years for the president to know enough to stay out of them.

A presidential chain of command may not always be in the national interest. During the Watergate crisis, to ensure that President Nixon ordered no domestic or foreign military operations outside established procedures, the secretary of defense and chairman of the Joint Chiefs of Staff instituted a command-control procedure (based on the statute creating the National Security Council) that required the president to pass all commands to the military through the secretary of defense. Secretary James Schlesinger later explained, "In keeping with my statutory responsibilities, I did assure myself that there would be no question about the proper constitutional and legislated chain of command, and there never was any question."[7] Should Schlesinger have established a "presidential" rather than a legislated chain of command had the president so ordered? Had Schlesinger relayed military orders that were illegal or unconstitutional on their face, should military commanders have obeyed them? One answer is provided by convicted Watergate conspirator Gordon Liddy, who upon being released from prison reaffirmed his commitment to the principle that "when the prince approaches the lieutenant, the proper response of the lieutenant to the prince is 'Fiat voluntas tua'—Thy will be done."[8]

Clearly situations can be imagined in which no prince or president should be obeyed by a subordinate: insanity, treason, criminal conspiracy, or subversion of the Constitution. Officials must pay more than lip service to the Nuremberg principle: following orders from a higher authority does not constitute a defense in a criminal prosecution for commission of an unlawful or unconstitutional act. Such situations stand at one extreme, but they are reminders of the limits one must place on the "chain of command" doctrine.

The Constitutional Framework

The Constitution confers neither the title nor the plenary authority of "chief executive" on the president. Article II grants the incumbent "The Executive Power of the United States," but no agreement exists on the meaning of these words. Following Hamilton and other "presidentialists" at the Constitutional Convention, most presidents claim power to superintend the departments on the basis of those opening words and their duty to take care that the laws be faithfully executed. "Congressionalists" take the phrase as a general term comprehending no more than the few and limited powers specifically enumerated in Article II. They argue that the "faithful execution of the laws" phrase should be read as an injunction against substituting presidential authority for legislative intent; it may narrow rather than broaden the meaning of "The Executive Power." The president "may require the opinion in writing" of department heads on the conduct of department business; read in conjunction with "The Executive Power" it implies the president's control over department business. But viewed through the doctrine of exclusion, the very limited grants of executive authority that are expressly enumerated imply the framers' decision to reserve the power to superintend departments to Congress under its various Article I powers of legislation, appropriation, and organization.[9]

The conflict between president and Congress over authority to superintend the departments has never been settled. Presidents assume that any power or responsibilities delegated by Congress to departments or bureaus become part of the president's authority and are subsumed under "The Executive Power" and the president's duty to execute the laws faithfully.[10] Congress assumes that when it delegates power directly to an official in an agency the president will keep his nose out of the business. The courts sometimes uphold Congress. Justice Oliver Wendell Holmes noted: "The duty of the President to see that the laws be executed is a duty that does not go beyond the laws or require him to achieve more than Congress sees fit to leave within his power."[11] Courts have ruled that officials charged by Congress, through laws, appropriations, and resolution, with taking certain actions, must obey these directions rather than presidential orders if the two conflict.[12] There seem to be two constitutionally established "chains of command," and the doctrine of coordinate powers makes it clear that neither Congress nor the president needs to subordinate its authority to the other branch.

Organizing the Executive

The power to organize and reorganize departments, including the Executive Office of the president, is assigned Congress under the "necessary and proper" clause of Article I. The legislature may exercise these powers or delegate them to the president through a law granting him authority to create or reorganize agencies. In wartime emergencies, Congress passes statutes that give the president power to create, reorganize, or even abolish agencies, subject to certain legislative restrictions.[13]

Existing statutes often provide the president with enough authority to create an agency without specific statutory approval. In 1971, when Nixon instituted a system of price controls, existing laws permitted assignment of responsibility for those controls to the Office of Emergency Preparedness. The General Services Administration provided office space, the Civil Service Commission transferred personnel from existing agencies, and the Internal Revenue Service and Agricultural Stabilization and Conservation Service provided branch offices to operate the program in the field. In the space of a few weeks a complete government "agency" had been created. All Nixon had needed to do was appoint a few top officials to set policy.

For routine organizational changes Congress passes reorganization acts. These normally provide (1) that presidentially proposed reorganization plans go into effect (2) if neither chamber of Congress disapproves by resolution within a specified period of time, usually sixty days.[14] Between 1939 and 1973, of 105 such plans submitted to Congress only 23 were disapproved: Truman gained 32 of 48; Eisenhower 14 of 17; Kennedy 6 of 10; Johnson 17 of 17; and Nixon 8 of 8. But in 1973, as part of the reaction against Watergate, the Democratic Congress refused to extend the reorganization authority and let the law lapse.[15] In 1977, with a Democratic president committed to major reorganization in power, the Democratic Congress passed a new reorganization act. It permitted the president to submit plans for individual agencies and departments, but allowed no "omnibus" plans for complete executive branch reorganization. Unlike the 1971 version, the 1977 act withheld permission for the president to propose creation or abolition of agencies, or termination of any statutory functions.[16]

To create new departments or agencies or to increase or decrease their authority, the president must submit legislative proposals to Congress. These are often defeated, as were Truman's planned Department of Welfare, Kennedy's proposed Department of Urban Affairs, Johnson's hybrid Department of Commerce and Labor, and Nixon's ingenious amalgamation of six departments into four. Carter's plan for a Department of Energy was substantially modified by Congress, which reduced the powers of the secretary of energy. Some units of the Executive Office of the President are created by executive order of the president based on his "Executive Power," and he organizes or reorganizes the White House office (consisting of his immediate aides) as he sees fit, since Congress approves these reorganization acts that he proposes as a matter of comity between branches. Other presidential agencies in the Executive Office of the President are created by statute, based on the "necessary and proper" clause of Article I; still others are created (or abolished) by reorganization plans. In addition, all sorts of temporary units are created by executive order and paid for out of the "unanticipated needs" appropriations granted to the White House: in recent years these have included the Presidential Clemency Board (to pardon Vietnam draft evaders or deserters); the Rockefeller Commission on the Central Intelligence Agency; and various task forces.

In the late 1970s Congress began considering proposals to create a "sunset" process in which (1) all federal agencies would be grouped by function, and each year Congress would conduct a full-scale review of a set of agencies so grouped; (2) congressional committees would conduct a "systematic evaluation . . . to determine if the merits of the program justify its continuation rather than termination"; (3) committees would evaluate spending and determine if agency goals had been achieved; and (4) would recommend elimination, consolidation, or reorganization of existing programs.[17] The General Accounting Office, Congressional Research Service, and Congressional Budget Office would aid committees in their work. Such program review would be required prior to passage of new budget authority or appropriations for the set of agencies whose turn it was to be examined. The Carter administration has gone on record in support of such a system, but most cabinet secretaries have found reasons why their own departments should be exempted from the process. Whether or not such a "sunset" bill passes Congress, it is symptomatic of the continued congressional involvement in executive branch reorganization. The bill providing for a Department of Energy passed the House with its own "sunset" provision limiting it to a five-year existence, but the provision was eventually dropped in the Senate. In recent years Congress has normally limited the authority of agencies to two- or five-year periods, which requires a full-scale congressional review prior to renewal of the authorization.[18]

Congress breaks into the "chain of command" of the departments and agencies it establishes. It specifies the authority of the departmental officials and may grant some autonomy to the bureaus. It may create independent agencies and commissions outside the departmental structure, whose autonomous status makes them "independent" of presidential supervision. It may establish public corporations and quasi-public corporations with independent boards of directors.

Congress may also specify the powers and duties of specific officials in the departments and bureaus. Presidents would prefer laws delegating such authority to them, because they desire maximum flexibility to assign responsibilities to subordinates, under the provisions of the Presidential Subdelegation Act of 1950.[19] But Congress often disregards the president and vests authority directly with departments and bureaus. Moreover, Congress vests state and local officials (or private-sector contractors) with primary operational responsibility to provide goods and services to the public under programs such as general revenue-sharing and the hundreds of categoric intergovernmental grant programs. State and local officials and private contractors are required to follow the provisions of the law, and they may challenge any administration policies in the courts if they believe them to be at variance with congressional intent or their own interpretation. Nothing limits the resourcefulness of legislators and their allies at the state and local level when they wish to insulate programs from administration control.[20]

In crisis situations, however, Congress grants the president what amounts to plenary authority over the bureaucracy.[21] Approximately 470 statutes passed over the years provided that "in case of emergency" or "in extreme emergency" or "in a state of public peril," each to be declared by the president, the administration may take extraordinary actions by executive order. Such delegations of legislative authority permit the president to control the economy in wartime by allocating the civilian labor force, detaining security risks, controlling imports and exports, rationing consumer goods, allocating industrial materials, regulating labor relations, seizing plants for war production, controlling excess profits, allocating credit, administering wage and price controls, supervising currency and banking institutions, imposing censorship, and controlling internal and international communications. Most such laws also provided that, by concurrent resolution, not subject to presidential veto, Congress could terminate a state of emergency. In 1976 the National Emergencies Act terminated four existing states of emergency, provided for the abolition of most emergency statutes, and created new procedures for delegating legislative power to the president in crises. The president could henceforth declare a state of emergency that would run for a year and could be renewed if the president provided Congress with ninety days' notice. Every six months Congress must vote to continue the state of emergency. The law also provided that a majority vote of the House and Senate through concurrent resolution could end a state of emergency.[22]

Staffing the Executive Branch

The president nominates and, by and with the advice and consent of the Senate, appoints civil and military officers. Congress may by law provide for the appointment of inferior officers, not all of which require Senate approval. The legislature has provided since passage of the Civil Service Act of 1883 for a Civil Service of career officials. Most of the approximately 2.8 million federal employees in the Competitive Service are hired, assigned, and promoted by departments and agencies under the general supervision of the Civil Service Commission (CSC). Most perform routine clerical or administrative tasks, but there are several categories of high-ranking civil servants with which an administration must work.[23] These include the following:

1. Competitive supergrades, consisting of approximately four thousand senior administrators operating at the top levels of the bureaus, regional offices, and field offices
2. P.L. 313 supergrades, consisting of scientific, technical, and professional officers performing specialized support functions in various departments and agencies
3. Supergrades in separate personnel systems, including the Foreign Service, Public Health Service, Atomic Energy Commission, and Tennessee Valley Authority

These are the officials of the "permanent government." They provide the government with expertise, experience, intelligence, and an "institutional memory" of what has worked in the past.

To work with these officials an administration may appoint officials from the "Excepted Service" of the Civil Service, so named because appointments are made without the use of competitive examinations. Approximately sixteen hundred such appointments are divided into two categories. Non-career appointments at supergrade levels (GS 16, 17, 18) are permitted under Executive Order 11315, and defined as positions "in which an incumbent is deeply involved in the advocacy of administration programs and support of their controversial aspects, participates significantly in the determination of major political policies of the Administration, or serves principally as personal assistant to or advisor of a presidential appointee or other key political figure." Many of the "in-and-outers" from the business and academic worlds who serve cabinet- and subcabinet-level officials in staff positions are given these appointments. Schedule C supergrade appointments (GS 16, 17, 18) are made by the president from the career service on a noncompetitive basis. The same executive order describes them as "positions of a confidential or policy determining character which are excepted from the competitive service to which appointments may be made without examination by the Commissioner."[24] There are approximately five hundred noncareer, 450 P.L. 313, and eleven hundred Schedule C appointments, which the president may make. The president relies on the expertise and experience of these administration officials and uses them to supervise the work of the career supergrade officials who manage the bureaus.

At the highest level, the president appoints without Senate consent approximately sixty White House aides with important responsibilities. He also appoints, with the advice and consent of the Senate, his choices for "Executive Level" positions: eight hundred or more secretaries, undersecretaries, deputy secretaries, and assistant secretaries of the departments, and the administrators and deputies for various independent agencies.[25] These eight hundred officials constitute "the administration," which exercises in the president's name both the constitutional power that he claims to superintend the departments and the legal authority that Congress delegates to them.

By law Congress determines whether a position falls under the competitive or noncompetitive service or is an "Executive Level" position requiring Senate confirmation. About three-fourths of the supergrade positions have been created by statute rather than by decision of the Civil Service Commission. Thus Congress, not the administration, to a large extent has determined the staffing patterns at the highest levels of the administration. In addition, approximately half the "excepted" positions in the Civil Service have been created by law rather than by the Civil Service Commission.[26] In short, Congress makes the final decision on whether political appointees or careerists control programs in the bureaus. By law Congress determines if a position requires the confirmation of the Senate. While it never required such confirmation for the director of the Bureau of the Budget, it amended the Budget and Accounting Act in 1974 to require that the Senate consent to the nominations of both the director and the deputy director of the Office of Management and Budget.[27]

Customarily the Senate follows a rule of comity in dealing with presidential nominees for executive-level positions. It allows the president to pick persons whom he wants and who have views compatible with his own, even when an antiadministration majority controls the chamber. Usually the Senate restricts itself by considering the "fitness" of the nominee (and possible conflicts of interest) rather than his politics.[28] But the Senate sometimes uses its power to give or withhold consent to presidential nominations to affect policymaking in the departments. It may delay confirmation by holding lengthy hearings to express its concern about the policy implications of a nomination. The committee may reach an "understanding" with the president as the price for clearing a nomination for a floor vote. For example, the independence of the special prosecutor conducting the Watergate investigations was at issue in the confirmation hearings for Attorney General Elliot Richardson. The senators and Richardson reached an agreement, approved by Nixon, to protect Prosecutor Archibald Cox from any interference with his duties. Nixon's subsequent order to Richardson to remove Cox led the attorney general to resign rather than dishonor his commitment to the Senate.

A close vote on confirmation may serve as a signal to the administration to proceed cautiously. The nomination of Paul Warnke as chief arms negotiator for the Carter administration was approved only after he had moderated his views on the strategy for negotiating an arms control agreement with the Soviet Union. As part of the "price" paid for confirmation, Carter assured the senators that the negotiating team at the arms talks would include a representative of the Joint Chiefs of Staff; later the president promised to keep the Senate "fully and currently informed" on all negotiations. Even so, the forty votes mustered against the nominee were a warning to the administration that a treaty with the Soviet Union might be defeated in the Senate unless it were acceptable to the "hawks" of the chamber.

The Senate cannot, under the Constitution, attach formal conditions to the consent it gives to presidential nominations. It may not instruct the nominee in his performance of his duties if confirmed. It may not attach reservations to its confirmation resolution. In this respect the power of advice and consent differs from the apparently similar power of advice and consent to treaties. The Senate may revise the draft of a treaty to which it gives its consent through amendments, or attach reservations to its resolution interpreting the obligations of the United States. But through its power to confirm or deny nominations, the Senate in fact attaches conditions to some nominations, which though not legally binding, are politically binding.

But it should be emphasized that most of the time the Senate takes pro forma actions on nominations. Of the fifty most significant Carter appointments, only one was withdrawn (Theodore Sorensen for the CIA), and only ten hearings on nominees lasted more than one day. There was little debate on most nominations in committees or the Senate, and there were recorded votes in the Senate for only six nominees. David Cohen, the president of Common Cause, charged that "the Senate confirmation process is a rubber-stamp machine with almost no serious attention given by senators to their constitutional responsibilities."[29]

The president may exploit a loophole in the law that prohibits an official from serving more than thirty days in an executive-level position without obtaining the consent of the Senate. Some officials have served in "acting" capacities for considerably longer periods: Nixon's choice for FBI Director, L. Patrick Gray, served for nine months before Nixon nominated him and Senate consideration could begin. Such a delay is a clear violation of the Vacancies in Executive Departments Act of 1868. But the act may not cover a situation in which a subordinate official whose appointment had been consented to by the Senate is appointed by the president to serve at a higher level in an "acting" capacity. Carter allowed Associate Director of OMB James McIntyre to serve for several months as acting director (after Bert Lance resigned) without sending his nomination to the Senate. Eventually, after Carter had satisfied himself that McIntyre could do the job, he sent the nomination to the Senate, and the official was confirmed. The use of this loophole may occur in the last months of a "lame-duck" administration as high-level officials return to private life and their subordinates carry on until the very end.

Nowhere does the Constitution expressly grant the president the power to remove senior civil officers. Andrew Jackson and Andrew Johnson fought the battles with Congress establishing the presidential prerogative to remove cabinet secretaries based on "The Executive Power" and "the faithful execution of the laws." But Congress and the careerists were never totally defeated. The president may dismiss career officials only for cause (i.e., misconduct, delinquency, inefficiency, disability, or criminal conduct), but he may transfer them, reassign them, or even demote them, subject to civil service regulations and the laws. The president may remove noncareer civil servants and reassign careerists in Schedule C positions. He has only the most limited powers of removal when dealing with regulatory agencies or commissions, or public corporations, and he cannot remove officials of these bodies for policy disagreements with his administration.[30] Congress by law provides for the removal of such officials. It may vest removal power with a board of directors or with the president, or it may exercise the power itself by concurrent resolution not subject to the veto power of the president.

The president's removal powers are often exercised as part of a set of transactions with state officials or members of Congress. Harold Seidman, a senior official with the Bureau of the Budget, has observed, "Probably more executive branch officials have been fired or reassigned as a result of pressure from the Congress than by the President."[31] As part of its price for support of antipoverty legislation, the North Carolina congressional delegation forced Lyndon Johnson to remove Adam Yarmolinsky from the task force planning the antipoverty program, and thus prevented him from becoming an official of the agency once it was established. Senator Jackson held a virtual "veto" over the composition of the delegation to the Strategic Arms Limitations Talks of 1972–73.[32]

II

The Triple Alliance

Career officials have their own policies to promote. These may place them in conflict with the administration and its political executives. Some bureau chiefs and program managers have spent twenty years or more working their way up the ladder, usually in one agency (especially after reaching the GS-13, middle-management level), and are strong advocates of their programs. By the time they reach the top they are likely to have spent between seventeen and twenty-five years in a single agency, making them fierce loyalists.[33] They are likely to be incrementalists, interested in preserving agency routines and standard operating procedures, and working within the repertoire of programs and techniques they have developed over the years.[34] They seek to preserve the mission of their agency, to serve its constituencies, and to maintain control and jurisdiction over its policy domain.

Congressional committee leaders similarly have spent many years working up the seniority ladder. Like the careerists, they view themselves as experts. Often they may have been instrumental in writing the statutes under which programs operate; in such cases as the "Fulbright" scholarship program they have even established programs named after them. Both careerists and legislators regard government service as their career; by contrast, many political executives, from business, law, and academia, regard service as temporary. Both lawmakers and careerists have similar educational and social backgrounds: both think similarly about public issues and use similar methods of analysis and conceptualization. No significant differences in liberalism and conservatism are apparent between the two groups.[35] Both work closely with lobbyists representing interest groups that benefit from programs. A resultant "triple alliance" of careerists, legislators, and lobbyists engages in transactions that directly affect the way programs are run:

1. *Bureau-interest group*: Interest groups want to write guidelines for programs, gain formal access to officials by instituting advisory committees, and win formal or informal vetoes over agency decisions. They expect to staff some noncareer positions at the top levels of the bureaus. Careerists expect interest groups that benefit from their programs to testify favorably at congressional committee hearings and to lobby at the department level for additional funds for the program.
2. *Bureau-committee*: Careerists want statutory language giving them maximum authority and discretion, expanding their jurisdiction, and funding more missions. They want better facilities, more personnel, and "grade-creep" (promotions for career personnel and more positions allocated to high civil service categories). Committee members want special treatment

for their constituencies and for interest groups. They want to influence the distribution of goods, services, patronage, and contracts.

3. *Committee-group*: Committee members want campaign contributions, help in their election campaigns, and honoraria for speeches. They rely on expertise of lobbyists in writing laws. Interest groups expect members of committees to provide them with formal and informal access to the bureaus and funds for programs that benefit them. They expect committee members to help them win the nomination of group members by the president to the department level.[36]

The president must confront this triple alliance (sometimes referred to as the "permanent government" or "subgovernment") when he attempts to institute a chain of command from the departmental to the bureau level.

Congressional Oversight

Congress has created by laws and by precedent a set of procedures that enable it to superintend the bureaucracy. Oversight is authorized by a provision of the Legislation Reorganization Act of 1946 requiring committees to "exercise continuous watchfulness of the execution by the administrative agencies concerned of any laws, the subject matter of which is within the jurisdiction of such committee."[37] For many years after passage of this provision, oversight was not a major function of committee members, who were more concerned with passing new laws than in implementing existing ones. But with the expansion of the intergovernmental grant and contract programs in the 1960s and the bloc grant programs in the 1970s, pressures from interest groups and state and local officials combined to encourage increased legislative oversight of bureaus providing goods and services in the congressional districts.

As the political stakes involved in oversight increased for members of Congress, they provided new resources to aid them in their responsibilities. The Legislative Reorganization Act of 1970 provided additional staffing for committees and funds to retain outside experts. It also increased the resources of the General Accounting Office and empowered it to make program evaluations:

The Comptroller General shall review and analyze the results of Government programs and activities carried on under existing law, including the making of cost benefit studies, when ordered by either House of Congress, or upon his own initiative, of when requested by any committee of the House of Representatives or the Senate, or any Committee of the two Houses, having jurisdiction over such programs and activities.[38]

The GAO hired economists, systems analysts, engineers, and management consultants to conduct these analyses. Approximately twelve hundred of the twenty-seven hundred professional staff members audit and evaluate Department of Defense programs, in spite of that department's strong opposition to congressional evaluation of weapons systems. In recent years the GAO has conducted major cost-benefit reviews of programs in the War on Poverty, the Agricultural Research Service, the Farmers Home Administration, the Smithsonian Institution, the Internal Revenue Service, the Occupational Health and Safety Administration, and the Nuclear Regulatory Commission. Sometimes Congress requires such a review as part of its renewal of authority for an agency or department. The 1970 Legislative Reorganization Act requires each agency to report promptly to the House and Senate Government Operations Committees actions taken with respect to any GAO recommendation made during such investigations.[39]

Standing committees and their subcommittees conduct routine oversight. The 1974 Committee Reform Amendments require each House committee to establish a separate oversight subcommittee. Increasingly, Congress renews agency authorizations for one-, two-, or five-year periods rather than permanently. Half the independent regulatory agencies must have Congress renew their authorizations periodically; so, too, must several of the independent corporations. At congressional hearings legislators may question officials "for the record" to get them to commit themselves to act (or discontinue acting) in certain ways. At times the careerists act in collusion with members of Congress, by feeding them information about agency activities, so they can put administration representatives on the spot and gain concessions or admissions from them in testimony. After hearings, the committee may "direct" or "suggest" that actions be taken in its report. Often understandings reached in hearings, or directives placed in reports, carry more weight with senior career officials (who frequently seek such directives) than the orders of the administration. The exchanges in hearings and the directives of the reports may also be used in the courts to clarify the "legislative history" of a law and the intent of Congress in passing it; thus interest groups can use the legislative history to challenge presidential orders that conflict with accommodations reached in the triple alliance.

Committee Clearance and Vetoes

Committees increasingly bind bureaus to themselves through statutory provisions that require officials to "come into agreement" with committee majorities prior to taking certain specified actions. In effect these provisions provide the committees with a formal "veto" over actions of the administration. The earliest known such provision was passed in 1895, giving the House Committee on Printing authority to approve the publication list of the public printer. Only a short step led from such "housekeeping" provisions to more substantive use of the veto. A typical example occurs in the Post Office Department Appropriations Act of 1971: it specifies that the locations of new postal facilities be approved by the

House and Senate Committees on Public Works.[40] In recent years the
Armed Services Committees have controlled the openings and closings
of military bases, the Public Works Committees have controlled contracts
for capital expenditures, the Interior Committees have controlled locations
of regional offices, the Post Office Committees have located postal buildings, the Agricultural Committees have approved various loan and grant
programs, all through similar veto systems. As another example, the Civil
Division of the Justice Department may engage private counsel to defend
former or present officials in lawsuits brought by private citizens alleging
violations of their civil rights only after the attorney general has obtained
the approval of the Senate and House Judiciary Committees.

Perhaps the most effective use of the veto was by the Joint Committee
on Atomic Energy (JCAE) in the 1950s. A provision of law required the
Atomic Energy Commission (AEC) to keep the JCAE "fully and currently informed" on its program of nuclear reactor development. In
effect that provision made the committee a "board of directors" that supervised the peaceful development of atomic energy. The committee
determined what technology would be advanced, the location of experimental facilities, and policies relating to the private development of
commercial power plants.[41]

Committee vetoes generally involve the distributive process. Even
more important are the "chamber vetoes," which may deal with major
administration policies. The chamber veto enables one house, by simple
resolution or both houses by concurrent resolution, to "veto" a proposed
action or terminate an existing state of affairs in the executive branch.
Such resolutions may override presidential impoundment of funds, or
end a presidential state of emergency. They can prevent agreement with
other nations to cooperate on nuclear development, prevent sale of nuclear
reactors abroad, and block arms sales to other nations. They can prevent
regulations from being implemented, such as auto-safety rules and
campaign finance regulations. Reorganization plans submitted by the
president and decisions of the Tariff Commission must also pass through
the "veto" process.[42] No complete count exists of these provisions, but the
Congressional Research Service discovered that between 1932 and 1975
Congress passed 196 such committee and chamber vetoes. Of these, 89
were passed between 1970 and 1975, including most of the important
chamber veto provisions.[43]

These vetoes are rarely used. Instead, their existence creates a bargaining situation between president and Congress. The Ford administration
proposed the sale of fighter aircraft to Egypt but never even made a
formal proposal (selling transport planes instead) because of the veto
system. Its proposed sale of missiles to Jordan ran into stiff opposition in
Congress, and the deal was withdrawn. Eventually the United States and
Jordan agreed on installation of missiles in fixed sites, which could be
used only for defensive purposes. The sale to Iran of advanced recon-

naissance aircraft equipped with the most sophisticated electronic equipment was withdrawn after congressional opposition; the sale was renegotiated, and the electronic equipment was not included in the second deal. While no arms sale has ever been vetoed, the existence of the provision has forced the administration to modify its proposals.

Presidents oppose both chamber and committee veto provisions. They claim that most of these provisions interfere with "The Executive Power." They argue that such provisions unconstitutionally delegate legislative authority away from the entire Congress to the chamber of one house or to committees. In effect, Congress passes a broadly worked law giving the president or departments discretion to act, then permits a chamber or a committee to fill in the details by overseeing officials through use of the veto. Since the chamber resolution or committee veto is not subject itself to a presidential signature or veto, it represents a way of bypassing the presidential veto in lawmaking and is therefore unconstitutional.

Sometimes presidents have vetoed bills containing the chamber or committee veto provision. Woodrow Wilson vetoed the first version of the Budget and Accounting Act in 1920 because it provided that the Comptroller of the General Accounting Office could be removed by concurrent resolution of Congress. Johnson and Ford vetoed several measures containing chamber vetoes. In vetoing the Foreign Assistance Act of 1976, Ford said that it would "seriously obstruct the exercise of the President's constitutional responsibilities for the conduct of foreign affairs."[44] Nixon vetoed the War Power Resolution containing a concurrent resolution provision that in his view interfered with his constitutional war powers. Carter lobbied successfully with the Senate to remove several chamber veto provisions from the bill establishing a Department of Energy and avoided the exercise of his veto.

But presidents have not taken a consistent position against either the chamber or committee veto system. Sometimes such a provision serves their purposes. Presidents have strongly supported various executive reorganization acts that delegate authority to them, even though their proposals must go through a chamber veto. They have pressed for emergency authority, even when it may be ended by concurrent resolution of Congress. Often the legislature attaches the chamber veto to a law simply to give itself ultimate jurisdiction, while at the same time delegating operational authority to the president (the case with the Tariff Commission). The chamber veto provision becomes a way to reassure reluctant members of Congress that the delegation of vast powers to the president is not unconditional. In conducting foreign relations several of the committee veto provisions may have their use: the State Department can always shift the onus on Congress for a refusal to provide allies with certain types of weapons they may seek or the sale of certain nuclear-reactor systems.

Presidents do not always veto laws with such provisions. Franklin

PREROGATIVE POWERS VS. THE LEGISLATIVE VETO

To the Congress of the United States:

In recent years, the Congress has strengthened its oversight of Executive Branch decisions. I welcome that effort. Unfortunately, there has been increasing use of one oversight device that can do more harm than good—the "legislative veto."

. . .

Such intrusive devices infringe on the Executive's constitutional duty to faithfully execute the laws. They also authorize congressional action that has the effect of legislation while denying the President the opportunity to exercise his veto. Legislative vetoes thereby circumvent the President's role in the legislative process established by Article I, Section 7 of the Constitution.

These are fundamental constitutional issues. The Attorney General is seeking a definitive judgment on them from the courts, but no immediate resolution is in prospect. Pending a decision by the Supreme Court, it is my view, and that of the Attorney General, that these legislative veto provisions are unconstitutional.

. . .

In sum, for both constitutional and policy reasons, I strongly oppose legislative vetoes over the execution of programs. The inclusion of such a provision in a bill will be an important factor in my decision to sign or to veto it.

I urge Congress to avoid including legislative veto provisions in legislation so that confrontation can be avoided. For areas where Congress feels special oversight of regulations or other actions is needed, I urge the adoption of "report and wait" provisions instead of legislative vetoes.

. . .

As for legislative vetoes over the execution of programs already described in legislation and in bills I must sign for other reasons, the Executive Branch will generally treat them as "report and wait" provisions. In such a case, if Congress subsequently adopts a resolution to veto an Executive action, we will give it serious consideration, but we will not, under our reading of the Constitution, consider it legally binding.

The desire for the legislative veto stems in part from Congress' mistrust of the Executive, due to the abuses of years past. Congress responded to those abuses by enacting constructive safeguards in such areas as war powers, and the budget process. The legislative veto, however, is an overreaction which increases conflict between the branches of government. We need, instead, to focus on the future. By working together we can restore trust and make the government more responsive and effective.

Jimmy Carter

The White House
June 21, 1978

Roosevelt signed the Lend-Lease Act and much wartime emergency legislation with chamber veto provisions. Eisenhower signed a defense reorganization act with provisions for committee vetoes. Nixon signed the Emergency Petroleum Allocation Act of 1973, and Ford the Presidential Recordings and Materials Preservation Act of 1974, both of which contained chamber veto provisions. Johnson, Nixon, and Ford also signed many laws with committee veto provisions; they did so because they believed these provisions to be insignificant, or because they needed the authority in the statutes and could not risk sending the measures back through the legislative process just to remove the veto provision.

Lawmakers defend veto provisions in several ways. They note that the oversight function is mandated in both the 1946 and 1970 Legislative Reorganization Acts, signed into law by presidents. Moreover, as the president may delegate his authority to subordinates, the veto system is a reasonable exercise of the parallel legislative power to delegate authority to committees or to one or both chambers. Congress has always had authority to pass laws requiring officials in bureaus to satisfy certain conditions prior to taking actions: at times these have included "come-into-agreement" provisions involving governors, state legislators, community planning boards, and even interest or clientele groups. Congress argues that the "committee veto" provision is simply another one of those requirements that an agency must satisfy before "The Executive Power" of the president can come into play. Are congressional committees, the argument goes, to deny themselves the same kind of "veto" that they routinely grant to state and local officials or private groups in dealing with national programs?

To defend chamber vetoes Congress argues that if it delegates vast legislative powers to the executive by majority vote, it should be able to take back these powers by the same majority vote. If the president could veto their "vetoes" lawmakers insist, it would take passage of a law, and then possibly an override of a presidential veto by a two-thirds vote, to remove what it had given to the president by a simple majority.

The Constitution does not restrict Congress to the exercise of legislative powers. Although all legislation must go to the president for signature or veto, not all acts of Congress are subject to the veto of the president. That is to say, acts of Congress are by no means limited to legislation and include Senate advice and consent to treaties and nominations, passage of proposed constitutional amendments, and passage of declarations of war —none of which involve the veto power. Nor is the impeachment power subject to the veto. Therefore, lawmakers argue, the mechanism by which powers that have been delegated to the president may later be removed from him need not be subject to the presidential veto. Nor must the committee veto be subject to a presidential veto to make it a constitutional exercise of congressional power.

In addition to the formal committee veto system, Congress has experimented with another technique that cuts into the presidential chain of command: the "no-appropriation" system. A substantive committee is given authority over future appropriations requests of an agency. Without agreement from the committee, the Appropriations Committee will not provide new funds for the bureau. Technically this system simply involves an agreement between two congressional committees and is not subject to presidential challenge on constitutional grounds. It may have the same function and effect as a formal committee veto measure.

Not all committee vetoes are written into law. Most of the time the "triple alliance" functions without using a formal committee veto, through what might be termed an "informal veto" system. Between 1975 and 1976, for example, the United States admitted 145,000 refugees from Indochina under the emergency parole authority of the attorney general. In practice such authority is never exercised on a large scale without the concurrence of Senate and House leaders. In 1976 the chairman of the House Judiciary Subcommittee on Immigration insisted that additional refugees be admitted by legislation rather than on the parole authority, and the Ford administration complied.

The effectiveness of the formal veto cannot be gauged by its actual use. It is written into law when the informal clearances no longer operate to the satisfaction of committee leaders. It is a sign that the bond between bureaus and committees has broken down. But the possibility that a committee can write such provisions into the statutes is always in the minds of officials in the bureaus, and makes it difficult for the president to induce them to follow his, rather than committee, priorities.

Reporting Requirements

In order to oversee the bureaucracies Congress must obtain information from them. It may ask the GAO to conduct an investigation, or insert reporting requirements in statutes. It may require that quarterly or annual reports be transmitted to specified committees or to the entire Congress.[45] It may require that proposals be sent to committees prior to implementation, a "report-and-wait" mechanism that enables Congress to block any decision through informal or formal veto provisions or through new legislation. The War Powers Resolution and the National Emergencies Act require the president to inform Congress under what combination of constitutional and statutory authority he bases his decisions to act. Similarly the president must report all executive agreements negotiated with other nations, all troop buildups, all impoundments, all fund transfers and reprogramming of funds over certain specified amounts, arms sales and reactor sales to other nations, contract renegotiations involving defense contractors, and Central Intelligence Agency covert operations. In some cases reports are public documents transmitted to the entire Congress; in other cases they are classified, transmitted to committees (like the Senate Select Committee on Intelligence), and may be made known to Congress or the public only after various complicated procedures involving votes of the legislative chamber.

Some reporting requirements are ineffective. Not all reports required by law are submitted, nor are all complete. Since many reports contain no meaningful information, they are not always read by members of committees or their staffs. Most reporting requirements have not been useful as mechanisms for effective oversight.[46] One conspicuous exception is the requirement that the administration keep the Senate Select Committee on Intelligence informed of covert operations. The resolution creating the committee not only referred to ongoing activities, but also mentioned "any significant anticipated activities."[47] The CIA Director reported orally to senators and briefed committee members on anticipated operations. But at the same time he urged that such reporting requirements be dropped to ensure the secrecy of covert operations. The committee, however, seemed satisfied that its briefings had enabled it to engage in effective oversight of agency operations.

Congressional Oversight Assessed

Although Congress's oversight role has increased in recent years, it should not be exaggerated. It is still intermittent, especially in the Senate, where members are spread too thin, serving on too many committees and subcommittees to develop expertise in agency operations. Most oversight still involves the distributive process rather than substantive issues. Bureaus may play a Senate committee off against its House counterpart, or play both off against the White House, to retain their freedom of action. Committees have a tendency to promote the interests of the bureau through the "triple alliance" rather than to oversee them effectively. Oversight is not continuous or effective, but one study concludes that it seems most likely to occur when (1) constituent interests are at stake; (2) issues are narrow and do not cross committee jurisdictional lines; (3) an important committee member takes a personal interest in the situation; (4) an official rubs a legislator the wrong way; (5) Democratic legislators can embarrass a Republican administration.[48] At times even the Republican minority, with the aid of the investigative media, can use committee hearings to put a Democratic administration on the defensive—the case in 1978 when Senators investigated an alleged cover-up and obstruction of justice in the Department of Justice relating to a former Republican U.S. attorney's investigation of political corruption in Philadelphia among Democratic officeholders.

III

The Presidential Perspective

In their election rhetoric many presidents run against "Washington," and each new incumbent pledges to clean up the "mess" left by his predecessor. Each intends to make government more efficient and responsive to the public, to cut its size and reduce the perquisites of the bureaucrats. As early as 1800 Jefferson made an issue of the power of careerists in campaigning against the Federalists, and in the 1830s Jackson and Van Buren capitalized on the sentiments of the public by introducing the spoils system and rotation in office rather than permanent tenure. In the 1880s and 1890s, successive presidents championed a permanent civil service as a reaction to the excesses of the spoils system. Theodore Roosevelt and William Taft encouraged the professionalization of the career service, and Republican presidents in the 1920s introduced management improvements to create a "businesslike" atmosphere in the bureaus.

More recently currents of social and political change have had an impact on the career service. The cold war led Truman and Eisenhower to institute "loyalty-security" programs to review the records of officials and recommend dismissals of individuals who were thought to be risks. In the 1960s Kennedy and Johnson emphasized citizen involvement in the running of intergovernmental grant programs through national advisory committees, community boards, and other decentralizing mechanisms. Programs to end racial discrimination in the federal service, stimulated by the civil rights movement, were instituted by the Civil Service Commission. In the 1970s Nixon, Ford, and Carter made an issue of bloated bureaucracy. Nixon reduced staffing in the departments by eighty thousand and Ford dropped close to one hundred thousand (although the size of independent agencies and commissions increased). Carter reminded officials that they were to serve rather than command the public, proposed sweeping new codes to prevent conflicts of interest, and issued well-publicized instructions to senior officials on the use and misuse of such perquisites of office as limousines. "I came to Washington with the promise, and the obligation, to help rebuild the faith of the American people in our Government," he told a news conference, adding that he wanted a government "that will be efficient, not mired in its own red tape; a Government that will respond to the needs of the American people and not be preoccupied with needs of its own."[49]

Well-publicized actions that affect the entire federal service provide useful themes for the president. He can make the careerists the whipping boys for the failure of his administration to solve problems, and he can play on the emotions of the public by appearing to take on the entrenched bureaucrats. He cannot gain the loyalty or cooperation of senior career officials, however, by attempting to whip them into line.

Manipulating the Career Service

The president must work with careerists. He needs their expertise and experience, and to obtain these things he must attempt to manipulate the career service so that officials sympathetic to his priorities are placed in command of programs. One method is to change job descriptions of positions from the career to the noncareer service. The altered descriptions must then be approved by the Civil Service Commission. The incoming assistant secretary for administration in each department works with personnel officials to write job descriptions for vacancies that allow assignment of particular officials known to be sympathetic to the administration. Favoritism in assigning careerists characterized the Nixon administration, even though at one point on the White House tapes Nixon was heard to explode, "We have no discipline in this bureaucracy. We never fire anybody. We never reprimand anybody. We never demote anybody. We always promote the sons-of-bitches that kick us in the ass."[50] Nixon assigned the Division of Executive Development and Labor Relations of OMB the task of "advising the President on the development of new programs to recruit, train, motivate, deploy, and evaluate the men and women who make up the top ranks of the civil service, in the broadest sense of that term."[51] Although this sounds straightforward, the kind of development Nixon had in mind is illustrated by the activities of the White House personnel office, which produced a "text" for personnel officials in the departments. The *Federal Political Personnel Manual*, authored by Frederick Malek, outlined ways in which the civil service system could be manipulated by the administration. Each department was to set up a personnel office headed by a special assistant to the secretary. This assistant would write job descriptions to fit particular individuals known to be sympathetic to the new administration. Other officials would receive transfers to undesirable locations, special assignments requiring travel, or trivial work.[52] The Nixon administration proposed to Congress that career executives be given positions at the discretion of the departmental or agency executive-level employees, but the House rejected this proposal. Nixon himself seems to have taken little part in the White House personnel operation or the work of the OMB; he generally merely approved their choices for management positions in the bureaus.

For some time the Civil Service Commission did not interfere with the activities of the administration. Ultimately, after Nixon had resigned, its Bureau of Executive Manpower fed documented information to the House Committee on the Post Office and Civil Service, which resulted in an investigation of the practices of the Nixon administration. When Ford

entered office, the commission pressured him to tighten up merit procedures, and the president exchanged letters with its chairman to the effect
that the civil service system would be strengthened. By October 1974, the
commission could require departments to report all new Schedule C
assignments to ensure that the noncompetitive appointments were made
only for positions exempted by the commission.[53]

But manipulation of the civil service system neither began nor ended
with Nixon. Presidents always reward careerists who loyally carry out
their programs. Carter proposed replacement of the Civil Service Commission with a "merit board" to protect employee rights, and a new
Office of Personnel Management that would supervise a Senior Executive
Service of supergrade officials. Careerists could be promoted to or removed from the service without the right of appeal, enabling the administration to staff the service with careerists of demonstrated loyalty.
Superiors could also award incentive bonuses to officials. These "reforms"
would enable the administration to fill top executive positions with
loyalists and end the secretive manipulation that had characterized prior
administrations.

The Bureaucratic Perspective

Careerists want the president's support. They resent his campaign
attacks on "bureaucracy" but applaud his acknowledgment of their
expertise and devotion to public service. They want him to recommend
pay raises and defend the "merit" system. They expect him to promote
careerists into the ranks of political executives, especially at the assistant
secretary levels. They expect that in each department the assistant secretary for administration (who handles personnel matters) will come from
their ranks. Foreign service officers pressure the administration to name
ambassadors from the service rather than from lists of "fat cat" contributors. Above all, careerists expect the president to support their budget
requests, grant them maximum autonomy in their operations, and protect
the missions of their bureaus. In all these expectations they are usually
disappointed.

To get what they want careerists use several strategies. The *organizational* strategy involves insulating the bureaus within the department or
making them autonomous agencies. The tiny Legal Services Division of
the Office of Economic Opportunity (OEO) spent several years attempting to win autonomy within the OEO. Then, during the Nixon administration, it convinced Congress to convert it into the Legal Services
Corporation, complete with a governing board not subject to presidential
control.

The president may employ the organizational strategy against a
bureau. When George McGovern served as director of the Food for

Peace Program during the Kennedy administration, he was made a White House assistant in order to bring the program into the presidential orbit. Similarly the War on Poverty was run from the Executive Office of the president during the Johnson administration. James Schlesinger was named energy advisor in the White House with authority to coordinate activities of all energy agencies pending their reorganization by the Carter administration into a new department. To take control of programs in scattered departments or agencies the president may assign a White House assistant to the policy area and have assistant secretaries in one or more departments report to the aide.

The bureau may use the *constituency* strategy to mobilize interest-group support of its autonomy. Department political executives grant the bureau its freedom because they calculate as unacceptably high the political costs to the president of any attempt to control it. Bureaus work closely with interest and clientele groups to convince congressional committees to enact the following provisions into law:

1. Professional qualifications are to be required for senior officials. This provision encourages promotions from the career service to top positions in the bureaus.
2. A professional career service, with its own code of ethics, must staff the bureau and run its programs. Examples include the Foreign Service, Public Health Service, Forest Service, P.L. 313 services, or military academy graduates in the armed forces.
3. Research, development, and evaluation are to be conducted by the bureau itself or contracted by it to professional associations and interest groups sympathetic to its mission.
4. Operating authority should be vested in bureau officials, and their actions should be subject to concurrence by interest and clientele groups represented on advisory committees. These committees are to develop written "guidelines" for bureau activities.
5. Detailed spending authorizations and specific itemized appropriations should be granted directly to the bureaus in order to prevent the department (or White House) from determining the allocation of resources for bureau programs.

Career officials in some agencies create their own professional associations, consisting of active and (at times) retired agency officials (e.g., the Federal Bar Association, the Foreign Service Association, the Association of the Army, and the Navy League). These organizations establish links with professional societies and interest groups in the private sector and may help mobilize them against presidential decisions. When Nixon attempted to dismantle many of the programs of the War on Poverty and reorganize the Office of Economic Opportunity, lawsuits brought by unions representing antipoverty workers in federal, state, and local agencies stopped the president.

When it leaks information to the press about an administration decision it believes to be unwise, the bureau uses a *media* strategy, calculating that it can make a national agenda item of the issue and force the president to retreat. Well-timed leaks, detailing how the "hatchet men" from the White House were planning to destroy the program, countered Nixon-proposed cuts in the food stamp program. Careerists cultivate the image of neutral, nonpartisan, nonpolitical "civil servants" to contrast their activities with those of administration executives who (they claim) inject "politics" into government. Careerists may also claim that the administration wants them to act unprofessionally: poverty lawyers argued that certain of Nixon's proposals, which would have prevented them from offering representation to the poor in some cases, violated the Canon of Ethics. Not all such efforts are successful. Poverty lawyers may not represent the poor in some types of cases. Staff members of the Voice of America launched an unsuccessful media campaign in the last days of the Ford administration to win autonomy from the U.S. Information Agency, arguing that they were professional journalists who could not present "objective" news, as required by their profession, if subordinated in a "propaganda agency."

Senior officials may use the *resignation* threat to keep the president out of the affairs of their bureaus. J. Edgar Hoover enjoyed such public prestige as director of the FBI that no president could afford the political costs to be incurred if he were actually to carry out such a threat. His bureau enjoyed virtual autonomy within the Justice Department. Threats to resign by career military officers appointed to the Joint Chiefs of Staff have influenced decisions about the size of the military budget and even the terms that American negotiators may offer or accept at arms control conferences.[54] But very few career officials enjoy the public prestige to make such threats credible. It is also rare for careerists to resign over a policy disagreement with the administration. Most, shunted aside to other assignments, either accept their "demotion" or leave government service quietly.

Officials may employ the strategy of *guerilla warfare*. They structure information they provide to political executives so that only the proposal they favor will seem viable to their superiors. They point out technical obstacles that prevent implementation of administration proposals. Officials may use their discretion in implementing direct orders to subvert administration intentions. During the Cuban Missile Crisis of 1962 the navy was ordered to "quarantine" Cuba. The particular procedures chosen by the chief of Naval Operations seemed intended to force the Soviet navy to back down and demonstrate American control of the seas. But Kennedy wanted to give the Russians room to maneuver and additional time to reach a compromise with him, so they could extricate themselves from the confrontation without loss of face. Eventually the president and Secretary of Defense McNamara had to issue new orders to the navy and take control of the quarantine to meet their objectives, over the strenuous opposition of the chief of naval operations.[55]

Often the most effective strategy is to adopt a *low profile*. There are approximately eight thousand senior careerists, among them five hundred bureau chiefs chosen from the career service. The White House cannot possibly superintend the hundreds of bureaus and thousands of programs run by these officials. If policy decisions can be camouflaged as routine administrative and managerial decisions, the president may find it difficult to catch on in time to alter them. *Low visibility* becomes the rule of the day for many savvy careerists.

Presidential Transactions with Bureaus

The president can reward or punish bureaus. He may occasionally use his powers to make an example of an agency: from the White House perspective no agency is entirely worthless, for it may always have its use as a horrible example. To punish a bureau the president may leave it to the tender mercies of his Executive Office agencies. They will monitor its internal management and personnel practices, propose fewer super-grade positions and possibly a reduction in personnel. Outside task forces and commissions will evaluate agency or bureau performance and recommend sweeping changes in its mission. They will propose reorganization plans to limit its jurisdiction or end its autonomy, and will "layer" it with assistant secretaries and special White House assistants. If necessary they will discredit the bureau with media leaks about its poor performance. They will pressure its personnel into early retirement by giving them unattractive assignments. They will slash its budget requests and shift funds to other bureaus in the same department.

To reward a bureau the president may consult with its chief about new programs and incorporate his ideas into the state of the Union address or a special legislative message. He can adopt agency budget proposals as his own. He can propose reorganizations that upgrade the status of the bureau and expand its jurisdiction. He can promote bureau chiefs and assistants from the permanent service, and even make careerists assistant secretaries of the department.

An outgoing administration often decides to "blanket" bureaus by filling senior positions with careerists. The purpose is to make it difficult for the new administration to place its political appointees at the head of the bureaus. Incoming department secretaries may ask these careerists to resign, and if necessary, will "fire" them by transferring them back to lower positions in the career service. In addition, a new administration places as many positions as it can in the Schedule C list for discretionary appointments, so that it can put its own people in charge. If necessary it will "layer" careerists with a new level of political executives to whom they must report.

IV

The Departments

Presidents cannot control the bureaus because the department secretaries cannot control them. The presidential chain of command breaks down because department secretaries lack incentives and resources—administrative and political—to control the bureaus. Secretaries have four functions: they must manage their departments and set priorities; represent constituencies to the president and the president to constituencies; help make administration policy and propose new policy initiatives; offer advice to the president. Most secretaries are least effective as managers.

One problem is that most cabinet appointments are not made on the basis of the administrative talents of nominees. Close political associates are almost always chosen to head the Department of Justice: Eisenhower picked his campaign manager, Herbert Brownell; Kennedy chose his brother and campaign manager, Robert Kennedy; Nixon picked his law partner and campaign manager, John Mitchell; and Carter picked his close political advisor, Griffin Bell. Some secretaries offer geographical balance, like westerners chosen for interior; others may be picked on the basis of race, sex, religion, or ethnicity—common for HEW and HUD. Many secretaries are picked to serve as "ambassadors" to various constituencies, especially the secretaries of Treasury, Commerce, Agriculture, and Labor. National security managers with experience in several administrations are often chosen for State and Defense: the former is likely to be a lawyer without administrative talent; the latter is likely to be picked precisely because he is an effective manager, becoming the exception to the general rule.

The president makes cabinet nominations to enhance his own political position; each nominee brings a "dowry" in the form of some constituent or bureaucratic support to the administration. But with one or two exceptions the president and his new secretaries do not know each other well. At the beginning of his administration the president has just finished two years of campaigning, and has had little time to get to know most of the people he has appointed to top positions. As John Kennedy remarked to John Kenneth Galbraith during the transition of 1960, "I must make the appointments now; a year hence I will know who I really want to appoint."[56] The president will pick a few people he knows personally, will choose from among candidates submitted by his transition "talent scouts" for most of his cabinet, and will then pick the top seventy-five or one hundred nominees for the most important positions. Most he will meet for the first time during the transition period when he interviews them for the job. The American system, then, is totally unlike a parliamentary one, where the prime minister fills his cabinet and lower-level positions with members of his parliamentary party, most of whom he has worked with for years. And with the weakening of party organizations and their declining influence in presidential campaigns, the president has less incentive than ever before to rely on the advice of national and state party leaders in filling the top positions.[57]

Approximately fifteen hundred political positions at the executive, noncareer, and noncompetitive civil service levels will be filled by the highest officials in the departments, working with the White House and transition teams, and once the administration has taken office, with the assistant secretary for administration, the Civil Service Commission, and the OMB. Other positions, including top jobs in regional offices, U.S. attorneys and U.S. marshalls, are filled by "senatorial courtesy" in one of several variations: (1) members of the president's party from the state in which the appointment will be made suggest nominees; (2) the president clears his own suggestions for the positions with senators of his own party from the state in which the appointment will be made; (3) these courtesies in exceptional cases may be extended to senators from the opposition party. In effect the president exercises his appointment power for the benefit of state party organizations that the senators represent. The loyalties of officials in regional or local offices may thus rest as much with their congressional sponsors and local party leaders as with the administration. The president also extends some of this patronage to leaders in the House. He also frequently nominates to executive positions at the subcabinet level several ex-legislators of his own party or even their senior staff assistants.

Most departments lack any "team" loyal to the secretary. Each subcabinet official, chosen through the recommendation of a different "sponsor," has his own constituency and develops his own allies in and out of government to secure his position and help him advance his career. Some assistant secretaries, such as Theodore and Franklin Roosevelt, Averill Harriman, and Nelson Rockefeller, were political leaders in their own right, not mere foot soldiers for their secretaries. Andrew Young, the ambassador to the United Nations in the Carter administration, and nominally under the supervision of the State Department, took pains in his first months in office to make it clear that he was not a spokesman for the department, prompting State within a period of two weeks to repudiate his pronouncements on Angola, Vietnam, and other issues. Young had direct access to the president, chose his Washington-based staff himself, and picked his own deputies in the Mission to the UN rather than using the Commission on Ambassadorial Appointments. In addition Young suggested the nominee for assistant secretary of state for international organizations, ensuring that the official would be an ally rather than supervisor of his work. Young sat with the National Security Council and the cabinet, functioning autonomously under the supervision of the president.

Secretaries and subcabinet officials are wasting assets whose value to the president depreciates during his administration. Their limited loyalty to him diminishes steadily as they are "captured" by the permanent government. They often "go native" by championing the interests of their bureaucratic and interest-group constituencies. As the first director of the Bureau of the Budget, Charles Dawes, pointed out, "Cabinet members are vice-presidents in charge of spending, and as such they are the natural enemies of the President."[58] In the first months of the Carter administration battles had already broken out between HUD and HEW on the one hand, and the White House on the other, over projected spending levels for the departments, with the president complaining that their requests would break his budget.

The life of a cabinet member who puts pressure on the president—to borrow words from the English political theorist Thomas Hobbes—is nasty, brutish, and (often) short. Truman fired Secretary of Commerce Henry Wallace for attacking his foreign policy. Secretary of Labor Martin Durkin lasted a year under Eisenhower, and Interior Secretary Walter Hickel was fired by Nixon. Secretary of Defense James Schlesinger was dropped by Ford after siding with the Pentagon in a budget dispute.

Few department secretaries stay the length of an administration. Their average tenure in office in recent years has been forty months. In the first five years of the Nixon administration the entire cabinet was replaced with a total of thirty cabinet appointments. In one eighteen-month period the Justice Department was headed by no less than five attorneys general.[59] The average tenure of cabinet members in the Nixon administration was only eighteen months. At the subcabinet level the average tenure in office in recent years has been eighteen months, with a drop to only twelve months during the Nixon administration.[60] Between 1960 and 1972 many officials averaged less than one year of service, including 16 percent of the secretaries, 16 percent of the undersecretaries, and 22 percent of the assistant secretaries.[61]

Political executives are hardly settled into office when they resign, get fired, or win promotions. They rarely gain the expertise to control their bureaus. With high turnover the normal pattern, the incentive for careerists is to "educate from below," to delay making ordered changes, and to manipulate their superiors. Bureau chiefs rely on "end runs" to Congress and their constituencies to evade the presidential chain of command. Each side blames the other for conflict and delay. In recognition of the problem, the Carter administration set as its goal a four-year term for its political executives; whether the traditional pattern will be broken remains to be seen.

Although turnover is high, most resignations are not attempts to influence administration policies. Between 1900 and 1970, of the 389 top officials who submitted their resignations to the president, 91.3 percent left with no public protest.[62] The norm is for officials to resign quietly if they disagree with administration policy. They may receive new assignments in different areas in the same administration, or they may be appointed in a new administration. Those who make a public fuss are usually consigned to oblivion, since presidents know that what the official does to one president he might be tempted to do to another. The few officials who "go public" in a national agenda appeal are likely to be former politicians themselves, used to appealing to mass audiences, such as William Jennings Bryan, Harold Ickes, Harold Stassen, Walter Hickel, George Romney, and Elliot Richardson. Appointees from business, law, finance, or academia are more likely to leave quietly.[63]

Secretaries and the Bureaus

Political executives have few resources to use in controlling the bureaus. They lack, with some rare exceptions, access to or influence with the president. Many departments have been little more than "holding companies" for a conglomeration of bureaus, agencies, offices, and administrations contained within them. Carter's Interior Secretary Cecil Andrus called them "little fiefdoms" and observed,

The policy here has been for the grazing interests to have their chunk here, for coal to have another chunk; lumber, mining, all with their own part of the department. This place was like a centipede with each little pair of legs scuttling off in its own direction.[64]

Various reorganization plans sometimes vest authority at the departmental level. In 1950 and 1953 two reorganization plans stimulated by the findings of the Hoover commission strengthened the office of the secretary in the departments, and various Defense Department reorganization laws have added to the responsibilities of the secretary at the expense of the various services and commands. Since the 1960s staffing of the secretaries' offices in the departments has increased: officials have the capability to apply centralized management and budgeting systems, institute timetables for program planning, conduct research and development and program evaluation, and establish legislative clearance procedures.

Most departments have not been able to use the new management techniques to gain control over the bureaus. Some departments were skeptical of new management and decision-making methods. Between 1965 and 1967 the State Department experimented with a "country program budget" system, but the innovation was not supported at the department's highest levels and eventually was dropped in favor of a government-wide "PPBS" budgeting system sponsored by the Bureau of the Budget. In turn that system was sabotaged by State officials resentful that their own approach had been discarded.[65] In Agriculture program analysts used the new budget system as "window dressing" to justify decisions made by the bureaus using more traditional methods. By the 1970s the "PPBS" system which had been introduced with such fanfare in the departments in 1965 had been abandoned by the OMB in favor of something called "Management by Objective"—an approach which emphasized decentralization of planning by letting bureaus establish their own goals.

Congress has not given much help to secretaries who want to control the bureaus, viewing such efforts as a threat to the "triple alliance" in which they exert great influence. Appropriations for the offices of the secretaries are low, and even though their resources have increased, most are still not fully staffed.

The Cabinet

The collective cabinet is of no use to the president in instituting a chain of command. In theory the cabinet can serve as a sounding board, an advisory body, a forum for debate, or even a source of innovation. But it is not really suited for any of these purposes, and is used more for public relations symbolism than for substantive governing.[66] The secretaries prefer to "boycott the agenda" at meetings. Each participant operates on the premise that his or her department's interests will best be served if none of the other secretaries comments on its affairs. Thus Jesse Jones, Franklin Roosevelt's secretary of commerce, asserted, "there was no one at the table who could be of help to me except the President, and when I needed to consult him I did not choose a cabinet meeting to do so."[67]

Cabinet unity is maintained not by exploring problems, developing a consensus on specific proposals, or maintaining a collective responsibility for decisions, but rather by muting interdepartmental disputes. Discussion focuses on partisan issues, legislative strategy, or public relations imagery. Carter, for example, used his first cabinet meeting to order that department executives use fewer limousines. He ordered that each secretary personally read every federal regulation issued by a bureau in their departments, an obviously unworkable command, which was soon rescinded. The importance of this kind of meeting was indicated when Carter's aide Hamilton Jordan informed the president that he wouldn't attend the weekly cabinet sessions since they were a "waste of time."[68] The cabinet is of such little use that some presidents, like Kennedy and

Nixon, held hardly any meetings (Kennedy held only six in three years). Others, such as Lyndon Johnson, used them to hold forth on things bothering them—in effect using the meetings as a form of group therapy for the administration. A more effective approach is for the president to meet with secretaries and agency heads on an ad hoc basis or in cabinet committees. As Kennedy complained, "Cabinet meetings are simply useless. Why should the Postmaster sit there and listen to a discussion of the problems of Laos?"[69]

Eisenhower tried to make the cabinet part of the chain of command. He established a "secretariat" under the direction of White House aide Maxwell Raab. Cabinet meetings had formal agendas, and position papers were debated. Indended to focus on department business, the agenda included important domestic issues and even national security matters. But the secretaries presented papers that were merely "puff pieces," highlighting the achievements of their departments. Important issues could not be resolved at the meetings, although there was much sounding off, especially by Treasury Secretary George Humphrey and Defense Secretary Charles Wilson. When the president made decisions (usually after cabinet meetings), the secretariat was supposed to ensure that the departments took action. But the cabinet secretary had no supervisory authority, nor did he have the prestige and clout to act in the president's name in dealing with the secretaries. Usually Eisenhower would not take action against "offenders," and gradually the secretariat system fell into disuse. Ford used a cabinet secretary in much the same manner and with much the same results. Carter named a campaign aide, Jack Watson, as cabinet secretary (complete with staff of twelve) but gave him the additional assignment of "domestic ambassador," which converted him into a public relations man for the administration rather than a coordinator of programs. Neither Watson nor his staff had much impact on department business. The post seems to have been created for him as a result of a power struggle (which he lost) with other White House aides—being cabinet secretary is, in one sense, the equivalent of exile from the centers of power on the White House staff.

Strong presidents have reason to downgrade the cabinet and prevent its institutionalization. A collective cabinet with its own staff could become a competitor for "The Executive Power" and come to function as a "council of state"—the system rejected at the Constitutional Convention. Because presidents reserve their prerogatives for themselves, they hold few meetings, permit no votes, and deny the cabinet any staff resources. But this means that there is no "administration" in the true, collective sense of the word. The secretaries do not constitute a government in the parliamentary sense: they do not stand or fall together, nor do they share a collective political responsibility for the policies (or even the politics) of the president.

Presidential-Secretarial Relations

Every president has his own way of dealing with cabinet members. Each wants loyalty and none likes to be undercut or pressured. Historian Arthur Schlesinger, Jr., has described one method, Franklin Roosevelt's:

His favorite technique was to keep grants of authority incomplete, jurisdictions uncertain, charters overlapping. The result of this competitive theory of administration was often confusion and exasperation on the operating level; but no other method could so reliably ensure that in a large bureaucracy filled with ambitious men eager for power, the decisions, and the power to make them, would remain with the President.[70]

Roosevelt counterbalanced a Public Works Administration run by Harold Ickes with a Works Progress Administration run by Harry Hopkins. He parceled out electrical power programs among Agriculture, Interior, and the newly created Tennessee Valley Authority. Planning for recovery he delegated to Treasury, Commerce, the National Recovery Administration, and the National Emergency Council. Roosevelt's personal emissaries and his assignment of Treasury officials for certain negotiations upstaged State Department diplomats. If they wanted to win jurisdictional battles, the departmental secretaries learned that they needed to form alliances with the president, to promote his interests, and to warn him of the plans of rivals.

This competitive system forced information and options upward to the White House, but it was chaotic and inefficient. Many talented individuals could not work for long in such an atmosphere and split with Roosevelt. His effort to foster rivalries created strains between the president and his secretaries. This pattern even continued during the Second World War, when the president insisted that each of the emergency agencies report directly to him. At one point forty-seven such agencies existed.[71] Ironically, however, although everyone in theory reported to the White House, no one in practice needed to do so for most department business. Eventually the rivals realized that no alliance with the White House was permanent. They then sought new allies among interest groups and congressional committees, or resolved conflicts among themselves, or simply went their own ways. The result was that Roosevelt lost influence in the departments—one of the reasons that the 1937 Brownlow commission recommended a major overhaul of the presidency and the creation of various staff agencies. Since Roosevelt's time no president his instituted a competitive system. Instead, most prefer to meet on an ad hoc basis with staff members and the most important secretaries, consigning the others to a sort of limbo. The "inner cabinet"—usually State, Defense, Treasury, and Justice—and the president's relationship to it account for most of the action in any administration. The members of the inner cabinet serve as advisors rather than as representatives of their departments or agencies when they counsel the president. But if the president wins the support of these secretaries he has merely changed the locus of his problem and not its nature: he may have won over the secretaries, but will their departments follow? For an effective chain of command the president cannot rely on the secretaries; rather, he must use the staff agencies of the White House.

V

The White House Staff

The White House Office consists of personal assistants to the president. Though it was once merely a small group of aides, it has itself grown into a large organization. Prior to 1939 there was no formal office: assistants came from the departments "on loan" to the White House.[72] Franklin Roosevelt's "brains trust" was assembled in this way: Thomas Corcoran came from the Reconstruction Finance Corporation, Raymond Moley and Adolph Berle from the State Department, and Rexford Tugwell from Agriculture. As late as 1938 the president had only a few personal assistants and had to put staff members on department budget lines. The undersecretary of the interior, for example, had traditionally been used as the White House liaison officer with Congress.

The Brownlow Commission recommended a change in the system. Its report argued,

The President needs help. His immediate staff assistance is entirely inadequate. He should be given a small number of executive assistants who would be his direct aides in dealing with the managerial agencies and administrative departments of government.[73]

Roosevelt subsequently submitted a reorganization plan to Congress that led to a White House office staffed by six senior aides. By the end of the Second World War the number of assistants had increased to forty-five. By the close of the Truman administration it had reached two hundred fifty; it passed four hundred under Eisenhower; and the staff had got up to six hundred forty at the end of the Nixon administration. It declined to four hundred eighty-five by the end of the Ford presidency. By July of his first year in office Carter had a staff of five hundred seventy-eight, of whom four hundred sixty-one were full-time, seventeen were part-time, and one hundred were detailees from the departments not officially listed as members of the White House office. Of this large total, perhaps seven counted as senior aides, another fifty or so were principal deputies to these aides, one hundred additional assistants had professional duties, and the remainder were primarily in clerical and administrative capacities.

Another way to describe the staff is in terms of salaries: approximately seventeen were ranked at executive level III to V, on a par with the undersecretaries and assistant secretaries of the departments. Forty-six in all were receiving salaries in excess of $40,000, according to the White House listing of April 1977. In Carter's first year the budget for the White House Office ran over $17.6 million, up considerably from the $3.6 million total in the last year of the Johnson administration.[74]

It is difficult for the president to control a White House Office that consists of high-powered executives who themselves supervise ambitious and energetic assistants. After extensive interviews with, and research on, the White House Office, political scientist Thomas Cronin noted:

The presidency has become a large, complex bureaucracy itself, rapidly acquiring many dubious characteristics of large bureaucracies in the process: layering, overspecialization, communications gaps, inter-office rivalries, inadequate coordination, and an impulse to become consumed with short-term, urgent operational concerns at the expense of thinking systematically about the consequences of varying sets of policies and about the important long-range problems.[75]

The president who surrounds himself with senior assistants may be tempted to close off the outside world and remain unresponsive to departmental, bureau, and interest-group pressures. Nixon used H. R. Haldeman as a barrier against outsiders: Haldeman himself remarked, "Every President needs a son of a bitch, and I'm Nixon's. I'm his buffer and I'm his bastard. I get done what he wants done and I take the heat instead of him."[76] These aides—characterized as a "palace guard" by outsiders unable to gain access to the president—may in turn join with the incumbent in a "seige" mentality, as they attempt to fend off unwanted but mounting outside pressures. The result may be what Irving Janis has called "groupthink": a consensus on critical issues that bears an ever-decreasing relationship to reality.[77] If such consensus yields policies that fail, the president may use his assistants as personal confidants or as amateur therapists, or even as whipping boys, to enable him to vent his frustration. Like Lyndon Johnson, he may tease, humiliate, browbeat, and emotionally drain his assistants, in which case turnover will be high and morale low.

Every president surrounds himself with aides personally loyal to him, who in Theodore Sorensen's words, have the "ability to serve the President's needs and to talk the President's language."[78] Kennedy had his "Irish Mafia," Johnson his Texans, Nixon his California advertising men (nicknamed "the Prussians"), Ford his colleagues from Michigan, and Carter his campaign crew from Georgia. Not by accident does a president surround himself with assistants from his home state, for Texan Bill Moyers, an aide to Lyndon Johnson, concluded that "any President has to have around him some people who are so unquestioningly loyal that their very loyalty is a source of strength to him."[79] But loyalists pose several problems to a president. They may take actions that damage him; or he may order actions that hurt them. In the Watergate case, for example, Nixon conspired with top aides in an obstruction of justice that destroyed not only all their careers but also the careers of several junior aides who followed orders without question. The testimony or memoirs of several staff members was the same; each believed that Nixon's orders were the law or superseded the law. Jeb Magruder recounts that he told himself, "Jeb, you're not going to screw this one up. You like this job and you're going to do what they tell you."[80] He admitted that when he was ordered to go after White House "enemies" he had no qualms about the actions he was expected to take: "Although I was aware they were illegal, and I am sure others did—we had become somewhat inured to using some activities that would help us in accomplishing what we thought was a cause, a legitimate cause."[81]

The president's political opponents wait for staff members to get into trouble and then attack. Eisenhower had to dismiss his "chief of staff," Sherman Adams, for accepting gifts from Boston industrialist Bernard Goldfine. Nixon dismissed several high-ranking aides in a vain attempt to end investigation of the Watergate cover-up. Carter accepted the resignation of OMB director and White House advisor Bert Lance after an investigation of his conduct as a Georgia bank director prior to joining the administration.

In each case the White House staff failed to protect the president's interests and instead looked out for its own. Instead of investigating initial allegations against individuals, the staff attempted to minimize them. For instance, White House counsel Lipshutz and his staff did not warn Carter that a report prepared by the comptroller of the currency in August 1977 not only did not clear Lance but also raised many charges about his performance as a banker. Carter aide Hamilton Jordan, spreading the rumor that Treasury Secretary Michael Blumenthal was behind the attempt to "get" Lance, succeeded in splitting the administration; he did no one—not Lance, not Jordan, not Blumenthal, and not Carter—any good. Only White House aide Midge Costanza managed to tell Carter what he had to hear, that Lance was a liability and should resign or be dismissed. It was perhaps no coincidence that she had earlier opposed the president's denial of federal funds for abortions. Her unusual tendency to speak her mind and oppose a president only underscored the unlimited quantities of agreeable yes-men usually found in the immediate vicinity of the Oval Office. Within the year her office was relocated to the White House basement. She later resigned.

A large staff does not make an effective presidency. That the incumbent can only deal personally with a limited number of assistants limits the number who can be considered senior advisors (perhaps a dozen) or who can speak in his name. Carter relied on a "committee of seven," filling lower staff levels with aides who lacked direct access to him. In Nixon's

A POLITICAL EXECUTIVE ASSESSES WHITE HOUSE
OVERSIGHT OF ADMINISTRATION

Confusion is created when men try to do too much at the top. In order to know what decisions are being made elsewhere in government, the White House tends either to spend time reviewing programs or to take more and more decisions on itself. The separate responsibilities of the White House, Executive Office, and the agencies are fudged, and the demarcations of who does what become uncertain. The result is a blurring of the distinction between staff and line, between program and policy. Decisions tend to be reviewed and reviewed, and operational delays increase accordingly.

As this confusion continues a curious inversion occurs. Operational matters flow to the top—as central staffs become engrossed in subduing outlying bureaucracies—and policymaking emerges at the bottom. At the top minor problems squeeze out major ones, and individuals lower down the echelons who have the time for reflection and mischief-making take up issues of fundamental philosophical and political significance.

Former HUD Undersecretary Robert Wood

Quoted in Richard Nathan, *The Plot That Failed*, New York: Wiley, p. 54.

White House John Dean served as "counsel to the president" for more than a year and a half without reporting to Nixon directly. Officials in the departments quickly distinguish between senior and junior staff members. The juniors will be outranked and outflanked by their counterparts in the departments, and the result will be conflict when the White House staff member tries to give orders to political executives or senior careerists.

Delegating administrative responsibilities to members of the White House staff, and allowing them to oversee departments and bureaus, becoming in effect "oversecretaries," runs counter to the advice of the Brownlow committee, which cautioned that senior aides should "not be interposed between the President and the heads of his departments, they would not be assistant presidents in any sense."[82] Roosevelt's Executive Order 8248 creating the White House office specified that "in no event shall the administrative assistants be interposed between the President and the head of any department or agency." But the tendency to assume operational control may be irresistible for these aides, who have access to the president and can sense his impatience with the performance of the bureaus. Soon the aides make suggestions to the departments, then give orders, prefacing them with the magic words, "The President wants. . . ." Thomas Cronin quotes one White House assistant who observes,

Everybody believes in democracy until he gets to the White House, and then you begin to believe in dictatorship because it's so hard to get things done. Every time you turn around, people just resist you, and even resist their own job.[83]

Senior aides may delegate administrative oversight to their assistants, who in turn may do positive harm out of ignorance of the issues. In communicating back to their bosses, assistants are likely to simplify and even distort the issues. Because they are young men and women on the way up, they are not likely to refuse an order, even if asked to violate the law or the Constitution. As John Dean admitted, "I soon learned that to make my way upward, into a position of confidence and influence, I had to travel downward through factional power plays, corruption, and finally outright crimes."[84] A junior aide such as Dean may even become the "fall guy": a large staff enables the president to claim that his orders were misinterpreted in the chain of command, and he can therefore disavow any actions taken by staff with whom he has not communicated personally.

   The Brownlow commission proposed that the president be assisted by a very small staff of senior aides, with extensive political and administrative experience. As the commission noted,

Their effectiveness in assisting the president will, we think, be directly proportional to their ability to discharge their functons with restraint. They would remain in the background, issue no orders, make no decisions, emit no public statements.[85]

In recent administrations staff members have become part of the problem rather than part of the solution. They make it more difficult for the president to institute a chain of command working in his interest, and they distort information up and down the executive hierarchy. They issue orders that may not be obeyed, make decisions that may not make sense, and "emit" enough public statements to bury an administration with hostile media coverage. Carter seems to have grasped the problem. He did not appoint a "chief of staff" to act as a buffer between him and officials in the administration. He did not staff his office with substantive experts, "counselors," or other policymakers. At one of his early press conferences he vowed,

I believe in Cabinet administration of our government. There will never be an instance while I am President where the members of the White House staff dominate or act in a superior position to the members of our Cabinet.[86]

In its reorganization plan for the Executive Office the Carter administration proposed to reduce the number of permanent positions in the White House office from 485 to 351, clearly a step in the right direction. It was, however, more symbolic than real, since the trimming involved moving White House mailroom, payroll, and other housekeeping operations from the White House Office to a newly created Central Administrative Unit in the Executive Office of the president. And some aides were placed on departmental payrolls to preserve the image of a reduced White House staff.

Staff Oversight of Bureaucracy

The White House office performs several functions. It plays a key role in policy initiation, either by clearing proposals among departments or actively taking sides. Aides may provide the president with a "back channel" to communicate directly to low-ranking officials so he can obtain information and options that might otherwise be blocked at the departmental level. Carter's senior aides, for example, were each given a small block of time to see the president each week, and were permitted to bring people in to see the president on their own initiative if they thought it advisable that he be exposed to their points of view.

The president may appoint an aide to act as a counterweight against an unresponsive department. When Eisenhower wished to prepare disarmament proposals prior to the 1955 Geneva Summit Conference, he made Nelson Rockefeller a special assistant and installed him and his staff in Quantico, Virginia, in order to develop proposals that the president knew would not be forthcoming from the State Department.

White House aides may oversee departmental business by doing any or all of the following:

1. Chairing interdepartmental committees to coordinate government policies
2. Drafting speeches to be made by political executives or clearing speeches these officials wish to deliver
3. Acting as "firefighters" in crisis situations by assuming direct operational control of agencies
4. Serving as line officials themselves, especially in sensitive national security assignments in which they replace the ambassador as the president's personal emissary to a foreign government

Each president has his own style of using aides. Kennedy, following Franklin Roosevelt's pattern, parceled out ad hoc assignments, usually in crises, to trusted aides. They served in effect as "desk officers" in making and implementing policies, displacing all officials in the departmental hierarchy and dealing directly with the line officers who would implement decisions made at the White House. Carter gave his regular aides specific orders *not* to interfere with the department chain of command, nor to serve as desk officers. The only exception, by design, was James Schlesinger. As energy aide he was expected to supervise all bureaus and agencies that would be incorporated into the Department of Energy.

Nixon attempted to centralize control of the departments through the Executive Office of the president.[87] Especially after his first term, he appointed managers rather than politicians to his cabinet, expecting them to execute his orders rather than represent interest-group constituencies or provide him with advice. He moved members of the White House office into departments as political executives; they were expected to handle such presidential business as patronage and distributions. The president combined the position of White House aide with that of department secretary to create several "doublehatters": in 1971 he appointed Treasury Secretary George Schultz as an assistant and chairman of the newly created Council on Economic Policy; HUD Secretary James Lynn became presidential assistant for community development; HEW Secretary Caspar Weinberger became assistant for human resources; and Agriculture Secretary Earl Butz was named assistant for natural resources. In 1973 Nixon gave a presidential aide, National Security Advisor Henry Kissinger, the additional position of secretary of state.

The doublehatter system was a reaction to Congress's refusal to reorganize the departments as Nixon had urged: in effect the president was accomplishing by executive order and White House reorganization what the legislature had refused to pass into law, reducing the number of cabinet secretaries reporting to him from eleven to seven. He hoped to end friction between the cabinet and the White House office by giving the "doublehatters" direct access to him, and to provide for coordination of programs across departmental lines. Each doublehatter had a council or other White House staff resource, enabling him to promote programs from a perspective broader than his own department's.

Nixon modified the system at the beginning of his second term.[88] There were now five senior assistants to the president: Haldeman as "chief of staff," Ehrlichman for domestic affairs, Kissinger for national security affairs, Ash (of OMB) for executive management, and Schultz (Treasury) for economic affairs. Three "counselors" with responsibilities for human resources, natural resources, and community development would report to the president through these aides. In effect, the members of the White House staff, the OMB director, and Schultz and Kissinger had constituted themselves as the "inner circle" while the doublehatters moved down one notch. The remaining secretaries of departments counted for next to nothing in the Nixon White House. By May 1973 the last vestiges of the "senior assistant" structure were abandoned after several top aides resigned. The department secretaries were now to have direct access to the president. But in fact Nixon so isolated himself during Watergate that he had little to do with any department business for the remainder of his time in office.

President Ford undercut the position of the doublehatters he inherited. Kissinger lost his position as assistant for national security affairs. (Asked later how much power the assistant should have, he quipped,

"At the moment I am very much opposed to the Assistant for National Security Affairs having any influence.")[89] Treasury Secretary William Simon chaired, but did not direct, the newly created Economic Policy Board, which Ford turned over to White House aide William Seidman. Agriculture Secretary Butz lost control over natural resources policies when the White House established the Federal Energy Office and later the Federal Energy Administration. For a brief period Interior Secretary Rogers Morton chaired an Energy Resources Council, but he was eventually displaced by a succession of White House energy "czars."

The doublehatter innovation seemed an ideal system for a president who wished to have as little as possible to do with departmental business or most cabinet secretaries. But in practice these "supersecretaries" (with the exception of Kissinger) were never able to coordinate several departments for presidential purposes. The system left the president too dependent on his principal advisors and cut down other sources of information or policy options. While it may have eliminated some friction between the secretaries and the White House office, new sources of friction opened between senior White House aides and the doublehatters. Ford was well advised to end the innovation, and the Carter administration went one step further and abolished many of the councils and offices within the White House that doublehatters had used as coordinating mechanisms.

The Office of Management and Budget

The Office of Management and Budget (OMB) introduces new budgeting, decision-making, and management techniques into the bureaucracy. It abandoned the "PPBS" budgeting system that had been introduced in 1965 by its predecessor, the Bureau of the Budget, because of stubborn resistance to its use by much of the career bureaucracy and many of the political executives.[90] But its own attempts at centralized management were no more successful. OMB Deputy Director Frederick Malek introduced the "Management by Objective" (MBO) technique: the White House, departments, and bureaus would all "track together" by having the bureaus develop their own goals, specify timetables for implementation, and then work with departments and OMB to adjust these goals to presidential priorities. Malek brought thirty "management associates" into the OMB to work with the assistant secretary for administration in each department. These assistant secretaries were former OMB officials or Nixon political appointees.

The OMB focused on departmental structure, research and evaluation capability, paperwork and procedures, and personnel management. The process of "management by objective" was supposed to work as follows:

1. Program managers and bureau chiefs would develop a list of objectives that they thought important and describe how their organizations could carry them out.
2. Internal management conferences would be held, with the participation of bureau chiefs and the assistant secretary for administration, to review the priorities of the bureaus and develop timetables for implementation.
3. The OMB deputy director would meet with department officials for quarterly sessions to monitor the progress of the bureaus in implementing departmental and presidential priorities.[91]

But the top level of the OMB gave the new system little support because of friction between Malek and OMB Director Ash. The director canceled his participation in scheduled meetings with department officials to discuss the system, a sure sign he was undercutting Malek's efforts. The newly installed management associates did not coordinate their work with budget or legislative specialists who had worked for the Bureau of the Budget for many years and were skeptical that the associates knew enough to suggest changes in bureau procedures. For their part, according to political scientist Richard Rose, who studied the system intensively, "Officials have an incentive to produce vague, ambiguous, or confusing statements, so that it will be impossible to show that an objective has not been achieved."[92] In any case, most careerists thought the MBO system was another harebrained scheme developed by the OMB, treated it in the same fashion as PPBS, and made little use of it. Internal management conferences were not held on schedule. In effect, the system "evaporated": without being formally abolished, it ceased to have any significance for the careerists, the department officers, or even OMB analysts.[93] As MBO unraveled, management personnel in the OMB were left with little to do, so they took ad hoc assignments or spent most of their time on nonmanagement matters, such as budget analysis.[94] The OMB was in turmoil, with budget examiners and legislative specialists working with careerists in the departments to undercut the "whiz kid" management specialists. By September 1976, political scientist Lawrence Berman reported the results of a questionnaire submitted to OMB employees: over half saw the OMB as "fair" to "poor" in fulfilling its function of overseeing department management; only 14 percent of OMB employees gave management function a higher priority than the budgeting function.[95]

The OMB also provided management assistance through its Evaluation and Program Implementation Division. After MBO evaporated, it developed a program of "Presidential Management Initiatives" with the departments. But as political scientist Stephen Wayne points out, "OMB provided a management service and the departments and agencies generally chose when and how to use it. Most of them did not use it very much."[96] In the Carter administration the emphasis within the OMB was on proposing plans for executive reorganization. The new

THE EXECUTIVE OFFICE OF THE PRESIDENT: 1939–1979

Management Agencies
Council on Personnel Administration   1939–40
Office of Government Reports   1939–42
Liaison Office for Personnel Management   1939–43
National Resources Planning Board   1939–43
Permanent Advisory Committee on Government
    Organization   1953–61
Bureau of the Budget   1939–70
Federal Property Council   1973–77
*Office of Management and Budget   1970–
*Central Administrative Unit   1977–

Economic Advisors and Offices
National Resources Planning Board   1939–43
Bureau of the Budget   1939–70
Council on International Economic Policy   1971–77
Council on Economic Policy   1973–74
Economic Policy Board   1974–77
Labor-Management Committee   1975–75
Cost of Living Council   1971–74
*Council of Economic Advisors   1946–
*Office of Special Representative for
    Trade Negotiations   1963–
*Council on Wage and Price Stability   1974–

Policy Advisors and Offices
National Aeronautics and Space Council   1958–73
Office of Science and Technology   1962–73
Economic Opportunity Council   1965–77
Office of Economic Opportunity   1964–75
National Council on Marine Resources and
    Engineering Development   1966–71
Council for Urban Affairs   1969–70
Domestic Council   1970–77
Office of Consumer Affairs   1971–73
Special Action Office for Drug Abuse Prevention   1971–75
Office of Telecommunications Policy   1970–77
Energy Policy Office   1973–74
Federal Energy Office   1974–75
Energy Resources Council   1975–77
*Council on Environmental Quality   1969–
*Domestic Policy Staff   1977–
*Office of Science and Technology Policy   1975–
Office of Drug Abuse Policy   1975–

National Security Advisors and Offices
Office of the Director of Mutual Security   1951–54
Board of Consultants on Foreign Intelligence
    Activities   1956–61
President's Foreign Intelligence Advisory Board   1961–77

*National Security Council	1947–
*Central Intelligence Agency	1947–
*Director of Central Intelligence	1947–
*Intelligence Oversight Board	1947–
Mobilization and Preparedness Agencies	
Office of Emergency Management	1940–54
Committee for Congested Production Areas	1943–44
Office of War Mobilization and Reconversion	1942–45
War Refugee Board	1944–45
National Security Resources Board	1947–53
Office of Defense Mobilization	1952–59
Office of Civil and Defense Mobilization	1958–62
Office of Emergency Planning	1962–69
Office of Emergency Preparedness	1965–73

position of executive associate director was created, and Carter appointed Harrison Wellford to it, a campaign and transition advisor who had concentrated on the structure of the executive branch.

The Executive Office of the President

As a result of the recommendations of the Brownlow commission, President Roosevelt created several staff agencies for his own assistance as part of the Executive Office of the President (EOP). These organizations come and go: some are created (or abolished) by law, others by executive order. They have several different functions:

1. Some are operating agencies that belong in the departments but have gained autonomous "presidential status," such as the Disarmament Agency (1950s) and the Office of Economic Opportunity (1960s).
2. Some represent the interests of particular constituencies, such as the Office of Consumer Affairs, the Office of Science and Technology, the Office of Drug Abuse Policy and the Office of Special Consultant to the President on Aging.
3. Some offices develop policies, such as the National Security Council, the Domestic Council, the Economic Policy Board, and the Council of Economic Advisors.
4. Some agencies have management functions, such as the Federal Property Council, the Office of Management and Budget, or the Central Administrative Unit (a housekeeping agency for the White House).

It might be added that Nixon used executive office agencies to undertake illegal actions and serve as "political police" for the administration—activities that the FBI, CIA, and Treasury Department refused to undertake. The White House Drug Enforcement Agency broke the law by engaging in break-ins and surveillance of various White House enemies.[97] Staff members of the Domestic Council were involved in the "plumbers" operation and the Watergate crimes. While this use of agencies may be unique, it corresponds to the principle that staff members close to the presidential orbit are likely to view his word as law—even when statutes must be violated as a consequence of the presidential orders.

The Carter transition task-force characterized the Executive Office as "a jumble of different kinds of entities which serve different purposes and exist for different reasons."[98] The president eliminated several units, especially those that developed minor policies or represented constituencies, to concentrate the office on management, economic policy-making, and national security affairs.

Although agencies have come and gone, certain fundamental problems remain constant. Since the 1943 abolition of the National Resources Planning Board, the presidency has lacked a real planning unit. Similarly no executive program evaluation unit can match the expertise of the General Accounting Office. Neither the BOB nor its successor, the OMB, effectively institutionalized central management programs or developed effective mechanisms for interdepartmental coordination.[99] There is no cadre of senior career officials working in many of these units; in others, such as the OMB, they are so "layered" by political executives that their advice may not reach the highest levels. Consequently there is no "institutional memory" in many executive office agencies: when a new administration comes into power, it seems that it is constantly reinventing the wheel, since it cannot draw on the experience of its predecessors. Study commissions, most notably the Heineman task force and the Ash council, have pointed out some of these problems and have proposed creation within the EOP of an office for management. These proposals have been defeated by a combination of pressures from the BOB (and later the OMB) and the cabinet.[100] The prospects for creation of a new presidential agency with management functions remain small, even though the OMB, nominally with jurisdiction, has failed to perform this function in the president's interests.

Reorganizing the Executive

Those who propose "reorganization" of the executive branch almost always have a bias. If they are "presidentialists," they want to strengthen the chain of command; if they are "congressionalists" or "careerists," they wish to subvert it. Presidentially oriented reforms include: replacement of the Civil Service Commission with a director of civil service who would be a political executive; expansion of the list of noncareer and supergrade positions; an increase in the staffing of, and resources for, the office of the secretary in the departments; limitation of Senate confirmation of political executives to the very top departmental positions (excluding members of the White House Office and Executive Office agencies); and delegation of statutory authority for program operation to the president or department secretaries rather than directly to the bureaus. Congressionalists and careerists propose different reforms. They would cut back on presidential reorganization authority; strengthen the powers of the Civil Service Commission, decrease the number of non-career positions; expand Senate confirmation to cover more positions on the White House Executive Office of the President (including directors and deputy directors of all units); expand Senate confirmation to more positions at the bureau level; create a Senate Office for Nominations to aid committees in screening nominees; delegate more authority for program operations directly to bureaus; and increase the use of chamber resolution, committee veto, report-and-wait, and sunset provisions in the laws.

For the conduct of government it is neither "good" nor "bad" that careerists are not always loyal to the president. Hierarchy in the executive branch is a means to an end, not the end itself. The "chain of command" principle implicit in the presidential reading of "The Executive Power" competes with the checks and balances principle in which Congress shares in the superintendence of administration based on its Article I powers. Not all presidential actions reflect a sense of the national interest, and not all congressional oversight is based on narrow, parochial, or constituency concerns. A pluralistic system may be chaotic and cumbersome, but it may also check presidential excesses. The president should have to deal with bureaucracies and their interest-group allies through persuasion and bargaining rather than fiat. If the president governs in the national interest, what better way to keep him accountable than to require him to engage in a continuous dialogue with his constituencies, using the bureaus as his intermediaries? Congress should play a strong role in oversight, for what other institution can require that the goals of an administration be compatible with the conditions existing in each region, state, or locality?

If the president becomes preoccupied with international crises, broad economic issues, or other matters, the presence of strong, autonomous subsystems accustomed to making and implementing policies and operating through consensus and adjustment, offers continuity and stability to the administration. Even when the president and the presidency cannot manage routine affairs, no vacuum need exist. In crisis situations Congress by statute and the president by custom have expanded administration powers so that the president can exercise vast, almost plenary powers to meet the emergency. When absolutely necessary, a chain of command can be instituted to cope with emergencies. But for politics as usual, or in moments of crisis when administrative issues are secondary, a bureaucracy with a good deal of autonomy and its own close relations with interest groups and Congress may serve the American people well.

The Budgetary

Process

To BUDGET is to govern. In a system of separated institutions that share power, the question is which institution, and by what authority, determines spending levels for the departments? The Constitution neither creates a budget process nor does it describe a role in budgeting for the president. The Framers intended that a Treasury Department would be established by Congress to manage finances, and that it would work closely with the legislature, much as the superintendent of finances had worked with the Continental Congress. Implicit in the provision that the president might recommend to Congress such measures as he thought expedient was the hint that he might propose a financial program, but there was no explicit grant of budget authority in Article II. Such taxing and spending powers as are mentioned in the Constitution are assigned to Congress by Article I.

But presidents attempt to control the budget process. In Gerald Ford's words, "the budget is the President's blueprint for the operation of Government in the year ahead."[1] If he can control spending levels, he can impose a chain of command in the executive branch, reward bureaus that carry out his programs, and punish those that are insubordinate. He can set priorities and influence the timing of new initiatives, and strengthen his position as legislative leader by using agency funds as "prizes" in the distributive process. He can also control aggregate spending levels, thus influencing fiscal policy. If the president loses control of the budget process—as he often does—he loses control of the government: the executive branch remains fragmented and directionless, policymaking remains decentralized and subject to control by the subgovernments, the legislative party considers him an "amateur" who cannot transact business with it, and his fiscal policy fails.

I

Competition for Power

Presidents rarely dominate the budget process. Departments and bureaus vie with the White House for influence over the Executive Budget that the president sends to Congress. The earliest practices in the executive branch centralized power with the Treasury Department. Its secretary, Alexander Hamilton, compiled budget estimates for the departments and submitted them to Congress as an administration program on behalf of the president. Tax and revenue measures were considered separately, but they were coordinated with estimates of expenditures; the Treasury program itself was part of a comprehensive program for industrial and commercial development to be financed in part by European investors.

Such a centralized system did not last long. In 1795, with Hamilton out of government, department secretaries began transmitting their spending estimates directly to Congress, bypassing both the Treasury and the president, a decentralization of power that lasted more than a century (although in 1878 the Treasury began compiling the department requests into a single volume for submission to Congress).

As part of the progressive movement in government to introduce rational management into the executive branch, President Taft proposed to Congress in 1912 that the president should submit an executive budget to Congress with his own estimates of expenditures for the departments. Taft argued,

The reason for urging that the budget should be submitted by the President is that the President is the only person who under the Constitution is responsible for the acts of the executive branch. . . . the President shall each year get before the country what it is that the administration desires to do; shall indicate in a budget message wherein action is necessary to enable the administration adequately to meet the public needs; shall indicate what definite legislation is desired and what funds are needed. . . .[2]

The Budget and Accounting Act of 1921 centralized some budget authority by providing that the president, assisted by a Bureau of the

Budget, would compile department estimates, revise them, and submit an executive budget to Congress. A section of the act provided,

No estimate or request for an appropriation and no request for an increase in an item of any such estimate or request shall be submitted to Congress or any committee thereof, by any officer or employee of any department or establishment, unless at the request of either House of Congress.[3]

The Bureau of the Budget sent circulars to the departments instituting a form of "budget clearance" so that neither authorizations nor appropriations could bypass its budget review process: requests for spending authority and funds would be submitted by bureaus to departments, and by departments to the BOB for consideration by the president.[4] Whereas in the nineteenth century the president generally stood aside when department budgets were compiled, the 1921 act and the procedures used by the BOB made him a central figure in the budget process. He must interact with bureaus and departments in preparing budget figures and then exercise leadership in Congress to get that branch to accept his proposals. He operates within a complicated process when he develops the executive budget, a process that takes almost a year to complete and makes it difficult for him to determine what funds will be requested in his name in "his" budget.

The Action-Forcing Process

The Executive Budget is prepared according to a timetable, through a sequence of steps arranged so that officials interact with each other in specified ways and through specific channels at particular times. Budgeting is an *action-forcing process*: decisions are made in a cycle, according to deadlines, so that the budget may be submitted to Congress at the beginning of the calendar year.

The following chart (figure 8-1) indicates the major activities of the president, Congress, and the bureaucracy prior to and during the fiscal year. Bureaus compile their initial estimates between January and July, twenty-two to fifteen months prior to the fiscal year. A fiscal year begins October 1 and ends September 30, and it is numbered for the year in which it ends. The president and his executive office agencies make decisions between May and December, fifteen to nine months prior to the start of the fiscal year. The president acts after bureaus and agencies have submitted estimates to departments, and departments have submitted proposed budgets to the Office of Management and Budget (OMB). The president's influence is at its lowest at the very beginning of the budget process and increases to its maximum point in the weeks prior to transmission of the budget to Congress.

The executive budget that the president submits to the legislature is a *request* for funds—the final decisions are made by Congress through

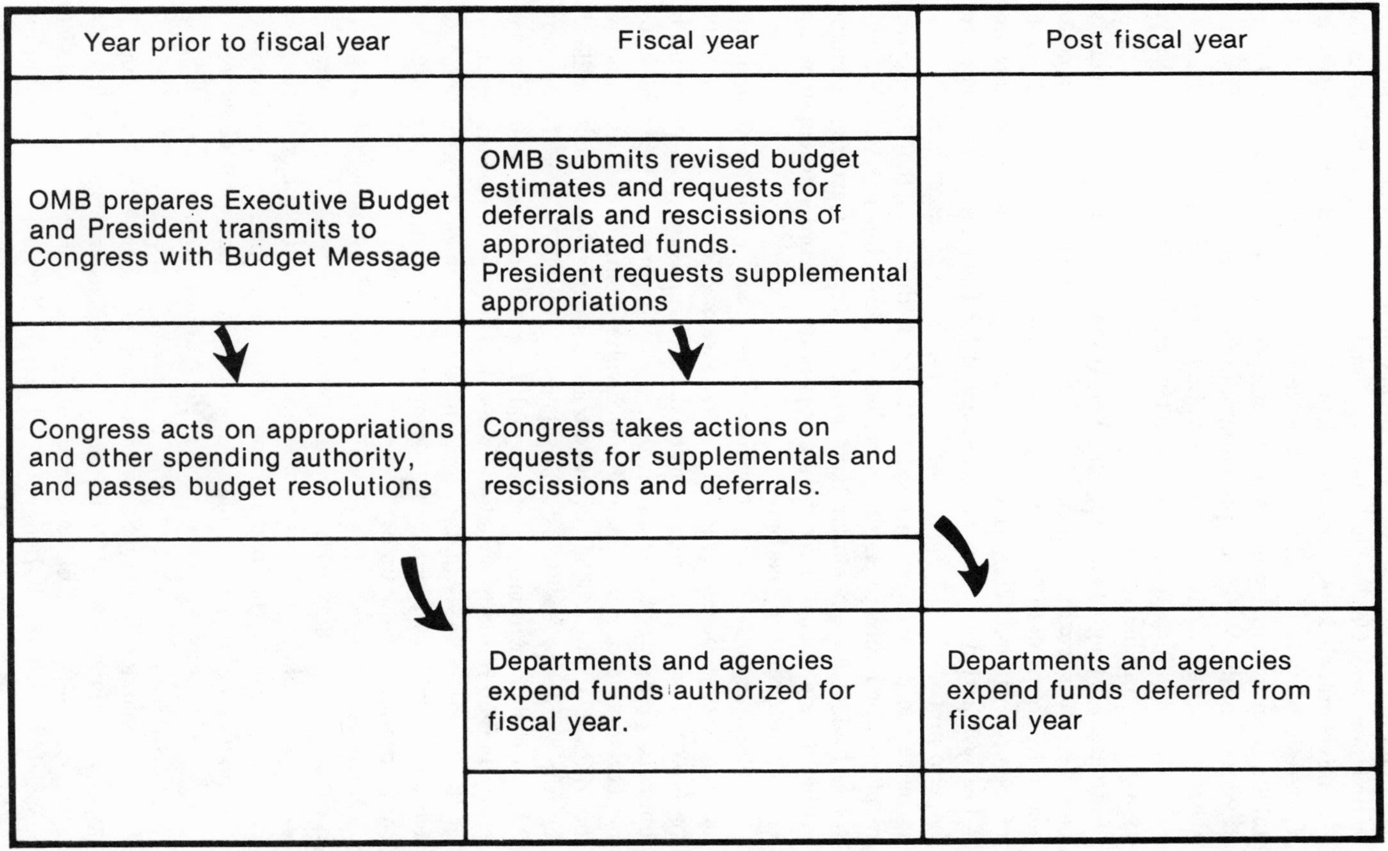

Year prior to fiscal year	Fiscal year	Post fiscal year
OMB prepares Executive Budget and President transmits to Congress with Budget Message	OMB submits revised budget estimates and requests for deferrals and rescissions of appropriated funds. President requests supplemental appropriations	
Congress acts on appropriations and other spending authority, and passes budget resolutions	Congress takes actions on requests for supplementals and rescissions and deferrals.	
	Departments and agencies expend funds authorized for fiscal year.	Departments and agencies expend funds deferred from fiscal year

FIGURE 8-1

laws and appropriations between January, when the president makes his submission, and October 1, when the fiscal year begins. Officials in the executive branch know that presidential requests may be changed by Congress, for as one official commented about Ford's plan to cut $17 billion from agency estimates in the summer of 1975, "Nobody is taking it very seriously. We're not preparing a budget that Congress will adopt, we're preparing what the Administration will send up for Congress to add on to."[5] (Since 1975 the president is required by law to submit revisions to his original requests in April and July.)

Program managers and bureau chiefs (especially if they are careerists) consider their current expenditure levels as their *base*: the amount necessary to spend in future fiscal years to maintain the existing activities of the organization. They view preservation of the base (which includes a yearly inflation adjustment) as essential for their programs. They also hope to protect the *fair share*: the fair proportion of increments that may come to the department in good times or of decreases that the department may be forced to endure in periods of retrenchment.[6] Many officials try to budget *incrementally*: they expect to replicate existing spending within a range of 10 percent (plus or minus) in order to continue the existing programs of the bureau.

Political executives at the department level are less likely to be incrementalists, or to be concerned about the base or fair share of bureaus and programs. They often propose major shifts of funds between programs in bureaus, or between bureaus within the department. These shifts are neither routine nor incremental but involve political choices based on priorities of senior officials in the administration.[7] Departmental officials use the budget process to establish their own authority over the bureaus. They use their own budget officers and comptrollers office to analyze and revise bureau requests. Friction always develops between budget officers at the different levels of the department. Both favor growth, but each has a different way of analyzing expenditures, and different priorities for the allocation of new funds.

In the 1950s most agency budgeting seemed to be based on incremental growth rates. But even in bureaus that grew incrementally, examination of program categories usually indicated major shifts from one fiscal year to the next. In the 1960s many bureaus and agencies expanded rapidly because of presidential commitments in a variety of policy areas. Some agencies, such as the National Aeronautics and Space Administration, the Department of Defense, and the Department of Energy, abandoned altogether the method of incremental budgeting in favor of various new methods.[8] Since the expansion of programs in the 1960s and the period of retrenchment in the 1970s, the incrementalism associated with much budgeting, although it remained an important factor for overall allocation of resources, cannot explain most of the variations in both bureau or program expenditures, in presidential budget requests, and in resulting congressional appropriations.[9] Most budget decisions are highly political and controversial, pitting bureaus against each other and against departments, and officials at all levels against a president who may think it necessary to cut back on many programs.

Managing the Defense Budget

The problems that the shift away from incrementalism has caused presidents is illustrated by the budget process in the Department of Defense. The president wants to control that budget because it is so large, because it involves immense distributions, and because without such control he cannot determine strategic policy or the kind of weapons the nation will procure.

Presidents have never been able to design a budget process that gave them the control they sought. Prior to the Korean War President Truman set expenditure ceilings for the Pentagon that amounted to approximately one-third of the estimated government expenditures as its "fair share." The Joint Chiefs of Staff (JCS) would then submit its recommendations, which were determined by logrolling and compromises between the services. These figures went much higher than Truman's ceiling. The secretary of Defense would pressure the JCS to lower its figures, but the JCS generally refused. Then civilian officials would make the cuts themselves in line with Truman's directives. The military might defend the budget in public, but it often undercut the administration in the hope that Congress would restore funds the president had cut.

In the Eisenhower administration the National Security Council (NSC) produced a Basic National Security Council Policy Memorandum as "guidance" for the JCS, which then produced its own Joint Strategic Operations Plan—a compilation of three separate military service plans. The NSC would then decide on a budget ceiling, which generally was calculated at 10 percent of the anticipated gross national product, and which took into account Eisenhower's attempts to submit a balanced budget to Congress. The JCS would ask for more as its "fair share" and refuse to lower its requests. The Defense comptroller, acting on instructions from the Bureau of the Budget, would then prepare the Defense Department budget. Eisenhower made most of the major decisions himself.[10]

Both Truman and Eisenhower set ceilings on expenditures that the services, the JCS, and military contractors opposed. The secretary of defense and the comptroller would function as intermediaries between the president and the JCS. Services preserved a united front in dealing with the administration by dividing up the "pie," which resulted in an air force share of about 46 percent, a navy share of 28 percent, and an army share of 22 percent. Each of the services relied on its own assessments of Soviet military capabilities and intentions on a "worst case" basis, ascribing to the Soviet bloc the worst of motives and the highest of capabilities. The president countered these assessments by using "intention analyses" prepared by the Central Intelligence Agency and the Department of State, which revealed a cautious and even defensive-minded Soviet military establishment. Truman generally stood firm against military pressure, but at times Eisenhower would raise his initial figure and compromise with the services and JCS.

Outside analysts who examined the budget system made several sharp criticisms. Interservice rivalries were accommodated through logrolling without any reference to strategic doctrines or coordination with diplomatic and economic objectives of the administration. Most budget decisions were expressed in terms of structure and organization rather than missions or strategies. The budget reflected the fair shares of some commands that already were obsolete.[11] Presidents were politically vulnerable, since they seemed to be acting against the advice of the professional military. Every so often, service leaders would "end run" the president and take their case to Congress. Truman faced the "Revolt of the Admirals" in 1949 over cancellation of their pet project, nuclear aircraft carriers, and fought with the air force over the number of bomber wings to be maintained .Eisenhower fought several battles against the army and faced pressure in Congress from legislators mobilized by the air force on issues ranging from nuclear planes to ballistic missiles. Neither the president nor the secretary of defense had the experts in the administration who could combine national security and economic goals into a coherent formulation that would justify the allocations in the defense budget.

President Kennedy installed Robert McNamara (former president of Ford Motor Company) as secretary of defense to overhaul the entire budget process. Kennedy did not fix a ceiling for expenditures and was prepared to increase spending sharply. McNamara created an Office of Systems Analysis (OSA) under the Defense comptroller, which introduced new techniques of systems analysis and cost-benefit analysis into the budget process. The secretary made decisions on proposed programs and weapons systems from options prepared by OSA, the JCS, the services and commands, and the Office of Director of Defense Research and Engineering (DDRE). By 1962 the head of the OSA, Alain Enthoven, had been upgraded to assistant secretary for systems analysis, a sign of the increased importance of the new techniques.

The services and JCS had to adopt the new budgeting methods. The secretary of the navy created the Office of Program Appraisal in 1965, and in 1966 the chief of Naval Operations organized a Systems Analysis Division. The secretary of the air force used the Air Battle Analysis Center, and the air staff relied on a Studies and Analysis Group. The army staff organized the Office of Planning and Program Analysis. In 1970 the Joint Chiefs created the Studies, Analysis and Gaming Agency.

McNamara centralized decision-making by using as an action-forcing process the preparation of the Draft Presidential Memorandum (DPM). This document was prepared by the OSA on a particular topic (i.e., air defense), reviewed by the services and the JCS, and then sent by the secretary with his recommendations for the president's approval. The drafting of DPMs involved debates on budgets and strategic doctrines, usually pitting OSA and the secretary against the services and the JCS. The president would generally approve DPMs that rejected three-quarters of the recommendations of the services.[12] Budget figures submitted by the JCS would run approximately 20 percent higher than Defense Department recommendations, and presidents Kennedy and Johnson would then cut between 10 and 25 percent of the original service recommendations in their requests submitted to Congress.[13]

The new system did not run smoothly. The services were skeptical of the new budgeting techniques, especially when favored weapons systems were rejected. The procurement of weapons was marked by cost overruns and technical problems, some of which the JCS blamed on the new budgeting techniques. McNamara had little public or congressional support and could be outmaneuvered by the services in Congress, especially when he recommended contract cancellations or revisions, or closings of bases. Kennedy and Johnson made some decisions that undercut the Secretary, especially on base closings, missile production, and development of the antiballistic missile system.

The Nixon administration dismantled most of the budget process. Defense Secretary Melvin Laird, himself a former congressional leader who had chafed under McNamara's system, introduced "participatory management" and instituted a triad to control budgets, consisting of himself, Undersecretary David Packard, and Director of DDRE John Foster. The DDRE, with its bias toward procurement of technologically sophisticated weapons, supplanted OSA as the major analyst of proposed weapons systems. OSA no longer initiated strategy, budget, or procurement studies, but was reduced to a review of options presented by the JCS and services. The triad also downgraded recommendations of the Defense comptroller and generally favored positions of the services and JCS. Each service once again pressed for a "fair share" of the total budget.[14]

But the services were no happier with Nixon than with his predecessors. In an October 1969 National Security Council decision memorandum Nixon ordered a reduction in preparedness from a "two and one-half" to a "one and one-half" war strategy, which meant reductions in the numbers of ships, planes, and troops to be maintained. Nixon instituted a review of proposed weapons systems centered in the National Security Council by establishing the Defense Program Review Committee, chaired by NSC Director Henry Kissinger. The committee, aided by its program analysis staff, reviewed weapons systems and made five-year strategic plans. It also influenced the fiscal plan for the Pentagon.[15]

The OMB also played a role in defense budgeting through its National Security Programs Division. Civilian analysts from OMB, the NSC, and the Defense Department worked together in the early stages of the budget process. The defense secretary provided the JCS with a fiscal guidance memorandum early in the budget cycle. The JCS then prepared its strategic operations plan based on the program objective memoranda of the services. Defense officials would then respond with program decision memoranda modifying the proposals of the services and commands. The JCS and services would then produce a force posture statement and joint force memorandum, which the secretary would review and modify. The JCS could then appeal to the OMB or to the NSC Program Review Committee. At times Kissinger and Nixon would restore some of the cuts made by the Defense Department.[16] By institutionalizing the conflict amongst Laird, the JCS, the services, and OMB, Kissinger and Nixon were left with the final decision on important issues. This system, which provided the president with a variety of options, was an improvement on Kennedy's practice of relying almost exclusively on McNamara's judgment about the Pentagon budget.

The Carter administration changed procedures in order to give fiscal guidance to the JCS and services very early in the budget process. A new deputy secretary was put in charge of the budget process. Preliminary ceilings set by the administration were revised throughout the budget cycle, leaving the president and defense secretary with maximum flexibility. Secretary Harold Brown, himself a former director of DDRE, sometimes sided with the professional military and against the OMB analysts in battles over procurement of advanced weapons systems such as the MX missile. At other times he made severe cuts in programs, such as the naval shipbuilding program. When Carter came into office he pledged to cut defense expenditures by billions of dollars, yet after several months in office the defense secretary announced that the administration intended to increase the defense budget by approximately 3 percent in real terms; following a review by OMB the presidential decision was to request a 2 percent increase. Pentagon officials pressured president and Congress for additional funds and costly new weapons systems.

Department Growth Patterns

Enough has been said to indicate that career officials will fight with department executives, and both will have quarrels with presidents, no matter what budget technique is employed. Neither bureau chief nor department secretary will exercise restraint or call for retrenchment in aggregate levels of spending; it is perhaps no coincidence that the greatest spurt in defense expenditures occurred in the Kennedy and Johnson administrations—even prior to the war in Vietnam—as a consequence of the new budgeting systems. A president who cannot make his own decisions will find his budget totals increasing exponentially.

Some departments will emphasize incremental growth to minimize conflict with the president. They will work closely with interest groups and Congress and present requests for small increases to OMB. Others, intent on major expansion, may choose a different strategy, attempting to put their activities before the public as vital to national security or well-being. Such departments will solicit presidential support for large increases, mobilize their supporters at the grass roots, and embark on a national agenda strategy to gain a public commitment from the president to request major funding of their new programs. They are likely to use task forces, national commissions and conferences, and the media to promote first-stage initiation.

Studies by political scientists indicate that agencies that ask for large, nonincremental funding increases, and adopt a strategy to mobilize political support, tend to receive larger increases in both presidential budget requests and congressional appropriations, than agencies that pursue an incremental approach.[17] As clashes between bureau and department levels grow more heated over the allocation of scarce resources, more bureaus may turn to overt political pressure on the administration to secure what they consider to be adequate funding. To deal with increased conflict within the executive branch the president must act as his own budget officer. To do so he needs staff assistance from agencies of the institutionalized presidency.

The Office of Management and Budget

To prepare the executive budget the president uses the Office of Management and Budget (OMB). Its predecessor, the Bureau of the Budget (1921–1970) generally avoided a policymaking role. As its first director, Charles Dawes, explained, "the Budget Bureau keeps humble, and if it ever becomes obsessed with the idea that it has any work except to save money and improve efficiency in routine business it will cease to be useful in the hands of the President."[18] For fifty years the BOB worked as the president's agency, serving his interests alone, operating from his perspective. Director Dawes established the norm that "the Budget Bureau must be impartial, impersonal, and non-political."[19] Director Harold Smith warned that "deciding basic policies is clearly outside the Bureau's role."[20] Director Kermit Gordon noted that the director is obligated to "use such secondary decision-making authority as the President allows him to exercise in accordance with the President's attitudes, values, and priorities as he discerns them—even when, on occasion, they may differ from his own."[21] The bureau applied the doctrine of "neutral competence," which according to political scientist Hugh Heclo, "consists of giving one's cooperation and best independent judgment of the issues to partisan bosses—and of being sufficiently uncommitted to be able to do so for a succession of partisan leaders."[22] But in practice the BOB was never entirely neutral. It participated in the creation of many New Deal agencies, and it eventually helped reorganize them into the modern departmental structure that evolved in the Truman and Eisenhower administrations. It participated in the task forces of the New Frontier and the Great Society. Its careerists emphasized incremental change and were sometimes resistant to radical innovations that might cut across depart-ment lines. Some budget officials served once with agencies they later examined, which created a connection between careerists in the depart-ment and the BOB that might prove counterproductive for the president.

The Nixon administration, committed to retrenchment in many fields and radical innovations in a few others, and hostile to many of the New Frontier and Great Society intergovernmental grant programs, did not believe that the bureau would be "neutral" or responsive to presidential priorities. The bureau was abolished and replaced with the Office of Management and Budget, whose director served as a presidential counselor and was installed in the west wing of the White House with other senior advisors. A cadre of political executives, the program asso-ciate directors, was placed in the OMB to control career division managers and budget examiners. The predictable result was erosion of staff morale and the resignation of many experienced budget officers. In 1960 three-fourths of the senior officials had been with BOB for more than six years, whereas by 1974 two-thirds of the heads of the OMB's major units had been with the agency for less than one year.[23]

Ford and Carter kept the OMB politicized with their own appointees, and their OMB directors served as principal presidential assistants. They emphasized responsiveness at the expense of "neutral competence" and experience. Since in periods of retrenchment budget decisions are likely to cause conflict in the administration, it well serves the president to have loyalists at the high levels of his budget agency. But he loses the "institu-tional memory" of the office, for career professionals have judgment and intuition that could benefit the administration. The installation of political executives who lack experience, long-range perspective, and expertise means that there is no one at senior levels who can "educate the president from below" by explaining to him the administrative or other consequences of decisions about agency budgets.

The OMB and the Departments

At the start of the budget cycle (early spring) the OMB informs the departments of the tentative fiscal outlook and of presidential spending priorities. Some departments are expected to come up with new initiatives, and others are asked to retrench. Later the OMB may impose specific ceilings. In some cases OMB examiners will offer suggestions or even participate in departmental review of bureau estimates. During the summer a detailed set of fiscal projections and spending guidelines are issued. Between September 15 and November 1 the OMB formally examines department budgets by holding hearings at which officials must justify their figures before senior examiners. Between November 1 and December 1 the OMB holds its "director's review" of the entire budget, and it invites participation by the National Security Council, the Council of Economic Advisors, and several White House aides. The OMB communicates decisions to departments, which may then appeal directly to the president. Most of the time the president will deny the appeal, for as Kermit Gordon observes,

If the President reverses his Budget Director fairly frequently, the latter's usefulness to the President will be gravely impaired, if not destroyed . . . and his desk will become only a temporary resting place for problems on the way to the President.[24]

Nixon would not permit domestic departments to appeal to him after the OMB had made its decisions. Other presidents may be more accommodating and flexible. Departments fear reprisals from the OMB if they appeal, since it may cut more from the budget or suggest major management changes in the next budget cycle. Department secretaries may prefer to appeal to Congress for restoration of cuts rather than to the president.

Sometimes Pentagon budget requests are treated differently: in the Kennedy and Johnson administrations the Defense Department budget was accepted by the president without review by the Bureau of the Budget—the BOB could then appeal to the president if it thought expenditure proposals for specific items were too high. The presumption of necessity rested with the Pentagon, and the burden of proof rested with the BOB—a reversal of the situation with other departments. Nixon scrapped that procedure and left final decisions with the NSC committee and the OMB, giving the Pentagon the right to appeal to him. Both Ford and Carter also used the OMB as a counterweight to the budget prepared by the secretary of defense, and both upheld the OMB rather than the department on several crucial issues.

Each president conducts his final review of the budget differently. Nixon spent hardly any time with his budget director and only concerned himself with aggregate totals rather than with specific departmental re-

PREPARING THE EXECUTIVE BUDGET

February–March

1. The executive branch begins work on the executive budget to be submitted to Congress the following January.
2. The Council of Economic Advisors makes economic forecasts and the Office of Management and Budget makes expenditure projections. The president confers with economic advisors on fiscal policy and overall expenditure levels for the next fiscal year.
3. Bureaus and agencies make budget estimates and submit them to department budget offices.

March–April

1. The president makes tentative decisions on overall spending levels for the next fiscal year.
2. Departments receive guidelines on overall spending levels in accordance with presidential decisions.
3. Departments review agency and bureau submissions and begin to prepare documentation and testimony to justify expenditures to OMB and the president.

May–August

1. The president revises his decisions on overall spending levels in consultation with his principal economic advisors. He makes tentative decisions on spending ceilings for departments.
2. OMB holds hearings with officials from each operating bureau and agency, and also holds discussions with department budget officials.
3. Departments prepare final budget requests in consultation with OMB officials.
4. White House aides, interest group lobbyists, and state and local officials may intervene to press their case on OMB and the president.

September–October

1. Departments make final submissions to OMB. The OMB director conducts the Director's Review of department budgets and confers with the president.
2. The president reviews fiscal policy with advisors and makes tentative decisions on overall expenditure levels.

November–December

1. OMB and CEA make final fiscal projections. The president makes fiscal policy and spending decisions.
2. The president conducts a final review of department budgets. He decides appeals made by department secretaries against the decisions of OMB.
3. OMB notifies departments of presidential decisions. Departments conform their plans and spending projections to OMB decisions.

January

1. The OMB finishes preparation of the executive budget.
2. The president prepares a budget message for transmittal to Congress. The budget and budget message are sent to Congress.
3. The Executive Branch begins to prepare the next budget to be submitted to Congress the following January.

quests. In contrast, Eisenhower spent a great deal of time on individual items, especially those from the Defense Department. Truman and Ford plunged into the details of domestic programs, and enjoyed making decisions on the "appeals" made by department secretaries against OMB decisions. Johnson used his first budget review to lower expenditures to under $100 billion in order to soften up Congress for his legislative initiatives and tax program. Carter's budget review focused on the impact of a proposed new urban program on his goal of achieving a balanced budget by 1981, a review that resulted in disapproval of most of the proposals submitted by his interdepartmental urban task force.

The president considers the executive budget primarily in political terms. He must be concerned with "packaging" it for Congress and the public. It must convey his priorities without splitting his party and playing into the hands of the opposition. To satisfy his party is almost impossible: Republican presidents project large deficits that outrage their conservative followers but do not satisfy Democrats who focus on proposed cutbacks. Carter's middle course left him open to criticism from Republicans that he had not reduced the size of the deficits, and from Democrats who claimed that he had not proposed any major new initiatives. In the general letdown of the post-Christmas season the president seems more Scrooge than Santa Claus as he submits his budget to Congress.

The president normally engages in buckpassing in order to project a frugal image. He underestimates the costs for payouts in some entitlement programs. He overestimates revenues by projecting a booming economy. The purpose of these maneuvers is to lower the anticipated budget deficit. It also enables the president to blame Congress for "irresponsible" spending proposals and for subsequent deficits.

The Executive Budget

The budget that the president submits to Congress each January consists of routine compilations of agency bases and increments, some provision for new programs or expansion in existing ones, provisions to abolish or cut back on some expenditures, and estimates for the costs of "uncontrollables," such as debt interest, pensions, salaries, contract payments, and transfer payments to individuals (social security, welfare, unemployment insurance, medicare, medicaid, food stamps). These uncontrollables accounted for 66.2 percent of the FY 1970 budget, 72.8 percent of the FY 1973 budget, and 75.1 percent of the FY 1974 budget. Since 1974 over three-fourths of the budget has become "uncontrollable" in the sense that payments must be made under existing laws, and there is no ceiling on these expenditures instituted through appropriations. Approximately half the budget outlays are for transfer payments to individuals, established by law, and it is less likely that these expenditures will be curtailed than it is that taxes will be raised or the debt increased to cover outlays. As much as nine-tenths of the requested increases in funding from one fiscal year to the next involve these "uncontrollable" items and payouts to individuals.

In the 1960s the executive budgets generally provided increments for most programs and significant expansion of various domestic social welfare programs. In the 1970s, with the exception of defense and energy, there are few major new initiatives proposed, and increments are matched by decreases in some areas. In recent budgets presidents may propose between $10 and $20 billion in new programs, and a like amount in terminations or decreases. Expenditure by *category* (lumping expenditures of several departments or agencies for overall national goals) shows incremental change. In Carter's fiscal year 1979 budget, for example, defense increased 0.8 percent, education and employment 3 percent, income security (transfer payments) 0.5 percent, transportation 1.7 percent, natural resources 1.6 percent, community development 2.3 percent, justice 2.4 percent, agriculture 1.8 percent; and commerce decreased 3 percent and health 1.1 percent. The only nonincremental change was for expenditures in energy, up 26.3 percent. Overall expenditure by department tends to rise incrementally as well. The most vulnerable targets for major changes are politically unpopular programs like foreign aid or manned space exploration, those benefiting the poor in urban areas, or those where "uncontrollable" payouts are getting out of hand, such as medicare and medicaid. Political scientist Lance LeLoup estimates that perhaps 10 to 15 percent of the entire budget is susceptible to change in a given fiscal year.[25] Since most uncontrollables and transfer payments are politically untouchable, and since the defense budget generally increases, the result is that major changes must be made within a few departments and agencies in which spending is controllable, and in which it is politically possible for the president to recommend cutbacks. What appears to be "small change" when viewed as a percentage of the entire executive budget actually involves significant fluctuations in bureau budgets and in spending for particular programs from one year to the next. The changes that the president proposes in his budget are then considered through the congressional appropriations process, in which bureaus that have suffered cutbacks win the opportunity to overturn the president's decision.

II

The Appropriations Process

Budget authority in Congress is decentralized. The principle rivals for power have been the House and Senate Appropriations Committees on the one hand and the standing committees on the other. At first appropriations bills were under the jurisdiction of various standing committees, but by the end of the Civil War the two Appropriations Committees had won jurisdiction over almost all spending measures. Between 1877 and 1899 the pendulum swung the other way, and they were stripped of bills dealing with rivers and harbors, agriculture, naval affairs, pensions, the post office, and the army. Then in 1921, as part of the budget reform being instituted, the House restored jurisdiction over all appropriations bills to its Appropriations Committee, and the Senate followed suit a year later. Authority was not completely centralized, however, because standing committees retained the power to write laws that bypassed the appropriations process and provided alternate sources of funds—the "back-door" provisions. By the mid-1970s such provisions accounted for approximately half of government expenditures. In 1974 Congress provided that most back-door funding provisions be renewed by the Appropriations Committees, a victory for them over the standing committees that provided for a considerable centralization of budget authority. At the same time Congress also created two new Budget Committees, with power to recommend overall expenditure ceilings and "category" ceilings, creating a new rivalry between appropriations committees, which provide funds for departments and bureaus, and budget committees, which have jurisdiction over congressional resolutions that set overall and category spending ceilings for the fiscal year.

In a parliamentary system the government submits its estimates of expenditures and revenues to a parliament, and then organizes its followers to pass its budget and tax proposals on a party vote. The cabinet proposals are rarely changed by the parliament. In the American system the president submits his executive budget to Congress, which then gives different committees jurisdiction over different aspects. Revenue proposals (and any specific requests for legislation that the Treasury submits throughout the year) are dealt with by the House Ways and Means and Senate Finance Committees. Proposals for changes in the laws to deal with "uncontrollables" are sent to standing committees with jurisdiction (generally Ways and Means and Finance), which have jurisdiction over almost half the federal outlays. Fiscal implications of the president's program are studied by the Joint Economic Committee, and budget resolutions are prepared by the House and Senate Budget

Committees (see chapter 9). Expenditure requests are sent to the House and Senate Appropriations Committees. In none of these committees does the administration command automatic majorities, and in none can it control the timing of decisions or the resolution of issues.

When the Appropriations Committees begin consideration of spending requests, they have several options. They have the figures in the president's budget, estimates from substantive committees of probable outlays of programs under their jurisdiction (which takes into account proposed changes in laws affecting these programs that are likely to pass in the congressional session), program options prepared by the Congressional Budget Office (CBO), and tentative spending guidelines for sixteen "functional categories" prepared by the Budget Committee in their chamber. The president also provides them with the current services budget, which indicates the amount that must be appropriated by Congress if the present level of services for each program is to be maintained in the next fiscal year.

The president must influence these committees if he is to convert his budget recommendations into spending authority for the departments and agencies. But the appropriations committees are among the most powerful in Congress, and their members are immune to presidential pressure. They are insulated from electoral competition, especially in the House. In 1972 committee Democrats were elected with an average of 73.8 percent, in 1974 with an average of 76.8 percent, and in 1976 with an average of 74.7 percent in the House; committee Republicans in those years were elected with averages of 60.4 percent, 60.3 percent, and 65.2 percent respectively, with no members defeated. Each committee member can maintain his position in his district through delivery of goods and services and patronage, from agencies eager to please him. The president cannot oust these members from his party, the committee, or the House by purging them if they cross him.

The House committee, in a process known as "cross-walking," transfers lines from the executive budget into thirteen separate appropriations bills, one for each subcommittee. These subcommittees act as miniature committees, and each defers to the others in its area of expertise. Members of the two parties may disagree with each other on specifics, but subcommittee norms emphasize bipartisan consensus-building based on certain shared values: respect for hard work and expertise, reciprocity among members, and a shared attitude that they are "guardians of the Treasury."[26] A majority are conservatives, and southern Democrats are overrepresented as subcommittee chairmen. The members are often disposed to cut increases requested by a Democratic president. During the Nixon and Ford administrations requests were sometimes so low that the subcommittees increased totals.

When a subcommittee "marks up" the bill to determine dollar amounts it will recommend to the full committee, it has several choices. It can make an across-the-board slash in agency expenditures by a specified percentage ("meataxe cut"). Or it can give the agency the amount appropriated in the preceding year, which in a period of high inflation has the impact of a cut. If it wishes to maintain the status quo it may appropriate the amount indicated in the current services budget. To reward an agency it may give it the amount recommended by the OMB in the executive budget (if that is an incremental increase) or if it is really generous, it may provide the amount that the agency requested from the OMB. In exceptional cases it will even tack on additional funds to provide for expenditures that the substantive committees will authorize through new legislation, in effect mandating activities that the administration has not planned for.

In the 1950s and 1960s subcommittees generally cut only part of the increments requested for agencies in the executive budget. This meant that in each successive year agencies would receive modest increases. Bureaus would generally defend the president's budget, since they expected to obtain some, if not all, of the increments he had recommended for them. In the 1970s the OMB protects neither the "base" nor "fair share" of bureau budgets, so there is less loyalty on the part of careerists to the president's recommendations. Bureaus have an incentive to "end run" the administration and appeal directly to Congress for additional funds. The irony is that administration attempts to use the OMB to establish a presidential chain of command for purposes of retrenchment or "zero-base" budgeting has led to disloyalty in the bureaus, which look to congressional subcommittees to restore the cuts. The nexus between Congress and the bureaucracy is strengthened, and the chain of command in the administration is weakened, when new management and budgeting techniques are introduced.

The Senate Appropriations Committee usually acts on bills after the House committee has completed its work, although this is not a constitutional requirement and should not be confused with the provision that the House must originate all revenue measures. The twenty-seven members of the Senate committee are joined by up to twenty-four other senators on various subcommittees, in accordance with Rule 16, clause 6, which provides that the eight appropriations subcommittees may name three additional senators to serve with each of them. Application of this rule means that over half the Senate deals with appropriations. Rather than broadening perspectives, this involvement narrows them. Each subcommittee adds subject-matter specialists from the standing committees with jurisdiction over the agencies to be funded, and these additional senators try to "boost" the programs under their jurisdiction by seeking high appropriations. This is especially true for military, space, atomic energy, public works, and agriculture appropriations. In contrast to their House colleagues, senators serve on several major committees and many subcommittees and have less time to understand the details of appropriations bills. They are more partisan and less deferential to subcommittee experts, and they do not consider themselves "guardians of the Treasury." Subcommittee decisions are often challenged and modified by the full committee, or even overturned by the Senate.

Senate subcommittees work with "sideslips" prepared by the staff, which contain the budget options given by the administration and results of House subcommittee and committee actions. The Senate often assumes that figures approved by the House are too low and is therefore disposed to entertain agency or department "appeals." The subcommittees may function as "courts of appeal" and restore funds cut by the House. Senators who champion particular agencies can expect grateful officials to be attentive to their concerns about agency operations. The deeper the cuts an agency suffers in the House, the more responsive it may become to members of the Senate.[27]

Both appropriations committees must be responsive to their chambers. If their bills exceed category ceilings established by the budget committees, they must explain their actions. Sometimes sharp controversy erupts between standing substantive committees that authorized major new programs and the appropriations committees that cut funds for them. In spite of differences in the chambers, most votes on appropriations bills involve high party cohesion and pass the chamber. This should not be taken as a sign that the administration has been successful. Coalitions are organized by congressional party and committee leaders, and whatever last-minute compromises are necessary to round up the votes are organized in the chamber itself, with the White House generally playing a secondary role. The conference committee that reconciles figures in each appropriations bill may listen to administration officials and the OMB director in making its final decisions—but it may also go off on its own. The final figures approved by the conference committee are usually closer to those contained in the Senate bill rather than those in the House version, and they are often closer to the president's original suggestions than the original action taken by the House. Cuts are restored because the Senate figures are more realistic and House members are willing to recede from what may have been punitive actions.[28] When both the Senate and House figures are higher than presidential recommendations, the two chambers are not likely to drop down to the presidential figures.

Administrative Oversight

Subcommittees use the hearings to engage in administrative oversight for several purposes. They have a "nickel and dime" mentality that induces them to focus on agency overhead such as office furnishings, limousines, and vouchered expense accounts. They scrutinize contracts for goods and services for evidence of irregularities or poor judgment. Subcommittees use the General Accounting Office to investigate agencies with reputations for poor financial management. The legislators make sure that they and their favored colleagues in the House are given preference when projects are planned, regional offices are constructed, or other facilities are built. They may also concern themselves with politically sensitive issues, such as federal funding for abortions, birth control, school busing, and they may place prohibitions on agency activities that have become unpopular.

The president not only wants his budget figures approved, he also wants complete discretion in spending the funds. The first appropriations act passed by Congress was drafted by Treasury Secretary Alexander Hamilton, and provides an illustration of what presidents seek:

That there be appropriated for the service of the present year, to be paid out of monies which arise, either from the requisitions heretofore made upon the several states or from duties on impost or tonnage, the following sums, viz. A sum not exceeding 216,000 dollars for defraying the expenses of the civil list, under the late and present government; a sum not exceeding 137,000 dollars for defraying the expenses of the department of war; a sum not exceeding 190,000 dollars for discharging the warrants issued by the board of Treasury and remaining unsatisfied; and a sum not exceeding 96,000 for paying pensions to invalids.[29]

In crisis Congress will pass general appropriations, often in the form the president seeks, as it did for Franklin Roosevelt in the early stages of the Depression and during the Second World War. But in normal times appropriations bills will run for many pages and involve detailed provisions: formulae specifying distribution of goods and services; eligibility standards for clientele receiving services; procedures for how services are to be rendered and agency activities conducted; prohibitions of activities; personnel ceilings and pay scales; and specific category ceilings for individual programs. Many appropriations bills require agencies to submit evaluations of the effectiveness of their programs or other specified data to congressional committees. Bills may also direct the General Accounting Office to conduct a detailed audit or a policy evaluation of specific programs for the committees.[30]

Committees need not place such provisions in the appropriations bills. They may write "directives" in their reports accompanying bills to the floor, which they expect agency officials to follow. Committee members maintain close consultation with officials and are given advance notice of many agency decisions. They can exercise an "informal veto" over some decisions. A detailed appropriation that ties an agency up is often a sign that the informal system of consultation no longer works. Conversely a general appropriation, far from being an abdication of legislative oversight, may indicate a close working relationship between committee and agency.

But appropriations committees are not particularly effective in using oversight to develop new policies. They are better at uncovering abuses of financial authority or at influencing the distributive process to their advantage than they are at policy initiation.[31] Some agencies are examined perfunctorily, and others not at all. Lawmakers often focus more on increments than on examination of agency bases.[32] Subcommittee jurisdictions do not logically follow the organization of departments, and often agencies are not examined in a broad perspective or in relation to activities of other departments. There are no systematic attempts to determine if activities could be performed better by the private sector or by state and local governments. Appropriations committees, like the substantive legislative committees, frustrate administration attempts to concentrate resources in a few states or urban areas to mount major attacks on problems. Poverty, transportation, housing, and community development funds must be distributed widely to meet committee requirements, so there is no way to concentrate effort on problems of the large urban centers. Funds are spread thin, and some programs become boondoggles.

Modification of the Executive Budget

Although Congress does not change overall spending totals much, it makes significant changes in funding for specific domestic programs, especially in distributive social welfare programs involving poverty, community development, housing, education, and transportation. Only a few agencies are immune to congressional action: these include the FBI, which is never cut below administration requests, and the CIA, whose budget is "hidden" in those of other agencies and not subject to the full scope of the appropriations process. Military budget requests are hardly changed in wartime, but in peace the aggregates are changed slightly, and there are major changes in programs for procurement of strategic weapons, capital construction of naval vessels, and research and development. For several years after the Soviet Union launched its Sputnik satellite, Congress used its appropriations powers to fund accelerated development of the Polaris missile and submarine program and to procure Atlas ICBM missiles. At times as much as 10 percent of the strategic weapons funding will be rearranged by congressional committees.[33] In most years a "subgovernment" of defense contractors, congressional committee leaders, and military officers in the Pentagon combine to increase spending totals to levels higher than figures recommended in the president's budget.[34] Occasionally, however, the Budget Committees and Appropriations Committees will work closely together to make large cuts in defense spending, as was the case in 1975 after the fall of the South Vietnamese government and the end of American military involvement in Indochina.[35] In the case of military spending, it often seems that the president is the "guardian of the Treasury" and not the members of the appropriations committees.

The president cannot control Congress when it revises the figures in his executive budget. Because the likelihood of successful White House intervention is low, the president is often reluctant to do more than stand behind the OMB and work discreetly in the conference committees to restore the worst of the cuts or trim the most excessive increases. As political scientist Stephen Horn noted, "With the exception of defense, foreign aid, and space programs, personal requests from the Chief Executive are few. Primarily this is a question of tactics. No President wants to commit his prestige and then suffer a rebuff."[36] National Agenda politics will not work, because consideration of bills is complex and drawn out over many months. Most decisions made by subcommittees are neither dramatic nor comprehensible to the public. The sheer quantity of figures guarantees that most changes could not be made issues by the White House. The president may threaten to veto appropriations bills, but prior to the Nixon administration this weapon was rarely used: between 1789 and 1966 there were only forty such vetoes, and of these ten were overridden (including eight for public works). The administration needs funds, and often finds it better to take what Congress offers rather than risk delay and possible further setbacks. Congress passes continuing resolutions to fund programs at existing levels until an appropriations measure is signed into law, but this hurts departments because of inflation and inability to receive increments. In many cases a presidential veto of funds for a popular program will be overridden. When Congress considered the 1976 Labor–Health, Education, and Welfare appropriation, many Republicans deserted President Ford and voted to override. Democrats passed measures with high spending totals that Ford vetoed, thus creating an election issue between the two parties. In spring 1976 Ford warned Congress that he would veto measures the entire summer if necessary to hold down spending totals; in the fall he was defeated in the election, and one of the issues Carter used effectively was Ford's veto of various antirecessionary public works and public employment measures. (Carter in 1978 issued similar warnings.) The president may win a victory in the appropriations process if his veto is sustained, and later wind up losing the political wars.

III

Impoundment Powers

Until 1974 and passage of new legislation, the presidential weakness in the appropriations process could be overcome, at least in part, by instituting prerogative government. Presidents claimed constitutional and statutory authority to *impound* funds appropriated by Congress, either by rescinding spending authority (and treating the appropriation as permissive rather than mandatory), or by deferring spending to future fiscal years, or by establishing reserves from existing appropriated funds for each program to meet contingencies. Like the veto power, impoundment power is a negative and defensive exercise of prerogatives, used out of weakness in the legislative process and working only to block congress, not to lead it.

As part of their "executive power" presidents claimed the right to defer spending to future fiscal years. In 1803 Thomas Jefferson deferred spending a $50,000 appropriation for gunboats in order to purchase more advanced ships the following year. He was careful to inform Congress of his actions and assure it that the funds would be expended.[37] Grant returned funds to the Treasury when public works projects could be completed for less money than Congress had appropriated, a power upheld by opinion of two attorneys general.[38] Congress eventually placed such authority on a statutory basis by passing Anti-Deficiency Acts of 1905 and 1906, and the Bureau of the Budget developed the policy, announced by Director Dawes in 1921, that "the President does not assume . . . that the minimum of government expenditures in the year is the amount fixed by Congress in its appropriations."[39] Harding considered appropriations a form of permission, as a ceiling, rather than as a mandate or directive to spend the full amounts. The Bureau of the Budget created reserves from appropriated funds to meet emergencies or to effect savings when they could be made without cuts in service.[40]

During the Depression Congress gave Hoover authority to cut the budget deficit by establishing reserves in accordance with previous practices. By 1932 Hoover had interpreted the Economy Act of that year as giving him authority to cancel projects funded by Congress, in effect a form of item veto giving him great power over the details of appropriations bills. Congress protested this interpretation. In 1933 Roosevelt used a different tack; he instructed the Bureau of the Budget to make quarterly allotments of appropriations to departments to keep them within spending limits. The BOB in turn created or increased reserves by deferring spending to future fiscal years.[41]

Congress has continued to provide presidents with statutory authority to make certain kinds of impoundments. The Anti-Deficiency Act of 1950 provides:

In apportioning any appropriation, reserves may be established to provide for contingencies, or to effect savings whenever savings are made possible by or through changes in requirements, greater efficiency of operations, or other developments subsequent to the date on which such apportionment was made available.[42]

But this law gave the president no authority to establish reserves in order to curtail or abolish programs, or to control aggregate spending levels as part of fiscal policy. The committee report accompanying the measures in the House found "no warrant or justification for the thwarting of a major policy of Congress by the impoundment of funds."[43] But the law was loosely drawn, and presidents could get around its intent. Nixon in 1971 used "other developments" mentioned in the statute; he asserted that if he intended to abolish a program (like the War on Poverty's Office of Economic Opportunity) he could then impound appropriated funds for it. In 1976 the Ford administration cut expenditures in the food-stamp program by changing administrative regulations to make eligibility more difficult—and then established reserves under the provisions of the act, a clear example of a policy decision announced as an administrative action. In 1978 President Carter signed a supplemental appropriation bill that provided for funds for an experimental nuclear reactor that the administration opposed. Carter announced that he would use the funds to terminate the project rather than continue with its construction. This prompted the comptroller general of the GAO to warn the president that the congressional intent in the appropriations was that the funds be used to construct the reactor, and that in the event the funds were used to terminate the project, such expenditures would be illegal, and federal officials involved "shall be held accountable for and required to make good to the United States the amount of any payment prohibited by law."[44]

Congress may provide by law that the administration cut off funds to state or local governments or to private contractors not in compliance with federal laws or court orders.[45] Since the 1960s, such impoundments have been used by presidents in cases involving race and sex discrimination, and against welfare and education agencies that have not complied with various laws or regulations. The OMB or a department will also impound funds where corruption at the local level makes effective use of the funds impossible. Congress may delegate authority to the president to make selective or across-the-board expenditure cuts. The Economy Act of 1932 gave Hoover authority to lay off federal workers, lower salaries, and reorganize agencies.[46] In 1945, after the Second World War ended, Congress ordered rescissions in military spending; in 1951 it ordered cuts of $550 million and in 1968 during the Vietnam War a congressional spending resolution mandated cuts in several domestic programs.

Some exercises of impoundment powers rest on a presidential claim of constitutional prerogative. Like most such claims, they are controversial and place the president in conflict with Congress—especially since no impoundment power is explicitly granted by the Constitution in Article II. The president creates the impoundment power by treating appropriations passed by Congress as permissive rather than mandatory, and by combining "The Executive Power" and the duty to faithfully execute the laws into a new *spending power.*

President Grant relied on the spending power when he began the practice, in 1876, of impounding funds for domestic distributions in the "pork-barrel" Rivers and Harbors Bill passed by Congress in each session. He impounded $2.7 million of a $5 million measure, and in his message to the House he warned, "Without enumerating, many appropriations are made for works of purely private or local interest, in no sense national. I cannot give my sanction to these, and will take care that during my term of office no public money shall be expended on them."[47] The Democratic House passed a resolution calling on Grant to justify his actions, but the president made no response. Since the appropriation was indefinite in term, the funding authority did not lapse, and within two years he and his successor released the funds.

Presidents also rely on the commander in chief clause for impoundment authority. Between 1942 and 1945 Roosevelt deferred more than $500 million in pork-barrel projects. Congress for its part passed in 1943 an amendment to the Public Roads Bill allowing impoundment only on certification by the War Production Board that the completion of the project would impede the war effort, a requirement easily met by the administration. The Senate passed, but the House rejected, a provision in the Rural Post Roads Bill placing impoundment authority with the commissioner of public roads rather than with the president. The Senate passed, and the House rejected, an amendment that would have required the president to obtain congressional approval for all impoundments.[48] Instead the Public Works Acts of 1944 and 1945 left impoundment authority with the president.[49]

Even in peacetime presidents impound funds for weapons systems. In 1949 Truman directed the Bureau of the Budget to impound $735 million to reduce the Air Force bomber wings from fifty-eight to forty-eight. He relied on language in the appropriation that made this particular expenditure permissive.[50] But the House Appropriations Committee, in a report the following year, argued,

. . . there is no warrant of justification for the thwarting of a major policy of Congress by the impounding of funds. If this principle of thwarting the will of Congress should be accepted as correct, then Congress would be totally incapable of carrying out its constitutional mandate of providing for the defense of the Nation.[51]

Truman impounded funds for a "supercarrier" favored by the navy, while Eisenhower impounded $137 million to prevent development of the Nike-Zeus antiaircraft missile system. Kennedy impounded $180 million of the funds appropriated to develop the B-70 strategic bomber. The House Appropriations Committee reported a tough bill that "directed, ordered, mandated and required" Secretary of Defense MacNamara to spend the funds, but Kennedy convinced the chairman to substitute softer language that "authorized" him to spend the money, in effect converting the appropriation into a permissive measure and avoiding a confrontation between president and Congress.[52] Subsequently the administration built two prototype bombers before the program was phased out. Later in 1966 the Senate softened language involving a contract for a nuclear powered frigate to give President Johnson discretion.

Presidents take statutes that give the administration general fiscal responsibility and interpret them expansively to justify impoundments. They rely on the Employment Act of 1946, which states:

The Congress declares that it is the continuing policy and responsibility of the Federal Government to use all the practicable means consistent with its needs and obligations and other essential considerations of national policy . . . to provide maximum employment, production, and purchasing power.[53]

But the law doesn't mention impoundments, and if Congress had intended to authorize presidential impoundments on fiscal grounds, surely it could have authorized them in the act. Instead, the president was given authority to make "such recommendations for legislation as he may deem necessary or desirable," indicating that Congress intended to have the final word on making fiscal policy.[54] Nixon relied on this law, and also on a provision of the Economic Stabilization Act of 1971, which gave the president authority "to stabilize prices, rents, wages and salaries."[55] This act did not mention impoundments either, but neither did it explicitly forbid them. Presidential interpretation of these and other laws carried his power to extremes: a president can use whatever statutes Congress passes that delegate economic authority to the executive branch, and then he can claim that because impoundment was not mentioned or prohibited in these statutes, it can be used to implement the legislation. If such an interpretation of the laws were valid, Congress would be forced to amend all existing economic legislation in force to deny the president impoundment authority.

Presidents often have used a combination of constitutional prerogatives and statutory powers to make impoundments on fiscal grounds. They fuse the "take care" clause with laws setting the debt limit and their authority under the Employment Act of 1946 to create a "resulting" impoundment power to stabilize the economy. But the "take care" clause is an obligation, not a separate grant of power, and Congress argues that

it is limited to the duty to execute the laws as Congress intended. Therefore, the president must execute appropriations acts as Congress intended,
and cannot interfere with the delegation of spending authority to subordinate officials in the executive branch.

A comparison between actions taken by Johnson and Nixon is instruc-
tive. Both used impoundment powers to control aggregate spending, but
each used a different political strategy. In 1966 Johnson announced impoundment of approximately $5.3 billion from appropriations for the
departments of HEW, Agriculture, Interior, and from the Highway Trust
Funds. Early in 1967 he released $1.5 billion to forestall congressional
criticism. He then asked Congress for an expenditure ceiling that would
give him authority to impound, and Congress passed the Revenue and
Expenditure Control Act of 1968, linking a reduction of $6 billion in out-
lays and up to $10 billion in new obligational authority (i.e. appropria-
tions) with a 10 percent surcharge asked by the administration.[56] Johnson
let Congress set priorities and determine the size of the cutbacks through
legislation. He relied on temporary deferrals rather than permanent
rescissions. He cut low priority programs, including some of his own
Great Society favorites. He used his cabinet secretaries to cool congressional tempers, and worked personally with committee leaders in the
House in framing the expenditure resolution. Johnson viewed appropriations as permissive rather than mandatory. Congress responded by
amending the laws dealing with the federal highway program to state
explicitly that its funds could not be impounded as an antiinflationary
economic stabilization measure.

Nixon also used impoundments, especially after his administration
seriously underestimated the size of the deficits, which jumped from $5.5
billion in FY 1969 to $13.1 billion in FY 1970 to over $29 billion in FY
1971 and 1972. This was due primarily to shortfalls in revenues caused by
a slumping economy, rather than by congressional spending measures.
Nixon made rescissions of $12.9 billion in FY 1971 and in the following
year; facing an estimated deficit of $34 billion, he made more drastic cuts,
which totaled $19 billion in impoundments.[57] But Nixon's methods were
controversial, because through selective impoundments he eliminated or
curtailed programs favored by the Democratic Congress. Hubert
Humphrey accurately pinpointed the problem:

Under policy impoundment, funds are withheld not to effect savings, not as
directed by Congress, not as Commander-in-Chief, but because the President has
unilaterally decided to impound money for programs that are not his priorities.
It is a method of substituting executive will for congressional purpose.[58]

The administration impounded funds when appropriations exceeded its
requests in the executive budget (as with additional public works funds
Congress added to his FY 1972 requests), when it opposed programs but
did not have votes in Congress to eliminate them, or when it planned to

ask for new legislation to fold existing programs into general revenue-sharing or bloc grants. Some impounded funds were then diverted to other programs. As political scientist Harvey Mansfield, Sr., pointed out at Senate hearings, "the object was not an overall reduction, but despite continuing inflationary pressures, a redistribution of emphasis in order to favor different constituencies from those the Johnson Administration had cultivated."[59] Impoundment had become a form of "item veto," with no possibility of override through the checks and balances system. Even worse, it could be used coercively, for Nixon demanded that Congress rewrite substantive laws for such programs as Rural Electrification and Federal Housing Administration loans—or suffer impoundment of funds. With these powers a president could become a legislature unto himself.

Conflict over Impoundment

In 1969 one of the most perceptive scholars of the budget process could write of impoundments that "the record of the past three decades suggests that Presidents exercised this power with considerable restraint and circumspection."[60] But between 1969 and 1974 the Nixon administration made impoundments in order to frustrate the legislative will. The Democratic Congress soon reacted to the institution of the presidential prerogative. At first individual members personally intervened with the White House to press their cases for restorations of funds for favored projects. By 1970 the chairmen of many subcommittees were upset at the pattern of impoundments, which threatened their control over the distributive process, and began to view the issue as an institutional question between the branches. The Appropriations Committees held hearings on administration impoundments of funds for low-income housing, and substantive committees also raised questions about Nixon's actions.

Congress began to chip away at the presidential prerogative through statutory actions. The Second Supplemental Appropriation Act of 1969 established an expenditure ceiling, but denied Nixon the impoundment power that had been granted to Johnson. On signing the measure Nixon warned, "I would prefer that Congress make these offsetting cuts in programs it considers of lesser priority. . . . If it does not do so, the duty of making such cuts clearly becomes mine."[61] In 1970 Congress again passed an expenditure ceiling, but again without explicit impoundment authority for the president. Several laws were passed to counter impoundments: the Foreign Assistance Authorization of 1971 provided that no funds could be expended for foreign aid programs until funds impounded in Agriculture, Housing and Urban Development, and Health, Education and Welfare were released; a 1970 hospital construction measure explicitly forbade impoundments; and a federal highways act was accompanied by a "sense of Congress" resolution opposing impoundments. In

March 1971 the Senate Subcommittee on the Separation of Powers, chaired by Sam Ervin, held hearings on proposals to pass a statute limiting the president's impoundment power.

The administration counterattacked. The White House threat of a veto of the fiscal year 1972 Labor-HEW appropriations measure forced Congress not only to cut spending totals, but also to add a provision requested by the administration to limit expenditures to 98 percent of the total appropriated, thus granting to Nixon authority to impound $347 million and affirming the principle that appropriations were permissive rather than mandatory. If Congress wished to tack on provisions making appropriations mandatory in new laws, it would provide the administration with the opportunity to argue that in all other appropriations bills in which such "mandatory" language did not appear, the intent of Congress was to leave expenditure levels at the discretion of the president. As Deputy Attorney General Joseph Sneed argued at Senate hearings,

There have been only a very few federal statutes in which the Congress has expressed an unequivocal intention to mandate spending for a particular program. Thus, history compels the conclusion that if the Congress wishes to mandate full spending for a particular program, it must do so in unmistakably clear terms.[62]

To avoid this trap the House deleted from most appropriations bills passed by the Senate the language requiring the president to spend appropriated funds. Instead, members of the House argued that *all* appropriations were mandatory, with only such exceptions as Congress might explicitly provide by law.

In October 1972 Congress handed Nixon a major defeat. The president requested impoundment authority in the expenditure ceiling being considered by Congress. The Senate and House versions of the resolution differed, and a conference committee routinely reported a version to both chambers for final passage. But the Senate balked, and at a second conference committee meeting it was decided to put in new language that established a presidential impoundment provision limited to one day only—and even on that day he could take no action—a complicated parliamentary maneuver that in effect would prevent the president from exercising impoundment authority granted in the resolution. The conference committee then included a provision establishing a joint committee to review the entire budget process, and added a section— Title IV, the Federal Impoundment and Information Act—requiring the administration annually to submit to Congress and to the General Accounting Office a complete listing of impoundments, the reasons for them, and the authority under which they were made.[63]

Nixon responded by viewing the measure as tacit congressional acknowledgment of his prerogative to impound funds. The new Impoundment and Information Act did not, after all, prohibit impoundments, but rather required the president to give Congress information on the actions he had taken. So Nixon in 1973 ordered new impoundments of funds for highways, rural services, school aid, public housing, rent supplements, homeowner mortgages, and pollution control. Congress in turn extended the Economic Stabilization Act, this time specifying explicitly that the president had *no* impoundment authority to carry out its provisions. In effect the act denied him authority to make impoundments for fiscal purposes, the very grounds Nixon had used to justify his policy impoundments.[64] The President and Congress were on a collision course.

Congress and the Courts

Some members of Congress now joined with state and local officials, public service unions, and interest and clientele groups to fight Nixon's impoundments through the courts. The administration challenged their right to sue, claiming that as the impoundment issue was a "political question"—involving the distribution of powers between the branches— it was not an issue suitable for judicial resolution. But the courts took as their prerogative the resolution of such a "boundary dispute" between the branches, for issues of statutory construction and constitutional interpretation were clearly subject to judicial review. Only two of the many cases brought before the federal judiciary were denied review because the plaintiffs lacked standing.

Federal courts generally rejected administration arguments that appropriations are simply ceilings, permissive rather than mandatory. The courts insisted that if the president relied on statutory powers, he could impound funds only when explicitly authorized under the law. Courts enjoined Nixon from dismantling programs authorized by Congress simply because he planned to eliminate them and had requested no funds for them in the future.[65] In over thirty lower court cases the judiciary overturned most Nixon impoundments, although occasionally judges found that Congress had, through statute, given the president power to effect savings (as with a HUD impoundment of $150 million and a moratorium on construction of new public housing).[66] In two cases the courts rejected the administration claim that it had constitutional power over expenditure levels in the bureaus. Courts rejected the argument that the administration could impound funds to prevent inflation or for any other general purpose —only impoundments that involved efficiencies would be allowed under the laws permitting presidents to establish reserves for contingencies.

Eventually the Supreme Court decided two cases involving impoundment of funds for water pollution control. The Court denied that the administration had statutory authority to impound funds where the intent of Congress was to require the executive to spend the funds. Even if Congress had used ambiguous or unclear language in the appropriation, the courts could find its intent. The Court determined that $18 billion in water pollution control funds had been obligated by the administration under the procedures of the act, and therefore none of the funds could be withheld at a later stage through impoundments—putting an end to an administration deferral of $9 billion.[67] The Court did not rule on whether or not the president had any inherent constitutional authority to make impoundments, restricting itself solely to the issue of statutory construction presented by the case.

Checking the President

By late 1973 Nixon had made so many impoundments in distributive programs that he had lost support from his natural congressional constituency, conservative Republicans and southern Democrats. Though not unsympathetic to administration arguments on fiscal policy, they were outraged that the president had challenged congressional control over the distributive process. Allen Ellender, chairman of the Senate Appropriations Committee—and one of the president's strong supporters on many issues—warned as early as 1971 that "the President is showing a complete and utter disregard for the expressed will of Congress."[68] Two years later a bipartisan group of congressional leaders prepared to meet what Sen. Frank Church referred to as "one of the crucial tests before us, if Congress and constitutional government are to survive."[69] In 1973 committees in both the House and Senate held hearings to consider impoundment legislation. The president, meanwhile, indicated that he would impound funds appropriated for water pollution control (the case eventually decided by the Supreme Court), which enraged Sen. Edmund Muskie, the major sponsor of the pollution program. Muskie testified at Senate hearings that "an executive who can refuse to fund—who can refuse to allot—can refuse to implement the law, and how are we to guess what rationale he will choose to justify his actions?"[70] Supporters of the president argued that since Congress had shown no capacity to control expenditures, the president in checking its irresponsibility was exercising his duty as manager of the economy. As OMB Director Roy Ash observed, defending administration actions, Congress should spend its "time and energy in constructing and adopting procedures which would enable it to effectively handle and control budget totals and the actions it must take to live within these totals."[71] Members of Congress responded that their actions had hardly increased expenditures, since they often cut programs; the real reasons for deficits were the failure of the administration to accurately forecast revenues, and the corresponding failure to manage the economy so that prosperity would provide revenues necessary to fund existing programs. In short, the legislators believed that the administration was shifting the blame onto Congress for its own poor performance in managing the economy through the false charge that the legislature had taken actions to increase the deficit beyond aggregate spending levels recommended by the administration.

An impoundment control statute passed the House and Senate in different versions in 1973 but was not passed into law. In the spring and summer of 1974, as the Nixon administration was collapsing, the bipartisan coalition maneuvered to pass a revised version of the legislation deadlocked in conference in the previous year. Democrats pressed for impoundment legislation and Republicans called for a complete reform of the budget process. Just before the Nixon administration fell, Congress passed the Budget Reform and Impoundment Act, which established expenditure control provisions (to satisfy Republicans) and new provisions limiting presidential impoundments (to satisfy Democrats). Nixon signed the measure because most members of Congress favored it, and because it would have passed over his veto in any event.[72]

Under provisions of the law, the president was explicitly forbidden to make policy impoundments. He could defer spending to a later fiscal year by submitting a list of deferrals that would go into effect unless either chamber passed a resolution (not subject to presidential veto) to reject the deferral. He could rescind expenditures only by submitting a request to Congress, which had forty-five days to pass a rescission bill empowering him to make the impoundment. All rescissions and deferrals had to be reported to Congress by the president. The comptroller general of the GAO reports all actions that impound funds without congressional notification, and triggers the forty-five-day period for congressional action. The comptroller general could reclassify a presidential impoundment as either deferral or rescission, and his reclassification would be conclusive. The phrase "other developments" was deleted from the 1950 antideficiency law, thus preventing impoundments on fiscal policy grounds.

The Ford administration did not accommodate itself gracefully to the new procedures. It contended that the law applied only to new deferrals, and not to those made in prior fiscal years. It submitted requests for either rescissions or deferrals on most items in appropriations bills that exceeded the original budget requests, especially in social welfare categories (but not in defense appropriations), forcing Congress to deal with 330 deferrals and 150 rescissions (including 120 policy deferrals and 133 policy rescissions). Congress responded by routinely rejecting most requests for rescissions: in fiscal year 1975 and the first half of fiscal year 1976 only $458.8 million were approved of the $4.5 billion of rescissions requested.[73] But over 90 percent of the requested deferrals were allowed without being vetoed by either chamber. Ford's impoundment requests gave conservatives in Congress a second chance to cripple new program initiatives. It also permitted the OMB and departments to delay spending at higher levels mandated by Congress until the forty-five-day period had elapsed and the rescission had been defeated.

The result of the conflict between president and Congress over the impoundment prerogative was an entirely new budget process that emphasized collaboration and checks and balances. Some flexibility in the use of impoundments remained, since neither courts nor Congress had dealt decisively with the presidential claim of *constitutional* impoundment authority based on the commander in chief clause. Stripped of power to make routine impoundments in domestic programs, presidents relied more heavily on the veto power as the remaining instrument of prerogative government.

The Carter administration tried to prevent unnecessary expenditures in several ways. Funds for various water development projects were removed from the fiscal year 1978 budget, bringing protests from legislators. The House Appropriations Committee restored funding for most projects, and the new administration then pledged to Congress that if the funds were voted, it would spend them. However, when Carter canceled the B-1 bomber and Minuteman III strategic missile system, he demonstrated an effective technique to bypass the new impoundment process. The president used his administrative authority to cancel contracts to procure new weapons, then notified Congress several weeks later, asking it to rescind the appropriations. Defense Secretary Harold Brown, striking a conciliatory note, observed that if Congress did not approve of the rescission within forty-five days, he would then negotiate new contracts to spend the funds previously appropriated. Although Congress approved the rescission after intensive lobbying by the administration, Carter and Brown's actions were criticized by many members of Congress. GAO Comptroller Elmer Staats pointed out that by canceling contracts before the rescission had been approved, Carter presented Congress with a fait accompli, making it difficult and expensive to overturn the decision, and violating the spirit of the law if not the letter.

IV

Spending Powers

Program management provides agency officials, department secretaries, and the president a final opportunity to make policy. As Louis Fisher observes, "What is done by legislators at the appropriations stage can be undone by administrators during budget execution."[74] Whereas most spending decisions are made by the bureaus in consultation with congressional committees and interest groups, the president uses the OMB and other agencies to review and influence developments in programs of interest to him.

The president may interpret authorizations and appropriations as permissive rather than mandatory, as Eisenhower did in 1959 when he simply did not establish a food-stamp program that had been passed into law by Congress. He may make rescissions and deferrals in collaboration with Congress when he has its support. He may issue executive orders that tighten eligibility requirements or that change procedures in distributive programs, thus delaying payouts and having the same impact on spending as a deferral. New programs may be set up slowly so that appropriated funds cannot be spent during the fiscal year: the 1975 summer employment program developed by Congress but opposed by the Ford administration was handled this way. The OMB may delay apportionment of funds from the Treasury to an agency, while at the same time proposing that agency's elimination or reorganization; by the time the agency can receive funds, its authority may have expired— which happened to the Community Services Administration in 1975.

The president may ask Congress for complete discretion for several budget items. The Disaster Relief Fund is administered from the Executive Office of the president without restrictions. Until 1973 the Emergency Fund of the Defense Department was used as a general-purpose White House account. Nixon used a presidential contingency fund to give Egyptian President Anwar Sadat a present of a $3 million helicopter during his visit to Egypt in 1974. For national security matters there are several confidential accounts not audited by Congress, including four in the White House, six in diplomatic agencies, and one each for atomic energy, space, the FBI, and the CIA.[75] For secret projects the president may ask congressional leaders for a general appropriation: the Manhattan Project to develop the atomic bomb required over $2 billion and was passed by Congress without even an inquiry as to the purpose of the appropriation.

Central Intelligence Agency expenditures are drawn on certificates from the agency director and are not made public or audited by Congress. According to law the funds "may be expended without regard to the provisions of law and regulations relating to the expenditure of Government funds."[76] Secret transfers to CIA accounts from other agencies may be made "without regard to any provisions of law limiting or prohibiting transfers between appropriations."[77] This provision enables the president to reduce funds for agencies to levels specified in his executive budget by transferring what he regards as the excess amounts appropriated by Congress to the CIA. Oversight is exercised by the Senate and House Select Committees on Intelligence, the Senate and House Armed Services Committees, and the Senate and House Appropriations Committees, but these units until recently have not concerned themselves with CIA expenditures. In 1974, following disclosure of CIA funding of covert operations overseas, Congress prohibited the agency from spending funds for those operations "other than activities intended solely for obtaining necessary intelligence."[78] But a loophole permitted covert operations if the president found such actions necessary for national security and reported to Congress on their size and scope after their termination. The Joint Committee on Intelligence, created in 1976 to oversee the CIA, was given authority to examine its budget requests, which was a first step toward giving Congress a role in influencing agency spending decisions.

Agencies request *transfer authority* from Congress so they may move funds from one account to another, in effect bypassing any detailed appropriations. Congress sometimes permits such transfers, but at other times it has either outlawed them altogether or provided strict conditions for them. At present, transfers are permitted, but committees with jurisdiction must be informed in advance and retain power to approve or block them—a form of committee veto.

The White House played a major role in financing the Cambodian intervention of 1970 with a $108.9 million transfer from military aid accounts for Greece, Turkey, Taiwan, Phillipines, and South Vietnam.[79] As a reaction, Congress in 1971 passed a law prohibiting transfers for Cambodia unless the president gave congressional leaders advance notice. In 1972 transfers of military aid from one nation to another were prohibited unless the president gave Congress notice.[80] The war in Cambodia in 1972–73 was then financed by over $750 million in existing Pentagon transfer authority from other accounts, bypassing the intent of the law if not its letter.[81] Such transfer authority has also been used to convert economic assistance into military aid. Between 1954 and 1971 over $1.6 billion in Food for Peace funds was transferred to military assistance accounts, while other funds went from development assistance to military aid.[82]

The president may also influence the *reprogramming* of funds: shifts within an agency account from one activity to another. The Department of Defense, for example, reprograms in order to develop new weapons systems, which enables it to counteract cuts made by the Appropriations Committees. At times the department will also use its authority to bypass the president and the OMB. Between 1956 and 1972 the average annual reprogramming in the Defense Department was $2.6 billion; in fiscal year 1971 it reached a high of $3.3 billion. Substantial reprogramming was permitted in fiscal year 1976 for new strategic-weapons research and procurement. Congressional committees used to permit departments to reprogram first and inform them afterwards. But as a result of abuses and bypassing of the intent of appropriations measures, Congress now requires semiannual notifications, and in some cases, prior clearance with committees.[83] Departments may not restore cuts in programs made by appropriations committees, but they may try to convince committee members that proposed reprogrammings are justified.

The president can use *contract authority* to circumvent the appropriations process. Under a 1958 law the president may modify any defense contract during a state of national emergency in order to authorize more weapons than Congress has funded. In 1971 the administration modified the Lockheed C5A and Cheyenne helicopter contracts, incurring additional expenses for these weapons. In 1973, in response, Congress modified the procedures: a new law limited such authority to $25 million contracts; for larger amounts the Senate and House must receive prior notification, and either chamber may "veto" the proposed contract modification.

The president may use *no-year funds* to determine spending levels. These are funds that, after being appropriated by Congress, remain available until expended, unlike other appropriations, which revert back to the Treasury at the end of the fiscal year. Much of this kind of spending authority is granted to the Defense Department; thus there is only a tenuous relationship between appropriations and expenditures in any given fiscal year, since outlays are based on a combination of spending authority for prior and current fiscal years. The president and the OMB may permit the Defense Department to spend prior year funds to make up for cuts imposed in the current fiscal year by reprogramming judiciously, especially for weapons development and procurement.[84]

V

Reforming the Budget Process

The president attempts to maintain some semblance of hierarchy in the executive branch by controlling the budget process. But many budgeting and spending decisions remain with permanent careerists, department budget officers, and congressional committee leaders. The process is so complicated, the number of participants so large, and the number of separate budget lines to be considered so great, that no administration can have more than a marginal impact on the budgetary process.

Reformers who wish to strengthen the presidency have proposed that the president be given an item veto on appropriations bills or the right to impound funds. Some suggest that impoundment be permitted unless Congress "overrides" with a joint resolution—itself subject to a presidential veto. They also argue for an end to restrictions on transfer and reprogramming authority so the president could add funds where Congress had made cuts. They want appropriations to be general rather than specific, permissive rather than mandatory, and no-year rather than limited to a specific fiscal year. If these "reforms" were implemented, the appropriations process would be symbolic: impoundments would prevent Congress from adding to totals in the executive budget; item vetoes would prevent congressional program initiation; transfer and reprogrammings would prevent Congress from cutting figures recommended in the president's budget. These proposals would strengthen the presidential chain of command by concentrating power in the OMB, which not only would propose a budget, but would also control the "spending power."

The very different reforms actually enacted by Congress emerged from its experience in attempting to impose oversight on the bureaucracy. They emphasize checks on arbitrary presidential prerogatives, but still permit the president to propose an executive budget, request rescissions and referrals, or propose transfers and reprogrammings. In each case the reforms have strengthened congressional participation in the budget process by ensuring that Congress disposes of suggestions that the president proposes. The legislature has created an action-forcing process not only for the preparation of the executive budget, but also for decisions on appropriations and outlays and for spending decisions in the bureaus. These action-forcing systems have evolved toward greater complexity as various mechanisms have been added requiring presidential innovation and a congressional response. They are systems involving a mix of values: continuity is represented by the incrementalism of the bureaus; rational management is championed by the OMB and department budget offices; constituency interests are represented by political executives in the departments; electoral values are considered by the White House staff and members of Congress; fiscal considerations are paramount in the thinking of the House and Senate Budget Committees.[85]

Reform of the budget process has transformed the confrontation between president and Congress over prerogative powers into a process placed on a firm statutory base, within the traditional system of checks and balances. Separate institutions share budgetary powers in action-forcing processes of mixed values and pluralistic decision-making. In a sense, developments in the budget process reflect what has happened between president and Congress in several areas of confrontation in the 1970s. However imperfect the system remains, its transformation is a sign of the power of regeneration that American political institutions seem always to exhibit after the collapse of prerogative government.

Economic Policymaking

THE BUSINESS of America, Calvin Coolidge observed, is business; similarly, the performance of the economy is presidential business. The list of incumbents defeated for reelection because of depressions stretches from Van Buren to Hoover, and a listless economy played a part in Ford's loss in 1976. The public expects the president to provide full employment, stable prices, and a rising standard of living. The opposition party makes economic conditions a major issue, as Lawrence O'Brien, then chairman of the Democratic National Committee, did when he quipped that "Nixonomics means that all the things that should go up—the stock market, corporate profits, real spendable income, productivity—go down, and all the things that should go down—unemployment, prices, interest rates—go up."[1] Just a few years later Republicans were giving Carter the same criticisms.

The Constitution seems to make economic policymaking a congressional responsibility, since Article II provides no enumeration of economic powers, while Article I grants a considerable number of powers. But whatever the intentions of the founding fathers, from the first days of the Republic presidents have used prerogative powers and political influence to make economic decisions. They have taken the lead in developing fiscal policies based on taxation and expenditure decisions. But fiscal policymaking has not been an effective instrument for presidents. Economists in presidential agencies use inaccurate information and rely on theoretical models of the economy whose predictive validity is weak. It has never been easy for presidents to win congressional approval of their tax and expenditure recommendations. In the late 1970s neither presidents nor their advisors seemed to know how to put the economy on even keel, and leading economists were questioning whether the tools of fiscal policy could be made to work.

I

Fiscal Policy

Fiscal policy involves decisions about aggregate levels of public expenditure and revenues in order to moderate the swings of the business cycle and provide high employment without excessive inflation. The tools of fiscal policy are tax rates, which increase or decrease revenues, and spending levels in government agencies, which increase or decrease outlays. By altering tax rates and outlays the government tries to correct imbalances in the private sector. In the absence of a planned economy, in which the government would make production, investment, consumption, and savings decisions, the fiscal policy of the government has two characteristics: it supplements private sector decisions, and it reacts to conditions in the private sector. When private investment and consumption decisions are too low, the government may increase expenditures or lower tax rates, which increases demand for goods and services and results in increased production and investment. When investment and consumption decisions are too high, the economy can be "cooled" by raising tax rates or decreasing government outlays, thus lessening demand and decreasing production and investment, at least in theory.

Such demand-management does not require centralized planning. Limited to incremental adjustments in existing levels of demand, to tinkering with a few variables in the public sector, it is based in large measure on *anticipated reactions*: on calculations by those in the private sector who make decisions of the impact of fiscal policy on their businesses. The president must convince people who make production and investment decisions to take actions in their own interest that will moderate the excesses of the business cycle and increase the growth rate. The president must give the right "signals," and economic managers must recognize these signals. For the system to work, the president must have a strategy to gain the confidence of the business community, and economic managers must believe that the government knows what it is doing.

Fiscal Theories

The use of fiscal theory by presidents to make economic decisions is a recent development. Prior to the 1930s there was no administration fiscal policy. In good times a president maintained the confidence of the business community by appointing financiers to the Treasury, by intervening on the side of management in strikes (if necessary with federal troops), and by keeping "hands off" the economy. In bad times presidents reassured the public that conditions would soon improve, maintained public order, and bailed out the banking system with the resources of the Treasury. The economy was supposed to be self-regulating. The only fiscal rule was the balanced budget: in recessions or depressions the president attempted to reduce expenditures to match the reduction in revenues. Even if a fiscal theory had existed, relatively low levels of government expenditure and taxation in proportion to the gross national product (GNP) would have meant that any changes would have had almost no impact.

Economists developed fiscal theories involving demand-management in the 1920s, but President Hoover made little use of them. Franklin Roosevelt campaigned for office in 1932 on a platform based on traditional practices, stressing reduction in expenditures and a balanced budget. His administration ran deficits because of its expenditures for various New Deal programs, but these deficits were an *outcome* of decisions taken to alleviate suffering rather than a set of fiscal policy decisions. The British economist John Maynard Keynes, whose fiscal theories were beginning to influence economists in the United States, came to America to study the impact of deficit spending on the economy; after meeting with President Roosevelt he remarked, disappointedly, "I'm afraid your president knows little about economics."[2] In 1937, disregarding the advice of the "Keynesians" in his administration, Roosevelt tried to reduce expenditures to cope with a new recession, and the situation deteriorated. But that was the last time a president would try to cut outlays when times were bad. The New Deal economists, especially those in the Fiscal Division of the Bureau of the Budget, abandoned the orthodoxy of the balanced budget. Some called for "pump-priming": massive injections of expenditures by the government that would stimulate demand to such an extent that the economy would recover. The analogy was to priming a pump so that it could resume normal operation. Other, more pessimistic economists argued that the private sector could no longer provide enough demand, so that in the future the government would have to make up the difference through demand-management on a continuing basis. One theory emphasized a temporary, ad hoc intervention; the other involved continuous demand-management.

As is so often the case with economics, events outpaced the theorists. When in 1946 President Harry Truman abandoned the sacred cow of the balanced budget and focused on demand-management, he used neither of the two theories that had been developed during the Depression. His problem involved the postwar boom and its attendant inflation. The president had to use a fiscal policy to restrain inflation and *reduce* demand in the private sector.[3] Eisenhower also abandoned the balanced budget orthodoxy (if not in rhetoric, then in practice). His problem was to maintain price stability in a period of growth and to moderate the excesses of the business cycle. Republican economists proposed a *compensatory* fiscal policy: in boom the government would reduce outlays and run a surplus; in recessions it would increase outlays and run a deficit. Some of the changes in outlays would be discretionary, but most would be automatic, through "built-in stabilizers": in hard times welfare payments and unemployment insurance outlays would increase and in good times they would decrease. The Republican economists argued that the budget need not be in balance every year—a break with traditional party principles—but only over the course of an entire business cycle, a period of several years. Expenditure policy would cushion the impact of recessions, and in good times prime reliance would be placed on raising interest rates to reduce investment and restrain a boom. At times Eisenhower followed the fiscal policies of his advisors, but in 1957 he veered back to a more orthodox line and proposed a cut in outlays. The economy went into its third recession of the decade, and was slumping in 1960 during the presidential election, giving the Kennedy campaign a potent issue.

Kennedy's economists wanted to increase the growth rate. According to Walter Heller, chairman of the Council of Economic Advisors (CEA), they sought to change fiscal policy from a "corrective" to a "propulsive" orientation.[4] Arthur Okun, another CEA member, observed that "the revised strategy emphasized, as the standard for judging economic performance, whether the economy was living up to its potential rather than merely whether it was advancing."[5] New Frontier economists calculated the GNP that would exist at "full employment" (using a 4 percent rate of unemployment) and compared it with the actual GNP achieved to find a "performance gap." The goal of the administration was to close that gap, making the American economic system the model for other nations seeking high rates of growth. From the revenues that a healthy economy would generate the administration could allocate resources for new domestic programs, and military ventures could be financed without increasing taxes or moving into the classic "guns or butter" situation. New Frontier economists convinced Kennedy that they could "fine tune" the economy. The annual report of the Council of Economic Advisors in 1962 argued,

To be effective, discretionary budget policy should be flexible. In order to promote economic stability, the Government should be able to change quickly tax rates or expenditure programs, and equally able to revise its actions as circumstances change. . . .[6]

Congress remained unconvinced, and neither Kennedy nor Johnson could win authority to raise or lower tax rates. Johnson's miscalculations about spending for the Vietnam War, and his reluctance to propose measures to curb excessive demand unleashed by the war, left a legacy of inflation for the Republicans to deal with when Nixon assumed office.

Nixon and Ford emphasized the use of fiscal policy for corrective purposes. They were willing to tolerate negative rates of growth if necessary to bring inflation under control. Republican economists abandoned the notion that the administration could "fine tune" the economy. The CEA Annual Report of 1970 warned that "business and labor cannot plan, and homebuyers cannot effectively manage their affairs, when Government alternates between keeping first the accelerator and then the brake pedal to the floor."[7] By 1975 the results of the corrective orientation were apparent: unemployment had peaked at a new postwar high of approximately 9 percent, industrial output was down 9 percent and the GNP 2 percent from the preceding year, and the nation was recovering from a 12.2 percent inflation rate. Fine-tuning was dead, not to be revived in Carter's administration, but alternative approaches to demand-management had yet to prove their utility. As the GNP went up and inflation went down in 1977, the Carter administration seemed as surprised as the rest of the nation; as inflation once again increased in 1978, the new administration might be pardoned if it wondered whether any theory at all could explain the fluctuations.

The State of the Art

"Economics has come of age in the 1960s," Walter Heller boasted to his colleagues in 1967, and most economists agreed. But for Robert Heilbroner, in his address as president of the American Economic Association in 1974, the major issue facing economists had become "a growing awareness of intellectual incompetence."[8] As early as 1970 Arthur Okun had ruefully observed, "Surely since the Second World War, the economy has jumped the track of stable growth more often and more severely as a result of government actions than autonomous shifts in private demand."[9] Heller, in his inaugural address as president of the American Economic Association, felt compelled to defend the competence of the profession against attacks by his fellow economists.[10] One of Nixon's advisors, CEA member William Fellner, evaluated government policies quite harshly in 1976:

Over a period of considerable length, policies have reflected the weakest and most outdated elements of an analytical structure that is in need of reconstruction rather than slight retouching. It has become impossible to continue along the policy lines of the past ten years.[11]

Arthur Okun, speaking in 1977 at the Economic Club of Chicago, noted that inflation and unemployment rates had become "intertwined and combined in a way that is historically unprecedented, and by the verdict of many economic textbooks, theoretically impossible."[12]

Within the government, economic advisors echoed the same themes. "There is a lesson to be drawn from past policy mistakes," noted the 1976 Report of the Council of Economic Advisors, adding, "the history of monetary and fiscal policies demonstrates that we have a great deal to learn about implementing discretionary policy changes."[13] Chairman Alan Greenspan admitted, "The economist is going to be wrong a large percentage of the time."[14] Carter's treasury secretary, (an economist himself) Michael Blumenthal, admitted that "the real cause of inflation is not properly understood yet in this country and elsewhere."[15] James Tobin, former CEA member, in reviewing the dismal record of economic management, noted that "economists have lost their short-lived reputation as pragmatic experts," and concluded that "the profession has lost confidence in its own premises and methods."[16] So, one might add, has the general public, the Congress, and several presidents.

The Collapse of Fiscal Theory

In the 1970s economists have challenged the predictive validity of several aspects of orthodox fiscal theory. They have argued that these theories do not accurately measure the impact of public policies on private-sector decisions; that some effects of government decisions produce results that are perverse (i.e., the opposite to what was intended); that others involve intertemporal substitutions (in which an effect occurs sooner rather than later without changing the overall impact on the economy); or that multiplier effects of government spending changes cannot be accurately calculated nor the magnitude of impact on the economy specified.[17] Some economists argue that fiscal theories do not adequately account for several key factors: state and local spending, taxing, and borrowing decisions; the monetary policies of the Federal Reserve Board; and international capital flows and the value of currencies when measured against each other.

The most fundamental tenet of fiscal theory has been questioned— the supposed trade-off between inflation and unemployment. According to the "Phillips curve," the stimulation of demand can produce lower rates of unemployment only at the cost of higher rates of inflation; restraining private sector demand will lead to price stability, but will also lead to higher rates of unemployment. If this curve worked (as many economists assumed it did), it would provide every administration with a set of alternatives: it could either reduce unemployment and accept higher prices, or it could promote price stability and accept higher rates of unemployment. Republicans would probably control inflation and Democrats would reduce unemployment, based on tendencies for electoral coalitions to form in part on economic lines.

But the supposed trade-off doesn't always work. In the 1970s inflation and unemployment at times increased simultaneously (1973–75) in what became known as "stagflation," and then dropped simultaneously (1975–77)—even while the size of government deficits was increasing. Prices in the late 1970s seemed to be cost oriented and fairly predictable, rising about 6 percent whether conditions were good or bad. Wage increases averaged around 8 percent whether demand for goods and services was high or low. Some inflation, then, seemed to be "built in" to a system in which high rates of joblessness and poor economic growth could be maintained, giving the system the worst of both possible worlds.[18] Former secretary of the treasury Henry Fowler called it "hesiflation"—a condition in which unacceptable levels of unemployment were combined with high rates of inflation, but in which growth rates were also unsatisfactory.

Economists of the right such as Alan Greenspan argued that stimulating the economy would produce only a temporary gain in employment, and that this gain would be wiped out later through rising inflation that cut down on capital investment. William Fellner argued that none of the fiscal models "have so far proved adequate tools for predicting future relations between inflation and unemployment."[19] Milton Friedman demonstrated that since World War II the trend in many Western nations has been for higher inflation to be accompanied by higher rates of unemployment, calling into question the trade-off of the Phillips curve for most industralized nations.[20] Economists of the left argued that increasing demand to create full employment would actually reduce rates of inflation, giving the best possible results. Their premise was that most prices are "administered" by corporations rather than set by market forces. Full employment stimulated by government expenditures would lead to more demand for goods, so that margins of profit could decrease while total corporate profits increased because of a higher volume of sales. But if unemployment increases and demand is reduced, they argue, profit margins can be increased by corporations so that they can maintain overall profits. In this theory unemployment, recession, and inflation all go together: if the government wishes to promote price stability and control inflation, it must increase rather than decrease demand, and must lower the unemployment rate rather than accept a rise in the rate as a "necessary evil." The ranks of both the right and the left are growing, while fewer economists now embrace the "trade-off" theory of the Phillips curve.

Economists cannot be sure of the impact that changes in tax rates will have on the economy. A small tax reduction or rebate may cost the government a great deal but have minimal impact on consumer demand, especially if the public uses the additional money to buy small items or splurge on luxuries (the windfall effect) rather than purchasing "big ticket" consumer durables. Manipulating tax rates may lead to perverse effects owing to the delay in passing laws to change rates, and the delay thereafter in collections. The impact of changing rates may be felt long after the conditions that gave rise to them have changed.

In theory, tax increases restrain consumer demand. But if the government taxes people who normally save additional income, while distributing additional transfer payments to those likely to use them for immediate consumption, demand in the private sector may increase. This occurs in periods of high inflation when wage earners are pushed into higher brackets and payroll taxes rise, while social security payments and other transfer payments that are "indexed" to a rise in the cost of living are increased. Similarly, an increase in the rate of business taxation intended to lower investment in new plant and equipment may actually increase investment if (1) the economic managers believe that the price of capital goods will rise in the near future and (2) depreciation of investment for tax purposes offers a high offset against corporate profits. After the corporate tax surcharge of 1968, for example, business investment increased, contrary to the expectations of the administration.[21]

Fiscal theory offers little help to the president when he makes expenditure decisions. An increase in outlays supposedly stimulates demand in the private sector. Whether or not a change in the size of the deficit is stimulative depends on how the increase in the deficit is financed. A deficit is stimulative if it does not reduce the supply of savings to a point where curtailing of new investment has a greater negative effect than the positive effect caused by additional outlays. If the deficit is financed by individuals who purchase Treasury bonds and pay for them by checks drawn on their accounts, then bank deposits will be reduced and the supply of money will fall. Private investment may be reduced as the money supply decreases and interest rates climb, resulting in stagnation rather than growth. But an increase in the deficit is stimulative if the Federal Reserve Board (the independent agency that regulates the supply of money) buys the new Treasury offerings from commercial banks, for in that case the board "pays" for its purchases by crediting the reserves of the banks. This system is known as "monetizing" the deficit, since the reserves that the board injects into the banking system will expand the currency, lower interest rates, and fuel an expansion of demand. But the decision as to how a deficit will be financed is not made by the president. It rests with the managers of the Federal Reserve Board, who always have the option of offsetting the president's fiscal policy by contracting or expanding reserves in the banking system.

The administration may find that its timing is out of phase with changes in the business cycle, so that stimulus comes in boom times and restraint during a downturn. Fiscal policy may aggravate the instability of the business cycle, which according to Paul McCracken, a CEA chairman under Nixon and Ford, "is apparently caused by the unliquidated fish-tail effects from prior monetary and fiscal policy changes made in response to economic developments too short-run to have been countered by these policies in any case."[22] George Perry, an economist at the Brookings Institution, has argued that "fiscal policy has contributed to the last three recessions," noting especially restrictive policies leading to the downturn of 1973–75.[23]

Decisions about expenditures, revenues, and borrowings made by states in the federal system often counteract national fiscal policy. State and local purchases from the private sector account for about 15 percent of the GNP, almost twice as much as the 8 percent accounted for by the federal government, so the fiscal impact is great.[24] During a recession the national government may run deficits to stimulate the economy, but state and local governments, required by state constitutions to run balanced operating budgets, will curtail expenditures and raise taxes, as in 1975–76. Many federal grant programs have no net effect because local officials substitute increased federal funding for cutbacks of their own funds in their operating budgets. In boom times or during the last stages of a recovery, when the national government exercises restraint, the state and local governments pressure Congress to continue the anti-recessionary programs as a form of increased federal intergovernmental assistance. And in good times state and local governments are most likely to increase expenditures, lower taxes, and borrow heavily for capital construction, thus increasing demand.

The pattern of international currency flows and the decisions of multinational corporations about investment and production may also counteract administration fiscal policy. An expansionary policy based on increases in the deficit may lead to a rise in interest rates if the Federal Reserve Board "leans against the wind" or if demand surges ahead of the currency supply. Higher rates in turn attract foreign funds, especially dollars held by foreigners (the Eurodollars and Petrodollars), because overseas investors may decide to take advantage of higher rates for short-term Treasury offerings. The dollar will be strengthened as a result of these currency flows, which makes American products more expensive in foreign markets while foreign imports become cheaper here. Eventually the export market shrinks and imports rise, both factors that slow down economic growth. In such a case export markets are lost, domestic markets are threatened, and unemployment will increase rather than decrease. This effect seems to have occurred between 1974 and 1976. On the other hand, deficit financing may lead to a glut of dollars abroad, resulting in a dramatic slide in the value of the dollar on currency markets. The resulting rise in the price of imports fuels inflation, as do decisions of domestic manufacturers to raise their prices. The result may be a sharp increase in inflation, possibly equaling the rate of decline in the value of the dollar when measured against a composite of other "hard" currencies. This form of inflation seemed to be occurring in 1978.

Obtaining Accurate Information

Not the least of the problems the president faces in trying to formulate a fiscal policy is the difficulty in obtaining useful information. What his advisors give him is not what he wants, for they offer technical advice based on fiscal models. What he wants is not what he needs, for "watered down" economic advice that he can understand and act upon may not be valid. What he needs is not what he will receive, because he needs accurate information based on economic models with good predictive validity—and such information and models do not exist.

Reporting systems in the private sector are incomplete. Even accurate statements of profits and losses, especially from the multinationals, are difficult to obtain, because corporations are adept at "cooking" books to show small profits at home, while concealing large profits from subsidiary operations abroad. The "preflow" data of orders, contracts, and investment and production intentions are considered by economic managers to be "trade secrets," and in a competitive system that is rightly so. Companies resist making detailed information about their intentions available to government economists. To gauge consumer demand and confidence, the government and private survey organizations use public opinion polls, based on the science of "psychological economics," but as the leading practitioner, George Katona of the Survey Research Center of the University of Michigan, notes, the prospects are for "a series of rapid fluctuations, periods of recovery alternating with recessions in fairly quick succession," to be brought about "by optimism or even elation that is shortly replaced by pessimism or even dejection."[25] No one can gauge what consumers will be thinking for more than a few months at a time.

Economists rely on various time-series as statistical indicators to forecast changes in the economy. The profession tinkers with a set of "leading indicators," hoping to find the right combination of time-series that will provide a six-month to one-year notice of a downturn. But the best of these indicators do not offer much advance notice and, more important, decision-makers don't really trust them. Most economists use the "rule of three" when dealing with the leading indicators: after three months of a downturn or an upturn they are ready to announce that the economy is moving in the direction of the indicators. This rule reduces the utility of the leading indicators, since it reduces the timeliness of advice economists can give based on them. And the time-series themselves often must be revised as more complete data becomes available, so what appears in one month to be a downturn may actually be "revised" later and become a slight upturn, a situation that makes it difficult to apply the "rule of three." Between 1948 and 1976 the leading indicators have accurately predicted a downturn six times, but on three occasions they declined for two months in a row without a corresponding downturn in the economy.

No one is sure what the unemployment rates are. The Bureau of Labor Statistics missed an estimated 1.5 million new jobs that had been added to the economy in the summer of 1976; then in 1977 it found another 300,000 new jobs added in the fall of 1976 that its earlier set of indicators had missed. Congress in 1977 created a National Commission on Employment and Unemployment Statistics to plan for a complete overhaul in the way the government collects this key statistic. At present the employment rate is calculated by dividing the number of jobholders by the total population; and in recent years, as more women and youth have entered the labor market, a larger proportion of the population is working, and the employment rate has gone up to its highest levels in history. But at the same time, the unemployment rate, measured as a percentage of those who want to work but are without jobs, divided by the total of those at work and those who want to work, has also increased. Thus, high rates of employment are coupled with high rates of unemployment. In the economic recovery that began in 1975 many new jobs were generated, but these often went to newly employed workers entering the labor market for the first time; the rate of unemployment between 1975 and 1977 hardly declined at all. Conservative economists emphasize the employment rate to demonstrate how well the economy is performing, whereas liberal economists, focusing on high rates of unemployment among youths and minorities, call for additional stimulus.

Economists are skeptical of their forecasts. Robert Eisner claims that "forecasters, in and out of Government, have repeatedly revised their estimates of the timing and results of anti-inflationary action."[26] The 1973 Report of the Council of Economic Advisors boasted that "by the end of 1972 the American anti-inflation policy had become the marvel of the rest of the world."[27] Yet the price of that report had jumped in one year from $1.50 to $2.25! Two months after it was issued the administration was compelled to devalue the dollar while inflation skyrocketed. In February 1975, Arthur Burns, chairman of the Federal Reserve Board, examined the forecasts prepared by administration economists and told the Joint Economic Committee of Congress, "I looked at those figures in astonishment. Why do people put out figures like that when they don't know what they're talking about?"[28] The assessment of Paul McCracken is still valid: "Our problems of estimating where the economy is going often have their origins in the fact that we do not even know where we have been."[29] Mathematical economists are now convinced that to the extent that economic forecasting can be considered scientific, it must move from deterministic cause-result models to develop "stochastic," or probabilistic, theories, so that its predictions will have some validity.[30] Such reconstruction of forecasting has not yet occurred in the federal government.

The early performance of Carter administration forecasters was poor. In February 1977 the OMB projected annual GNP growth at 5.4 percent and inflation at 5.1 percent for the year; by April these projections were revised to 4.9 percent growth and 6.2 percent inflation. The CEA forecasts were challenged within the administration by planners for the new Department of Energy on the question of whether administration tax proposals might have a fiscal "drag" on the economy. Economists from previous Democratic administrations argued with the CEA about the size of the deficit and its effect on stimulating the economy. Arthur Burns, testifying in May before the Senate Banking Committee on the projections of administration economists put the entire matter into perspective when he stated, "I say I don't know and I think they don't know either."[31]

Administration economists operate under constraints that make it unlikely that their forecasts will be accurate. They must assume that the president's budget will be an accurate representation of expenditures of the government in the next fiscal year—even though everyone knows that Congress may make significant changes. They must assume that his tax program will be adopted on time and *in toto*—even though Congress rarely gives the president what he wants. They generally estimate that revenues will be high because they must assume economic conditions will be good; for fiscal years 1970 through 1972 the difference between estimates and actual receipts averaged more than $9 billion per year. Like Dr. Pangloss, administration economists never refer to adverse conditions until the country is already aware that a recession has occurred. In 1975 CEA and Treasury spokesmen were under presidential orders not to refer to conditions as a downturn, even though the downturn had lasted for months. Wilfred Lewis observed, "As a rule, administrations have delayed public acknowledgment of a recession until the evidence was overwhelming—well into the period of decline."[32]

The Council of Economic Advisors does not accurately predict federal revenues or outlays for any given fiscal year. Early in 1968 it estimated a deficit of $8 billion, but the final figure was $29 billion. The fiscal year 1972 deficit was revised upward by $27 billion in the middle of the fiscal year to take account of new conditions. The fiscal year 1976 deficit, in contrast, was overestimated by about $10.4 billion, and the fiscal year 1978 deficit was overestimated by $12 billion. In most years the changes in the GNP are greater than CEA predictions. Between 1947 and 1972 the actual change in federal expenditures was 4 percent higher than CEA forecasts; in those same years the annual change in federal revenues was 6 percent, with CEA figures bearing no relationship to actual changes from one year to the next. William Niskanen, the Budget Bureau official who reached these conclusions, has observed,

For the entire post-World War II period, the actual federal surplus or deficit . . . has been unrelated to the surplus or deficit forecast in the president's budget. This suggests that the executive branch has also had little ability either to control or forecast the net fiscal restraint or stimulus on the federal budget.[33]

Under Eisenhower forecasts were relatively accurate, but beginning with the Kennedy administration the gap between predictions and outcomes increased. It was ironic that those economists who had the most confidence in their ability to "fine tune" the economy seemed least able to predict events.

Because presidents cannot make accurate forecasts they may abandon their policies abruptly. Upon taking office Ford emphasized control of inflation, yet just a few months later, with the economy in a tailspin, he was calling for a tax cut as a stimulative measure. Similarly the Carter administration began with a tax cut proposal as part of an antirecessionary stimulative package, and several months later dropped the idea of a tax rebate, called the recovery well under way, and emphasized an anti-inflationary program. Abrupt "179-degree" turns have become the chief characteristic of presidents.

Administrations cannot be certain of how much money they spend. Accurate estimates of Defense Department outlays is impossible because (1) outlays bear only a tenuous relationship to new obligational authority, since prior-year and no-year funds may be used; (2) estimates of costs of military operations are unpredictable and are usually underestimated for limited interventions; (3) procurement decisions are affected by actions taken by allies and adversaries, as well as by results of arms limitation agreements. Central Intelligence Agency funds hidden in the budgets of other agencies may be spent abroad, eliminating their fiscal impact on the domestic economy. Transfer payments for welfare, unemployment insurance, social security, pensions, and medical programs can be estimated but not precisely controlled. Various subsidies to farmers are based on farm prices, which in turn are based on output of crops. Harvests are directly dependent on weather conditions, which account for almost all the variation in output from one year to the next. Not all funds appropriated in the intergovernmental grant and contract system will be spent by state and local governments on schedule.

All these variables make it impossible to predict how much the government will spend each quarter or in the fiscal year. During the first nine months of 1976 the national government spent $11.9 billion less than the OMB had projected, and the final figure for the fiscal year was $7.1 billion, prompting Arthur Okun to comment on "a most remarkable bi-partisan display of ignorance," since no one seemed to know why the money had not been spent.[34] The Ford and Carter administrations could not even determine (1) if the money had simply "disappeared" or (2) if it would be spent later by various agencies. Thus, no one could even determine if the shortfall would have a serious fiscal impact. For fiscal year 1977 federal outlays came to $404 billion, about $9.4 billion less than Carter's February budget projection. The administration explained that intergovernmental "red tape," impoundments, and overoptimistic projections from the departments had caused "spending underruns."[35] Carter's second try at projecting expenditures was even worse. His January 1978 budget indicated that spending for fiscal year 1978 would total $462.2 billion; less than two months later he submitted revised figures totaling $453.5 billion—a correction of $8.7 billion in the projections.[36] Spending underruns for FY 1978 totaled almost $20 billion.

The forecasts of an outgoing administration should never be taken seriously. The budget submitted in January by the outgoing president is primarily a political document. Truman's last budget, for example, contained many new programs that he knew incoming Republicans had no intentions of adopting. Eisenhower's last budget projected a surplus of $1.3 billion, in spite of the fact that during his eight years in office he hardly ever had a balanced budget. Johnson's outgoing budget had a surplus forecast of $3.4 billion—something he had never achieved while in office. Ford proposed large program cuts, combined with a massive tax cut, and specified that by following his proposals the budget would be balanced within two years—in spite of the fact that his administration had run the largest deficits in history. The outgoing president always presents a budget and an economic report that paints a rosy picture of the progress he has made. An incoming president usually paints a grim picture of problems he must tackle, for as Paul McCracken wisely notes, "The worse [the problems] can be made to seem at the outset, the better the record will seem to be at the end."[37] The new administration predicts lower unemployment and inflation rates, higher growth rates, and increased corporate profits—all achieved while making progress toward a balanced budget. Whatever else may be said about presidents, they never lack for optimism when making economic forecasts.

II

The Advisory System

The president receives economic advice from councils, boards, departments, and task forces. Each government agency has a different operational responsibility, which colors its forecasts and advice. The president rarely obtains a consensus. Departments take a programmatic perspective and call for more spending. The OMB is concerned with rational allocation of resources in accordance with presidential priorities, and it would resist a fiscal policy that called for either massive increments or decreases if it thought departments could not function effectively. The Treasury must manage the debt and concern itself with international monetary issues. The CEA concentrates on moderating the business cycle and promoting high growth rates. The Labor Department may call for additional stimulus to deal with the problems of the unemployed, whereas the Commerce Department must consider the perspective of business.

Tax measures always create conflict in the advisory system. Departments oppose tax reductions that would lower revenues so much that new spending measures might have to be scrapped. The CEA proposes tax cuts to stimulate the economy, claiming that the immediate loss in revenues will be more than offset by improved business conditions that will lead to increases in the GNP and in tax receipts in succeeding years. The Treasury is concerned with regulatory and "tax expenditure" issues (i.e., the use of tax laws to provide incentives for certain activities through reductions in, or exemptions from, taxes), as well as with the impact of reduced revenues on debt financing. HEW may call for higher payroll taxes for its social security trust funds just as the CEA is calling for lower income taxes to stimulate the economy. White House aides counsel the president on the political impact of tax proposals.

The president makes the final decision. In 1954 the CEA called for a tax cut and Treasury opposed it; Eisenhower decided in favor of the cut. In 1961 the CEA proposed a tax cut to stimulate investment, and both the Treasury and Defense Departments opposed it. The White House staff eventually tipped the balance toward the CEA, and in 1963 Kennedy submitted legislation to Congress. In 1966, however, when the CEA recommended a tax increase to control inflation caused by the Vietnam war, the White House staff opposed it. Not until 1968 did the CEA convince Johnson to adopt its proposals. In 1969 Nixon's advisors split three ways: a Treasury plan was opposed by the White House staff on political grounds and by the CEA on economic grounds. In 1975, when the Democratic Congress passed a tax reduction, the CEA and the OMB urged Ford to sign it while the Treasury unsuccessfully pressed for a veto. The CEA in 1977 convinced Carter to offer a "rebate" on taxes; eventually the Treasury and the OMB convinced Carter to scuttle it. Economists in the Treasury squared off against Carter's energy advisor over the fiscal implications of tax proposals contained in the president's package of energy legislation.

Economic advisors play three roles. They are professional economists who can provide expert advice; they are public officials with operational responsibilities who protect the missions and the jurisdictions of their organizations; they are public spokesmen for the administration. Edwin Nourse, the first chairman of the CEA, emphasized the role of expert. He observed in a letter to Truman,

The Council of Economic Advisors is conceived as a scientific agency of the Federal Government. . . . There is no occasion for the Council to become involved in any way in the advocacy of particular measures or in the rival beliefs and struggles of the different economic and political interest groups.[38]

Nourse was reluctant to testify before congressional committees or to speak out for Truman's program. The president was turned off by Nourse's habit of lecturing to him on economics as if he were a college freshman. Upset that his advice was ignored, Nourse later offered a bitter assessment of Truman in his memoirs: "The President has no philosophy, doesn't think, doesn't read the things he would have to read if he were trying to understand the problems he's up against."[39]

Presidents prefer advisors who combine professional expertise with political sense. Truman named Leon Keyserling, a New Deal activist (and a lawyer, not an economist) as chairman of the CEA and used him to defend his policies before Congress. Kennedy made Chairman Walter Heller the "point man" for the administration; Heller would argue positions that the president, for political reasons, could not yet adopt publicly. When Heller made some progress in convincing Congress and the business community, the president could then embrace the CEA proposals as his own.[40] Advisors must translate their expertise into language the president can understand, without any trace of condescension. Arthur Burns, chairman of the CEA under Eisenhower, held weekly sessions with the president to explain economic developments and offer advice; from all accounts these meetings were more successful than those held by Truman and Nourse.[41] Former CEA members testify that no advisor can remain detached from presidential politics and policies. Arthur Okun points out that "political economists necessarily move in the realm of social values, and that is the way they become the most useful, especially as advisors to the President," and Gardner Ackley warns that "if his economic advisor refrains from advice on the gut questions of policy, the president should and will get another one."[42]

Several advisors speak for the administration. The CEA prepares the analysis that forms the basis for the annual economic report and the budget message the president sends to Congress each January. The secretary of the treasury is the chief spokesman in defending the budget before several committees. In recent years the OMB director has testified before congressional committees as well. Having several visible spokesmen is not always an advantage. Some department secretaries (especially the secretaries of Labor and Commerce) may depart from the administration "line" under questioning by press or legislators. The president may then have the White House issue a "clarification" that undercuts their position. The press then pursues the principals in order to magnify divisions in the administration. The most a president can hope for is an agreement among his advisors to keep their disagreements in closed forums.

Every president has his style of economic decision-making. Some prefer a principal advisor, almost always the secretary of the treasury, to shield them from conflict. Nixon relied on treasury secretaries John Connally and George Schultz to make major decisions, for according to speechwriter William Safire the president was prone to "MEGO" (my eyes glaze over) when economic issues were considered. On the other hand, Kennedy encouraged debates between advisors, and set the CEA against the Treasury. He created a Cabinet Committee on Economic Growth (chaired by the CEA) and matched it against a Cabinet Committee on the Balance of Payments (chaired by Treasury) to focus debates.

The Ford administration attempted to institutionalize the advisory system through creation of an Economic Policy Board.[43] Membership consisted of all cabinet secretaries (except the secretary of defense and the attorney general) and also included the CEA, the OMB, and the Council for International Economic Policy (CIEP). Invitees included the directors of the Federal Energy Administration, the National Security Council, and the Domestic Council. As one participant noted, "A measure of whether something works is whether the top guys attend. The top guys attend faithfully."[44] Policies were set by its executive committee, consisting of the treasury secretary (who chaired the board), a principal White House aide, the CEA chairman, and the secretaries of State, Labor and Commerce, the OMB director, and the CIEP director. A twenty-five-member staff worked on specific issues. The board, after considering various options, would present memoranda for the president (with boxes he could check) on proposed courses of action. Ford might meet with the executive committee before making his final decision.

In effect Ford instituted a "collective presidency" to make fiscal policy. But the board did not work successfully. Its staff was small, and it had to rely on cooperation from the Treasury, the OMB, and other departments. It briefly succeeded in coordinating the energy program, because existing departments wanted to control the new agencies. The board was most effective in limiting "end runs" to the president and in preventing any one department from controlling all access to him. It forced issues into channels, so Ford could not be "captured" by a single advisor or department secretary. The board gave the impression that the government spoke with one voice, and it was particularly effective in forcing White House review of speeches made by Secretary of State Kissinger on international economic policy. But those with private lines to the president occasionally tried to bypass the board. Agriculture Secretary Earl Butz boasted, "I feel free to call up the President. I don't do it very often. When any cabinet member has to go to the President, it means that the mechanisms of government have broken down."[45] As economic policymaking dominated the Ford administration, other advisory bodies, such as the Domestic Council, attempted to influence policymaking by preparing their own staff studies or making their own proposals.[46] These attempts to "crowd" the presidential advisory system resulted in conflict within the advisory system during the Ford administration.

The Carter administration abolished several economic and domestic policy units, including the Council on International Economic Policy and the Domestic Council. It also abolished the Economic Policy Board, replacing it with an Economic Policy Group. Treasury Secretary Michael Blumenthal chaired the group, which met weekly, and which also contained the chairman of the CEA, the director of OMB, the director of the NSC, the secretaries of Energy, Commerce, Labor, and Housing and Urban Development, and the undersecretary of state for economic affairs.

This group performs essentially the same functions under Carter as the board did for Ford. Most successful as a clearinghouse for proposals and a forum for debate, it is least influential as a manager or coordinator of economic policies. Departments still try to undercut the group. When the CEA proposed a set of "economic impact statements" to be issued by each department promulgating new regulations, it was opposed by Secretary of Labor Ray Marshall, who explained to reporters, "So long as you ultimately have a chance to explain your position to the President, you don't get as disturbed about what happens in any group such as the Economic Policy Group," and added, "That's not the end of the line. The President is the end of the line."[47]

All presidents rely on an "inner circle" of senior advisors. The treasury secretary, the OMB director, and the CEA chairman arrange luncheons or dinners on a regular basis to discuss issues and try to compromise on their positions. These officials are known as the "triad," and when joined by the chairman of the Federal Reserve Board, as the "quadriad." If they can agree on an economic measure, it is not likely that any other combination of officials will convince the president to turn down their recommendations. The Carter administration seemed unique in giving Vice-President Mondale a major role in economic policymaking, although on several occasions he has been on the losing side of issues.

The Federal Reserve Board

The Federal Reserve Board (or Fed) is an independent agency that regulates the nation's monetary supply and banking system. It has a major impact on fiscal policy. Increasing the supply of money and thus lowering its cost to borrowers encourages investment and consumption, but by stimulating demand this increase may erode price stability. Some argue that each 1 percent increase in the money supply yields a 0.75 percent increase in the GNP. But economists differ on whether the "lift" in the GNP is permanent; some claim that when inflation occurs, the stimulus will be "washed out" and no greater effect will have been produced. To decrease the money supply, or to limit its increase, raises interest rates and therefore should slow investment and consumption, thus restraining excessive demand. But a rise in interest rates is itself inflationary, since it represents an increase in the cost of money, and therefore a restrictive monetary policy may not maintain price stability. Higher rates of interest may actually stimulate investment if economic managers expect that rates will rise even higher in the near future. And lower rates of interest may not stimulate investment if firms, anticipating that they can borrow on even better terms in the near future, defer investment decisions. The process is not mechanical, with an interest rate "pedal" that can be pressed to spur investment or lifted to restrain it. Instead, it is psy-

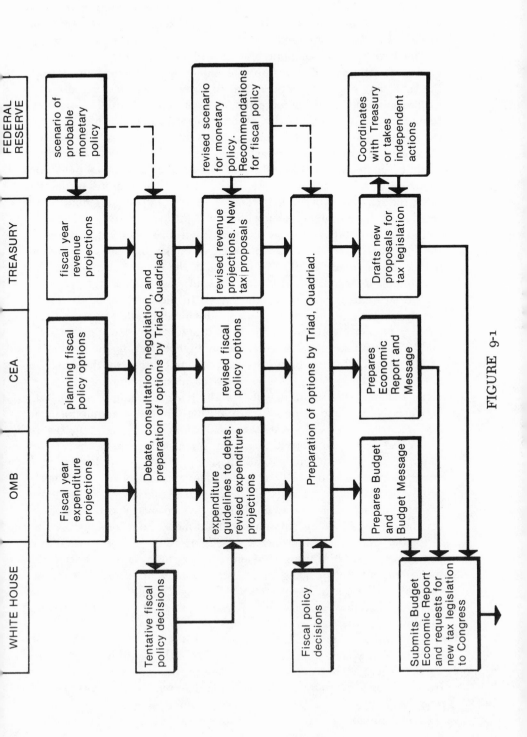

WHITE HOUSE	OMB	CEA	TREASURY	FEDERAL RESERVE

Fiscal year expenditure projections

planning fiscal policy options

fiscal year revenue projections

scenario of probable monetary policy

Tentative fiscal policy decisions

Debate, consultation, negotiation, and preparation of options by Triad, Quadriad.

expenditure guidelines to depts. revised expenditure projections

revised fiscal policy options

revised revenue projections. New tax proposals

revised scenario for monetary policy. Recommendations for fiscal policy

Fiscal policy decisions

Preparation of options by Triad, Quadriad.

Prepares Budget and Budget Message

Prepares Economic Report and Message

Drafts new proposals for tax legislation

Coordinates with Treasury or takes independent actions

Submits Budget Economic Report and requests for new tax legislation to Congress

FIGURE 9-1

chological, having to do with the confidence that the business community has in the board, and the signals that the board sends to economic managers in the private sector.

The Fed has only an imprecise idea of how fast the money supply grows. Its estimates of the supply of money held by commercial banks (i.e., checking deposits) is poor, and its weekly estimates are subject to major revisions. In 1976 the prestigious Conference Board (an organization of economists) suggested abolishing the estimates, which it described as "statistical noise."[48] Monetary theorists disagree on which indicator of money is crucial in forecasting a change in business conditions: quantity, circulation, or interest rates. There are at least seven definitions of quantity from which to choose. If the theorist concentrates on interest rates, there are short-term, long-term, or "swap" rates (the federal funds rate banks charge each other for the overnight loan of excess reserves).

In theory the Federal Reserve Board controls interest rates by setting the "discount" rate on its loans to member banks. In practice its actions may lead to perverse results. An increase in the interest rate may lead to transfers of Eurodollars and Petrodollars into the United States, actually increasing funds available for investment. In the early 1970s the money supply available for investment increased while interest rates were rising. In 1977 foreign investment in the United States soared while short-term and long-term interest rates were sharply higher than the year before.

The Federal Reserve Board may also attempt to control the supply of money directly, through its power to set reserve requirements for its member banks—the requirement that the bank maintain a certain ratio between its loans and its deposits. By raising the reserve requirement the Fed decreases the bank's ability to make new loans; lowering the requirement makes more credit available. But membership in the Federal Reserve system is declining, and these requirements no longer affect enough commercial banks to provide adequate control over the money supply. And if bank credit is not readily available on favorable terms, corporations in boom times can finance investment by issuing stock or commercial paper or by obtaining loans directly from foreign investors.

Finally, the Fed uses "open market" operations: it buys and sells government securities from commercial banks to expand or contract the money supply. But in doing so it must also maintain short-term interest rates at a level that will not attract either too little or too much foreign currency. The flow of such currencies can affect the exchange rate for the dollar and the balance of payments.

The president cannot control the Federal Reserve Board, because Congress in its 1935 amendments to the law made the board an independent agency that is not subject to his will. The president nominates the chairman of the board for a four-year term that does not coincide with his own. The seven board members each serve a fourteen-year term, and the president cannot remove them. In each presidential term the incumbent nominates only two members, and all nominations must be confirmed by the Senate.

The problem for the president is that the Treasury may want low interest rates so that its bonds will yield low interest just when the board may want high interest rates to lower demand. Thus, when the Treasury must finance large deficits the board may decide on a policy of monetary restraint to counterbalance administration actions. After World War II just such a conflict occurred. The Treasury proposed that the Fed "peg" interest rates at low levels to support its bond offerings, as it had done during the war. But in the postwar period such a policy would have increased the money supply and fueled inflation. In 1947 the Fed abandoned its support for Treasury bond offerings. During the Korean War the Treasury again pressured the Fed for low interest rates. In January 1951 President Truman called both sides to the White House, and after the meeting the Treasury announced that the Fed had agreed to support low interest rates. The Fed denied that such an agreement had been reached, and released a transcript of the meeting to back its contention. With Truman on the defensive, the two sides finally worked out a written "accord"—similar to a treaty of peace—which was favorable for the Fed.[49] Ever since that time presidents have been wary of tangling openly with the board, for when they do so they lose the confidence of the business and financial communities.

The CEA and Fed often disagree on fiscal policy. The Fed may use its open market operations to "lean against the wind" and counterbalance administration actions. In 1931 it raised the discount rate and refused to monetize the debt or expand the money supply; Herbert Hoover then felt compelled to raise taxes and balance the budget, thus inhibiting the economic recovery. Had the Fed been more accommodating to Hoover's wishes the economy might have done better.[50] In 1957 the Fed took actions to moderate the expansionary course proposed by the CEA, as it did in 1966–69 and 1974–75. In 1977 Chairman Arthur Burns testified against the Carter administration's tax cut proposals, again raising fears that the Fed would oppose administration policies. The Fed's actions in reducing the rate of growth of the money supply and encouraging a rise in the interest rate provoked OMB Director Bert Lance to charge that the policies of the Fed itself were fueling inflation.[51] George Perry, who has studied the Federal Reserve Board, observes that "there is no statistical evidence of fiscal policy and monetary policy working systematically together."[52]

The president negotiates with the Fed chairman. He may include him in an informal "quadriad" of advisors. He may agree to keep the deficit below a certain figure if the Fed agrees to support Treasury bonds. In 1937 Chairman Marriner Eccles made such a deal with Roosevelt, and in 1953 the Treasury and Fed worked together cooperatively; in 1961–65 there was coordination on an expansionary fiscal policy. In 1970 Chairman

Arthur Burns demanded that Nixon make some budget cuts before he would ease the tight money policy, and in 1971 he pressured the administration to institute wage and price controls (but insisted that the Fed, rather than the Price Commission, determine interest rates and regulate corporate dividends). The Fed pursued an "easy money" policy in the election year, increasing the money supply 7.9 percent for the year and 8.7 percent in the final quarter of 1972. This provided a temporary stimulus but fueled subsequent inflation. The following year the monetary "brakes" were applied and the expansion of the currency slowed to 5.8 percent. In response to charges by critics of the Fed that it had made a "deal" with Nixon to help him win reelection, Burns (himself a former Nixon "counselor" in the White House) has claimed that he warned off two Nixon emissaries in 1971 and refused to make deals with the president. He further claims that White House aide Charles Colson then took charge of a Nixon operation to smear Burns and pack the board with his own nominees. Burns thereupon confronted Nixon with evidence of improper pressure tactics and forced the president to apologize and call off Colson.[53] Whatever the truth in the charges of "deals" and countercharges of "pressure," in 1976 Chairman Burns and the board went out of their way to act circumspectly and exercised monetary restraint in the election year.

Although the Carter administration made it clear that it disagreed with Burns's policies, it went out of its way to praise the chairman and held out the possibility of a reappointment to get Burns to be cooperative. But Burns and the board raised interest rates in October 1977, and argued before Congress that the administration should rethink its tax and energy programs and not pressure the Fed to change its monetary policies. The president eventually dropped Burns and made a new appointment, Textron chairman William Miller, to become chairman of the Fed. Carter and Miller then struck a deal to coordinate monetary and fiscal policy. The administration reduced the size of the projected deficit for FY 1979 by decreasing its tax cut proposals from $25 billion to less than $15 billion. In turn the Fed supported Carter's opposition to a proposed reduction in the capital gains tax. Miller indicated that as the size of the budget deficits decreased, the Fed would lower interest rates—these were proposals timed to provide a small deficit and low rates of interest by 1980, when presumably Carter would be running for a second term.

Congress has never *required* the board to coordinate monetary policy with the fiscal policy of the administration. Fed Chairman William McChesney Martin stated, "I am accepting the Employment Act of 1946 as national policy and as being applicable to the Federal Reserve System."[54] Since the act sets no ranking for its goals, and does not require monetary authorities to take any specified actions to meet the goals, such a statement means nothing. The board is made the scapegoat by the

White House for adverse economic conditions. White House aides credit fiscal policy for all successes and monetary policy for most problems. Buck-passing is endemic in the system: the president can take politically popular but economically unsound measures, trusting the board to make the necessary corrections by "leaning against the wind." In 1965 Johnson refused to follow the recommendations of his economic advisors to propose a tax increase, and the Fed felt constrained to adopt a tight monetary policy to dampen inflation. After the board raised the discount rate, Johnson remarked at a news conference,

The Federal Reserve Board is an independent agency. Its decision was an independent action. I regret, as do most Americans, any action that raises the cost of credit, particularly for homes, schools, hospitals, and factories.[55]

Had Johnson fought for the politically unpopular but necessary tax increase, there would have been no need to blame the board for its action.

Congress expects the board to take the advice of its two banking and currency committees. The board is required to keep the committees informed of its actions and release to Congress the minutes of its meetings. Occasionally committees warn the board to take certain actions or drop certain policies. But proposals that the board keep monetary growth at levels defined by Congress have never passed, and thus far Congress has taken no action on the recommendation of the Joint Economic Committee that the board be "obliged to agree with the White House each year on economic goals and ways to achieve them."[56]

Presidential Decision Making

The president must put his economic program in a political context to win congressional and public support for it. He must pay lip service to promoting full employment, but he need not develop a fiscal policy to achieve it. The unemployment rate has no direct correlation with presidential popularity in public opinion polls. In both the Kennedy and Johnson administrations the popularity of the incumbent increased just as the unemployment rate also increased. The public seems to have been impressed that both presidents tried to ameliorate hardship and made proposals to meet the recession and stimulate the economy.[57] The president is under no statutory obligation to promote full employment. The 1946 Employment Act is sometimes misleading referred to as the "*full employment act*," but that is neither its title nor its purpose. Its goals are threefold: maximum employment, production, and purchasing power —and tradeoffs between these goals are permitted. The statute sets no targets to define maximum employment. In practice, administrations change the unemployment rate considered permissible under the condition of "maximum employment" (it has risen from 3.5 percent to 4.9 percent in three decades). The initial draft of the 1946 law mentioned full

INITIAL DRAFT: FULL EMPLOYMENT ACT

. . . it is the responsibility of the Federal Government to pursue such consistent and openly arrived at economic policies and programs as will stimulate and encourage the highest feasible levels of employment opportunities through private and other non-Federal investment and expenditure; (e) to the extent that continuing full employment cannot otherwise be achieved, it is the further responsibility of the Federal Government to provide such volume of Federal investment and expenditure as may be needed to assure continuing full employment.

FINAL VERSION: EMPLOYMENT ACT OF 1946

The Congress hereby declares that it is the continuing policy and responsibility of the Federal Government to use all practicable means consistent with its needs and obligations and other essential considerations of national policy, with the assistance and cooperation of industry, agriculture, labor, and state and local governments, to coordinate and utilize all its plans, functions, and resources for the purpose of creating and maintaining, in a manner calculated to foster and promote free competitive enterprise and the general welfare, conditions under which there will be afforded useful employment opportunities, including self-employment, for those willing, and seeking to work, and to promote maximum employment, production, and purchasing power.

60 Statute 24, February 20, 1946.

employment, but by the time the bill was sent to the floor of the Senate that phrase had disappeared, and Robert Taft could reassure his Republican colleagues, "I do not think any Republican need fear voting for the bill because of any apprehension that there is a victory in the passage of the full enployment bill, because there is no full employment bill anymore."[58]

The president follows policies that, over the course of his term, should have the effect of lowering the unemployment rate and the inflation rate. Most presidents choose the "quick fix" to boost employment and raise income in an election year, accepting the possibility that a new round of inflation will occur after the elections. All postwar presidents (except Eisenhower) relied on an expansionary fiscal policy in the fourth year of their first term. Several accepted large deficits and proposed tax cuts in the fourth year, including Johnson (serving out Kennedy's term), Nixon, and Ford. They have also urged the Fed to ease restraints in the election year. When Ford proposed a massive tax cut in 1975, Sen. Henry Bellmon, a Republican member of the Senate Budget Committee, remarked, "If I had an evil political mind—and I have—I might think that there was some political motive in this timing," and added, "it would be very convenient to have a tax cut early in the political year and an expenditure cut very late in the year."[59]

Presidents often announce decisional rules for the executive budget to further their fiscal policies. To stabilize the business cycle they choose the countercyclical rule: deficits and surpluses must balance out over the course of the cycle. To stabilize prices they propose a restrictive budget that tolerates high unemployment. To emphasize economic growth they may utilize the concept of the "full-employment balanced budget": receipts and expenditures are calculated as if the nation were already at full employment; this calculation projects higher revenues than will actually be collected; future government expenditures are set at the same total as the hypothetical revenues, leaving the budget in hypothetical "balance"—although in reality an actual deficit will be run. In effect this rule provides a way to measure the size of the deficit an administration should run as it attempts to move toward full employment. (The concept was developed by New Frontier economists, used briefly by Nixon and then discarded, and has not been applied since.)

Presidents pay lip service to balancing the budget, since opinion polls show about two-thirds of the public consider it "very important" and about one-quarter consider it "fairly important." Since 1961 there has been only one year in which a deficit was not run. The concept of "full-employment balanced budget" may become a convenient device in the future to enable the president to run large deficits yet retain the politically popular slogan. Another ploy, used by Carter, is to project a balanced budget in the future. He presented the midyear review of the fiscal year 1978 budget with a projection of a balanced budget for fiscal year 1981, a goal that most economists and the Congressional Budget Office found incompatible with other administration goals. The OMB forecast that by 1981 there would be a "full-employment surplus" of $42.1 billion and in 1982 a surplus of $75.5 billion.[60] The president and his economic advisors argued that costly new initiatives should be delayed for a year or more until the improved performance of the economy was reflected in additional revenues, which then could be allocated for new programs. It was rather reminiscent of Alice in Wonderland—jam tomorrow, jam yesterday, but never jam today.

All presidents respond similarly to recessions. They rely primarily on New Deal programs already in place, such as social security, unemployment insurance, and welfare, to stabilize the economy through increased payouts. Then they take some or all of the customary counterrecessionary measures:

1. Propose to Congress increased payouts for social security, unemployment insurance, food stamps, and welfare.
2. Speed up tax refunds, propose tax rebates and lower tax rates, and increase veteran's benefits or bonuses.
3. Increase capital expenditures through area redevelopment, small-business.

loans, accelerated public works, accelerated federal construction, and accelerated payment on contracts for work in progress.

4. Increase funding of the intergovernmental grant system by advance payments of revenue sharing to states and counties, advance payments for grant-in-aid programs, and increased funding for bloc grant programs.

5. Aid specific sectors through research and development grants, procurement contracts, tax legislation, government-insured loans, and subsidies.

6. Establish or expand job training programs, public-employment programs, and incentives for private-sector employment of the low-skilled labor force.

These techniques are more symbolic than effective. They demonstrate concern for people who are suffering, provide relief for those fortunate enough to obtain scarce jobs, and provide benefits to various corporations participating in programs. Presidents who fight to enact or expand these programs gain popularity, even if the economy does not rebound dramatically.[61] But according to economists who have studied these programs, their net fiscal impact is small, and the stimulus they provide does not affect the overall timing or magnitude of recovery in the business cycle. Wilfred Lewis, a leading scholar of these programs, concludes that "it seems doubtful that the discretionary counterrecessionary actions can be assigned much importance in limiting the duration or severity of the postwar recessions."[62]

No presidential candidate or president relishes giving the public a dose of hard economic medicine. In 1976, while *candidate* Ford stumped the nation promising that full employment would be a major goal of his administration if he were elected, *President* Ford submitted a fiscal year 1977 budget that anticipated high levels of unemployment to achieve price stability. *Candidate* Carter called for a balanced budget achieved within four years and lower rates of unemployment and inflation, yet *President* Carter submitted budgets with continued high levels of unemployment projected for the first part of his term. Presidents did not propose countercyclical personal tax increases during the business cycles of 1946–48, 1949–54, 1954–58, and 1958–61. Lyndon Johnson hesitated more than a year before recommending a tax increase in 1967 that was too late to restrain runaway inflation. Nixon rejected the increase his advisors recommended in 1972–73. But no president should be judged harshly for acting on political grounds. Given the state of the "science" of economics, flying by the presidential "seat of the pants" is not an altogether irrational way to deal with his uncertainties.

III

Congress and Fiscal Policy

The Constitution vests Congress with plenary powers in domestic and foreign economic matters. Article I provides a specific enumeration of congressional powers: taxation, regulation of currency, and tariffs. The Federal Reserve Board receives its authority and maintains its autonomy through statutes, and even the Council of Economic Advisors and Office of Management and Budget have statutory bases.

Congresses establishes procedures that force the president to propose an economic program, present his budget, and report on developments affecting the budget at specific times during the year. Congress sets overall revenue and expenditure targets through concurrent resolutions and passes specific tax and appropriations measures. In each case the initiative rests with the administration, and the disposition of fiscal policy rests with the legislature.

Congress delegates its consideration of the presidential program to several committees, which are among the most powerful in each chamber. Each has a large professional staff that works closely with units in the presidential advisory system. The committees can prepare their own legislative proposals, and are likely to do so in periods of split government. No president can rely on party discipline to control the committees. Eisenhower faced intense opposition to his program from Republican conservatives who pressed unsuccessfully for large budget cuts and a tax reduction for business. Kennedy was reluctant to propose the program the CEA recommended because of the opposition of Democratic committee leaders to a tax cut. Johnson routinely negotiated with Wilbur Mills, chairman of the House Ways and Means Committee, not only on tax proposals, but also on the size of the proposed deficit, and he could not obtain a tax surcharge bill from Mills's committee until he agreed to an expenditure cut. Ford's tax cut proposal met with opposition from Republicans on the newly created Budget Committee in the Senate. Carter's $31 billion counterrecessionary program was criticized by the Democrats on the Joint Economic Committee as being $11 billion too small, and the House and Senate substantially rewrote his tax proposals. The tax rebate idea was dropped, and so were taxes proposed in the energy bill.

Congress guards its prerogatives and will not surrender them to the president. In 1961 the Commission on Money and Credit proposed that the president be given standby authority to raise or lower taxes for countercyclical purposes (up to 5 percent), such action to be subject to concurrent veto within sixty days. Though the 1962 CEA Report asked for similar authority, no action was taken. Some economists have suggested that the president should be permitted to levy a positive or negative surtax.[63] In 1976 the Joint Economic Committee proposed that Congress prepare a "standby" tax program to take effect whenever Congress passed, and the president signed, a joint resolution. But neither a system of presidential discretionary action nor a contingency program triggered by Congress have ever become law. Wilbur Mills, a leading congressional authority on these matters, argued that "taxes should not be raised and lowered from season to season like the hemline of women's skirts and dresses."[64] Nor have presidents gained authority to raise or lower social security or unemployment insurance payroll taxes or the distribution of public works funds. Congress insists on authorizing each action, as it did in passing the jobs and public works programs of 1976 and 1977. Although economists like Arthur Okun have argued that "our legislators must face up to the challenge either by improving their record or by delegating authority to the president," Congress has increased its influence in fiscal policymaking, and it has not granted new discretionary authority to the president.[65]

Decision Making Prior to Fiscal Year 1977

Until 1977 tax legislation and appropriations were considered by committees without reference to fiscal policy. Taxes were dealt with primarily as redistributive issues (the question of progressivity) or as distributions, through various special "Christmas tree" presents for favored interest-groups. Any tax measure proposed by the administration had to run a legislative obstacle course. The timing and magnitude of changes proposed for fiscal purposes were considered by committees that had higher priorities. The result was a delay between a presidential request and a congressional action: the 1963 tax cut proposals were enacted a year later; the investment tax credit suspension was delayed for ten weeks in 1966; the proposed surcharge of 1966 was not enacted; the restoration of the investment tax credit in 1967 took fourteen weeks; the surcharge of 1967 was delayed ten months; the tax program of 1969 was not enacted; the tax program of 1975 was ignored by Congress, which passed its own measure; the tax rebate of 1977 was dropped by the administration. Tax reform, a high priority for Carter, was stalled in Congress in 1978. If a president made a proposal for a tax increase, it was usually ignored, so the inclination of the administration was to let inflation occur: as incomes rose during the inflationary period, people would be pushed into higher tax brackets, which became an "invisible" increase in taxes on their income without any legislative action.

The Appropriations Committees that made expenditure decisions concentrated on distributions, increments requested by departments, and administrative oversight, paying little attention to fiscal policy. The total amount of new obligational authority given to the administration was simply the sum of the separate appropriations bills, and represented an *outcome* rather than a deliberate policy on expenditures. The level of spending in any fiscal year was determined by administration actions based on old and new obligational authority, and therefore had only a tenuous relationship to actions taken by the committees. But it also had only a tenuous relationship to the CEA program or the OMB budget presented to Congress.

The haphazard system of congressional decision-making on taxes and spending left presidents and their advisors unable to predict accurately the impact of government actions on the economy. New Frontier and Great Society economists were confident that fiscal policy could work, but only if the president could take discretionary tax and expenditure actions to "fine tune" the economy. Congress ignored the proposals for discretionary tax authority and paid lip service to proposals for expenditure authority. After a brief flurry of impoundments Lyndon Johnson and Congress compromised: the president would propose a spending ceiling that Congress would pass in the form of an expenditure resolution. In return, the House Ways and Means Committee would report a tax bill containing administration requests for a surcharge. This arrangement was a stopgap measure. Johnson received "impoundment authority" in the expenditure resolution so that he could remain within the ceilings, but even so, several program categories were exempted and overall spending for fiscal year 1969 was $4.5 billion over the original limit. The 1970 and 1971 resolutions were ineffective, since the Democratic Congress would not grant Nixon impoundment authority, and Congress could go beyond any limit it had previously enacted simply by subsequently passing additional appropriations: the overruns for fiscal year 1970 and fiscal year 1971 were $4.7 billion and $6.3 billion. No one took the resolutions seriously, and they were no aid to forecasters in and out of government.

Other proposals were rejected by Congress. One would have taken all administration requests for increments above existing spending levels and presented them as a single "Annual Expenditure Increment Appropriation." Congress could then have made decisions about the increase in expenditures from year to year, which would have permitted it to focus on fiscal considerations. Another proposal was for an automatic link between expenditure increases and tax rates: one such "rule" proposed that Congress should set the size of surplus or deficit by resolution, and any marginal expenditures that exceeded the ceiling would be matched by an equivalent revenue increase so the fiscal impact of increased spending would be neutralized. Marginal expenditures would come from tax dollars rather than from "deficit dollars."[66]

Decision Making Transformed

With passage of the Budget and Impoundment Control Act of 1974 Congress created an action-forcing process for fiscal policymaking. The act scrapped the ineffective system of expenditure resolutions and provided instead for passage of budget resolutions that would embody decisions about revenues and expenditures. It also created House and Senate Budget Committees with jurisdiction over the budget resolutions, and a Congressional Budget Office (CBO) as a pooled resource for the two new committees.

The CBO gives Congress expertise to aid it in making fiscal policy. Its director is appointed jointly by the Speaker of the House and the president pro tem of the Senate for a four-year term. Assistant directors administer divisions dealing with fiscal policy, budget analysis, and tax policy.[67] It analyzes the president's executive budget and CEA report, and its director testifies before the Joint Economic Committee and the budget committees to challenge administration forecasts and assumptions. By April each year the CBO submits its own report on the executive budget, and develops, on a nonpartisan basis, its own forecasts and sets of alternative options for Congress to consider.[68] It also submits information to committees that involves "scorekeeping", keeping track of administration and congressional actions throughout the year that affect fiscal policy. Congress does not always rely on CBO expertise. In the first two years the Budget Committees often ignored CBO special studies; warned it against duplicating committee, CRS, or GAO research; and denied one-quarter of the staff positions it requested.[69]

The House and Senate Budget Committees hold hearings on the president's budget. These begin with the "chairman's mark," a set of revenue and expenditure figures prepared by committee staff for consideration by the members. The committees then determine figures for expenditures and revenues, which they recommend to their chambers. Each chamber passes a version of the First Budget Resolution, and then a conference committee reconciles the different versions. By May 15 Congress passes its First Concurrent Budget Resolution, which provides (1) an overall expenditure ceiling and (2) sixteen category ceilings (i.e., defense, natural resources, etc.) to be used by the Appropriations Committees. Over the summer the appropriations bills are prepared, and they are passed between September 1 and 10. Once Congress has passed these bills, it must reconcile its actions (and any tax law it has passed) with the original budget resolution. It may modify the original resolution or trim spending totals to stay within the original guidelines. The mechanism for making these decisions is the Second Concurrent Budget Resolution, which is passed by September 15. This resolution, unlike the first, is binding on Congress. Under its provisions no law or appropriation that would

1. Congress receives reports and messages including: *Current Services Budget*, submitted November 10 by the Office of Management and Budget, which projects expenditures necessary to maintain programs in the next fiscal year at existing levels or at levels required by law; a report from the Joint Economic Committee assessing the *Current Services Budget*, submitted late December; the *Report of the Council of Economic Advisors*, together with the *President's Economic Message*, submitted late January; and the *Budget of the United States Government*, submitted late January.

2. Standing legislative committees, the Appropriations Committees, the Senate Finance Committee, and the House Ways and Means Committee, report spending plans indicated by authorizations, appropriations, or entitlements, to the House and Senate Budget Committees by March 15.

3. The Congressional Budget Office submits an annual report analyzing presidential budget proposals and suggesting options, to the House and Senate Budget Committees by April 1.

4. The Budget Committees report their versions of the First Concurrent Budget Resolution to their chambers by April 15. A Conference Committee reconciles these versions. Congress passes the First Budget Resolution by May 15. It sets overall targets for outlays, new budget authority, revenues, budget surplus or deficit, and the size of the debt. Spending targets are also set for the functional categories used in the *Budget of the United States Government* and for the thirteen appropriations bills.

5. Legislative committees must report bills authorizing new budget authority by May 15. Bills are later passed and sent to the president for signature or veto.

6. The Congressional Budget Office issues periodic reports on budget authority, outlays, and debt legislation, which compares changes authorized by legislation with the First Concurrent Budget Resolution.

7. Appropriations bills reported by the Appropriations Committees are passed by Congress no later than the seventh day after Labor Day and are sent to the president for signature or veto.

8. The Budget Committees report their versions of the Second Concurrent Budget Resolution to their chambers. A Conference Committee reconciles the versions, and Congress adopts the Second Concurrent Budget Resolution by September 15. This resolution reconciles the budget by changing one or more of the following: appropriations and entitlements (outlays), revenue measures, public debt legislation. It also directs legislative committees to report the necessary legislative changes to the Budget Committees, which then report these changes in the form of the Reconciliation Bill. (In the event agreement is not possible on the Second Resolution, the Conference Committee reports continuing resolutions to authorize expenditures). The Reconciliation bill is passed by September 25.

9. The Reconciliation Bill is sent to the president for signature or veto. The adjustments in this bill supersede all previously passed appropriations, entitlements, revenue, or debt legislation.

10. The Fiscal Year begins October 1.

modify its fiscal impact may be passed during the fiscal year without triggering a set of procedures that forces Congress to reconsider the Second Budget Resolution. Any programs proposed by the president or the standing committees during the fiscal year can only be enacted after consideration of their fiscal impact—and it is Congress, rather than the administration, that makes the final decision through its reconsideration of the Second Budget Resolution.

The two Budget Committees are strong enough to force serious consideration of fiscal policy by the tax and appropriations committees. The House Budget Committee has twenty-five members, who are chosen as follows: one by the speaker, one by the minority leader, five from Appropriations, five from Ways and Means, and thirteen from other committees. Most members are senior leaders who owe little to the White House, and some are veterans of long service on the other powerful economic committees. The Senate committee has thirteen members picked through normal procedures, many of whom are influential leaders. On both committees the Democrats tend to be liberal and the Republicans conservative.

The Budget and Appropriations Committees are natural rivals in each chamber. The Senate Budget Committee has challenged the Appropriations and Finance Committees, claiming that tax or expenditure measures would violate Second Budget Resolutions. The House Appropriations Committee has criticized the House Budget Committee for the "generally superficial and nonanalytical manner" in which fiscal policy has been developed, and also criticized it for its line by line reviews of specific program estimates. But these committees may work with the Budget Committee at times in attempts to hold down spending proposals recommended by the standing legislative committees.[70]

The danger in the new process is that the majority party will split on fiscal issues. In the first "trial run" in fiscal year 1976, the House Budget Committee initially failed to report a resolution because of differences between liberal and conservative committee Democrats. Only after two Republicans switched their votes did the committee report its resolution. In May the First Resolution passed the House only after party leaders rounded up the votes of members and pressured some into supporting "the new budget process" by voting for a resolution with which they disagreed; the vote in favor was a narrow 200 to 196. Similarly in November the Second Resolution passed the House after leaders applied pressure. In the spring 1977 First Resolution the Democratic liberals and conservatives were again at odds, almost losing its passage (on one vote by a lopsided 84 to 320). In 1978 House Democrats held together, but at one point a center-right alignment of Republicans and Democrats joined to defeat a proposal from liberal Democrats to shift $4.8 billion from defense into job programs.

The most serious problem with the new process occurs in periods of split government. For fiscal year 1977 President Ford submitted a restrictive budget that emphasized price stability rather than growth. The Budget Committees set guidelines in the First Resolution that called for increases in domestic spending, and the Appropriations Committees made modest increases over the president's requests in many program categories. Democratic committee leaders also proposed new public works and employment programs. Congress passed a First Budget Resolution with expenditures $17 billion higher than totals proposed in the executive budget. The Second Budget Resolution was $13.1 billion higher than figures Ford proposed in his midyear Budget Revision.[71] Ford had offered a budget that might appeal to Democratic conservatives. He also proposed a $10 billion cut in taxes if his budget were adopted in order to put Democrats on the defensive in an election year. He vetoed several appropriations bills in 1976, and in the presidential primaries charged that Democrats were pursuing a policy "that inevitably leads to ruin." To undercut the new budget process Ford demanded that Congress adopt the figures in his budget for its resolutions. He submitted rescission or deferral requests whenever Congress appropriated funds exceeding the figures he had requested for specific programs. The Democratic Congress denied these requests, shelved his proposed increase in payroll taxes, raised figures in appropriations, and prepared its own tax program. Ford eventually signed the Democratic tax bill. He then made fiscal policy an issue in the elections, but his defeat was an indication that Congress could retain the power to make final decisions about fiscal policy.

Carter's victory did not end friction between the president and Congress. The Joint Economic Committee found his economic stimulus package too small. The natural rivalry between the OMB and the CBO on program options, and between the CEA and the CBO on fiscal options, continued strong. The stimulus package was accepted by Congress in the form of a special resolution that modified the Second Budget Resolution, but the Carter tax program was gutted. When Carter dropped his rebate proposal, the Senate Budget Committee felt that he had cut the ground from under it, since the committee had incorporated his plan in the modification of the Second Budget Resolution it had offered to accommodate the new administration, and had, together with the House leadership, gone out on a limb to challenge and defeat the leaders of the Appropriations Committee on spending totals in the revised resolution.

The White House almost lost the resolution in the House. Its revised budget called for FY 1978 spending authority for defense of $120.1 billion. The House Armed Services Committee called for spending of $120.9 billion. But the House Budget Committee reported a resolution with a figure of $116 billion. In the House the administration supported the Burleson amendment, offered by the conservatives, to restore $4.1 billion. The Republicans, sensing their opportunity, voted for the amendment restoring the funds (passed 225 to 184), but then turned around and voted with the liberal Democrats to kill the entire amended budget resolution (84 to 320). The Republicans had been able to split the Democrats and had thrown the budget process into temporary disarray. House Budget Committee chairman Giaimo, furious with the administration, observed tartly, "I don't expect the president or Mr. Brown [secretary of defense] to write the budget for us."[72] Speaker O'Neill, Muskie, and Giaimo then met with the president, and later told a news conference, "his cabinet will not be interfering with budget resolutions."[73] Eventually a new compromise on the Defense budget was worked out by the Budget Committee and House leadership, and a First Budget Resolution passed with 192 Democrats combining with 29 Republicans in favor, and 70 Democrats voting with 107 Republicans opposed.

The most interesting aspect of the entire fiasco was the point made by Speaker O'Neill, who remarked somewhat incredulously after conferring with Carter, that "the Cabinet members had no idea what the budget process was."[74] The process of fiscal policymaking had become so complex that it would take Washington newcomers, presidents and cabinet secretaries alike, at least one year of experience through the cycle to understand how the system worked. In the future a new administration, with its new fiscal program and expenditure priorities, will clash with the Budget Committees, antagonize committee and party leaders, and intervene in untimely and counterproductive ways. By the second or third year the president and his OMB director and cabinet secretaries will have become accustomed to the system and will work better with Budget Committees in making necessary compromises. This prediction is borne out in the Carter administration's experience the second time around the cycle. The First Resolution for the fiscal year 1979 budget made hardly any changes in the budget authority requested by the administration.

Party voting is high for the two budget resolutions in the House, with approximately two-thirds or more Democrats voting for the resolutions, and between four-fifths and all of the Republicans voting against them. As Louis Fisher points out, the resolutions in the House "have become instruments of the majority leadership of the Democratic caucus."[75] The Budget Committee is highly partisan and the reports of its majority and minority members serve to sharpen debate and heighten awareness of fiscal choices. The new budget process has instituted a form of "party government" in the fiscal policymaking process. In the House, party cohesion is high because of efforts of committee and party leaders, without presidential leadership. As the intervention by the Defense Department in the First Resolution of 1977 indicates, the administration may do more to split its party than to promote unity, even if it is done inadvertently. In the Senate, Democrats have given high support to the resolutions, whereas the Republicans have split. A successful president will work closely with the Speaker and the Senate majority leader to develop not simply an administration fiscal program, but a *party* program which unites the congressional and presidential wings. With the two parties opposing each other on the recorded votes for the resolutions, their differences will be clearly visible to the electorate in presidential election campaigns, and the preconditions for a responsible party system will have been met.

The beginnings of such a system can be discerned in the partisan maneuvering over the First Resolution for fiscal year 1979. With California's Proposition Thirteen tax cut a major national agenda issue, Republicans proposed tax cuts coupled with cuts in nondefense spending. Their resolution was defeated, 203 to 197, with 139 Republicans and 58 Democrats in support, and 1 Republican and 202 Democrats opposed. Although the Democrats had the votes to control the budget process, the Republicans had used the budget mechanism to put their fiscal proposals before the nation, in preparation for the upcoming congressional campaigns. By 1980, in a presidential election year, the budget process will become an integral part of the preelection maneuvering by the parties.

IV

When Fiscal Policy Fails

When fiscal policy fails the president can take many actions to keep the economy healthy. To provide more jobs he may propose various countercyclical employment and public works programs or tax credits for companies that employ those out of work, unskilled, or entering the labor market for the first time. To control inflation he may propose "deregulation" of certain sectors, vigorous antitrust action in others, and changes in tariff rates or marketing agreements with other nations. He may also resort to one or more of the following approaches to influence wage rates and prices:

1. Jawboning: a public appeal to labor and management to keep wage demands and price increases down, especially during contract negotiations.
2. Prenotification: an agreement with managers that they will give advance notice to the government before raising prices, permitting the administration to try to persuade them to rescind their decision.
3. Guideposts: administration targets for wage settlements and price increases that unions and management may agree to consider in their negotiations.
4. Transactions: government provision of a benefit for an industry (such as a higher tariff), which is tied to a specific wage settlement or pricing decision.
5. Sector stabilization: establishment of labor-management committees to develop guidelines for settlements to keep price and wage increases at specified limits.

6. Wage-price controls: authority given to the president by Congress to impose controls, which are usually administered by a tripartite pay board (consisting of representatives from labor, management, and the public) and a price board consisting of public members.

Kennedy relied on jawboning to deal with the steel industry, but it disregarded his plea for price restraint and forced him into a major confrontation with the industry that eroded business confidence in his administration and sent the stock market plunging. Guideposts were also ineffective: Kennedy's 3.2 percent target for wage increases was exceeded by labor unions, which preferred to bargain without political pressure. Carter's Council on Wage and Price Stability (COWPS) irked both management and labor by instituting an "advance notice" system to monitor proposed wage and price increases. The AFL-CIO opposed the extension of COWPS by Congress in 1977, so upset was it with the monitoring of collective bargaining agreements. A labor-management group consisting of eight leading corporations and unions pressured the administration throughout 1977 to drop proposals for standards, guidelines, or prenotification.[76]

Sector stabilization attempts also work poorly. In 1971 the Nixon administration established the Construction Industry Stabilization Committee to facilitate settlements. When such committees are created, they serve as a "signal" to economic managers that the president may soon ask for across-the-board wage and price controls. Labor presses for higher wages and industry raises prices, as both attempt to beat the imposition of controls. To calm such fears Ford established a labor-management committee for the construction industry that had no authority to impose settlements. Carter's decision to establish a labor-management committee instead of promoting sector stabilization was taken as a signal that he would *not* impose controls.

The administration may use transactions with economic managers to control prices. In 1977 U.S. Steel announced a price increase of up to 6 percent on various products, which effectively forced a rollback of even higher price increases previously announced by other major companies. Prior to the decision, steel executives met with CEA chairman Schultz, Treasury Secretary Blumenthal, and OMB Director Lance to discuss the possibility that steel imports had been unfairly priced by foreign companies and should be penalized by the administration. Just as the U.S. Steel pricing decision was announced, the adminstration began investigating the possibility of imposing new import quotas that would favor American domestic steel producers. Industry and government were moving to accommodate each other's interest through a specific quid pro quo.[77]

The most drastic measure a president can take is to impose wage-price controls. In wartime such measures are expected, but if a president imposes controls in peacetime, it is admission of administration failure to manage the economy properly. In 1970, in spite of Nixon's opposition, the Democratic Congress put him on the spot by passing an Economic Stabilization Act, which gave him standby authority to impose controls.[78] Although Nixon did not wish to use that authority, the rising inflation rate induced him to apply it to the construction industry in March 1971 and to the entire economy (the first peacetime imposition of controls in American history) in August 1971.

The effectiveness of Nixon's controls is disputed. Phase I applied a ninety-day freeze to all wages, prices, and rents. Phase II then established a system of mandatory wage controls administered by a tripartite pay board, and price and rent controls administered by a price commission. Nixon's goals were to keep inflation to between 2 and 3 percent, by keeping wage increases to no more than 5.5 percent. Phase III was instituted in January 1973 and abolished both the board and the commission, replacing them with a Cost of Living Council. Controls were replaced by a set of "standards" administered by employers, and all rent controls ended.[79] In July 1973 Nixon instituted Phase IV, which eliminated "standards" on a sector-by-sector basis in exchange for commitments to limit price increases in the succeeding year. Authority for wage-price controls expired in April 1974, with no administration proposal for their extension. The Ford administration subsequently proposed, and Congress passed, a measure establishing an eight-member presidential board, the Council on Wage and Price Stability, with no mandatory control authority, but with responsibility to conduct presidential "jawboning." In 1975 Congress extended COWPS for two years, and in 1977 the Carter administration received an additional two-year extension even though organized labor opposed the measure.

Both management and labor oppose wage-price controls, but the record of the Nixon administration indicates that the burden falls most heavily on labor. During Phase I wages and prices were tightly controlled; in Phase II wage increases were not generally permitted but prices were allowed to rise to reflect increased costs. The way Phases III and IV were administered proved beneficial to business: corporate profits had declined 12 percent per year between 1968 and 1970, but under the system of controls they rose an average of 15 percent annually between 1970 and 1973.[80] Price controls did not squeeze profit margins; owing to increased labor productivity between 1970 and 1973, the profit margins actually increased, according to Marvin Kosters, one of the top officials of the Cost of Living Council.[81] Dividends, interest payments, and corporate profits were left uncontrolled: wage earners bore the brunt of inflation control while those people whose incomes were derived primarily or exclusively from investments made no sacrifice. Labor representatives in the program protested its policies and administration and eventually ended their participation.

The Nixon program simply postponed inflation until after the presi-

dential elections. In 1973 the inflation rate climbed to 11.5 percent, and
eight months after the last controls were removed it soared to 12.2
percent.[82] The Democrats passed the standby authority in 1970 hoping
that Nixon would not impose controls and would leave himself open to
criticism. Instead, Nixon called the Democrats' bluff, imposed controls,
and managed to keep inflation in check until he won his reelection.

The failure of fiscal policy and the ineffectiveness of controls led to
new emphasis by the two congressional parties for ways to stimulate the
economy. Republicans emphasized private-sector incentives, such as tax
credits, dividend and capital gains exclusions, depreciation allowances
and write-offs, to provide incentives for investors to finance an expansion
of the productive capacity of industry. Some Democratic liberals proposed
further tinkering with the Employment Act of 1946. One such proposal,
the Equal Opportunity and Full Employment Act (also known as the
Humphrey-Hawkins Bill) went through several versions and picked
up the lukewarm support of President Carter in 1977 (although it was
opposed by the CEA). In November 1977 the administration endorsed a
new version of the measure, now retitled the Full Employment and
Balanced Growth Act. It would require him to set forth plans in his
economic report to achieve a 4 percent unemployment rate (3 percent for
adult workers) within five years. The Federal Reserve would be required
to submit a report within thirty days of each economic report outlining
measures it would take to conform to the president's plans. The Joint
Economic Committee would evaluate the proposals of the president and
Fed, and would make recommendations in the form of a concurrent
resolution that would approve or disapprove the goals and policies in the
president's report. The resolutions would then be used by the Budget
Committees for their First Budget Resolution several months later. Title II
of the measure provided that if the programs fail to bring unemployment
down within two years, the government must institute a program of
"reservoir jobs" making the government the employer of last resort for the
unemployed.[83]

The measure had become largely symbolic. Dropped from earlier
versions were provisions that the president had to submit annually a
separate Full Employment and Balanced Growth Plan, and had to administer various specific job-training and employment programs. Also dropped
was a provision establishing an Economic Planning Board to assist the
president in recommending measures to create jobs. No specific public-
employment measures were included in the bill. The measure had
become a gesture, complete with an "advisory board" consisting of business, labor, agriculture, and consumer representatives. It would have
little economic impact if adopted, but the measure was good politics,
since the electorate generally gives the Democrats high marks for
attempting to combat joblessness, even when unemployment rates remain
high.

It seems ironic that, in the 1960s, when confidence in fiscal theories was great, there were no effective mechanisms to enable the president and Congress to implement fiscal decisions, whereas in the 1970s, when the core of fiscal theory is under attack by economists, the political system has created processes to implement fiscal decisions. Economists who advise presidents and Congress are no longer sure of their prescriptions, but whatever they suggest, the political system can now implement it.

The new collaborative mechanisms provide creative friction between president and Congress and between Democrats and Republicans. The legislative parties can offer the electorate a choice based on positions taken in roll-call votes on the two budget resolutions. Should a version of Humphrey-Hawkins pass, still another resolution will also highlight the differences between the two parties. For the first time fiscal decision-making has become central and visible in domestic policymaking by Congress.

Informed of a dog that danced badly, Ben Jonson observed that the wonder was not that the dog danced poorly, but that he danced at all. Until recently, the wonder was not that presidential fiscal policy worked badly, but that presidents had the nerve to take responsibility for developing any fiscal policy at all. The new collaborative mechanisms that Congress has developed will, perhaps, enable more rational decisions to be proposed by administrations and enacted into law by congressional parties, and will permit the public to hold Congress and the president to much higher standards of performance.

Foreign Policymaking

PRESIDENTS have always relied on prerogative government to make foreign policy. They have successfully advanced their interpretation of their constitutional powers to justify their actions. Rarely has Congress dominated foreign policymaking although it has at times checked presidential initiatives. The major problem for presidents has not been the absence of authority or institutional conflict with Congress: it has been the weakness of the president as a *manager* of foreign relations. There is no unity of purpose within the executive branch. Often the national security "communities"—diplomatic, military, and intelligence—are rivals, working at cross-purposes or against the White House.

The president finds it difficult to deal with the foreign affairs bureaucracies because they have their own close connections to congressional leaders and interest groups. Most policymaking is conducted in "closed" forums, and much information is classified. It is hard for the president to maintain some measure of popular understanding for his policies, and win the trust of a people ill informed about foreign affairs. If the president fails to win popular and congressional support, the various "communities" will take the initiative from him, set boundaries for him, and apply an effective veto over his policies. The president may then become little more than clerk, using his formal powers for the benefit of one or more of the "communities." Unless the president can lead the nation, the government will have no policy, but merely the aggregate of smaller decisions made by the rival bureaucracies. Allies will doubt his leadership, adversaries will exploit the situation, and partisan opponents will await the opportunity to make the mismanagement of foreign affairs an issue in the next elections.

I

The Powers

The Constitution does not contain a "power to conduct foreign relations."[1] Few provisions deal with foreign affairs, and in the aggregate they do not constitute plenary authority; many powers are not mentioned or assigned to particular branches. Is, then, the power of the United States to conduct foreign relations plenary? May the national government do all that any sovereign nation may do, or is it restricted to powers delegated to it by the Constitution? Presidents use the *plenary powers* theory to argue that the United States may exercise any power in foreign affairs that any sovereign nation may exercise, based on the provisions of the Constitution, treaties and executive agreements, international compacts, and the customs, usages, and doctrines of international law.[2] In crises the government may even act in violation of the laws, or even of the Constitution itself, in order to preserve the nation.[3]

Presidents construe enumerated powers assigned to Congress narrowly, and use the doctrine of exclusion to argue that unless authority is expressly enumerated in Article I, Congress has no jurisdiction. They assert that the power to declare war is limited to the declaration itself, and does not include communication with foreign nations that might lead to war. The power to regulate foreign commerce is conceded, but presidents press for delegations of congressional authority to enable them to control tariff and trade policies. Other powers, such as annexation of territories, naturalization, immigration, and expulsions, are also conceded to Congress, but they are peripheral powers. Presidents consider the general congressional lawmaking, appropriations, treaty, and confirmation powers to be useful in completing and perfecting executive policies, and they expect Congress to support them under the subordinate powers doctrine. They will involve Congress only when they need its laws, appropriations, resolutions, or consent.

The president claims the silences of the Constitution. He finds a general "power to conduct foreign relations" for the nation. Then he assumes that whatever has not been expressly assigned to Congress is to be exercised by the executive. His grants of authority, such as "The Executive Power" and the commander in chief title, are expanded through rules of construction to their limits. His powers when combined "result" in additional powers: sole organ of communication with foreign governments, alliance powers, war powers, peace powers. He also claims inherent power as commander in chief to take emergency action to save the nation. He argues that acts he takes are conclusive on his own authority, except in the clear case in which the Constitution requires congressional action or Senate consent.[4]

Sole Organ

The president claims the power of sole organ of communication with other nations. As Secretary of State Thomas Jefferson explained to "Citizen Genêt," the ambassador of the French Republic,

He being the only channel of communication between this country and foreign nations, it is from him alone that foreign nations or their agents are to learn what is or has been the will of the nation; and whatever he communicates as such, they have the right, and are bound to consider, as the expression of the nation.[5]

The president has legal authority to control the activities of the secretary of state, and all communications of officials representing the United States. The president also claims constitutional power to control all communications with other nations. They communicate to the United States through documents addressed to the president or to officials in the Department of State. Other nations are not required to consider communications from Congress as representations of the nation's position. What they communicate to congressional delegations need not be considered by the president as representations to the U.S. government.

The power to communicate can be used by the president to make commitments or create de facto alliances. Presidents may make commitments unilaterally or through declarations and communiques with one or more foreign heads of state or heads of government, such as the Atlantic Charter issued by Roosevelt and Churchill cementing the Anglo-American alliance in World War II. The Shanghai Communique led to a de facto "alliance" between the United States and Communist China for certain limited purposes, concluded after Nixon's visit to Peking in 1972. Though it is not mentioned in the Constitution, the president may mediate, arbitrate, or offer good offices in disputes between other powers. Such mediation in the Russo-Japanese War brought Theodore Roosevelt the Nobel Peace Prize and American influence to the northern Pacific. In the 1970s American mediation and good offices in the Middle East conflict restored the nation's standing in the region and eclipsed Soviet influence; attempts to play a similar role in the Cyprus dispute brought condemnation from both Greece and Turkey and a weakening of the NATO alliance.

Alliance Powers

The president takes the initiative in proposing formal alliances with other nations. Some are based on historic ties, on language and culture or common political traditions, and still others involve economic links or strategic considerations. Alliances may split a president's party and weaken his own government. Washington's de facto alliance with the British in 1793 antagonized Secretary of State Jefferson and led eventually to his resignation from the government. Disagreement over the extent to which the United States should make commitments to Communist China and transfer sophisticated technology to it split officials in the State Department and brought Defense Department opposition. NATO commitments to Western Europe are supported by the public, but various alliances with dictatorships in Asia and Latin America are more controversial. The de facto alliances with Israel and various conservative Arab governments have been forged by presidents without benefit of treaties.

There is no "alliance power" in the Constitution. Presidents can make commitments to other nations based on various enumerated provisions, from which the president claims implied or resulting powers to make alliances. The president claims the power of *recognition* from the provisions that he receives ambassadors from other nations and nominates and (by and with the advice and consent of the Senate) appoints ambassadors and ministers to other nations. The decision to recognize another nation is the president's; the Senate simply concurs (or does not) in his choice of a person as ambassador. The president's decision to recognize a regime, and the level of representation agreed upon, can create a de facto alliance. Presidential recognition of Israel in 1948 was highly controversial, pitting most officials in the State Department, including Secretary of State Marshall, against the president's political advisors (who favored the action). Much later Carter's decision to recognize the "interests" of the Palestinians in a settlement of the West Bank issue represented a certain decision on a fundamental question of Middle Eastern politics. A president may recognize "rights" of peoples not yet politically organized. He may recognize insurgent or guerrilla movements. He may deny recognition to a regime that has assumed power through revolution or coup d'état. He may recall ambassadors for consultations or break relations with a regime to show American displeasure with it.

Treaty Powers

The framers anticipated that alliances would be created through treaties, ensuring participation by the Senate in major foreign policy decisions.[6] Notwithstanding their hopes, and in the interpretation of the treaty power they offered at the state ratifying conventions and in *The Federalist Papers*, President Washington established the precedent that the executive negotiates treaties without the prior advice of the Senate. At first he tried to consult with that body. He informed the chamber that he wished their advice on a proposed Indian treaty, and then appeared in the Senate with Secretary of War Knox. A motion to postpone debate was carried, which infuriated Washington, since he assumed that the senators did not wish to discuss the treaty in his presence. He stormed out of the chamber vowing that he would never return. Several days later, in a tense atmosphere, Washington came back and the Senate offered some advice, but never again did he repeat the procedure.[7] When he negotiated the Jay Treaty, Washington consulted closely with Senate leaders, and then submitted the complete treaty to the chamber —the practice followed ever since.

Presidents may consult with committee leaders, make them members or observers of negotiating teams, and allow them to monitor the progress of negotiations through briefings. Some senators may be permitted an informal "veto" over the composition of the negotiating team, and often the principal negotiators must receive Senate confirmation. Presidents may even encourage Senators to consult with foreign officials, and during these discussions the senators may indicate the terms under which the Senate might consent to the treaty.

Truman used these techniques successfully during the negotiations with Japan at the end of World War II for a treaty of peace. He chose Republican John Foster Dulles as his chief negotiator to give the treaty a bipartisan cast. Dulles collaborated with the Senate Foreign Relations Committee members and sought their advice during the negotiations. He took members of its Far Eastern Affairs Subcommittee to Japan on one of his trips, and he worked closely with its staff director, Francis Wilcox. Senators played a part in the negotiations, convincing the Japanese that their proposed recognition of Communist China would harm chances of passage in the Senate. At the signing ceremony the chairman and the ranking minority member of the Foreign Relations Committee served as members of the American delegation, and there were six alternates and nine observers from Congress. With the support of Senate leaders the treaty was given sympathetic hearings and sailed through the Senate with no reservations.[8]

A textbook example of how *not* to negotiate is provided by the negotiations to abrogate the one-sided Hay–Buneau–Varilla Treaty of 1903 that governed American-Panamanian relations. The negotiations had dragged on since the 1964 disturbances near the Canal Zone. They were to be based on the "Eight Principles" signed by Secretary of State Henry Kissinger in 1974, one of which indicated the American intention of providing the Panamanian government with full control of the canal and the Canal Zone. When Carter assumed office he named Sol Linowitz and Ellsworth Bunker as negotiators; neither of them had close ties to the thirty-one senators who had gone on record in 1975 in support of Senate Resolution 97, which expressed opposition to yielding American sovereignty in the Canal Zone. The negotiating delegation did not include any senators. Instead of consulting closely with committee leaders, the negotiators proceeded on their own, and members of Congress were given briefings as things progressed. Administration lobbyists Robert Bedel and Douglas Bennet from the State Department briefed senators just as agreement was being reached. Then the chief negotiators and Pentagon lobbyists briefed seventy-five senators just prior to the August 1977 "Agreement in Principle," which marked successful completion of a set of draft treaties. Other briefings for forty-five senators were held by the State Department and the White House. To mobilize "opinion leaders" the White House held nineteen briefings for fifteen hundred persons from twenty-five states; participants were chosen from lists supplied by senators. Chairman of the Joint Chiefs of Staff George Brown spoke out in support of the treaties before groups of retired military officers. The chiefs of staff informed their commands about the terms of the treaties, and ensured that the officer corps would either echo the administration line or maintain a discreet silence.

Opponents of the treaties organized at the grassroots, and an informal coalition of conservative organizations (the Conservative Caucus, the American Conservative Union, Citizens for the Republic, the Committee for the Survival of a Free Congress, the National Conservative Political Action Committee, the American Security Council, and the Young Republicans) combined into the Emergency Coalition to Save the Panama Canal. To counter the direct mail appeals of these groups, the administration used a media strategy. The signing ceremony was a public relations extravaganza, including a bipartisan cast of notables such as Gerald Ford, Nelson Rockefeller, Dean Rusk, William Rogers, Henry Kissinger, and Lady Bird Johnson. Secretary of State Cyrus Vance and Secretary of Defense Harold Brown made speaking tours. Six "town meetings" addressed by Carter (by telephone) were organized by the Foreign Policy Association. The president gave a "fireside chat" to the public.

The major problem for the administration was not lack of public support; senators could be expected to vote for the national interest and take political heat from conservatives at the grassroots. But the administration left itself vulnerable because the language of the treaties was unclear at several crucial points, and initially the two sides interpreted it differently. To take one point, Article VI of the Neutrality Treaty provided that after the year 2000 and the transfer of sovereignty to Panama, both parties would "agree to maintain the regime of neutrality established in this treaty." But how would that neutrality be maintained? Who would determine if it were violated? Could the United States defend the canal unilaterally? Secretary Vance argued in testimony before the Senate Foreign Relations Committee that the language meant there was no limit on the freedom of the United States to assure the neutrality of the canal. But Panama's chief treaty negotiator, Dr. Romulo Escobar Betancourt, argued that the United States had no right to intervene since that word had been discussed in treaty drafts and eliminated. Another Panamanian negotiator, Carlos Lopez Guevara, argued that Panama could not agree to any American right of intervention.

With the American Senate being told one thing and the Panamanian National Assembly being told another, treaty opponents demanded a clarification. At first the State Department simply defended its interpretation of the language of the treaties. Then under American pressure Panamanian leader Omar Torrijos joined with Carter in issuing a "Statement of Understanding" that actually was based on language suggested by moderate senators. Torrijos pressured Escobar to endorse the statement at a news conference. Senators Robert Byrd and Howard Baker then sponsored a "leadership amendment" with seventy-eight senators, which defined certain American rights to defend the canal. Meanwhile some Senate conservatives rallied around John Stennis and Barry Goldwater in a bipartisan coalition that attempted further amendments. The leadership of the Senate had to acquiesce in the DeConcini Reservation (giving the United States the right to use force to reopen the canal or restore its operations) and the Nunn Reservation (permitting the United States to negotiate with Panama to station American forces there after the year 2000). Eventually the two treaties passed the Senate by slim margins, 68 to 32, and then only because a number of Republicans supported the president on a bipartisan basis. Carter had to make several deals with some senators for their votes, and had to accept an amendment from the leadership and two reservations. Even though the treaties passed, the president had bungled his dealings with the Senate, antagonized Panama and other Latin American nations, and suffered political damage at home. Although the treaties never would have been popular, some of the problems could have been avoided had the Senate been brought in at an early stage; the language problems would then have been clarified *before* the negotiations were completed.

Presidents expect the Senate to acquiesce in the presidential initiative. Woodrow Wilson, analyzing the treaty process when he was a political scientist at Princeton, concluded,

The President cannot conclude a treaty with a foreign power without the consent of the Senate, but he may guide every step of diplomacy, and to guide diplomacy is to determine what treaties must be made, if the faith and prestige of the government are to be maintained. He need disclose no step of negotiation until it is complete, and when in any critical matter it is completed the government is virtually committed. Whatever its disinclination, the Senate may feel itself committed also.[9]

But Wilson had misread recent events. McKinley had barely won the approval of the Senate for the Treaty of Paris ending the war of 1898; he had received the vote of ten northern Democrats only after offering them patronage and the votes of four "silverites" and two populists only after working with William Jennings Bryan to convince them to support the treaty. The lesson that Wilson should have drawn was that a president must negotiate, bargain, and transact business with the Senate, which otherwise is likely to obstruct his treaty.

Wilson put his own theory to the test when he attempted to win consent to the Treaty of Versailles ending World War I. In negotiating the treaty, the president did not include a single senator from either party on the delegation—unlike McKinley, who had three senators on his negotiating team in Paris. Wilson refused to provide the Senate with information on the progress of the negotiations. Republican leaders offered fourteen "reservations," which were an affront to the president, since they involved his constitutional prerogatives. One provided for American withdrawal from the proposed League of Nations by concurrent resolution of Congress—which would not be subject to Wilson's veto. Another provided that the president could not direct troops in peacekeeping operations voted by the League, which was an attack on his powers as commander in chief. Still another would have prevented him from making interim appointments to an international organization when the Senate was recessed. The "irreconcilables" who opposed the treaty joined with a bipartisan group that supported it with reservations to pass the treaty with the reservations included. After Wilson directed his supporters to vote against the new version, the "irreconcilables" combined with them to vote down the amended treaty. The seventeen "irreconcilables" managed to defeat the treaty, even though Wilson could have formed a two-thirds majority to pass it with reservations. For the first time in history the Senate had rejected a peace treaty.

Wilson is not the only president to have been frustrated by the Senate. Between 1789 and 1844, five treaties were lost of the seventy-seven submitted to the Senate. Between 1844 and 1969, one hundred eighteen were submitted and eighteen lost, including a treaty to annex Texas and several treaties submitted by Andrew Johnson. After the Civil War, Senate consent was even harder to obtain than before. Between 1869 and 1919 the Senate defeated several presidential attempts to add territory to the Union, but passed the Treaty of Paris by a close margin. Various arbitration treaties proposed by Roosevelt and Taft, treaties negotiated with several Latin American nations, and the Treaty of Versailles were all defeated.[10] Between 1919 and 1939 Republican Senate leaders prevented American entry into the Permanent Court of International Justice, blocked general arbitration treaties, and kept America from joining the League of Nations.[11]

The Senators who used the treaty power to block presidential initiatives after World War I were not simply isolationists. They were interested in creating a "balance of power" system involving arms limitations incorporated into various treaties to be negotiated by the great powers. The same senators who blocked American participation in international organizations also promoted and directed the negotiations that led to the Five Power Treaty limiting naval armaments, the Four Power Treaty regulating spheres of influence in the Pacific, and the Nine Power Treaty regulating the Open Door in China.

Since 1939 most treaties negotiated by the president have encountered little Senate opposition, including the postwar collective security agreements such as NATO, SEATO, and the Rio treaties. In the 1970s, however, the Panama Canal Treaty was almost defeated, and the arms limitations negotiations with the Soviet Union were colored by what negotiators on the American side calculated the Senate might be willing to accept.

Whenever the Senate defeats treaties, proposals are made to lower the approval requirement to three-fifths or an absolute majority or to a simple majority of those present. Another proposal is that no amendments or reservations to treaties could be proposed by the Senate. But such reforms would require constitutional amendments, and they have no chance of adoption for the obvious reason that the Senate would never consent to them. But amending the Constitution is not necessary, for if the Senate becomes recalcitrant, the president may bypass it by using his commitment powers.

Commitment Powers

The president may take a treaty that does not pass the Senate and submit it to Congress for legislative action requiring simple majorities. When the treaty annexing Texas was defeated in 1844 President Tyler sent a resolution of annexation, which Congress passed. Or the president may take the terms of a treaty blocked by the Senate and convert it into an executive agreement to be implemented unilaterally. In 1905 Theodore Roosevelt negotiated the Dillingham-Sanchez Protocol, which provided for American operation of the customs houses in Santo Domingo. Because of Senate criticism the agreement was converted into a treaty requiring Senate approval. When Senate Democrats then blocked its consideration, Roosevelt announced that he would implement it as an executive agreement until the Senate gave its consent to the treaty.

In theory there is a distinction between a treaty, which expresses a continuing obligation undertaken between nations, and an executive agreement, which merely facilitates a particular arrangement during a limited period of time between governments. In practice, as Louis Henkin points out, this traditional distinction of international law has not been observed, so that no difference between the two types of instruments can be maintained.[12] There are far more executive agreements in force than treaties. Between 1946 and 1971, the United States entered into 361 treaties and more than 5,559 executive agreements. Of the 4,359 agreements in force in 1972, the majority involved some form of collaboration with Congress: either the agreements had been authorized by prior legislation, or the agreement itself required congressional approval or the passage of laws to implement it. But 3 percent of these agreements had been negotiated unilaterally by the president and implemented without congressional participation.[13] About 400 of these agreements were classified and kept from Congress, and some of these were major commitments and de facto alliances with other nations—arrangements that bypassed both the treaty powers of the Senate and the legislative powers of Congress. Prerogative government had been substituted for the collaborative process established by the Constitution.[14]

The president can make commitments without formalizing them as executive agreements. He can issue communiques or doctrines that ally the United States with other nations. He can give "understandings" in the form of memoranda of agreement when negotiators conclude agreements for military bases or installations; he can make oral commitments that are recorded in the form of an aide memoire during summit conferences. Even a presidential letter may create a commitment: when Nixon convinced South Vietnam's President Thieu to back the Paris Peace Agreement, he wrote to Thieu, "You have my assurance of continued assistance in the post-settlement period and that we will respond with full force should the settlement be violated by North Vietnam."[15]

Presidents argue that regardless of subject matter or congressional jurisdiction, they may negotiate on any subject not prohibited by the Constitution. Anything the president and Senate can accomplish by treaty, the president alone can accomplish by executive agreement. The role of the Senate in the treaty power is the exception to the general responsibility of the president to conduct foreign relations.[16]

In periods of split government the potential for conflict between president and Senate over the treaty power is high. In the early stages of the American involvement in Vietnam, neither Kennedy nor Johnson faced congressional questioning of their commitment powers. It was only after Nixon was inaugurated that the Democratic Congress turned to a general investigation of these powers. In February 1969 Congress created an Ad Hoc Subcommittee on U.S. Security Agreements and Commitments Abroad. The first product of its labors was the "National Commitments Resolution," expressing the sense of the Senate:

That a national commitment by the United States results only from affirmative action taken by the executive and legislative branches of the U.S. Government by means of a treaty, statute, or concurrent resolution of both Houses of Congress specifically providing for such commitment.[17]

The Nixon administration disregarded the resolution, since it had no force of law, and in 1970 concluded a military base agreement with the Spanish government that contained various security guarantees. The Senate countered by passing a resolution indicating that the agreement was not a national commitment, notwithstanding anything the executive branch might have communicated to the Spanish government.[18] The following year the administration exchanged notes with Portugal and Bahrain when it obtained new facilities for military installations. The Senate then tried to cut off funds for the facilities, but the House supported the administration and the attempt failed. The Senate then passed a resolution requiring the administration to submit the two agreements to the Senate as treaties, which Nixon refused to do.[19] Congress then passed a law that provided that

the Secretary of State shall transmit to the Congress the text of any international agreement, other than a treaty, to which the United States is a party as soon as possible after such agreement has entered into force with respect to the United States, but in no event later than sixty days thereafter.[20]

Secret agreements were to be submitted to the House Foreign Affairs and Senate Foreign Relations Committees.

Congress refused to pass stronger measures. The House did not pass a measure adopted by the Senate in 1974 that would have provided that executive agreements come into force unless both houses of Congress disapproved by concurrent resolution. The Senate defeated an amendment to the 1974 State-USIA authorization bill providing that no funds could be expended for military base agreements unless the Senate gave its advice and consent, or Congress approved such agreements by concurrent resolution. And Congress did not pass bills providing that either chamber could determine by resolution that an international agreement must be submitted as a treaty or law, and that such agreements would not go into effect until the treaty or law were approved.[21] Since Congress has defeated all these proposals, the commitment powers of the president remain a formidable resource for his diplomatic efforts.

II

Secrecy Systems

The greatest resource the president has in dealing with Congress, the public, and his own bureaucracies is his control of secret information involving national security matters. The president may decide key issues with a handful of aides, freeze out of his councils those in the government who oppose his policies, and spring faits accomplis on the cabinet, the careerists, and Congress. The secrecy system inhibits critics of his policies from challenging him, for they realize that they lack his information and may be discredited if he reveals aspects of the situation they knew nothing about. It is no small thing to challenge what Arthur

Schlesinger, Jr., calls the "religion of secrecy" promoted by the executive branch.[22]

It is necessary and proper to keep secrets about military preparedness and mobilization, strategic and contingency plans, deployment of forces for military operations, and the conduct of diplomacy where disclosure could lead to disruption of an alliance or hostilities against the United States and its allies. It is necessary to maintain the integrity of codes, intelligence sources, and communications channels. It is legitimate to maintain secrets about scientific, engineering, and production developments with military applications.

But most administrations extend secrecy systems far beyond the legitimate purposes in order to cover up actions that would embarrass them politically, or reveal nonfeasance, misfeasance, or malfeasance. Sen. Edward Kennedy summed up the case of the critics of secrecy systems when he observed that

government secrecy breeds deceit, that executive privilege nurtures executive arrogance, that national security is frequently the cover for political embarrassment, and that the best antidote to official malfeasance, misfeasance, and nonfeasance is the sunshine and fresh air of full public disclosure of official activities.[23]

Secrecy systems are used by the president to keep information from the military, diplomatic, and intelligence agencies, and by these agencies to keep information from the White House. The administration routinely uses secrecy systems to keep Congress uninformed or misinformed. As Rear Adm. (ret.) Gene LaRoque pointed out regarding the classifying of information:

Classification is made for a variety of reasons. First, to prevent it from falling into the hands of a potential enemy; this is legitimate but accounts for only a small portion of the material classified. Other reasons for classifying material are: to keep it from the other military services; from civilians in their own service; from civilians in the Defense Department; from the State Department; and of course from the Congress.[24]

In most cases the White House classifies information for its own purposes, to "manage" news about foreign affairs. If lies are necessary, White House spokesmen release false information, based on a "cover story" with surface plausibility: U-2 reconnaissance flights conducted over the Soviet Union in the 1950s were covered up by claims that the planes were engaged in weather research and strayed over Soviet territory by accident. It was not until the Soviets shot down a plane and captured its pilot, Francis Gary Powers, that President Eisenhower admitted ordering the flights. After the failure of the Bay of Pigs invasion of Cuba, White House spokesmen put out a story that only a small landing party had been involved in an attempt to reach the mountains and begin guerrilla warfare: that lie was punctured when Cuban Premier Fidel

Castro paraded thousands of prisoners in a stadium in Havana. The president may offer a misleading interpretation of facts by hiding his real intentions: the steady buildup of combat forces in South Vietnam in 1964 and 1965 was masked as a series of ad hoc reactions to events initiated by the Viet Cong, rather than as part of long-range American policy, and the public was not informed that fifty thousand combat troops had begun to initiate firefights as early as 1965.

Secrecy systems create a Catch 22 situation: legislators and the media are denied information, so they have no idea what questions to ask to find out what is going on. When CIA director Richard Helms was asked under oath at congressional hearings whether his agency was involved in the Watergate burglary, he could truthfully say no. But he felt no obligation to volunteer to the committee the information that the CIA had assisted White House aides in planning and preparing for the operation, and had acted under presidential orders to aid in its cover-up. Administration officials can testify before members of Congress and inform them of conditions in other nations and the American response to those conditions, yet not reveal crucial points, which prevents the checks and balances system from working properly.

The president selectively releases information to promote his version of events and discredit his critics. Lyndon Johnson would declassify information at news conferences (even at his ranch) in dramatic gestures to convince reporters he was "leveling" with them. In 1968 when Robert Kennedy was deciding whether to run for president, Johnson leaked a memo, written in 1963 by Roger Hilsman, then a State Department official (and in 1968 a foreign policy advisor to Robert Kennedy) supposedly linking Hilsman's policy recommendations to the assassination of South Vietnamese Premier Ngo Dinh Diem. This leak was calculated to discredit Hilsman (who had resigned from the State Department in protest against Johnson's escalation of the war) as well as Robert Kennedy; it exemplifies the misuse of the classification system for purely political purposes.[25]

The government allows former officials to obtain access to classified information when it believes that their articles, books, or memoirs will support the government line. White House aide Theodore Sorensen was permitted to take seven boxes of classified documents from the White House, enabling him to complete his book on Kennedy. The State Department routinely grants access to its files to senior officials who have left the government. Henry Kissinger relied on taped telephone conversations involving classified information in writing his memoirs. Yet the use of such material is also routinely denied to ex-officials who intend to write critical accounts, especially if they have resigned in policy disagreements with the administration.[26]

The president may co-opt publishers, editors, and columnists by feeding them classified information in certain circumstances, or appealing to them to withhold dissemination of information obtained from other sources. Kennedy asked the publishers of the *New York Times* to delay publication of a story that the invasion of Cuba was imminent so that the exile forces would not be endangered. In other cases an administration drops the carrot and uses the stick. When the *New York Times* printed parts of the *Pentagon Papers*, a set of classified Defense Department volumes analyzing American involvement in Indochina, the Nixon administration went to court and won a temporary restraining order preventing continued publication of the articles—the first order of its kind in American history. Eventually the Supreme Court overturned the order. Six justices, writing for the majority, agreed that the government had not met the burden of showing justification for enforcement of prior restraint. But the court rejected the view that prior restraints are never permissible; instead, it recognized that Congress should legislate conditions for any exercise of such restraint, while also insisting that the judiciary, not the executive, would determine both the standards that the government would have to meet, and the facts of each case (i.e., whether the government had met such standards).[27] Had Congress legislated a system of prior restraint for classified information, a majority of the Court might have upheld it, and the media would not have been able to disseminate the Pentagon Papers. Proposals for an "Official Secrets Act" providing for criminal penalties for publication of classified material were supported by the Nixon administration, but dropped by later administrations. However, several agencies, including the CIA, still support such a law.

The president may harass "leakers.' 'Nixon proposed a law that would have provided criminal penalties of up to seven years in jail and fines of up to $50,000 for any person, "if, being or having been in authorized possession or control of classified information, or having obtained such information as a result of his being or having been a federal public servant, he knowingly communicates such information to a person not authorized to receive it."[28] (Of course, under the provisions of such a law most ex-presidents, presidents, and other senior officials could be found guilty of leaking information to the media.) Similar proposals have been made in the Carter administration by CIA Director Stansfield Turner, but have not yet won the backing of the president, owing in part to opposition from Vice-President Mondale. At present officials face only the loss of their security clearances, or official reprimands, transfers, or dismissal.

The president may also employ "dirty tricks" against leakers. When Daniel Ellsberg, former special assistant to the assistant secretary for international security affairs in the Department of Defense, leaked the Pentagon Papers to the media, the Nixon "plumbers" burglarized the office of his psychiatrist to try to find damaging materials in the files. Ellsberg was prosecuted by the Justice Department for alleged violation of the espionage laws and for "stealing government property" because he had made reproductions from a copying machine off the premises of the Rand Corporation, which had been authorized to keep copies of the papers on its premises. Not only was Ellsberg tried on trumped-up charges, but Nixon himself seems to have tampered with the case. He offered the presiding federal judge, Matthew Bryne, the directorship of the FBI while the trial was in progress. Bryne eventually declared the case a mistrial because government prosecutors did not reveal that some of their evidence had been obtained as a result of the illegal wiretap placed on the home of Morton Halperin.

Officials who work in the intelligence or defense communities may be required as a condition of employment to sign agreements or contracts stating that they will not discuss or write about policies involving their agencies without obtaining prior agency clearance. In 1972 the CIA went to court to censor portions of a book written by Victor Marchetti, a former staff assistant to the director. A lower federal court forbade publication of the book without agency approval; this was the first successful prior restraint suit. The federal court held that Marchetti had waived his rights under the First Amendment by signing statements that he would not disseminate information relating to agency activities. The court of appeals affirmed the injunction, but limited it to matters that the CIA had classified.[29] Upon completion of the book Marchetti submitted the manuscript to the agency, which insisted that 168 passages be deleted. Marchetti went to court with his publisher, and in a second case the federal district court permitted 140 of the passages to be published (although the book was published with all 168 passages deleted during the course of the litigation).[30] The court of appeals then decided that the court would not review the reasonableness of the classification system, but would remand the case to the federal court for trial, where each separate document could be disputed between agency and author on the issue of whether or not it was properly classified.[31] The Supreme Court declined to review the case, Marchetti decided not to litigate on the classifiability of particular documents, and the permanent injunction remained in effect.[32]

In 1978 President Carter and the Department of Justice initiated a lawsuit to uphold the constitutionality of the CIA agreements. A former agent, Frank Snepp, did not submit to the CIA prior to publication his manuscript about a CIA station and the fall of the South Vietnam government. In its civil suit the Justice Department asked for punitive damages equivalent to the royalties Snepp would make on the book, and also asked for a restraining order to prevent Snepp from talking about the CIA or disseminating further information about it. Although Carter referred in a news conference to the need to protect classified information, neither the government nor author claimed that the book was based on classified documents. In fact, the issue involved nonclassified material. Snepp was not accused of a criminal act, but only of violating a contract with the agency. Did such a contract violate the First Amendment right of freedom of speech? As the case was being litigated in 1978, no one could be sure what the courts would do. But one thing was clear: the president had come down, just as Nixon had before him, on the side of the CIA rather than on the side of those who would attempt to improve its operations by describing its inadequacies.

Classification Systems

Presidential control of information is based partly on laws, which give the executive the power to classify military plans, mobilization plans, and atomic secrets.[33] By law the executive need not disclose certain classified information: the Federal Register Act of 1935 made it mandatory for the president to publish executive orders and presidential proclamations, but a provision allowed him to issue orders in the form of memoranda that may be classified; the Administrative Procedures Act of 1946 permitted departments to withhold information from the public when "there is involved (1) any function of the United States requiring secrecy in the public interest or (2) any matter relating solely to the internal management of an agency."[34] Until 1958 departments relied on a series of laws passed between 1789 and 1872, known collectively as the "housekeeping statutes," which, as codified in 1875, provided that each department head was authorized to prescribe regulations for "the custody, use, and preservation of its records, papers, and property appertaining to it."[35] In 1958 Congress passed a provision that stated that the housekeeping section "does not authorize withholding information from the public or limiting the availability of records to the public."[36] The Freedom of Information Act of 1966 specifically exempted matters that were "specifically required by executive order to be kept secret in the interest of national defense or foreign policy."[37] The Supreme Court, in a lawsuit brought under the act, made it clear that when an agency classified information according to this law, the courts would not inquire into how a particular document was classified under its provisions.[38] Congress in 1974 then amended the law regarding the national security exemption so that only those documents "specifically authorized under criteria established by executive order . . . are in fact properly classified pursuant to such executive order."[39] Under this amendment courts could determine through in camera inspections whether or not documents were properly classified or could be released under provisions of the Freedom of Information Act, thus giving the judiciary the last word rather than the executive.

But the president relies primarily on his constitutional prerogatives, as he defines them, rather than on statutes, to create and administer most classification systems. The first such systems were created by the War Department prior to and during the First World War, and the modern system was developed after Franklin Roosevelt issued Executive Order 8381 in 1940 classifying War and Navy Department information. After American entry into the Second World War, Executive Orders 9103 and 9182 established an overall classification system administered by the Office of War Information. That office issued Regulation 4, which established procedures to store, protect, and disseminate information classified as *secret, confidential,* and *restricted.* After the war President Truman issued Executive Order 10104 updating the military system, and Executive Order 10290 for nonmilitary agencies. The second system permitted classification of "official information the safeguarding of which is necessary in the interest of national security," and created categories of *top secret, secret, confidential,* and *restricted.* The loose language gave a blank check to the careerists and political executives. There were no limits on which agencies could classify, no accountability for misuse of the system, no penalties for misclassification, and no time limits. Whereas formerly the secrecy systems were used to safeguard military secrets, the new system could be used in the conduct of diplomacy to keep Congress uninformed or misinformed.

Eisenhower and Kennedy made minor changes in the system. In 1953 Eisenhower's Executive Order 10501 created the Interagency Committee on Internal Security to oversee the system, limited the number of agencies with classifying authority to forty-seven, and limited the number of officials who could classify documents to approximately 1.5 million. Downgrading and declassification procedures were established, and the "restricted" category was eliminated. Kennedy issued Executive Order 10964, which provided for automatic declassification of certain materials after twelve years unless the department requested a continuation. But Kennedy's secretary of defense did not implement the recommendations of a congressional committee that penalties be instituted for misuse of the system.

Although the Nixon administration used secrecy to shield its own initiatives from lower levels of the departments, and from Congress and the media, it also proposed and implemented major reforms in the system at the departmental level. Executive Order 11652 and the National Security Council memorandum that implemented it in 1972 reduced the number of agencies that could classify information top secret from thirty-four to thirteen, and the total number of agencies with classification authority to thirty-five. Administrative penalties were provided for misuse of authority and overclassification, including reprimands, suspension without pay, or removal. New criteria for classification were introduced, although the test for top secret remained vague: "whether its unauthorized disclosure could reasonably be expected to cause exceptionally grave damage to the national security." Automatic declassification of documents on a twelve and thirty year schedule was instituted, with the burden of proof on the agency to demonstrate the need to continue secrecy if a request to declassify was made by outsiders.[40] The National Security Council regulations provided that

in no case shall information be classified in order to conceal inefficiency or administrative error, to prevent embarrassment to a person or department, to restrain competition or independent initiative, or to prevent for any other reason the release of information which does not require protection in the interests of national security.[41]

But the new procedures were not designed to end abuses of the system. No criminal penalties were provided for misclassification to cover up malfeasance. Departments were not required to identify which officials classified documents, but only the officials who authorized classification and the kinds of documents that were classified. Without knowing who requested that a particular document be classified, or who acceded to the request, it would be impossible to determine who was violating the guidelines. Several loopholes permitted agencies to withhold information from each other, or even from the White House. The practice of limiting distribution to a few officials (the limdis system), thus limiting information and debate within an agency or department to those with a "need to know" (i.e., those who would support the administration), was provided for under Regulation 9 of the NSC memorandum:

The originating department or other appropriate authority may impose, in conformity with the provisions of this order, special requirements with respect to access, distribution, and protection of classified information and material, including those which presently relate to communications, intelligence, intelligence sources and methods and cryptography.[42]

The White House and National Security Council staff limited distribution of information to favored officials, thus setting off a scramble for limdis memoranda among outsiders. It was a standing joke in Washington that the Joint Chiefs of Staff had to plant "spies" in NSC offices to find out what Kissinger was planning. The director of Central Intelligence had his own "Specat" system to limit the distribution of intelligence reports to a few senior officials in the CIA and a handful of White House aides, freezing out military intelligence and State Department officials. Other agencies used "administrative control designations," of which there were at least sixty-three at that time, for the same purpose. The "top secret" clearance was held by almost a half million officials of the permanent government, and many members of Congress, and obviously was of no use to agencies or the White House in controlling access to information. The limdis, Specat, and administrative control systems were used by agencies against each other, and also against the White House. As Daniel Ellsberg, who had a dozen special Pentagon clearances, warned a Senate committee,

Could there be clearances the President doesn't know about? Of course, certainly, without any doubt, because of the physical nature of generating these things is such that they can multiply and proliferate in a way that no individual has any way of knowing about.[43]

Although such a situation is conceivable, the president can take prudent precautions. He can use his national security advisor and senior administration political executives to ensure that career officials cannot institute limdis systems that freeze out his loyalists.

The White House creates its own secrecy systems to prevent departments from finding out about its plans. These are organized by the national security advisor for the president. In 1963 Kennedy set up his own channel to communicate directly to his arms control negotiator, Averill Harriman. The purpose of the channel was to keep the Pentagon and Joint Chiefs of Staff in the dark until the terms of a test-ban treaty had been negotiated. Only six officials in the administration had access to Harriman's cables from Moscow. Kissinger also controlled information so that it could be kept from careerists in the various departments and agencies, and especially from the State Department until he became secretary of state.

Officials who have access to the most important information about American foreign policy based on special clearances form a small community that cannot exchange ideas or information freely with other officials in the executive branch, members of Congress, or outside experts. They discount the value of intellectual exchanges with persons who are not "cleared" and lack access to their secret information. As Ellsberg points out, "You have the information, they don't; they don't even have the wisdom to know what they don't know; therefore they have no legitimate role."[44] Officials with clearances manipulate those without them, lie to Congress, and turn the oversight system into a farce. They also monopolize access to the president and prevent him from discussing issues with outsiders. The president and his principal aides form a tight little band of "believers" in their policy, because they can console each other that their critics would support them, if only they were in a position to understand the situation. Thus the top levels of the administration tend to discount criticism of their policies from those who are "uninformed."

Members of Congress have proposed placing the secrecy systems on a statutory basis. A subcommittee of the House Government Operations Committee has made recommendations that involve the following: the number of officials who could classify would be limited to the head of departments and agencies and their principal deputies; each official would be accountable for decisions; criteria would be established by law to limit classification to national security matters, with specific enumeration of categories; administrative and criminal penalties for misuse would be instituted; all distribution channels and Specats would be made known to an interagency board monitoring the system; automatic downgrading would occur after three years unless an agency requested continuation; members of Congress and their aides could be given access to limdis documents; the onus would be on the administration to justify withholding of information from Congress in each case. Other proposals would establish an independent board, nominated by the president and confirmed by the Senate, which would "arbitrate" when Congress requests, and the executive denies, access to information.[45]

At present there is no way short of impeachment and removal from office that Congress can strike back at an administration that refuses to furnish it with classified information. For if it retaliates by passing laws or appropriations that restrain agencies from taking actions or spending funds, the secrecy system can be used to violate restrictions in the laws or even to transfer funds to make up for the cuts. Congress might never know that its sanctions had been nullified. A combination of an independent oversight board, coupled with judicial review of classifications under the Freedom of Information Act, might prevent some of the most unfortunate examples of misuse of the system.

Executive Privilege

The president may claim "executive privilege" to withhold information from Congress or the judiciary. In the nineteenth century presidents withheld information about diplomatic or military ventures, but all eventually provided Congress with information it sought or relied on statutory authority to withhold it. When Washington refused to supply the House with information about the Jay Treaty, it was because he claimed such information should properly be submitted to the Senate. When Jackson refused to provide the Senate with information about a nomination to office, the Senate retaliated by refusing to consent to the nomination, and no precedents were set. The modern practice of withholding information was instituted by President Taft, who issued Executive Order 1062, which provided:

In all cases where, by resolution of the Senate or House of Representatives, a head of a Department is called upon to furnish information, he is hereby directed to comply with such resolution, except when, in his judgment, it would be incompatible with the public interest, in which case he should refer the matter to the president for his direction.

Prior to the Second World War refusals to furnish Congress with information were rare. During the war Roosevelt refused to turn over to congressional committees the investigative files of the FBI dealing with the background of strikers at war plants. Truman later ordered that congressional requests to departments for personnel records (involved in congressional loyalty-security investigations) be submitted to him for final approval. Eisenhower refused to turn over personnel records of military officers to a Senate investigation led by Joseph McCarthy. At that time, while McCarthy was smearing the loyalty of career military and diplomatic officials with underhanded tactics, giving the name *McCarthyism* to the language to describe a set of dirty tricks used to destroy the careers of innocent persons, Eisenhower developed the prerogative of executive privilege.[46] Congress and the courts were sympathetic to Eisenhower in his battle against McCarthy, and were indisposed to sound the alarm that the president was asserting a power found nowhere in the Constitution. Several years later Attorney General William Rogers argued that Eisenhower need not disclose candid advice from assistants, or provide Congress with interdepartmental memoranda, advisory opinions, or informal working papers, as part of the concept of executive privilege.[47]

Successive presidents have broadened the scope of the privilege. Kennedy invoked it to prevent congressional oversight of foreign policy. He ordered Gen. Maxwell Taylor, his military advisor, to refuse to testify before a House Subcommittee on Defense Appropriations, which was holding hearings on the failure of the Bay of Pigs operation. Johnson made almost no use of executive privilege, relying primarily on the classification systems to keep Congress from discovering his intentions in Vietnam. Nixon permitted the Defense Department to refuse to supply documents to the House Armed Services Committee when it tried to investigate unauthorized bombing raids ordered by General LaValle against North Vietnam. The president prevented Congress from exercising oversight in a situation in which the White House and Defense Department had been unable to control the actions of senior military commanders in the Air Force, who themselves had determined bombing targets during the war. When Nixon made cabinet secretaries into White House assistants, it enabled the "doublehatters" to invoke executive privilege on the grounds that they acted as advisors to the president. Nixon could prevent Congress from obtaining testimony on sensitive issues from secretaries, even when the issues involved departmental responsibilities. Carter not only dismantled the last vestiges of the "doublehatter" system, he also made almost no use of executive privilege. Only once in his first fifteen months in office did he apply it, and that was in a lawsuit that involved application of the Trade Act of 1974. The government submitted certain papers to the courts, which after an *in camera* inspection agreed that the government need not disclose the information in the course of the judicial proceedings.

Corresponding to the expansion of executive privilege has been the assertion of "department" and "agency" privilege. Officials in the Kennedy and Johnson administrations sometimes disregarded congressional requests for information or testimony. In the Nixon administration committees would be given summaries rather than original documents, or else they would be given an incomplete record—the case with investigation of

THE NIXON ADMINISTRATION ON EXECUTIVE PRIVILEGE

Senator Muskie: . . . the Congress in your view, has no power to command the production of testimony or information by anyone in the executive branch under any circumstances?

Mr. Kleindienst: If the President of the United States so directs. . . .

Senator Muskie: So our power to command [the production of information] is in the President's hands?

Mr. Kleindienst: Well, your power to get what the President knows is in the President's hands. Your power to get information from citizens is in your hands.

Senator Muskie: Does that apply to every one of the employees of the [executive] branch of the United States?

Mr. Kleindienst: I think if the President directs it, logically, I would have to say that is correct. . . .

Senator Ervin: Your position is the President has implied power under the Constitution to deny to the Congress the testimony of any person working for the executive branch of the Government or any document in the possession of anybody working for the Government?

Mr. Kleindienst: Yes, sir, and you have a remedy, all kinds of remedies, cut off appropriations, impeach the President.

U.S., Congress, Senate, Hearings before the Subcommittee on Intergovernmental Relations, et al., *Executive Privilege, Secrecy in Government, Freedom of Information,* 93rd Cong., 1st sess. April 10, 1973, vol. I, pp. 20, 45–6, 51.

the alleged involvement of the International Telephone and Telegraph Company in the overthrow of the government of Chile, and the circumstances involving the grain sale to the Soviet Union. The Defense and State Departments delayed the submission of documents to the Senate Foreign Relations Committee for several months when Senator Fulbright conducted hearings critical of administration policies. Secretary of State Rogers refused to testify on the progress of the Paris Peace negotiations. Secretary of the Army Stanley Resor claimed that Congress had no need of his testimony (a novel argument) and declined to appear before the Senate Subcommittee on Constitutional Rights when it investigated army surveillance and spy activities against American citizens.

Departments may refuse to furnish information to create a bargaining situation with congressional committees. They may agree to testify in executive session if they are permitted to censor the hearings and reports the committee issues and delete classified information. They may furnish summaries of documents or abridged versions with the consent of the committee. Legislators often scale down their demands for information rather than continue the confrontation. The General Accounting Office also has problems: the Department of Defense often refuses to supply it

with information about weapons systems and costs, in spite of the clear
direction of the Budget and Accounting Act of 1921, which directs departments to furnish the GAO with "such information regarding the powers,
duties, activities, organization, financial transactions, and methods of
business of their respective offices as he [the comptroller general] may
from time to time require of them."[48]

Congress has yet to deal effectively with the claim of executive and
department privilege. It can threaten to impound funds, but when it
passes provisions providing for cutoff of funding if information it requests
is not furnished, the provision is not enforced. The president, the
attorney general, the secretary of the treasury, and the director of OMB
all refuse to make the impoundments on the grounds that the provision
of the law is unconstitutional.[49] Congress cannot do much to challenge a
president who claims executive privilege in national security matters. But
it may take actions in the future against officials who assert "department"
privilege or refuse to cooperate with committees engaged in the oversight
function.

III

Executive-Congressional Relations

The White House and departments initiate most foreign policies, and
Congress rarely plays a major role in their formulation.[50] Typically the
legislature acts to meet the commitments made by the executive; after the
"Yom Kippur" War of 1973, the executive policy of strengthening Israel
was perfected by Congress, which passed bills providing for over $2.2
billion in aid to that nation. Later the "shuttle diplomacy of Secretary of
State Kissinger was supported by Congress, which passed bills to provide
authority and funding for American observers to monitor the Sinai
Accords between Israel and Egypt.[51]

Congress concentrates on administrative oversight of particular programs, making marginal and incremental adjustments. The Food for
Peace Program, a congressional initiative designed to dispose of surplus
agricultural stocks, operates today under many congressional restrictions:
some prevent food aid from being used as a political weapon, others require that most aid be targeted to nations with the lowest per capita
income, still others set out factors to be considered in determining
recipient nations, including human rights violations. Congress requires
annual reports on the program, and notification of major administration
decisions must be submitted to the Agriculture and Foreign Relations

Committees. Congress also plays a major role in formulating and administering the foreign assistance programs of the Agency for International Development. It generally appropriates much less than the president recommends, then mandates that a certain percentage of goods and services be supplied by American contractors or transported on American ships. It closely superintends personnel policies and the perquisites of administrators. It places restrictions on use of funds by multinational agencies, especially lending institutions, and inserts "human rights" provisions that go beyond what presidents have recommended. In the 1960s Congress completely revamped the program, changing its emphasis from industrialization to rural development, and in 1978 it began consideration of a comprehensive reorganization plan devised by the late Sen. Hubert Humphrey.

Congress has most influence when it focuses on particular programs, especially those involved in international assistance, lending, or cultural exchange. In recent years committees have made increased use of staff experts, the General Accounting Office, the Office of Technology Assessment, and the Congressional Budget Office to deal with international economic and environmental issues.

Congress has also developed new "committee veto" and "chamber veto" systems. It has virtually eliminated the military assistance program. In response, the Pentagon developed a military sales program that encourages other nations to purchase expensive equipment. Congress gave itself a "veto" by chamber resolution of arms sales over $25 million, which has influenced the terms under which sales to Egypt, Jordan, Saudi Arabia, and Iran have been negotiated. In 1976 Congress required the administration to issue "human rights reports" for each nation that receives military assistance, and provided for a cutoff of aid to any nation by joint resolution. After violations were reported by the State Department, Carter himself cut off aid to Uruguay and Ethiopia, and lowered aid to Argentina. Meanwhile, reacting to the reports, Argentina, Brazil, Guatemala, and El Salvador all refused new American military assistance.

Presidents argue that committee and legislative vetoes on foreign aid, arms sales, arms assistance, and export of nuclear reactors are not useful mechanisms to make foreign policy. At best they force the president to modify, or even retract, commitments to other nations. At worst they undercut his position, cause a disruption in alliances, and contribute to instability in various regions. They are not mechanisms that enable Congress to set policy or to develop policy in collaboration with the executive branch. In a sense they are a substitute, developed through the checks and balances system, for real influence in decision making.

Congress serves, in the words of Holbert Carroll, as a "barometer of public feeling" on foreign affairs.[52] The reluctance of several presidents to recognize the governments of Cuba and mainland China seems to have been based in part on a calculation of what effects such actions would have on their domestic position. Senate reluctance for several months to consider the Panama Canal Neutrality Treaty was due in large measure to public opposition to its terms; the reservations and amendment that accompanied the treaty's passage were due to its lack of public support. Congressional cuts in foreign aid programs are popular and reflect the widely held view that such funds are better spent in the United States. Congressional cutoff of arms aid to Turkey after that nation invaded Cyprus also reflected the views of some constituencies. Congress places pressure on presidents to provide "protection" to industries against what they consider to be unfair foreign competition that involves "dumping" goods on the American market.

Because it lacks access to classified information, Congress is likely to be unsure of itself when dealing with issues involving alliances, commitments, and overall strategy. At the same time, it rushes into particular situations, prompted by concerns of constituents and interest groups, usually acting in a parochial fashion. It oscillates between high moralizing, when it legislates "human rights" provisions, and its typical distributive and transactional methods of doing legislative business for favored individuals and interest groups. It is given little credit by the public for wisdom or foresight in foreign affairs; and its record of isolationism prior to World War II, acquiescence in presidential war-making in the 1960s, and involvement in "Koreagate" scandals involving kickbacks and bribery of members in the 1970s, is not one to engender public support.

The president is tempted to rely on prerogative government for his most important diplomatic initiatives, because he suffers the same disadvantages as a party and legislative leader in foreign as in domestic affairs. He cannot count on the support of either congressional leaders or rank-and-file members. Wilson's congressional leaders were isolationists who opposed his entry into World War I. Theodore Roosevelt and Taft lost arbitration treaties because of the opposition of Republican senators, and Coolidge and Hoover could not convince Republican isolationists to let the United States enter the World Court. Eisenhower had to defend his treaty and commitment powers against the assault in the Senate of his own majority leader, while in the House conservatives deserted his party on foreign economic issues and reciprocal trade legislation. Lyndon Johnson faced major opposition to his Vietnam policies from Democratic Senate leaders Fulbright and Mansfield. Carter had to contend with "hawkish" senators who influenced arms negotiations with the Soviet Union, and "doves" who undercut his aggressive African policies. More than half the Democratic senators voted *against* his proposal to sell arms to Saudi Arabia; the deal was "saved" by the Republicans.

Presidents often ignore their party platform and the sentiments of congressional leaders and strive for a bipartisan coalition. The lack of party discipline in Congress can work for, as well as against, the president. Truman won crucial Republican support for the Marshall Plan. Lyndon Johnson won congressional approval for his war policies and for his assistance to Israel, in spite of the opposition to his policies from Mansfield and Fulbright. Carter received the support of Minority Leader Baker for the Panama Canal Treaty, and he overcame defections by several Democratic senators when he won the support of ten Republicans. The president need not postpone decisions to unify his party and need not consult its leaders prior to making decisions. He suffers no dire consequences if he fails to keep his party informed during crises—unlike the result in a parliamentary system when a prime minister may actually be stripped of party leadership.[53]

To deal with Congress the president relies on persuasion, transactions, or national agenda techniques. As Richard Neustadt points out, Truman's success in gaining Republican support for the Marshall Plan of postwar economic reconstruction in Europe depended on specific transactions between him and one of the leading Senate Republicans, Arthur Vandenberg. Truman permitted Vandenberg to name the administrator for the new program and agreed that it would be an independent agency rather than a State Department bureau, and that "businessmen" rather than diplomats would administer it.[54] Eisenhower could also make deals: in 1953, when his Senate leader William Knowland wanted to offer an appropriations rider cutting off American contributions to the United Nations if it admitted Communist China, the president persuaded him to offer a nonbinding resolution instead; in return, Eisenhower agreed to ask for a foreign aid authorization for one year instead of three and dropped a proposal for foreign aid to certain communist nations.[55] Lyndon Johnson warned members of Congress that he would retaliate against critics of his Vietnam policies, and he is said to have warned Sen. Frank Church that the next time he wanted a dam constructed in Idaho, he could "ask Ho Chi Minh."

There is strong sentiment on Capitol Hill that presidents should consult more with members on foreign affairs.[56] Such consultation is being institutionalized by committees that require more reports, more information, and more advance notification of decisions by officials in each of the three "communities." As oversight of routine activities increases, and as more members of Congress are participating in subcommittees that deal with some aspect of foreign relations (often economic affairs), the confidence of legislators, especially the newer members, that they have a constructive role to play in making foreign policy will increase. At some point the "post-Vietnam" and "post-Watergate" generation of legislators will come to dominate both chambers, and Congress may yet mount a serious assault on the secrecy system. Until that day comes, however, most major foreign policy initiatives will continue to come from the executive branch, and Congress will play a reactive role, either in support or in opposition to presidential proposals.

IV

Management of Foreign Relations

The success presidents have had in instituting prerogative government in foreign affairs and in dominating policymaking against congressional interference is somewhat offset by their difficulty in controlling the national security bureaucracies. They are disappointed by the performance of the State Department, subjected to pressure by the Defense Department and military services to "militarize" foreign policy, and tempted by the intelligence community to substitute covert operations for more conventional diplomacy. Careerists in the departments—the foreign service officers, the military officers, and the "spooks" of the intelligence agencies—have their own policies to promote. They work with private interest groups, members of Congress, and even their opposite numbers in foreign governments to influence the range of choice and the options of the president. Careerists may play off the political executives who are their nominal superiors, and subvert, delay, or modify presidential initiatives in the guise of obeying his orders. They may have a "guardianship" ethos, thinking of themselves as the defenders of the permanent and fundamental interests of the nation, and they may view the president and his entourage as temporary interlopers and as "amateurs" whose will must be shaped to their own.

The Problem with State

Some of the problems that a president has with "the communities" may be demonstrated by examining his relationship with the Department of State. In the nineteenth century the major problem for the president was that a secretary of state might believe himself to be so much more knowledgeable than the president about statecraft that he would try to run the government as a "prime minister." Secretaries who were former congressional party leaders and contenders for the presidency were particularly susceptible to the temptation to try to run the government. None managed to pull it off, but several, such as Webster and Seward, exerted much influence and caused much friction in the cabinet until they were checked by the president or Congress.

In modern times the problem is the weakness of the secretary and his department in the government. Presidents often choose secretaries whom they can dominate or ignore; such was the case when Franklin Roosevelt chose Cordell Hull, an amiable nonentity, and kept him on for much of the New Deal and wartime period while the White House and the military made foreign policy. Nixon used William Rogers, a lawyer with some high-level experience but no congressional or public following and little diplomatic experience, so that he might control foreign policy-making himself. The atypical pattern is for the president to pick someone of experience and ability to work with closely: Truman and Marshall, Eisenhower and Dulles, Nixon and Kissinger, Carter and Vance.

The secretary of state and the top officials in the department hope to control the conduct of diplomacy, with the secretary serving as "chief negotiator" for the government. They also intend to initiate new policies by identifying emerging issues and proposing diplomatic solutions for them. They may serve as key presidential advisors in crises and control the interagency groups in Washington that make policy and the "country teams" abroad that administer them. Then again, the top officials in State may not have much influence in negotiations, policy formulation, or even the management of crucial aspects of foreign relations.

While presidents often rely on secretaries of state for advice, they rarely permit them to manage foreign relations. Presidents in the post–World War II period have ignored the recommendations of no less than seven study groups that have urged a "state-centered" foreign policy apparatus.[57] Presidents complain about the department and have little confidence in it. They are suspicious about the careerists, and most sympathize with Truman when he explained about an action he had taken, "I wanted to make it plain that the President of the United States, and not the second or third echelon in the State Department, is responsible for making foreign policy."[58] This attitude is also shared by some of the political executives the president appoints. Charles Frankel, an assistant secretary of state in the Johnson administration, explains that "those career officials have minds of their own, professional pride and an esprit de corps. They have seen Presidents come and go, and they have seen Presidents' appointees come and go faster."[59] Political executives view State as poorly administered, slow to respond to their directives, and bogged down in red tape. As former Ambassador to India John Kenneth Galbraith explained to Frankel by way of an introduction to the department, "You'll find that it's the kind of organization which, though it does big things badly, does small things badly too."[60]

Careerists complain of interference by presidential advisors and of "political considerations" when the president makes decisions with which they disagree. Many at State never forgave Truman and his advisors for recognizing Israel against the advice of Secretary of State Marshall and the careerists who counseled him. They complain of the high turnover of assistant secretaries, and as John P. Davies put it, of the "gypsy-encampment atmosphere along the banks of the Potomac," caused by a "constant coming and going of crusading amateurs," which leads to "diplomatus interruptus" in the department.[61] Careerists condemn White House aides who form a "palace guard" of well-meaning but inept amateurs, who interfere with diplomacy without facing the consequences, and who lack responsibility to administer the policies they pressure the president into approving.[62]

While complaining of presidential interference, careerists also are upset that the White House does not protect them against congressional "witch-hunts" instigated by right-wing congressmen convinced that the department is riddled with communists and fellow travelers. During the McCarthyite onslaught against the department, the patriotism and integrity of careerists was impugned, and neither Truman nor Eisenhower seemed able to put a stop to excesses committed in the name of "loyalty-security" investigations. Many careers were ruined, and senior careerists since then have had little faith in the ability of the administration to protect them from smears. As a consequence, the department is riddled with officials who sugarcoat their recommendations through excessive caution. Finally, officials resent it when the White House claims that they sabotage administration initiatives. As the chairman of the Foreign Service Officers Association pointed out, "This is a tired old line, repeated during every administration, by people seeking to explain away their own failures and to justify the hiring of their friends."[63]

Careerists argue that the president's lack of experience in world affairs, and his failure to perceive conditions abroad, causes him to make excessive commitments abroad. Various problems are associated with "presidential diplomacy" as careerists see it:

1. Presidents espouse general principles through declarations, communiques, and doctrines, which often are rhetoric and have little impact on diplomatic relations. They are no substitute for negotiations to solve disputes.
2. Presidential initiatives involve "media diplomacy" with little preparation at the foreign minister level. Expectations are raised for political purposes without any corresponding achievements. Consequently most summits are failures, with a negative impact as the public is disillusioned.
3. Presidents rely too much on general principles in dealing with other heads of state, rather than seeking solutions by means of case-by-case adjustments through traditional diplomatic efforts.

Careerists point to Eisenhower's summits with Khruschev and Kennedy's conferences with DeGaulle and his Vienna summit with Khruschev as examples of negotiations that achieved nothing. After Kennedy visited Ottawa, anti-Americanism among Canadians increased, and the government of Canada imposed new regulations against American business investment. Ford's economic summit of 1974 resulted only in the French president, Valery Giscard d'Estaing, referring to the president as "an imbecile," since Ford seemed to know little of the issues under discussion; Carter's forays with world leaders seem to have left the same impression with German Chancellor Schmidt, thus souring relations between the two nations. Carter's junket to various nations in the winter of 1977 was an example of presidential electioneering, designed merely to convince the home folks that the president was a world leader. The only major exceptions to the summit-as-junket was Nixon's visit to Communist China in 1972, and the Camp David negotiations.

However much the secretary of state may become involved in crisis management, presidents often keep high-level State Department officials in the dark when military operations or covert operations are planned: such was the case in the Bay of Pigs invasion of Cuba and in the invasion of Cambodia. Careerists argue that their advice should be sought when these kinds of decisions are made, yet experts are kept out of the inner circle during the deliberations, and the limdis channeling of memoranda usually does not include them.[64]

The White House may subvert the chain of command in the department. The president may establish direct links to a few ambassadors, such as Kennedy had with Galbraith in India. Or he may communicate directly with a foreign ambassador, as Nixon did with Soviet ambassador Dobrynin during negotiations for an arms limitations agreement, thus bypassing the State Department completely. Career diplomat Charles Yost complained that "foreign ambassadors in Washington and American ambassadors abroad are even at times encouraged to believe that they can obtain satisfaction of their requirements more easily from the National Security Advisor than from the Secretary of State. This is both petty and scandalous."[65] The White House may "raid" the State Department and detail its talented careerists to duty on the National Security Council staff.

The various interdepartmental committees that make policy are weighted against State, for as a former official argued, they "institutionalize at every level majority representation by military and intelligence officials."[66] State's careerists complain that in crises, greater weight is given to military options than to diplomatic solutions and that they are cast in the role of devil's advocates who are allowed to speak but are not really listened to. They are portrayed by the White House and other agencies as negative, cautious, and unimaginative when they oppose interventionist schemes of the other "communities." Careerists may even assume that the president wants to promote crises, and that he underestimates the risks of military and covert interventions.[67]

The State Department never seems to be able to control the "country teams" in other nations, even when the ambassador is nominally in charge of the CIA station and military mission. After Carter signed an order giving ambassadors authority to supervise all U.S. "officers and employees" in their countries, the CIA issued its own guidelines to station chiefs providing for exceptions and the continued limits on information the ambassador would be permitted to obtain from the CIA. Its exceptions included the covert operations that might be carried out. When CIA station chiefs and ambassadors argue, the disputes must be resolved at the White House, for the State Department cannot enforce its will by itself. The same situation holds true when the ambassador has problems with the military mission.

The State Department is relegated to chairing committees on peripheral issues in which the White House has little interest. When Johnson created the Senior Interdepartmental Group in 1966, chaired by the undersecretary of state, and established corresponding Regional Interdepartmental Groups chaired by assistant secretaries of state, it was understood by officials in all the communities that the purpose was to have State concentrate on issues for which the White House had no time, so that he could deal with Vietnam, the Middle East, and summitry with the Soviet Union.

The National Security Council

The president uses a "president-centered" system to manage foreign relations. He does so in order to keep the military and intelligence communities under control by using the resources of the institutionalized presidency.

Ironically, the major unit of the institutionalized presidency, the National Security Council (NSC), was foisted upon Truman by Congress in 1947, in spite of his objections. Partly it was a reaction to the way Roosevelt and the military chiefs had dominated policymaking during the war, and partly it was "Forrestal's revenge," since Adm. James Forrestal, who dreamed up the idea for the council, opposed Truman's plans to unify the armed services and pressed his plan in order to dilute the president's authority. The NSC consisted initially of the president, the secretary of war, the secretary of the navy, and the chairman of the National Security Resources Board. In 1949 the service secretaries were dropped, and the vice-president, the secretary of state, and the secretary of defense were added. The NSC then became a council embodying the highest diplomatic and military officials of the administration, rather than simply a military coordinating body. The statutory advisors to the NSC are the director of Central Intelligence, the chairman of the Joint Chiefs of Staff, and the director of the Arms Control and Disarmament Agency. Invitees to meetings normally include the secretary of the Treasury, the Director of the Office of Management and Budget, and other agency heads as appropriate.

The NSC does not function as a "council of state" for foreign affairs. Such a council would assume the constitutional authority of the president and place the management of foreign relations in commission. But the president retains all his constitutional authority. The NSC functions within the advisory system, as part of the Executive Office of the President, and not as an independent "branch" of government. Its function involves "advising the President with respect to the integration of domestic, foreign and military policies relating to the national security."[68] The president chooses the assistant for national security affairs, who runs the NSC staff, as his personal assistant, and he and the staff function for the White House rather than for the council as a collectivity. The president controls the frequency of meetings and the agenda. He calls for no votes and need not be bound by a consensus of participants. He generally does not make decisions at the meetings. When he does give orders, it is in his constitutional capacity as commander in chief, by virtue of his authority as president. The NSC itself has no authority to make decisions, although presidential decisions may be expressed in the form of NSC directives or memoranda.[69]

The president uses the NSC to legitimize decisions that he and his advisors may take in informal settings. He may label the group of advisors the "Executive Committee of the NSC," as Kennedy did; or hold a "Tuesday Lunch" of principal advisors, as Johnson did; or create a "Washington Special Action Group," as Nixon did. In crises the president can use NSC symbolism to reassure the nation that the challenge is being met. The actual "machinery," however, consists of the senior advisors, in and out of government, to whom the president turns for counsel. As Secretary of State Dean Rusk once observed, "The real organization of government at higher echelons is not what you find in textbooks or organization charts. It is how confidence flows down from the President. That is never put on paper. People don't like it. Besides, it fluctuates. People go up—and people go down."[70]

The president uses his assistant for national security affairs and the NSC staff to manage important foreign policies. Kissinger once noted that "the outsider believes a presidential order is consistently followed out [sic]. Nonsense. I have to spend considerable time seeing that it is carried out and in the spirit the President intended."[71] The staff may monitor department compliance, or issue instructions and act as "desk officers." It may coordinate activities that cross departmental lines. It can support a bureau against its opponents, and create "back channels" so that lower-level officials can communicate directly to the president. It can assign missions to agencies and strip others of jurisdiction. It may assume the role of "budget examiner" and ally itself with the OMB to deal with the military, especially in decisions involving procurement of strategic weaponry. The NSC staff may bring in outside consultants, or hire "in-and-outer" academics to serve a brief stint and manage a particular policy. The staff may preside over interdepartmental committees, running them as "shops" in the president's interest. The departments may offer their own alternatives, which results in friction between careerists and the NSC staff. Often departments leak classified information to Congress or the media in attempts to undercut the NSC staff.

Each president organizes the NSC differently, for as Eisenhower once said, "organization and procedures, save where they are rigidly fixed by law, should conform to each President's experience, desires, and methods of work."[72] Each president tries to compensate for the problems he observed in his predecessor's use of the NSC; there is a "fishtail effect" as each overcompensates for previous defects. There is little continuity or institutional memory in the system, and new staff members have no experience in operating the machinery of foreign policymaking. The noncareer staff members bring with them energy, enthusiasm, and fresh ideas, but they seriously underestimate the difficulties they face in dealing with departments. The president and his national security advisor constantly improvise and experiment with new policies and procedures, but what seem to them to be innovative approaches may appear to the careerists to be meddlesome interference.

Truman often ignored the NSC and attended only twelve of its fifty-one meetings prior to the onset of the Korean conflict.[73] During the war he used it for ceremonial purposes, and he made decisions with a small group of advisors from the departments. The NSC had a small staff, which was overshadowed by the Policy Planning Staff of the State Department, a unit created in 1947, which played a major role in developing the foreign policies of the administration. Together the State and Defense Departments shaped the most important policy documents of the NSC. The NSC executive secretary was a White House assistant with nowhere near the prestige or influence in government of Secretary of State George Marshall or his successor, Dean Acheson. The staff did not superintend the departments nor take a role in implementing presidential decisions.[74]

Eisenhower paid considerable attention during the transition period to revamping the NSC procedures, and it was organized under his supervision to serve as his "general staff," functioning for him as his staff had done when he was a top-ranking general during World War II. The president held weekly meetings of the NSC and attended regularly. He used it as a forum for debate during crises, and to consider economic issues, global strategy, diplomacy, and military operations. The president invited the secretary of the Treasury and director of the Bureau of the Budget to attend meetings. He built up the staff, drawing primarily on careerists from the departments. They produced position papers that were debated by the NSC Planning Board and ultimately adopted as administration policy in NSC papers and NSC memoranda. The special assistant for national security affairs managed this system, but he was neither a policy advisor nor an overseer of the departments. The NSC staff played a minor role in coordinating and implementing decisions through the Operations Coordinating Board, but the departments retained primary responsibility for management of policies. The State Department rather than the NSC staff initiated most of the position papers that the NSC considered.

Eisenhower's system worked poorly. Instead of clear choices, NSC papers often represented "treaties" negotiated between departments, which were broad simplifications, resulting in the lowest common denominator of agreement rather than hard choices from different options.[75] Decisions were not always operationally meaningful, since they were not tied directly into the budgetary process, nor could they be implemented by the NSC staff. New policies might be announced that had little effect on the operations, programs, or budgets of departments. Contingency plans might become outdated by later events, and much staff work became obsolete rapidly. NSC meetings had too many participants, so officials talked "for the record" and defended their vested bureaucratic interests, rather than speaking candidly to provide the president with counsel. The Operations Coordinating Board was ineffective, and it left the White House with the false sense of security that its decisions were being implemented.

In 1959 a Subcommittee on National Policy Machinery of the Senate Committee on Government Operations (known as the Jackson subcommittee after chairman Henry Jackson) studied the Eisenhower NSC system. It eventually recommended that the system be scrapped, that the State Department chair NSC committees and implement decisions, and that its Policy Planning Staff once again be restored as the primary initiator of new policies. The NSC was to be "deinstitutionalized" and serve as a forum for debate.[76]

When president-elect Kennedy met with Eisenhower during the transition period, the president told Kennedy that the NSC meetings were "the most important weekly meeting of the government."[77] But Kennedy decided to create an ad hoc system to make national security decisions. He dismantled the Planning Board and Operations Coordinating Board, as well as most of the NSC committees. He rarely convened the NSC, but relied instead on small groups of cabinet secretaries and White House aides. He also relied on "in-and-outers" and a group of "wise men," senior-level ex-officials from previous administrations. He installed his own people for key negotiations, such as Averill Harriman and Arthur Dean in dealing with the Soviet Union, and they acted as presidential agents with direct lines of communication to the White House. The president relied on Defense Secretary McNamara to formulate defense strategy, and the Pentagon's Bureau of International Security Affairs rivaled its opposite number at State, the Bureau of Political-Military Affairs, for influence in the administration. The national security advisor and his staff of academic "in-and-outers" played a role in developing policy options and challenging departmental policies. NSC task forces were established to deal with crises involving Laos, Berlin, and Cuba;

and Vietnam policymaking was handled not at State, but by the NSC interagency group, the Vietnam Special Group for Counterinsurgency. Kennedy installed a "situation room" in the basement of the White House so that he could monitor crises and so that he or NSC officials could communicate directly with officials of operating agencies in crises.[78]

Kennedy's system was flexible and responsive to presidential direction. Kennedy was given various options and made decisions in the form of National Security memoranda, Defense Department draft presidential memoranda, or State Department national policy papers. But the system was chaotic. Not all issues were fully briefed or debated. In the case of the harebrained Bay of Pigs invasion, the president fumed after the disaster that never again would he be taken in by the intelligence community. Kennedy and his advisors gave little direction to departments on routine issues, so in noncrisis situations the vacuum was filled by careerists or political executives acting on their own.[79] Crisis decision-making had a built-in bias toward using military or covert operations as solutions. Careerists at State felt isolated, and their cautions against military adventures went unheeded. Top officials did not clear problems with all agencies and officials affected at lower levels, thus cutting themselves off from sources of technical advice. They plunged ahead with risky operations and made expansive commitments. The crisis mentality led to a preoccupation with immediate events and left little time or energy for attending to long-range planning or developing policies for emerging problems. It was difficult for decision-makers to use the "ad hoc" system to manage more than one crisis at a time.[80]

Johnson ignored the NSC as a forum for debate. Instead he convened the "Tuesday lunch" with the secretaries of State and Defense, the assistant for national security affairs, the director of the CIA, and the chairman of the Joint Chiefs. The NSC staff increased in size and influence, representing the White House on interdepartmental committees. The assistant for national security affairs became a key presidential advisor, pressed his own views on Vietnam and other issues, and eventually eclipsed Secretary McNamara in influence with the president. The ad hoc system now choked off dissent, and advisors became a "palace guard," able to shield the president and reinforce his conviction that he was pursuing the right policies.

Nixon entered office determined to combine the best features of Eisenhower's staff and Kennedy's ad hoc system, and to fashion an instrument that would enable him to manage foreign affairs from the White House. His assistant for national security affairs, Henry Kissinger, wrote an analysis of the NSC system just prior to his appointment in which he argued that "the organizational problem seems to be to combine the procedural regularity of Eisenhower with the intellectual excitement of Kennedy."[81] The Central Research Program of the Institute for Defense Analysis, a private think tank commissioned to study the NSC system during the transition, reported that many officials in Kennedy's system believed that the president had dismantled too much.[82] Relying on recommendations made by Kissinger, the president convened the NSC in formal session, but only to serve a ceremonial function in ratifying decisions already made. Power was centralized in the White House, where Kissinger presided over a staff of one hundred twenty—three times the size of the staff in the Johnson administration. The assistant functioned as chief presidential agent for diplomacy, as a policy initiator, and as coordinator and implementer of presidential decisions.

The mechanisms for centralizing power were various NSC committees, chaired by Kissinger: for policy formulation there was the Senior Review Group; for negotiations with the Soviet Union, the Verification Panel; for the war in Indochina, the Vietnam Special Studies Group; for military procurement, the Defense Program Review Committee; for covert action, the "Forty Committee"; for intelligence, the "Intelligence Committee"; and for crises, the Washington Special Action Group. There were also a series of interdepartmental committees organized at the assistant-secretary level and presided over by the State Department, which provided supporting assistance to these committees.

Kissinger would put formal questions to the bureaucracy. Responses would then be "graded" by the former Harvard professor, who would call for revisions until the careerists had provided him with the information he wanted. He would, in a sense, pass or flunk officials, moving some to important positions and putting others on the shelf. He would also keep departments busy dealing with secondary issues or supplying him with information, while important policy decisions were handled in the NSC committees or between him and the president.

The system was designed to develop options for the president in the form of National Security Study memoranda. It was supposed to eliminate the logrolling and compromising that had plagued the Eisenhower system. The NSC staff focused on disagreements among the departments and played various officials against each other. Ultimately the president was given sharply contrasting options, and his choices were then implemented in National Security Decision memoranda. As Nixon described the idea, "The new NSC system is designed to make certain that clear policy choices reach the top, so that various positions can be fully debated in the meeting of the Council," adding, "I refuse to be confronted with a bureaucratic consensus that leaves me no options but acceptance or rejection, and that gives me no way of knowing what alternatives exist."[83]

In his second term Nixon named Kissinger secretary of state. In the aftermath of the 1973 Yom Kippur War he became the intermediary between Arab states and Israel through his shuttle diplomacy. His great success in winning disengagement agreements made him a national hero: "Super-K" had a higher standing in the polls than Nixon. Kissinger became a "prime minister" for the government, rallying support in Congress for the perfection of executive initiatives developed within the NSC system, shuttling over the globe to conduct State's diplomacy, and serving as a symbol of continuity and stability while Nixon and his aides were pre-occupied with Watergate. Kissinger and Defense Secretary Schlesinger even managed the various crises with the Soviet Union, only referring matters to Nixon for final approval. In the transition between the Nixon and Ford administrations he served as a surrogate for the "com-mander in chief" who no longer commanded the confidence of the nation. In what constituted a reversal of normal parliamentary practice, the head of government, Nixon, fell from office by losing the confidence of Congress, while the "prime minister," Kissinger, continued to run the government until a new head of state was installed.

Initially Ford welcomed "Super-K" and relied upon him for instruction in foreign affairs. Gradually the White House staff and the Defense Secretary convinced him that a more balanced system was desirable. Over Kissinger's strenuous objections the president removed him as assistant to the president for national security affairs and installed his deputy, Gen. Alexander Haig, in his place. As counterweights to the secretary of state the president relied on Treasury Secretary William Simon and Defense Secretary Donald Rumsfeld. As Kissinger's standing in Congress declined because of charges that he was involved in various wiretappings ordered during the Nixon administration, the president found it easier to treat the secretary as an advisor rather than as his "prime minister."

Carter took office determined that no "supersecretary" would run foreign policy. He maintained the separation of the NSC apparatus from the State Department. The NSC staff was reduced in size and functioned as a think tank for special studies rather than as an overseer of departments, although it won influence over the Defense Department's budget by working closely with the OMB in the early stages of the budget cycle. Instead of committees established by Kissinger, the new system relied on a Policy Review Committee (consisting of the secretaries of State and Defense, the director of central intelligence, and the national security advisor) and the Special Coordinating Committee. The new name for documents embodying Carter's decisions was "presidential decision memoranda," reflecting Carter's views that the president, not the NSC, made decisions in the administration.

Carter set up various "shops" to handle various aspects of foreign affairs: some were run from the NSC by his advisor, Columbia University professor Zbigniew Brzezinski; others were run out of the State Depart-ment; still others were run from the White House directly by chief aides or the vice-president. Carter appointed special negotiators to handle SALT, Cyprus, Panama, and Law of the Seas negotiations, and he appointed a special representative for trade negotiations to work out of the White House. Each shop connected back to the president, often though not always through Brzezinski. Like Franklin Roosevelt and John Kennedy, Carter preferred to dispense with formal hierarchy and departmental structure and deal directly with senior officials in whom he had confidence and to whom he had given a specific assignment. Neither the NSC nor the White House imposed a priori "solutions" on career officials, and the president did not "grade" officials in terms of whether or not they knew the "answers" to his questions. Unlike Kissinger, who operated the system in accord with the grand design that he and Nixon had fashioned, the Carter administration seemed to be feeling its way through a free-wheeling administrative structure that had no coherent intellectual underpinnings to it.

Improving the Advisory System

The NSC system fails to effectively integrate diplomatic, military, and intelligence concerns with international, economic, and scientific considerations. To remedy this problem a group of Carter transition advisors recommended that the NSC, the Domestic Council, and the Economic Policy Board be abolished, and that they be replaced by a cabinet committee, "ExCab," consisting of State, Treasury, HEW, a new Department of Commerce and Labor, and Defense. The ExCab would coordinate domestic and economic policies, particularly crucial issues of international economics that cut across department boundaries. A single unified staff would be drawn primarily from careerists to give them a broader "White House perspective" that they could take back to the departments when their tour of duty ended. The White House senior aides would number four, one of whom would be responsible for the management of foreign affairs, and would utilize ExCab staff for his activities.[84]

Carter ignored the central recommendations of various transition groups. The NSC system was retained, and no ExCab was established. Domestic departments remained outside of the formal NSC structure. No unified staff was created, nor were careerists brought into the NSC staff in large numbers. There was no emphasis on integrating economic and national security issues by merging staff units.

Other proposals have concentrated on improving the quality of debate in the administration. To break through the "palace guard" some political scientists suggest that policy-formulating boards be created or strengthened in each of the departments. They have in mind the "golden age" of the State Department in the immediate postwar period, when the Policy Planning Staff of the State Department developed many of the foundations for American foreign policy in the 1950s. In the words of political scientist Alexander George, the advisor to the president for national security matters should be a "custodian of debate," and the president "must define his own role as that of a *magistrate* who evaluates, judges, and chooses among the various policy options articulated by advocates."[85]

Kennedy's use of the ExCom during the Cuban Missile Crisis is the classic example of the "multiple advocacy" system. Protocol was suspended, and officials debated without consideration of rank or even of department interests. Lower-level officials offered advice and options (unlike the situation during the Bay of Pigs or the Vietnam escalations). Different options with strikingly different consequences were proposed, and there was no tendency to settle for a lowest common denominator to develop a consensus. At times Kennedy absented himself from deliberations so as not to influence the debators or prematurely commit himself. Ultimately the president made his own choices from among the various options, and modified his policy as he saw fit. It should be noted, however, that the major criticism of Kennedy's NSC system was that in most situations it did *not* operate through multiple advocacy and did *not* permit consideration of all options. The trick would be to institutionalize the system that Kennedy stumbled onto during the missile crisis and make it a regular feature of NSC deliberations.

A drastic proposal has been made to scrap the National Security Council entirely, use the cabinet as the forum for debate, and make the National Security Advisor a principal deputy for foreign affairs on the White House staff. He would direct and supervise department officials and take responsibility for implementing foreign policy.[86] Although such a proposal seems radical, several presidents have "abolished" the NSC by simply not convening it, or by absenting themselves from it and relying on informal groups of senior officials for advice. But it is not likely that Congress will abolish its creature or that presidents will wish to forego the council as a useful bit of symbolism.

Some analysts propose a bifurcated system in which the president and the NSC would make policy and the State Department would have primary responsibility to implement it. Richard Neustadt explored this line in Jackson subcommittee hearings, proposing that the Office of Secretary of State should function as a "budget bureau" for national security affairs, handling issues according to action-forcing processes. State would not actually manage all policies but would superintend other agencies and take a leading role in management of foreign affairs.[87] The Murphy Commission on the Organization of the Government for the Conduct of Foreign Policy took a similar approach in 1975, by recommending that the supersecretary innovation be ended after Kissinger's tenure was up (a recommendation President Ford seized upon immediately.) The president would make policy and the State Department would play the major role in carrying it out. To restore the bureaucratic balance State would create the position of undersecretary for political and national security affairs, and assign that official the job of challenging the Defense Department in its efforts to militarize foreign policy. The NSC, State, and the OMB would join forces and combine staff resources to see that NSC decisions were better integrated into the Pentagon budget process.[88] Carter did implement the last recommendation by establishing a new undersecretary position, but it was in the Defense Department and served as a focal point to enable civilian Pentagon officials to work with the NSC staff and the OMB in making procurement decisions. Instead of carrying out the other recommendations, Carter fragmented the management of foreign affairs by creating his "shops" and establishing direct links to many officials rather than working through State. Carter thus joins a long line of presidents who have rejected the recommendations of study groups and opted instead for perpetuation of the "president-centered" system to manage foreign affairs.[89]

Presidential War-making

WHO MAKES the decision for peace or war? Does the president follow the Constitution when he uses armed forces in hostilities without a declaration of war? In the great wars we have fought, the nation rallied around the presidency as the instrument of the national will: in struggles for independence, national unity, and national security, prerogative government was used without serious political backlash. And in minor incidents there has been little need to consider the constitutionality of presidential war-making. The controversy over the presidential prerogative involves neither great wars nor minor incidents, but rather the use of intelligence agencies or the armed forces for covert and overt interventions in the affairs of other nations, or the use of the armed forces for protracted "limited" wars. It also involves presidential disposition of forces in nuclear confrontations, such as the Berlin, Cuban, and Middle East crises of 1961, 1962, and 1973. Unless the president wins the support of Congress and the nation for his exercise of prerogative powers, he will face a split in his own party, a drop in public support, and pressure to end hostilities on disadvantageous terms.

I

Uses of Force

Most uses of the armed forces in hostilities have not involved a congressional declaration of war, ever since the early days of the Republic, when armies fought Indians and helped settlers annex parts of West Florida, and when naval squadrons fought French frigates and Barbery pirates. The president has always deployed the military forces in confrontations and "shows of force": the annexation of Texas was accompanied by naval maneuvers near Mexico; Japan was opened for foreign trade when an American naval squadron appeared off her shores, Admiral Dewey commanled a fleet near Venezuela to warn off the German navy, which was coming to collect debts from Venezuela. Between 1945 and 1975 there were 215 such demonstrations, including two threats of nuclear action.[1]

The armed forces are used for "police actions" that protect Americans against pirates and bandits, drug traffickers, smugglers, and guerrillas and terrorists. Forces may be ordered to cross borders and make limited incursions into other nations. Wilson sent General Pershing into Mexico with an expeditionary force to pursue Pancho Villa and his followers, but since this action was not directed against the Mexican government there was no need for a declaration of war. The president may send the military into other nations to put down mobs threatening American lives and property, or to participate in missions to rescue nationals of various nations. The armed forces may remain for a period of time to police a town or region, or participate in a military occupation according to terms negotiated with the foreign government.

The military may be used to extend American territory or administrative zones. Parts of West Florida were annexed by American settlers who were assisted by nearby military units; American settlers in Hawaii overthrew the native government and applied for territorial status. The navy claimed several Pacific islands for fueling stations. In 1903 the navy was deployed near the province of Panama to prevent Colombian forces from crushing the rebellion that led to Panamanian independence. None of these actions required congressional assent or a declaration of war.

Presidents may order the military to administer affairs of other nations. American occupations of Cuba (1906–09), Nicaragua (1912–25), and Haiti (1915–34) were ordered to place the financial affairs of these nations in the hands of American banks and Treasury officials so that foreign creditors could be paid. Or the military may be used to establish regimes friendly to the United States. Wilson ordered an American landing at Vera Cruz in order to favor one side in the Mexican civil war. Lyndon Johnson ordered American marines into Santo Domingo to prevent what

he considered to be a leftist government from assuming power. Wilson
sent American troops to Russia after the First World War to aid non-
communist forces against the Bolsheviks. Eisenhower sent marines to
Lebanon in 1958 to install a set of leaders friendly to the United States.
The Central Intelligence Agency may attempt to bolster or overthrow
foreign regimes: successful interventions have occurred in Iran, Guate-
mala, and Indonesia; some of the more spectacular failures included the
Bay of Pigs invasion of Cuba by exile forces trained and financed by
the CIA and intervention in the civil war in Angola.

Military forces have also been used in wars limited geographically,
when the president upholds principles of collective security against what
he considers to be communist aggression, or to uphold specific treaty or
other national commitments. Of over two hundred cases in which the
president has committed the armed forces abroad, most have been minor
incidents, with only a few limited or large wars. But in ninety-three cases
hostilities have lasted more than thirty days, and even then Congress
has not been asked to declare war. There have been declarations of war
made only five times: 1812, 1846, 1898, 1917, and 1941. And no one
expects Congress to be able to declare war prior to a nuclear exchange.

II

Theories of Presidential War-making

Critics of presidential war-making agree with the White House that
the declaration of war is outmoded and unsuited for certain conditions.
But they disagree with the argument that prerogative government must
be instituted to take the place of the constitutional requirement that the
president collaborate with Congress in declaring and making war. To
develop new collaborative mechanisms it would first be necessary to define
the problem: why do presidents involve the nation in limited wars?
Several theories of presidential war-making exist.

Strategic Considerations

The first theory focuses on strategic assumptions of American diplomatic and military strategists as they view political developments on the
"rim" separating Communist from non-Communist nations. These decision-makers saw a "line of containment" that must be held by "the
free world." Political instability in nations on the rim was a threat to all
non-Communist nations. Such instability was caused by Communist
elements as part of a coordinated offensive directed by the Soviet Union

and China against the strategic interests of the United States. As the Joint Chiefs of Staff warned in 1950, "The fall of Indochina would undoubtedly lead to the fall of other mainland states of Southeast Asia," which in turn would affect "the balance of power" between the United States and the Soviet Union.[2]

The United States intervenes to prevent Communist takeovers on "our" side of the "line." In addition, it protects vital military interests, such as lines of communication and sea and air lanes. The National Security Council warned in February 1952, "Communist domination of mainland Southeast Asia would place unfriendly forces astride the most direct and best developed sea and air routes between the Western Pacific and India and the Near East."[3] Just as significant, American intervention preserves the credibility of our commitments to other nations to maintain collective security against Communist aggression. As General Maxwell Taylor warned in a memorandum to Secretary of State Dean Rusk, "If we leave Vietnam with our tail between our legs, the consequences of this defeat in the rest of Asia, Africa, and Latin America would be disastrous."[4] Just prior to American escalation in Vietnam in the spring of 1964, Secretary of Defense McNamara pointed out to President Johnson that "the South Vietnam conflict is regarded as a test case of U.S. capacity to help a nation to meet a Communist war of liberation," and in the fall of 1964, an assistant secretary of defense, John McNaughton, in attempting to define American war aims placed at the top of the list actions "to protect U.S. reputation as counter-subversion guarantor."[5]

Related to the "credibility" doctrine is the "domino" theory. As expressed by John Kennedy, "If South Vietnam went, it would not only give them an improved geographic position for guerrilla assault on Malaya, but would also give the impression that the wave of the future in Southeast Asia was China and the Communists."[6] Kennedy was echoing the sentiments of a memo from Secretary of Defense Louis Johnson to President Truman, in which the secretary warned, "The choice confronting the United States is to support the legal governments in Indochina or to face the extension of Communism over the remainder of the continental area of Southeast Asia and possibly west-ward."[7]

In this theory of decision making the response of the president is almost automatic. The only decision that needs to be made concerns the level of the response, which is determined by the president, the secretary of defense, and the Joint Chiefs of Staff. Decision-makers, using new techniques of game theory, cost-benefit analysis, counterinsurgency warfare, and new technological "tools," can "manage" conflict and fight limited wars for limited objectives. When the Communists are convinced of the American resolve to assist other nations against aggression, they will be willing to negotiate at the conference table—if indeed they have not already suffered a military defeat.

But local Communist parties may not be taking orders from Peking or Moscow. Their struggle to attain power may be primarily an indigenous struggle rather than part of a great geopolitical game. Great-power intervention by the United States may unite Communist and non-Communist elements against the Americans. In addition, military interests of the United States may be *protected* at times by Communist states, as with Yugoslavia. American credibility is hardly enhanced when it spends its treasure and its blood and fails to secure military victories, for such failure may provide *incentives* for such activities to begin in other nations. If the United States has been drawn into conflict in one area, how can it maintain its credible commitments elsewhere? Even the "domino" theory lacks credibility, for many nations along the rim have been able to maintain non-Communist regimes without great-power intervention after one of their neighbors had become a Communist state.

The theory fails to explain why the United States intervenes on certain occasions and not on others. Why was it not in the national interest to use military force in China in 1948, but in the national interest to use force in Korea in 1950? Why did the Kennedy administration attempt a peaceful settlement of the Laotian conflict at Geneva just at the time it was making new commitments for a military solution in Vietnam in 1961–62? Why did the United States attempt covert intervention in Cuba in 1961 rather than launch a military invasion, as it did in Santo Domingo in 1965? In short, there seems to be nothing *automatic* about the response of the government to crises. The whole notion of "limited" war, for example, has never been accepted enthusiastically by the Joint Chiefs of Staff, which in its initial recommendations always seems to include a wide theater of operations (often involving mainland China) and a wide range of military options—often including the use of nuclear weapons.

If presidents believed they were launching military operations to win some "geopolitical game" with the Soviet Union or China, then the way to limit such interventions in the future would be to convince them that such a "game" was (1) not being played in a particular country by the other side, or (2) not always worth the cost to our own. Some scholars who studied developments in the postcolonial Third World attempted to demonstrate that most political conflict in these nations did not involve the "free world" against a Sino-Soviet conspiracy, but rather involved the working out of relationships between postcolonial and nationalist forces in the new nations. Therefore, they argued, the United States was intervening in civil wars rather than a global struggle. Critics in Congress and in the executive branch, such as Senator Fulbright and George Ball, took a different tack, arguing that such interventions placed a great burden on the military and the economy, and that they were unnecessary interventions in remote parts of the world where our "vital" interests were not at stake. For both sets of critics, presidential intervention in rim wars was primarily due to an *intellectual failure*: the failure to understand the world as it really is, to understand the nature of American vital interests, and to understand the limits to American power.[8] The solution to the problem of presidential war-making was to *limit* new American commitments to rim nations in the future, and to concentrate once again on our traditional collective security arrangements with Western European and Western hemisphere nations.

Alliance Politics

A second theory of decision making takes into account not only the American national interest, but also the national interest of other nations. In one variation the other nation intervenes in the affairs of our own to develop a policy in its favor. The Jeffersonians explained the American decision to engage in a naval war with France in 1798 by charging that the Federalist government was in the pay of the British. In World War I the isolationists charged that bankers and munitions makers, the "war profiteers," were in league with the Allies from the very beginning, and that American intervention was in the interests of the European governments and American bankers. The Korean Central Intelligence Agency may have given payoffs to some members of Congress in an effort to prevent planned withdrawals of American ground combat units from South Korea.

One explanation for the American decision to intervene in Vietnam focuses on the interests of our French allies. *The Pentagon Papers* makes the assumption that Truman's decisions to provide economic and military aid to the French for their war in Indochina was made in order to obtain French support for the European Defense Community (a proposal to rearm West Germany as part of a collective security arrangement) and to keep French moderates and rightists pro-American.[9] But such an explanation overlooks several facts. As early as 1945 the State Department determined to remain neutral in the struggle between the French and the forces of Ho Chi Minh, to keep the United States from becoming embroiled in a colonial war. Even after Truman decided to aid the French, it was made clear to them that the American interest was in a process of decolonization. As the American ambassador stated to the French Foreign Minister, the United States would not provide aid "unless real progress is made in reaching a non-Communist solution in Indochina based on cooperation of true nationalists of that country."[10] The United States warned the French that they could not simply install a puppet government to meet the requirements set by the United States. The Americans pressured France to create an autonomous state, affiliated within the French Union. As the military situation worsened, the interests of the two Western powers continued to diverge. The French eventually opted for a negotiated settlement at Geneva, looking toward a coalition government, but this policy was opposed by the United States. A National Security Council memorandum prior to the final French military defeats warned, "The French desire for peace in Indochina almost at any cost represents our greatest vulnerability in the Geneva talks."[11] The United States attended Geneva not to facilitate French interests, but rather, in the words of another NSC memorandum, "to maintain and support friendly non-Communist governments in Cambodia and Laos, to maintain a friendly non-Communist South Vietnam, and to prevent a Communist victory through all-Vietnam elections."[12] American pressure produced a partition plan that enabled Washington to replace the French as the dominant military (and economic) presence in the military regroupment zone that was later to become South Vietnam. Key to the American success was the installation of Ngo Dinh Diem, which resulted in American acceptance of the Geneva Accords.

While the initial decisions to aid the French in Indochina were probably associated more with American concerns about collective security in Europe than in Southeast Asia, the later decisions to create and prop up a government in South Vietnam were not due to the subordination of American interests to those of our French allies. Instead, the Americans pressured the French at each step into (1) remaining in an untenable conflict and (2) initiating a process of decolonization. Once the French "tapped out" of the game, the Americans continued the process of decolonization by installing their own allies and replacing the French influence in the area with their own.

Economic Interests

This theory of decision making focuses on elites that occupy important positions in the national security bureaucracies, the cabinet, and the White House staff. Because many of them have served at high levels in the banking, corporate, or legal world, their presence as national security policymakers is taken as evidence that their motive is not to protect the national interest, but rather to advance the economic interests of the financial or corporate groups they represent. Some critics charge that they operate on behalf of investment houses that make loans to foreign regimes, or on behalf of multinational corporations that invest in foreign nations.[13]

The theory does *not* require that American investments in the particular nation be large in order to justify American intervention. Instead, the "economic domino" theory applies: the fall of the nation may endanger American interests in other, more important nations. Although direct American investment in Indochina was small in the late 1940s, the theory argues that intervention was necessary to protect American interests in the rest of Southeast Asia, and to prevent Japan, the "superdomino," from falling.[14] As Richard Nixon warned in 1953, "If this whole part of Southeast Asia goes under Communist domination or Communist influence, Japan, who trades and must trade with this area in order to exist, must inevitably be oriented towards the Communist regime."[15]

Intervention may cost the United States a great deal more than the net worth of its investment in that nation. But critics who apply the economic-interest model point out that what might seem an "irrational" expenditure for the nation may be quite "rational" for the elites who make decisions in their own interest. As Nina Adams points out about the Indochina war fought by the French through 1954, "Although the war cost the French and American taxpayers ten times the value of French investments in Indochina, the private interests which had made most of the investments kept reaping profits right to the bitter end."[16] The war becomes a subsidy, paid by taxpayers from general revenues of the nation, to protect the economic interests of those who have invested in the foreign nation and the surrounding region. The nation as a whole may assume an economic loss, but if the financial elites are still able to make a profit on their investment, they will use their control over the national security apparatus to continue hostilities.

The problem with this theory is that it may reveal an association between economic interests of the United States and presidential war-making without actually proving that the economic elites forced the presidential decision. Key positions in the national security bureaucracies are filled by Wall Street lawyers, investment bankers, and industrialists from the "military-industrial complex."[17] But by no means do such officials constitute a majority of the national security managers in any single administration. Nor do most such officials have personal economic interests in the decisions that are made. The internal memoranda of the National Security Council reveal that economic considerations *were* significant in decision making in Vietnam, but they view economic interests from the standpoint of the nation as part of the geopolitical game, rather than from the standpoint of particular investment groups. National security managers seemed concerned in the 1950s with preserving the natural resources of Southeast Asia so that the West, Japan, and India could develop trade patterns with the region, and with denying these natural resources to Communist nations. To argue from these memoranda that specific investment "circles" were manipulating American foreign policy for their own narrow interests, without offering any documentary evidence for the case, is a perversion of the historical record.[18]

National security managers make "economic interests" of the nation a factor in their calculations as part of their geopolitical strategic arguments. In part their development of a national economic interest to justify intervention is a ploy designed to gain support from major economic-interest groups and from the American people for decisions that may make little economic sense but that these managers calculate should be taken as part of the "game" played against the Communist nations. To find the machinations of a set of financial elites behind every decision to intervene will create more problems for the analyst than it will solve. How can such a theory explain why the United States intervened in Korea in 1950, yet failed to intervene in China just two years earlier? How can the economic-interest theory account for limited wars on the one hand, and the investment and trade that occur between multinational corporations and Communist regimes around the globe on the other? What economic-interest theory can account for the curious situation in Angola, where a Marxist government deploys its Cuban advisors to protect oil fields in Cabinda, which are run by American oil corporations, while a supposedly "pro-Western" guerrilla movement with ties to the CIA has made several attempts to blow those fields sky-high?

National Security Managers

Ideological factors may also account for presidential war-making. National security officials have an ideology that leads to the "militarization" of American foreign policy. They are used to taking risks and managing crises. They have, according to Richard Barnett, "a standard way of looking at the world, a set of shared unchallengeable assumptions."[19] These managers want to preserve and increase America's military and economic strength, and project American force in order to influence events abroad. They apply force or threaten force against Communist movements in the Third World and convince the president to approve their proposed course of action.

The problem with operating with preconceived notions about events in other nations is illustrated in Lyndon Johnson's decision to intervene in the Dominican Republic in 1965.[20] After the coup that overthrew the government, neither the military nor the various political factions could establish order. American embassy officials encouraged military officers who called for a junta to take over, and offered to mediate between them and civilian groups. Meanwhile Secretary of State Dean Rusk, who knew next to nothing about the political situation in the country, thought the Communists were attempting to take over.[21] His concerns became a "clue" for the ambassador, the military, and the CIA: an American decision to intervene could be taken if top-level decision-makers were convinced that a Castroite takeover of the country was about to occur. Ambassador Bennet reported in his cables to the State Department that "Castro elements" were gaining ground in dominating civilian opposition to the military. The CIA concentrated, in its reporting, not on the political situation, but on the activities of a handful of supposed "Communist agents." The Dominican military requested that American marines be landed to aid in quelling a "Communist takeover." Newly installed CIA Director Raborn emphasized the Communist connections of the rebel leaders, based on reports from his CIA station chief.

President Johnson, after consulting with Secretary of State Rusk, Undersecretary of State Ball, Secretary of Defense McNamara, and National Security Advisor Bundy, authorized a contingent of marines to evacuate American civilians. He then ordered the military to review its operational plans to ensure that it could prevent a "takeover" by Communist elements. McNamara joined with the JCS to request that more troops be sent in, and the president agreed. The chairman of the JCS told the general commanding the troops, "Your announced mission is to save American lives. Your unstated mission is to prevent the Dominican Republic from going Communist."[22] In spite of the opposition of the military, which hoped to crush the antijunta forces holding the city, the president acceded to the position of the State Department, which organized an "Inter-American Peacekeeping Force" to restore order in Santo Domingo. The junta established its political authority as the civilian forces capitulated.

The ideology of the national security managers was a significant factor in Johnson's decision to send in the marines. The embassy and the CIA magnified the possible risks in permitting the civilian politicians to establish a government. They focused on the activities of the Communists and Castroites and exaggerated their influence among the various factions. They relied on a misleading analogy (Cuba) to condition their responses. The CIA and the embassy focused on the kind of information the State Department wanted—evidence of Communist infiltration—rather than on the information the State Department needed—political information that could have been used to mediate between the two sides. Abraham Lowenthal finds a "syndrome of miscalculation" throughout the crisis, so that all events are viewed in terms of a Communist "takeover," and "another Cuba."[23] In such circumstances, the use of force becomes inevitable.

To argue that American national security managers possess an "ideology," even if true, would not necessarily explain presidential war-making. Why did the United States not intervene militarily in Vietnam in 1954, as Nixon and members of the Joint Chiefs of Staff urged? Why did the United States choose to attempt a political rather than a military solution of the Laotian conflict in 1962? If foreign policy is so militarized, why was there no significant pressure on the president to use threats of military intervention during the Arab oil embargo of 1974? National security managers give the president different recommendations in different crises. Most opposed military intervention in China in 1948. The Joint Chiefs have always opposed engaging in "limited" wars on the periphery of Asia, and at the lower levels CIA officials have often provided pessimistic assessments of the prospects for successful American interventions. The Joint Chiefs at times have urged restraint in various crises rather than a military response. As the war in Vietnam developed, army generals became increasingly pessimistic about their ability to achieve a military solution.[24] The administration was divided on the response to take to several North Korean provocations in 1969, including the downing of an American reconnaissance plane and the seizure of the electronic intelligence ship Pueblo. Most of the key national security managers did not favor militarization of the dispute and convinced Nixon to take a diplomatic approach. The actions of the Ford and Carter administrations in negotiating with the Panamanian government over the future status of the Panama Canal also undercuts the notion of an inflexible ideology of interventionism.

Nor does it seem to be true that national security managers "surround" the president and draw him into their ideological consensus. Kennedy, Johnson, Nixon, and Ford all hired and fired key military and national security advisors, or transferred them from one assignment to another, in order to determine national security policies. In the Korean War Truman controlled the pace and goals of the military effort by firing General MacArthur and winning the backing of his chief national security advisors for his own decision. Kennedy brought into the Pentagon the crisis managers who developed limited-war strategies, and brought in the chief proponent of American assistance to Vietnam, General Maxwell Taylor, as his principal military advisor and later chairman of the Joint Chiefs of Staff. After Johnson decided to escalate the war, he developed an entire "team" of diplomatic, military, and intelligence officials who shared his views, and he installed many of them in missions in Vietnam to administer the stepped-up American military programs. When McNamara no longer supported Johnson's war policies he was replaced and given an assignment as president of the World Bank. Rather than making the president into a "clerk" who will take actions agreed to by the national security elites, the record indicates that it is the president who makes the key decisions and then surrounds himself with advisors who have views compatible with his own.

Coalition Building

Some decision-making theories, developed by political scientists and organizational behaviorists, argue that the "consensus" that is developed by the national security managers rests not on ideology but on the missions and organizational interests of the national security agencies. Each agency has a mission to perform, which gives each an incentive to propose actions that require its unique services. In turn the information that is passed along to top levels of the administration is colored by the vested interests of the officials. Either the defense secretary or the secretary of state takes the lead in developing a coalition of principal advisors: if the consensus is for force or for diplomatic efforts, the president is likely to follow it.

The period immediately after Kennedy's assassination provides a useful case study. Although Kennedy had intervened in Vietnam to test the new tools of counterinsurgency and to preserve the credibility of the American commitment to non-Communist governments in the Third World, his administration had never resolved the issue of the extent of this commitment: did the U.S. government intend to use limited force to *assist* other governments to resist aggression? Or did it intend to use whatever force was necessary to *defeat* Communist military forces and maintain non-Communist regimes? In late 1963 Kennedy had taken several actions, against the advice of the Joint Chiefs of Staff and the secretary of defense, to limit the American commitment to South Vietnam. He rejected a plan for covert operations to be launched against North Vietnam (CINCPAC OPLAN 34-63) proposed by the Joint Chiefs. He called for a reduction of one thousand advisors and authorized planning for such a reduction in National Security Council memorandum 263. This withdrawal was to be accelerated as a result of a decision taken by the administration at the Honolulu Conference of November 20. The purpose of the administration actions seemed to be either (1) to prod the Diem government and its successor into taking necessary reforms to win the allegiance of the peasants or (2) to move toward a political settlement and possibly a coalition government along the lines of the Laotian settlement of 1962. But two days after Kennedy's assassination these plans were changed. President Johnson held a meeting with top national security advisors on November 24, which resulted in National Security memorandum 273: "both military and economic programs, it was emphasized, should be maintained at levels as high as those in the time of the Diem regime."[25] The central objective was no longer to assist South Vietnam in its struggle—the political objective of the Kennedy administration; it had now become an American commitment to "win" the fight against the Communists, an open-ended military commitment. Johnson's decision was due to the coalition that had been created by Secretary of State Rusk, Secretary of Defense McNamara, and Chairman of the Joint Chiefs Taylor. As a result of that initial decision, the national security advisors pressured the president to approve various escalations, secret operations, and commitments. The losing coalition consisted of middle-level officials with a great deal more knowledge of conditions in Southeast Asia but far less bureaucratic "clout": Assistant Secretary of State Roger Hilsman, Assistant Secretary Averill Harriman, Ambassador to India John Kenneth Galbraith—and significantly, Attorney General Robert Kennedy. A short time later, for a variety of reasons, all found themselves out of the administration.

In the Cuban Missile Crisis of 1962 the evidence suggests that President Kennedy did not make his decisions on the basis of a consensus of his advisors. In spite of American warnings to the Soviet Union not to place offensive missiles in Cuba, and in spite of assurances that such missiles would not be located there, American reconnaissance flights discovered missile emplacements and missiles. Kennedy assembled a group of thirteen present and former officials to help make crucial decisions, the so-called ExCom (Executive Committee) of the National Security Council. He absented himself from meetings so that he could in no way "bias" deliberations. There seemed to be several actions the administration could take: (1) downplay the matter and after making a diplomatic protest let the incident drop; (2) establish a blockade around the island to prevent military supplies from being delivered and call for a negotiated settlement to the dispute; (3) launch an invasion of the island for the limited objectives of destroying the missile sites or overthrowing the Castro regime; (4) have the air force destroy the missile sites.

To the extent that a coalition formed, it did not seem to control presidential decision-making. At one point seven of the thirteen advisors were in favor of some sort of military action against the Cuban regime. It was the minority group, including Attorney General Robert Kennedy and speechwriter Theodore Sorensen, who searched for other options. President Kennedy leaned toward them. He made nonmilitary choices whenever possible. He took the least bellicose military option open to him, the blockade of Cuba, and referred to it as a quarantine. The president relied on his own diplomatic intermediaries and on direct communication with the Soviet leadership in an attempt to "cool" the crisis.[26] There is some evidence that Kennedy, working through intermediaries, struck a secret bargain with the Soviet Union, providing for eventual American removal of missiles from Greece and Turkey and a pledge to respect the integrity of the Castro government in exchange for immediate Soviet removal of the missiles.

The consensus model fails to account for many crucial presidential decisions. In 1954 it was the consensus of most senior officials that the United States should relieve the siege of Dien Bien Phu in Indochina and commit American forces to the conflict. President Eisenhower took a different course of action. The 1961 decisions to begin escalation in Vietnam ran counter to the suggestions of the professional military. The 1966 bombing of Hanoi was as much of a surprise to most national security managers as it was to the North Vietnamese, since the decision was made by Johnson at his ranch in almost complete solitude. The 1968 bombing halt was also made by Johnson without a consensus. The Nixon decisions to bomb Hanoi and blockade Haiphong, and to invade Cambodia, were made without significant participation by most of the national security bureaucracy, and amidst charges that the major problem of the Nixon presidency was the increasing isolation of the incumbent when such crucial decisions were made.

The consensus model fails to account for the possibility that parts of the national security apparatus may initiate actions on their own to force the hand of the president. Consider the role of the CIA in attempting to sabotage the Geneva Agreement on Laos. The CIA backed right-wing forces during the conflict and felt, even after the 1962 agreement, that these forces could win a military victory against the Pathet Lao. It recommended various actions to the administration without success. But its field operatives encouraged the right-wing army groups to violate the accords and overthrow the coalition government. The new government then launched a military offensive, which failed, prompting it to charge that the North Vietnamese and even the Red Chinese had invaded Laos, all in a vain attempt to force an administration response of American troops to prop its sagging fortunes.

The CIA also attempted to escalate the war against the North Vietnamese in 1963, in spite of the fact that Kennedy throughout the summer had not yet made a decision on requests for actions against North Vietnam. In June General Harkins approved South Vietnamese commando operations against North Vietnam, and in September the CIA pressed for resumption of its Laos operations directed into North Vietnamese territory. Some analysts believe that before his death Kennedy had lost control of decision making involving covert operations and planning.[27]

Other instances exist of agencies attempting to force the administration to take certain actions. In the Cuban Missile Crisis the navy attempted to administer the quarantine line in its own way: the placement of the line and the orders given to commanders indicated that the navy intended to force a confrontation with the Soviet Union in order to demonstrate its naval superiority. McNamara and the president had to regain control of the Navy Department and the fleet, and issue a different set of orders, so that their goal of a negotiated settlement could be achieved.[28] The American commander in the intervention in the Dominican Republic attempted to convince the president that the military position of the troops was untenable unless they were permitted to advance into the city and crush the rebellion. Instead, the president issued orders that the forces were to advance, but only for very limited tactical disposition of the forces, and were not to engage in conflict in the city.[29] In neither case does it seem that military commanders shared the "consensus" of civilian authorities.

Alternatively, important national security decisions may be made without presidential participation. During the Arab-Israeli conflict of 1973, major decisions involving management of the crisis in American-Soviet relations were made by Secretary of State Kissinger and Secretary of Defense Schlesinger. Nixon, preoccupied with the Watergate affair and the reaction to the "Saturday Night Massacre" at the Department of Justice, seemed unable to participate effectively in deliberations, and for the most part he remained in his private White House quarters. When decisions were made, the president was telephoned for his assent.[30]

This case, which is so atypical, cannot be considered evidence for a coalition model of decision making, but rather for the proposition that if the president is unable to function as commander in chief, he will become a clerk for the cabinet members who are prepared to act in his name and function as "prime ministers."

Quagmire Theory

Implicit in the books written by some of the journalists who covered the escalation of the war in Vietnam is the notion that America blundered into a major conflict through a series of decisions, none of which were made with the ultimate idea of fighting a major conflict. The war, in this view, was an *outcome* rather than a *policy*. The CIA provided poor intelligence. The Defense Department's "Whiz Kids" and its senior political officials had unjustified confidence in their ability to "manage" a limited war in Asia. The Defense, National Security, and State Department officials formed a coalition that sold the president on incremental steps and promised him that the next step would be the one that would provide success in the war. As Arthur Schlesinger argued, "Each step in the deepening of the American commitment was reasonably regarded at the time as the last that would be necessary. Yet in retrospect, each step led only to the next, until we find ourselves entrapped in that nightmare of American strategists, a land war in Asia."[31]

The quagmire theory takes presidents off the hook. Faulty intelligence and bad advice of the national security officials caused the president to escalate. No one can be blamed for the decision to go to war, since no such decision was made. It is no accident that those who worked for Presidents Kennedy and Johnson have embraced the quagmire theory or contributed to its exposition at the time of the escalation; it not only seemed to explain the facts as these officials understood them, but it also provided a convenient scapegoat—the same scapegoat that had been used to shift blame from the Kennedy administration onto the intelligence agencies for the Bay of Pigs debacle.

But the quagmire theory cannot account for the decision to intervene in Vietnam, especially for certain crucial events in 1964. During the Gulf of Tonkin incident the administration released a version of events sharply at variance with the facts, relying on its classification system to deceive Congress, so that a resolution in support of the presidential decision to escalate hostilities would receive congressional support. The administration version of the incident was that on August 2, 1964, three North Vietnamese torpedo boats approached the U.S.S. *Maddox* in international waters, in a threatening manner. The *Maddox* fired warning shots and then fired directly at the boats; they released torpedoes, which the destroyer evaded. Fighter planes from the U.S.S. *Ticonderoga* then

damaged two of the P T boats. On August 4, the U.S.S. *Maddox* and
U.S.S. *Turner Joy* were on patrol sixty-five miles from land, and their
radar picked up five vessels approaching. Believing themselves under
torpedo attack, the destroyers returned fire and sunk two of the craft.
The following day American warplanes attacked the P T boat base,
destroying or damaging twenty-five boats and petroleum storage facilities.
Fifteen minutes after the president made the decision to bomb the base,
he invited sixteen congressional leaders in for a briefing. All agreed to
support a proposed Gulf of Tonkin Resolution the president planned to
introduce to Congress, which would back his actions. On August 6
Secretaries McNamara and Rusk and JCS Chairman Wheeler testified
before a closed joint session of the Senate Armed Services and Foreign
Relations committees, and then at a session of the House Foreign Affairs
Committee. The resolutions, as reported to Congress, were then debated
for nine hours and passed by overwhelming margins in each chamber.[32]
Not only did Congress back the president in his capacity as commander
in chief to use whatever force was necessary to repel aggression against
American forces, but in the Senate an amendment offered by Senator
Nelson, urging that "except when provoked to greater response, we should
continue to avoid a direct military involvement in the Southeastern Asian
conflict," was defeated.[33]

In 1968 Chairman J. William Fulbright of the Senate Foreign Relations
Committee organized hearings to investigate the Gulf of Tonkin incident.
The conclusions of the committee were (1) that the *Maddox* was not on
a routine patrol in international waters, but rather on an intelligence
mission; (2) that the *Maddox* was between eight and nine miles from
North Vietnam when fired upon, within the twelve-mile limit claimed by
North Vietnam as its territorial waters; (3) that a South Vietnamese
operation against North Vietnam that involved naval landings was taking
place at the same time; (4) that the U.S. Navy had intelligence information that indicated that the North Vietnamese were under orders to treat
U.S. patrols as part of that South Vietnamese operation; (5) that American
ships were deployed in the Gulf of Tonkin to reinforce the *Maddox* prior
to the first incident, indicating that the navy expected some trouble from
the North Vietnamese; (6) that the *Maddox* was patrolling very close
to a North Vietnamese base that had been under attack by the South
Vietnamese.[34]

The administration presented the incident as if it involved unprovoked
aggression on the part of the North Vietnamese. In fact, Lyndon Johnson
had participated in a deception. Johnson had permitted the navy to send
a patrol into North Vietnamese waters, in the midst of offensive operations conducted against North Vietnam by the South Vietnamese. He had
suckered the North Vietnamese into the incident, which provided a
pretext for the Gulf of Tonkin Resolution, and for the subsequent
escalation of the war.

The "quagmire" view of American involvement in Vietnam cannot account for the exaggerated American response to the minor Gulf of Tonkin incident, for the secrecy that surrounded the administration version of events, or for the deliberate distortions involved. It cannot account for plans made in late November 1963 to escalate the war against North Vietnam. It cannot account for plans made in the summer of 1964 to send more than one hundred thousand troops, in staged increments, into the fighting. And it cannot account for the fact that presidential decisions to escalate the war were made in spite of pessimistic assessments of the prospects for victory that were issued by the intelligence agencies. Escalation seems to have been decided upon at the highest levels of government, through conscious choice, and not as a consequence of erroneous intelligence assumptions or recommendations made by middle-level officials.

Presidential Decisions

The president determines where, when, and how the armed forces will be used based on his prerogative power. It is not the middle-level officials, the national security managers, the economic interest-groups, or the coalition of department secretaries that make the ultimate decision for peace or war, or the subsequent decisions to escalate or de-escalate.

One theory of presidential decision making was developed by Daniel Ellsberg, the Pentagon official who participated in the study that became known as *The Pentagon Papers* and who eventually leaked these documents to the *New York Times* in 1971. Ellsberg was not satisfied with the orthodox explanation that the United States had stumbled into a quagmire, because he knew from his study of the official records that both Kennedy and Johnson had received accurate assessments of the conflict from the CIA and other agencies, and that many national security managers were pessimistic about the American goal of creating a stable non-Communist government in South Vietnam. In spite of fairly good intelligence, a succession of American presidents had made commitments to South Vietnam and had escalated the American involvement. Why, Ellsberg wondered, would presidents choose to act in ways that ran counter to assessments of the national security bureaucracies?

The answer, he determined, could be found through analysis of the *domestic political situation* that presidents found themselves in after the Second World War: America had become "number one," the president was the leader of the free world, and the "fall" of any non-Communist nation (such as China) led to a backlash against the party in the White House that had permitted the Communists to achieve their success. To permit South Vietnam to "fall" would expose any incumbent president as a weak leader, would turn his congressional party and the public against him, and would lead to the defeat of his party in the next elections. No president could be the first to permit a Communist flag to fly over Saigon. Even if his national security managers could not guarantee him a way to win the Vietnam War, they could stave off the defeat of the South Vietnamese government. A succession of presidents escalated the American commitment in the conflict in order not to "lose" Vietnam.[35]

The political situation meant that a president had to operate within certain constraints: there could be no political solution involving a coalition with the Communists in the government of South Vietnam; there could be little pressure on the South Vietnamese government to institute major reforms; a Communist takeover must be resisted at all costs. Ellsberg codified two "rules" that presidents seemed to follow in making their decisions:

Rule 1.   Do not lose the rest of Vietnam to Communist control before the next election.
Rule 2.   Do not, unless essential to satisfy Rule 1 in the immediate or an earlier crisis [take a series of military actions, including the use of ground troops, bombings in South and North Vietnam, invasion of North Vietnam, or the use of nuclear weapons.][36]

At each step of the Vietnam War, the president escalated to preserve a stalemate in a war he could not win, primarily to preserve his own political position at home, secondarily to preserve his credibility as a world leader with America's allies abroad.

The political model fits very well the "Vietnamization" of the war involved in Nixon's decision to withdraw American ground combat troops during his first term in office. American casualties ran high, and public opinion, although sharply divided, was turning against the conduct of the war when Nixon took office. In spite of the recommendations by national security managers that the effort be continued and that a decision be made to commit forces necessary to "win" the war, the administration decided to withdraw combat forces and at the same time increase the bombing throughout Indochina. The punitive bombing of Hanoi and the blockade of Haiphong were designed to force the North Vietnamese to the bargaining table under circumstances that would make it look as if the allied side had preserved South Vietnam. The Paris Accords permitted an American disengagement from the ground war, on terms that seemed to promise continuation of Ellsberg's "rule 1," since bombings in South Vietnam, Laos, and Cambodia could be continued.[37]

There are other cases in which the political model has applicability: one is the decision of the Kennedy administration in 1961 to attempt a political solution to the Laotian conflict. In the spring the Defense Department had completed contingency plans to send American troops to Laos, but Kennedy decided instead on an effort to negotiate a coalition government among the rival Communist, neutralist, and rightist factions. The decision was based on a combination of factors: the rightist army was weak, the Pentagon was unenthusiastic about a limited land war in Laos and cautioned that manpower reserves were limited, congressional leaders did not support an intervention, and American allies were opposed to an escalation.[38] Provided rule 1 could be adhered to through creation of a neutralist government, there was no need to escalate. The administration stuck to its course in spite of CIA support for the right-wing forces and its desire to resume hostilities.

Perhaps the most significant crisis in which political considerations played a role was the Cuban Missile Crisis of 1962. Throughout the summer Republican legislators had warned that the Soviet Union was placing offensive missiles in Cuba. The administration, on the defensive, pointedly warned the Soviet Union not to do so and received assurances from the Soviet ambassador to the United States that no such weapons had been introduced. Once the existence of the weapons was confirmed by U-2 flights, Kennedy exploded. "He can't do this to me," the president complained. What made the placement of missiles a "crisis" for Kennedy was *not* the military significance of the move. Secretary of Defense McNamara discounted the military threat, since even at that time the Soviets had submarines and surface vessels armed with nuclear weapons quite close to American shores, even closer to vital targets than the missiles in Cuba. In the event of war these weapons could do more damage and were less vulnerable to either a retaliatory or preemptive strike than the weapons in Cuba. But the missiles were a *political* threat to the administration, which had staked its prestige on Soviet denials that the weapons were in Cuba. Not to respond to the placement would have made the administration look weak in the eyes of the world, friend and foe alike. The Republicans could confront the president with charges of duplicity (claiming he had known over the summer that the weapons were in Cuba) or cowardice (for failing to confront the Soviets). Kennedy, according to some observers, even thought that he could be impeached if he did nothing about the missiles. Whether or not the placement of missiles was a military threat to the United States, it was clearly a political crisis for the president.

Each of the decision-making models provides a different assessment of the function of the president. The geopolitical and ideological models focus on the perceptions of national security elites about the nature of communism and of political movements in the Third World; since these perceptions are faulty the president receives poor advice and, attempting to act in the national interest as he sees it, takes the nation into war. If the economic interest model is applied, the president becomes a "clerk" for an elite group that dominates the national security bureaucracies in its own interest. Whichever of these models is applied by the critic, the focus is neither constitutional nor institutional: to deter presidential war-making it would be necessary to replace the present national security elites with officials having different ideologies, more realistic assessments of developments in the Third World, and no links to the dominant financial institutions. Some critics argue that either peaceful, or even violent, overthrow of the entire American political system would be necessary to replace the influence of the elites and end American intervention.

Journalists who apply the quagmire theory focus on the shortcomings of the national security bureaucracy and on the arrogance of "the best and brightest" of the highest political officials in the administration who relied on their advice.[39] The intelligence agencies must provide more accurate assessments of political situations. The military and its civilian managers must have a more realistic notion of what American power is capable of achieving against movements of national liberation. The president must not isolate himself or rely on a single set of officials. He must not permit a "palace guard" to shield him from honest criticism of his policies. He must consult widely within the executive branch, with congressional leaders, and with a variety of "wise men" with experience in foreign affairs.[40]

Although economic interests, ideologies, and strategic gamesmanship may play some role in the presidential decision to engage in limited wars, the actual decisions occur under one of two conditions: (1) when a political coalition of senior advisors can convince the president of the need to use the military to salvage an American position of influence abroad; (2) when the president himself believes that his political stakes at home and his reputation as a leader abroad are at issue in the conflict. To the extent that coalition and political theories provide an explanation for presidential decision making, the critic of presidential war-making may focus on the "institutional anxiety" of the president, the anxiety that comes to the incumbent who is held responsible for all the setbacks to "the free world" in areas that no president can dominate with military force. To check presidential decisions about peace or war one might propose fundamental restructuring of his relationship to Congress. Procedural changes could be instituted that might make it less likely that the president could use secrecy, deception, and faits accomplis. If the president were required to collaborate with Congress in the decision to engage in limited warfare, he would be required to deal with legislators, and with the American people, in different ways. As his vantage point shifted he might choose nonmilitary options. If Congress played a large role in making and in honoring American commitments, if it shared in the "alliance power," the scope and number of such commitments might more realistically reflect American vital interests.

III

The War-making Prerogative

By what authority does the president decide upon peace or war, and how can his prerogative be squared with the provision in Article I of the Constitution granting Congress the power to declare war? The president asserts, through the doctrine of concurrent exercise, that his authority as commander in chief enables him to meet certain domestic and foreign obligations by ordering American armed forces to engage in hostilities.

For minor interventions the president claims an "interposition" power to protect American lives and property abroad. He combines the commander in chief clause with the duty to faithfully execute the laws, in order to enforce various consular or diplomatic agreements, treaties, or executive agreements. He may even pressure foreign governments to respect the terms of contracts under which American citizens and corporations conduct business.

Jefferson's actions against the Barbery pirates provides an example of presidential war-making under the *police powers*. The American policy had always been to negotiate treaties with the pirates and to pay tribute in return for safe passage and harbor. Jefferson had the navy issue instructions to a squadron to proceed to the Port of Algiers and offer $30,000 to the regent, proceed to Tripoli and offer $10,000 to the dey, and if these payments were refused, the commodore was given the following orders:

> But should you find on your arrival in Gibralter that all the Barbery Powers have declared war against the United States, you will then distribute your forces in such a manner, as your judgment shall direct, so as best to protect our commerce and chastise their insolence—by sinking, burning, or destroying their ships and vessels wherever you shall find them.[41]

Tripoli declared war and the U.S.S. *Enterprise* sank a pirate vessel. Jefferson sent a message to Congress (which did not include mention of his instructions to the squadron commander) asking Congress for authority to order ships to defend themselves. Three months later Congress passed legislation, after Jefferson had used secrecy, deception, and a naval fait accompli to maneuver Congress into ratifying his initiative. Eventually the Barbery powers concluded a treaty with the United States that ended the practice of requiring tribute, a major success for the Jefferson administration.

Such presidential authority may be directed not only against politically unorganized bandits and guerrillas and pirates, but also against sovereign governments. In 1854 the Nicaraguan town of Greytown was destroyed by naval bombardment for failure to pay reparations after the destruction of American property, an action that was upheld by the federal courts.[42]

To cite another example, in 1900 President McKinley, on his own authority and without prior or subsequent congressional authorization, sent five thousand American troops to China as part of the expeditionary force that crushed the Boxer Rebellion. In a 1901 protocol, negotiated by McKinley and ratified without participation of the Senate, the United States received from the Chinese Imperial Government the same concessions to do business in China as had been granted to the European powers.

The president may exercise an "international police power" to execute the laws of nations: the rights and privileges of any nation asserted against any other nation—even where the United States is a third party not immediately involved in the dispute. Theodore Roosevelt and several other presidents used the principles of the Monroe Doctrine to act as "policeman for the hemisphere" in disputes between Latin American and European nations. As Roosevelt expressed these principles in his annual message to Congress in 1904,

Chronic wrongdoing, or an impotence which results in a general loosening of the ties of a civilized society, may in America, as elsewhere, ultimately require intervention by some civilized nation, and in the Western Hemisphere the adherence of the United States to the Monroe Doctrine may force the United States, however reluctantly, in flagrant cases of such wrongdoing or impotence, to the exercise of an international police power.[43]

The United States occupied Cuba, Nicaragua, the Dominican Republic, and Haiti in the exercise of such police powers. At times American banks and Treasury officials operated the customs houses or took charge of the central banking operations of these nations, while military authorities exercised municipal governing power. These powers were repudiated by Franklin Roosevelt, who enunciated a "good neighbor" policy, and they were replaced by doctrines of collective security based on the Rio Pact of 1947 and establishment of the Organization of American States. Nevertheless such unilateral presidential authority to intervene in the affairs of other nations still exists, as the invasion of Santo Domingo in 1965 illustrates.

Presidents claim that the commander in chief clause permits them to dispose the armed forces as they see fit. A president may place the armed forces in situations in which hostilities are likely to occur, and once an incident has taken place he can either ask for a declaration of war or continue hostilities on his own authority.

President James Polk used his authority as commander in chief to pursue his policy of expansion. At the time of his inaugural Texas had just joined the Union, Mexico was threatening war, and Polk placed three thousand troops on alert near the disputed border. Polk reinforced naval units in the Pacific, to be in a position to take the Mexican province of Upper California with its excellent harbor at San Francisco. He sent agents to California to work closely with American settlers. The president then ordered Gen. Zachary Taylor into the territory disputed by the United States and Mexico, while at the same time offering to pay up to $40 million to Mexico for California. Congress tried to restrain Polk by refusing an administration request for funds for the purchase. The opposition Whig party proclaimed that the Texas border with Mexico was on the Nueces river, which undercut Polk's claim to territory up to the Rio Grande. Nevertheless Polk persisted in his policy, and Taylor's troops occupied high ground overlooking the Mexican village of Matamoros and trained its artillery on the town square. Mexico then declared "defensive war," and some American troops were killed in an engagement. Just prior to learning of the clash Polk and his cabinet had already decided to ask Congress for a declaration of war; news of the incident enabled the president to claim that Mexico had invaded Texas. Because of Polk's deception many opposition Whigs joined the Democrats and voted for a declaration of war. Although in his second annual message of 1847 Polk claimed that "the existing war with Mexico was neither desired nor provoked by the United States," the Whigs eventually realized that they had been taken in.[44] In his maiden speech to the House of Representatives, Abraham Lincoln, then a first-term representative from Illinois, attacked the president and exposed fully the deception in his presentation of the border incident to Congress.[45] Although victories by American forces enabled the United States to obtain California and territories in the Southwest, the Whigs forced Polk to settle for less territory in the negotiations than he wanted, by threatening to cut army appropriations if the war were resumed. During the peace negotiations the House even passed a resolution condemning Polk for a war "unnecessarily and unconstitutionally begun by the President of the United States."[46]

In modern times presidents have relied on the commander in chief clause to place American forces into hostilities without a declaration of war.

When North Korean forces advanced into South Korea in June 1950, President Truman ordered American forces in Japan to aid the government of South Korea in repelling the aggression. Truman did so even though there had been no attacks on American forces or citizens, no mutual defense treaty with the South Korean government existed, there was no immediate request for intervention from the South Korean government, there was no call for such intervention from the United Nations, and there was no American commitment to defend the territorial integrity of South Korea. The day after Truman's decision to go to war, the American action was reported to the United Nations Security Council, which then approved an American-sponsored resolution that "the members of the United Nations furnish such assistance to the Republic of Korea as may be necessary to repel the armed attack and to restore international peace and security in the area."[47] Although the administration later argued that American actions were undertaken to meet this commitment to the United Nations, in fact the actions were based, as the State Department noted, on the "traditional power of the president to use the Armed Forces of the United States without consulting Congress."[48] In fact Congress had provided by statute for a method by which the United States would meet its commitments to the United Nations. Congress had passed the United Nations Participation Act, which provided, in section 6, that the president could negotiate agreements with the Security Council to make American forces available for peacekeeping purposes, *subject to approval of Congress by act or by joint resolution.*[49] And the Senate Foreign Relations Committee had suggested, in its report accompanying the bill, that "it is appropriate to specify that the military agreement or agreements should be submitted for approval of the Congress."[50] Once hostilities had commenced, however, Congress provided Truman with appropriations for the war, authority for a massive rearmament program, selective service legislation, and domestic laws to facilitate mobilization of the economy, all indications of support for the decision. The Supreme Court upheld the presidential prerogative, for it noted that "it is not the function of the judiciary to entertain private litigation . . . which challenges the legality, the wisdom, or the propriety of the Commander-in-Chief in sending our armed forces abroad or to any particular region."[51] Similarly the judiciary refused to intervene when Lyndon Johnson relied on his authority as commander in chief to send forces to Vietnam, for a federal district court judge pointed out that "the fundamental division of authority and power established by the Constitution precludes judges from overseeing the conduct of foreign policy or the use and disposition of military power; these matters are plainly the exclusive province of Congress and the Executive."[52]

The Nixon administration also used the prerogative of troop deployment when it invaded Cambodia in 1970. Nixon justified the invasion by pointing to the withdrawal of American forces from Indochina carried out since he took office, and to his intention of withdrawing an additional 150,000 forces in 1970–71. He claimed the Cambodian sanctuaries for the North Vietnamese and Viet Cong were a clear and present danger to the safety of the remaining American forces; therefore the president relied on his authority as commander in chief to protect and defend his forces by attacking the enclaves. This tactical authority—to send forces into another nation without a declaration of war—was upheld, as usual, by the judiciary.[53]

Presidents assert the prerogative of unilaterally deciding whether or not to use the armed forces to discharge American treaty or executive agreement obligations to other nations. The power flows from combining the commander in chief clause, "the Executive Power," the obligation to faithfully execute the laws, and the oath of office. In collective security agreements an attack against one nation is considered to be an attack against all signatory nations. Since the original constitutional understanding left the president free to repel attacks against the United States without asking for a declaration of war, the president argues that an attack against another nation may be repelled by American forces based on his own constitutional authority. The Rio Treaty of 1947 provides that "an armed attack by any state against an American State shall be considered as an attack against all the American States." The NATO agreement provides that "an armed attack against one or more [of the parties] shall be considered as an attack against all of the parties." But Article V of the NATO Treaty makes it clear that the use of force in such circumstances is not automatic, for it states that each party will take "such action as it deems necessary, including the use of armed force." During the debate over the treaty the secretary of state made it clear that the provisions of the treaty were not self-executing, and that Congress could still play its constitutional role. The Southeast Asian Treaty Organization agreement was even more explicit: if aggression occurred within the treaty area, each party "agrees that it will in that event act to meet the common danger in accordance with its constitutional processes." But such language is vague: Congress will argue that it involves a declaration of war; the president will counter that it involves his prerogatives as commander in chief to deploy the armed forces. Not only have presidents relied on the language of treaty commitments; they have also used executive agreements, and even letters to heads of state of foreign governments.

The president may take action to support collective security agreements. The Cuban quarantine of 1962, for example, was backed by the Organ of Consultation of the Organization of American States, which recommended measures "to ensure that the Government of Cuba cannot continue to receive from the Sino-Soviet powers military material and related supplies. . . ."[54] But under Article 53 of the United Nations Charter there is a provision that "no enforcement action shall be taken under regional arrangements or by regional agencies without the authorization of the Security Council." This provision has become a dead letter when presidents have used their war powers.

The power of the president to defend the United States against a nuclear attack without waiting for a congressional declaration of war is subsumed under the commander in chief clause and is a logical extension of the original constitutional understanding regarding the power of the president to repel invasions. The president may deploy American forces in order to protect them against an enemy first-strike, and to maintain deterrent capability so that our conventional and nuclear forces can withstand such a strike and still retaliate. It might also be necessary for the president to order a preemptive first strike in certain circumstances.[55] In the midst of the Cuban Missile Crisis President Kennedy asserted the nuclear prerogative when he warned that any missile launched from Cuba against any nation in the Western hemisphere would be regarded as a nuclear attack launched by the Soviet Union against the United States—

an attack that would require a full retaliatory response. If necessary, then, the president will fuse the commander in chief clause with emergency prerogatives, to provide a set of "nuclear war powers" enabling him to launch a first strike to protect and defend the nation.

Congress and War Powers

Until recently Congress acquiesced in presidential war-making by passing facilitative legislation and appropriations, and even providing "retroactive" legitimacy if the president acted prior to a congressional session. Presidents have been given joint resolutions to back them in crises, including the Formosa Resolution of 1955, the Mideast Resolution of 1957, the Cuban Resolution of 1962, the Gulf of Tonkin Resolution of 1964, and the Santo Domingo Resolution of 1965. In the Mideast, Cuba, and Tonkin resolutions Congress did not state that it was delegating its own war powers to the president; instead, it left implicit in the language of the resolutions the notion that the president is using his own constitutional authority and that Congress is simply expressing its support. In the Gulf of Tonkin Resolution, for example, "the Congress approves and supports the determination of the President, as Commander-in-Chief, to take all necessary measures to repel any armed attack against the Forces of the United States and to prevent further aggression. . . ."

Under a "Whig" interpretation of the Constitution, Congress would declare war, and the president would then exercise powers delegated to him by Congress in prosecuting the war it had authorized. In the absence of a formal declaration of war, the statutes and joint resolutions of Congress would delegate authority to the president. Thus Congress could determine the aims of a war, control its scope and pace, and have ultimate authority over the deployment of forces. Congress could determine how the war powers were to be exercised in its initial declaration, in subsequent legislation or appropriations, or in a joint resolution.[56]

But presidents view this approach as unworkable. While they concede that Congress has a concurrent power to determine for peace or war, they argue that the commander in chief clause provides them with a full set of war powers. Congressional resolutions in crises, therefore, do not add or subtract from these powers. The president may enter hostilities, determine strategy and tactics and control deployments, decide on war aims, arrange truces and armistices, and negotiate peace treaties—all on his own authority. In the Vietnam conflict President Johnson argued that the Gulf of Tonkin Resolution merely placed Congress on record in support of his actions as commander in chief; in 1971, when Congress repealed the resolution, President Nixon disregarded it. Even the repeal of the resolution did not direct the president to end hostilities, or in any other way interfere with presidential war-making.[57]

Was the Vietnam War Constitutional?

The Johnson administration argued that since South Vietnam was a sovereign state, recognized by over sixty nations, and a participant in over thirty international organizations (including twelve specialized organs of the United Nations), it was a state under international law. The State Department claimed that South Vietnam had been attacked by North Vietnam, which had infiltrated forty thousand troops into the fighting by 1964. Such aggression was covered by the protocol to the SEATO Treaty. Moreover, the United States had made various commitments to South Vietnam through letters to its heads of state and through executive agreements. Johnson argued that presidential and treaty commitments required him to apply the principles of collective self-defense and aid the South Vietnamese government. He claimed that he could act on his own authority as commander in chief. Congress supported him through passage of the Gulf of Tonkin Resolution and through legislation and appropriations. As commander in chief the president simply executed the obligations of the nation to Vietnam, to SEATO, and to the United Nations.

But critics of presidential war-making pointed out that South Vietnam was not a state under international law. The French in 1945 had recognized the Democratic Republic of Vietnam under Ho Chi Minh as the legitimate government of Vietnam. After the French lost their colonial war, the Geneva Accords of 1954 established two separate "military regroupment zones" pending elections to unify the country. The Americans helped to set up a South Vietnamese government, which in 1956 refused to hold such an election, since even President Eisenhower admitted that Ho Chi Minh's followers would have won it.

The resulting conflict between North and South Vietnam should be viewed as a civil war between rival factions of one nation. In that case the American obligation to the United Nations is covered under Article 33, which calls on nations to attempt a peaceful resolution of disputes. Between 1961 and 1966 the United States made no attempt to negotiate with the North Vietnamese, in spite of pleas by De Gaulle, U Thant, and leaders of several Asian nations, who wanted the issue brought before the United Nations. The American obligation to SEATO would be covered by Article 4(a), which provided that if "the inviolability or the integrity of the territory or the sovereignty or political independence" of a nation covered under the SEATO protocol were threatened "in any way other than by armed attack or is affected or threatened by any fact or situation which might endanger the peace of the area, the parties shall consult immediately in order to agree on the measures which should be taken for the common defense."

If the conflict in Vietnam were a civil war, it would fall under the definition of a "fact or situation which might endanger peace of the area." The United States would be obliged to consult with all other SEATO signatories prior to taking military action unilaterally. These SEATO signatories would have to agree on "measures which should be taken for the common defense." The president was under no obligation to respond with force to protect South Vietnam. In any event, nothing in the SEATO Treaty would permit the president, on his own authority, to use force, for even if the signatories agreed on measures proposed by the United States, such action would have to be authorized by the U.N. Security Council under Article 53 as an enforcement action of a regional organization.

The Gulf of Tonkin Resolution was not "the functional equivalent of a declaration of war," though that is what administration spokesman Nicholas Katzenbach had called it at a Senate hearing.[58] The legislative history of the resolution does not support the notion that Congress was supporting a presidential war in Indochina. Senator Brewster indicated that he viewed "with dismay" the suggestion that American troops might be sent to Vietnam, and was reassured by Senator Fulbright, the manager of the resolution, that "there is nothing in the resolution, as I read it, that contemplates it," adding, "that is the last thing we would want to do."[59] In the House, Thomas Morgan, chairman of the House Committee on Foreign Affairs, argued in the debate,

The resolution is definitely not an advance declaration of war. The Committee has been assured by the Secretary of State that the constitutional power of Congress in this respect will continue to be scrupulously observed.[60]

At no point in the escalation of the American commitment to Vietnam was the United States in any grave and present danger. At every stage the president had the opportunity to ask Congress for a declaration of war, if indeed there was "aggression" by North Vietnam. Assuming that the conflict was a civil war, no treaty obligations or other commitments required the president to use the armed forces. If he wished to do so, he should have secured the concurrence of SEATO allies and of the Congress.

The Role of International Law

Whatever kind of strategic or geopolitical case can be made for the American intervention in Vietnam, the legal case for the kind of action Presidents Kennedy and Johnson took remains weak. As in the case of most interventions, the president makes the decision and then calls upon counsel at the White House, in the State Department, and in the Justice Department to defend his actions. In the case of the intervention in the Dominican Republic, for example, the State Department legal advisor was not consulted on the action, but was asked a week after the landings to prepare a brief defending them.[61] The State Department legal advisor played no role in decisions involving interventions in Vietnam, Laos, or

Cambodia, and only defended actions subsequent to their implementation. Perhaps the only recent case in which considerations of international law played some role was the Cuban Missile Crisis: those who argued for a quarantine rather than for immediate military action relied on arguments prepared by the State Department legal advisor, and it was at the request of the State Department that the Organization of American States issued its resolution in support of Kennedy's actions.[62]

Some observers have argued that the president needs a legal advisor on international affairs reporting directly to him, so that the conduct of foreign relations would be influenced by doctrines of international law. But it is doubtful that such a legal advisor would be able to restrain a president intent on using force, and far more likely that he would function as an apologist for administration action. In any event, the role of the legal advisor in the Cuban Missile Crisis was limited to the application of international law to the dispute: the constitutionality of Kennedy's actions in deploying forces or in threatening the Soviet Union with a nuclear strike seems never to have been an issue. To restrain presidential war-making would require a set of checks and balances, *not* some new mechanisms in the presidential advisory system, for only procedures that involved Congress would introduce constitutional considerations and the values of collaboration and consultation between branches into the decision-making process.

IV

Congressional Checks

During President Nixon's first term in office the Democratic Congress attempted to force the administration to extricate itself from combat in Indochina. Between 1966 and July 1973, Congress took 113 roll call or teller votes on measures to limit or end combat activities, with 94 votes occurring during the Nixon administration.[63] Almost all of these resolutions failed to pass, with the administration putting together a coalition of Republicans and Democratic "hawks" against the liberal Democrats.

Antiwar forces in Congress passed the Cooper-Church amendment to the Department of Defense appropriation bill of 1970, providing that "none of the funds appropriated by this act shall be used to finance the introduction of American ground combat troops into Laos or Thailand."[64] But this did not prevent the administration from bombing in Laos or from using mercenary and CIA-equipped paramilitary forces in these nations. After the Cambodia invasion Congress passed the Cooper-Church Amendment to the Special Foreign Assistance Act of 1971 Supplemental Appropriation, which provided that none of the funds authorized or appropriated pursuant to that or any other act "may be used to finance the introduction of United States ground combat troops into Cambodia, or to provide United States advisors to or for Cambodian military forces in Cambodia."[65] The Defense Department violated the act by arranging for "military equipment delivery teams" to take on advisory functions, such as providing staff assistance, logistics and supply services, and assistance in planning bombing missions for the Cambodian armed forces. The General Accounting Office detailed these violations of the law, which prompted this response from an embassy official: "I think the GAO inspectors are working from a different philosophy than we are. . . . The kinds of things they regard as advisory, we regard as having a statutory or regulatory obligation to do, such as seeing that our military equipment is put to good use."[66] In spite of provisions of the amendment, the bombings of Cambodia were coordinated by American military planes, while the equipment delivery teams provided advice to field commanders on the battlefield.

Antiwar legislators made several attempts to end the bombings in Indochina. In 1971 the Gravel amendment to a defense procurement authorization bill would have ended the bombing in Indochina except as necessary to provide for safe withdrawal of American forces from Indochina, but it was rejected by the Senate, nineteen to sixty-four. In 1972 the Proxmire amendment to a defense appropriation bill would have barred funds for bombing in Indochina, but it too was rejected, twenty-two to fifty-five. Finally, in the spring of 1973 the Democratic Senate caucus put itself on record against military operations in Cambodia, and the House Democratic caucus approved a motion sponsored by the Steering Committee to bar the transfer of funds in the Defense Department for Cambodian bombings. The House Democrats then attached an amendment barring bombing throughout Indochina to an appropriations measure late in June. To avoid a presidential veto of this essential bill the Democrats reached a compromise with Nixon that provided for an August 15 cutoff of funds for bombing in Indochina. On August 3, as the cutoff date approached, Nixon for the first time acknowledged congressional authority to use its power of appropriations as a war power, by observing,

By legislative action the Congress has required an end to American bombing in Cambodia on August 15. The wording of the Cambodia rider is unmistakable; its intent is clear. The Congress has expressed its will in the form of law and the administration will obey that law.[67]

But Congress only took this action *after* the Paris Accords had been signed and American combat involvement in Vietnam had ended. It was only then that the antiwar legislators could muster the votes to stop senseless bombings throughout Indochina.

All the "end the war" amendments introduced in Congress were defeated. The Hatfield-McGovern amendment of 1970 offered to the Military Procurement Act of 1971 would have provided that after April 30, 1971, funds appropriated might be expended "only to accomplish the orderly termination of military operations there and the safe and systematic withdrawal of remaining armed forces by December 31, 1971."[68] The measure was defeated by the Senate in 1971, and the following year, when the Senate did vote to cut off funds in a procurement authorization bill, the amendment was deleted in conference at the insistence of the House, and deleted from another bill by floor action in the House.

The only success for antiwar forces through 1973 was the Mansfield amendment of 1971 to the Military Procurement Authorization Act of 1972, which provided that the policy of the United States was to terminate all military operations in Indochina at the earliest practicable date, provide for prompt and orderly withdrawal of all American armed forces from Indochina subject to the release of all U.S. and allied prisoners and an accounting for the missing in action. Congress called on the president to announce a firm withdrawal date and to negotiate an immediate ceasefire and subsequent exchange of prisoners with the North Vietnamese. After the amendment became law, Nixon warned at the signing ceremony that "the so-called 'Mansfield Amendment'—does not represent the policies of this administration," and added, "it is without binding force or effect."[69] Viewing the amendment as an unconstitutional infringement upon his powers as commander in chief to deploy forces or decide when peace powers should be exercised, Nixon refused to announce a withdrawal date or negotiate under the procedures established by Congress.

Congress never exercised its own war powers to check presidential war-making. It never approved a particular date for withdrawal of American forces from Indochina. It never cut off funds for forces in combat. It never used the appropriation power to require evacuation of American forces. The first effective funding cutoff did not pass Congress until after the Paris Peace Accords had ended direct American combat activity against the North Vietnamese.

When antiwar forces finally obtained the votes for a funding cutoff, the president was, predictably, prepared to veto the measure. But the reason why Nixon chose to accept a compromise and signed the bill into law on July 1, 1973 is to be found in a related development occurring in Congress—the consideration of a general resolution that would affect presidential war powers. To head off passage of such a resolution Nixon decided to accept a bill with specific restrictions on the Indochina war. But in the fall of 1973, in the midst of the crisis with the Soviet Union over hostilities in the Middle East, and at the very moment the president was embroiled in the "Saturday Night Massacre" at the Justice Department, Congress passed a War Powers Resolution, which became law over Nixon's veto. Congress overrode the veto as part of the general sentiment that something must be done about the "imperial presidency."

Passage of the act brought to a head the conflict between president and Congress over war powers. In his veto message Nixon warned that the resolution would "seriously undermine this nation's ability to act decisively and convincingly in times of international crisis," and he claimed that it would "attempt to take away, by a mere legislative act, authorities which the president has properly exercised under the Constitution for almost 200 years."[70] But some members of Congress thought the resolution as finally enacted was too weak, and that it would, for the first time, give congressional sanction to presidential war-making. Thomas Eagleton complained, "By failing to define the president's powers in legally binding language, the bill provided a legal basis for the president's broad claims of inherent power to initiate a war."[71]

The War Powers Resolution

The joint resolution that Congress passed is designed to provide more adequate mechanisms of reporting and consultation by the executive branch to Congress, and to provide for a checks and balances system that permits Congress to overturn a unilateral presidential decision for war. Section (2)(a) spells out the goals:

To ensure that the collective judgment of both Congress and the President will apply to the introduction of United States Armed Forces into hostilities, or into situations where imminent involvement in hostilities is clearly indicated by the circumstances, and to the continued use of such forces in hostilities or in such situations.[72]

In the purpose and policy section, the conditions under which the president may order the use of force are listed in Section (2)(c):

The constitutional power of the President as Commander-in-Chief to introduce United States Armed Forces into hostilities, or into situations where imminent involvement in hostilities is clearly indicated by the circumstances, are exercised only pursuant to (1) a declaration of war (2) specific statutory authorization, or (3) a national emergency created by attack upon the United States, its territories or possessions, or its armed forces.[73]

The first condition is the one set forth in Article I of the Constitution, but the language of the resolution indicates that such a declaration does not delegate congressional war powers to the president, but simply provides him with an opportunity to exercise his own prerogatives as commander in chief. The language of the joint resolution takes the "presidentialist" view rather than the "Whig" view of war powers: war-making is a presidential power under the Constitution, and therefore Congress may not place restrictions or conditions on the exercise of such war powers once hostilities ensue. The third condition is based on the original constitutional understanding that the president could repel invasions on his own authority. But it also permits him to use force if the armed forces of the United States are attacked, without specifying what kind of attack or otherwise restricting the location to American territory or possessions. The language sanctions presidential war-making to defend armed forces located in a foreign country during violent revolution or civil war. It might apply during the Gulf of Tonkin incident in 1964, or whenever the North Koreans make one of their periodic attacks on American forces. In short, the resolution does not distinguish between a major attack and an incident. It permits the president to deploy forces in such a way as to create an incident and then take the nation into war. Presumably if troops are attacked by enemy forces operating from "sanctuaries," the president may invade a neutral nation without obtaining a declaration of war—the situation involved in Nixon's decision to invade Cambodia in 1970.

The second condition, requiring specific statutory authorization, can always be obtained by the president at the beginning of a crisis. When Johnson escalated the war in Vietnam he obtained statutory authority and specific appropriations. In a crisis atmosphere the nation rallies around the president and accepts his interpretation of events. His popularity rises as he defends the nation against aggression. It is highly unlikely that Congress will refuse his request for statutory authorization to conduct hostilities.

The major problem with Section (2)(c) is that it has no binding force or effect. It is located in the purpose and policy section of the resolution. Such sections are usually regarded as general statements of congressional intent rather than as operative sections of the law. In most codifications of law, for example, such sections are omitted. Even the House Committee on Foreign Affairs, in its report accompanying the resolution, noted that "subsequent sections of the joint resolution are not dependent on the language of this subsection."[74] Another section of the resolution even contemplates that the president will not restrict himself to the three conditions, since it requires him to provide Congress with an explanation of his constitutional authority for commitment of forces "without prior legislative approval."[75]

Presidents do not regard themselves as bound by the conditions of Section (2)(c). When they report the use of armed forces they ignore this section and rely on their constitutional authority as commander in chief. In testifying before a House subcommittee on the operation of the resolution, the legal advisor to the State Department in the Ford administration, Monroe Leigh, claimed

that the President has the Constitutional authority to use the Armed Forces to rescue American citizens abroad . . . to protect U.S. embassies and legations abroad, to suppress civil insurrection, to implement and administer the terms of an armistice or cease fire designed to terminate hostilities involving the United States, and to carry out the terms of security commitments contained in treaties.[76]

But no list, however exhaustive, could be drawn by president or Congress, for Leigh added that "we do not believe that any single definitional statement can clearly encompass every conceivable situation in which the

President's commander in chief authority could be exercised."[77] The administration still claimed concurrent authority in war-making, denied the constitutionality of any enumerated listing of conditions in a war powers resolution, and reaffirmed that the president had unilateral authority to honor treaty commitments.

The War Power Resolution also provides the manner in which the president is to consult with Congress in the exercise of war powers. It states that "the President, in every possible instance, shall consult with Congress before introducing United States Armed Forces into hostilities."[78] The legislative history, contained in the Report of the House Committee on Foreign Affairs, indicates what Congress had in mind:

> . . . consultation in this provision means that the decision is pending on a problem and that the members of Congress are being asked by the President for their advice and opinions and, in appropriate circumstances, their approval of the action contemplated.
> . . . the President himself must participate and all information related to the situation must be made available.[79]

But this consultation provision is not required "in all cases" but only "in every possible instance," and presidents have not provided an opportunity for members of Congress to participate in the decision-making process. Nor does the bill indicate whom the president consults: the entire membership of both Houses would be an unwieldy body and could endanger the security needed for planned operations. The bill as presently written does not provide for designated committees or congressional leaders with whom the president must consult. The bill requires him to consult "regularly" thereafter. But it does not indicate whether continuous consultation is intended.

The president must submit a written report to Congress within forty-eight hours of the introduction of armed forces into hostilities or where imminent involvement of hostilities is indicated, or into territory, airspace, or waters of a foreign nation when equipped for combat, and he must report any substantial enlargement of the armed forces equipped for combat in any foreign nation.[80] Only in the case where hostilities have occurred, or imminent involvement in hostilities is indicated, is consultation with Congress required and the sixty-day cutoff provision (to be discussed below) is triggered. This reporting requirement is incomplete. It does not cover the following: military alerts; naval quarantines or blockades in international waters; the use of naval vessels for convoys; the training, equipping, or transporting of mercenaries or guerrillas for combat on foreign territory; or the supply, financing, training, or transporting of forces of another nation into combat on foreign territory. Thus, had such a resolution been in effect in 1941, Roosevelt would not have been required to report his decision to use American patrols near Allied convoys; in 1962 Kennedy would not have had to make a report on the American role in the Bay of Pigs invasion of Cuba, and in 1962 he would not have had to report on the imposition of a quarantine line around Cuba.[81]

In his report the president must indicate the circumstances of the deployment and the constitutional and legislative authority on which the decision was based, and he must estimate the scope and duration of the hostilities or involvement. Every six months thereafter he must submit a similar report. Although the president might claim that he decides when a report is necessary, the congressional view, as expressed by Sen. Jacob Javits, prime sponsor of the resolution, is that "the minute he puts troops into hostilities or imminent danger of hostilities, the act begins to operate. And he does not have to tell us he is doing it, because the sixty-day clock starts to tick if a report is required, even if he fails to do a report."[82]

The War Powers Resolution provides for a "checks and balances" system by enabling Congress to enact *subsequent restraints* after the president has introduced troops into hostilities or into a situation in which hostilities are imminent. These restraints are limited to situations involving hostilities (imminent or actual) and do not cover cases involving buildups or deployments in other nations.[83] Section (5)(c) creates an automatic cutoff of a presidential war: within sixty days of the introduction of forces into hostilities or imminent hostilities, Congress must, by declaration of war or specific statutory authorization, or by concurrent resolution, provide for the continuation of hostilities. The president must terminate the use of the armed forces unless Congress has taken such action within the sixty-day period, or is physically unable to meet as a result of an armed attack. The onus is on the administration to obtain legislative approval, for congressional inaction or stalemate requires the president to terminate hostilities.

Section (5)(c) also provides that "such force shall be removed by the President if Congress so directs by concurrent resolution." Such a resolution is not subject to presidential veto. Once Congress has voted such a resolution, the president must start removing the armed forces. He does not comply with the concurrent resolution simply by negotiating a cease-fire or a disengagement in the immediate fire zone. But whenever forces are required to be withdrawn, either by concurrent resolution or at the end of a sixty-day period if Congress has not approved an extension of hostilities, the president has a thirty-day period to withdraw forces if he determines that there is a situation of "unavoidable military necessity respecting the safety of the United States Armed Forces."[84]

The concurrent resolution provision has often been misinterpreted by analysts. The language specifically states that

at any time that United States Armed Forces are engaged in hostilities outside the territory of the United States, its possessions and territories without a declaration of war or specific statutory authorization, such forces shall be removed by the President if Congress so directs by concurrent resolution.[85]

The provision may be applied only in the absence of a declaration of war or specific statutory authorization by Congress. But if Congress has declared war, or a resolution giving authority to wage war is passed, or a specific statutory authorization has been enacted into law—*then the concurrent resolution procedure to terminate hostilities cannot be used.* Since it is quite likely that in the initial stages of conflict Congress will vote to authorize hostilities, it would seem that the concurrent resolution provision will quickly become a dead letter.

To get around this problem—the nullification of the concurrent resolution provision through prior statutory authorization—some commentators have argued that Congress could insert language in its authorization saying in effect that the concurrent resolution procedure for cutting off the war would remain in force, notwithstanding the passage of authorization for hostilities.[86] Or Congress could put a "sunset" provision in its legislation, limiting the authorization to a specified time period (such as a fiscal year). It could even provide in the statutory authorization, repeal of the authorization by a concurrent resolution, thus paving the way for a concurrent resolution terminating presidential authority in hostilities.

The president could disregard any of these provisions. He could claim that once warfare had begun the commander in chief clause gave him constitutional authority to prosecute it, whether or not Congress provided for or later repealed its statutory authorization. He could interpret the language of Section (5)(c) to mean that the concurrent resolution could be used only *prior* to the first statutory authorization, and could not be applied if such an authorization were later repealed. He could argue that any provision in statutory authorization involving "sunset" or a concurrent resolution to repeal, or language maintaining the cutoff resolution, was inconsistent with the plain meaning of Section (5)(c), and he could then disregard a concurrent resolution cutting off hostilities by claiming it had been invalidated by the prior passage of statutory authorization. What is needed is an amendment to the War Powers Resolution that broadens the use of the concurrent resolution and permits its application at any stage of presidential war-making, even after statutory authorization for a war.

Another provision of the resolution that has confused some commentators is the six-month reporting provision of Section (4)(c). It has been argued that each six-month report is followed by a new sixty-day period, in which congressional inaction would lead to termination of hostilities under Section (5). Thus, every six months the president would be required to convince Congress to authorize or resolve a continuation of hostilities.[87] This interpretation is incorrect. The only sixty-day period in the resolution is the period of time that begins after the president initially introduces forces into hostilities, under the provision of Section (4)(a)(1). The six-month reporting requirement stands alone. It triggers no new sixty-day period, and Congress need not take any action on the report submitted for the war to continue.

The concurrent resolution and the sixty-day cutoff provisions have a much more limited impact on presidential war-making than some commentators have assumed. There are other problems with these provisions. What, for example, constitutes specific legislative authorization to conduct hostilities? Clearly a declaration of war, a concurrent resolution approving a specific use of force, or a law authorizing particular hostilities meets the definitional test. On the other hand, general appropriations for defense do not, and neither do foreign aid measures or other laws involving a foreign nation. Section (8)(a) specifically states,

Authority to introduce United States Armed Forces into hostilities . . . shall not be inferred from any provision of law . . . including any provision contained in any appropriation act, unless such provision specifically authorizes the introduction of United States Armed Forces into hostilities.

But in both the Korean and Indochinese conflicts, specific appropriations were passed for use of the armed forces in those hostilities. In future engagements it is likely that the president can obtain funds, for as Sen. Frank Church pointed out during Senate hearings,

I cannot imagine a situation where the President would take us into a foreign war of major proportions under circumstances that would not cause both the public and Congress to rally around the flag, at least for sixty days.[88]

During the initial sixty-day period the president should be able to obtain a specific appropriation, since it is almost impossible for Congress to refuse such a request once troops are involved in fighting. To deny funds leaves the legislators open to charges that they were abandoning American boys who were fighting and dying overseas.

Presidents have in the past applied collective security agreements and other national commitments on their own authority as commander in chief. Section (8)(a) specifies that no national commitment to use force can be inferred "from any treaty . . . unless such treaty is implemented by legislation specifically authorizing the introduction of United States Armed Forces into hostilities." If the forces are already in foreign nations, however, the president may deploy them, and if they are fired upon, he has authority under the resolution to engage in hostilities. Moreover Section (8)(d)(1) states that no provision of the resolution "is intended to alter . . . the provisions of existing treaties." Since these provisions are interpreted by the president to justify an automatic response to aggression, it is not clear how Section (8)(d) may be reconciled with Section (8)(a). Either the president may apply the doctrine of collective self-defense and use the armed forces on his own authority to meet treaty commitments, or he may not do so unless Congress passes implementing legislation. Congress at present has confused rather than clarified matters through passage of these inconsistent provisions.

Section (8)(a) does not define national commitments precisely. Although treaties are not to be construed as commitments without implementing legislation, there is no mention of concurrent resolutions passed by Congress, such as the Berlin Resolution of 1961. Nor is there any mention of executive agreements. This provides the president with a "loophole," so that he may define such instruments as national commitments; he may then claim that these commitments are prior authorization to use force. What is needed is specific language in the resolution that defines statutory authorization to conduct hostilities in such a way that no resolution, treaty, executive agreement, law, appropriation, or any other legislative enactment made prior to the introduction of troops constitutes statutory authority to conduct hostilities. And it must be specified that any concurrent resolution that requires the president to end hostilities supersedes any authority he may claim to have to conduct hostilities.

Even if these changes in the War Powers Resolution were enacted—and some of them were being considered by Congress in 1977—the president might still ignore a concurrent resolution requiring him to withdraw forces. Monroe Leigh stated the position of the Ford administration when he warned,

I think it would be unconstitutional on the simple logic that if the President had the power to put the men there in the first place that power could not be taken away by concurrent resolution because the power is constitutional in nature. There might, however, be all sorts of reasons as to why the political process would force him to wish to comply with that concurrent resolution.[89]

But a president might also take his chances by relying on prerogative government and ignoring such a resolution while he continued hostilities. If Congress passed a resolution, the president might continue to make expenditures using appropriated but unexpended and unobligated funds that total billions of dollars. In the following exchange between a congressman on the House International Relations Committee and the legal advisor to the State Department, the Ford administration position was made clear:

Mr. Solarz: . . . would the Congress have the authority in your judgment, to pass a law cutting off funding for the troops, and thereby, in effect, requiring the president to withdraw them? . . .
Mr. Leigh: If he has used up all the money appropriated and then Congress refuses to provide any more, I think the Congress has effectively stopped the president from continuing the military action. I don't know how he can go on. If, on the other hand, we still had moneys that were unexpended, he could continue to spend those until such time as there was a court challenge and the court found that he was acting illegally.[90]

As Solarz pointed out in 1977 Senate hearings, if the president acts on his prerogative authority, "all he has to do is draw on previously appropriated funds from the Defense budget and keep them there anyway, then we have accomplished nothing."[91]

410 THE AMERICAN PRESIDENCY

Some reformers have proposed prohibiting by law the expenditure of funds beyond the sixty-day limit or after the adoption of a concurrent resolution requiring withdrawal of forces.[92] Based on its constitutional authority to appropriate funds Congress may specify the uses to which funds are put. It has appropriated funds subject to conditions or contingencies, or subject to various standards of performance. And it has done so in various foreign aid, military sales, and military procurement programs—areas close to the president's authority in diplomatic, national security, and defense policymaking. There is no reason why Congress could not use its appropriation power and the procedures of the Budget and Impoundment Act of 1974 in order to (1) provide for an automatic cutoff of funds after sixty days if Congress has not authorized the war; or (2) provide by concurrent resolution a rescission of funds for warmaking, to be attached to the concurrent resolution requiring a withdrawal. Others have proposed a different method: a precise enumeration of presidential authority to conduct hostilities, coupled with an automatic funding cutoff if the president engages in unauthorized or unenumerated actions.[93]

The Resolution in Operation

Presidents have had no incentive to make the resolution work. They believe it weakens the presidency, infringes on its constitutional prerogatives, erodes the confidence of allies that he will honor our national commitments, and saps the concept of collective self-defense. As Secretary of State William Rogers expressed the position of the Nixon administration in 1971 when Congress was considering an early version of the resolution,

To circumscribe—or even appear to weaken—presidential ability to act in emergency situations would run the grave risk that an enemy might miscalculate the ability of the United States to act in a crisis. This might embolden another nation to provoke a crisis or take other actions which undermine international peace and security. [94]

The resolution has been used several times since its passage, and in each case presidents have taken actions that have reduced its effectiveness, minimized its scope, and established important precedents. The first case occurred during the Da Nang sea evacuation of sixty-five thousand Americans, South Vietnamese, and other nationals, begun on April 3, 1975, in the last days of the Vietnam conflict. President Ford ordered naval units, marines, and other armed forces to assist in the evacuation. He then notified Congress on April 4 "in accordance with my desire to keep Congress fully informed on this matter," but did not concede in his two-page report that he was required to furnish the information.[95] He claimed that the use of the armed forces involved a Section (4)(a)(2) situation, *not* a situation of "imminent involvement in hostilities" and therefore the sixty-day limit did not apply to the evacuation. He argued that the action was taken "pursuant to the President's constitutional authority as Commander-in-Chief and Chief Executive in the conduct of foreign relations, pursuant to the Foreign Assistance Act of 1961, which authorizes humanitarian assistance to refugees." The constitutional claim was, once again, a broad interpretation of the commander in chief clause, while the statutory claim involved a *prior* legislative authorization for the use of the armed forces. But the particular law upon which the president relied did not authorize the use of force. Furthermore, between 1973 and 1975 Congress had passed seven statutory provisions into law that expressly prohibited the expenditure of funds for "combat activities" or for "military or para-military operations in, over, or off the shores of" the nations of Indochina.[96] Whether or not such provisions would prohibit the armed forces from protecting U.S. citizens was not clear.

Ford asked a joint session of Congress on April 10 for action that would "clarify immediately its restrictions on the use of U.S. military forces in Southeast Asia." In particular he asked for a bill that would state that none of the seven funding prohibitions "shall be construed as limiting the availability of funds for the use of the Armed Forces of the United States to aid, assist, and carry out humanitarian evacuation, if ordered by the President."[97] Some members of Congress then proposed bills that would have given the president a legislative authorization, from congressional powers, to evacuate citizens and foreign nationals, and that would have required him to furnish Congress a Section (4)(a)(1) report and subject his action to the sixty-day cutoff or concurrent resolution provisions. But the House passed no such provision because other members feared that any grant of authority for an evacuation might be used by the president as a pretext to resume hostilities and save the crumbling position of the South Vietnamese.

On April 12 Ford ordered an evacuation in Phnom Penh, Cambodia. Although the forces were equipped for combat, the president claimed that they were involved in a situation that did not start the sixty-day clock running. On April 30 Ford ordered the evacuation of Saigon, with nine hundred marines participating in the two-day operation. The same set of constitutional justifications were repeated in both operations when the president made brief reports to Congress.[98]

Congressional failure to pass an evacuation authorization left it looking ridiculous. Obviously the president was not going to permit Americans to be taken prisoner by the invading armies, and was going to mount a major rescue operation, no matter what limitations had been placed in the laws. He clearly intended to use the commander in chief clause to assert a traditional "rescue power."[99] The president had to act or face political suicide and the disintegration of morale in the armed forces. By taking resolute action, the president not only evacuated Americans, but he also established the precedent that, notwithstanding the provisions of the War Powers Resolution, he could proceed without prior consultation of Congress, with the most limited reporting, and with no regard for either the "purpose and policy" section of the resolution or for specific laws prohibiting military action in Indochina. At his discretion the president could label reports in ways that could avoid the consultation requirements or the triggering of the sixty-day clock. Congress missed the opportunity to place all evacuations of American citizens on a statutory basis subject to the controls of the resolution. In the evacuation of Americans from Lebanon during the civil war of 1976, president Ford did not even find it necessary to report to Congress under the provisions of the resolution, setting yet another precedent to weaken the reach of the act.

The *Mayaguez* incident provides further evidence that the Ford administration did not intend to change the way in which presidents decide to use force. On May 12 the *Mayaguez* was intercepted by a Cambodian torpedo boat, boarded, and taken to the island of Kho Tang, where its crew was detained for questioning. The Cambodians were concerned that the ship might be on a surveillance mission, although it was in international waters in the Gulf of Siam. The White House issued an announcement that it considered the seizure "an act of piracy" and the State Department demanded an immediate release of the merchant ship, adding that "failure to do so would have the most serious consequences."[100] After meeting with the National Security Council, President Ford ordered naval vessels into the area and reconnaissance flights to determine the exact whereabouts of the ship. A message was sent to the Communist Chinese government asking for its intercession with the Cambodians for the release of the ship. A naval group blockaded the island, sank three Cambodian patrol boats, and damaged four others. On May 13 the White House briefed ten House and eleven Senate members, but Ford did not provide an opportunity for consultation. Meanwhile the NSC discussed various options in four different meetings over the next two days.

On May 14 Ford ordered eight hundred troops to Thailand. The Senate Foreign Relations Committee and the House International Relations and Armed Services Committees were briefed by the White House, but again there was no prior consultation on decisions to use force. The president then authorized operations on May 14 to rescue the crew (which had secretly been transferred to the mainland), bomb targets in Cambodia (including an airfield and refinery), and recapture the ship. Half an hour before the mission began the crew of the ship was released and sent across the border into Thailand. But without knowledge of the release, the operation commenced: marines stormed ashore in Kho Tang, encountered stiff resistance and heavy fire, and in the ensuing hostilities forty-one marines were killed and fifty more were wounded. Naval aircraft destroyed Cambodian planes and ships in the operation. An hour after the mission was underway Ford briefed seventeen congressional leaders and asked for their support in the crisis. Again, there was no meaningful consultation, for as Senate Majority Leader Mansfield later testified, "I was not consulted, I was notified after the fact about what the Administration had already decided to do."[101] The Senate Foreign Relations Committee, after receiving a briefing from a deputy assistant secretary of state, issued a statement supporting the president "in the exercise of his constitutional powers within the framework of the War Powers Resolution to secure the release of the ship and its men."[102]

On May 15 Ford sent his report to Congress. He based his actions on his authority as commander in chief, although none of the situations contemplated in the purpose and policy section of the resolution had been involved. He ignored the funding prohibitions on military actions in and around Cambodia. His report failed to mention a related military buildup in Thailand, as required by Section 4(a)(3). His retaliatory actions were far in excess of the measures necessary to safeguard American lives and property (even assuming any military action was necessary), and they were in excess of the limited measures recommended by the Joint Chiefs of Staff.[103]

Although in his report Ford claimed that he had "previously advised" Congress of his intention to use force, the president never consulted with Congress in the crisis; even James Eastland, president pro tem of the Senate, denied that he had been advised or informed of the president's intentions. As Senator Jacob Javits observed, "consultations with the Congress prior to the *Mayaguez* incident resembled the old, discredited practice of informing selected members of Congress in advance of the implementation of decisions already taken within the executive branch," and added that "a distinction must be made between the historic custom of giving advance notice to the congressional leadership of major presidential decisions, and the prior consultation requirement of the law."[104] Representative John Sieberling argued that Congress could have been consulted, "since the President had time to consult with the NSC four separate times, surely he could have found time to seek the advice and counsel of the Congress on this matter, had he so desired."[105] Had the president consulted with Congress, he might have delayed his retaliatory action until further word was obtained from the Communist Chinese government. Then the president would have learned that the Cambodians were prepared to negotiate about the release of the crew, and were interested in a peaceful settlement. Implicit in the report of the General Accounting Office that studied the president's actions was the conclusion that it had been unnecessary for the president to order bombings or the landing of marines since the Cambodians had already decided to release the crew and the ship. The consultation provision, had it been used properly, might have saved American lives.[106]

If Congress intends to play a role in crises, it must change the consultation provisions of the resolution. As Pat Holt, former chief of staff of the

Senate Foreign Relations Committee points out, the "executive branch has a long history of using 'inform' synonymously with 'consult.' "[107] Congress must create an action-forcing consultation mechanism by designating the congressional leaders with whom the president must communicate (party leaders, committee leaders, a particular select or standing committee in each chamber) and the forum in which communication takes place (the White House, the legislative chamber, a committee hearing, a meeting of the NSC). The existing process is symbolic since the president can issue incomplete reports and give "briefings" instead of engaging in genuine consultations. As Senator Javits summed up his experience with the reports issued by the president, "they do not suggest a readiness within the Executive Branch to provide the full and timely disclosure of relevant facts and judgments which the reporting provisions of the law were designed to elicit," while Clement Zablocki, chairman of the House subcommittee that has jurisdiction over implementation of the resolution, was even blunter when he claimed, "the executive branch proclivity is toward evasive and selective interpretation of the War Powers Resolution."[108]

Carter and the Resolution

The attitude of the Carter administration toward the resolution has been formulated by the legal advisor to the Department of State in Senate hearings held in 1977. The administration, according to Herbert J. Hansell, "acknowledges the constitutional responsibility of the Commander-in-Chief to act, expeditiously when necessary, to preserve the security of our Nation."[109] Hansell pledged that the administration would consult fully with Congress in crises, and would "follow the letter and spirit of section 5," acknowledging that if Congress voted a withdrawal by concurrent resolution, the administration would comply.[110]

But the Carter administration left itself maximum flexibility if faced with a crisis. Hansell opposed any changes in the law that might provide for a funding cutoff, specification of consultation procedures, or a precise enumeration in Section (2) of the president's constitutional authority to engage in hostilities.[111] As the following colloquy in the hearings indicates, the Carter administration was not prepared to concede that the War Powers Resolution was constitutional, thus leaving the way clear for the administration to take whatever actions it deemed necessary:

Senator Clark: I don't see what would be unproductive about this administration going on record as saying that they think the War Powers Resolution is constitutional.
Mr. Hansell: Please don't misunderstand, Senator. What we said is that the administration does not challenge the constitutionality of it.
Senator Clark: I understand that.
Mr. Hansell: And I think that is the critical question.

Senator Clark: It may be the critical question, but it is really not the question I am asking.

Mr. Hansell: That is right. I understand that. I am not, I guess, prepared to say that in all respects the administration would render an affirmative determination that yes, it is constitutional.[112]

Javits later asked Hansell to formalize agreed-upon consultation procedures, through a letter from the president to the speaker and president pro tem of the Senate. But no letter had been sent as of the summer of 1978.[113]

The Future of Presidential War-making

The War Powers Resolution may not have transformed the way in which America goes to war, but that is not to say that it has had no impact at all. It forces Congress on record about the wisdom and legality of hostilities at an early stage. Every six months it sparks a debate when the president issues his required report. The new process might induce a president to redefine his war aims or make new diplomatic initiatives in order to retain support within his party. For every six months Congress might attempt to cut off funding or repeal the specific authorization of the war, leading the way for an attempt to pass a concurrent resolution requiring the withdrawal of forces. Such an action would undercut the president and destroy him politically. On the other hand, in a war that commanded widespread support, each six-month reporting period would provide the president with the opportunity to demonstrate congressional support, which in turn might convince an enemy to negotiate. While the six-month reporting period does not automatically trigger congressional action, it does provide the opportunity for the president to consult with Congress and to come to agreement on the terms on which the war will continue to be prosecuted. Through congressional hearings on the president's report a forum would be created for prowar and antiwar forces to continue the national debate.

Although prospects for American intervention in limited wars seem to have lessened in the late 1970s, the political risks of any intervention that does occur may impel a president to act with overwhelming force in the early stages in the hopes that hostilities can be ended quickly. No president wants to risk another Korea or Vietnam, especially not with all the procedural issues involved in the operation of the War Powers Resolution. Other nations must calculate, therefore, that if a president does use his prerogative power as commander in chief to intervene with military force, such intervention is likely to escalate quickly—a prospect that makes it even more difficult for "crisis managers" to prevent the nuclear holocaust that haunts the future of mankind.

Conclusion:

The Presidency in

the 1980s

PRESIDENTIAL scholars make poor forecasters. Creators of the
office were convinced by the end of the eighteenth century that incumbents would either subvert the Constitution or prove too weak to preserve it. Prior to the Civil War, constitutional lawyers, reacting to the
presidencies of Jefferson and Jackson, argued that the office was the chief
defect of the governmental system and should be checked by Congress
or by a council of state. Few realized that the real danger to the Union
would lie in a succession of weak incumbents incapable of uniting the
sections to a common purpose. Near the turn of the nineteenth century
the public-law scholars in the graduate schools of political science
thought that the presidency was evolving into a ceremonial office, and
would be displaced by an emerging parliamentary system. Most recently
we had political scientists, using case-study and behavioral methods,
claiming that incumbents governed in the national interest primarily
through their powers of persuasion rather than by command—just at a
time when several presidents used veto and impoundment prerogatives
for domestic affairs and war-making powers for their foreign policies.

It is clear that the only certain forecast about the presidency is that no forecast is certain. With this caution in mind I should like to conclude with some words about present trends and possible developments in the next decade.

The Accountability of Power

Presidents are not likely to become popular or party leaders. The mean turnouts of eligible voters will remain low and may decrease in the next several elections. Media techniques used during campaigns raise public expectations, whereas subsequent performances of incumbents in office result in a disillusioned and cynical electorate. The increase in the number of primaries and the changes in party rules leave incumbents vulnerable to intraparty challenges, and midterm policy conventions may embarrass the administration and provide ammunition for partisan opponents. Legislators will remain disassociated from the presidential electoral system, and the White House will be unable to purge dissidents or use the caucuses to impose party discipline.

Presidents will be tempted to appeal to the people. They will emphasize their expertise, their unique "vantage point," and equate their proposals with the national interest. But incumbents are not experts; worse, they are not perceived by legislators as effective politicians, nor by the public as competent managers. Interest groups all challenge the president when he attempts to define a national agenda. The media delight in putting incumbents on the defensive, and relish serving up the evidence of double-talk or double-dealing in the executive branch. The legacy of Watergate is wolfpack journalism, which will confirm the worst fears of the public. The White House will remain in a state of siege, as the normal transactions of the political system are unearthed, magnified, and then distorted by the media. Presidential attempts to control the national agenda seem destined to fail on most issues.

The Locus of Power

Presidents will continue the decentralization of domestic policymaking and program management. Bureau chiefs and program managers will maintain their ties with congressional committees and subcommittees, and with interest and clientele groups. Presidents are not likely to take more than a passing interest in struggles between departments and bureaus, or between state and federal officials, for in most cases their stakes are limited. Executive Office agencies, particularly the Office of Management and Budget and the domestic staff in the White House Office, will continue to participate in departmental business, thus maintaining the appearance, if not the reality, of intense presidential participation in domestic program planning. But the major stakes for the White House will be political and economic rather than programmatic or managerial: to retain some influence in the distributive process to build support in Congress and with state parties; to influence the magnitude and timing of national commitments so that aggregate spending levels do not exceed White House targets.

Presidential domestic priorities will involve management of fiscal and natural resource policymaking. In both areas Congress has traditionally played a major role, and it has created mechanisms in the budget, impoundment, and fiscal processes that require the administration to collaborate with it. There are substantial differences between the two parties in these areas, and a president who could capitalize on these differences might succeed as a legislative leader. But the problem for a Democratic president is that he might be tempted to rely on national agenda politics and so split his party on ideological or sectional lines. For a Republican president the danger is that party differences will be expressed institutionally through the checks and balances system, with an antiadministration majority in Congress dominating policymaking through the new fiscal and budget mechanisms. Split government might produce deadlock, followed by presidential subversion of the spirit or letter of the new mechanisms. It is likely that instead of party government, decentralized policymaking in the executive branch will be matched by autonomous legislative leaders working closely with interest groups to develop policies, which will then pass Congress through transactional methods. That is why prospects that the White House can develop, for example, serious energy and natural resource policies for long-term development without relying on emergency powers are not good.

The Limits of Power

Presidents will not be able to manage foreign relations well. The various foreign policy communities remain at odds with one another and with the White House: Defense wants more funds for advanced weapons systems and opposes concessions in arms limitation negotiations; the CIA remains demoralized as a result of cutbacks in personnel and increased White House supervision; State does not receive the authority it requests to manage foreign policy, and friction between it and the National Security Council staff seems to have become an institutionalized feature of the foreign policy machinery. The situation will not improve, because foreign affairs in the next decade will center on economic negotiations, and both State and the NSC staff remain poorly equipped to deal with these matters. In the resulting vacuum the Treasury, special White House aides, the ambassador to the United Nations, and even the vice-president, all stake out their "turf," or meddle in the business of State and the NSC. There are too many rhetorical flourishes, too many "policies" enunciated in too many speeches—and too little policy, direction, or coherence. Camp David successes remain sweet, and rare.

Presidents will continue to rely on their prerogative powers. Nixon, Ford, and Carter all argued that their powers as commander in chief could not be diminished by the War Powers Resolution. Each used constitutional authority to expend the functions of the intelligence community, strengthen secrecy systems, and make commitments to foreign nations. Presidents argue that they cannot be held legally liable by the judiciary for violations of constitutional rights of citizens in national security matters.

But presidents must contend with the "backlash" effects produced by Vietnam and Watergate. Congress has passed laws designed to provide it with more information about executive branch activities. These may require the president to specify the constitutional or legal authority for his actions, or provide Congress or its committees with information. Even when such information is classified or closely held, some committees have arranged to be briefed on a regular basis by administration officials. Each year Congress passes more laws that require briefings or formal reports. It is not clear, however, that presidents will provide timely or complete information to Congress. Nor is it certain that legislators have the time, the interest, or the ability to digest and act upon massive amounts of information that they now require be transmitted to them by the executive branch.

Congress has also legislated action-forcing mechanisms that limit or affect statutory presidential authority. These include requirements for the concurrence of committees or one or both chambers before action may be taken, concurrence if action is to be continued past a specified deadline, "vetoes" of actions already taken, and termination of an existing situation or repeal of presidential authority by concurrent resolution. These systems have not always worked well. Congress sometimes acts perfunctorily and acquiesces in important matters without thorough review of executive action. In other circumstances it uses these mechanisms to dominate the distributive process rather than to make policy. Occasionally the legislature uses these mechanisms as part of the checks and balances system, to require constructive modifications of administration proposals, as in the cases of arms sales to Iran and Saudi Arabia. The constitutionality of some of these mechanisms has been challenged by the White House, especially in circumstances where they seem to infringe on the constitutional prerogatives of the president. It is possible that some committee vetoes and concurrences will be struck down by the courts. Congress might then respond by tying its systems of administrative oversight directly to the appropriations process. What seems certain is that

Congress intends to legislate more veto and concurrence systems, especially in national security affairs.

Presidents have at times evaded the letter or spirit of some of the action-forcing systems. Ford worked grudgingly within the impoundment system but tried to overload Congress with trivia. He avoided full compliance with the reporting provisions of the War Powers Resolution. Carter tied various arms sales to nations in the Middle East in a single package, pressuring Congress to approve all components by threatening to withdraw all sales if a single element were disapproved. He canceled the B-1 bomber in a way that evaded the mechanisms of the impoundment process. He did not concede the constitutionality of some of the provisions of the War Powers Resolution. He also questioned the constitutionality of several committee and chamber veto systems.

In the future presidents will continue to oppose such provisions, especially in national security matters. They argue that the government can speak no longer with one voice, since the executive may make promises or commitments that Congress will delay, modify, or refuse to honor. Foreign leaders will charge presidents with bad faith, or will conclude that the White House can neither make nor carry out a foreign policy. These leaders may be tempted to deal directly with members of Congress rather than confine their official representations and negotiations to the Department of State and the president. They will attempt to influence Congress not only by force of argument, but if past history is any guide, by national agenda politics and through transactions or corruption.

Presidents will be tempted to pass the buck and blame Congress for all setbacks in foreign policy. The stage seems set for a replay of the period just prior to World War II, when attempts by Congress to restrict presidential freedom of maneuver—which succeeded all too well—ultimately led the generation that assumed power in the postwar period to conclude that Congress was incapable of sharing power in foreign policymaking. However poorly some presidents have performed in recent years as world leaders, there is little evidence to suggest that Congress, as it presently operates, is in a position to formulate better policies. There is some evidence to suggest that without executive leadership, Congress is likely to blunder terribly in alliance politics. The challenge for Congress is to demonstrate that it can collaborate effectively with the executive in making foreign policy and in managing foreign relations, for if it fails to do so, its use of the new action-forcing mechanisms simply to check the president will leave it discredited, and a backlash will set in against the mechanisms it has created. In major crises the White House is likely to institute some form of prerogative government and disregard provisions of the mechanisms Congress has legislated; such seem to be the lessons of the *Mayaguez* incident and the evacuations in Indochina.

The Uses of Power

Like generals who plan for the next war around the lessons of the last one, presidential scholars have focused attention on the "dirty tricks" of the recent past. Preventing another Watergate by decreasing the size of the White House staff, preventing political police from functioning in the Executive Office, extending public financing of elections, providing for fuller disclosure of lobbying activities, and establishing mechanisms for a special prosecutor to investigate charges of malfeasance involving the White House—these are commendable reforms, and some will probably be instituted. But they do not address the central problem of presidential power: how to make collaborative government work.

Congress must demonstrate that the action-forcing collaborative mechanisms it has created can work in crises, and that they are a viable alternative to prerogative government. Collaboration means more than sharing superintendence of the departments with the executive branch in order to control the distributive process for the benefit of constituents, interest groups, and voting blocs. It involves more than dominating bureaus that administer routine programs. Rather, it involves interactions between the branches that result in important national policies; and it calls for effective use of mechanisms that require the president to inform, consult, and propose, and require Congress to concur, perfect, and if necessary veto presidential initiatives within a limited period of time. Perhaps the most important use of collaborative mechanisms is to keep presidents in a consultative and persuasive frame of mind, which involves a purpose as much psychological as institutional.

Presidents do their part when they invite full and timely consultation within the executive branch, permitting careerists to work closely with political executives in formulating options. They act in the spirit of the system when they give advance notice of their intentions to legislative leaders, provide them with adequate and relevant information, and allow congressional thinking to influence their own deliberations.

Congress does its part when it uses its pooled resources and staffs to obtain its own information and develop its own options. It then can evaluate presidential proposals against alternatives, prior to concurring, perfecting, or vetoing his initiatives. But as yet Congress has not demonstrated that it is prepared to assume a major role in a collaborative system. Incentives for legislators to take the initiative in making policy are lacking. Congress is still not committed to using advanced techniques in the budgetary process. It does not interact early enough with the departments to make a significant impact on overall expenditure levels or on program options. It continues to react, and therefore continues to acquiesce, while making "paper" policies or legislating irresponsible amendments in its budget resolutions. In some policy areas, such as taxation and energy, the committees go their own way; the net result is that the executive controls the resolution of some issues by default, while on other issues the chaotic, decentralized, patterns of committee government are maintained.

Americans want presidents to solve problems. But the party system, the legislature, and the subgovernments each deny the White House the political power or legal authority necessary to manage public affairs. Because we emphasize the limits to power rather than the uses of power, incumbents must substitute rhetoric for achievement. In real or manufactured crises they institute forms of prerogative government, and such crises will continue to occur precisely because presidents remain too weak to manage most problems until they get out of hand. Prerogatives are still seen by the White House as the antidote to paralysis.

There are no easy answers to the problems of a presidential office that remains the major destabilizing factor in the political system by oscillating between too little and too much power. Decentralizing responsibility for most domestic programs to subgovernments and the federal system, strengthening collaborative mechanisms for management of the economy and foreign affairs, and setting new and stricter standards for the exercise of prerogative powers in genuine national emergencies—these might be steps toward placing presidential power and accountability in better constitutional balance.

APPENDIX A

The Presidency in the Constitution

ARTICLE I

Section 3

6. The Senate shall have the sole power to try all impeachments. When sitting for that purpose, they shall be on oath or affirmation. When the President of the United States is tried, the Chief Justice shall preside; and no person shall be convicted without the concurrence of two-thirds of the members present.

7. Judgment in cases of impeachment shall not extend further than to removal from office, and disqualification to hold and enjoy any office of honor, trust, or profit under the United States; but the party convicted shall, nevertheless, be liable and subject to indictment, trial, judgment, and punishment, according to law.

Section 7

2. Every bill which shall have passed the House of Representatives and the Senate shall, before it becomes a law, be presented to the President of the United States; if he approve he shall sign it, but if not he shall return it, with his objections, to that house in which it shall have originated, who shall enter the objections at large on their journal and proceed to reconsider it. If after such reconsideration two-thirds of that house shall agree to pass the bill, it shall be sent, together with the objections, to the other house, by which it shall likewise be reconsidered, and if approved by two-thirds of that house it shall become a law. But in all such cases the votes of both houses shall be determined by yeas and nays, and the names of the persons voting for and against the bill shall be entered on the journal of each house respectively. If any bill shall not be returned by the President within ten days (Sundays excepted) after it shall have been presented to him, the same shall

be a law, in like manner as if he had signed it unless the Congress by their adjournment prevent its return, in which case it shall not be a law.

3. Every order, resolution, or vote to which the concurrence of the Senate and
House of Representatives may be necessary (except on a question of adjournment)
shall be presented to the President of the United States; and before the same shall
take effect, shall be approved by him, or being disapproved by him, shall be repassed
by two-thirds of the Senate and House of Representatives, according to the rules
and limitations prescribed in the case of a bill.

ARTICLE II

Section 1

1. The executive power shall be vested in a President of the United States of
America. He shall hold his office during the term of four years, and, together with
the Vice President, chosen for the same term, be elected as follows:

2. Each state shall appoint, in such manner as the legislature thereof may direct,
a number of electors, equal to the whole number of Senators and Representatives to
which the State may be entitled in the Congress; but no Senator or Representative,
or person holding an office of trust or profit under the United States, shall be appointed an elector.

3. The electors shall meet in their respective states and vote by ballot for two
persons, of whom one at least shall not be an inhabitant of the same state with
themselves. And they shall make a list of all the persons voted for, and of the
number of votes for each; which list they shall sign and certify, and transmit sealed
to the seat of the government of the United States, directed to the President of the
Senate. The President of the Senate shall, in the presence of the Senate and House
of Representatives, open all the certificates, and the votes shall then be counted. The
person having the greatest number of votes shall be the President, if such a number
be a majority of the whole number of electors appointed; and if there be more than
one who have such a majority, and have an equal number of votes, then the House
of Representatives shall immediately choose by ballot one of them for President; and
if no person have a majority, then from the five highest on the list the said House
shall in like manner choose the President. But in choosing the President the votes
shall be taken by states, the representation from each state having one vote; a quorum
for this purpose shall consist of a member or members from two-thirds of the states,
and a majority of all the states shall be necessary to a choice. In every case, after
the choice of the President, the person having the greatest number of votes of the
electors shall be the Vice President. But if there should remain two or more who
have equal votes, the Senate shall choose from them by ballot the Vice President.
[*This paragraph was superseded by the Twelfth Amendment*]

4. The Congress may determine the time of choosing the electors and the day
on which they shall give their votes, which day shall be the same throughout the
United States.

5. No person except a natural born citizen, or a citizen of the United States at
the time of the adoption of this Constitution, shall be eligible to the office of President;
neither shall any person be eligible to that office who shall not have attained to the
age of thirty-five years, and been fourteen years a resident within the United States.

6. In case of the removal of the President from office, or of his death, resignation,
or inability to discharge the powers and duties of the said office, the same shall
devolve on the Vice President, and the Congress may by law provide for the case of
removal, death, resignation, or inability, both of the President and Vice President,
declaring what officer shall then act as President, and such officer shall act accordingly until the disability be removed or a President shall be elected. [*See also the
provisions of the Twenty-fifth Amendment*]

7. The President shall, at stated times, receive for his services a compensation, which shall neither be increased nor diminished during the period for which he shall have been elected, and he shall not receive within that period any other emolument from the United States or any of them.

8. Before he enter on the execution of his office he shall take the following oath or affirmation:

> I do solemnly swear (or affirm) that I will faithfully execute the office of the President of the United States, and will to the best of my ability preserve, protect, and defend the Constitution of the United States.

Section 2

1. The President shall be Commander-in-Chief of the Army and Navy of the United States, and of the militia of the several states when called into the actual service of the United States; he may require the opinion, in writing, of the principal officer in each of the executive departments, upon any subject relating to the duties of their respective offices, and he shall have power to grant reprieves and pardons for offenses against the United States, except in cases of impeachment.

2. He shall have power, by and with the advice and consent of the Senate, to make treaties, provided two-thirds of the Senators present concur; and he shall nominate, and, by and with the advice and consent of the Senate, shall appoint ambassadors, other public ministers and consuls, judges of the Supreme Court, and all other officers of the United States, whose appointments are not herein otherwise provided for, and which shall be established by law; but the Congress may by law vest the appointment of such inferior officers, as they think proper, in the President alone, in the courts of law, or in the heads of departments.

3. The President shall have power to fill up all vacancies that may happen during the recess of the Senate, by granting commissions which shall expire at the end of their next session.

Section 3

He shall from time to time give to the Congress information of the State of the Union, and recommend to their consideration such measures as he shall judge necessary and expedient; he may, on extraordinary occasions, convene both houses, or either of them, and in case of disagreement between them with respect to the time of adjournment, he may adjourn them to such time as he shall think proper; he shall receive ambassadors and other public ministers; he shall take care that the laws be faithfully executed, and shall commission all the officers of the United States.

Section 4

The President, Vice President, and all civil officers of the United States shall be removed from office on impeachment for and conviction of treason, bribery, or other high crimes and misdemeanors.

ARTICLE IV

Section 4

The United States shall guarantee to every State in this Union a republican form of government, and shall protect each of them against invasion; and on application of the legislature, or of the executive (when the legislature cannot be convened) against domestic violence.

ARTICLE VI

2. This Constitution, and the laws of the United States which shall be made in pursuance thereof, and all treaties made, or which shall be made, under the authority of the United States, shall be the supreme law of the land; and the judges in every State shall be bound thereby, anything in the Constitution or laws of any State to the contrary notwithstanding.

AMENDMENT XII (1804)

The electors shall meet in their respective states and vote by ballot for President and Vice President, one of whom, at least, shall not be an inhabitant of the same state with themselves; they shall name in their ballots the person voted for as President, and in distinct ballots the person voted for as Vice President, and they shall make distinct lists of all persons voted for as President and of all persons voted for as Vice President, and of the number of votes for each; which lists they shall sign and certify, and transmit sealed to the seat of the government of the United States, directed to the President of the Senate. The President of the Senate shall, in the presence of the Senate and House of Representatives, open all the certificates and the votes shall then be counted. The person having the greatest number of votes for President shall be the President, if such number be a majority of the whole number of electors appointed; and if no person have such a majority, then from the persons having the highest numbers not exceeding three on the list of those voted for as President, the House of Representatives shall choose immediately, by ballot, the President. But in choosing the President the votes shall be taken by states, the representation from each state having one vote; a quorum for this purpose shall consist of a member or members from two-thirds of the states, and a majority of all states shall be necessary to a choice. And if the House of Representatives shall not choose a President whenever the right of choice shall devolve upon them, before the fourth day of March next following, then the Vice President shall act as President, as in the case of the death or other constitutional disability of the President.

The person having the greatest number of votes as Vice President shall be the

Vice President, if such number be a majority of the whole number of electors appointed; and if no person have a majority, then from the two highest numbers on the list the Senate shall choose the Vice President; a quorum for the purpose shall consist of two-thirds of the whole number of Senators, and a majority of the whole number shall be necessary to a choice. But no person constitutionally ineligible to the office of President shall be eligible to that of Vice President of the United States.

AMENDMENT XX (1933)

Section 1

The terms of the President and Vice President shall end at noon on the 20th day of January, and the terms of Senators and Representatives at noon on the 3rd day of January, of the years in which such terms would have ended if this article had not been ratified; and the terms of their successors shall then begin.

Section 2

The Congress shall assemble at least once in every year, and such meeting shall begin at noon on the 3d day of January, unless they shall by law appoint a different day.

Section 3

If, at the time fixed for the beginning of the term of the President, the President elect shall have died, the Vice President elect shall become President. If a President shall not have been chosen before the time fixed for the beginning of his term, or if the President elect shall have failed to qualify, then the Vice President elect shall act as President until a President shall have qualified; and the Congress may by law provide for the case wherein neither a President elect nor a Vice President elect shall have qualified, declaring who shall then act as President, or the manner in which one who is to act shall be selected, and such persons shall act accordingly until a President or Vice President shall have qualified.

Section 4

The Congress may by law provide for the case of the death of any of the persons from whom the House of Representatives may choose a President whenever the right of choice shall have devolved upon them, and for the case of the death of any of the persons from whom the Senate may choose a Vice President whenever the right of choice shall have devolved upon them.

AMENDMENT XXII (1951)

No person shall be elected to the office of the President more than twice, and no person who has held the office of President, or acted as President, for more than two years of a term to which some other person was elected President shall be elected to the office of the President more than once. But this article shall not apply to any person holding the office of President when this article was proposed by the Congress, and shall not prevent any person who may be holding the office of President, or acting as President, during the term within which this article becomes operative from holding the office of President or acting as President during the remainder of such term.

AMENDMENT XXIII (1961)

Section 1

The District constituting the seat of government of the United States shall appoint in such a manner as the Congress may direct:

A number of electors of President and Vice President equal to the whole number of Senators and Representatives in Congress to which the District would be entitled if it were a State, but in no event more than the least populous state; they shall be in addition to those appointed by the States, but they shall be considered, for the purposes of the election of President and Vice President, to be electors appointed by a State; and they shall meet in the District and perform such duties as provided by the twelfth article of amendment.

AMENDMENT XXV (1967)

Section 1

In case of the removal of the President from office or of his death or resignation, the Vice President shall become President.

Section 2

Whenever there is a vacancy in the office of the Vice President, the President shall nominate a Vice President who shall take office upon confirmation by a majority vote of both Houses of Congress.

Section 3

Whenever the President transmits to the President pro tempore of the Senate and the Speaker of the House of Representatives his written declaration that he is unable to discharge the powers and duties of his office, and until he transmits to them a written declaration to the contrary, such powers and duties shall be discharged by the Vice President as Acting President.

Section 4

Whenever the Vice President and a majority of either the principal officers of the executive department or of such other body as Congress may by law provide, transmit to the President pro tempore of the Senate and the Speaker of the House of Representatives their written declaration that the President is unable to discharge the powers and duties of his office, the Vice President shall immediately assume the powers and duties of the office as Acting President.

Thereafter, when the President transmits to the President pro tempore of the Senate and the Speaker of the House of Representatives his written declaration that no inability exists, he shall resume the powers and duties of his office unless the Vice President and a majority of either the principal officers of the executive department or of such other body as Congress may by law provide, transmit within four days to the President pro tempore of the Senate and the Speaker of the House of Representatives their written declaration that the President is unable to discharge the powers and duties of his office. Thereupon Congress shall decide the issue, assembling within forty-eight hours for that purpose if not in session. If the Congress, within twenty-one days after receipt of the latter written declaration, or, if Congress is not in session, within twenty-one days after Congress is required to assemble, determines by two-thirds vote of both Houses that the President is unable to discharge the powers and duties of his office, the Vice President shall continue to discharge the same as Acting President; otherwise, the President shall resume the powers and duties of his office.

APPENDIX B

The Presidents of the United States of America

	Term of Office	Political Party	State of Residence	Inauguration Age	Sessions of Congress
George Washington	1789–1797	Fed.	Va.	57	1– 4
John Adams	1797–1801	Fed.	Mass.	61	5– 6
Thomas Jefferson	1801–1809	Dem.–Rep.	Va.	57	7–10
James Madison	1809–1817	Dem.–Rep.	Va.	57	11–14
James Monroe	1817–1825	Dem.–Rep.	Va.	58	15–18
John Q. Adams	1825–1829	Dem.–Rep.	Mass.	57	19–20
Andrew Jackson	1829–1837	Dem.	Tenn.	61	21–24
Martin Van Buren	1837–1841	Dem.	N.Y.	54	25–26
William Harrison	1841	Whig	Ind.	68	27
John Tyler	1841–1845	Dem.*	Va.	51	27–28
James K. Polk	1845–1849	Dem.	Tenn.	49	29–30
Zachary Taylor	1849–1850	Whig	La.	64	31
Millard Fillmore	1850–1853	Whig	N.Y.	48	31–32
Franklin Pierce	1853–1857	Dem.	N.H.	50	33–34
James Buchanan	1857–1861	Dem.	Pa.	65	35–36
Abraham Lincoln	1861–1865	Rep.	Ill.	52	37–38
Andrew Johnson	1865–1869	Union†	Tenn.	56	39–40
Ulysses Grant	1869–1877	Rep.	Ohio	46	41–44
Rutherford Hayes	1877–1881	Rep.	Ohio	54	45–46
James A. Garfield	1881	Rep.	Ohio	49	47
Chester Arthur	1881–1885	Rep.	N.Y.	50	47–48
Grover Cleveland	1885–1889	Dem.	N.Y.	47	49–50
Benjamin Harrison	1889–1893	Rep.	Ind.	55	51–52
Grover Cleveland	1893–1897	Dem.	N.Y.	55	53–54
William McKinley	1897–1901	Rep.	Ohio	54	55–56
Theodore Roosevelt	1901–1909	Rep.	N.Y.	42	57–60
William Taft	1909–1913	Rep.	Ohio	51	61–62

* Elected on Whig ticket, affiliated with congressional Democrats.
† Elected on Unionist and Republican slates.

	Term of Office	Political Party	State of Residence	Inaugu- ration Age	Sessions of Congress
Woodrow Wilson	1913–1921	Dem.	N.J.	56	63–66
Warren Harding	1921–1923	Rep.	Ohio	55	67
Calvin Coolidge	1923–1929	Rep.	Mass.	51	68–70
Herbert Hoover	1929–1933	Rep.	Calif.	54	71–72
Franklin Roosevelt	1933–1945	Dem.	N.Y.	51	73–78
Harry Truman	1945–1953	Dem.	Mo.	60	79–82
Dwight Eisenhower	1953–1961	Rep.	N.Y.	62	83–86
John Kennedy	1961–1963	Dem.	Mass.	43	87–88
Lyndon Johnson	1963–1969	Dem.	Texas	55	88–90
Richard Nixon	1969–1974	Rep.	Calif.	56	91–93
Gerald Ford, Jr.	1974–1977	Rep.	Mich.	61	93–94
James E. Carter	1977–	Dem.	Ga.	52	95–

APPENDIX C

Guide to Research on the Presidency

I. EXECUTIVE BRANCH

A. The texts of speeches, news conferences, proclamations, executive orders, messages transmitted to Congress, and other White House papers are printed in the *Weekly Compilation of Presidential Documents* (National Archives and Records Service). Presidential orders and proclamations are reported daily (except Monday) in *The Federal Register* and are codified in the *Code of Federal Regulations* (National Archives and Records Service). (Consult the Supplement to Title 3: The President, for the period June 2, 1943–December 31, 1958, and the *List and Index of Presidential Executive Orders* for the period 1789–1941.)

Presidential powers are interpreted in the *Opinions of the Attorney General* (Vols. 1–41, Department of Justice) and in briefs prepared by the Office of Counsel, Department of State, reprinted in *Department of State Bulletin* (1939–).

Texts of treaties ratified and in force, and of executive agreements negotiated solely by the president, are contained in *Treaties and Other International Acts Series* (1946–). Also see the *Treaty Series* (1908–1945), *Executive Agreement Series* (1929–1946), and *Treaties, Conventions, International Acts, Protocols and Agreements Between the United States of America and Other Powers* (1776–1937). All are issued by the Department of State.

A useful compendium of materials involving the prerogatives of the presidential office is contained in William M. Goldsmith, *The Growth of Presidential Powers*. 3 vols. (New York: Chelsea House, 1974).

B. A listing of the published writings of presidents is contained in Donald H. Mugridge, *The Presidents of the United States, 1789–1962, A Selected List of References* (Library of Congress, 1963).

Important collections of presidential papers include: Jared Sparks, ed., *The Writings of George Washington* (New York: Harper and Brothers, 1847–52); John C. Fitzpatrick, ed., *Writings of George Washington*. 39 vols. (Washington, D.C.: U.S. Government Printing Office, 1931–44); Charles F. Adams, ed., *The Works of John Adams*. 10 vols. (Freeport, New York: Books for Libraries Press, 1969); Julian P. Boyd, ed., *The Papers of Thomas Jefferson* (Princeton: Princeton University Press, 1950–); Gaillard P. Hunt, ed., *Writings of James Madison* (New York: G.P. Putnam's Sons, 1900–1910); Stanislaus Murray Hamilton, ed., *The Writings of James Monroe* (New York: AMS Press, 1969); Charles F. Adams, ed., *The Memoirs of John Quincy Adams* (Philadelphia: J.B. Lippincott, and Co., 1874–1877); John Spencer Bassett, ed., *Correspondence of Andrew Jackson* (Washington, D.C.: Carnegie Institution of Washington, 1926–1935); Martin Van Buren, *The Autobiography of Martin Van Buren* (New York: A.M. Kelley, 1969); Lyon G. Tyler, *The Letters and Times of the Tylers* (New York: Da Capo Press, 1970); Milo M. Quaife, ed., *The Diary of James K. Polk* (Chicago: A.C. McClurg and Co., 1910); Frank Severence, ed., *The Millard Fillmore Papers* (Buffalo: Buffalo Historical Society, 1907); J.B. Moore, ed., *The Works of James Buchanan*; J.G. Nicolay and J. Hay, eds., *Complete Works of Abraham Lincoln* (Harrogate: Lincoln Memorial University, 1927); Charles Williams, ed., *Diary and Letters of Rutherford Birchard Hayes* (Columbus: The Ohio State Archeological and Historical Society, 1922–1926); George F. Parker, ed., *Writings and Speeches of Grover Cleveland* (New York: Kraus Reprint Co., 1970); Grover Cleveland, *Presidential Problems* (New York: The Century Co., 1904); Benjamin Harrison, *This Country of Ours* (New York: Scribner's Sons, 1901); Hermann Hagedorn, *The Works of Theodore Roosevelt* (New York: Scribner's Sons, 1926); Theodore Roosevelt, *An Autobiography* (New York: Macmillan, 1919); William Howard Taft, *Our Chief Magistrate and His Powers* (New York: Columbia University Press, 1916); R.S. Baker and W.E. Dodd, eds., *The Public Papers of Woodrow Wilson* (New York: Harper and Brothers, 1925); Woodrow Wilson, *Constitutional Government in the United States* (New York: Columbia University Press, 1908); Calvin Coolidge, *The Autobiography of Calvin Coolidge* (New York: Cosmopolitan Book Co., 1929); William Myers, ed., *The State Papers and Other Public Writings of Herbert Hoover* (Garden City, N.Y.: Doubleday Doran and Co., Inc., 1934); Herbert Hoover, *Memoirs*. 2 vols. (New York: Macmillan, 1951); Samuel Rosenman, ed., *The Public Papers and Addresses of Franklin D. Roosevelt* (New York: Random House, The Macmillan Co., Harper Brothers, 1938–1950); Harry Truman, *Memoirs*. 2 vols. (Garden City, N.Y.: Doubleday, 1955–1956); Dwight Eisenhower, *The White House Years* (Garden City, N.Y.: Doubleday, 1965); Lyndon Johnson, *The Vantage Point* (New York: Holt, Rinehart & Winston, 1971); Richard Nixon, *RN* (New York: Grosset & Dunlap, 1978). Also see James D. Richardson, ed., *A Compilation of the Messages and Papers of the Presidents, 1789–1897* (Washington, D.C.: U.S. Government Printing Office, 1896–1899); *Public Papers of the Presidents of the United States* (Washington, D.C.: Federal Register Division, 1958–).

C. Deposits in the National Archives System include: Herbert Hoover Library, West Branch, Iowa; Franklin D. Roosevelt Library, Hyde Park, New York; Harry S. Truman Library, Independence, Missouri; Dwight Eisenhower Library, Abilene, Kansas; John F. Kennedy Library, Cambridge, Massachusetts; Lyndon B. Johnson Library, Austin, Texas; Gerald R. Ford Library, University of Michigan, Ann Arbor, Michigan. The use of materials in presidential libraries is discussed in several journal articles, including: G.L. Cole, "Presidential Libraries," *Journal of Librarianship*, Vol. 4, 1972, pp. 115–129; Clement Vose, "Presidential Papers as a Political Science Concern." *PS*, Winter, 1975, pp. 8–18.

D. Useful annual bibliographies on the presidency are prepared by The Center for the Study of the Presidency, 926 Fifth Avenue, New York, N.Y. The most comprehensive bibliography of the modern presidential office, consisting of 2,500 works, is Fred Greenstein, et al., *Evolution of the Modern Presidency: A Bibliographical Survey* (Washington, D.C.: American Enterprise Institute for Public Policy Research, 1977).

II. THE LEGISLATIVE BRANCH

A. Publications of Congress are listed in a monthly index, *CIS/Index* (Congressional Information Service). Bills and resolutions introduced by members are found in the *Digest of Public General Bills and Selected Resolutions*, issued in five cumulative volumes for each session of Congress. Proposed constitutional amendments are compiled in Herman Ames, *The Proposed Amendments to the Constitution of the United States During the First Century of its History* (54th Cong., 2nd Sess., H. Doc. 353, part 2), covering 1789–1889; Michael Musmanno, *Proposed Amendments to the Constitution* (70th Cong., 2nd Sess., H. Doc. 551) covering 1889–1928; Richard D. Hupman, *Proposed Amendments to the Constitution of the United States* (Washington, D.C.: Government Printing Office, 1970) covering 1926–1969.

B. Hearings held by congressional committees are listed in library holdings by legislative chamber, name of committee, and name of subcommittee. They are listed in the *CIS/Index*, the Commerce Clearing House *CCH Congressional Index*, and the *Monthly Catalogue of United States Government Publications* (1963–). The *Cumulative Index of Congressional Committee Hearings* lists hearings held between 1935 and 1963, and the *Checklist of U.S. Public Documents* provides a listing for hearings between 1789 and 1909 on pp. 1532–1652. Also see W.W. Buchanan and E.A. Kanely, *Cumulative Subject Index to the Monthly Catalogue of United States Government Publications: 1900–1971* (Washington, D.C.: Carrollton Press, 1973–).

C. Committee reports are listed, by name of issuing committee, in the *Monthly Catalogue of United States Government Publications*. Some reports are reprinted in *United States Code Congressional and Administrative News* (West Publishing Company). Since 1970, Congressional Information Service (CIS) has abstracted hearings, reports, and documents in Volume I and provides an index to the legislative histories of public laws in Volume II. *The Congressional Set* contains the bound volumes, arranged by committee, of reports issued since 1817. To locate the volume in which a particular report is found, consult the *Monthly Catalogue of United States Government Publications* and locate the special report number accompanying the listing. Then consult the *Numerical List of Reports and Documents*, which indicates the bound volume corresponding to the special report number.

D. Presidential messages to Congress, texts of legislation considered, proposed constitutional amendments, debates and votes on legislation, and other congressional business are contained in *The Congressional Record*, published daily when either chamber is in session, since 1873. Its predecessors are *Annals of Congress* (1789–1824), *Register of Debates* (1824–1837) and *Congressional Globe* (1833–1873).

E. Laws of the United States are bound by date of passage in *United States Statutes at Large* (1789–). Laws are arranged by subject matter and codified in the *United States Code* (General Printing Office). A private version of the code, *United States Code Annotated* (West Publishing Co.), adds judicial decisions and executive orders related to the legislation. The *United States Code* contains a table that indicates the relationship of each section of the laws to the *Code of Federal Regulations* (General Printing Office). By using the two codes, one can find the executive orders that implement the legislation.

F. *Decisions of the Comptroller General*, issued irregularly, deals with the legality of expenditures within the executive branch, and therefore at times with presidential authority. It is published by the General Accounting Office.

III. THE JUDICIAL BRANCH

A. The cases decided by the United States Supreme Court appear in *United States Law Week* (Washington, D.C.: Bureau of National Affairs). Monthly and yearly cumulations of decisions are contained in *Lawyer's Edition, U.S. Supreme Court Reports* (Washington, D.C.: Lawyers Cooperative Publishing Company). Most cases decided by the Federal Courts of Appeals are contained in *Federal Reporter, 2nd Series* (West Publishing Company). Selected cases from Federal District Courts are reported in the *Federal Supplement* (West Publishing Company).

B. Legal encyclopedias provide full annotations to relevant cases, statutes, and executive actions. Annual Supplements are provided. Two useful editions are *Corpus Juris Secundum*, Volume 16: Constitutional Law (West Publishing Company) and *American Jurisprudence, 2nd*, Volume 16: Constitutional Law (Lawyers Cooperative Publishing Co.).

C. A citator determines the status of a decision. It indicates whether the case is still controlling, or whether it has been modified, distinguished, or reversed by subsequent decisions. *Shepard's United States Citations, First Section: The United States Constitution*, lists all federal cases concerned with the Constitution.

D. The work of the Supreme Court is reviewed annually by the *Harvard Law Review* and the *Supreme Court Review* of the University of Chicago, and in the first editions of *U.S. Law Week* each October.

E. The *Index to Legal Periodicals* lists law review articles by author and subject (1908–). The *Index to Legal Periodical Literature* (Vols. I–III) is used for the period 1791–1908. *Law Books in Print* (1965) and its supplements are arranged by author and subject.

IV. RESEARCH GUIDES

Laurence F. Schmeckebier and Roy B. Easton, *Government Publications and Their Use*, 2nd rev. ed. (Washington, D.C.: The Brookings Institution, 1969); John B. Mason, *Research Sources, Annotated Guide to the Social Sciences, II* (Santa Barbara: ABC–CLIO, 1971); Clement Vose, *A Guide to Library Sources in Political Science* (Washington, D.C.: The American Political Science Association, 1975); J. Myron Jacobstein and Roy M. Mersky, *Fundamentals of Legal Research* (Mineola: The Foundation Press, Inc., 1977).

FOR FURTHER
REFERENCE

The Classics: Augustus B. Woodward, Considerations on Executive Government in the United States (Flatbush, N.Y.: I. Riley, 1809) and The Presidency of the United States (New York: D. Van Veighton, 1825); Henry Lockwood, The Abolition of the Presidency (New York: R. Worthington, 1884); James Bryce, The American Commonwealth (London: The Macmillan Co., 1888); Henry Jones Ford, The Rise and Growth of American Politics (London: The Macmillan Co., 1898); Wilfred Binkley, The Powers of the President (New York: Doubleday and Doran, 1937); Pendleton Herring, Presidential Leadership (New York: 1940); Harold Laski, The American Presidency (New York: Harper and Brothers, 1940).

Significant Modern Works: Richard Hofstadter, The American Political Tradition (New York: Alfred A. Knopf, 1948); Louis Brownlow, The President and the Presidency (Chicago: Public Administration Service, 1949); Clinton Rossiter, The American Presidency (New York: Harcourt, Brace and World, 1956); Edward Corwin, The President: Office and Powers, 4th ed. (New York: New York University Press, 1957); Rexford Tugwell, The Enlargement of the Presidency (New York: Doubleday, 1960); Richard Neustadt, Presidential Power (New York: John Wiley and Sons, 1960); Louis Koenig, The Chief Executive (New York: Harcourt, Brace, Jovanovich, 1975); James MacGregor Burns, Presidential Government (New York: Avon, 1965); Joseph Kallenbach, The American Chief Executive (New York: Harper and Row, 1966); James Barber, The Presidential Character (Englewood Cliffs: Prentice-Hall, 1972); Erwin Hargrove, The Power of the Modern Presidency (Philadelphia: Temple University Press, 1974); Henry Steele Commager, The Defeat of America: Presidential Power and the National Character (New York: Simon and Schuster, 1975); Arthur M. Schlesinger, Jr., The Imperial Presidency (Boston: Houghton Mifflin, 1973).

Executive Power in Provincial and State Governments: Evarts B. Greene, The Provincial Governor in the English Colonies of North America (New York: Longman's Greene and Co., 1898); William C. Morey, "The First State Constitutions," The Annals of the American Academy of Political and Social Science, Vol. 4 (Philadelphia, American Academy of Political and Social Science, 1894); George Bancroft, History of the United States (New York: D. Appleton and Co., 1892); Edward Channing, A History of the United States (New York: The Macmillan Co., 1912).

The Executive Power in Continental and Confederation Government: Edward Corwin, "The Progress of Constitutional Theory Between the Declaration of Independence and the Meeting of the Philadelphia Convention," *American Historical Review*, Vol. 30, 1925; Edmund C. Burnett, *The Continental Congress* (New York: W.W. Norton and Co., 1941); Merrill Jensen, *The Articles of Confederation* (Madison, Wisc.: The University of Wisconsin Press, 1940); Jennings B. Sanders, *The Presidency of the Continental Congress* (Gloucester, Mass.: Peter Smith Publishers, 1961) and *Evolution of the Executive Departments of the Continental Congress* (Chapel Hill, N.C.: University of North Carolina Press, 1935).

Creation of the Presidency: Max Farrand, *The Records of the Federal Convention of 1787* (New Haven: Yale University Press, 1937); Charles Thach, *The Creation of the Presidency* (Baltimore: The Johns Hopkins Press, 1922); Charles Warren, *The Making of the Constitution* (Boston: Little Brown, 1937); Gordon Wood, *The Creation of the American Republic: 1776–1789* (Chapel Hill, N.C.: University of North Carolina Press, 1969); James Flexner, *George Washington and the New Nation* (Boston: Little Brown, 1969); Max M. Mintz, *Gouverneur Morris and the American Revolution* (Norman, Okla.: University of Oklahoma Press, 1970); Charles Smith, *James Wilson* (Chapel Hill, N.C.: University of North Carolina Press, 1956); Clinton Rossiter, *Alexander Hamilton and the Constitution* (New York: Harcourt, Brace and World, Inc., 1964); Irving Brant, *Madison*, Vol. III, (New York: Bobbs-Merrill Co., 1941).

Ratification Controversies: Jonathan Elliot, *The Debates of the Several State Conventions* (Philadelphia: J.B. Lippincott, 1896); Jackson Main, *The Anti-Federalists* (Chapel Hill, N.C.: University of North Carolina Press, 1961); Paul Ford, *Pamphlets on the Constitution of the United States* (Brooklyn: Historical Printing Club, 1888); Michael Riccards, "The Presidency and the Ratification Controversy," *Presidential Studies Quarterly*, Vol. VII, No. 1, Winter, 1977; Cecilia Kenyon, "Men of Little Faith," *The William and Mary Quarterly*, Vol. XII, No. 1, January 1955.

Prerogative Powers: Edward Corwin, *The President: Office and Powers*, 4th ed. (New York: New York University Press, 1957); Clinton Rossiter, *Constitutional Dictatorship* (New York: Harcourt, Brace and World, 1963); Louis Henkin, *Foreign Affairs and the Constitution* (Mineola: The Foundation Press, 1972); Arthur M. Schlesinger, Jr., *The Imperial Presidency* (Boston: Houghton Mifflin, 1973); James G. Randall, *Constitutional Problems Under Lincoln* (Urbana, Ill.: University of Illinois, 1964); Louis Koenig, *The Presidency and the Crisis* (New York: King's Crown Press, 1944); Maeva Marcus, *Truman and the Steel Seizure Case* (New York: Columbia University Press, 1977); Michael Benedict, *The Impeachment and Trial of Andrew Johnson* (New York: W.W. Norton, 1973); Irving Brant, *Impeachment* (New York: Alfred A. Knopf, 1972); Raoul Berger, *Impeachment* (Cambridge: Harvard University Press, 1973); Charles Black, *Impeachment* (New Haven, Yale University Press, 1974); "Symposium: United States v. Nixon," *UCLA Law Review*, Vol. 22, No. 1, October 1974; House of Representatives, *Impeachment of Richard M. Nixon, President of the United States, Final Report* (New York: Bantam Books, 1975); David Wise, *The American Police State* (New York: Random House, 1976); Morton Halperin and Daniel Hoffman, eds., *Freedom vs. National Security* (New York: Chelsea House, 1977); Theodore Sorensen, *Watchman in the Night* (Cambridge: MIT Press, 1975); Paul Halpern, ed., *Why Watergate?* (Pacific Palisades, Calif.: Palisades Press, 1975).

Presidential Elections: Gerald Pomper, *Elections in America* (New York: Dodd Mead, 1973); Donald Matthews, *Perspectives on Presidential Selection* (Washington, D.C.: The Brookings Institution, 1973); James Barber, *Choosing the President* (Englewood Cliffs: Prentice-Hall, 1974); Nelson Polsby and Aaron Wildavsky, *Presidential Elections*, 4th ed. (New York: Charles Scribner's Sons, 1975).

Primaries: Louise Overacker, *The Presidential Primary* (New York: Macmillan, 1926); William Keech and David Matthews, *The Party's Choice* (Washington, D.C.: The Brookings Institution, 1976); James Davis, *Presidential Primaries* (New York: Thomas Y. Crowell, 1967); Gerald Pomper, *Nominating the President* (Chicago: Northwestern University Press, 1963); Edward Merriam, *Primary Elections* (Chicago: University of Chicago Press, 1908); Austin Ranney, *Participation in American Presidential Nominations, 1976* (Washington, D.C.: The American Enterprise Institute, 1977).

Conventions: Paul David et al., *The Politics of National Party Conventions* (New

York: Random House, 1964); Judith Parris, *The Convention Problem* (Washington, D.C.: The Brookings Institution, 1972); Jeffrey Pressman et al., *The Politics of Representation* (New York: St. Martins Press, 1974); Denis Sullivan et al., *Explorations in Convention Decision-Making* (San Francisco: W.H. Freeman and Co., 1976); Jeane Kirkpatrick, *The New Presidential Elite* (New York: Russell Sage, 1976).

Election Campaigning: Theodore White, *The Making of the President, 1960* (New York: Atheneum, 1961); Lewis Chester et al., *An American Melodrama* (New York: The Viking Press, 1969); Joseph McGinnis, *The Selling of the President, 1968* (New York: Trident Press, 1969); Hunter Thompson, *Fear and Loathing on the Campaign Trail* (San Francisco: Straight Arrow Press, 1973); Martin Schramm, *Running for President, 1976* (New York: Stein and Day, 1977); Clifford Brown and the Ripon Society, *The Jaws of Victory* (Boston: Little Brown, 1974).

Media Politics: Stanley Kelley, *Professional Public Relations and Political Power* (Baltimore: The Johns Hopkins Press, 1956); Harold Mendlsohn and Irving Crespi, *Polls, Television and the New Politics* (Scranton: Chandler Publishers, 1970); Melvyn Bloom, *Public Relations and Presidential Campaigns* (New York: Thomas Y. Crowell, 1973); Robert Agranoff, ed., *The New Style in Election Campaigns* (Boston: Holbrooke Press, 1972); Thomas Patterson and Thomas McClure, *The Unseeing Eye* (New York: Putnam's Sons, 1976).

Campaign Finance: Louise Overacker, *Presidential Campaign Funds* (Boston: Boston University Press, 1946); Alexander Heard, *The Costs of Democracy* (Chapel Hill, N.C.: University of North Carolina Press, 1960); Herbert Alexander, *Financing the 1968 Election* (Lexington, Mass.: D.C. Heath, 1971); Delmer Dunn, *Financing Presidential Campaigns* (Washington, D.C.: The Brookings Institution, 1972); David Adamany and George Agree, *Political Money* (Baltimore: The Johns Hopkins Press, 1975).

The Electoral College: Lucius Wilmerding, *The Electoral College* (New Brunswick, N.J.: Rutgers University Press, 1958); Laurence Longley and Alan Brown, *The Politics of Electoral College Reform* (New Haven: Yale University Press, 1972); Wallace Sayre and Judith Parris, *Voting for President* (Washington, D.C.: The Brookings Institution, 1970).

Succession Procedures: Ruth Silva, *Presidential Succession* (Ann Arbor, Mich.: University of Michigan, 1951); John Feerick, *From Failing Hands* (New York: Fordham University Press, 1965) and *The Twenty-Fifth Amendment* (New York: Fordham University Press, 1976); Allen Sindler, *Unchosen Presidents* (Berkeley: University of California Press, 1976).

Party Government: E.E. Schattschneider, *Party Government* (New York: Holt, Rinehart and Winston, 1942); Stephen Bailey, *The Condition of Our National Political Parties* (New York: The Fund for the Republic, 1959); James Macgregor Burns, *The Deadlock of Democracy* (Englewood Cliffs, N.J.: Prentice-Hall, 1963); Austin Ranney, *The Doctrine of Responsible Party Government* (Urbana, Ill.: University of Illinois Press, 1954) and *Curing the Mischiefs of Faction* (Berkeley: University of California Press, 1975); Charles Hardin, *Presidential Power and Accountability* (Chicago: University of Chicago Press, 1974); Hugh Bone, *Party Committees and National Politics* (Seattle: University of Washington Press, 1958); Cornelius Cotter and Bernard Hennessy, *Politics Without Power* (New York: Atherton Press, 1964); V.O. Key, *Politics, Parties and Pressure Groups* (New York: Thomas Y. Crowell, 1964); David Broder, *The Party's Over* (New York: Harper and Row, 1972); Edward Flynn, *You're the Boss* (New York: Viking Press, 1947); James Farley, *Jim Farley's Story* (New York: McGraw-Hill, 1948); Lawrence O'Brien, *No Final Victories* (New York: Doubleday, 1974); Hugh Scott, *Come to the Party* (Englewood Cliffs: Prentice-Hall, 1968).

Program Innovation: Stephen J. Wayne, *The Legislative Presidency* (New York: Harper and Row, 1978); James Macgregor Burns, *Presidential Government* (New York: Avon, 1965); Lawrence Chamberlain, *President, Congress, and Legislation* (New York: Columbia University Press, 1946); David Truman, *The Governmental Process* (New York: Alfred A. Knopf, 1951); Theodore Lowi, *The End of Liberalism* (New York: W.W. Norton, 1969); John Kessel, *The Domestic Presidency* (Belmont: Wadsworth, 1975); James Sundquist, *Politics and Policy* (Washington, D.C.: The Brookings Institution, 1968); Henry Laurin, *Presidential Transitions* (Washington,

D.C.: Public Affairs Press, 1960); Norman Thomas and Hans W. Baade, eds., *The Institutionalized Presidency* (Dobbs Ferry, N.Y.: Oceana, 1972).

Congressional Innovation: Ronald Moe, ed., *Congress and the President* (Pacific Palisades, Calif.: Goodyear, 1971); John Johannes, *Congress and Policy Innovation* (Morristown, N.J.: General Learning Press, 1972); David Price, *Who Makes the Laws?* (New York: Schenkman, 1972); Frederic Cleaveland, *Congress and Urban Problems* (Washington, D.C.: The Brookings Institution, 1969); David Truman, *Congress and America's Future* (Englewood Cliffs, N.J.: Prentice-Hall, 1965); Harvey Mansfield, ed., *Congress Against the President* (New York: Praeger, 1976); Gary Orfield, *Congressional Power* (New York: Harcourt, Brace, Jovanovich, 1975).

Legislative Leadership: Randall Ripley, *Congress* (New York: W.W. Norton, 1975); Lewis Froman, *The Congressional Process* (Boston: Little, Brown, 1967); Bertram Gross, *The Legislative Struggle* (New York: McGraw-Hill, 1953); Pendleton Herring, *Presidential Leadership* (New York: Rinehart, 1940); Norman Ornstein, ed., *Congress in Change* (New York: Praeger, 1975); Donald Matthews, *U.S. Senators and Their World* (Chapel Hill, N.C.: University of North Carolina Press, 1960); Randall Ripley, *Power in the Senate* (New York: St. Martins Press, 1969); Joseph Clark, *The Senate Establishment* (New York: Hill and Wang, 1963); Neil McNeill, *The Forge of Democracy* (New York: David McKay, 1963); Richard Bolling, *House Out of Order* (New York: Dutton, 1965); Randall Ripley, *Party Leaders in the House of Representatives* (Washington, D.C.: The Brookings Institution, 1967); Nelson Polsby et al., "The Institutionalization of the U.S. House of Representatives," *The American Political Science Review*, Vol. 62, No. 1, March 1968.

Congressional Committees: Lauros McConachie, *Congressional Committees* (New York: Thomas Y. Crowell, 1898); Woodrow Wilson, *Congressional Government* (New York: Houghton Mifflin, 1885); James Robinson, *The House Rules Committee* (Indianapolis: Bobbs-Merrill Co., 1963); Richard Fenno, *Congressmen in Committees* (Boston: Little Brown, 1973); George Goodwin, *Little Legislatures* (Amherst, Mass.: University of Massachusetts Press, 1970).

Congressional Voting: Lewis Froman, *Congressmen and Their Constituencies* (Chicago: Rand McNally, 1963); David Mayhew, *Party Loyalty Among Congressmen* (Cambridge: Harvard University Press, 1966); John Kingdon, *Congressmen's Voting Decisions* (New York: Harper and Row, 1973); W. Wayne Shannon, *Party, Constituency, and Congressional Voting* (Baton Rouge, La.: Louisiana State University Press, 1970); Aage Clausen, *How Congressmen Decide* (New York: St. Martins Press, 1975).

National Agenda Politics: Elmer Cornwell, *Presidential Leadership of Public Opinion* (Bloomington, Ind.: Indiana University Press, 1965); Edward Chester, *Radio, Television and American Politics* (New York: Sheed and Ward, 1969); Bernard Rubin, *Political Television* (Belmont: Wadsworth Publishing Co., 1967); Newton Minow et al., *Presidential Television* (New York: Basic Books, 1973); James Pollard, *The Presidents and the Press* (Washington, D.C.: Public Affairs Press, 1964).

Veto Powers: Carleton Jackson, *Presidential Vetoes: 1792–1945* (Athens, Ga.: University of Georgia Press, 1967); Edward Mason, *The Veto Power* (Harvard Historical Monograph No. 1, 1890); Charles Zinn, *The Veto Power of the President* (Washington, D.C.: Government Printing Office, 1951); U.S. Senate, Committee on the Judiciary, Subcommittee on the Separation of Powers, "Constitutionality of the President's Pocket Veto Power," Hearings, 92nd Cong., 1st Sess., 1971 (Washington, D.C.: Government Printing Office, 1971).

Administrative Leadership: Thomas Cronin, *The State of the Presidency* (Boston: Little, Brown, 1975); Graham Allison, *Essence of Decision* (Boston: Little, Brown, 1971); Harold Seidman, *Politics, Position and Power* (New York: Oxford University Press, 1974); Harold Smith, *The Management of Your Government* (New York: McGraw-Hill, 1945); Richard Fenno, *The President's Cabinet* (Cambridge: Harvard University Press, 1959); Patrick Anderson, *The President's Men* (Garden City, N.Y.: Doubleday, 1968); Edward Hobbes, *Behind the President* (Washington, D.C.: Public Affairs Press, 1954); Louis Koenig, *The Invisible Presidency* (New York: Holt, Rinehart & Winston, 1960); Richard Johnson, *Managing the White House* (New York: Harper and Row, 1974); Richard Rose, *Managing Presidential Objectives* (New York: The Free Press, 1976); Richard Nathan, *The Plot that Failed* (New York:

John Wiley and Sons, 1975); Stephen Hess, *Organizing the Presidency* (Washington, D.C.: The Brookings Institution, 1976).

Political Executives and Careerists: Anthony Downs, *Inside Bureaucracy* (Boston: Little Brown, 1967); William Niskanen, *Bureaucracy and Representative Government* (Chicago: Aldine, 1971); Wallace Sayre, ed., *The Federal Government Service* (Englewood Cliffs, N.J.: Prentice-Hall, 1965); John Corson and Paul Shale, *Men Near the Top* (Baltimore: The Johns Hopkins Press, 1966); David Stanley et al., *Men Who Govern* (Washington, D.C.: The Brookings Institution, 1967); Hugo Heclo, *A Government of Strangers* (Washington, D.C.: The Brookings Institution, 1977); Edward Weisband and Thomas Franck, *Resignation in Protest* (New York: Grossman, 1975).

Congressional Oversight: Joseph Harris, *Congressional Control of Administration* (Washington, D.C.: The Brookings Institution, 1964); Louis Fisher, *President and Congress* (New York: The Free Press, 1972); Alfred deGrazia, ed., *Congress: The First Branch* (New York: Doubleday, 1967); Morris Ogul, *Congress Oversees the Bureaucracy* (Pittsburgh, Pa.: University of Pittsburgh Press, 1976); House of Representatives, Committee on Government Operations, "Extent of the Control of the Executive by the Congress of the United States," Committee Print, 87th Cong., 2nd Sess., 1962 (Washington, D.C.: Government Printing Office, 1962).

Studies on Organization of the Executive Branch: President's Committee on Administrative Management, *Report with Special Studies* (Washington, D.C.: Government Printing Office, 1937); Commission on the Organization of the Executive Branch of Government, *General Management of the Executive Branch* (Washington, D.C.: Government Printing Office, 1949); The President's Task Force on Government Reorganization, *Report: The President and his Executive Office* (Washington, D.C.: Government Printing Office, 1967); Committee on Post Office and Civil Service, *Report on the Growth of the Executive Office of the President, 1955–1973*, House of Representatives, 93rd Cong., 1st Sess. (Government Printing Office, 1973); Transition Study Team, White House Study Project, "Analysis of the Executive Office of the President," Report No. 2, December 3, 1976; President's Reorganization Project, *Report: Reorganization of the Executive Office of the President*, July, 1977.

The Budgetary Process: William Willoughby, *The National Budget System* (Baltimore: The Johns Hopkins Press, 1927); Arthur Smithies, *The Budgetary Process in the United States* (New York: McGraw-Hill, 1955); Aaron Wildavsky, *The Politics of the Budgetary Process*, 2nd ed. (Boston: Little Brown, 1974); William Niskanen, *Structural Reform of the Federal Budget Process* (Washington, D.C.: The American Enterprise Institute, 1973); Lance LeLoup, *Budget Politics* (Brunswick, Ohio: King's Court Press, 1977).

Agency and Department Budgeting: Samuel Huntington, *The Common Defense* (New York: Columbia University Press, 1961); Ralph Sanders, *The Politics of Defense Analysis* (New York: Dunellen Publishing Co., 1973); Frederick Mosher and John Harr, *Programming Systems and Foreign Affairs Leadership* (New York: Oxford University Press, 1970); Randall Ripley and Grace Franklin, eds., *Policy-Making in the Federal Executive Branch* (New York: The Free Press, 1975).

Presidential Budgeting: Charles F. Dawes, *The First Year of the Budget of the United States* (New York: Harper and Brothers, 1923); Fritz M. Marx, "The Bureau of the Budget: Its Evolution and Present Role," Parts I, II, *The American Political Science Review*, Vol. 39, No. 4, August, 1945, pp. 653–84, No. 5, October, 1945, pp. 869–98; Allen Schick, "The Budget Bureau that Was," *Law and Contemporary Problems*, Vol. 35, No. 3, Summer 1970, pp. 519–39; Percival Brundage, *The Bureau of the Budget* (New York: Praeger, 1970); Hugh Heclo, "OMB and the Presidency —the Problem of 'Neutral Competence,'" *The Public Interest*, Vol. 38, Winter 1975, pp. 80–98; Bureau of the Budget, "Steering Group Evaluation of the Bureau of the Budget," Vols. I–III (Washington, D.C.: Office of Management and Budget, 1967); President's Reorganization Project, "OMB Report and Survey" (Washington, D.C.: Office of Management and Budget, 1977).

Congressional Appropriating Powers: Richard Fenno, *The Power of the Purse* (Boston: Little, Brown, 1966); Stephen Horn, *Unused Power* (Washington, D.C.: The Brookings Institution, 1970); Robert Wallace, *Congressional Control of Federal Spending* (Detroit: Wayne State University Press, 1960); Joseph Harris, *Congressional*

Control of Administration (Washington, D.C.: The Brookings Institution, 1964); Allen Schick, "The Battle of the Budget," in Harvey Mansfield, Sr., ed., *Congress Against the President* (New York: Praeger, 1976); Edward Kolodziej, *The Uncommon Defense* (Athens, Oh.: Ohio State University Press, 1966).

Impoundment Powers: Warren Archer, "Presidential Impoundment of Funds," *University of Chicago Law Review*, Vol. 40, Winter, 1973, pp. 328–57; Ralph Abascal and John Kramer, "Presidential Impoundment," Part II, *Georgetown Law Journal*, Vol. 63; October, 1974, pp. 149–185; Law Note, "Protecting the Fisc: Executive Impoundment and Congressional Power," *The Yale Law Journal*, Vol. 82, No. 8, July 1973, pp. 1636–1658; Allen Schick, "Budget Reform Legislation: Reorganizing Congressional Centers of Fiscal Power," *Harvard Journal of Legislation*, Vol. 11, No. 2, February, 1974, pp. 303–350; Senate Subcommittee on the Impoundment of Funds, Committee on Government Operations, Subcommittee on the Separation of Powers, Committee on the Judiciary, *Joint Hearings*, January 30, 31, February 1, 6, 7, 1973, Vol. I, 93rd Cong., 1st Sess. (Washington, D.C.: Government Printing Office, 1973); House Committee on Rules, "Impoundment Reporting and Review," Hearings, Parts I–II, 93rd Cong., 1st Sess. (Washington, D.C.: Government Printing Office, 1973); House Committee on Government Operations, "Presidential Impoundment of Congressionally Appropriated Funds," Committee Print, 93rd Cong., 2nd Sess. (Washington, D.C.: Government Printing Office, 1974).

Spending Powers: Lucius Wilmerding, *The Spending Power* (New Haven: Yale University Press, 1943); Louis Fisher, *Presidential Spending Power* (Princeton: Princeton University Press, 1975).

Fiscal Policy-Making: Gordon Bach, *Making Monetary and Fiscal Policy* (Washington, D.C.: The Brookings Institution, 1971); Lawrence Pierce, *The Politics of Fiscal Policy Formation* (Pacific Palisades, Calif.: Goodyear Publishing Company, 1971); Herbert Stein, *The Fiscal Revolution in America* (Chicago: University of Chicago Press, 1969); Lewis Kimmel, *Federal Budgets and Fiscal Policy, 1789–1958* (Washington, D.C.: The Brookings Institution, 1959); Wilfred Lewis, Jr., *Federal Fiscal Policy in the Postwar Recessions* (Washington, D.C.: The Brookings Institution, 1962); James Sundquist, *Politics and Policy: The Eisenhower, Kennedy and Johnson Years* (Washington, D.C.: The Brookings Institution, 1968); R.L. Miller and R.M. Williams, *The New Economics of Richard Nixon* (New York: Harper's Magazine Press, 1972); Leonard Silk, *Nixonomics* (New York: Praeger, 1973).

The Economic Advisory System: Edward S. Flash, *Economic Advice and Presidential Leadership* (New York: Columbia University Press, 1965); Corinne Silverman, "The President's Economic Advisors" (Syracuse, N.Y.: Inter-University Case Program, 1959); Edwin Nourse, *Economics in the Public Service* (New York: Harcourt, Brace and Co., 1953); Walter Heller, *New Dimensions of Political Economy* (New York: W.W. Norton, 1967); Arthur Okun, *The Political Economy of Prosperity* (New York: W.W. Norton, 1970); James Tobin, *The New Economics: One Decade Older* (Princeton, N.J.: Princeton University Press, 1974); Arthur Burns, *The Management of Prosperity* (New York: Columbia University Press, 1966).

Guideposts and Controls: Crauford Goodwin, *Exhortation and Controls* (Washington, D.C.: The Brookings Institution, 1975); Marvin Kosters, *Controls and Inflation* (Washington, D.C.: The American Enterprise Institute, 1975); Arnold Weber, *In Pursuit of Price Stability* (Washington, D.C.: The Brookings Institution, 1973); J. Sheahan, *The Wage-Price Guideposts* (Washington, D.C.: The Brookings Institution, 1972).

Congressional Fiscal Policymaking: Senate Committee on Rules and Administration, "Federal Budget Control by the Congress," Hearings, 93rd Cong., 2nd Sess. (Washington, D.C.: Government Printing Office, 1974); U.S. Congress, Joint Study Committee on Budget Control, House Report No. 747, 93rd Cong., 1st Sess. (Washington, D.C.: Government Printing Office, 1973); Senate Committee on Government Operations, "Improving Congressional Control of the Budget," Hearings, Parts I, III, 93rd Cong., 1st Sess. (Washington, D.C.: Government Printing Office, 1973); House Committee on Rules, "Budget Control Act of 1973," Hearings, 93rd Cong., 1st Sess. (Washington, D.C.: Government Printing Office, 1973).

Diplomatic Powers: Louis Henkin, *Foreign Affairs and the Constitution* (Mineola: The Foundation Press, 1972); Arthur Schlesinger, Jr., *The Imperial Presidency*

(Boston: Houghton Mifflin, 1973); Edward S. Corwin, *The President's Control of Foreign Relations* (Princeton, N.J.: Princeton University Press, 1917); Daniel Cheever and H. Field Haviland, *American Foreign Policy and the Separation of Powers* (Cambridge: Harvard University Press, 1952); Francis Wilcox and Richard Franck, eds., *The Constitution and the Conduct of Foreign Policy* (New York: Praeger, 1976); Sidney Warren, *The President as World Leader* (New York: McGraw-Hill, 1967); Phillippa Strum, *Presidential Power and American Democracy* (Pacific Palisades, Calif.: Goodyear, 1972); Doris Graber, *Public Opinion, the President, and Foreign Policy* (New York: Holt, Rinehart and Winston, 1968).

Alliance Powers: W. Stull Holt, *Treaties Defeated by the Senate* (Baltimore: The Johns Hopkins Press, 1933); D. F. Fleming, *The Treaty Veto of the American Senate* (New York: G. Putnam's Sons, 1930); Wallace McClure, *International Executive Agreements* (New York: Columbia University Press, 1941); Bernard Cohen, *The Political Process and Foreign Policy* (Princeton: Princeton University Press, 1951).

Secrecy Systems: Richard Franck and Edward Weisband, eds., *Secrecy and Foreign Policy* (New York: Oxford University Press, 1974); David Wise, *The Politics of Lying* (New York: Random House, 1973); Norman Dorsen and Stephen Gillers, eds., *None of Your Business* (New York: The Viking Press, 1974); Morton Halperin and Daniel Hoffman, eds., *Freedom vs. National Security* (New York: Chelsea House, 1977); House Committee on Government Operations, "Availability of Information to Congress," Hearings, 93rd Cong., 1st Sess. (Washington, D.C.: Government Printing Office, 1973); House Committee on Foreign Affairs, "Executive Classification of Information," Report 93–221, 93rd Cong., 1st Sess. (Washington, D.C.: Government Printing Office, 1973); Senate Committee on Government Operations, Committee on the Judiciary, "Executive Privilege, Secrecy in Government, and Freedom of Information," Vols. I–III, Hearings, 93rd Cong., 1st Sess. (Washington, D.C.: Government Printing Office, 1973); Senate Committee on Foreign Relations, "Security Classification as a Problem in the Congressional Role in Foreign Policy," Committee Print, 92nd Cong., 1st Sess. (Washington, D.C.: Government Printing Office, 1971); House Committee on Government Operations, "U.S. Government Information Policies and Practices," Hearings, 92nd Cong., 1st and 2nd Sess. (Washington, D.C.: Government Printing Office, 1971–1972); Raoul Berger, *Executive Privilege: A Constitutional Myth* (Cambridge: Harvard University Press, 1974); Arthur Breckenridge, *The Executive Privilege* (Lincoln, Neb.: University of Nebraska Press, 1974).

State-centered Diplomacy: John Campbell, *The Foreign Affairs Fudge Factory* (New York: Basic Books, 1971); John P. Davies, *Foreign and Other Affairs* (New York: W.W. Norton, 1964); Stanley Hoffman, *Gulliver's Troubles* (New York: McGraw-Hill, 1968); Charles Yost, *The Conduct and Misconduct of Foreign Affairs* (New York: Random House, 1972); Norman Graebner, *An Uncertain Tradition: American Secretaries of State in the Twentieth Century* (New York: McGraw-Hill, 1961); Don K. Price, *The Secretary of State* (Englewood Cliffs, N.J.: Prentice-Hall, 1960).

National Security Machinery: Edward Hobbes, *Behind the President* (Washington, D.C.: Public Affairs Press, 1954); I.M. Destler, *Presidents, Bureaucrats and Foreign Policy* (Princeton, N.J.: Princeton University Press, 1974); Morton Halperin, *Bureaucratic Politics and Foreign Policy* (Washington, D.C.: The Brookings Institution, 1974); Keith Clark and Laurence Legere, *The President and the Management of National Security* (New York: Praeger, 1968); Graham Allison and Peter Szanton, *Remaking American Foreign Policy* (New York: Basic Books, 1977); R. Gordon Hoxie, *Command Decision and the Presidency* (New York: Readers Digest Press, 1977); Roger Hilsman, *To Move a Nation* (Garden City, N.Y.: Doubleday, 1967); Richard Neustadt, *Alliance Politics* (New York: Columbia University Press, 1970).

Presidential Warmaking: Richard Barnett, *The Roots of War* (New York: Atheneum, 1972); Arthur Schlesinger, Jr., *The Imperial Presidency* (Boston: Houghton Mifflin, 1973); Noam Chomsky, *American Power and the New Mandarins* (New York: Pantheon, 1969); Daniel Ellsberg, *Papers on the War* (New York: Simon and Schuster, 1972); Gabriel Kolko, *The Roots of American Foreign Policy* (Boston: Beacon Press, 1969); Phillippa Strum, *Presidential Power and American Democracy* (Pacific Palisades, Calif.: Goodyear, 1972); Irving Janis, *Victims of Groupthink* (Boston: Houghton Mifflin, 1972); Merlo Pusey, *The Way We Go to War* (Boston: Houghton

Mifflin, 1969); Ernest May, ed., *The Ultimate Decision* (New York: George Braziller, 1960).

War in Indochina: Richard M. Pfeffer, *No More Vietnams?* (New York: Harper and Row, 1968); Chester Cooper, *The Lost Crusade* (New York: Dodd Mead, 1970); David Halberstam, *The Best and the Brightest* (New York: Random House, 1969); Townsend Hoopes, *The Limits of Intervention* (New York: David McKay, 1969); Peter D. Scott, *The War Conspiracy* (Indianapolis: Bobbs-Merrill, 1972); Doris Kearns, *Lyndon Johnson and the American Dream* (New York: Harper and Row, 1975); Noam Chomsky and Howard Zinn, eds., *The Pentagon Papers, Senator Gravel Edition, Vol. V, Critical Essays* (Boston: Beacon Press, 1972).

War Powers: Clarence Berdahl,*War Powers of the Executive in the United States* (Evanston, Ill.: University of Illinois Press, 1921); James G. Rogers, *World Policing and the Constitution* (Boston: World Peace Foundation, 1945); Edward Corwin, *The President: Office and Powers*, 4th rev. ed. (New York: New York University Press, 1957); Francis Wormuth, *The Vietnam War: The President vs. the Constitution* (Santa Barbara, Calif.: Fund for the Republic, Center Occasional Paper, 1968); Edward Corwin, *Total War and the Constitution* (Westminster, Maryland: Knopf, 1947); Louis Henkin, *Foreign Affairs and the Constitution* (Mineola, N.Y.: The Foundation Press, 1972).

War Powers Legislation: Jacob Javits, *Who Makes War?* (New York: William Morrow and Co., 1973); Thomas Eagleton, *War and Presidential Power* (New York: Liveright, 1974); Gerald Angst, "1973 War Powers Legislation," *Loyola University of Chicago Law Journal*, Vol. 5, No. 1, Winter 1974; Michael Glennon, "Strengthening the War Powers Resolution," *Minnesota Law Review*, Vol. 60, No. 1, November 1975; Comment, "The War Powers Resolution," *Harvard Journal on Legislation*, Vol. 11, No. 181, 1974; Committee on Foreign Relations, *Documents Relating to the War Powers of Congress, the President's Authority as Commander-in-Chief and the War in Indochina*, 91st Cong., 2nd Sess. (Washington, D.C.: Government Printing Office, 1970); Committee on Foreign Relations, U.S. Senate, *War Powers Legislation Hearings*, 92nd Cong., 1st Sess. (Washington, D.C.; Government Printing Office, 1971); Committee on Foreign Affairs, House of Representatives, *War Powers Legislation*, Hearings Before the Subcommittee on National Security Policy and Scientific Developments, 92nd Cong., 1st Sess. (Washington, D.C.: Government Printing Office, 1971); Committee on Foreign Affairs, House of Representatives, *Congress, the President and the War Powers*, Hearings Before the Subcommittee on National Security Policy and Scientific Developments, 93rd Cong., 1st Sess. (Washington, D.C.: Government Printing Office, 1973); Committee on International Relations, House of Representatives, *War Powers: A Test of Compliance*, Hearings Before the Subcommittee on International Security and Scientific Affairs, 94th Cong., 1st Sess. (Washington, D.C.: Government Printing Office, 1975); Committee on International Relations, House of Representatives, *Seizure of the Mayaguez*, Hearings Before the Subcommittee on International Political and Military Affairs, 94th Cong., 1st Sess., Parts I, II, III, IV (Washington, D.C.: Government Printing Office, 1975); Committee on Foreign Relations, United States Senate, *War Powers Resolution*, Hearings, 95th Cong., 1st Sess. (Washington, D.C.: Government Printing Office, 1977).

Notes

Introduction

1. *New York Post*, February 15, 1977.
2. U.S. Congress, House, Hearings before a Subcommittee of the Committee on Government Operations, *Expenditure of Federal Funds in Support of Presidential Properties*, 93rd Cong., 1st Sess. (Washington, D.C.: Government Printing Office, 1974), p. 485.
3. The Former Presidents Act of 1958, P.L. 85–745; the Presidential Transition Act of 1963, P.L. 88–277.
4. This concept is developed by John W. Chambers in "The Transformation of the Ex-Presidency" (paper delivered to the Annual Meeting of the Organization of American Historians, 1977).
5. Alexis de Tocqueville, *Democracy in America* (New York: Schocken Books, 1961), 1:214.
6. C. Vann Woodward, *Responses of the Presidents to Charges of Misconduct* (New York: Delacourt, 1974), pp. xiv–xxvi.
7. U.S. Congress, *Congressional Record*, 85th Cong., 1st Sess., vol. 103, part 2, February 4, 1957, p. 1458.
8. P.L. 93–526.
9. David Easton and Jack Dennis, eds., "The President as a Focal Point of Political Socialization," in *Children in the Political System* (New York: McGraw-Hill, 1969); Dean Jaros et al., "The Malevolent President," *The American Political Science Review*, 62, no. 1 (March 1968): 64–75; F. Christopher Arterton, "The Impact of Watergate on Children's Attitudes Toward Political Authority," *Political Science Quarterly*, 89, no. 2 (June 1974): 269–288.
10. Paul B. Sheatsley and Jacob I. Feldman, "The Assassination of President Kennedy," *Public Opinion Quarterly* 28, no. 2 (Summer 1964): 192.
11. Roberta Sigel, "An Exploration into Some Aspects of Political Socialization," in *Children and the Death of a President*, eds. Martha Wolfenstein and Gilbert Klisen (New York: Peter Smith, 1965), p. 51.
12. Fred Greenstein, "College Students' Reaction to the Assassination," in *The Kennedy Assassination and the American Public*, eds. Bradley E. Greenberg and Edwin B. Parker (Stanford, Calif.: Stanford University Press, 1965), p. 25.

13. Wilbur Schram, "Communication in Crisis," in Greenberg and Parker, *The Kennedy Assassination and the American Public*, p. 14.

14. Harold Orlansky, "Reactions to the Death of President Roosevelt," *The Journal of Social Psychology* 26, no. 4 (November 1947): 239, 243; also see Dorothea Johanssen, "Reactions to the Death of President Roosevelt," *The Journal of Abnormal and Social Psychology* 41, no. 2 (April 1946): 221.

15. James MacGregor Burns, *Roosevelt: The Soldier of Freedom* (New York: Harcourt, Brace, Jovanovich, 1970), p. 610.

16. *The Gallup Opinion Index*, Report No. 139, February 1977.

17. *The Gallup Opinion Index*, Report No. 127, February 1976.

18. Theodore White, *Breach of Faith* (New York: Atheneum, 1975), p. 332.

19. Ibid., p. 21.

20. United Press International, *The Impeachment Report* (New York: 1974), p. 274.

21. Ibid., p. 237.

22. White, *Breach of Faith*, pp. 297–298; Robert G. Lehnen, "The Congress and Public Opinion," *American Institutions, Public Opinion ad Public Policy* (Hinsdale, Ill.: The Dryden Press, 1976), pp. 153–177; Scott quoted by Robert Woodward and Carl Bernstein, *The Final Days* (New York: Simon and Schuster, 1976), p. 155.

23. Lehnen, "The Congress and Public Opinion," p. 167.

24. *Newsweek*, vol. 84, August 19, 1974, p. 15.

25. Walter Mondale, *The Accountability of Power* (New York: David McKay, 1976), p. xv.

26. White, *Breach of Faith*, p. 340.

27. Russell Baker, "Letter From Washington," *The New York Times Magazine*, February 15, 1976, p. 64.

28. Arthur H. Miller, "Political Issues and Trust in Government, 1964–1970," *The American Political Science Review* 68, no. 3 (September 1974): 951–972.

29. William Watts and Lloyd Free, *State of the Nation, 1974* (Washington, D.C.: Potomac Associates, 1974), pp. 72–74.

30. Ex Parte Milligan, 71 U.S. 125 (1866).

31. Henry Adams, *The Education of Henry Adams* (Boston: Houghton Mifflin, 1929), p. 206.

32. "A President Unfit to Rule," *The Spectator*, vol. 230, June 9, 1973, p. 1.

33. Haynes Johnson, *The Working White House* (New York: Praeger, 1975), p. 34.

34. Arthur Schlesinger, Jr., *The Imperial Presidency* (Boston: Houghton Mifflin, 1973), p. 411.

35. Adams, *The Education of Henry Adams*, p. 418.

36. Theodore Sorensen, *Watchman in the Night* (Cambridge: MIT Press, 1975), p. xv.

37. Clinton Rossiter, *The American Presidency* (New York: Harcourt Brace and World, 1960), pp. 102–103.

38. Eric Goldman, *The Tragedy of Lyndon Johnson* (New York: Knopf, 1969), p. 330.

39. For discussion of the benevolent president see Thomas Cronin, "The Textbook Presidency and Political Science," reprinted in U.S. Congress, *The Congressional Record*, vol. 116, Appendix, 91st Cong., 2nd Sess., 1970, pp. 517102–517105.

40. For discussion of the malevolent president see Amaury de Riencourt, *The Coming Caesars* (New York: Coward, McCann, 1957), and Schlesinger, *The Imperial Presidency*.

41. On the irrelevant president see C. Wright Mills, *The Power Elite* (New York: Oxford University Press, 1956); on the role of national security managers see Richard Barnet, *The Roots of War* (New York: Penquin, 1973), pp. 76–137.

42. The concept of the amateur president who becomes a "clerk" and uses formal presidential powers for the benefit of others is developed by Richard E. Neustadt, *Presidential Power* (New York: John Wiley and Sons, 1961); the phrase "executive clerkship" was used in much the same way by Henry Campbell Black, *The Relation of the Executive Power to Legislation* (Princeton: Princeton University Press, 1919);

similarly, James Garfield confided to a friend, "It had better be known in the outset whether the president is registering clerk of the Senate or the Executive of the United States," quoted in T.C. Smith, ed., *Life and Letters of James Garfield* (New Haven: Yale University Press, 1925), 2:1109.

Chapter One

1. Jonathan Elliot, ed., "Madison to Randolph, February 25, 1787," *The Debates of the Several State Conventions*, 2nd ed. (New York: Franklin, Burt Publishers, 1888–96), 5:107.

2. John C. Fitzpatrick, ed., *Journals of the Continental Congress* (Washington, D.C.: U.S. Government Printing Office, 1904–37), 31:692; 32:39–40.

3. Harold Syrett, ed., *The Papers of Alexander Hamilton* (New York: Columbia University Press, 1962), 3:309–10.

4. Fitzpatrick, *Journals of the Continental Congress*, 31:698–700, 739, 886–896.

5. Jared Sparks, ed., "Washington to Lee, October 31, 1786," *The Writings of George Washington* (New York, 1902), 9:204.

6. Julian Boyd et al., eds., "Washington to Jefferson, May 30, 1787," *The Papers of Thomas Jefferson* (Princeton, N.J.: Princeton University Press, 1955), 9:389.

7. Charles P. Smith, *James Wilson* (Chapel Hill: University of North Carolina Press, 1956), p. 158.

8. Library of Congress, Washington Papers, Series 4, George Washington, "Sentiments of Mr. Jay, Gen. Knox, and Mr. Madison on a Form of Government, Previous to the General Convention held at Philadelphia in May, 1787."

9. Merrill Jensen, *The Articles of Confederation* (Madison: University of Wisconsin Press, 1940), p. 136.

10. Ibid., pp. 269–270.

11. Syrett, "Hamilton to Duane, September 3, 1780," *The Papers of Alexander Hamilton*, 3:404.

12. Fitzpatrick, *Journals of the Continental Congress*, 3:233–525; 4:8–9; see Jennings B. Sanders, *Evolution of the Executive Departments of the Continental Congress, 1774–1789* (Chapel Hill: University of North Carolina Press, 1935), pp. 3–17.

13. Quoted in Clinton Rossiter, *1787, The Grand Convention* (New York: Macmillan, 1966), p. 50.

14. John Locke, "The Legislative, Executive and Federal Powers of the Commonwealth," and "Of the Subordination of the Powers of the Commonwealth," *Second Treatise of Civil Government*, ed. J.W. Gough (Oxford: B. Blackwell, Co., 1946); Baron de Montesquieu, "Of the Laws Which Establish Political Liberty with Regard to the Constitution," *The Spirit of the Laws*, trans. Thomas Nugent (New York: Hafner Publishing Co., 1965).

15. This section relies heavily on Evarts B. Greene, *The Provincial Governor in the English Colonies of North America* (New York: Longmans, Greene and Co., 1898).

16. Max Farrand, ed., *The Records of the Federal Convention, 1787*, rev. ed. (New Haven: Yale University Press, 1966), 1:99.

17. William Webster, "A Comparative Study of the State Constitutions of the American Revolution," *The Annals of the American Academy of Political Science*, 9 (Philadelphia, 1897), pp. 380–419.

18. John Adams, *The Defense of the Constitution of the United States Against the Attacks of Mr. Turgot* (London: Printed for J. Stockwell, 1794).

19. Syrett, "Washington to Hamilton, March 31, 1783," *The Papers of Alexander Hamilton*, 3:309–10; on the mutiny itself see Richard H. Kohn, "Inside History of the Newburgh Conspiracy," *The William and Mary Quarterly*, 28, no. 2 (April 1970), pp. 187–220.

20. Farrand, *Federal Convention*, 1:65.

21. Henry Cabot Lodge, ed., *Hamilton, Works* (New York, 1904), 1:289.

22. Farrand, *Federal Convention*, 2:35.

23. Ibid., 1:20–22.
24. Ibid., p. 101.
25. Ibid., pp. 235–237.
26. Ibid., 2:29.
27. Ibid., p. 29.
28. Ibid., p. 31.
29. Ibid., p. 58 describes one vote on June 19 that favored an electoral college, because small states were given more representation in the plan than they had anticipated. The next week the Convention reversed itself and returned to the original plan of legislative election.
30. Ibid., pp. 493–494.
31. Ibid., p. 525.
32. Ibid., 1:244.
33. Ibid., 2:177–189.
34. Charles Thach, *The Creation of the Presidency, 1775–1789* (Baltimore: Johns Hopkins University Press, 1922), pp. 110–112.
35. Farrand, *Federal Convention*, 2:499.
36. Ibid., 1:65–66.
37. Ibid., 2:301.
38. Ibid., pp. 342–344.
39. Ibid., p. 65.
40. Ibid., p. 52.
41. Ibid., p. 65.
42. Ibid., p. 68.
43. Ibid., p. 550.
44. Ibid., p. 551.
45. Raoul Berger, "Crimes and Misdemeanors," *Impeachment* (Cambridge: Harvard University Press, 1973).
46. The Articles of Confederation provided the following in Article 3: "The said states hereby severally enter into a firm league of friendship with each other for their common defense, the security of their liberties and their mutual and general welfare; binding themselves to assist each other against all forces offered to, or attacks made upon them, on account of religion, sovereignty, trade, or any other pretense whatsoever." It was not clear from this language whether states were bound to assist each other against domestic insurrection, or whether the Continental Congress was bound to assist a state in such an insurrection.
47. *The Federalist Papers*, no. 74.
48. Farrand, *Federal Convention*, 2:318.
49. Ibid., p. 318.
50. By no means did the framers contemplate that the power to declare war would be shared between Congress and the president, or that the president could unilaterally determine on war or peace; see Abraham Sofaer, *War, Foreign Affairs and Constitutional Power* (Cambridge: Ballinger Publishing Co., 1976), p. 56; see Charles Lofgren, "Warmaking Under the Constitution: The Original Understanding," *Yale Law Journal* 81, no. 4, (March 1972): 672–702. Madison and Wilson both stated at the convention that executive powers "do not include the right of war and peace" (Farrand, *Federal Convention*, 2:319).
51. Farrand, *Federal Convention*, 2:319.
52. Cromwell's document reprinted in G. B. Adams and H. M. Stephens, eds., *Select Documents of English Constitutional History* (London: Macmillan and Co., 1902), pp. 407–416.
53. William Blackstone, "Of Parliament" and "Of the King's Prerogative," *Commentaries on the Laws of England*; compare with Hamilton's address, June 18, 1787, Farrand, *Federal Convention*, 1:282–293. On Hamilton's use of Blackstone's *Commentaries* during the Revolutionary War, see Gerald Stourz, *Alexander Hamilton and the Idea of Republican Government* (Stanford, Calif.: Stanford University Press, 1970), pp. 13–21.
54. Farrand, *Federal Convention*, 1:66–67, 70.
55. Elliot, *Debates of the Convention*, 2:54, 58, 220–221, 484. On the position of the anti-Federalists, see Cecilia Kenyon, "Men of Little Faith," in *The Reinterpreta-*

tion of American Government: 1763–1789, ed. Jack P. Greene (New York: Harper and Row, 1968).

56. Cato, "Various Fears Concerning the Executive Department," *The New York Journal,* November 8, 1787.

57. Elliot, *Debates of the Conventions,* 2:448.

58. Ibid., p. 348.

59. *The Federalist Papers,* no. 51.

60. Note the difference between Hamilton's convention speech and his argument in *The Federalist Papers,* no. 69; on the use of the papers as propaganda, see Frederick W. Marks III, "Foreign Affairs: A Winning Issue in the Campaign for Ratification," *Political Science Quarterly* 86, no. 3 (September 1971): 444–69.

61. But for an alternative view see the argument that "The Executive Power" was not intended to include prerogatives, made by Raoul Berger, *Executive Privilege* (Cambridge: Harvard University Press, 1974), pp. 64–66. Berger takes the arguments in *The Federalist Papers* literally, rather than viewing them as tactical ploys misrepresenting the position of the authors on prerogative powers.

62. Boyd et al., "Madison to Jefferson, September 6, 1787," *Papers of Thomas Jefferson,* 12:103.

63. Syrett, "Memo of September 17–30, 1787," *Papers of Alexander Hamilton,* 4:275; just two years before his death Hamilton wrote to a friend, "Perhaps no man in the United States has sacrificed or done more for the present Constitution than myself; and contrary to all my anticipations of its fate, as you know from the very beginning, I am still laboring to prop the frail and worthless fabric." (Quoted in Adrienne Koch, *Power, Morals, and the Founding Fathers* [Ithaca: Cornell University Press, 1961], p. 76.)

64. *Inaugural Addresses of the Presidents of the United States* (Washington, D.C.: U.S. Government Printing Office, 1965), p. 3.

Chapter Two

1. Theodore Roosevelt, *Letters,* Elting E. Morison, ed. (Cambridge: Harvard University Press, 1951–1954), 1:1087.

2. Woodrow Wilson, *Constitutional Government in the United States* (New York: Columbia University Press, 1908), p. 68.

3. Theodore Roosevelt, *An Autobiography* (New York: Charles Scribner's Sons, 1931), p. 388.

4. James Buchanan, *Works,* John Bassett Moore, ed. (Philadelphia: J.B. Lippincott, 1908–1911), 10:400.

5. Charles F. Adams, ed., *The Works of John Adams* (Boston: Little, Brown, 1856), 11:302.

6. William Howard Taft, *Our Chief Magistrate and His Powers* (New York: Columbia University Press, 1916), p. 53.

7. Adams, *Works of John Adams,* 10:47.

8. This debate is discussed by Edward S. Corwin, *The President's Control of Foreign Relations* (Princeton: Princeton University Press, 1917), especially Chapter One, "Pacificus and Helvidius."

9. *The Annals of Congress,* 5:771 (1796).

10. *Opinions of the Attorney General,* 39:484 (1941).

11. James Richardson, ed., *The Messages and Papers of the Presidents, 1789–1897* (Washington, D.C.: Government Printing Office, 1896–1899), 7:3189.

12. Quoted in Harold Hyman, *A More Perfect Union* (New York: Knopf, 1973), p. 46.

13. *The Inaugural Addresses of Presidents of the United States* (Washington, D.C.: Government Printing Office, 1965), p. 126.

14. Richardson, 7:3215–3519.

15. Appropriations Act of August 6, 1861, 12 U.S. Stat., 326.

16. The Prize Cases, 2 Black 635 (1863).

17. Richardson, 3:1139–1154.

18. U.S. Congress, *Senate Journal*, 23rd Cong., 1st Sess., p. 197.

19. Quoted by Leonard White, *The Jacksonians* (New York: The Free Press, 1965), p. 22.

20. *The Writings and Speeches of Daniel Webster* (Boston: Little, Brown, 1903), 7:188.

21. Kendall v. Stokes, 12 Peters 524 (1838).

22. Abel Upshur, *A Brief Inquiry Into the Nature and Character of Our Federal Government* (New York: Da Capo Press, 1971), p. 116.

23. U.S. Congress, *The Congressional Globe*, 27th Cong., 1st Sess., pp. 3–5.

24. Quoted in Oliver Chitwood, *John Tyler* (New York: Russell and Russell, 1939), p. 270.

25. Maeva Marcus, *Truman and the Steel Seizure* (New York: Columbia University Press, 1977), p. 9.

26. Edward Corwin, *The President: Office and Powers*, 4th ed. rev. (New York: New York University Press, 1957), pp. 408–410.

27. Edward Berman, "Labor Disputes and the Presidents of the United States" (Ph.D. diss., Columbia University, 1924).

28. Marcus, *Truman and the Steel Seizure*, p. 156.

29. Ibid., p. 92.

30. Quoted in Alan Westin, *The Anatomy of a Supreme Court Case* (New York: Macmillan, 1958), p. 62.

31. Quoted in Marcus, *Truman and the Steel Seizure*, p. 121.

32. Ibid., pp. 176–177.

33. Youngstown Sheet and Tube v. Sawyer, 343 U.S. 579 (1952).

34. 343 U.S. 637.

35. 343 U.S. 653.

36. Quoted in Harold Hyman, *A More Perfect Union* (New York: Knopf, 1973), p. 417.

37. This discussion follows Hyman, *A More Perfect Union* and Michael L. Benedict, *The Impeachment and Trial of Andrew Johnson* (New York: W.W. Norton, 1973).

38. Woodrow Wilson, *Congressional Government* (New York: Houghton Mifflin, 1885); also Woodrow Wilson, "Cabinet Government in the United States," *The International Review* 7 (August 1879): 146–163.

39. U.S. Senate, Civil Service and Retrenchment Committee, Sen. Rep. 576, 47th Cong., 1st Sess. (Washington: Government Printing Office, 1883).

40. Henry C. Lockwood, *The Abolition of the Presidency* (New York: R. Worthington, 1884).

41. Albert Hart, "The Speaker as Premier," *Atlantic Monthly*, March 1891; also Mary P. Follett, *The Speaker of the House of Representatives* (New York: Longman's Green and Co., 1896).

42. Henry Jones Ford, *The Rise and Growth of American Politics* (New York: Macmillan, 1898), especially Chapter 28: "The Ultimate Type."

43. Nixon released a version of the tapes entitled *Submission of Revised Presidential Conversations* to the House Committee on the Judiciary. Not only did this material omit several crucial conversations, but it also had a significant eighteen-minute erasure in the midst of one conversation. There were also deletions throughout the transcript—at least 340 examples. For a full discussion of the places in which the tape transcripts were "doctored," see William Todd, "The White House Transcripts," *The Papers of the Bibliographic Society of America* 68, no. 3 (1974): 267–296.

44. Nixon to Ervin, July 6, 1973.

45. Oral argument before Judge John Sirica, August 22, 1973.

46. Brief submitted August 7, 1973.

47. Brief submitted August 7, 1973.

48. 38 Fed. Reg. 30739, 32805; 28 U.S.C. 316.

49. Senate Resolution 105 (May 1, 1973).

50. Guidelines of the Attorney General, May 19, 1973. On the independence of the Attorney General from the president, and of the Special Prosecutor from the Attorney General, see especially the discussion between Elliot Richardson and John

Tunney in U.S. Congress, Senate, Committee on the Judiciary, "Nomination of Eliot L. Richardson to be Attorney General," Hearings before the Commitee on the Judiciary, 93rd Cong., 1st Sess. (Washington, D.C.: Government Printing Office, 1973), pp. 176–177.

51. Brief submitted June 21, 1974.

52. Brief submitted July 1, 1974.

53. Nixon v. Sirica, 159 U.S. App. 58 (1973), p. 69.

54. United States v. Nixon, 418 U.S. 683 (1974), p. 695.

55. 418 U.S. 713.

56. House Committee on the Judiciary, *Report: The Impeachment of Richard M. Nixon* (Washington, D.C.: Government Printing Office, 1974), pp. 359–360. The original tapes were not released, but copies were made available. For the argument that these tapes and transcripts may also have been doctored by the White House, see Todd, "The White House Transcripts," p. 280.

57. Elizabeth Drew, *Washington Journal* (New York: Random House, 1974), p. 14.

58. Press conference, February 25, 1974.

59. Staff analysis, February 28, 1974, as cited in Drew, *Washington Journal*.

60. Staff Memorandum, House Committee on the Judiciary, "Constitutional Grounds for Presidential Impeachment," February 20, 1974.

61. *Selected Materials Published by the House Judiciary Committee*, 93rd Cong., 1st Sess. (Washington, D.C.: Government Printing Office, 1973), p. 11.

62. House Committee on the Judiciary, *Debate on Articles of Impeachment*, 93rd Cong., 2nd Sess. (Washington, D.C.: Government Printing Office, 1974), p. 337.

63. Ibid., pp. 341–342.

64. *New York Times*, May 19, 1977.

65. U.S. Congress, Senate, Committee on Foreign Relations, *Dr. Kissinger's Role in Wiretapping*, 93rd Cong., 2nd Sess. (Washington, D.C.: Government Printing Office, 1974), p. 23 (hereinafter cited as Wiretapping Hearings).

66. "Deposition by Richard M. Nixon," *The Civil Liberties Review*, June/July 1976, p. 22.

67. Wiretapping Hearings, p. 5.

68. "Deposition by Richard M. Nixon," p. 19.

69. Kissinger's responses to interrogatories were made available by David Wise to David Friend and cited in Friend, "The Kissinger Wiretaps" (senior essay, Columbia College, 1977), p. 2.

70. The White House Tapes, February 28, 1973.

71. Wiretapping Hearings, p. 208.

72. Ibid., p. 117.

73. Ibid., p. 117.

74. U.S. Congress, Senate, Committee on Foreign Relations, *Nomination of Henry A. Kissinger*, 92nd Cong., 2nd Sess. (Washington, D.C.: Government Printing Office, 1973), p. 2.

75. For a discussion critical of the Senate action see George D. Aiken, *Aiken: Senate Diary* (Brattleboro, Vt.: The Stephen Greene Press, 1976), pp. 302–303.

76. Omnibus Crime Control and Safe Streets Act of 1968, Title III, 18 U.S.C. 2510–20.

77. Halperin et al. v. Kissinger et al., 424 F. Supp. 838 (D.C. Circuit, 1976).

78. 424 F. Supp. 845.

79. As reported by *New York Times*, August 6, 1977.

80. *New York Times*, February 11, 1978.

Chapter Three

1. *Inaugural Addresses of the Presidents of the United States: 1789–1965* (Washington, D.C.: Government Printing Office, 1965), p. 14.

2. *Inaugural Addresses*, p. 1.

3. *New York Times*, May 9, 1954.

4. *New York Times*, November 5, 1976. The "clear majority" was 50.06 percent of votes cast.

5. William Keech and David Matthews, *The Party's Choice* (Washington, D.C.: The Brookings Institution, 1976), pp. 14–19; on the process by which major contenders emerge prior to the primary season, see Arthur Hadley, *The Invisible Primary* (Englewood Cliffs, N.J.: Prentice-Hall, 1976).

6. Herbert Alexander, *Financing the 1968 Election* (Lexington, Mass.: D.C. Heath, 1971), p. 13.

7. *Congressional Quarterly Weekly Reports*, 34, no. 39 (September 25, 1976): 2606.

8. On the provisions of the law, see David Adamany and George Agree, "Election Financing: The 1974 Reforms," *Political Science Quarterly* 90, no. 2 (Summer 1975): 201–220.

9. Buckley v. Valeo, 424 U.S. 1 (1975). Contributors could spend unlimited amounts on behalf of candidates, provided they did not contribute funds to candidates' campaigns or coordinate their efforts with the campaigns.

10. Joseph Napolitan, *The Election Game and How to Win It* (New York: Doubleday, 1972), p. 65.

11. Quoted in Michael Novak, *Choosing Our King* (New York: Macmillan, 1974), p. 49.

12. Kandy Stroud, *How Jimmy Won* (New York: William Morrow and Co., 1974), p. 49.

13. Napolitan, *The Election Game and How to Win It*, p. 11; also see Joseph Lelyveld, "The Selling of a Candidate," *The New York Times Magazine*, March 28, 1976.

14. *New York Times*, May 4, 1977.

15. The concept originates with Daniel Boorstin, *The Image* (New York: Atheneum, 1962), p. 38.

16. Theodore White, *The Making of the President, 1968* (New York: Atheneum, 1969), p. 339.

17. James Beniger, "Winning the Presidential Nomination: National Polls and State Primary Elections," *Public Opinion Quarterly* 40, no. 1 (Spring 1976): 31–37; also see Michael Robinson, "T.V.'s Newest Program: The Presidential Nominations Game," *Public Opinion*, May/June, 1978, p. 42. Between 1936 and 1964, seven of ten nonincumbent nominees were poll front-runners. But five of the last seven Democratic nominees, including the last three, were not front-runners. Humphrey picked up 22 percent in Gallup polls in 1968, McGovern picked up 27 percent in 1972, and Carter picked up 49 percent in 1976.

18. Herbert Asher, *Presidential Elections and American Politics* (Homewood, Ill.: The Dorsey Press, 1976), p. 279.

19. Austin Ranney, *Participation in American Presidential Nominations, 1976* (Washington, D.C.: The American Enterprise Institute, 1977), p. 6.

20. Leonard Weinberg and Joseph Crowley, "Primary Success as a Measure of Presidential Election Victory," *Midwest Journal of Political Science* 14, no. 3 (August 1970): 506.

21. Ranney, *Participation in American Presidential Nominations, 1976*, p. 19.

22. For recent developments in primary turnouts, see Richard Rubin, "Presidential Primaries" (paper presented at the American Political Science Association Convention, Washington, D.C., 1977).

23. Austin Ranney, "Turnout and Representation in Presidential Primary Elections," *The American Political Science Review* 66, no. 1 (March 1972): 27–36.

24. For differences in turnout rates between parties, see Richard Rubin, *Party Dynamics* (New York: Oxford University Press, 1976), p. 152. Ranney, in *Participation in American Presidential Nominations, 1976*, cites the decline in Democratic participation in 1976, while Rubin, in "Presidential Primaries," argues that as electorates become "socialized" to vote in primaries turnouts will increase. Democratic turnouts in the 20 states that held primaries both in 1972 and in 1976 dropped from 15,829,070 to 14,386,371, and in eight closed primary states in 1976, Republican turnout of registered voters exceeded the Democratic percentages.

25. Rubin, "Presidential Primaries," p. 19.

26. *New York Times*, March 11, 1976.

27. Winning (or doing better than expected) in New Hampshire is important. Approximately 30 percent of network stories on the first eight primaries in 1976 dealt with New Hampshire. See Michael J. Robinson, "The T.V. Primaries," *The Wilson Quarterly*, Spring 1977, pp. 80–83.

28. William Lucy, "Polls, Primaries and Presidential Nominations," *The Journal of Politics* 35, no. 4 (November 1973): 830–848.

29. Keech and Matthews, *The Parties Choice*, p. 247. For a discussion of proposals to "federalize the legal machinery" of primaries by passage of congressional legislation, see Austin Ranney, *The Federalization of Presidential Primaries* (Washington, D.C.: The American Enterprise Institute, 1978).

30. William Crotty, "Correspondence," *New York Times*, September 22, 1977.

31. Ranney, *Participation in American Presidential Nominations, 1976*, p. 15.

32. Susan Tolchin and Martin Tolchin, *To the Victors* (New York: Random House, 1972), p. 4.

33. Denis Sullivan et al., *The Politics of Representation* (New York: St. Martin's Press, 1976), pp. 44–62.

34. On the 1972 election, see Jeane Kirkpatrick, *The New Presidential Elite* (New York: Russell Sage, 1976), p. 46; on the 1976 election, see Jeane Kirkpatrick, *Dismantling the Parties* (Washington, D.C.: The American Enterprise Institute, 1978), p. 10.

35. Committee on Political Parties, "Toward a More Responsible Two-Party System," *The American Political Science Review* 44, no. 3, part 2 (September 1950): 1–96.

36. Gerald Pomper, *Elections in America* (New York: Harper and Row, 1973), pp. 181–189.

37. Hugh Scott, *Come to the Party* (Englewood Cliffs, N.J., Prentice-Hall, 1968), p. 37.

38. Herbert Alexander, *Financing Politics* (Washington, D.C.: Congressional Quarterly, Inc., 1976), p. 20.

39. *New York Times*, November 25 and December 11, 1975; *Wall Street Journal*, November 17, 1975.

40. *New York Times*, December 11, 1974.

41. Alexander, *Financing Politics*, p. 204.

42. *New York Times*, February 19, 1976.

43. U.S. Senate, *The Final Report of the Senate Select Committee on Presidential Campaign Activities*, "Milk Fund" (New York: Dell, 1975), vol. 2.

44. For the complete listing of contributors who received ambassadorships see U.S. Senate, *Final Report*, 2:65.

45. U.S. Senate, *Final Report*, vol. 2, "Campaign Financing," provides a discussion of methods used to solicit corporate contributions.

46. These techniques are described in Alexander Heard, "Group Involvement Through Giving," *The Costs of Democracy* (Chapel Hill: University of North Carolina Press, 1960).

47. Adamany and Agree, "Election Financing: The 1974 Reforms," pp. 201–202.

48. Quoted in John Kessel, *The Goldwater Coalition* (New York: Bobbs-Merrill, 1968), p. 161.

49. On the nineteenth-century "militant" style of disciplined electioneering, see Richard Jensen, "American Election Campaigns" (paper presented at the Midwest Political Science Association Meeting, Chicago, 1968).

50. Reprinted in Martin Schramm, *Running for President, 1976* (New York: Stein and Day, 1977), p. 263.

51. Democrats in the 1950s had an initial advantage of about 8 percent based on party identifiers, and in the 1970s this advantage has been maintained. See Philip Converse, "The Concept of the Normal Vote," in *Elections and the Political Order*, Angus Campbell et al., eds. (New York: John Wiley, 1966).

52. Gerald Pomper, *The Election of 1976* (New York: David McKay, 1977), p. 61.

53. Thomas Patterson and Thomas McClure, *The Unseeing Eye* (New York: G.P. Putnam's Sons, 1976), pp. 1–22.

54. Center for Political Studies, *ISR Newsletter* 6, no. 1 (February 1978): 5.

55. Patterson and McClure, *The Unseeing Eye*, p. 111.

56. C. Vann Woodward, *Reunion and Reaction* (New York: Little, Brown, 1956), pp. 225–226.

57. The Ripon Society and Clifford W. Brown, Jr., *The Jaws of Victory* (New York: Little, Brown, 1974), p. 4.

58. Ibid., pp. 14–22.

59. *New York Times*, July 9, 1973.

60. The classic formulation of nonissue-oriented voting behavior is found in Angus Campbell et al., *The American Voter* (Chicago: University of Chicago Press, 1961), pp. 120–145, 295–380, 441–521.

61. In 1968, many voters found it difficult to distinguish the positions of the major candidates on the war in Vietnam. See Benjamin Page and Richard Brody, "Policy Voting and the Electoral Process: The Vietnam War Issue," *The American Political Science Review* 66, no. 3 (September 1972): 983.

62. Lyndon Johnson won 64 percent of the dove and 52 percent of the hawk vote in the 1964 election; see Kessel, *The Goldwater Coalition*, p. 290.

63. Seymour Lipset and Earl Raab, "The Election and the National Mood," *Commentary* 55, no. 1 (January 1973): 43–50.

64. If each cluster of issues were unrelated to all others, the probability that a voter and candidate would agree on all clusters would be $1/2^n$ where n $=$ the number of issue clusters. But in many elections, several clusters can be placed on a liberal-conservative dimension, considerably increasing the probability that a voter and a candidate would agree on a number of issue clusters. On the tendency for candidates and issues in recent elections to be located along such a dimension, see Norman H. Nie, "Mass Belief Systems Revisited," *The Journal of Politics* 36, no. 3 (August 1974): 540–91.

65. Asher, Chapter Three, "Party Identification" and Chapter Four, "The Issue Voting Controversy," *Presidential Elections and American Politics*.

66. Mark A. Schulman and Gerald M. Pomper, "Variability in Electoral Behavior," *The American Journal of Political Science* 19, no. 1 (February 1975): 7–9; for the increased importance of issue voting, see Gerald M. Pomper, "From Confusion to Clarity: Issues and American Voters, 1956–1968," *The American Political Science Review* 66, no. 2 (June 1972): 415–28; and David RePass, "Issue Salience and the Party Choice," *The American Political Science Review* 65, no. 2 (June 1971): 389–400.

67. On the increased importance of candidate image between 1952 and 1972, see Samuel Kirkpatrick, William Lyons, and Michael Fitzgerald, "Candidates, Parties and Issues in the American Electorate," *American Politics Quarterly* 3, no. 3 (July 1975): 247–83.

68. *New York Times*, January 28, 1977.

69. Institute for Survey Research, *Newsletter*, Winter 1977, "Post-Election Analysis."

70. Gallup Poll released October 26, 1977.

71. The Constitution does not require a winner-take-all system. Until the 1830s, other methods were used, including selection by the legislature or contests in special districts or congressional districts. Maine alone now chooses half its electors from congressional districts.

72. Steven Brams and Morton Davis, "The 3/2s Rule in Presidential Campaigning," *The American Political Science Review* 68, no. 1 (March 1974): 113–34.

73. Joseph Kallenbach, "Our Electoral College Gerrymander," *Midwestern Journal of Political Science* 4, no. 2 (May 1960): 162–91.

74. *New York Times*, April 1, 1976.

75. Harvey Zeidenstein, "Protecting Urban Interests—Myth or Reality?" *Direct Election of the President* (New York: Lexington Books, 1973).

76. Quoted by Neal R. Pierce in *The People's President* (New York: Simon and Schuster, 1968), p. 64.

77. Ibid., p. 100.

78. For a full account, see Joseph Kallenbach, "The Presidency and the Constitution," *Law and Contemporary Problems* 35, no. 3 (Summer 1970): 19–34.

79. One such measure, H.J. Res. 681, passed the House in 1969 but was defeated

by a filibuster in the Senate in 1970. The Senate passed another measure, S. Res. 1, in 1977.

80. For a complete discussion, see Arthur Schlesinger, Jr., "On the Presidential Succession," *Political Science Quarterly* 89, no. 3 (September 1974): 475–506.

81. John Feerick, *The Twenty-Fifth Amendment* (New York: Fordham University Press, 1976), p. 130.

82. Ibid., pp. 137–38.

83. Ibid., pp. 169–79.

84. Quoted in Schlesinger, "On the Presidential Succession," p. 476.

Chapter Four

1. Martin Tolchin, "An Old Pol Takes on the New President," *The New York Times Magazine*, July 24, 1977, p. 43.

2. Archibald Butts, *Taft and Roosevelt* (Port Washington: Kenniket Press, 1971), 2:645.

3. C.S. Olcott, *Life of William McKinley* (New York: Anns Press, 1916), 2:296; Theodore Roosevelt, *Presidential Addresses and State Papers, 1905* (New York: P.F. Collier, 1905), 3:320; Franklin Roosevelt, *Public Papers and Addresses of Franklin D. Roosevelt* (New York: Russell and Russell, 1969), 7:570; Dwight Eisenhower, *Public Papers of the Presidents, 1953* (Washington, D.C.: Government Printing Office, 1954), p. 701.

4. Jeane Kirkpatrick, *The New Presidential Elite* (New York: Russell Sage, 1976), p. 126.

5. *New York Times*, May 8, 1977.

6. Joseph Califano, Jr., *A Presidential Nation* (New York: W.W. Norton, 1976), p. 159.

7. Sherman Adams, *Firsthand Report* (New York: Greenwood, 1961), p. 18.

8. Diane Wallerstein, "Target '76" (senior scholar essay, Barnard College, 1977).

9. *New York Times*, February 12, 1978.

10. For a general discussion of developments in the party system, see William Chambers and Walter Burnham, eds., *The American Party Systems*, 2nd ed. (New York: Oxford University Press, 1975).

11. Kirkpatrick, *The New Presidential Elite*, p. 10.

12. The 162-member Republican National Committee consists of a chairperson and a national committeeman and committeewoman from each state, the District of Columbia, Guam, Puerto Rico, and the Virgin Islands. The Democratic National Committee consists of a chairperson and next highest party official of the opposite sex from each state, the District of Columbia, and Puerto Rico. In addition, the Democrats apportion two hundred delegates to state parties on the basis of their apportionment at the national convention, and there are three representatives from the Democratic Governors Conference, three from the Democratic Mayors Conference, four from the congressional party, and three from the Young Democrats.

13. Califano, *A Presidential Nation*, p. 151.

14. P.L. 88–277; P.L. 94–499. Carter received an appropriation of $2 million for the transition and spent approximately $1.02 million. See General Services Administration, "Nixon-Carter Expenses: Transitions" (Washington, D.C.: 1977).

15. Califano, *A Presidential Nation*, p. 153.

16. Michael J. Malbin, "New Party Chairmen Face Different Problems," *The National Journal* 9, no. 6 (February 5, 1977): 214.

17. Rowland Evans and Robert Novak, *Nixon in the White House* (New York: Random House, 1971), p. 31.

18. John Saloma and Frederick Sontag, *Parties* (New York: Random House, 1973), p. 100.

19. Lawrence O'Brien, *No Final Victories* (New York: Doubleday, 1974), p. 108.

20. *New York Times*, December 11, 1977.

21. James Farley, *Jim Farley's Story* (New York: McGraw-Hill, 1948), p. 68.

22. Saloma and Sontag, *Parties*, p. 103.

23. For the argument that national party organs have been significantly strengthened by these developments, see Gerald Pomper, "The Decline of Party in American Elections," *Political Science Quarterly* 92, no. 1 (Spring 1977): 37.

24. Jeffrey Pressman, Denis Sullivan, and F. Christopher Arterton, "Cleavages, Decisions and Legitimation: The Democratic Mid-Term Convention, 1974," *Political Science Quarterly* 91, no. 1 (Spring 1976): 89–107.

25. *New York Times*, June 11, 1977.

26. Adams, *Firsthand Report*, p. 9.

27. Herbert Alexander, *Financing Politics* (Washington, D.C.: Congressional Quarterly, 1976), p. 210.

28. See "Statement of Republican Principles and Objectives" (February 6, 1950) and "Aims and Purposes" (December 5, 1945). (From files of the Republican National Committee.)

29. Hugh A. Bone, *Party Committees and National Politics* (Seattle: University of Washington Press, 1958), p. 216.

30. Herbert Parmet, *The Democrats* (New York: Macmillan, 1970), p. 152.

31. Hugh Scott, *Come to the Party* (Englewood Cliffs, N.J.: Prentice-Hall, 1968), p. 58.

32. William Riker and William Best, "Presidential Action in Congressional Nominations," in *The Presidency*, ed. Aaron Wildavsky (Boston: Little, Brown, 1969).

33. Farley, *Jim Farley's Story*, pp. 146–147.

34. Robert Erikson, "The Advantage of Incumbency in Congressional Elections," *Polity* 3, no. 3 (Spring 1971): 345–405; Warren Kostroski, "Party and Incumbency in Postwar Senate Elections," *The American Political Science Review* 67, no. 4 (December 1973): 1213–1234.

35. John Ferejohn, "On the Decline of Competition in Congressional Elections," *The American Political Science Review* 71, no. 1 (March 1977): 166–175.

36. Albert Cover and Donald Mayhew, "Congressional Dynamics and the Decline of Competitive Congressional Elections," in *Congress Reconsidered*, ed. Lawrence Dodd and Bruce Oppenheimer (New York: Praeger, 1977).

37. Walter Burnham, *Critical Elections* (New York: W.W. Norton, 1970), p. 109. But in 1976 the figure dropped to 28.5 percent due to Carter's sweep of most southern congressional districts. For data on ticket splitting between 1920 and 1976, see *Congressional Quarterly Weekly Reports*, April 22, 1978, p. 972.

38. David Mayhew, "Congressional Elections: The Case of the Vanishing Marginals," *Polity* 6, no. 3 (Spring 1974): 295–317.

39. Alfred Steinberg, *Sam Rayburn* (New York: Hawthorn, 1975), p. 252.

40. *Congressional Quarterly Weekly Reports* 35, no. 12 (March 19, 1977): 489.

41. Gary Jacobson, "Presidential Coattails in 1972," *Public Opinion Quarterly* 40, no. 2 (Summer 1976): 196.

42. Edward Tufte, "Determinants of Outcomes of Midterm Congressional Elections," *The American Political Science Review* 71, no. 1 (March 1977): 817.

43. Samuel Kernell, "Presidential Popularity and Negative Voting," *The American Political Science Review* 71, no. 1 (March 1977): 46–59.

44. David Brady and Naomi Lynn, "Switched-Seat Congressional Districts," *The American Journal of Political Science* 17, no. 3 (August 1973): 528–543.

45. On the recent increase in turnover that may alter careerist patterns, see Lawrence Dodd and Bruce Oppenheimer, "The House in Transition," in *Congress Reconsidered*, ed. Dodd and Oppenheimer (New York: Praeger, 1977). Just prior to the 1978 midterm congressional elections, a record number of retirements of incumbents for the last two decades was announced.

46. Samuel Huntington, "Congressional Responses to the Twentieth Century," in *Congress and America's Future*, ed. David B. Truman (Englewood Cliffs, N.J.: Prentice-Hall, 1974).

47. See, for example, Robert Dole's complaints as Republican National Chairman during the Nixon administration, in Clark Mollenhoff, *Game Plan for Disaster* (New York: W.W. Norton, 1976), p. 200.

48. *New York Times*, July 14, 1977.

49. *New York Times*, July 1, 1977.

50. Robert Huckshorn, *Party Leadership in the States* (Cambridge: University of Massachusetts Press, 1976), p. 207.

51. Adams, *Firsthand Report*, p. 166.

52. Ibid., p. 57.

53. Hugh Heclo, *A Government of Strangers* (Washington, D.C.: The Brookings Institution, 1977), pp. 71–75.

54. Susan Tolchin and Martin Tolchin, *To the Victor* (New York: Random House, 1971), p. 251.

55. For reform proposals, see "Toward a More Responsible Two-Party System," *The American Political Science Review* 44, no. 3, part 2 (September 1950).

56. For a critique of the reforms in the Democratic Party see Austin Ranney, *Curing the Mischiefs of Faction* (Berkeley: University of California Press, 1975).

57. Charles M. Hardin, *Presidential Power and Accountability* (Chicago: University of Chicago Press, 1974), pp. 183–189.

58. Parmet, *The Democrats*, pp. 65–66.

59. Adams, *Firsthand Report*, p. 460.

60. Ibid., p. 29.

61. The Ripon Society and Clifford Brown, Jr., *The Jaws of Victory* (Boston: Little, Brown, 1974), p. 236.

Chapter Five

1. For the argument that the president is an effective social planner, see James Macgregor Burns, *Presidential Government* (New York: Avon Books, 1965), pp. 326–327; for a more skeptical appraisal, see Thomas Cronin, "Presidents as Chief Executives" in *The Presidency Reappraised*, eds. Rexford Tugwell and Thomas Cronin (New York: Praeger, 1977), p. 237.

2. Richard Neustadt, "The Presidency and Legislation: Planning the President's Program," *The American Political Science Review* 49, no. 4 (December 1955): 1015.

3. Ibid., p. 1014.

4. These tactics are discussed by John Johannes, *Congress and Policy Innovation* (New York: General Learning Press, 1972).

5. Theodore White, *The Making of the President, 1968* (New York: Atheneum, 1969), p. 147.

6. Richard M. Pious, "Nationalizing the Welfare System," *Current History* 64, no. 385 (August 1973): 66–70.

7. Richard M. Pious, "The Phony War on Poverty," *Current History* 61, no. 363 (November 1971): 266–72.

8. *New York Times*, August 21, 1977.

9. Doris Kearns, *Lyndon Johnson and the American Dream* (New York: Harper and Row, 1976), pp. 65–68.

10. For a discussion of Johnson's style of leadership, see David Mayhew, *Party Loyalty in Congress* (Cambridge: Harvard University Press, 1966), pp. 167–168.

11. On Ford's style, see ibid., pp. 150–160.

12. Frank Friedel, *Franklin D. Roosevelt: Launching the New Deal* (Boston: Little, Brown, 1973), p. 305.

13. James D. Barber, *The Presidential Character* (Englewood Cliffs, N.J.: Prentice-Hall, 1972), p. 42.

14. The discussion of public policies makes use of concepts presented by Randall Ripley and Grace Franklin, *Congress, the Bureaucracy and Public Policy* (Homewood, Ill.: The Dorsey Press, 1976).

15. The task force reports are reprinted in M. B. Schnapper, ed., *New Frontiers of the Kennedy Administration* (Washington, D.C.: Public Affairs Press, 1961).

16. James Sundquist, *Politics and Policy: The Eisenhower, Kennedy and Johnson Years* (Washington, D.C.: The Brookings Institution, 1970), p. 415.

17. Henry Campbell Black, *The Relation of Executive Power to Legislation*

(Princeton: Princeton University Press, 1919), Chap. 3: "Executive Initiative in Legislation."

18. Fred Israel, ed., *The State of the Union Messages of the Presidents*, vol. 3 (New York: Chelsea House, 1966), pp. 3026–3521.

19. Bureau of the Budget Circular No. 44.

20. Bureau of the Budget Circular No. 49.

21. Bureau of the Budget Circular No. 336.

22. Richard Neustadt, "The Presidency and Legislation: Planning the President's Program," *The American Political Science Review* 49, no. 4 (December 1955): 980–1021.

23. Robert Gilmour, "Central Legislative Clearance: A Revised Perspective," *Public Administrative Review* 31, no. 2 (March/April 1971): 150–158.

24. William Leuchtenburg, "The Genesis of the Great Society," *The Reporter* 34, no. 8 (April 21, 1966): 38.

25. Robert Gilmour, "Policy-Making and the National Forests" (Ph.D. diss., Columbia University, 1968), p. 184.

26. Norman Thomas and Harold Wolman, "Policy Formulation in the Institutionalized Presidency: The Johnson Task Forces," in *The Presidential Advisory System*, eds. Thomas Cronin and Sanford Greenberg (New York: Harper and Row, 1969).

27. Lyndon Johnson, *The Vantage Point* (New York: Holt, Rinehart and Winston, 1971), p. 326.

28. Stephen J. Wayne, *The Legislative Presidency* (New York: Harper and Row, 1978), pp. 102–103.

29. Arthur Burns, "Heller's New Dimensions of Political Economy," *The National Banking Review* 4, no. 4 (June 1967): 374.

30. Reorganization Plan No. 2, July 1, 1970.

31. *U.S. Government Organization Manual* (Washington, D.C.: Office of the Federal Register, 1976), pp. 90–91.

32. William Carey, "Presidential Staffing in the Sixties and Seventies," *Public Administration Review* 29, no. 5 (Sept./Oct. 1969): 450–458.

33. Louis Maisel, "High-Level Domestic Advising" (Paper presented to the Annual Meeting of the Southern Political Science Association, Atlanta, Georgia, Nov. 4–6, 1976), p. 21.

34. Raymond Waldman, "The Domestic Council: Innovation in Presidential Government," *Public Administration Review* 36, no. 3 (May/June 1976): 266; also Wayne, *Legislative Presidency*, p. 185.

35. Wayne, *Legislative Presidency*, p. 121.

36. For a general discussion of the Domestic Council, see John Kessel, *The Domestic Presidency* (North Scituate: Duxbury Press, 1975); also Ronald Moe, "The Domestic Council in Perspective," *The Bureaucrat* 5, no. 3 (October 1976): 258.

37. Wayne, *Legislative Presidency*, p. 123.

38. For a general discussion see David Beckler, "The Precarious Life of Science in the White House," *Daedalus* 103, no. 3 (Summer 1974): 115–135.

39. Norman Thomas, "Presidential Advice and Information," *Law and Contemporary Problems* 35, no. 3 (Summer 1970): 161.

40. Robert Sherwood, *Roosevelt and Hopkins* (New York: Harper, 1948); Arthur Schlesinger, Jr., *A Thousand Days* (Boston: Fawcett World, 1975); Theodore Sorensen, *Kennedy* (New York: Harper and Row, 1965); William Safire, *Before the Fall* (Garden City, N.Y.: Doubleday, 1975).

41. Patricia S. Florestano, "The Characteristics of White House Staff Appointees from Truman to Nixon," *Presidential Studies Quarterly* 7, no. 4 (Fall 1972): 186.

42. On the history of the ninety-nine commissions from Truman through Nixon, see Thomas R. Wolanin, *Presidential Advisory Commissions* (Madison: University of Wisconsin Press, 1975).

43. Ibid., p. 144.

44. Peter Lyon, *Eisenhower: Portrait of the Hero* (Boston: Little, Brown, 1974), p. 675.

45. *New York Times*, September 29, 1977.

46. Sundquist, *Politics and Policy*, p. 489.

47. Quoted in Johannes, *Congress and Policy Innovation*, p. 1.

48. Samuel Huntington, "Congressional Responses to the Twentieth Century" in *Congress and America's Future*, ed. David Truman (Englewood Cliffs, N.J.: Prentice-Hall, 1973), p. 31.

49. Gary Orfield, *Congressional Power* (New York: Harcourt Brace Jovanovich, 1974), pp. 260–261; but Democratic initiatives may then be vetoed by the president, as indicated by Demetrios Caraley, "Congressional Politics and Urban Aid," *Political Science Quarterly* 91, no. 1 (Spring 1976): 19–46.

50. For a discussion of policy entrepreneurs, see David Price, *Who Makes the Laws?* (New York: Schenkman Publishing Co., 1972).

51. Frederic Cleaveland et al., *Congress and Urban Problems* (Washington, D.C.: The Brookings Institution, 1969), p. 351.

52. On the role of the Joint Committee on Atomic Energy, see Alan Rosenthal and Harold Green, *Government of the Atom* (New York: Atherton Press, 1963).

53. General Accounting Office, *Annual Report, 1971*, p. 18.

54. See Harrison W. Fox and Susan W. Hammond, *Congressional Staffs* (New York: The Free Press, 1977) and especially Chapter 8, "Congressional Support Staffs."

55. Nelson Polsby, "Policy Analysis and Congress," *Public Policy* 18 (Fall 1969): 65.

56. On one such improvement, see Richard M. Pious, *Puerto Ricans and the New York State Literacy Test* (Masters essay, Columbia University, 1966).

57. Richard M. Pious, "Congress, the Organized Bar and the Legal Services Program," *The Wisconsin Law Review* 72, no. 2 (April 1972): 418–446.

58. Lawrence Chamberlain, *President, Congress and Legislation* (New York: Columbia University Press, 1944) studied ninety bills passed by Congress between 1880 and 1940, finding the president the preponderant influence in nineteen cases, Congress in twenty-nine, and equal influence in twenty-nine, with pressure groups initiating the remainder. Seventy-seven of the measures had been introduced in Congress prior to their becoming administration bills. Ronald Moe and Steven Teel, "Congress as Policy Maker," *Political Science Quarterly* 85, no. 3 (September 1970): 443–470, found that Congress had more influence than the president in policy initiation. The only recent study that concedes the president a predominant role is William Goldsmith, *The Growth of Presidential Power: A Documentary History* (New York: Chelsea House, 1974), which found the president the preponderant influence in passage of twenty-six laws, Congress in seven, and joint collaboration in twenty-eight, for the period 1945–1964, pp. 1400–1402.

Chapter Six

1. Franklin Roosevelt, *Public Papers and Addresses of Franklin Roosevelt* (New York: Random House, 1936), 5:215.

2. Theodore Sorensen, *Kennedy* (New York: Harper and Row, 1965), p. 352.

3. *New York Times*, March 12, 1977.

4. On the broad delegations of authority by Congress to the executive, see Louis Fisher, *President and Congress* (New York: The Free Press, 1972), Chapter 3, "Delegation of Power"; also Theodore Lowi, *The End of Liberalism* (New York: W.W. Norton, 1969), Chapter 8, "Interest Group Liberalism and Poverty."

5. Robert Peabody, *Leadership in Congress* (Boston: Little, Brown, 1976), p. 493; for a general treatment, see Randall Ripley, *Party Leaders in the House of Representatives* (Washington, D.C.: The Brookings Institution, 1967).

6. Peabody, *Leadership in Congress*, p. 477; in situations in which the Speaker is from the opposition party the president obviously does not consider him a lieutenant.

7. *New York Times*, March 27, 1977.

8. For a discussion of these events see Joseph Clark, *Congress: The Sapless Branch* (New York: Harper and Row, 1964), Chapter 7, "Prologue to Reform."

9. See the argument of Stephen Balch, "Do Strong Presidents Really Want Strong Legislative Parties?", *Presidential Studies Quarterly* 7, no. 4 (Fall 1977): 231–237.

10. *New York Times*, October 21, 1977.

11. Aage Clausen, *How Congressmen Decide* (New York: St. Martin's Press, 1975), p. 196; John Kingdon, *Congressmen's Voting Decisions* (New York: Harper and Row, 1973), pp. 169–170; but on Nixon's ability to win Republican support for some domestic measures they opposed when Democratic presidents first introduced them, see Demetrios Caraley, "Congressional Politics and Urban Aid," *Political Science Quarterly* 91, no. 1 (Spring 1976): 26.

12. Mark Kesselman, "A Note: Presidential Leadership of Congress on Foreign Policy," *Midwest Journal of Political Science* 5, no. 3 (August 1961): 284–289; Mark Kesselman, "Presidential Leadership in Congress on Foreign Policy," *Midwest Journal of Political Science* 9, no. 4 (November 1965): 401–406.

13. Kingdon, *Congressmen's Voting Decisions*, pp. 17–21; see also John Schwarz and Earl Shaw, *The United States Congress in Comparative Perspective* (Hinsdale, Ill.: The Dryden Press, 1976), p. 171.

14. Kingdon, *Congressmen's Voting Decisions*, p. 179.

15. David Mayhew, *Party Loyalty Among Congressmen* (Cambridge: Harvard University Press, 1966), pp. 148–168; Demetrios Caraley notes that support for urban programs depends primarily on party affiliation, since the average rural Democrat in Congress had urban support scores twice as high as those of the average urban Republican, and even southern Democrats in the House scored higher than all but eastern Republicans, which seems to support Mayhew's argument; cf. Demetrios Caraley, "The Carter Congress and Urban Voting," in *American Politics and Public Policy*, ed. Walter Dean Burnham and Martha Wagner Weinberg (Cambridge: MIT Press, 1978).

16. Schwarz and Shaw, *Congress in Comparative Perspective*, p. 120.

17. *Congressional Quarterly Almanac*, 32, 1976, p. 1008.

18. Demetrios Caraley, "Congressional Politics and Urban Aid," *Political Science Quarterly* 91, no. 1 (Spring 1976): 19–47.

19. Charles Jones, *Minority Party Leadership* (Boston: Little, Brown, 1970), p. 79.

20. Lyndon Johnson, *The Vantage Point* (New York: Holt, Rinehart and Winston, 1971), p. 159.

21. William Safire, *Before the Fall* (Garden City, N.Y.: Doubleday, 1975), p. 685.

22. Schwarz and Shaw, *Congress in Comparative Perspective*, pp. 48–49; see also Norman Ornstein, Robert Peabody, and David Rohde, "The Changing Senate," *Congress Reconsidered*, ed. Lawrence Dodd and Bruce Oppenheimer (New York: Praeger, 1977).

23. Richard Bolling, *House Out of Order* (New York: E.P. Dutton, 1966), p. 39.

24. Abraham Holtzman, *Legislative Liaison* (Indianapolis: Bobbs-Merrill, 1973), p. 1.

25. Lawrence F. O'Brien, Jr., "The Invisible Bridge," (Harvard College senior thesis, 1967); also G. Russell Pipe, "Congressional Liaison: The Executive Branch Consolidates its Relations with Congress," *Public Administration Review* 26, no. 1 (March 1966): 14–24.

26. Ralph Huitt, "White House Channels to the Hill," in *Congress Against the President*, ed., Harvey C. Mansfield (New York: Praeger, 1976), p. 83.

27. Holtzman, *Legislative Liaison*, pp. 251, 254.

28. See Richard Pious, "Congress, the Organized Bar, and the Legal Services Program," *Wisconsin Law Review*, 1972, no. 2, pp. 418–447.

29. On mobilization at the grassroots level, see Morton Grodzins, *The American System* (Chicago: Rand McNally, 1966), especially Chapter 9, "The Mobilization of Public-Private Influence."

30. *Time*, September 1, 1961, p. 14.

31. Johnson, *The Vantage Point*, p. 28.

32. Doris Kearns, *Lyndon Johnson and the American Dream* (New York: Harper and Row, 1976), p. 226.

33. "Text of Bryce Harlow Keynote Address at Nashville Symposium" in *Center House Bulletin* 4, no. 1 (Winter 1974).

34. Johnson, *The Vantage Point*, Chapter 9, "Bite the Bullet."

35. Charles Clapp, *The Congressmen* (Washington, D.C.: The Brookings Institution, 1963), p. 182.

36. Doris Kearns, *Lyndon Johnson and the American Dream*, p. 182.

37. Richard Neustadt, *Presidential Power* (New York: John Wiley, 1961), pp. 52–53.

38. Kearns, *Lyndon Johnson and the American Dream,* p. 185.

39. John E. Moore, "Controlling Delinquency," in *Congress and Urban Problems,* ed. Frederic Cleaveland (Washington, D.C.: The Brookings Institution, 1969), pp. 145–146.

40. Johnson, *The Vantage Point,* p. 458.

41. *New York Times,* February 15, 1978.

42. Johnson, *The Vantage Point,* p. 457.

43. Lawrence O'Brien, *No Final Victories* (Garden City, N.Y.: Doubleday, 1974), p. 118.

44. Sorensen, *Kennedy,* p. 344.

45. Robert Sickels, *Presidential Transactions* (Englewood Cliffs, N.J.: Prentice-Hall, 1974), p. 117.

46. *New York Times,* March 10, 1976.

47. *New York Times,* March 10, 1976.

48. *New York Times,* September 15, 1977.

49. A discussion of the strategy of widening arenas is contained in E.E. Schattschneider, *The Semi-Sovereign People* (New York: Holt, Rinehart and Winston, 1960).

50. Johnson, *The Vantage Point,* p. 450.

51. Robert Donovan, *Eisenhower: The Inside Story* (New York: Harper and Brothers, 1956), p. 230.

52. Johnson, *The Vantage Point,* p. 74.

53. Most presidential addresses are not keyed to pending measures. The ninety-five speeches Hoover made were devoted to restoring confidence, and Roosevelt made radio "fireside chats" that summed up the accomplishments of his administration, since half were given when Congress was out of session. See Edward W. Chester, *Radio, Television and American Politics* (New York: Sheed and Ward, 1969), p. 33.

54. Eisenhower was refused time on NBC and CBS in 1958 during the Quemoy crisis. In 1961, Kennedy was given a 10:00 p.m. (EST) time slot rather than the 6:00 p.m. time he requested during disturbances over racial integration at the University of Mississippi. In 1967 ABC and CBS did not televise one of Johnson's speeches on Vietnam. In 1975, CBS and NBC refused Ford's request for air time to discuss his tax reform measures, claiming that the speech was political and would subject them to demands for equal time from the opposition. In 1977 Carter's energy speech was broadcast by CBS only after a special White House appeal.

55. Newton Minow et al., *Presidential Television* (New York: Basic Books, 1974), pp. 126–159.

56. *New York Times,* February 14, 1978.

57. In May 1977, Carter's aides proposed a television blitz for his energy program, which would have included endorsements by Hollywood stars and various media events. Instead, the president chose a low-key strategy while his proposals went smoothly through the House and only "went public" with one major address while the bills were in the Senate. On the Carter media options, see *New York Times,* May 19, 1977.

58. Elmer Cornwell, *Presidential Leadership of Public Opinion* (Bloomington: University of Indiana Press, 1965), pp. 180–181.

59. Donovan, *Eisenhower: The Inside Story,* p. 150.

60. Neustadt, *Presidential Power,* pp. 65–67.

61. Transcript of remarks of President Franklin D. Roosevelt, May 8, 1933.

62. Alonzo Hamby, *Beyond the New Deal* (New York: Columbia University Press, 1973), p. 74.

63. Gerald Benjamin, "Nixon and the Press in Perspective" (unpublished), p. 15.

64. Pierre Salinger, *With Kennedy* (Garden City, N.Y.: Doubleday, 1966), p. 120.

65. For a general discussion see William Porter, *Assault on the Media* (Ann Arbor: University of Michigan Press, 1976); on surveillance of reporters, see David Wise, *The American Police State* (New York: Random House, 1976), pp. 3–31.

66. Hugh Sidey, *A Very Personal Presidency* (New York: Atheneum, 1968), p. 88.

67. Arthur Krock, *The Consent of the Governed* (Boston: Little, Brown, 1971), pp. 228–242; William Safire, *Before the Fall* (Garden City, N.Y.: Doubleday, 1975), pp. 49–50.

68. Johnson, *The Vantage Point*, p. 80.

69. Presidents begin with very high ratings: (Truman) 77, (Eisenhower) 69, (Kennedy) 76, (Johnson) 76, (Nixon) 61, (Ford) 47, (Carter) 62 were the averages from Gallup Polls for the first year; cf. *Gallup Opinion Index* No. 152 (March 1978), p. 4. On the parabolic curve, see James Stimson, "Public Support for American Presidents: A Cyclical Model," *Public Opinion Quarterly* 40, no. 1 (Spring 1976): 1–22. Other studies have shown a high correlation between presidential popularity and foreign affairs measures, and a low—even negative—correlation between popularity and success in passing domestic legislation; cf. George Edwards III, "Presidential Influence in the House: Presidential Prestige as a Source of Presidential Power," *The American Political Science Review*, 70, no. 1 (March 1976): 101–113; on the kinds of foreign crises that raise or lower presidential popularity, see Jong R. Lee, "Foreign Policy Events and Presidential Popularity," *Presidential Studies Quarterly* 7, no. 4 (Fall 1977): 252–256.

70. Through the Lincoln administration, special sessions were called only nine times. Taft called one special session in 1909, Wilson in 1913 and in 1917, Harding in 1921, Hoover in 1929, and Roosevelt in 1933. These sessions were called because Congress did not normally meet until December following the inauguration of the president, and the special sessions enabled the administration to present Congress with a program in the spring of its first year in office. The adoption of the Twentieth Amendment provided that Congress would convene just prior to the inauguration of the new president, ending the need for special sessions in the first year. Since then the only sessions have been called by Harry Truman in 1947 and 1948.

71. See James Patterson, *Congressional Conservatism and the New Deal* (Lexington: University of Kentucky Press, 1967).

72. Jong R. Lee, "Presidential Vetoes from Washington to Nixon," *Journal of Politics*, 37, no. 2 (May 1975): 526–540.

73. The Pocket Veto Case, 279 U.S. 653.

74. Kennedy v. Sampson, 511 Federal Reporter, 2nd Series 430 (1974).

75. *New York Times*, April 14, 1976.

76. Hollingsworth v. Virginia, 3 Dallas 378 (1798).

77. Stephen Wayne, *The Legislative Presidency* (New York: Harper and Row, 1978), p. 76.

78. Ibid., p. 81.

79. Ibid., pp. 86–87.

80. Clement Vose, "The Memorandum Pocket Veto," *Journal of Politics* 26, no. 2 (May 1964): 397–405.

81. North Pacific Railway Co. v. Kansas, 248 U.S. 276 (1919).

82. Between 1917 and 1976, there were 127 votes for cloture, of which 38 were successful. In recent years there have been several mini-filibusters led by one or two senators to dramatize a point, with no real chance of success; far fewer major filibusters have occurred.

83. For a similar discussion, see Pendleton Herring, *Presidential Leadership* (New York: Farrar and Rinehart, 1940), especially Chapter 6, "The Limits of Presidential Responsibility."

Chapter Seven

1. President's Committee on Administrative Management, *Report with Special Studies* (Washington, D.C.: Government Printing Office, 1937), p. 5.

2. Arthur Schlesinger, Jr., *A Thousand Days* (Boston: Houghton Mifflin, 1965), p. 981.

3. Joel Aberbach and Bert Rockman, "Clashing Beliefs Within the Executive Branch," *The American Political Science Review* 70, no. 2 (June 1976): 456–468.

4. Quoted in Marriner Eccles, *Beckoning Frontiers* (New York: Knopf, 1951), p. 336.

5. Commission on the Organization of the Executive Branch of Government, *General Management of the Executive Branch* (Washington, D.C.: Government Printing Office, 1949), p. 7.

6. Quoted in Richard Neustadt, *Presidential Power* (New York: John Wiley, 1961), p. 7.

7. *New York Times*, August 24, 1974.

8. *New York Times*, September 9, 1977.

9. Leonard White, *The Federalists* (New York: Macmillan, 1948), Chapter 8, "Federalist and Republican Theories of the Executive Power."

10. The greatest of the constitutional scholars on the presidency, Edward Corwin, summed up the position of the "presidentialists" thus: "The Constitution knows only one 'executive power,' that of the President, whose duty to 'take care that the laws be faithfully executed' thus becomes the equivalent of the duty and power to execute them himself according to his own construction of them." Cf. Edward Corwin, *The President: Office and Powers*, 4th ed. rev. (New York: New York University Press, 1957), p. 84.

11. Myers v. United States, 272 U.S. 52 (1926).

12. Kendall v. Stokes, 12 Peters 524 (1837).

13. Such acts include the Lever Food and Fuel Control Act, P.L. 65–41 (1917) and the National Recovery Act, P.L. 73–67 (1933).

14. Harvey C. Mansfield, Sr., "Reorganizing the Federal Executive Branch," *The Institutionalized Presidency*, ed. Norman Thomas and Hans W. Baade (Dobbs Ferry, N.Y.: Oceana Publications, 1972), pp. 35–69.

15. Clifford L. Berg, "Lapse of Reorganization Authority," *Public Administration Review*, 35 (March/April 1975): 195–200.

16. P.L. 95–17.

17. In the Ninety-Fifth Congress Senator Edmund Muskie (D. Maine) introduced the Program Evaluation Act of 1977, cosponsored by fifty-nine Senators, providing for sunset review of all government programs. S 600, introduced by Senator Charles Percy (R. Illinois) and Senator Abraham Ribicoff (D. Connecticut), provides for review of all regulatory agencies. Several bills have also been introduced in the House. For a general discussion, see Allen Schick, "Zero-Base Budgeting and Sunset," *The Bureaucrat* 6, no. 1 (Spring 1977): 12–33; Robert D. Behn, "The False Dawn of Sunset Laws," *The Public Interest* 49 (Fall 1977): 13–19; and Anthony R. Licata, "Zero-Base Sunset Review," *Harvard Journal of Legislation* 14, no. 3 (April 1977): 505–541.

18. Most agencies would probably survive a sunset review. A study conducted by political scientist Herbert Kaufman for the Brookings Institution sampled 175 agencies that existed in 1923 and found that, in 1973, 85 percent still existed, and 62 percent had the same organizational status. Cf. Herbert Kaufman, *Are Government Organizations Immortal?* (Washington, D.C.: The Brookings Institution, 1976), p. 134.

19. P.L. 81–873 (1950).

20. Literature on the relationships between public officials and private groups in the intergovernmental system is extensive. See Harold Seidman, *Politics, Position and Power* (New York: Oxford University Press, 1970), p. 138; Emmette Redford, *Democracy in the Administrative State* (New York: Oxford University Press, 1969), p. 42; Frederick Mosher, *Democracy in the Public Service* (New York: Oxford University Press, 1968), Chapter Four, "The Professional State"; Edward Weidner, "Decision-Making in a Federal System" in *Federalism: Mature and Emergent*, ed. Arthur W. MacMahon (New York: Russell and Russell, 1955).

21. See J. Malcolm Smith and Cornelius P. Cotter, *Powers of the President During Crises* (Washington, D.C.: Public Affairs Press, 1960); and Robert S. Rankin and Winfried R. Dallmayr, *Freedom and Emergency Powers in the Cold War* (New York: Appleton-Century-Crofts, 1964).

22. P.L. 94–412.

23. A comprehensive account of the civil service system is contained in Hugh Heclo, *A Government of Strangers* (Washington, D.C.: The Brookings Institution, 1977).

24. U.S. Civil Service Commission, "Statutory Exceptions to the Competitive Service" (Washington, D.C.: Government Printing Office, 1973), p. 12.

25. Heclo, *A Government of Strangers*, p. 38.

26. Ibid., p. 32.

27. P.L. 93-250.

28. The Senate rarely blocks a presidential appointment. Since World War II only Lewis Strauss was formally rejected by the Senate (for Secretary of Commerce in 1959). Presidents sometimes withdraw nominations after opposition develops. Theodore Sorensen, Carter's nominee for Director of Central Intelligence, withdrew after a majority of the Senate Select Committee on Intelligence indicated opposition to his nomination. The power of the Senate is often inhibitory, although it is rarely employed on formal votes.

29. *New York Times*, November 13, 1977.

30. Presidential removal power was affirmed by the Supreme Court in Myers v. United States, 272 U.S. 52 (1926); it does not include members of independent regulatory agencies, Humphrey's Executor v. United States, 295 U.S. 602 (1935); under certain circumstances due process or other conditions may be required for removals, Weiner v. United States, 357 U.S. 349 (1958).

31. Seidman, *Politics, Position and Power*, p. 50.

32. Elizabeth Drew, "A Reporter at Large," *The New Yorker*, April 4, 1977, pp. 99-117.

33. Eugene B. McGregor, Jr., "Politics and Career Mobility of Civil Servants," *The American Political Science Review* 68, no. 1 (March 1974): 24.

34. This discussion of organizational behavior is adapted from Graham Allison, *Essence of Decision* (Boston: Little, Brown, 1971), especially Chapter 3, "Model II: Organization Process."

35. Joel Aberbach and Bert Rockman, "The Overlapping Worlds of American Federal Executives and Congressmen," *British Journal of Political Science* 7, no. 1 (January 1977): 27-42.

36. On relationships between interest groups and executive officials see David Truman, *The Governmental Process* (New York: Knopf, 1951); also Grant McConnel, *Private Power and American Democracy* (New York: Knopf, 1967). A model of the "triple alliance" is contained in J. Lieper Freeman, *The Political Process* (New York: Random House, 1955).

37. P.L. 79-601.

38. P.L. 91-510, sec. 204(a).

39. See Joseph Pois, "Trends in General Accounting Office Audits," and Ira Sharkansky, "The Politics of Auditing," both in *The New Political Economy*, ed. Bruce L.R. Smith (London: Halsted Press, 1975).

40. P.L. 91-422.

41. Alan Rosenthal and Harold Green, *Government of the Atom* (New York: Atherton Press, 1963).

42. H. Lee Watson, "Congress Steps Out: A Look at Congressional Control of the Executive," *California Law Review* 63, no. 4 (July 1975): 983-1094.

43. C. Norton, "Congressional Review, Deferral and Disapproval of Executive Actions," (Congressional Research Service, 1975), p. 8. Forty-eight provisions passed Congress between 1974 and 1978, *New York Times*, June 22, 1978.

44. *Weekly Compilation of Presidential Documents* 12 (May 10, 1976); 828. Issues involving legislative vetoes were being litigated in 1978. Former President Nixon sued the General Services Administration, contending that the provision of law giving Congress a one-chamber "veto" over regulations issued by the General Services Administration involving access to the White House tapes was unconstitutional. Nixon argued that the function of approving or disapproving regulations was executive and should have been delegated by Congress to the president under the Presidential Recordings and Materials Preservation Act. Carter warned Congress that he would consider vetoing bills with legislative veto provisions, and his Department of Justice filed a brief in the Nixon suit agreeing with some of the former president's contentions that the legislative veto was unconstitutional.

45. House Document 31, "Reports to be Made to Congress," 91st Cong., 1st Sess. (Washington, D.C.: Government Printing Office, 1967).

46. Morris Ogul, *Congress Oversees the Bureaucracy* (Pittsburgh: University of Pittsburgh Press, 1976), pp. 177-179.

47. Sen. Res. 400 (1976).

48. Ogul, *Congress Oversees the Bureaucracy*, p. 21.

49. *New York Times*, March 3, 1978.

50. Quoted in Stephen Wayne, *The Legislative Presidency* (New York: Harper and Row, 1978), p. 187.

51. Executive Order 11541.

52. U.S. Congress, House, Committee on Post Office and Civil Service, Subcommittee on Manpower and Civil Service, *Final Report on Violations and Abuses of Merit Principles in Federal Employment*, 94th Cong., 2nd Sess. (Washington, D.C.: Government Printing Office, 1976).

53. Bernard Rosen, "A Plus for Effective Government," *Civil Service Journal* 15, no. 2 (October/December 1974): 1–5.

54. Morton Halperin, *Bureaucratic Politics and Foreign Policy* (Washington, D.C.: The Brookings Institution, 1974), p. 227.

55. Graham Allison, *Essence of Decision* (Boston: Little, Brown, 1971), pp. 129–131.

56. John Kenneth Galbraith, *Ambassador's Journal* (Boston: Houghton Mifflin, 1969), p. 7.

57. Richard Neustadt, *Presidential Power Revisited* (New York: John Wiley and Sons, 1976), p. 7.

58. Richard Neustadt, *Presidential Power* (New York: John Wiley and Sons, 1961), p. 39.

59. Thomas Cronin, *The State of the Presidency* (Boston: Little, Brown, 1975), pp. 180–189.

60. Heclo, *Government of Strangers*, p. 103.

61. Arch Patton, "Government's Revolving Door," *Business Week* 2298 (September 22, 1973), p. 12.

62. Thomas M. Franck and Edward Weisband, *Resignation in Protest* (New York: The Viking Press, 1976), p. 59.

63. Ibid., p. 144.

64. *New York Times*, February 4, 1977.

65. Frederick Mosher and John Haar, *Programming Systems and Foreign Affairs Leadership* (New York: Oxford University Press, 1970), pp. 111–119.

66. The best general treatment of the cabinet is contained in Richard Fenno, Jr., *The President's Cabinet* (Cambridge: Harvard University Press, 1959).

67. Quoted in Rexford G. Tugwell, "The President and His Helpers," *Political Science Quarterly* 82, no. 2 (June 1967): 262.

68. *New York Times*, March 2, 1977.

69. Schlesinger, *A Thousand Days*, p. 688.

70. Arthur Schlesinger, Jr., *The Coming of the New Deal* (Boston: Houghton Mifflin, 1958), pp. 527–528.

71. Richard T. Johnson, *Managing the White House* (New York: Harper and Row, 1974), p. 34.

72. Hoover's payroll included four secretaries, two military aides, and several clerical aides. Cf. Patrick Anderson, *The President's Men* (Garden City, N.Y.: Anchor Books, 1969), pp. 54–55. In some ways, little has changed since the nineteenth century. Consider the letter President Garfield sent to John Hay, attempting to convince him to become Secretary to the President: "The Secretary of the President ought to rank with any of the seven members of the Cabinet. In a thousand ways, the President needs a trusted and capable friend at hand, one who can see the moves on the chess-board more clearly than the players can." Quoted in T.C. Smith, *Life of James Abram Garfield* (New Haven: Yale University Press, 1925), 2:1070.

73. President's Committee on Administrative Management, *Report With Special Studies*, p. 5.

74. *The Budget of the United States Government, Fiscal Year 1978* (Washington, D.C.: Government Printing Office, 1977), p. 815. An accurate count is made difficult by the practice of using consultants, detailees from departments still on department payrolls, and White House aides placed on department payrolls.

75. Thomas Cronin, "The Swelling of the Presidency," *Saturday Review of Society* 1, no. 1 (February 1973): 30–36.

76. Jeb Stuart Magruder, *An American Life* (New York: Atheneum, 1974), p. 58.

77. Irving Janis, *Victims of Groupthink* (Boston: Houghton Mifflin, 1973).

78. Theodore Sorensen, *Decision-Making in the White House* (New York: Columbia University Press, 1963), p. 71.

79. Patrick Anderson, *The President's Men* (Garden City, N.Y.: Doubleday, 1969), p. 53.

80. Magruder, *An American Life*, p. 56.

81. Ibid., p. 306.

82. President's Committee on Administrative Management, *Report with Special Studies*, p. 5.

83. Thomas Cronin, *The State of the Presidency* (Boston: Little, Brown, 1975), p. 17.

84. John Dean, *Blind Ambition* (New York: Simon and Schuster, 1976), p. 30.

85. President's Committee on Administrative Management, *Report with Special Studies*, p. 5.

86. Dom Bonafede, "Carter's White House Staff Heavy on Function, Light on Frills," *The National Journal* 9, no. 7 (February 12, 1977): 234. A year later, a special meeting of cabinet members and senior staffers was called by Carter at Camp David, in order to discuss how decision-making in the administration could be coordinated by the White House.

87. For a general discussion, see Richard Nathan, *The Plot that Failed* (New York: John Wiley and Sons, 1975).

88. Seidman, *Politics, Position and Power*, pp. 116–118.

89. *New York Times*, November 14, 1976.

90. Allen Schick, "A Death in the Bureaucracy: The Demise of Federal PPB," *Public Administration Review*, 33, no. 2 (March/April 1973): 146–155.

91. For a general discussion, see Richard Rose, *Managing Presidential Objectives* (New York: The Free Press, 1976).

92. Ibid., p. 90.

93. Richard Rose, "Implementation and Evaporation: The Record of MBO," *Public Administraion Review* 37, no. 1 (Jan./Feb. 1977): 69.

94. Rose, *Managing Presidential Objectives*, p. 102.

95. Lawrence Berman, "The Office of Management and Budget that Almost Wasn't," *Political Science Quarterly* 92, no. 2 (Summer 1977): 302–303.

96. Wayne, *The Legislative Presidency*, p. 192.

97. Edward Jay Epstein, *Agency of Fear* (New York: G.P. Putnam's Sons, 1977).

98. White House Study Project, Report No. 2.

99. Richard Rose, "The President: A Chief But Not an Executive," *Presidential Studies Quarterly* 7, no. 1 (Winter 1977): 14.

100. For the complicated story of the proposed reforms and their derailment, see Berman, "The Office of Management and Budget that Almost Wasn't," *Political Science Quarterly*, 281–303.

Chapter Eight

1. Gerald Ford, "Budget Message of the President," *The Budget of the United States Government, Fiscal Year 1978* (Washington, D.C.: Government Printing Office, 1977), p. M-3.

2. Message from the President of the United States, "The Need for a National Budget," *Report of the Commission on Economy and Efficiency*, House Document 854, 62nd Cong., 2nd Sess., 1912, pp. 143–144.

3. 42 Stat. 20, sec. 206.

4. Bureau of the Budget, Circular No. 49: "All requests or recommendations for legislation, the effect of which would be to create a charge upon the public treasury or commit the government to obligations which would later require appropriations to meet them, should first be submitted to the President before being presented to Congress . . . it shall first be submitted to the Director of the Budget, who shall

make recommendations with respect thereto, to the President. And no such request shall be submitted to either House of Congress, or to any committee thereof, without having first been approved by the President."

5. Joel Havemann, "Budget Report/ Ford, Congress Seek Handle on 'Uncontrollable Spending,'" *The National Journal* 7, no. 48 (November 29, 1975): 1624.

6. Aaron Wildavsky, *The Politics of the Budgetary Process* (Boston: Little, Brown, 1974), p. 17; also Otto Davis, Michael Dempster, and Aaron Wildavsky, "A Theory of the Budgetary Process," *The American Political Science Review* 60, no. 3 (September 1966): 529–548.

7. Peter Natchez and Irvin Bupp, "Policy and Priority in the Budget Process," *The American Political Science Review* 67, no. 3 (September 1973): 951–963.

8. Paul Schulman, "Nonincremental Policy Making: Notes Toward an Alternative Paradigm," *The American Political Science Review* 69, no. 4 (December 1975): 1354–1370.

9. William B. Moreland, "A Nonincremental Perspective on Budgetary Policy Actions," in *Policy-Making in the Federal Executive Branch*, ed. Randall Ripley and Grace Franklin (New York: The Free Press, 1975).

10. Lawrence J. Korb, "The Secretary of Defense and the Joint Chiefs of Staff: The Budgeting Process," in *The Military-Industrial Complex*, ed. Sam Sarkesian (Beverley Hills: Sage Publishers, 1972); also James Roherty, "The Office of Secretary of Defense: The Laird and McNamara Styles," in *New Civil-Military Relations*, ed. John Lovell and Phillip Kronenberg (New Brunswick, N.J.: Transaction Books, 1974).

11. For a study of the problems with Pentagon budgeting in this period, see Samuel Huntington, *The Common Defense* (New York: Columbia University Press, 1961).

12. Ralph Sanders, *The Politics of Defense Analysis* (New York: Dunellen Publishing Company, 1973), p. 73.

13. On presidential consideration of service budget requests, see Arnold Kantor, "Congress and the Defense Budget: 1960–1970," *The American Political Science Review* 66, no. 1 (March 1972): 131 (especially Table 1).

14. Robert Bender, "The Defense Budget and Civil-Military Relations," in *Civil-Military Relations*, ed. Charles Cochran (New York: The Free Press, 1974), p. 107.

15. Sanders, *The Politics of Defense Analysis*, p. 84.

16. Korb, "The Secretary of Defense and the Joint Chiefs of Staff: The Budgeting Process," p. 262.

17. Lance LeLoup, "Agency Policy Actions: Determinants of Nonincremental Change," in *Policy Making in the Federal Executive Branch*, ed. Ripley and Franklin.

18. Gary Bombardier, "The Managerial Function of OMB," *Public Policy* 23, no. 3 (Summer 1975): 317.

19. Bureau of the Budget, Circular No. 1, June 29, 1921.

20. Harold D. Smith, "The Bureau of the Budget," *Public Administration Review* 1, no. 2 (Winter 1940/41): 106–115.

21. Kermit Gordon, "Reflections on Spending," *Public Policy* 15 (1966): 12.

22. Hugh Heclo, "The Presidency and OMB," *The Public Interest* no. 38 (Winter 1975): 81–82.

23. Ibid., p. 84.

24. Gordon, "Reflections on Spending," p. 12.

25. Lance LeLoup, *Budgetary Politics* (Brunswick, Ohio: Kings Court Communications, 1977), p. 13.

26. For a study of the House Appropriations Committee, see Richard Fenno, *The Power of the Purse* (Boston: Little, Brown, 1966).

27. The appellate role of the Senate Appropriations Committee is discussed by Wildavsky, *The Politics of the Budgetary Process*, p. 52; the committee is the subject of Stephen Horn, *Unused Power* (Washington, D.C.: The Brookings Institution, 1970).

28. Fenno, *The Power of the Purse*, pp. 666–667; on military budgets, see Kantor, "Congress and the Defense Budget: 1960–1970," p. 139.

29. The text of this measure is reproduced in Edward Corwin, *The President: Office and Powers*, 4th ed. rev. (New York: New York University Press, 1957), p. 128.

30. Keith Marvin and James Hedrick, "The GAO Helps Congress Evaluate Programs," *Public Administration Review* 34, no. 4 (July/August 1974): 327–332.

31. Horn, *Unused Power*, p. 180.

32. In 1978, Congress began serious consideration of proposals for "zero-base" budget review for the appropriations process. Every five or six years a program would be examined thoroughly by standing committees, which would then have to report their findings before the appropriations committees could consider agency budget requests. See Allen Schick, "Zero-Base Budgeting and Sunset," *The Bureaucrat* 6, no. 1 (Spring 1977): 12–33; and Anthony R. Licata, "Zero-Base Sunset Review," *Harvard Journal of Legislation* 14, no. 3 (April 1977): 505–541.

33. Edward Kolodziej, *The Uncommon Defense and Congress, 1945–1963* (Athens: University of Ohio Press, 1966), p. 137.

34. On the operation of the "triple alliance" in the Defense Department, see Gordon M. Adams, "Disarming the Military Subgovernment," *Harvard Journal of Legislation*, 14, no. 3 (April 1977): 459–503.

35. Louis Fisher, "Congressional Budget Reform: The First Two Years," *Harvard Journal of Legislation* 14, no. 3 (April 1977): 429.

36. Horn, *Unused Power*, p. 195.

37. James Richardson, ed., *Compilation of the Messages and Papers of the Presidents, 1789–1897* (New York: Johnson Reprint Co., 1969), 1:360–361, 372.

38. *Opinions of the Attorney General*, (1896) pp. 392–393, (1899) pp. 295–296.

39. Bureau of the Budget Circular, No. 4, July 21, 1921.

40. Bureau of the Budget Circular, No. 51, December 21, 1921.

41. Executive Order 6166.

42. 64 Stat. 595, sec. 3679. A 1961 memorandum from the Bureau of the Budget to Kennedy also took a narrow view of the antideficiency act, as did Assistant Attorney General William Rehnquist in a 1969 Justice Department memorandum to Nixon. See U.S. Congress, Senate, Committee on the Judiciary, *Comptroller General's Opinion of the Legality of Executive Impoundments of Appropriated Funds*, 93rd Cong., 2nd Sess. (Washington, D.C.: Government Printing Office, 1974), with portions of the 1961 memo reprinted on p. 19. The 1952 edition of the Budget Examiner's Handbook noted that "reserves must not be used to nullify the intent of Congress with respect to specific projects or levels of programs," cited in *Comptroller General's Opinion of the Legality of Executive Impoundments of Appropriated Funds*, p. 18.

43. House Report No. 1797, 81st Cong., 2nd Sess., p. 311.

44. *New York Times*, March 13, 1978.

45. 42 U.S.C. Title VI, sec. 2000d–3.

46. 42 Stat. 382.

47. James Richardson, *Messages and Papers of the Presidents: 1789–1897* (Washington, D.C.: Government Printing Office, 1896–99), p. 377.

48. Second Supplemental National Defense Appropriations Act of 1943, P.L. 77-763.

49. 58 Stat. 887, 59 Stat. 11.

50. Louis Fisher, "Presidential Spending Discretion and Congressional Controls," *Law and Contemporary Problems* 37 (Winter 1972): 161.

51. House Report No. 1797, p. 311.

52. Gerald W. Davis, "Congressional Power to Require Defense Expenditures," *Fordham Law Review* 33 (October 1964): 39–60.

53. 15 U.S.C. Title V, sec. 1021.

54. Ibid.

55. 84 Stat. 799, sec. 202.

56. P.L. 90–364, Title II.

57. Fisher, "Congressional Budget Reform," p. 414.

58. U.S. Congress, *Congressional Record*, February 20, 1973, 119: 2873.

59. U.S. Congress, Senate, Committee on the Judiciary, *Impoundment of Appropriated Funds by the President*, Joint Hearings before the Ad Hoc Subcommittee on Impoundment of Funds of the Committee on Government Operations and the Subcommittee on the Separation of Powers of the Committee on the Judiciary, 93rd Cong., 1st Sess. (Washington, D.C.: Government Printing Office, 1973), pp. 172–173. Hereinafter cited as 1973 Senate Hearings.

60. Louis Fisher, "Funds Impounded by the President: The Constitutional Issues," *George Washington Law Review* 38, no. 1 (October 1969): 137.

61. *Public Papers of the Presidents of the United States, 1969* (Washington, D.C.: Federal Register Division, 1971), p. 538.

62. 1973 Senate Hearings, pp. 367, 841.

63. 92 Stat. 1324, P.L. 92-599.

64. P.L. 93-28 sec. 4(j): "Nothing in this title may be construed to authorize or require the withholding or reservation of any obligational authority provided by law or of any funds appropriated under such authority."

65. State Highway Commission of Missouri v. Volpe, 347 F. Supp. 950 (1971).

66. Cases overturning Nixon impoundments include: Local 2677 The American Federation of Government Employees v. Phillips, West Central Missouri Rural Development Corp. v. Phillips, and National Council of OEO Locals v. Phillips, all at 358 F. Supp. 60 (D.C., 1973); Gaudmuz v. Ash, 368 F. Supp. 1233 (1973), and Pennsylvania v. Lynn, 362 F. Supp. 1362 (1973).

67. Train v. City of New York, 420 U.S. 35.

68. *U.S. News and World Report*, 70, no. 16 (April 19, 1971): 42.

69. U.S. Congress, Senate, Committee on Government Operations, Ad Hoc Subcommittee on the Impoundment of Funds, *Hearings* (January 30, 31, February 1, 6, 7), 93rd Cong., 1st Sess. (Washington, D.C.: Government Printing Office, 1973), p. 72. Hereinafter cited as 1973 Ad Hoc Hearings.

70. 1973 Ad Hoc Hearings, p. 151.

71. Ibid., p. 233.

72. Budget and Impoundment Act of 1974, P.L. 93-344.

73. *Congressional Quarterly Almanac* 31 (1975): 783.

74. Louis Fisher, *Presidential Spending Power* (Princeton, N.J.: Princeton University Press, 1975), p. 7. This section relies heavily on Fisher's work.

75. Ibid., p. 207.

76. 50 U.S.C. 403(d)(6).

77. 50 U.S.C. 403(f).

78. 88 Stat. 1804, sec. 32 (1974).

79. Fisher, *Presidential Spending Power*, p. 107.

80. Ibid., p. 104.

81. Ibid., p. 111.

82. 7 U.S.C. 1704(c) sec. 614; on Food for Peace Transfers, see Fisher, "Presidential Spending Discretion," p. 146.

83. Fisher, *Presidential Spending Power*, p. 87.

84. Timothy H. Ingram, "The Billions in the White House Basement," *The Washington Monthly* 3, no. 11 (January 1972): 42.

85. A proposal to increase congressional influence in the budget process suggests reducing the forty-five-day period given to the president after a deferral or rescission request has been denied, so that the administration would have to spend the funds immediately after Congress made its decision. The appropriations committees may yet introduce a computerized information retrieval system so that budget information about transfers and reprogrammings can be obtained instantly; committees could then intervene if appropriations laws were being circumvented. The Congressional Budget Office has conducted a study of "advance budgeting" to place programs on a two-year or longer appropriation cycle. Such a cycle would commit departments to program expenditures for several years in advance and lock in a new administration for almost half its first term. See Congressional Budget Office, "Advance Budgeting" (February 24, 1977).

Chapter Nine

1. Rowland Evans and Robert Novak, *Nixon in the White House* (New York: Random House, 1971), p. 177.

2. Arthur Schlesinger, Jr., *The Coming of the New Deal* (Boston: Houghton Mifflin, 1958), p. 406.

3. Lewis Kimmel, *The Federal Budget and Fiscal Policy: 1789–1958* (Washington, D.C.: The Brookings Institution, 1959), especially Chapter 6, "Fiscal Policy Since 1940."

4. Walter Heller, *New Dimensions of Political Economy* (Cambridge: Harvard University Press, 1966), p. 62.

5. Arthur Okun, *The Political Economy of Prosperity* (New York: W.W. Norton, 1970), p. 40.

6. Council of Economic Advisors, *Annual Report, 1962* (Washington, D.C.: Government Printing Office, 1962), p. 17.

7. Council of Economic Advisors, *Annual Report, 1970* (Washington, D.C.: Government Printing Office, 1970), p. 10.

8. Robert Heilbroner, "The Clouded Crystal Ball," *American Economic Review,* 64, no. 2 (May 1974): 124.

9. Okun, *The Political Economy of Prosperity*, p. 111.

10. Walter Heller, "What's Right with Economics," *American Economic Review,* 65, no. 1 (January 1975): 1–26.

11. William Fellner, *Towards a Reconstruction of Macroeconomics* (Washington, D.C.: The American Enterprise Institute, 1976), p. 113.

12. Arthur Okun, "The Great Stagflation Swamp," *The Brookings Bulletin* 14, no. 3 (Fall 1977): 1. By 1978, referring to the theory that a 3 percent rate of growth in the GNP could reduce unemployment by 1 percent (known as "Okun's law"), Arthur Okun admitted, "Okun's Law has been repealed," adding, "what we've got now is the biggest puzzle in the behavior of the economy that I've seen in years." *New York Times,* May 13, 1978.

13. Council of Economic Advisors, *Annual Report, 1976* (Washington, D.C.: Government Printing Office, 1976), p. 20.

14. *New York Times,* April 28, 1977.

15. *New York Times,* March 20, 1977.

16. James Tobin, *The New Economics: One Decade Older* (Princeton, N.J.: Princeton University Press, 1974), p. 6.

17. Alan Blinder and Robert Solow, "Analytical Foundations of Fiscal Policy," in *The Economics of Public Finance,* Blinder et al. (Washington, D.C.: 1974).

18. Okun, "The Great Stagflation Swamp," p. 2.

19. Fellner, *Towards a Reconstruction of Macroeconomics,* pp. 47–50.

20. Milton Friedman, "Inflation and Unemployment," *Journal of Political Economy* 85, no. 3 (June 1977): 451–472; see Phillip Cagan, "The Reduction of Inflation and the Magnitude of Unemployment," *Contemporary Economic Problems, 1977* ed. William Fellner (Washington, D.C.: American Enterprise Institute, 1977).

21. William L. Springer, "Did the 1968 Surcharge Really Work?", *American Economic Review* 65, no. 4 (December 1975): 644–659.

22. Paul McCracken, "An Appraisal of Economic Policy" (address delivered to the American Statistical Association, Washington, D.C., December 27, 1967), p. 11.

23. George L. Perry, "Stabilization Policy and Inflation," *Setting National Priorities,* ed. Henry Owen and Charles Schultze (Washington, D.C.: The Brookings Institution, 1976).

24. Attiat Ott and David Ott, *Projections of State-Local Expenditures* (Washington, D.C.: American Enterprise Institute, 1976).

25. George Katona and Burkhard Strumpel, "A New Economic Era," *Public Opinion,* March/April 1978, p. 9.

26. Robert Eisner, "What Went Wrong?", *Journal of Political Economy* 79, no. 3 (May/June 1971): 638.

27. Council of Economic Advisors, *Annual Report, 1973* (Washington, D.C.: Government Printing Office, 1973), p. 63.

28. *New York Times,* February 8, 1975.

29. Paul McCracken, *Reflections on Economic Advising* (Los Angeles: International Institute for Economic Research, 1976), p. 9.

30. James B. Ramsey, "Economic Forecasting—Models or Markets?" Hobart Paper No. 74 (London: Institute of Economic Affairs, 1977).

31. *New York Times,* May 4, 1977. The inflation rate for the year was actually 6.8 percent.

32. Wilfred Lewis, Jr., *Federal Fiscal Policy in the Postwar Recessions* (Washington, D.C.: American Enterprise Institute, 1973), p. 20.

33. William Niskanen, *Structural Reforms of the Federal Budget Process* (Washington, D.C.: American Enterprise Institute, 1973), pp. 14–15.

34. *New York Times*, October 12, 1976.

35. *New York Times*, September 18, 1977.

36. *New York Times*, March 14, 1978.

37. *Wall Street Journal*, January 17, 1977.

38. Quoted in Edward Flash, Jr., *Economic Advice and Presidential Leadership* (New York: Columbia University Press, 1965), p. 15.

39. Edwin G. Nourse, *Economics in the Public Service* (New York: Harcourt Brace and Co., 1953), p. 377.

40. Hugh S. Norton, *The Council of Economic Advisors, Essays in Economics*, no. 27, May 1973 (Bureau of Business and Economic Research, 1973).

41. Neil H. Jacoby, "The President, the Constitution, and the Economist in Economic Stabilization," *History of Political Economy*, 3, no. 2 (Fall 1971): 398–414.

42. Okun, *The Political Economy of Prosperity*, p. 23; Gardner Ackley, "The Contribution of Economists to Policy Formation," *Journal of Finance*, 21, no. 2 (May 1966): 176.

43. On the workings of the Board, see Daniel Balz, "Juice and Coffee and the GNP—the Men Who Meet in the Morning," *The National Journal* 8, no. 14 (April 3, 1976): 426–433; also Joseph Kraft, "Right, for Ford," *The New York Times Magazine*, April 25, 1976, pp. 26, 106–116.

44. Balz, "Juice and Coffee and the GNP," p. 428.

45. Ibid., p. 432.

46. On the competition between staff units of the Executive Office in making economic policy, see John Helmer and Louis Maisel, "Analytical Problems in the Study of Presidential Advice: The Domestic Council Staff in Flux," *Presidential Studies Quarterly* 8, no. 1 (Winter 1978): 59–60.

47. *New York Times*, May 9, 1977.

48. The Conference Board, *Across the Board*, October 1976.

49. Gordon Bach, *Making Monetary and Fiscal Policy* (Washington, D.C.: The Brookings Institution, 1971), p. 82.

50. Herbert Stein, *The Fiscal Revolution in America* (Chicago: University of Chicago Press, 1969).

51. *New York Times*, June 2, 1977.

52. George L. Perry, "Stabilization Policy and Inflation," p. 295.

53. *New York Times*, July 14, 1977.

54. Cited by Gerhard Colm, "The Executive Office and Fiscal and Economic Policy," *Law and Contemporary Problems* 21 (Autumn 1956): 710–723.

55. Council of Economic Advisors, *Annual Report, 1975* (Washington, D.C.: Government Printing Office, 1975), p. 134.

56. *New York Times*, September 25, 1977.

57. Henry Kenskie, "The Impact of Unemployment on Presidential Popularity from Eisenhower to Nixon," *Presidential Studies Quarterly* 7, nos. 2–3 (Spring/Summer 1977): 114–126.

58. Quoted in Nourse, *Economics in the Public Service*, p. 349.

59. *New York Times*, October 22, 1975.

60. Office of Management and Budget, "Midyear Budget Review," July 1, 1977. Later, OMB Director James McIntyre, Jr. admitted that the budget for the fiscal year 1981 would have a deficit of at least $20 billion.

61. Kenskie, "The Impact of Unemployment on Presidential Popularity from Eisenhower to Nixon," pp. 114–126.

62. Lewis, *Federal Fiscal Policy in the Postwar Recessions*, p. 22.

63. Bach, *Making Monetary and Fiscal Policy*, p. 5.

64. Wilbur Mills, address to the American Enterprise Institute, April 20, 1967, p. 5.

65. Okun, *The Political Economy of Prosperity*, p. 19.

66. Aaron Wildavsky, *The Politics of the Budgetary Process*, 2nd ed. (Boston: Little, Brown, 1974), pp. 235–240.

67. *The Congressional Budget Office: Responsibilities and Organization* (Washington, D.C.: Government Printing Office, 1976).

68. Congressional Budget Office, "Budget Options for Fiscal Year 1977" (Washington,, D.C.: Government Printing Office, 1976).

69. For criticisms of the Congressional Budget Office, see Senate Report No. 1201, 94th Cong., 2nd Sess., 1976; House Report No. 645, 94th Cong., 1st Sess., 1975; House Document No. 20, 95th Cong., 1st Sess. 1977.

70. See "Views and Estimates of Standing Committees of the House on the Congressional Budget for Fiscal Year 1978" (March 15, 1977), p. 41; also John W. Ellwood and James Thurber, "The New Congressional Budget Process," in *Congress Reconsidered*, ed. Lawrence Dodd and Bruce Oppenheimer (New York: Praeger, 1977); Louis Fisher, "Congressional Budget Reform: The First Two Years," *Harvard Journal on Legislation* 14, no. 3 (April 1977): 435.

71. Congressional Budget Office, "Congressional Budget Scorekeeping Report," Report No. 3, October 1, 1976, p. 1.

72. *New York Times*, April 29, 1977.

73. *New York Times*, May 3, 1977.

74. Ibid.

75. Fisher, "Congressional Budget Reform: The First Two Years," p. 437.

76. *New York Times*, September 28, 1977.

77. *New York Times*, May 9 and 10, 1977.

78. P.L. 91–379.

79. Executive Order 11695.

80. Marvin Kosters, *Controls and Inflation* (Washington, D.C.: American Enterprise Institute, 1975), p. 47.

81. Ibid., p. 53.

82. Ibid., p. 1.

83. U.S. Congress, House, Subcommittee on Employment Opportunities of the Education and Labor Committee, *Hearings on S. 50*, 95th Cong., 2nd Sess., January 18, 1978; also see American Enterprise Institute Legislative Analysis, *Full Employment and Balanced Growth Act: An Update* (Washington, D.C.: American Enterprise Institute, 1978).

Chapter Ten

1. Louis Henkin, *Foreign Affairs and the Constitution* (Mineola, N.Y.: The Foundation Press, 1972), p. 16.

2. Raoul Berger, "The Presidential Monopoly of Foreign Relations," *Michigan Law Review* 71, no. 1 (November 1972): 28; Henkin, *Foreign Affairs and the Constitution*, pp. 22–23.

3. On emergency prerogatives, see Arthur Schlesinger, Jr., *The Imperial Presidency* (Boston: Houghton Mifflin, 1973), pp. 321–322.

4. Justice Sutherland summed up the "presidentialist view" by alluding to the "very delicate, plenary, and exclusive power of the President as sole organ of the federal government in the field of foreign relations," in *United States v. Curtiss-Wright Export Corporation*, 299 U.S. 304 (1936). But Sutherland's opinion was dicta, not necessary to decide the case, which involved the question of whether Congress had the power to legislate an arms embargo by joint resolution, and, if so, whether it could then delegate that power to the president. The case did not involve inherent presidential powers, nor the extent to which the president may constitutionally control foreign policy. Needless to say, it was also descriptively inaccurate then, as now.

5. *American State Papers, Foreign Relations* 1 (November 22, 1793): 184.

6. Berger, "The Presidential Monopoly of Foreign Relations," pp. 6–11.

7. W. Stull Holt, *Treaties Defeated by the Senate* (Baltimore: Johns Hopkins University Press, 1933), pp. 29–32.

8. Bernard Cohen, *The Political Process and Foreign Policy* (Princeton, N.J.: Princeton University Press, 1951).

9. Woodrow Wilson, *Constitutional Government in the United States* (New York: Columbia University Press, 1908), pp. 77–78.

10. Holt, *Treaties Defeated by the Senate*, p. 119.

11. D.F. Fleming, *The Treaty Veto of the American Senate* (New York: G.P. Putnam's Sons, 1930), p. 272.

12. Henkin points out that while there must be distinctions between treaties and executive agreements, the courts "have not told us which are which," *Foreign Affairs and the Constitution*, p. 179.

13. John B. Rehm, "Making Foreign Policy Through International Agreement," in *The Constitution and the Conduct of Foreign Policy*, ed. Francis Wilcox and Richard Franck (New York: Praeger, 1976).

14. Berger, "Presidential Monopoly of Foreign Relations," p. 34.

15. Richard Nixon to Nguyen Thieu, dated January 5, 1973; reprinted in *New York Times*, May 1, 1975.

16. Wallace McClure, *International Executive Agreements* (New York: Columbia University Press, 1941), p. 343.

17. Senate Resolution 69.

18. Senate Resolution 469.

19. Senate Resolution 214.

20. Public Law 92–404.

21. U.S. Congress, Senate, *Congressional Oversight of Executive Agreements*, Hearings before the Subcommittee on the Separation of Powers of the Committee on the Judiciary, 94th Cong., 1st Sess. (Washington, D.C.: Government Printing Office, 1975).

22. Schlesinger, *The Imperial Presidency*, p. 330.

23. U.S. Congress, Senate, Hearings before Committees on Government Operations and Judiciary, *Executive Privilege, Secrecy in Government, Freedom of Information*, 93rd Cong., 1st Sess., vol. 2, p. 209 (Washington, D.C.: Government Printing Office, 1973); also see the earlier critique of secrecy systems by the Committee on Government Operations, U.S. Congress, House of Representatives, Report No. 1884, 85th Cong., 1st Sess. (Washington, D.C.: Government Printing Office, 1958).

24. U.S. Congress, House, Hearings before the Committee on Government Operations, *U.S. Government Information Policies and Practices*, 92nd Cong., 2nd Sess. (Washington, D.C.: Government Printing Office, 1972), pp. 2909–2910.

25. David Wise, *The Politics of Lying* (New York: Random House, 1973), p. 173.

26. Ibid., pp. 143–147.

27. *The New York Times Company v. United States*, 403 U.S. 713 (1971).

28. See provisions of S. 1400, introduced March 27, 1973.

29. United States v. Marchetti, No. 540–72–A (E.D. Va., 1972), 466 F. 2nd 1909 (1972).

30. *Knopf Inc. v. Colby*, No. 540–73–A (E.D. Va., 1974).

31. *Knopf Inc. v. Colby*, 509 F. 2nd 1362 (1975).

32. *Knopf v. Colby*, cert. denied, 421 U.S. 992 (1975). For a full discussion, see Morton Halperin and Daniel Hoffman, *Freedom vs. National Security* (New York: Chelsea House Publishers, 1977), pp. 109–112.

33. For a compendium of statutes and the texts of relevant sections, see Halperin and Hoffman, *Freedom vs. National Security*, pp. 115–138.

34. Administrative Procedures Act of 1946, P.L. 79–404 secs. 3(1) and 3(2).

35. 5 U.S.C.A. Section 22; in several court cases between 1895 and 1955 courts interpreted these laws to provide secretaries with authority to withhold information in national security matters.

36. 72 U.S. Stat. 542.

37. P.L. 90–23, sec. 552(4)(b)(1).

38. *Environmental Protection Agency v. Mink*, 410 U.S. 73 (1973).

39. 5 U.S.C. Section 522(b)(1).

40. *Federal Register*, 37, p. 10053; "Progress Report: Implementation of Executive Order 11652," Interagency Classification Review Committee (1973), p. 3.

41. Ibid.

42. Ibid.

43. 1973 Senate Hearings, p. 430.

44. 1973 Senate Hearings, p. 428.

45. William S. Moorehead, "Operation and Reform of the Classification System in the United States," *Secrecy and Foreign Policy*, ed. Thomas Franck and Edward Weisband (New York: Oxford University Press, 1974).

46. Attorney General Herbert Brownell coined the phrase in a memorandum submitted to a congressional subcommittee, which accompanied a letter from Eisenhower to Defense Secretary Charles Wilson directing senior department officials not to testify before the subcommittee. Brownell's memo in turn consisted of excerpts from an article written several years before by a Justice Department attorney, developing the argument of an "executive privilege"; cf. Herman Wolkinson, "Demands of Congressional Committees for Executive Papers," *Federal Bar Journal* 10 (April, July, October, 1949).

47. William P. Rogers, "Constitutional Law: The Papers of the Executive Branch," *American Bar Association Journal*, 44 (1958): 941–945.

48. 42 Stat. 20, sec. 313. Between 1964 and 1974, departments refused the GAO and Congress in 225 cases, including 130 requests for documents and 47 for testimony, according to *The National Journal*, September 7, 1974.

49. Franck and Weisband, *Secrecy and Foreign Policy*, p. 83.

50. James A. Robinson, *Congress and Foreign Policy Making*, rev. ed. (Homewood, Ill.: Dorsey, 1967), p. 65, indicates that in twenty-two cases studied, Congress initiated only three policies.

51. Marvin Feurwerger, "The Emergency Security Assistance Act of 1973 and American-Israeli Relations," *Midstream*, August/September 1974, pp. 32–33.

52. Holbert Carroll, *The House of Representatives and Foreign Policy*, rev. ed. (Boston: Little, Brown, 1966), p. 10.

53. For an interesting discussion of presidential power placed in comparative context, see Kenneth Waltz, *Foreign Policy and Democratic Politics* (Boston: Little, Brown, 1967), Chapter 5, "National Legislatures."

54. Richard Neustadt, *Presidential Power* (New York: John Wiley and Sons, 1961), pp. 51–53.

55. Malcolm Jewell, *Senatorial Politics and Foreign Policy* (Lexington, Ky.: University of Kentucky Press, 1962), p. 49.

56. Commission on the Organization of Government for the Conduct of Foreign Policy, "Appendix M: Report of a Staff Survey of Congressional Views on the Organization of Government for the Conduct of Foreign Policy," p. 126, indicates that of the 106 members surveyed, 76.2 percent wished for more consultation by the executive branch and 72.4 percent wanted to strengthen the oversight system.

57. I.M. Destler, *Presidents, Bureaucrats and Foreign Policy* (Princeton, N.J.: Princeton University Press, 1974), p. 8.

58. Harry Truman, *Years of Trial and Hope* (Garden City, N.Y.: Doubleday, 1956), p. 165.

59. Charles Frankel, *High on Foggy Bottom* (New York: Harper and Row, 1968), p. 56.

60. Ibid., p. 11.

61. John P. Davies, *Foreign and Other Affairs* (New York: W.W. Norton, 1964), pp. 175, 180, 196.

62. Stanley Hoffman, *Gulliver's Troubles, Or the Setting of American Foreign Policy* (New York: McGraw-Hill, 1968), p. 285.

63. *New York Times*, December 12, 1977.

64. John F. Campbell, *The Foreign Affairs Fudge Factory* (New York: Basic Books, 1971), pp. 51–55.

65. Charles Yost, *The Conduct and Misconduct of Foreign Affairs* (New York: Random House, 1972), p. 144.

66. Campbell, *The Foreign Affairs Fudge Factory*, p. 269; Yost, *The Conduct and Misconduct of Foreign Affairs*, p. 89.

67. Campbell, *The Foreign Affairs Fudge Factory*, pp. 51–54; the first warnings about military influence within the NSC system came from two former assistant Secretaries of State, Harvey Bundy and James Rogers, in the Hoover Commission

Study, *Task Force Report on Foreign Affairs*, "Appendix H: Report with Recommendations" (Government Printing Office, 1949); for a different perspective on the problems, see Richard Barnet, *The Roots of War* (New York: Atheneum, 1972).

68. P.L. 80-253, sec. 101(a).

69. Edward Hobbes, *Behind the President* (Washington, D.C.: Public Affairs Press, 1954), p. 135.

70. Quoted in Morton Halperin, *Bureaucratic Politics and Foreign Policy* (Washington, D.C.: The Brookings Institution, 1974), p. 219.

71. Ibid., p. 245.

72. R. Gordon Hoxie, *Command Decision and the Presidency* (Pleasantville, N.Y.: Readers Digest Association, 1977), p. 229.

73. I.M. Destler, "National Security Advice to U.S. Presidents," *World Politics* 29, no. 2 (January 1977): 147.

74. Keith Clark and Laurence Legere, *The President and the Management of National Security* (New York: Praeger, 1969), p. 59.

75. Ibid., p. 221.

76. U.S. Congress, Senate, Hearings before the Subcommittee on National Policy Machinery of the Committee on Government Operations, *Organizing for National Security*, 86th Cong., 2nd Sess., Parts 1–3 (Washington, D.C.: Government Printing Office, 1960).

77. Hoxie, *Command Decision and the Presidency*, p. 243.

78. Destler, *Presidents, Bureaucrats and Foreign Policy*, Chapter 5, "Strategies of Presidents."

79. Clark and Legere, *The President and the Management of National Security*, pp. 243–245.

80. Ibid., p. 243.

81. Henry Kissinger, "Bureaucracy and Foreign Policy Making," in *Readings in American Foreign Policy*, ed. Morton Halperin and Arnold Kantor (Boston: Little, Brown, 1973).

82. Clark and Legere, *The President and the Management of National Security*, p. 11.

83. Richard M. Nixon, "U.S. Foreign Policy for the 1970s: A New Strategy for Peace," February 18, 1970, p. 22.

84. Graham Allison and Peter Szanton, "Organizing for the Decade Ahead," in *Remaking Foreign Policy* (New York: Basic Books, 1976).

85. Alexander George, "The Case for Multiple Advocacy in Making Foreign Policy," *The American Political Science Review* 66, no. 3 (September 1972): 761.

86. James L. McCamy, *The Conduct of the New Diplomacy* (New York: Harper and Row, 1964), pp. 121–222.

87. U.S. Congress, Senate, Subcommittee on National Security Staffing and Operations, Committee on Government Operations, *Report*, March 25, 1963 (Washington, D.C.: Government Printing Office, 1963).

88. Commission on the Organization of the Government for the Conduct of Foreign Policy, *Final Report* (Washington, D.C.: Government Printing Office, 1975), pp. 5–39.

89. Other proposals include a Department of Foreign Affairs with subdepartments for political, economic, and cultural affairs and the establishment of a "first secretary" for foreign affairs to coordinate all implementation of foreign policies; see Arthur MacMahon, *Administration in Foreign Affairs* (University, Alabama: University of Alabama Press, 1953); similarly, Senate Committee on Foreign Relations, *United States Foreign Policy*, 86th Cong., 2nd Sess. (Government Printing Office, 1960), p. 3; Eisenhower's proposals for a Secretary for International Coordination are described by Clark and Legere, p. 69, and by Hoxie, p. 229.

Chapter Eleven

1. Information compiled in Barry M. Blechman and Steven S. Kaplan, *Force Without War* (Washington, D.C.: The Brookings Institution, 1978).

2. The Senator Gravel Edition, *The Pentagon Papers: The Defense Department History of United States Decisionmaking on Vietnam* (Boston: Beacon Press, 1972), 1:186–187 (hereafter cited as Gravel).

3. NSC 124/1, in Gravel, 1:375–381.

4. Gravel, *Pentagon Papers*, 2:336.

5. Ibid., 3:500, 598.

6. Ibid., 2:828.

7. Ibid., 1:195.

8. J. William Fulbright, *The Arrogance of Power* (New York: Random House, 1966), pp. 1–23.

9. Gravel, *Pentagon Papers*, 1:79–80, 405–407.

10. Ibid., p. 33.

11. Ibid., p. 452.

12. National Security Council 5429/2, August 10, 1954.

13. On the theory that an economic elite dominates foreign policy, see Gabriel Kolko, *The Roots of American Foreign Policy* (Boston: Beacon Press, 1969).

14. Gravel, *Pentagon Papers*, 1:82, 375–381.

15. Joyce Kolko and Gabriel Kolko, *The Limits of Power* (New York: Harper and Row, 1972), p. 685.

16. Nina S. Adams, "The Last Line of Defense," in Gravel, 5:149.

17. On national security elites and their origins, see Richard Barnet, "The National Security Managers and the National Interest," *Politics and Society*, 1, no. 2 (February 1971): 257–268.

18. See, for example, Richard B. DuBoff, "Business Ideology and Foreign Policy: The National Security Council and Vietnam," in Gravel, 5:16–32.

19. See Richard Barnet, *The Roots of War* (New York: Atheneum, 1972), especially Chapter 5, "The Operational Code of the National Security Managers."

20. See Abraham Lowenthal, *The Dominican Intervention* (Cambridge: Harvard University Press, 1972) for the general account on which this section relies.

21. Ibid., p. 82.

22. Ibid., p. 116.

23. Ibid., pp. 155, 162.

24. Douglas Kinard, *The War Managers* (Hanover: University Press of New England, 1977).

25. Peter D. Scott, "Vietnamization and the Drama of the Pentagon Papers," in Gravel, *Pentagon Papers*, 5:211–248. This section relies heavily on Scott's analysis.

26. Graham Allison, *Essence of Decision* (Boston: Little, Brown, 1971).

27. Scott, p. 230.

28. Allison, *Essence of Decision*, p. 131.

29. Lowenthal, *The Dominican Intervention*, pp. 118–121.

30. Marvin Kalb and Bernard Kalb, *Kissinger* (Boston: Little, Brown, 1974), p. 490.

31. Arthur Schlesinger, Jr., *The Bitter Heritage* (Boston: Houghton Mifflin, 1967), p. 47; also David Halberstam, *The Making of a Quagmire* (New York: Random House, 1964).

32. John Galloway, *The Gulf of Tonkin Resolution* (Rutherford, N.J.: Fairleigh Dickinson University Press, 1970).

33. Ibid., p. 89.

34. U.S. Congress, Senate, Committee on Foreign Relations, *The Gulf of Tonkin: the 1964 Incidents*, 90th Cong., 2nd Sess. (Washington, D.C.: Government Printing Office, 1968).

35. Daniel Ellsberg, "The Quagmire Myth and the Stalemate Machine," in *Papers on the War* (New York: Simon and Schuster, 1972).

36. Ibid., p. 105.

37. By the time North Vietnam completed its military victory, only 28 percent of the American public thought it would be a serious setback for the United States, a 74 to 17 percent majority of the public opposed Ford's request for additional military aid to South Vietnam, and 79 to 21 percent were opposed to American involvement in future "guerrilla-type" wars. Ellsberg's "rules" no longer seemed to be

a requirement for presidents. Poll data from *New York Post*, March 20, 1975, reporting a Louis Harris poll.

38. Walt Haney, "The Pentagon Papers and the United States Involvement in Laos," Gravel, 5:262.

39. David Halberstam, *The Best and the Brightest* (New York: Random House, 1969).

40. On tests for presidential consultation see Arthur Schlesinger, Jr., *The Imperial Presidency* (Boston: Houghton Mifflin, 1973); for a critique of nonconstitutional standards, see Richard M. Pious, "Is Presidential Power Poison?", *Political Science Quarterly*, 89, no. 3 (Fall 1974): 627–643.

41. Lawrence Goldsmith, *The Growth of Presidential Power* (New York: Chelsea-Bowker, 1974), 1:375–376.

42. Durand v. Hollins, 8 F. Cas. 111.

43. Theodore Roosevelt, Annual Message to Congress, December 6, 1904, reprinted in James D. Richardson, ed., *A Compilation of the Messages and Papers of the Presidents, 1789–1897* (Washington, D.C.: Government Printing Office, 1896–1899), 15:6923.

44. James K. Polk, Second Annual Message to Congress, in Richardson, *A Compilation*, 5:2322.

45. Abraham Lincoln, *The Congressional Globe*, 30th Cong., 1st Sess., January 12, 1848, pp. 154–155.

46. *The Congressional Globe*, 30th Cong., 1st Sess., January 3, 1848, p. 95.

47. S/1505/Rev.

48. *Department of State Bulletin*, 23, no. 578 (July 31, 1950): 173.

49. P.L. 78–267; see Merlo Pusey, *The Way We Go to War* (Boston: Houghton Mifflin, 1969).

50. Senate Report No. 717, 79th Cong., 1st Sess., November 8, 1945 (Washington, D.C.: Government Printing Office, 1945).

51. Johnson v. Eisentrager, 339 U.S. 763.

52. 373 F. 2d 664.

53. Mottola v. Nixon, 318 F. Supp. 538 (N.D. Calif.).

54. Abram Chayes, "Law and the Quarantine of Cuba," *Foreign Affairs* 41, no. 3 (April 1963): 550–558.

55. Louis Henkin, *Foreign Affairs and the Constitution* (Mineola, N.Y.: Oceana, 1972), pp. 52–54.

56. See Henkin, *Foreign Affairs and the Constitution*, p. 108 for an interesting discussion of this point.

57. Leonard Ratner, "The Coordinated Warmaking Power," *Southern California Law Review* 44:474.

58. 78 Stat. 384; Senate Committee on Foreign Relations, *United States Commitments to Foreign Powers*, Senate Report No. 797, 90th Cong., 1st Sess. (Washington, D.C.: Government Printing Office, 1967), p. 82.

59. U.S. Congress, *Congressional Record*, 110, no. 18, p. 403.

60. Ibid., p. 539.

61. Thomas Erlich, "The Legal Process in Foreign Affairs: Military Intervention—A Testing Case," *Stanford Law Review* 27, no. 3 (February 1975): 644.

62. Richard Falk, "Law, Lawyers and the Conduct of American Foreign Relations," *The Yale Law Journal* 78, no. 6: 920.

63. *Congressional Quarterly Weekly Reports*, August 11, 1973, p. 2205.

64. 83 Stat. 469, sec. 643.

65. 84 Stat. 1942, sec. 7.

66. *New York Times*, October 29, 1973.

67. Richard M. Nixon to Speaker Carl Albert, August 3, 1973.

68. 84 Stat. 905.

69. 85 Stat. 430; *Weekly Compilation of Presidential Documents* 7 (November 22, 1971): 1531.

70. *Weekly Compilation of Presidential Documents* 9 (November 24, 1973): 1285.

71. Thomas Eagleton, *War and Presidential Power* (New York: Liveright, 1974), p. 203.

72. P.L. 93–148, sec. (2)(a).

73. P.L. 93–148, sec. (2)(c).

74. U.S. Congress, House, Report No. 93–287, Subcommittee on International Security and Scientific Affairs, Committee on International Relations, *The War Powers Resolution, Relevant Documents, Correspondence, Reports*, 94th Cong., 1st Sess. (Washington, D.C.: Government Printing Office, 1975). Hereafter cited as House Documents.

75. P.L. 93–148, sec. (4)(a)(B).

76. U.S. Congress, House, Hearings before the Subcommittee on International Security and Scientific Affairs, Committee on International Relations, *War Powers: A Test of Compliance*, 94th Cong., 1st Sess. (Washington, D.C.: Government Printing Office, 1975), p. 90. Hereafter cited as Compliance Hearings.

77. Compliance Hearings, p. 91.

78. P.L. 93–148, sec. 3.

79. Conference Report No. 93–547, October 4, 1973, pp. 13–14.

80. P.L. 93–148, secs. 4(a)1,2,3.

81. Note, "The War Powers Resolution: Statutory Limitation on the Commander-in-Chief," *Harvard Journal of Legislation* 11 (1974): 190–194.

82. Compliance Hearings, pp. 63–65.

83. Conference Report No. 93–547, p. 15.

84. P.L. 93–148, sec. 5(c).

85. Ibid.

86. Michael J. Glennon, "Strengthening the War Powers Resolution: The Case for Purse-Strings Restrictions," *Minnesota Law Review* 60, no. 1 (1975): 37.

87. See the analysis based on this mistaken assumption by Graham Allison, "Making War: The President and Congress," in *The Presidency Reappraised*, 2nd ed., ed. Thomas Cronin and Rexford Tugwell (New York: Praeger, 1977), pp. 238, 245.

88. U.S. Congress, Senate, Hearings before the Committee on Foreign Relations, *War Powers Resolution*, 95th Cong., 1st Sess. (Government Printing Office, 1977), p. 172. Hereafter cited as 1977 Hearings.

89. Compliance Hearings, p. 91.

90. Compliance Hearings, p. 92.

91. 1977 Hearings, p. 17.

92. Glennon, "Strengthening the War Powers Resolution," discusses these proposals.

93. 1977 Hearings, pp. 12, 71.

94. William P. Rogers, "Congress, the President, and the War Powers," *California Law Review* 59, no. 5 (September 1971): 1211.

95. House Documents, pp. 40–41.

96. Citations for these provisions: P.L. 93–431, sec. 839; P.L. 93–238, sec. 741; P.L. 93–52, sec. 108; P.L. 93–50, sec. 307; P.L. 93–189, sec. 30; P.L. 93–115, sec. 806; P.L. 93–126, sec. 13.

97. U.S. Congress, *Congressional Record*, 121, April 10, 1975, p. H 2684.

98. House Documents, p. 42; see also Gerald R. Ford, "Statement of Evacuation of Mission in Phnom Penh, *Weekly Compilation of Presidential Documents*, 11 (April 12, 1975), "Statement of Evacuation of all Personnel from Saigon," *Weekly Compilation of Presidential Documents* 11 (April 29, 1975).

99. For a defense of presidential actions, see J. Terry Emerson, "The War Powers Resolution Tested," *Notre Dame Lawyer* 51, no. 2 (December 1975): 192.

100. *New York Times*, May 13, 1975.

101. 1977 Hearings, p. 67; for a discussion of the problems with the consultation provision, see Robert Zutz, "The Recapture of the S.S. *Mayaguez*: Failure of the Consultation Clause of the War Powers Resolution," *International Law and Politics* 8 (1976): 457–478.

102. Pat Holt, *The War Powers Resolution* (Washington, D.C.: The American Enterprise Institute, 1978), p. 17.

103. Compliance Hearings, p. 67.

104. Compliance Hearings, p. 45.

105. Ibid.

106. *Report of the Comptroller General of the United States*, October 4, 1976,

p. 69. Ford denied that he was bound by the resolution in these incidents. Nor did he concede that the resolution was constitutional. He also argued that the prior consultation provision was unworkable: the Da Nang evacuation took place during congressional recess, Congress had adjourned for the day of the Lebanese evacuation, and some key legislators could not be reached. See Gerald Ford, "The War Powers Resolution," the John Sherman Cooper Lecture of the University of Kentucky, reprinted in *Report No. 69*, The American Enterprise Institute, June 1977, especially pp. 4–5. It might be noted that although Ford claimed that he had used the procedures of the resolution in two Lebanese evacuations in 1976, no written reports were ever received. Instead, the State Department gave informal briefings to selected leaders. See Holt, *The War Powers Resolution*, p. 11.

107. Holt, *The War Powers Resolution*, p. 31.

108. Compliance Hearings, pp. iv, 69.

109. 1977 Hearings, "Statement of Hon. Herbert J. Hansell, Legal Advisor to the Department of State," p. 188.

110. 1977 Hearings, p. 190.

111. 1977 Hearings, pp. 190–194.

112. 1977 Hearings, p. 207. In a similar development, Attorney General Griffin Bell claimed that arms sales to foreign nations were not subject to a legislative veto provision. He warned that he "would not be bound" by the law but then said that "under a spirit of comity" he would abide by it. See his remarks quoted in *New York Times*, June 22, 1978.

113. 1977 Hearings, p. 204.

INDEX